5 20 X

Date

```
D1307541
```

GENERAL EDITOR

T. LYNN SMITH
UNIVERSITY OF FLORIDA

Societies

Prepared at the University of Kentucky by:

IRWIN T. SANDERS, Editor
Professor of Sociology

RICHARD B. WOODBURY, Asst. Editor
Associate Professor of Anthropology

FRANK J. ESSENE
Associate Professor of Anthropology

THOMAS P. FIELD
Associate Professor of Geography

JOSEPH R. SCHWENDEMAN
Professor of Geography

CHARLES E. SNOW
Professor of Anthropology

Around the World

VOLUME TWO: THE CHINESE PEASANT • THE
COTTON SOUTH • THE ENGLISH MIDLANDS

THE DRYDEN PRESS • PUBLISHERS • NEW YORK

For the past seven years, a group of social scientists—sociologists, anthropologists, and geographers—at the University of Kentucky has been developing a new approach to the study of society—one that presents, from an interdisciplinary point of view, the essential characteristics of a society, in terms of both its everyday workings and its organization.

We have sought to build in the minds of beginning students a clear, meaningful concept of the social universe as an area of scientific study. Convinced that such a conception best prepares students for further work in history, government, social anthropology, and other fields, we have stressed society as the chief subject matter of the social sciences. The work does not try to teach the social sciences *per se*; the intention is rather, to prepare the student for later study. It does not attempt to teach Principles of Government, for example, but it does explain the role of government and its various forms in different societies. Even those students who do not go on to specialize in the social sciences, however, will gain, from the study of this material, in their understanding of the society in which they live and of the other societies of the world.

Societies Around the World, the outcome of our undertaking, treats societies comprehensively—not in piecemeal fashion with discrete and disparate discussions in terms of one discipline or another, but as dynamic wholes. Through selections from many authoritative sources representing a wide variety of approaches, methods, and points of view, each of the societies can be seen as a "going concern." Because each selection is an entity and because each is related to the basic study plan, the student can read purposively and intensively—and can develop in intellectual maturity.

The selections are supplemented by a few original articles and are knit together by brief transitional comments and explanations. As the student compares one society with another, he will discern not merely the differences among six societies that are widely diverse geographically and encompass virtually the entire range of complexity known in human social groupings; more important, he will identify and understand the main characteristics of society in general.

The Introduction to Volume One makes clear to the beginning student some of the elementary concepts useful in studying man, whether biologically or socially; in visualizing and understanding the habitat and economy of a group; and in analyzing social organization and sociocultural change. An outline, "How to Study a Society" (Vol. I, p. 5), orients the student and provides a basis for his use of the comparative method.

Volume One presents, first, the Eskimo, whose adaptation to a rigorous arctic habitat has been ingenious and complex but whose social patterns are relatively simple. Next, the Navajo are shown to have made another kind of environmental adjustment, to a semi-arid climate; their social organization illustrates the operation of a matrilineal clan system. The Baganda of equatorial

Africa, the third society studied, had a well-defined system of kingship long before their culture contact with Europeans; in recent generations they have undergone profound economic, political, and social change.

Social change, one of the underlying themes of *Societies Around the World*, is illustrated with especial clarity in the three societies that comprise Volume Two. That volume opens with a study of the Chinese Peasant, who exemplifies the chief traits of a peasant society—the form of social grouping in which most of the world's population now lives. The Cotton South is then presented as an area undergoing swift economic and social change because of the industrialization of what was, only a century ago, an almost wholly agrarian society. The English Midlands, the last society studied, affords insight into the organization and problems of a contemporary industrial society.

Volume Two closes with a brief overview of the methods and content of the various fields of social science, in the expectation that the student will have new interests to satisfy and new questions for which to seek answers.

ACKNOWLEDGMENTS

Thomas P. Field prepared materials which were used as a basis for the maps and for the photographic sections.

During the past seven years, many people, chiefly at the University of Kentucky, have contributed to the courses from which these two volumes have resulted. The co-authors listed on the title page are the major contributors to the project, which included several planographed editions. In addition, valuable contributions have been made by twelve other instructors who have taught the course. These valued colleagues are: C. Arnold Anderson, Percy Black, James W. Gladden, David L. Hatch, Catharine K. Haynes, James W. Hughes, Harry K. Hutter, Gordon Lewis, Willard E. Ruggles, Bernard H. Schockel, Willis A. Sutton, Jr., and Richard L. Tuthill.

We have had the benefit of seminar and other discussions with a number of people who possess a first-hand knowledge of the six habitats and societies chosen. These include, for the Eskimo, George A. Dale, the late W. Elmer Ekblaw, Margaret Lantis, and E. S. Lusby; for the Navajo, Father Berard Haile and Clyde Kluckhohn; for the Baganda, Thomas Cullen, William S. Kajubi, and C. Amory Ross; for the Chinese Peasant, George B. Cressey, Francis L. K. Hsu, and Lewis S. C. Smythe; for the Cotton South we have drawn heavily upon the University of Kentucky staff members specializing in this area; and for the English Midlands, Jacqueline Tyrwhitt and, especially, Catharine K. Haynes, who, during a year recently spent in England, devoted a great deal of time to gathering source material through interviews and library research; W. Warren

Haynes also has made many helpful suggestions. We were also aided by W. P. MacLean.

We have had the benefit of extensive collaboration by our colleagues Professor C. Arnold Anderson and Dr. Mary Jean Bowman through the intermediate stages of this project; they withdrew before the final versions were published.

Nathalie F. S. Woodbury collaborated professionally and assisted in the technical details of preparing the manuscript. Arthur M. Grove contributed cartographic materials used in the early phases of the habitat study. Mary Hatch and Kyllikki Lassi translated several passages from the German.

A list of all of those at the University of Kentucky who have been connected in other ways with the preparation of materials leading up to these published volumes would prove too extensive to present here. For example, without the support of Martin M. White, Dean of the College of Arts and Sciences, this course would never have been successfully launched and continuously improved. Professor W. S. Webb, former Head of the Department of Anthropology, and Dr. Howard W. Beers, Head of the Department of Sociology, though not officially connected with this writing project, aided it in many ways. Dr. Richard L. Tuthill, University Registrar and Professor of Geography, has contributed much to the planning and concept of these volumes. Various staff members in allied social science departments have also made invaluable suggestions. For example, Professor Merton C. England, of the History Department and Managing Editor of the *Journal of Southern History,* provided valuable help on the Old South. Especial thanks are due Evelyn Louise Midkiff, secretary of the Sociology Department, who has frequently gone far beyond the call of duty in taking care of innumerable details in the preparation of the manuscript.

An expression of gratitude is also due to the publishers and authors who permitted us to make extensive use of their materials, as well as to the students at the University of Kentucky who volunteered many worth-while comments and often taught the instructors who, in turn, were teaching them.

February 1953   I.T.S., R.B.W., F.J.E., T.P.F., J.R.S., C.E.S.

NOTE

With a few exceptions, footnotes and references contained in the original selections that make up these volumes have been omitted; those retained appear in parentheses in the text. Many subheads have been deleted or revised by the editors to fit the material actually quoted. The omission of a paragraph or more in a selection is indicated by the use of three asterisks.

THE AUTHORS OF THE SELECTIONS

Contents: Volume Two

THE COTTON SOUTH

THE ENGLISH MIDLANDS

Societies Around the World

THE CHINESE PEASANT

THE COTTON SOUTH

THE ENGLISH MIDLANDS

Introduction

Introduction

>>>

Social Change on a Worldwide Scale

We live in a time of spectacular social changes. Every continent has areas where old patterns are yielding to the new, frequently with much discomfiture to many people. Social forces are working at so accelerated a pace that people everywhere wonder what the morrow will bring. A major purpose of this book is to present three case studies of societies that are experiencing varying degrees and kinds of change so that, by comparing them with one another and with our own society, we can gain an understanding of how societies change. Before we turn to a study of the Chinese peasant, the Cotton South, and the English Midlands, we should first examine briefly five of the major social forces at work behind the news items of press and radio throughout the world.

THE STRUGGLE FOR A HIGHER STANDARD OF LIVING

Most of the people of the world go to bed at night still hungry—not through choice but through lack of an adequate food supply. In the past, hunger and fam-ine have been regarded as expected difficulties, to be faced as courageously or resignedly as possible. Even in England before the Industrial Revolution, people continued to starve in one part of the country while there was plenty of food in another part, simply because of inadequate transportation facilities. But now, through gossip spreading from market towns, through articles in newspapers and in short-wave broadcasts, rural people everywhere are being told that famine and undernourishment need not forever be considered normal. Although any solution of their problems is far in the future, people are beginning to hope. They hear of the standard of living in America, or of the claims of advancement in the Soviet Union, and they wonder why they also cannot have the things they hear about. This yearning is of itself a potent social force when it leads to action.

This desire for higher standards explains the widespread appeal of agrarian reform in which the land from large estates is distributed among the landless or the small holders. The United States occupation force has recently carried out such a land reform in Japan in the hope of providing a more solid base for the rural society of that country. The Communist-dominated governments also initiate land reforms, but in almost every case to date these have been a prelude to a collectivization of the land which removes it eventually from the ownership of the peasant to whom it was originally distributed.

The Middle East, including the great bloc of Arab states, faces acute agrarian problems because of the ownership of much of the land by a few people, some of them described as feudal in practice and point of view. Land hunger is real and is growing more acute as people increase in numbers and require more food and other items.

Health is said by public-health authorities to be "a purchasable commodity." More and more people around the world want better health for themselves and their children, though a great number still lack an understanding of basic health principles. Unfortunately, where the need is greatest the financial problems are often most serious.

To speak of automobiles, refrigerators, and television sets in connection with the world's standard of living is, to put it mildly, premature. As our study of the Chinese peasant will show, the demands of most peasant people are minimal, from the American point of view. Those who are being caught up in the vortex of change ask simply for food, a new plowshare, common medicines, and a book or two from which their children can learn to read. They want clothing to keep them warm in winter and sufficient income to meet the incidental—though often heavy—expenses of ceremonial occasions. But each generation, largely stimulated by the impact of Western ideas and technology, wants more than the preceding generation. Dreams of plenty and promises of better days ahead are working like leaven among millions of people who hardly dared to dream before. This is a social force not to be taken lightly, especially among people who have recently become conscious of their meager material existence in comparison with the fabulous achievements in other parts of the world.

THE SPREAD OF INDUSTRIALIZATION

A second force of worldwide significance is the spread of industrialization in countries which are trying to catch up with the output of the West. What happens when a peasant countryside becomes part of an industrial society is well described for the English Midlands in pages which follow. In reading this, we may wonder whether China and other countries will undergo the same stages.

From the standpoint of the people involved, the auspices under which industrialization comes and the social philosophy of those responsible for it are also tremendously important. The factory system of our day requires that workers leave their handicrafts in home or small shop and place themselves under the supervision of plant managers; family patterns change with new work schedules and with the receipt of wages, which give independence to the single individual. In other words, industrialization of even a part of a country—whether Mexico, Pakistan, or the Cotton South—means great social change for those involved.

Is industrialization the answer to the acute problem of overpopulation, about which many statesmen feel deep concern? Professor Warren S. Thompson, in his article on the population of China quoted later, points out that the industrialization of Europe and America proceeded as it did because there were new frontiers and unsettled lands to which surplus people could go. This provided new markets and new sources of raw materials, and also eased the pressure of increasing population upon a rising standard of living. But where will the people of India and China go if modern, scientific agricultural practices make their farm labor no longer necessary and if industry does not expand fast enough to give them jobs? Will a higher stand-ard of living ever be obtainable? J. Lossing Buck, Hsiao-t'ung Fei and Chih-i Chang examine in later selections the role that industrialization may play in the development of such countries as China.

The conclusions and decisions of scholars may or may not be put into prac-tice, but many governments the world over are doing all in their power to promote new industries to meet the needs of their people. In imitation of Europe and America, there is a growing tendency to make the machine a fetish and to look to it for progress in terms of material gains.

We of the West started this Industrial Revolution, which is now making its force felt around the world—not only in manufacturing but also in agricultural technology, communications, and transportation. Its power for promoting human happiness is tremendous provided wise heads guide its development.

THE STRUGGLE FOR NATIONAL INDEPENDENCE

In the nineteenth century, in the Balkans, the idea of nationalism was strik-ingly illustrated where one small country after another imbibed the heady wine of independence and, with Russian help, successfully pushed back the Ottoman Empire, in which the idea of a nation state played almost no part. Before World War I, the Austro-Hungarian Empire was foundering on the stubborn rocks of national aspirations of its minority groups, such as the Czechs, the Croatians, and the Slovenes. In a sense, World War I and Wilson's Fourteen Points won the day for the nation state in Europe. Later on, the concept of statism was developed to so menacing a degree by the Nazi and Fascist regimes that most of the Western World, with other allies, fought World War II to end—among other things—this perversion of the ideal of political freedom.

Is it any wonder, then, that this virus of nationalism, which in its extreme form is recognized as socially disorganizing in a family of nations, should spread to India, Indonesia, the Arab World, and to Africa as it had spread to Latin

America almost one hundred years ago? These large areas of the world which have been under the control of, or at least the influence of, Europeans are seeking for themselves the national independence which has already been accepted in the West. This accent on national independence is couched in many slogans and phrases, such as "Asia for the Asiatics," "a drive against imperialism," or "an end to colonialism."

A glance at any day's headlines is apt to show, therefore, some leader in a seemingly faraway country berating those in other lands who have in the past or are in the present supposedly curtailing his nation's independence, whether through economic measures or through a political arrangement of long standing. This drive to be free of outside interference is a social force out of which social changes are being fashioned. To be sure, in many countries people's loyalties are still centered in their family and local village; they have not yet been initiated into the cult of nationalism, but that will happen sooner than most of us realize. It will take considerable time for recently freed countries to realize what other countries are finding out—that patriotism or enlightened love of country is different from the brand of narrow nationalism that makes the nation the supreme value in life.

THE STRUGGLE FOR POLITICAL DEMOCRACY

As we take a worldwide view of social forces at work, we hear many highly articulate leaders demanding for their countries national independence; but far in the background are the almost muted sounds of those who want *individual* independence—or political democracy—too.

In discussing political democracy, we must frankly face the fact that we are apt to take it for granted or credit it with too wide an acceptance. To most of mankind Western democracy is still a rather novel idea, but it is an idea of tremendous power when it is understood by sufficient people in a country. The English Revolution (1688–1689), the American Revolution (1775–1783), and the French Revolution (1789–1799) testify to the power of the ideals of "liberty, equality, and fraternity." Although they did not occur simultaneously, we can, for convenience, combine these three revolutions into what might be called the Western Revolution and describe its political genius as its attitude toward the *importance* and *uniqueness* of the individual. Its heirs became *citizens* rather than *subjects*.

Western political democracy, however, should not be confused with the Marxist brand of economic "democracy," which has always proved unworkable in any extreme form. At times, to be sure, governments must act to safeguard the interests of their citizens in economic as well as other matters, but the democratic test of such action is the rendering of service to the individual and the preservation of his "inalienable rights."

In most of the world, "the dignity of the common man" remains a lofty and unattained ideal. Even though the common man may be given the right to vote, he cannot rise in dignity as long as he is chained to hunger or relegated to a rejected, inferior status because of occupation, religion, or the color of his skin. But the Western Revolution, as long as it is true to its democratic tradition, will continue to champion the dignity of the common man, and those who take it seriously will keep on feeling twinges of conscience as they see violations of this ideal at home or abroad. This is why the Commission on Human Rights of the United Nations has devoted great efforts to drafting a charter of principles toward which all mankind can move, though it be at uneven pace.

A political democracy is not created simply by the drafting of constitutions, the meeting of national assemblies, or the casting of ballots by a large proportion of its people. The satellite countries of Eastern Europe under Soviet influence do all of these things and call themselves the "people's democracies." They lack one indispensable ingredient: respect for the rights of the individual.

It would be wrong indeed to believe that political democracy can assume only the governmental forms fashioned here in America to meet our own needs almost two hundred years ago. Each people will have to use those political forms which, in their own cultural setting, best transform into reality the democratic ideals about which we speak. After all, democracy is more a spiritual force than a political organization. Furthermore, numerous social changes will have to occur before large masses of people become educated enough to understand the role that each must play in the establishment of political democracy as a meaningful force in their lives. There will be many false starts, much misuse of the word "democracy" from an American's standpoint, but broad social changes may eventually result. This is a social force to watch.

THE SECULARIZATION OF DAILY LIFE

Professor Howard Becker, of the University of Wisconsin, makes use of a sacred-secular continuum in viewing the behavior of societies. At one extreme, or pole, he places those societies in which people behave traditionally, in which custom is sacred, in which the past dictates to the present. In these societies most behavior is nonrational and largely emotional. At the other extreme of the continuum he places the secular societies, those in which the scientific spirit has so permeated the thinking of the people that they subject every phase of life to minute investigation and try to base their conduct on logic, on cold reason. Of course, no actual society exists at either extreme, for each society lies somewhere in between, and the differences are largely those of degree.

Western societies tend toward the secular pole. Accompanying the changes in political ideology of the English, American, and French Revolutions were changes in the attitudes toward time-honored traditions. People who had deposed and beheaded those monarchs who claimed the God-given right to rule could also question other "sacred" traits of their society. This led to various contradictions and controversies in Western society as science and religion began to out-argue each other before realizing that there was a place for both, even in a modern age.

Whereas we of the West have had a century for the accommodation of the science-religion controversy, other societies, feeling the impact of Westernization, face the problem almost overnight. For example, in most sacred societies the father's word is law; he is not only respected but usually implicitly obeyed. What happens to the parent-child relationship when a son in a Lebanese village, for example, realizes that he has learned far more about the world than his father can ever learn, that many of his father's commands violate good farming practices and sound health procedures and are at times just outright "superstitious"? Such a son is becoming secularized, as is the society of which he is a part.

Secularization, a truly powerful social force, is coming rapidly to many areas of the world, bringing with it the danger that the old forms of social control may be discredited and discarded before new types of control have been created as a substitute. In such cases, grave social disorganization is apt to result, giving rise to political vacuums to be exploited by aggressive leaders intent on a rise to power through a local revolution.

Thus, we are being reminded that social changes, though considered commonplace in the West, can reach cataclysmic proportions in other societies, where one innovation sets up a chain reaction of effect and countereffect. Is it any wonder, then, that we stress *social change* as the underlying theme of this book and hope that our tracing of change in the three societies to be studied will give us some insight into the revolutionary character of the age in which we live?

The Approach Used in This Book

As was pointed out in the preface, this is a source book of selections chosen so as to provide a sampling of the outstanding authorities on the topics being discussed. We can appreciate the individual flavor of each writer—Martin Yang, an American-trained anthropologist, describing the Chinese village in which he was reared; Hodding Carter, a Mississippi newspaper man, telling of his religious upbringing in the South; or J. B. Priestley, the well-known English novelist, candidly characterizing the Midlands on a trip through that area. Some of the selections are written with objective, scientific detachment; others are more colorful and impressionistic. Some articles may seemingly contradict one another here and there, but this should stimulate us to inquire more deeply into the real state of things.

The fundamental approach of this book is a combination of the case study and the comparative method. For each of the three societies studied, we have sufficient material to enable us to look at the society as a whole—to see its many aspects (such as the family, government, and the rest) and to note how these are all interrelated to form a social system. Each should become vivid as related facts fall into place.

But these three societies (plus our own) are not to be examined as *separate* units; they are treated in such a way that they can be *compared*. Because our treatment of all three follows the same general topical scheme, we can examine the societies point by point. This enables us to formulate generalizations which discussion with other people may prove to be true or perhaps in need of rephrasing. As we do this, we shall begin to see something of the methodology of the social scientist, who, after collecting his facts and then classifying them, looks for generalizations which can be stated as hypotheses to be tested by further research. The five major topical headings covered in each unit and summarized below form a good basis for comparison.

Five Aspects of Each Society

Habitat

Every society is located in space, and its members must make adjustments to their physical surroundings. The Cotton South, the English Midlands, and most of China are located in the North Temperate Zone, but differences in size and shape will be seen to be very important influences.

Habitat also involves the *surface features,* such as mountains, plains, and valleys, rivers and lakes. In both China and the Cotton South the importance of alluvial flood plains is striking.

Climate includes temperature, precipitation, and wind. Differences among the three habitats studied will be readily apparent, as will their influences upon such matters as agriculture and fuel requirements.

Resources, including soil, minerals, natural vegetation, wild animals, and water, are important to any society, even to the more technologically advanced, which use a much wider variety of resources. It was natural resources along with other advantages that caused England to lead the world in the Industrial Revolution. The authors of this book hold that geographic factors *influence* many economic and social adjustments, although they do not accept the thesis sometimes advanced that the habitat *determines* the kind of society which must develop.

The people

In this volume we are concerned more with dynamics of population growth than with the anthropological classification of people into racial types, to which we devoted some attention in Volume I. At the turn of the nineteenth century, Robert Malthus was alarming the people of England with his theory that a population tended to reproduce geometrically (1, 2, 4, 8, 16, 32, 64, and so on) and would greatly outstrip the food supply, which, he thought, increased arithmetically (1, 2, 3, 4, 5, 6, 7, and so on). This would mean that the lowest economic group would forever be on a mere subsistence, or even a starvation, diet. This, of course, does not hold true for most industrialized societies. Does Malthusianism apply, however, to peasant societies? What about migrations of people to less crowded regions in these countries? Do the poorer people reproduce faster than the richer? If so, does this lead to a deterioration in the quality of the population, or is the biological stock unimpaired? The comparative method should prove particularly helpful in arriving at some answers to these questions.

Maintenance institutions (economy)

In order to understand the lifeway of a people, we need to know how they make their living through the utilization of resources at hand or obtainable by trade, and how they distribute the goods that are produced. We also want to know about the kind of property system that determines ownership, inheritance, and the right to dispose of certain possessions. In connection with an economy, we must also consider the occupational specialization and the division of labor.

The Chinese peasant, as we shall see, has traditionally been inclined toward self-subsistence, or producing primarily for his own needs. He trades any surplus crops at the market town and buys the few necessities in return. The study of his economy will also reveal his close association with the soil, the degree to which the land is worked by owners or tenants, and the numerous village organizations created by the peasant to help him face his economic crises.

The Cotton South represents a modified plantation economy, in which the emphasis is on the production of a major crop—cotton—for cash sale. Here the planter has set the social pattern, although the small-scale farmers, or yeomanry, have been an important segment among agricultural producers. After the Civil War, slavery gave way to sharecropping, and many whites as well as Negroes found it hard to make ends meet. The New South, however, has been changing more rapidly economically than most Americans realize. Agriculture is becoming diversified and mechanized, and in some areas commercial farms employing wage workers predominate. Industry is growing at a rapid pace, and in most respects the economy of the South is becoming more like that of the nation as a whole.

The English Midlands has been chosen as the representative of industrial society for the obvious reason that it was the cradle of the Industrial Revolution. A study of its economy reveals a complexity not only in the manifold problems of manufacturing but also in the mechanics of obtaining raw materials and of distributing the finished products to consumers around the world. Banking, storage, insurance, transportation, and wholesaling and retailing establishments, to mention but a few, are essential to an industrial society. The factory system employs large numbers of workers, who organize into unions to deal with management; the government becomes more active in passing and enforcing labor legislation and business and stock-exchange regulations, and in trying to protect the consumer while satisfying the demands of various pressure groups.

Thus, by a careful comparison of the three types of economy described in this volume, we should be able to trace the multiplication of economic groupings as the consumer demand moves from that of the Chinese peasant to the level of the British middle-class housewife trying to obtain what she considers to be the necessities for her family.

SOCIAL ORGANIZATION

The analysis of social organization in this volume centers around a few elementary but very important concepts which can best be understood as they are applied to specific societies. Here, however, they will be stated in the abstract with the expectation that the reader will make his own application later on.

A society consists of social relationships. These, rather than people, are the units of a society.

A social relationship consists of statuses and roles. That is, two or more individuals occupy statuses, such as father, son; salesman, customer; or teacher, pupil, and interact by playing roles appropriate to the specific statuses. For example, an individual while in the role of a salesman shows deference to customers, even those much younger than himself. But at another time the same individual, in the role of father, will expect his son and son's friends to show toward him the respect or deference that their roles require. Thus, there are prescribed roles for particular statuses, and they are followed in specific social situations, but every individual occupies a large number of different statuses at different times.

We can list and classify a wide variety of statuses into definite patterns of association, such as the family pattern (father, mother, son, daughter, father-in-law, grandmother, etc.) or the local-government pattern (mayor, city councilman, policeman, voter, judge, fire chief, etc.). These *patterns* and many others together make up the parts of the *structure* of a society.

We can list and classify the possible roles in a society. First, we can classify them on the basis of what the people were actually doing—that is, as to kinds of activities. As we go through the streets of any town we see some people selling and others buying; we see adults taking care of children, at home or perhaps at a school; we see others enforcing the law or, if in an Arab country, calling the faithful followers of Islam to prayer. In order to establish a classification, we can label some roles economic, some educational, some political, some familial, and so on. If we were to do this, we would set up approximately the same classification that we use in the patterns of association just described.

But there is a second way of classifying what we see people do. We can say that some of them are competing with one another (in business, athletics, or the classroom); some are cooperating with one another; and a minority may even be performing roles that place them in conflict with one another. Later on, we may see this conflict change to accommodation, as each party gives in a little, or to assimilation, if one group of people absorbs another. This classification is based on the type of interaction or social process involved.

A third classification of roles views their motivational aspect. By what psychological and social processes are people guided into the learning of life's important roles to the point that they want to do what others expect them to do? By what forms of social control are people who are prone to deviate from the expected ways held in check so that society can maintain some degree of equilibrium? Thus, we can list some roles as conforming, meaning that people are doing what they are supposed to do under given situations. Other roles we observe could be called deviant, since they are not those which persons of a given status should be performing at the time, according to the expectation of most of the members of the society.

But the culture, or social heritage, surrounds social relationships in at least two ways. (1) It provides a set of *values* by which statuses are ranked in importance so that we can arrange the statuses of many *patterns* into a hierarchy of prestige or authority and we can determine what is considered important and unimportant. (2) It provides a set of *norms*, or rules, of the game, which guide the individual in the performance of his roles and even set limits to what can and cannot be done. These will be illustrated in the societies described.

These, then, are some basic steps in understanding the nature of a society. We study the chief *patterns of association* and the *system of social values,* the *basic processes by type of interaction* and the *motivational processes of socialization and social control.* Finally, we note for each society some of the *norms* to which well-behaved members of the society conform in the performance of their many roles. Patterns of association, processes, values, and norms are not usually so labeled when they appear in the selections, but transitional passages will indicate how we can identify them.

SOCIOCULTURAL CHANGE

Since the major theme of this book is *sociocultural change,* this term deserves clarification. We begin with the word *culture,* which, in keeping with Ralph Linton's usage, we define as *social heritage.* We also think of it as anything manmade, the opposite of *natural.* To analyze what is manmade, even in the case of one society, we must have some rough way of grouping the *traits* observed. This we do by a threefold classification:

ARTIFACTS. These are material things. They can be seen and handled; they can be made, used up, or destroyed. Examples are an ax, a shoe, a telephone, a pair of chopsticks. Each artifact is used according to specific techniques.

SOCIOFACTS. These are the traits covered under social organization. A woman's club, for instance, is a sociofact, as is a class system or a football team.

MENTIFACTS. These embrace the psychosocial side of man's heritage, such as the values and norms previously mentioned, as well as beliefs, ideas, myths, and ideologies commonly held by the people.

Culture, then, is the combination of artifacts, sociofacts, and mentifacts, all intricately interrelated. Sociocultural change, therefore, would be any alterations in these three aspects—*e.g.*, substitution of the automobile for the horse and buggy, a change from a monarchy to a republic, or the acceptance of new beliefs, such as the germ theory of disease, by a large number of people.

Since our focus in this book, however, is upon society (the realm of the socio-facts), most of our analysis in later selections will deal with the effect upon social relationships of the adoption of new practices or the acceptance of a new set of beliefs by members of the society.

This is but a brief introduction to the concept of sociocultural change but should at least suggest to us what to look for in reading about the societies which follow. By now the reader should have some foretaste of the approach used in this book as well as some idea of its contents. If he will bear in mind the five topical headings, and even some of the subtopics mentioned, and use them for comparative purposes, his study should prove creative and rewarding.

THE CHINESE PEASANT

Above: China is predominantly a land of farmers, even though it also contains some of the world's greatest cities. Most Chinese peasants rent or own many tiny patches of land, which they farm by primitive methods. The cultivation of rice, which is possible where fields can be flooded, produces an enormous return in food value per acre. *Below:* Farm families are not completely self-sufficient, and for millennia China has had a system of many small village markets, where people in the vicinity may buy and sell.

The enormous population of China has always made manpower abundant and inexpensive, and the high cost of feeding animals has also tended to make man the chief beast of burden. *Above:* The yoke is one of the most common means of carrying heavy loads in China, and when the two baskets are properly balanced, a man can carry a considerable weight. *Below:* To many Chinese the machine-age has meant such small-scale improvements as the sewing machine rather than vast industrial projects, which have been slow in coming.

China's contacts with the Western world have been mostly through her ports, where many innovations such as modern buildings, electricity, and telephones (*above*) make parts of the coastal cities quite occidental in superficial appearance. But the struggle to take advantage of western technological ingenuity is costly and comes mainly where foreign capital has been invested. Traditional techniques of hulling rice (*below*), for example, use cheap and abundant manpower instead of machinery imported from abroad. China is not rich in most of the natural resources important to industrial growth.

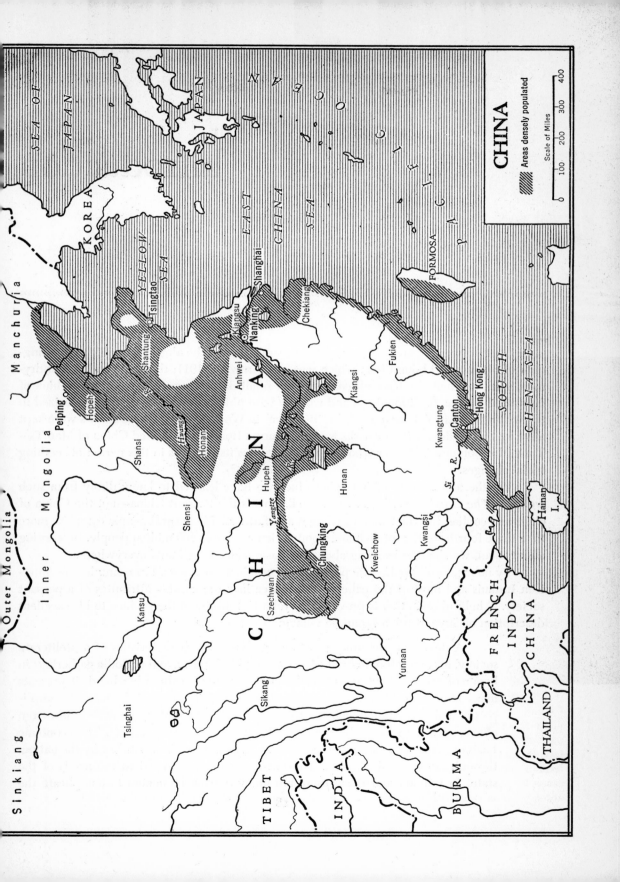

CHINA

Areas densely populated

Scale of Miles

0   100   200   300   400

Sinkiang

Outer Mongolia

Inner Mongolia

Manchuria

SEA OF JAPAN

KOREA

YELLOW SEA

Tsingtao

Shantung

Peiping

Hopeh

Shansi

Kansu

Tsinghai

TIBET

Sikang

Szechwan

Shensi

Honan

Hwang

Chungking

Yangtze

Hupeh

Kweichow

Yunnan

BURMA

INDIA

THAILAND

FRENCH INDO-CHINA

Kwangsi

Kwangtung

Si R.

Canton

Hong Kong

Hunan

Kiangsi

Fukien

Chekiang

Anhwei

Kiangsu

Nanking

Shanghai

C H I N A

EAST CHINA SEA

JAPAN

PACIFIC OCEAN

FORMOSA

SOUTH CHINA SEA

Hainan I.

Introduction

>>

The Western world knows vaguely about several Chinas: the almost feudal Manchu kingdom of pigtails and bound feet, which was overthrown in 1911; the homeland of laundrymen, who, incidentally, have all come from a small district around Canton; the China of cultivated leisure, traditional art, and worldly-wise philosophy successfully popularized in the writings of Lin Yutang; one of the "Big Five" in World War II, whose sinews were kept alive by the traffic moving over the tortuous Burma Road; and the Red China of Mao Tse-Tung, the Communist leader who supposedly guides its fortunes in this period of seething social changes.

Yet there is another China, whose face we have learned to know dimly from such works as *The Good Earth* by Pearl S. Buck. This is the Peasant China—not the China of cities and coolies, but the China of villages and farmers. These rural people comprise more than three fourths of the total Chinese population of almost 400 million people. In learning about them, we shall be learning about the basic traits of peasants everywhere.

By no means all nonliterate peoples are considered peasants. For example, the American Indians and most of the tribesmen of Africa lack the specific attributes of a peasant society. A helpful definition is provided by John F. Embree in the preface to his excellent description of Suye Mura, a Japanese village:

> A peasant community possesses many of the characteristics of a preliterate society, e.g., an intimate local group, strong kinship ties, and periodic gatherings in honor of some deified aspect of the environment. On the other hand, it presents many important differences from the simpler societies; each little peasant group is part of a larger nation which controls its economic life, enforces a code of law from above, and, more recently, requires education in national schools. The economic basis of life is not conditioned entirely by the local requirements but by the nation, through agricultural advisers. The farmer's crop is adjusted to the needs of the state. In religion and ritual there are many outside influences to complicate the

18

simple correlation of rites and social value, festivals and agricultural seasons. While full of local variations, the rituals and festivals are not indigenous to the community nor is the community spiritually self-sufficient.

A longer interpretative discussion of peasant societies is found in Selection 1. This Chinese unit does not attempt to be encyclopedic; rather it serves as an introduction to the ways in which ordinary people live and think, not as statistics but as human beings.

• 1 • Characteristics of Peasant Societies
IRWIN T. SANDERS

The majority of the people in the world today live in folk societies.* These "little people" of the world fill the teeming villages of the Orient, they form the bulk of the population in southern and eastern Europe, and they pass on from one generation to another the colorful costumes and customs of the Latin Americas. In North America evidences of the folk society are numerous: in the French-Canadian villages, among the peons of Mexico, and even in the more isolated areas of the Appalachian mountains.

At first glance it would seem ridiculous to lump together people of so many languages, of so many creeds and colors. However, underneath their apparent divergencies are many ways in which they are much alike. . . .

FOLK SOCIETY A SURVIVAL

One of the most important features of the folk society is that it has stood the test of time. For centuries it has been a way of life to countless millions, carrying with it the au-

* *Folk.* The simpler, uneducated, and less sophisticated members of a population, the masses of a population who by sheer weight of numbers determine the character of the group and preserve and perpetuate its culture traits; also a tribe or group of kindred people. (E. B. Reuter, *Handbook of Sociology,* The Dryden Press, New York, 1941.)

thority of past successes. But now the various folk of the world are finding that they must adjust in part to a twentieth-century mode of living which is as yet virtually untried. It is rather an adventure of man's spirit into the unknown, an adventure which invariably involves a casting away from the moorings that formerly gave the greatest feeling of security. No wonder, then, that peasants look with suspicion and reservation at the new world dawning about them. The folk society represents the tried and true, a survival. The new ways have yet to prove themselves.

*   *   *

Thus one must appreciate the historical continuity of a folk society if one is to understand its nature. It was centuries in the building and it still has a strength that hurried Westerners often fail to grasp. Although breaking down in places, like a windmill perhaps rusting and squeaking, it can still prove more than a match for modern Don Quixotes battling with more self-righteous enthusiasm than social wisdom.

ROOTED IN THE SOIL

Members of a folk society are of the earth, earthy. They vary from climate to climate and country to country in the fervor with which

[From "Characteristics of Peasant Societies," *Farmers of the World: the Development of Agricultural Extension,* edited by Edmund de S. Brunner, Irwin T. Sanders, and Douglas Ensminger, Columbia University Press, New York, 1945. Pp. 37-45. Used by permission.]

they till the soil, but basic to their way of life is the security which agriculture affords. When they choose to work, providing the powers that be are propitious, they know they will reap the fruit of their labors.

In most folk societies much is made of fertility rites, which emphasize fertility of soil as well as fertility of women. Where the cultivation of crops is laborious and where the pressure of population upon food supply is great, land hunger grows and society becomes even more deeply rooted in the soil. This is not to say that labor per se is necessarily glorified, but rather the object of the labor—the soil. Few peasants are sophisticated enough to think of labor as one of the factors of production. Labor is a constant which is taken for granted, whereas the quality of the soil and the caprices of the weather are the variables which interest the people.

Life follows the cycle of the seasons. Because of this, the year has an accentuated variety. The tedium of monotony is periodically broken. The tasks of spring differ from those of fall; the leisure of winter is in striking contrast to the demands of summer.

Thus all of life is strongly colored by the man-land relationship in a folk society. Whether one owns the land oneself, or works for years for those who do, one develops a sense of proprietorship, at times mystical and at times strikingly realistic. Under the Czars the Russian serfs had a saying which combined both mysticism and realism and showed that the peasants felt they had the best of the bargain: *My vashi, zemlia nasha.* "We belong to you but the land belongs to us."

USUALLY FAMILISTIC

Ancestor worship in China may seem to have little in common with a feud in the Kentucky mountains, but in reality both are evidences of the same fundamental belief that the family (with little or no help from the government, from business, from the church) is capable of carrying on the important affairs of life. In a folk society the family tends to occupy two spheres of dominance: over other institutions and over the individual.

The Family Is the Central Institution. In most folk societies the family is the chief economic unit. It produces not only the food but it also makes the soap, the homespun cloth, and the crude furniture; the family frequently constructs the home. In the person of some elder relative acting as midwife or doctor it brings infants into the world and treats the sick with mysteriously concocted remedies. In other words, the economy of the home is largely self-contained. Provision is usually made, however, for specialization along lines which serve the interests of the group as a whole. A wagonmaker, a tanner, a tinsmith, a master builder, a wood carver—these and many more illustrate the contribution of artisans to the physical welfare of the folk society. As the money economy began its encroachment, specialists in money-lending and merchandising became a part of the picture. Despite their coming, the family group was still considered fundamental and these artisans a mere matter of convenience.

Nor was formalized government of much importance in years gone by. Elders, representing large family groupings, conducted the affairs of the community in what they considered to be the best interests of all. In familistic societies throughout the world the people still look with resentment upon the imposition of outside officials who try to enforce laws and local regulations alien to the folkway of rule by older family representatives. Local leaders who are related by blood to the villagers have much more influence in the formation of public opinion than do the officials acting in the interest of a centralized government which the people feel they had no part in creating.

Religion, too, has its place in a familistic society but proves a bulwark rather than a competitor of the family system. Quite often the religious leader does little more than officiate when family crises arrive. In areas where Christianity has been accepted by large numbers of people, the Roman Catholic Church has tended to preserve the folk society while Protestant influences have tended to tear it down, moving it in the direction taken by Euro-American society in general. Islam and the other religions of the East are chiefly protectors of the status quo in which loyalty to one's family seldom conflicts with loyalty to one's religious duty.

Educational agencies and organized sources of recreation are little developed in a folk society. Much training is given in the home, and recreation is supervised by the family or by community opinion in general. Where school systems have been established by outside authorities—governmental or religious—they have tended to neglect the values of a folk society, emphasizing the values of Western society in which the school has an important role.

The Family Comes First, the Individual Second. The individualism of the West contrasts strikingly with the familism of the folk society. In the latter, customary controls still govern family relationships, although the conjugal family, made up of parents and children, is displacing the consanguineal family, comprising, in addition, many relatives of one of the parents. The kinship group traditionally guides the selection of mates by the young, and those earning money outside the home must turn these wages over to the family treasury; in turn, individuals wishing vocational training or education can count upon the support of their relatives, providing their plans follow the family decision. There is also a well-defined division of labor which is based not only on one's sex and age but also upon one's status in the family. Traditionally, the father maintains his dignity by being distant from his children; the mother expects a life of constant toil and frequent childbearing; the children expect little consideration, and they early learn to avoid those things which bring down swift punishment upon their heads.

Linked to this subservience to family roles is the fact that one's status in the community largely depends upon the status of one's family. An erring individual reflects upon the family, because in a folk society there has been no attempt to place the burden of moral training upon the school or the religious organization. It remains a family responsibility. Thus,

in the community at large, who you are (what family name you bear) is more important than what you are as an individual. Nevertheless, relationships remain personal, in contrast to the impersonality of the West, where what you have is frequently more important than what you are, or even the family to which you belong.

CONSERVATISM OF FOLK SOCIETY

The conservatism of peasants is rooted in their social values. Because their way of life provides what they consider their most important needs they are satisfied with it. To be sure, social inertia is present too. It is far more comfortable to cling to the old than to embrace the new. Furthermore, in a folk society individuals who seek to adopt a new practice frequently face the ridicule or even the hostility of their fellow peasants, primarily because of what has been called the strain toward consistency, or the tendency to pull all exceptional individuals down to the level of the average. Individual initiative, which is an important element in innovation, is discouraged by the less ambitious. If a person finds such an environment too restrictive he may migrate to the city and become a part of the urban world, with its different set of values and its impatience with the peasant way of doing things.

The folk society still lacks many of the agencies of communication which make modern life so dynamic. Automobiles and good roads, which encourage extreme mobility, are not yet a part of the folk culture; neither are private radio sets, or family subscriptions to daily papers or memberships in monthly book distributing societies. Communication is oral; the printed page is of little importance even though the literacy rate may be high among certain groups of peasants.

Whether it be a cause of his conservatism or its result, the member of a folk society lives in the present. Of course, the dead hand of the past controls his movements to the extent that it points the way through custom to one activity after another, such as putting blue beads around a donkey's neck or eating a prescribed dish at a particular feast. But in any event there is little apparent concern with the future. The peasant, unless influenced by modern commercialism, cannot conceive of investing a sum of money now in order to get back twice as much years later. This is why it is difficult to put across a forestry program. Individuals see nothing wrong in letting their hungry goats strip the young trees of leaves, for they are not accustomed to looking ahead ten years. They take each day as it comes.

This trait explains as well why members of the folk society will traditionally practice soil conservation where they can see the results in this year's or next year's crops but will do little to build up the soil for benefits to be derived at some more distant time. It is only as one begins to translate courses of action into monetary terms that one begins to sacrifice for the years to come. A barter economy therefore is one centered in the present; only in a money economy can one deal in "futures" whether on the grain exchange or in the speculation of land. By and large, the folk society is a barter economy, where "futures" come low.

SPATIAL AND MENTAL ISOLATION

Part and parcel of this conservatism is the peasant's isolation, spatially and mentally. Roads, for example, exist primarily for use between village and field or between village and market. Good roads in and of themselves rate low in the scale of values. So does going somewhere just for the sake of going. If a pilgrimage is customary then the person will take a pilgrimage. He does not hanker after the strange sights and experiences of a traveler and, in fact, he usually finds these disconcerting, unenjoyable, and even terrifying. But, upon returning to his native haunts, he does bask in the limelight of being called a Hadji, or by some other title which shows that he has followed a time-honored tradition.

In some societies the people believe that the soul of a deceased person must retrace within a matter of days all the earthly journeys of a lifetime. This proves a difficult chore for the spirit of a much-traveled wanderer. While it reflects the social pressure toward permanence of residence, it does not mean that some individual who has been to a distant place loses status upon his return. His tales enliven the neighborhood gatherings and, since he usually casts aspersions upon the food, dress, and manners of people abroad, he strengthens the ethnocentric beliefs of his fellows in the superiority of their own way of life. He does lose status, however, if he compares his own folk or society unfavorably with the "outside world," for to that extent he becomes a nonconformist, a disloyal member of the local group.

There is a marked cleavage between the village, the perpetuator of traditional folkways, and the city, the culture-carrier of the scientific age. For one thing, many city dwellers of peasant origin who have accepted the newer social values of the West have the zeal of new converts in ridiculing the life from which they have come. Although familiar with what the peasants do and why they behave as they do, these converts develop a bias which makes them highly unreliable as social interpreters. Government bureaus in many capitals are filled with these erstwhile peasants zealously struggling for urban status. Then, again, those whose families have been city dwellers for decades have lost touch with the rural people; they regard them as objects of idle curiosity or as fit subjects for exploitation.

Therefore, where the folk society still maintains a pristine vigor, the peasants build up a psychological barrier between themselves and the city dweller which frequency of urban contacts may actually strengthen. The peasant, in other words, does not succumb to the advertising patter which implies that because a thing is new and up-to-date, it is necessarily superior. He evaluates a new article or a new proposal in terms of the accustomed or conventional rather than on the basis of its novelty.

COMPARATIVELY LOW STANDARD OF LIVING

If one should seek an illustration of the changes wrought in Western society by the machine in the past one hundred years let him look first to a folk society. Using this as a starting point modern man can measure his material advancement. Because agrarian societies have an abundance of labor and think seldom in terms of profits, they have little incentive to mechanize their practices in home and field. In many ways they consider the machine a threat and find numerous pretexts for resisting its introduction. They praise what has been made by hand and hunt for flaws in machine-made products.

They produce, where agricultural conditions and size of farms permit, enough for home consumption, with a small surplus to exchange at the market for absolute necessities (such as salt and nails). Living conditions are crude and unsanitary; death rates are high. But this waste of health and life is a part of the fatalistic creed to which most of them subscribe. They have long ago shifted the responsibility to the supernatural and thus are able to adjust to the numerous bereavements that befall them. What the Westerner most frequently associates with a low level of living—unscreened windows, unsanitary handling of meat, improper disposal of sewage, impure and insufficient water, over-crowded houses, raw-boned animals, improper diet—seem relatively unimportant to a peasant. He is more concerned about having sufficient quantities of the kinds of food he likes, having a place to sleep, protection from the weather, and the wherewithal to observe the year's festivities in the recognized fashion. He wants to have enough fuel to see him through the winter, enough provender to keep his animals alive. In some societies, for example in India, many peasants follow an economy of scarcity, calculating how little they will need to grow for the year ahead and concentrating on producing this amount.

* * *

AN INTEGRATED SYSTEM

Robert Redfield has effectively stressed the unity found among the various phases of the folk society. In fact, he points out that the ways the group meets its problems "constitute a coherent and self-consistent system." He goes on to point out:

> Thus it is not enough to say that in the folk society conventional behavior is strongly patterned; we must also say that those patterns are interrelated in thought and action, so that one tends to evoke others, and to be consistent with others. We may add to this that the more remote ends of living are taken as given. The folk society exists not so much in the exchange of useful functions as in common understandings as to the ends given. In the trite phrase the folk society has a "design for living."

Because of this design, large numbers of people who differ from one another in many minor patterns nevertheless feel a sense of belonging to a peasant class. True enough, most of their association is in the primary groups of family and neighborhood or in the larger unit of the village community. But where one goes as a son-in-law or a daughter-in-law to a village many miles away one can readily adjust to such differences in plowing, breadmaking or embroidering a shirt. This is because the social values learned in the early home hold good for the new locale. This awareness of or identification with a peasant class is often vaguely defined among the members of a folk society. Its latent presence, however, is convincingly shown whenever there is an issue between peasants and nonpeasants. The villager will usually stick with other villagers even though they are strangers to him. One can thus accurately speak of the peasant mass and partially understand its staying power in the face of depressions or changing governments.

This unity of the folk society has another important implication. Changes which vitally affect one phase of life have their repercussions all along the line. Nowhere today does the folk society described here exist as a pure type. Everywhere it has taken on some of the characteristics of the Western society. It operates more and more on a money economy, its members are increasingly being drawn into the orbits of centralized governments, commercial interests are making the peasants trinket and gadget conscious, young people grow restive under the age-old conventions, especially when cities present attractive alternatives. These changes would not necessarily destroy the folk society, which still retains much assimilative power, but their effects deserve careful weighing in terms of each so-ciety. Those who seek to change, bear a responsibility that cannot lightly be cast aside, for each innovation launches a train of events which in the long run may produce results not originally desired. This does not mean that the only policy is a "hands off policy," but it does call for careful study of the society one wishes to change. Change there will be. Much will be impersonal and seemingly beyond control. But the consciously planned program of reform, uplift, or regeneration must be thought out and executed against the background of the social fabric, which in a folk society comes all of a piece.

The People and the Habitat

>>

A peasant society is a survival. China's antiquity is a well-known fact. We speak of Chinese history in millennia instead of in centuries and are impressed by its uninterrupted existence. Modern archaeologists are revising some of the earliest dates in the light of new finds and are moving closer to our own day some of the developments toward "civilization"; but even these revisions do not deny the fact that China is an old, old land, where people have long been struggling for existence in time-honored ways.

The theme of the next selection is this historical development. Such an article has the disadvantage of attempting to telescope topics which deserve much more extended treatment. Fortunately, it can be supplemented by information from any standard history or reference work. It does at least indicate something of the sweep of many periods and without this we are not ready to interpret properly the later sections of this book. Confucius, Mencius, Lao-Tse, and Mo Ti are Chinese sages frequently mentioned in this and later selections. Further information about them can be found in an encyclopedia or other reference work. The systems of thought and the cults to which Confucius and Lao-Tse gave rise are described briefly on page 88.

• 2 • Chinese Continuity
DANIEL H. KULP, II

To a student of things Chinese, their most impressive trait is continuity. One cannot travel in China today, from Shanghai to a small village in the most rural region, without wonder at the age-old devices, at the antiquity of the proverbs, the ceremonies, and the rituals —in short, without feeling that he walks through the ages.

Equally impressive to him are the long horns blown by the priests in the Lama Temple of Peiping, the symmetrical beauty of the altar of the Temple of Heaven, the

[From "Chinese Continuity," *The Annals of the American Academy of Political and Social Science,* Vol. 152, Philadelphia, 1930. Pp. 18-29. Used by permission.]

Temple or the Tomb of Confucius, the astronomical instruments, the Great Wall, the camel caravans, the two-wheeled carts, the deep-cut roads, the simple plow, the sea-going junk on the Yangtze, the towering water-wheels of Szechwan, the religious processions of Ningpo or Canton, the looms of Nanking or Huchow, the stacks and stacks of volumes of state history, or the proverbs on the lips of a common coolie—quotations from the Odes or from Confucius, Mencius, or Mo Ti.

Behind the wheelbarrow or the springless cart, the student sees the potter's wheel; back of the plow and the hoe, the primitive digging stick; beyond the tomes of historical records, the simple picture writing when a circle with a dot meant the sun. It seems just a step from China today to the era of beginnings. This long continuity ties the modern Chinese to an ancient past as the bamboo rope leashes a junk struggling to escape with the outgoing tide.

*   *   *

THE TIME FACTOR

Hoary antiquity is the outstanding characteristic of Chinese culture. No other people of the world have had such an ancient origin coupled with a continuous history reaching into the present.

China is a land wherein the fundament of culture was established by transmission from the region northeast of the Caspian Sea, so early that it is identical with that of Europe. In the course of time, war contact with the nomadic Turks on the north and the aboriginals of Asia on the east and the south improved upon this fundament of culture and elaborated it to such a high point that it included not only the technology that could support an ever-increasing population, but also an ideology which included an ethics of societal organization as high as any in the world up to the time of the rise of modern science in the Occident, a religion which was monotheistic, and a philosophy which was monistic and based upon both social ethics and a rudimentary science of astronomy.

*   *   *

THE LAND FACTOR

To appreciate the full importance of the land factor in Chinese continuity, one must remember that topography may work for or against contact. On the one hand, the very location of the geographic area in relation to Europe and the Mediterranean Basin has made for isolation, which accounts in part for the peculiarities of Chinese culture in contrast with the Europeo-American. On the other hand, that same location, being contiguous to the plains on the north and the west, has made for contact with the fighting nomads—to the south, for contact with the uncivilized tribes; while the Pacific Coast afforded opportunity for shipping. These latter conditions operated for a similarity of culture throughout eastern Asia—China, Japan, and Korea.

Not only locus but also size of land mass has made for continuity. With its southern extremity in Hainan, China extends as far north as the Amur; with its western end in the Pamirs, it reaches the Pacific. It contains nearly four and a half million square miles with a climatic range from the subtropical regions of the south to the cold-temperate, almost subarctic, areas of the north.

Though there is a difference of thirty-five degrees in latitude between the northern and southern extremities, the climate is greatly affected by topographic features. The cold of the high mountains in the west and the south, the heat and the moisture of the Yunnan jungles, the aridity of Turkestan, the constancy of the Han and Yangtze, and the unreliability of the Hwai and Yellow Rivers, all show that any climate of the world may be found somewhere in China.

Then to locus and size must be added fertility, for the wide coastal plains built up by the great rivers flowing into the ocean and revived by frequent floods, or covered with the rich loess deposited by the winds from the Gobi Desert, have been capable of supporting some of the most congested areas of the world.

This same land mass has been the home of

the races of China for approximately the last ten millennia.

RACES

China has always been occupied by a variety of races. The picture one gets at the dawn of history is somewhat as follows: on the north the Mongols, the Turks, the Manchus, the Koreans, the Tungus, and minor tribes of Buriats, Goldi, and Dahurs; on the northwest the Sarts and the Hindus; on the west the Tibetans, the Lolos, and the Mantzu; and on the south the Shans, the Miao, the Yao, and the Tung Chia, or cave dwellers. The ancestors of these modern peoples possessed the whole area now known as China. They were aboriginal tribes, whose origins are obscure in prehistory and are yet to be unraveled by archeological researches. They are frequently referred to as the Miao, the Man, the Ti, and the Yueh in ancient literature. They were the barbarians through whose conquest and by whose tribute the glory that was China was built.

But who were the Chinese? They were invading tribes not racially Chinese at all. They came from Central Asia in successive waves of migration, pushed out by economic competition due to the gradual desiccation of great inland seas, on whose shores once flourished a high civilization. Entering from the northwest, they penetrated the upper reaches of the Yellow River and settled permanently in the lower reaches or what is generally the area now occupied by Chihli, Shansi and Shantung. Continuous conquest by war enabled the descendants of these invaders to establish a political hegemony over the aboriginals, although the nomads of the north and the Miao of the southwest long retained their independence.

By sending out members of the royal family to rule over the conquered peoples, governmental centers were set up. These later became city-states and centers from which radiated the culture brought in by the invaders. Meanwhile, these rulers and their descendants intermarried with the aboriginals, developed new ruling houses, and merged the weaker city-states into kingdoms, until, by 1122 B.C., the House of Chou emerged supreme in the center of ancient culture and government. During this dynasty, political power was extended to the far south and was organized under a feudal system.

Thus there is much evidence both direct and indirect to support the theory that the modern "Chinese" are (1) the heirs of the invading culture bearers, who themselves were gradually amalgamated out of existence, but (2) racially, descendants of aboriginal tribes.

At any rate, the Chou Dynasty represents an era of nearly nine centuries during which the barbarians were gradually assimilated into the "Chinese" culture, although the name China does not attach to land or people generally until Chin Shih Hwang Ti, the first emperor, 221 B.C.

CULTURE

The adaptation of peoples to the various conditions of topography and climate, with a concomitant supply of food resources, through time produces characteristic culture complexes.

. . . In terms of material traits, North and South China represent two great culture areas with differences in their racial bases, the South China complex being fundamentally aboriginal and the North China complex being introduced by invaders.

THE LEGENDARY PERIOD

Even before the establishment of the Chou Dynasty, these northern culture bearers had achieved a high civilization. [The legendary history given here is partly supported by archeological findings, but some of these dates are many centuries too early. Iron, for example, actually appears first in the seventh century B.C.] They had agriculture and, as early as the twenty-third century, a Minister of Agriculture; certain use of iron as early as 1844 B.C.; and an acquaintance with such metals as gold, silver, copper, mercury, and lead. Horses date from the twenty-second century, as do also such animals as oxen, sheep, swine, and dogs. The people engaged in weaving silk, linen, and hair cloth and practiced dyeing in various colors—red, yellow, blue, and black. They used vessels of bronze and had bows, arrows, spears, battle axes, shields, and armor. Knives, hatchets, and plows were the principal tools. Language was in written form, as is evidenced by the famous bamboo books. Knowledge of music was very high. They possessed eight kinds of musical instruments—wind and string instruments, drums, cymbals, bells, musical stones, and the rattle, as well as pitch pipes, which according to Sinologues evidence a knowledge of mathematics. They used carts drawn by horses for transportation, and chariots in battle. Government was highly organized into a feudal monarchy with five grades of rank—duke, marquis, earl, viscount and baron—even as in Europe. The monarch was assisted by a premier and a cabinet of six ministers of religion, education, agriculture, works, justice, and communication, with subordinate ones for astronomy, music and forestry.

The monarch's governmental robes were decorated with emblems of the sun, the moon, the constellations, the dragon, the phoenix, and mountains on the upper garment. On the lower were the sacrificial cup, the aquatic plant, the flame, grain, the battle axe and *fu*. These indicated the various functions of the monarch and were worn by rulers of China until 1912, when the Republic was established. Even then, some of them were preserved in the seal of the new Government.

There is reasonable evidence of the existence of an elementary science and possibly of the establishment of schools. The people had a knowledge of astronomy and used a lunar-solar calendar. Astrology flourished because of their belief in the power of the stars to determine human affairs. There was a definite body of law and a code of punishment. A whole hierarchy of religious beings was worshipped under the leadership of the monarch. Worship was characterized by music and by a dance which was a rhythmic swaying of the body and a waving of palms and battle axes.

Their ethical teachings were high, as for example from the *Shu King:*

> Go not to excess in pleasure. Put away evil without hesitatiton. . . . Study to have all your purposes in accord with reason. . . . Calamities sent by Heaven may be averted; from those brought upon a man by himself there is no escape. . . . It is not the knowing, but the doing that is difficult.

Any one more or less familiar with China will recognize that with few exceptions these various forms of cultural achievements have continued down to recent times and, as noted before, reach back in their origins beyond these eras to the time when the ancestors of the invaders lived in Central Asia. Such is the general outline of the culture which had been achieved previous to the establishment of the Chou Dynasty in the twelfth century B.C.

CHOU DYNASTY—THE GOLDEN AGE

With the achievements previously attained, it is not surprising that the Chou Dynasty, during its nine hundred years of sway, created what is known as the Golden Age. It was during this period that the main features of Chinese thought and practice were crystallized and stereotyped in such forms that they have continued to the present.

It would be impossible to consider in detail all of the achievements which have continued in one form or another to recent times, but a few will suffice to support the fact of long cultural continuities.

In government, the feudalistic system which was begun during the Hsia and Shang Dynasties continued as the basis of organization and control. The government itself was on a familistic basis with all of the feudal lords at the beginning of the dynasty near relatives to the king. By it, political power was tremendously expanded.

In 684 B.C. the Marquis of Ch'i established a government monopoly in the manufacture of salt and iron in order to increase his wealth. This was the origin of the famous Salt Gabelle, still one of the principal sources of revenue. The border tariffs, or what is known now as *Likin,* were established during this period also as a source of revenue. Also one finds the system of tithing, in which the unit of organization was ten households—a system that was retained by the late Manchu Dynasty. Over a tithing were the headmen or village elders, who represented their villages in relation to the government. They were the first census takers and were responsible to the government for the conduct of the villagers and for the upkeep of the physical condition of the villages, such as walls, streets, lighting, police, and village temple and theater. They provided schools, built markets, and adjudged local disputes. They also protected the villagers from the exploitation of the officials, paid the customary taxes, and protested extra impositions. Thus in very early times was established the general scheme of social organization which rendered revenue to the central government and yet provided a high degree of local autonomy—the true basis of the modern democratic movement in China.

During this same period one finds the first effort at a League of Nations. In 545 B.C. Hsiang Hsu, a minister of the state of Sung, invited the ministers from fourteen different states to convene and draw up a covenant to put an end to war. While this covenant did not last long, it did establish a precedent which from time to time since then has been imitated.

By this time also the practice of revolution was firmly rooted. Already, the great cycle of political power had been amply revealed. A powerful lord skilled in fighting enlarged his sway and finally overthrew the last of a decadent dynastic line. He established a new house which waxed in power and glory, only to fall after a period of decadence and corruption to the vigor of some newly emergent leader who listened to the voice of the people, which is "the voice of Heaven." . . .

SOCIAL CLASSES

In a highly paternalistic system, the common people were grouped in nine classes, according to their occupations: (1) farmers, (2) gardeners, (3) woodmen, (4) herdsmen, (5) artisans, (6) merchants, (7) women weavers of silk and linen, (8) servants, (9) unskilled laborers with a superintendent in charge of each group.

Life was highly schematized, at least theoretically, though probably in practice the rigidity of the scheme broke down. That the general stereotype, or theory of organization of life continued is shown by the fact that even today, it is customary to classify people into (1) scholars, (2) landworkers, (3) artisans, (4) merchants, (5) housewives, (6) menials and unskilled workers, and (7) soldiers. Such classes are not to be considered as castes, for any one could become a scholar and a scholar could become an official. Only outcasts, convicts, slaves, actors, ragpickers, barbers, and prostitutes were not eligible to rise in the social scale.

MARRIAGE AND THE FAMILY

The institutions of marriage and the family were established in a form in which they have continued to the present. The marriage broker or go-between, the gifts, the reception of the proposal of marriage in the ancestral temple, and the practice of concubinage were common among the nobility and were imitated by those of lower rank.

Familist ethics of filial piety were stereotyped and put into record and have been influential from that period down to today.

MATERIAL CULTURE

In the buildings of the well-to-do, the characteristic architecture was already developed both in floor plan and decoration. The poor, then as now, lived in mud huts or shacks with walls and roofs made of interwoven reeds. Chairs were not used at that time, though furniture was decorated with mother of pearl, as is common today.

Cookery was highly developed. Food was served in dishes of bamboo, earthenware, and bronze, and eaten with chopsticks.

The dress of the ancient people was quite similar to that common up to the close of the Manchu Dynasty, generally made of silk and linen. The poor people grew fat in winter when they added their many quilted garments, for, then as now, their houses were not heated except with braziers. Jade ornaments were common and combs were instruments of decoration as well as for arranging the hair. The chief amusements were archery, music, drinking, fencing, cockfighting, and hunting.

This period also saw the invention of the compass.

Money was in use, which argues for commercial practices beyond the barter type. It was made of bronze in the form of a conventionalized spade and sword or knife. From the round hole at the end of the latter evolved the [perforated Chinese coin known as the] "cash."

LITERATURE AND PHILOSOPHY

To the Chinese scholar of today, the Chou Dynasty is the Golden Age not because of these various cultural achievements just indicated, but because of the work of the great scholars and philosophers, Confucius, Mencius, Lao Tze, Chuang Tzu, Mo Ti, and Hsün Tzu. Confucius gathered and edited the fragmentary records of early times and thus put into permanent form the accumulations of philosophy, ethics and government. Then it was that the Four Books and the Five Classics took form and through the influence of Confucius' disciples became the basis of Chinese ideology. Of such influence was Confucius that his teachings had become so sacrosanct within two centuries that when Chin Shih Hwang Ti wanted to do away with the feudalism of Chou he was opposed by the conservative scholars because the Master had approved of it. The emperor ordered the classics burned and the scholars put to death, but to no avail.

LATER CULTURAL ACHIEVEMENTS

Among the inventions important in the culture of China today and achieved subsequently to Chou are: modification of ancient script, invention of the brush pen and ink, and beginning of the building of the Great Wall, in the Chin Dynasty; sacrificing at the tomb of Confucius (195 B.C.), rise of alchemy, invention of paper, the great history of Sse-ma Ch'ien—a model for all official histories since —introduction of Buddhism, change of Taoism from philosophy to religion, and civil service examinations, in the Han Dynasty (206 B.C.-220 A.D.); a commercial colony of Arabs and Indians at Canton (300 A.D.) and commissions from Rome by sea, the first Buddhist pagoda built about 250 A.D. and the flourishing of Buddhism and Buddhist art, the use of chairs, and the first record of tea-drinking as a social custom, during the period of the Three Kingdoms and the Sui Dynasty (221-618 A.D.); and during the T'ang Dynasty, Christianity brought by Nestorians and Mohammedanism by the Arabs, rise of the secular theater under the influence of the "Pear Garden," and most important, the invention of printing and the first book, movable type (1041-1049 A.D.), and the issuance of paper money.

THE TECHNIQUES OF CONTINUITY

The techniques by which these culture complexes and behavior patterns were transmitted are to be found in the institutions of Chinese life, which represent the same sociological features as institutions anywhere. While certain phases of them in one historical period or another were raised to the level of statute laws, they operated mainly as common law and were administered not so much through the control of provincial or central governments as through the administrative functions of the elders or familistic heads.

In any analysis of Chinese society, one can secure a clear understanding of the processes and organizations only by appreciating the basic aspect of familism—a type of society in which all values are referred to family welfare. Furthermore, family welfare in this instance must be defined not only in terms of present generations but more emphatically in terms of family continuity and the welfare of the ancestral spirits. Thus one finds in the functioning of the total familist complex not only the biological continuity of the folk but also the concomitant maintenances, material and spiritual.

The bulk of the Chinese population resides in villages scattered throughout the country-side and these villages generally are occupied by one familist organization or sib. Within the village as a unit of social organization, all the principal institutions may be found—eco-nomic, religious, political, judicial, and recre-ational. The mechanisms of transportation are for the bulk of the population limited to the village and the surrounding fields, which makes the rate of mobility very low.

*   *   *

Thus the land factor, the race factor, and the culture factor through time have com-bined to produce a milieu especially effective for social continuity. Life is organized on an intimate, personal, blood basis. It is made sacrosanct by the ideals of filial piety and the practices and attitudes of ancestral worship.

ANCESTRAL WORSHIP

Aside from the general condition of isola-tion of China from the culture currents of the Occident, and aside from the effects of a uni-versal governmental language, the peculiar features that operated for the high degree of continuity in China can be found in ancestral worship. The Chinese youth feels himself constantly surrounded by a world of spirits, who harm or help him according to his atti-tude and behavior in respect to them. Let him honor them and worship them, and fortune will be his. He holds the same attitude in re-lation to his immediate progenitors, not only because the principle of filial piety prescribes it, but also because he knows that in time they too will be ancestral spirits. Thus the young are made highly suggestible to values which inhere in the family complex; values which make for the prestige of elders, for obedience, conformity, and social harmony. To depart from the folkways is, therefore, to lose status in the familist group—an event very rare except during the last few decades, when, under the impact of Western cultures,

individualization has tremendously increased.

*   *   *

FAMILIST GROUP PRACTICES

There is evidence that from time immemo-rial, the great majority of the people have been relatively poor, so that the struggle for exist-ence has always been hard. In order to meet these needs, the familist group developed certain mutual aid features which were based partly upon the religious institutions. Usually, each village has a group of voluntary associa-tions through which the members help one another in their economic practices, such as watering fields, harvesting crops, making sugar, repairing dikes, and the like. Connected with the ancestral hall of each village is a certain parcel of land, the income to be used for the upkeep of the hall, the expenses con-nected with rites and ceremonies of ancestral worship, and the care of the aged and the needy. Normally, therefore, one does not find in Chinese society the need for public charita-ble aid as in other societies. The beggars and needy folk are usually kin-wrecked, or are small family groups whose economic bases have been destroyed by catastrophic phenom-ena, such as plagues or floods.

Unless pressed by economic necessity, fami-list groups continue in one place for long periods of time. The lands are owned by the heads of immediate families, who have in-herited them from their immediate fathers and who will in turn parcel them out equally to the male offspring. Thus, through owner-ship and inheritance, residence is very con-tinuous. This makes for a stable kind of life by reducing contacts and enhancing conti-nuity.

With the exception of some factory pro-duction in such cities as Shanghai, Hankow, Tientsin, and Wusih, Chinese industry is do-mestic handicraft. Masters work in their own home-shops, assisted by apprentices whose families are either relatives or friends of the artisan. Both belong to the same trade guild. The guilds not only have control of standards of work, prices, and apprentices, but also frequently develop their own educational and recreational services. Thus the economic techniques are transmitted under conditions most favorable to continuity, i.e., personal instruction of a practical kind by the masters, and an organization that guarantees the maintenance of sanctioned standards through group pressures.

The persistence of home industry is amazing to a Westerner. Along the road from Shanghai to Woosung, within walking distance of Yangtzepoo, the greatest modern textile manufacturing district in China, one may still see old women spinning cotton and reeling the warp for the weaving of cotton cloth. The daughters of these same old women are working in the factories tending power reels and looms, yet frequently clothed in homespun! Ancient practice supports domestic thrift. One may well doubt, however, whether such continuity can survive another generation of industrialism.

EDUCATION

The political autonomy of Chinese villages accentuates the foregoing conditions, because it centers responsibility and authority within the village itself.

One responsibility which in time became a matter of pride was the education of the youth in the literature and philosophy characteristic of the country as a whole. This made for the continuity of the national ideology. Each long-established village aimed to produce scholars who could successfully compete in the civil service examinations and thereby become eligible to enter officialdom.

The examinations were based upon the classical literature and philosophy and were judged in terms of literary excellence crystallized in the standards of the famous eight-legged essays. To be able to quote profusely and to comment upon the writings of the sages and historians of early ages, particularly of the T'ang and Chou Dynasties, according to the stereotyped standards, was the key to success.

The village scholar conducted his school with methods of rote memory and strict ad-

herence to the literary language and products of the past. In forms of composition, thought, and methods of writing, each generation imitated the great literary products and thus transmitted the standard patterns from generation to generation.

In addition to the schools, which were the chief formal agents of transmitting these continuities, well-established villages usually included scholars' halls, dedicated to those who had successfully passed state examinations—places where scholars could congregate and converse on philosophy and religion. The effect of all this was to place the scholar first in social rank, giving to literary capacity a prestige second only to the worship of ancestors. Leadership tended to fall into the hands of those who combined the status of family elders and holders of degrees plus natural capacity; all of which tremendously enhanced the prestige of literary learning and accentuated the continuities effected through the traditional forms of education.

As an outgrowth of the literary tradition, there appeared in China those who corresponded to the minnesingers of Europe; poor, wandering scholars who traveled from village to village, or local village scholars, who would repair to village tearooms and there recount the tales of ancient folklore, recite poems, or detail the exploits of the great heroes. Thus, much of the learning was informally transmitted to the lower classes in the form of tales and proverbs. Both types suggested definite behavior patterns, for the tales as well as the proverbs always had their moral and ethical implications.

AESTHETICS

Art, too, reenforced the continuities of Chinese life in the use of the brush and ink, in the fine forms of calligraphy and also in the creation of symbolic art highly conventionalized and adapted to achievements with the brush, under the limitations of the oblong mural hangings. Even today, one will find in the scholars' hall or ancestral hall of almost any village, color paintings of the famous ancestors of the family.

But the art of lacquer with the paintings and decorations flourishes ubiquitously in connection with ancestral worship. For not only in the village ancestral hall or the village temple, but also in the ancestral hall of the large homestead, one will find beautiful cabinets ornately decorated. Within these are placed the tablets of the ancestors of the present sib, arranged in a hierarchy, generation after generation, some of them extending back a thousand years or more. The family lore is replete with the deeds of these ancestors. They serve as standards of behavior to the young, who are urged to emulate them.

In the Buddhist and Taoist temples art has flourished in statuary, architecture, paintings and calligraphy. The pictorial decorations of houses, particularly in the South, representing heroic deeds or famous people of tradition, constantly remind the youth of a glorious past and fill him with pride of ancestry, race, and culture.

Music is common in every village, for the truly cultured scholar, the ideal gentleman of Confucian standard, is skilled in the use of musical instruments as in poetry and philosophy. Traveling musicians constantly go about entertaining the patrons of teahouses, and skilled performers always accompany the dramatic presentations. Wandering theatrical troupes go from village to village and present the ancient historical plays and tales in the village theater. In all their forms, the aesthetic arts derive their techniques and standards of excellence from the past and are effective means not only of transmitting the ancient ideologies but also of reenforcing the prestige of that past.

ANTIQUITY SHAPES THE PRESENT

Thus, through their units of political and social organization, through their imitation of economic practices—"farmers of forty centuries"—in their worship of ancestors, in their filial piety and respect for elders, in their literary traditions, in their aesthetics, and even in their recreations, Chinese institutions trace their origins and find their perennial inspiration in antiquity.

So in general have the races of China, locked in a great land mass, through forty centuries evolved a culture predominantly organized to secure continuity of practices, attitudes, and ideals. Innovations and reforms might occur, rebellions might overturn dynasties, foreign nations might intrigue for control, yet the general current of life in the familist agricultural villages swept on, bearing into the present the vigor of an ancient heritage.

The continuity of Chinese life, as we have seen above, is based in part on China's geographical factors of location, size, topographic features, and soil. The next two selections examine these more closely. The first, by J. R. Schwendeman, looks at China as a whole and provides an over-all view of the Chinese peasant's adjustments to many problems of his habitat. The second, by George B. Cressey, which deals with the regional differences between North and South China, will enable us quickly to locate geographical references made in later selections.

• 3 • Geographic Features of the Habitat of the Chinese Peasant

J. R. SCHWENDEMAN

Nearly one-fourth of all the people in the world live in China Proper. By another comparison, more people live in China Proper than live in the vast lands of North America, South America, Africa, and Australia combined. But these astounding comparative statements only introduce still more incredible facts about the world's most densely occupied habitat.

Most people think of China as a vast empire teeming with people. China is a vast empire, it is true, of 4,516,934 square miles, and larger than the United States by more than one million square miles, but only the seaward fringe teems with people. Here on the coastal deltas and flood plains of China's great rivers live at least eighty per cent of the Chinese. This land they occupy so densely would only extend over the approximate area of the Cotton Belt of the United States. It would approach 400,000 square miles and be approximately ten per cent of the Chinese Empire.

A second impressive association, from the geographic point of view, is that the Chinese habitat is among the least desirable of the larger, highly cultured and densely occupied lands of the world. The Chinese are plagued by more problems from the physical environment than most well-occupied lands. Regardless of the tremendous industry of the Chinese peasant, he has succeeded no better in overcoming these vicissitudes of nature than mankind in general and excels the rest of mankind only by enduring suffering in famine, violent death, and destruction of property.

Most of China's land is rough, mountainous, and dry. The fertile plains are almost entirely river-made and largely subject to flood; there are no producing upland plains, such as in the United States and Europe. Loessland, the only exception in China

Proper, is relatively small and is being eaten away by erosion.

China's rainfall is subject to the unpredictable droughts which have been so severe and extensive as to create severe famine conditions. Over North China the rainfall comes almost entirely in the summer months. This feature of the precipitation regime creates serious water supply problems during the winter, and summer floods which destroy growing crops. The year round rainfall of western Europe and eastern United States is vastly more dependable and more evenly distributed.

Moreover, China is poorly supplied with forest products and lacks adequate quantity and quality in many important minerals, especially iron.

Finally, regardless of these many natural difficulties, China's millions strive to live by farming. Three-fourths of the population are peasant farmers. China's cropped lands are little more than half of those of the United States and are not supplemented by the extensive or desirable pasture lands found in the United States and Europe.

The Chinese peasant has taken his well-watered and fertile river valleys and has worked out a system of existence. Perhaps his major failure has been in achieving a balance and diversity in his economy.

POSITION

The people we have referred to as the Chinese peasant, and which we propose to study, live in a large habitat of one and one-half million square miles called China Proper. Politically, China Proper is composed of eighteen provinces located in eastern Asia. While one and one-half million square miles is a huge living space, it is by comparison but a doorstep to the vast interior of Asia, the world's largest continent covering one-third the earth, or 16,494,217 square miles.

Of China's position throughout the ages, already touched upon briefly in the preceding selection, George B. Cressey says,

> Southeastern Asia is almost an oasis, largely self-sufficient and isolated from the rest of mankind. Until the era of modern travel, the most perfect barriers surrounded China on all sides. Towering plateaus, arid deserts, tropical forests, and the widest of the oceans all helped to preserve the unity of China. Nowhere near by was there an equal neighbor, except in India which was months away. It is but natural that the Chinese thought of themselves as living in the "Middle Kingdom."

Even today with modern transport facilities, China's isolated position is one of the most secure in the world and her dominantly rough terrain will retard the development of effective communication. Here Cressey says,

> Overland travel has been confined to cart roads and flagstone trails, roughly characteristic of the North and the South respectively. Two-wheeled springless carts with narrow iron-studded wheels grind the earth into dusty ruts in the dry season and churn it into deep mud after the rains. Under such conditions one does not travel for pleasure. Sedan chairs are scarcely more comfortable. Where animals are not available long lines of coolies carry salt, tea, cloth and kerosene. . . . Since the means of travel are slow and inefficient, commerce requires an abnormally large number of people. Where man is so numerous and lives so close to the minimum, coolie carriers work for a pittance. It is thus cheaper to wear men down than to keep roads up.

So China remains the most inaccessible of all highly cultured and densely populated areas.

LANDSCAPE

China Proper is mainly a mountainous country. Over much of the area slopes are so steep that normal agriculture is impossible. The most significant mountain range is the Tsingling Shan. This is the mountain range that separates the North from the South, and it is the barrier on which the moist winds from the Pacific lose much of their moisture and against which the cold and dusty northwest winter winds break their force. It separates the moist agricultural lands of Central and South China from the brown and dusty but rich soils of the Northwest so that even the casual visitor to China is struck by these fundamental differences. Soils, crops, natural vegetation, houses and even the habits of the peoples themselves are different. Thus everywhere in China the mountains are a major factor in farming, in erosion control, in floods, and in communication.

Encircling China on the west are such vast mountain walls as the all but impenetrable Tibet, the rugged plateau of Yunnan, and the arid Mongolian Plateau. Access to the interior is only through such occasional passes as the famous Jade Gate near Lanchow.

China Proper has practically no intermediate landscape in the form of low plateaus and upland plains. Opposed to the extreme of rough, hilly and mountainous areas are the low river flood plains and deltas. The largest of these is the combined delta of China's two greatest rivers, the Yangtze and the Yellow. This delta plain is called the Chinese Plain and borders the Yellow Sea in southern extent to the Gulf of Pohai in its northern limits. Its area is about 125,000 square miles. This plain is the heart of classical China and is considered the most occupied land on earth. The present population is approximately 80 million people and 650 persons per square mile.

The alluvial plains of the Yangtze Valley are similar to those of the Chinese Plain but because the Yangtze River is navigable by ocean vessels this plain is commercially more important. This plain is about 75,000 square miles in extent and has a population of nearly 70 million people.

The other plains of China, including the Chengtu Plain of Czechwan, are alluvial in origin and mainly flood plains. They lie mostly along the Chinese coast south of the Yangtze including the large delta and valley plains of the Si Kiang, or are along the inland streams of the great Yangtze-Kiang basin. Together these plains provide the homelands for roughly eighty per cent of China's population, for on these plains productive soil, water supply, water transport, and climate combine to make possible the intensive agrarian economy evolved by the Chinese peasant.

CLIMATE

China Proper extends south-north from the tropics through most of the temperate zone and, therefore, has a wide climatic range. This part of China lies between the twentieth and forty-second parallels north—twenty-two degrees and something over 1500 miles. In North America this would extend from southernmost Cuba to New York.

In addition to this important north-south variation in climate, there are two other major features every student must note. First, there is the continental influence from the world's largest land mass, which is expressed in the monsoonal rhythm greatly intensifying the seasonal distribution of rainfall and temperature. For instance, winter temperatures in China's interior are colder than any other place in the world of equal latitude; and rainfall is largely confined to summer over most of China. Second, the climate is sufficiently temperate to admit of intensive culture but unpredictable and intense extremes in drought and floods occur.

Broadly speaking, China is divided into two climatic provinces, North and South. North China is generally considered the area north of the Tsingling Shan and its extension, the Hwaiyang Shan ranges. In this northern province the winters are cold, windy, dry, and dusty. The average January temperature is 23.5°F. at Peiping in the same latitude as Philadelphia, where the January average is 34.4°F. Philadelphia is subject to extreme continental influences in winter but the continental monsoonal influence of Asia

is far more intense. Practically no rain and little snow falls on the average from late September to late May at Peiping, thus creating severe seasonal moisture and water supply problems. The rainy season is mainly restricted to the summer months of June, July, and August. The average July rainfall of nine inches is twice that for any one month of the year in eastern United States. Moreover, the annual fluctuation of summer rainfall is terrific, varying from practically nothing to as much as two feet in a single month. Indeed, a report of twenty-three inches in thirty-three hours is on record. Summer rainfall in the eastern United States is rarely disastrously erratic, either wet or dry.

South of the Tsingling Shan are two distinct types of climate, that of central China of the Yangtze basin and that of the subtropical south. Both show the monsoonal influence in marked seasonal ranges in temperature and rainfall, although both are far from the extremes of North China in this respect. At Shanghai winters are cool to cold, with January averages at 37°F. Summers are hot at 80°F. for July. Rain falls the year round but varies from 1.3 inches for December to 7.4 inches in July. Hence, summer river stages are high and, at times, with excessive rainfall, reach terribly destructive stages.

While subtropical China shows mild winters (60°F.) and hot summers (82°F.) and marked seasonal rainfall distribution (1.1 inches to 15.1 on the average), the erratic tendencies of drought to flood are practically absent. This is true also for the protected inland basin of Szechwan of the upper Yangtze.

The monsoons are the seasonal winds of Asia which are unique among world winds for their seasonal reversal and persistence. In China the prevailing direction is northwest in winter making them cold, dry and dust-laden. In summer they prevail from the southeast, making them hot and moisture-laden.

Kendrew says, in *Climates of the Continents* (Oxford, 1942),

In winter atmospheric pressure is very high over Central Asia and the gradient over China steep. Strong winds blow out from the deserts of the interior, which are very cold at this season, and descend as a great cataract over the plateau edge, which is here undefended by mountain ramparts to China. Their descent warms them somewhat but they are still felt as icy blasts, especially in northern China, and they are so strong that they carry clouds of dust and on the China Sea navigation is often interrupted by bad visibility. . . . The winter monsoon is at its strongest in December, January, and February. . . . In May the summer low pressures are already developed over the interior of the continent and they deepen in June and July. The prevailing winds over all China are **south and southeast**, warm and rainy. . . . The summer monsoon, the season of rain and cloud and damp enervating heat, comes to an end in September. . . .

And many are the ways by which the Chinese peasant adjusts his routine of living to this monsoonal rhythm.

According to *China, Land of Famine,* published by the American Geographical Society:

Without doubt the worst famines in China have been caused by a lack of sufficient rainfall for a long period. Lack of rain occurs most often in northern and central China. While most other natural disasters result in only a partial destruction of the crops, a drought makes a normally flourishing countryside a barren waste. When it is remembered that in China almost the entire population exists by agriculture, it can be imagined what effect a dry period has, especially if it continues for two or three years, as sometimes happens. In time of drought it is only in those districts where irrigation is practiced that any crop at all can be harvested. . . .

It has been estimated by Dwight W. Edwards in his report *The North China Famine 1920-21* that in the great drought of those years, 500,000 people perished and nearly twenty million people were made destitute.

Floods in China are especially destructive since they occur in summer and since the greatest density of population is on the flood plains. Flood disasters occur in both the Yellow and Yangtze basins. The Yellow River is especially a problem since its current has to be contained by dikes for the river bed has been built up by silt until the river flows between its man-made dike banks above the countryside. When a flood occurs and the dikes break, hundreds of square miles—often thousands—are inundated. Sometimes the Yellow River changes its course and disaster results. Such an instance is the flood of 1887-1889 when a break occurred in the southern dike in the province of Honan. According to Chinese official records, more than 2,000,000 people lost their lives either from drowning or from starvation during the resulting famine, and nearly the whole province of Honan south of the river was inundated.

Typhoons and locusts are other calamities which are climatic or arise from climatic conditions. The typhoons are localized to the coastal areas and occur in the fall. Occasionally they are terrifically destructive. Inland they cause torrential rains but the winds lose their violence.

The locusts are listed as one of the three principal natural causes of famine along with flood and drought. This pest, which consumes the growing crops, leaves the countryside as barren as does a protracted drought. They are known to attack and absolutely ruin even trees. In this respect they are more damaging than drought or flood.

NATURAL RESOURCES

From the foregoing accounts it can be readily stated that China's greatest natural assets are her soil, level land, rivers, and other water supply and certain phases of climate. Her greatest handicaps lie in lack of forests and grasses and in the prevalence of mountains and recurring natural calamities.

On the basis of her natural advantages the Chinese provide more food directly from the land than is being accomplished by any other people in the world in a similar area. But it is not quite fair to say that the story of crops tells their sole adjustment to their habitat. In addition, they have a finely adjusted domestic animal economy which provides nonhuman power, a valuable supplement to diet, and moreover these animals subsist as scavengers, feeding upon waste and other inedible products which would otherwise be lost. The story of China's near half-billion fowl—chickens, ducks, geese, and turkeys, 75 million pigs, or 20 million water buffalo and oxen is a fascinating facet of peasant economy and a remarkable geographic adjustment. The Chinese also have some cattle, horses, mules, sheep, goats, and burros.

These resources and resource adjustments are major but among such a dense population such mineral resources as salt, clay and stone are vital and such a plant as bamboo is indispensable. Only a brief survey can be given of these many but essential resources.

Because of China's vegetable diet, salt is probably her most vital mineral. Eighty per cent of her supply comes from evaporating sea water and is one of the several important geographic contributions of the sea to China —fish, transportation, especially coastwise, protection, climatic control, and the dilution of continental wastes being other important benefits. Other sources of salt are from the inclosed lakes of Mongolia and the 26 districts of salt wells in Szechwan. Incredible as it may seem, the total number of these wells is estimated at 70,000 and they have been dug by native methods, some to depths of two to three thousand feet!

Sand, clay, and stone for homes, as well as pottery, tile, china, and domestic implements are invaluable in the Chinese Peasant stage of economy. Bamboo, used for every conceivable domestic implement from chop sticks to sedan chairs and musical instruments, would also rank in this category along with wood used for charcoal and weeds and dried stalks of the field used for fuel.

As to economic minerals such as coal, iron, and copper, China ranks as a minor nation. Of these, coal is uppermost. It is widespread over China, but 90 per cent is in the Loess Highlands (Ordos) with the second district in the Red Basin (Szechwan). China uses 40 million tons annually which is small compared to such an industrial nation as the United States which uses nearly 600 million tons. Even so, Chinese industries now use 15 million tons, a good beginning, and Chinese homes use 12 million tons for fuel. Coal in China has additional significance since she has practically no petroleum and must import such products as kerosene, which is widely used.

Iron, the world's most important industrial mineral, is very limited, which is a most serious deficiency. Most important deposits are along the Yangtze Valley with Tayeh in Hupei the leading center. Smaller localities are in Honan and Shantung. (Note these are in China Proper and do not take into account the important deposits in Manchuria.) Iron does not occur near good deposits of coking coal which adds to its use problems. Much as the Chinese peasant uses iron in such simple but universally found implements as the sickle and the hoe, the total annual consumption per capita is only three pounds as compared to 550 pounds per capita in the United States.

Other minerals of significant occurrence are tin, Kochin district in Yunnan; antimony, almost a world monopoly, mainly at Hsikwangshan, Hunan; followed at some distance lower in world rank by manganese and mercury.

While China is not a great producer of silver, she is normally the world's second largest consumer of this metal.

CONCLUSION

Thus it can be discerned that the habitat of the Chinese peasant is complex indeed and cannot be easily evaluated. It is neither a land of extremes such as that of the Eskimo, Navajo, or Baganda, nor yet a land of the many natural advantages enjoyed by the Cotton South or British Midlands.

• 4 • The Geographic Regions of China
GEORGE B. CRESSEY

China is a land of very diverse environments. Vegetation types range from desert to jungle, and the agriculture of the humid South has little in common with that of the semi-arid North. Even the dialect, the temperament, and the physique of the people differ widely in different areas. Behind many of these contrasts lie factors of the geographic environment. In this paper the principal geographic regions are outlined and suggestions are presented as to the relationship between physical conditions and human activities.

The major division of China is in two regions, the North and the South. Some writers have suggested a three-fold division, following the major river valleys; but such a grouping leaves out Manchuria and other areas and does not recognize the essential unity of the central and southern provinces. When Marco Polo visited China he noticed these two contrasting regions and gave them separate names. Both parts have many qualities in common, but the division serves to emphasize essential contrasts in the human environment.

South China is a land of abundant rainfall. There are many hills but every bit of level land is intensively cultivated. This is the land of canals and paddy fields, of rice and bamboo, of teeming populations crowded into cities with narrow streets. Here the people are somewhat shorter in stature than elsewhere in China and they speak a multitude of dialects. The South tends to be radical and revolutionary, while the North is stolid and conservative.

North China is a land of limited and uncertain rainfall, with large areas of level land but with precarious agriculture and frequent famines. In place of rice and the wet agriculture of the South, the standard crops are millet kaoliang [the grain sorghum; literally, "tall grain"], and beans. In place of the greenness of the South, this region is brown and dust-blown for much of the year. In place of canal boats and coolie carriers, there are two-wheeled carts and draft animals. The people are taller and speak a uniform dialect—the Mandarin. Most important of all, the growing season in the North is but four to six months, while in the South it is nine months to a year. Thus, while the North raises one crop or in some places two, the South produces two and three.

These differences are so distinct that they divide China into two great geographic areas, as dissimilar as many countries. Out of these contrasts have developed social, economic, political, and even racial contrasts. The boundary between these two Chinas lies midway between the Yangtze Kiang and the Hwang Ho, and is indicated on the map by the northern edge of the Central Mountain Belt.

NORTH CHINA PLAIN

The North China Plain is one of the most clearly defined geographic regions in the world. On all sides except the southeast the boundary is well marked by mountains or the sea. Toward the southeast the topographic plain merges with that of the Yangtze, but the limit of the cultural plain is marked by a distinct change in climate, soil, and agriculture.

This great expanse of level land is the gift of the Hwang Ho and the other streams which flow out of the encircling mountains. These rivers have built out a great delta into what was once an arm of the sea. Where they enter the plain from the loess-clad hills of the West, they are so heavily loaded with silt that they are not able to carry all of their

[From "The Geographic Regions of China," *The Annals of the American Academy of Political and Social Science,* Vol. 152, Philadelphia, 1930. Pp. 1-9. Used by permission.]

burden to the sea, and they deposit some of it along the way. By this process the beds of the rivers have been built higher and higher, and through man's attempts to control the rivers this deposition has been confined within artificial embankments which themselves continually need to be raised. In many places, the beds of the streams are now many feet above the level of the surrounding country, so that one may stand on the plain and look up at the sails of passing junks. When these dikes fail, vast areas are flooded and famine ensues.

This region is the home of a crowded and industrious agricultural population. With an area of 125,078 square miles, considerably smaller than that of California, the post-office estimates for 1926 show a population of 80,979,025. This gives a population density of 647 people per square mile, probably eighty-five per cent of whom obtain their living directly from the soil. Man lives very close to nature in this fertile plain. His chief concern is food, and that is dependent upon rainfall. Unfortunately, the precipitation is limited and uncertain, the average amounting to but twenty inches a year. Often the total falls much below this or comes too late to be of value for crops or is so concentrated as to produce floods. Agriculture is thus precarious and crop failures are frequent. Man has so crowded the land that little margin can be accumulated for the bad years.

The principal crops are wheat, *kaoliang* or grain sorghum, millet, soy beans, cotton, tobacco, and vegetables. With the exception of the last, none of these crops are commonly irrigated. On acount of the dryness of the winters, one crop per year is the rule in the northern portion of the plain, but south of Shantung, two crops are common. Rice is rarely grown and millions of people eat it only once a year or so, at feasts. Mules, oxen, and donkeys are used on the farms and for hauling two-wheeled carts.

This region has played a leading role in China's history. It has been the seat of most of the great dynasties, and the home of Confucius and the sages.

LOESS HIGHLANDS

The Loess Highlands lie between the North China Plain and the deserts of Central Asia, and thus have climatic characteristics which are intermediate between those of these two regions. Most of the region is semiarid, with a rainfall of from ten to fifteen inches.

The distinctive feature of the topography is the thick mantle of loess which is spread over hills and valleys alike. This loess is a fine silt dust which has been blown outward from the Gobi and Ordos Deserts and sprinkled over the country as though by a giant flour sifter. In general, it covers all of the country, except the highest mountains, between the Great Wall and the Tsinling Mountains. The thickness of the loess has often been exaggerated, and it probably nowhere averages over three hundred feet.

The steep slopes of the mountains and the dissected loess topography which characterize the Loess Highlands cause human activity to be concentrated in the valley bottoms, which are commonly narrow and capable of but limited cultivation. The loess hills are often terraced, but on account of the scarcity of water they are not irrigated, and crops mature only in the more favorable years. The only areas of green are the thread-like strips along the streams. While most of the region is hilly, there are several plains of considerable extent, notably around Tai-yuanfu and Sianfu, where conditions resemble the North China Plain. Cultivated land amounts to only seventeen per cent of the entire area, in contrast to sixty-six per cent in the North China Plain. . . . [Famines have recently struck this region.]

In addition to wheat, millet, and *kaoliang* —the principal food crops—there is an extensive cultivation of the opium poppy. On account of the difficulty of transportation, opium is about the only cash crop which can be exported through the mountains, so that opium occupies a position somewhat similar to that of moonshine whisky in the southern Appalachians.

Cart roads connect the principal cities, but most of the region is without wheeled vehicles and depends upon pack animals. In the absence of railroads, which penetrate only the borders of the region, isolation is a dominant factor in the human geography.

It is estimated that the Loess Highlands contain eighty per cent of China's entire coal reserves, with the major portion in the province of Shansi.

MOUNTAINS OF SHANTUNG, LIAOTUNG, AND JEHOL

This region consists of three separate areas grouped around the Gulf of Chihli. These areas form a geologic as well as a geographic unit, for they are made up largely of hard, ancient rocks which have been eroded into bare mountains with steep slopes. Overlying these older formations are, here and there, softer beds, which make islands of more gentle relief.

Although this is one of the smaller of the natural regions of China, its position next to the sea and its proximity to two of the most important agricultural plains give it an increased importance. The cities of Dairen and Tsingtao are among the most important seaports of the country, and, together with Tientsin in the North China Plain, form the principal gateways to North China.

Coal and iron ore are both mined on a large scale, but agriculture is still the dominant occupation, with twenty per cent of the land under cultivation.

MANCHURIAN PLAIN

No other portion of China so closely resembles the United States as does Manchuria. The Mountains of Eastern Manchuria correspond in a way to the Appalachians, the Manchurian Plain may be regarded as a compressed section similar to one across the Mississippi Valley with increasing dryness to the west as in North America, and the Khingan Mountains take the place of the Rockies, although they are much lower and less rugged. Farther west there are deserts in both continents.

The Manchurian Plain is a pioneer land of rapidly expanding agriculture, and in this respect likewise has certain historical similarities to the United States. Although the region south of Mukden has been occupied by the Chinese for many years, a great migration into northern Manchuria has been in progress since 1925. This movement of farmers from old China, south of the Great Wall, reached one million immigrants in 1927, but dropped to two hundred thousand in 1929. This migration from the overcrowded lands of Shantung, Chihli now known as Hopei, and Honan has been due to the attraction of free or cheap land and to the devastation of the North China Plain by wars, bandits, and famine. The extent to which these colonists moved northward because of the pull of the pioneer urge as compared to the push of circumstances in their old homes is an important question, for it has a bearing on the future of this new land.

Kaoliang, millet, and wheat are raised as elsewhere in the North, but it is the soy bean which has been responsible for the marked prosperity of the region. The world-wide sale of beans, bean cake, and bean oil has made this the only region in China where exports exceed imports. The prosperity and the progressiveness of Manchuria are shown in the fact that it has a greater mileage of railways than all of China south of the Great Wall put together. It is likewise the only area where active railway construction is in progress.

Manchuria forms a fascinating geographic laboratory of huge proportions, with potentialities somewhat similar to those which faced the Pilgrims. Nature has provided a favorable environment; will the Chinese use the opportunity to develop a new and better civilization, or will the land become as overcrowded and famine-threatened as old China? The world may well judge the fundamental ability of the Chinese race by what it accomplishes here.

* * *

CENTRAL MOUNTAIN BELT

The Central Mountain Belt is made up of a series of ranges extending from Tibet almost to the Pacific. The topography is rugged in the west, where the elevations rise to three miles, but becomes more gentle toward the east. These mountains cut directly across central China and separate the country into two very diverse parts.

This is a transitional region, which marks the southward limit of loess, cold winters, and dry crops such as millet and *kaoliang,* and the northward extent of water buffalo, rice, tea, and bamboo.

These mountains have likewise had a political significance, for they have formed a barrier to armies and rebellions. In 1860 they prevented the Taiping rebels from coming north of the Yangtze Valley, and in 1875 they similarly limited the southward advance of the terrible Mohammedan uprising in the northwest.

YANGTZE PLAIN

This region is largely made up of the alluvial plain of the Yangtze Kiang below Ichang, although there are some areas of hills which are necessarily included. The lower part of the Hwai Ho and the area around Hangchow Bay are also included. This is a land of canals, with a length of over thirty thousand miles in the delta alone.

The Yangtze is the largest river in Asia and of foremost importance to China. It is navigable for ocean steamers to Hankow, 630 miles from the sea, and by smaller steamers for a thousand miles more. In some sections the banks are diked, but the flood menace is very much less than with the Hwang Ho.

Although this is one of the smallest regions, it has a population second only to that of the North China Plain, with a density of 897 people to the square mile, the highest in all China. This is a region of intensive agriculture, with rice, silk, wheat, beans, cotton, and oil seeds as the principal crops. A large amount of hand labor is used in cultivating the soil. Climatic conditions are favorable and two crops per year are the rule. The rainfall exceeds forty-five inches.

The Yangtze Plain is the social, political, and economic heart of the new China. Modern factories, electric lights, telephones, and imported goods are found in all of the larger cities. The chief industrial cities of the country are found here.

The city of Shanghai now has a population of 2,712,032, placing it next to Paris as the sixth city of the world. Two hundred million people live in its hinterland and it is growing rapidly. The tonnage of ships entering the port in 1928 was 34,583,369, so that it follows New York and London in this respect.

Although this region is excellently supplied with water transportation, there are few railroads. Airplane mail service has recently been opened between Shanghai and Hankow.

RED BASIN OF SZECHWAN

The Red Basin is one of the most enthusiastically praised regions in China. It is said that everything which can be grown anywhere in China may be produced here, for the climate is favorable, the soil productive, and the people energetic.

This basin is surrounded on all sides by high and rugged mountains, so that access is difficult. The only entry of importance is through the gorges of the Yangtze, which lie in the Central Mountain Belt. Fourteen-knot steamers now regularly navigate the rapids, but it was formerly necessary to travel on native junks which were towed up the river by long lines of trackers. Despite its isolation from the outside world, this region has a population of 43,860,118.

Most of the Red Basin is made up of hills of red sandstone, which are more extensively terraced than in any other section of China. There is also a remarkably fertile plain around the city of Chengtu.

Transportation is largely dependent upon man power, to pull junks, push wheelbarrows, carry sedan chairs, or transport loads. As Beech has said, man is "the universal animal, the omnibus of commerce, and the pack mule of the race. It is cheaper to wear men down than to keep roads up. When he falls, few care and still fewer pity, for others are eager to fill his place." Such is the value of human life where man permits himself to overcrowd the land.

SOUTH YANGTZE HILLS

All of China south of the Yangtze is distinctly hilly or mountainous, and forms a super-region which is known as the South China Highlands. Level land is strictly limited, and there are no broad plains such as those which characterize the North. The South Yangtze Hills include that part of the region which is tributary to the Yangtze Plain.

Cultivation is restricted to the valley floors and the lower slopes of the hills. Rice is the dominant crop, but only limited areas of the hills are terraced. There is normally a surplus for export to the industrial districts along the Yangtze. Tea is an important cash crop and is grown more extensively here than anywhere else in China. Although the capacity of the land to support agriculture is low, the favorable climate causes a dense concentration of people along the rivers.

SOUTHEASTERN COAST

The Southeastern Coast consists of a rocky and irregular shore line backed by picturesque mountains, roughly parallel to the sea, through which swift rivers have cut narrow canyons. Each of these streams has a delta and an important city at its mouth, and these cities and tributary rivers dominate the economic life. Travel is by boat along the rivers or by sea from one city to another, rather than overland.

Fishing is an important industry along the coastal fringe. The building of junks is aided by supplies of timber which are brought down from the mountains. The maritime interests of the region have led the people to migrate to the South Seas in large numbers and the stream of remittances sent back to relatives by these adventurers plays an important part in maintaining the dense population.

This is the typhoon region, with the worst storms from July to September.

HILLS OF LIANGKWANG

This is the tropical region of China, with abundant rainfall and a year-round growing season. The year may be divided into two seasons, a long, hot, humid summer and a short, dry winter. The rainfall exceeds sixty inches. The perpetual greenness is in direct contrast to the brownness of the North during so much of the year.

Agriculture is carried on under intensive conditions and might better be termed gardening than farming, because of the excessive amount of hand labor which is involved. Draft animals are relatively less important than farther north, for the demand for human food is such that there is no land available for forage crops. The water buffalo is the principal farm animal. Two crops of rice per year are the rule, and a third crop of vegetables may also be raised. Other products are sugar cane, tobacco, palm leaves for fans, excellent oranges and other fruits, and mulberry for silk.

On account of the large amount of hilly land unsuited for occupation, the population density of the region as a whole is not particularly high. The real crowding may be seen in the statistical tables, which indicate that the farm land per capita is but 0.18 acre, and that there is the amazing total of 3495 people to each square mile of cultivated land. High standards of living are impossible under such conditions.

Rivers and canals are used for transportation wherever available, while away from the waterways, coolie carriers are employed. There are no cart roads and only three short railways.

Hongkong is the great distributing center for south China, and has one of the finest harbors in the world. Canton is located up the shallow Pearl River and is the political rather than the economic rival of Hongkong.

The people of this region, particularly those from the Canton delta, are among the most progressive in China. Large numbers have gone overseas. . . .

SOUTHWESTERN TABLELAND

This region is a dissected plateau, cut by deep canyons and crossed by high mountains. The average elevation is above a mile, so that although it lies near the tropics it has a delightful, temperate climate. There are several broad plains, and these areas together with the valley bottoms are intensively tilled. Rice is the dominant summer crop, and the opium poppy is conspicuous during the winter.

The Southwestern Tableland is an anthropological museum. Only about half of the people are real Chinese, and the remainder comprise a great variety of primitive peoples. In all cases, the standard of living is low. Difficulties of transportation will doubtless keep this a backward region for some time to come.

One of the world's outstanding population experts is Warren S. Thompson, who for many years has been interested in the study of China's population problems. Like any research worker in this field, he is baffled by the lack of knowledge about the topic, but he is qualified to make good "guesstimates." Whether or not we agree with his opinions as to what should be done to ameliorate the population pressure, we are likely to be impressed with the magnitude of the problem and be critical of those who propose easy solutions.

• 5 • The Population of China: Present and Future
WARREN S. THOMPSON

THE SIZE OF THE POPULATION

. . . Any discussion of the population of China must be prefaced by saying that little is *known* about it. There has never been a census as we ordinarily use that term, nor has any reliable register been maintained either by the local governments or by the central government within the past century. The so-called "censuses" are at most merely the sum of the guesses of local officials, and usually they cover only a part of the country. Any more or less official figure for China's population must therefore be treated as a guess. This does not mean, however, that one "census" is as good as another; a critical evaluation of these "censuses" may result in a better guess than any one "census."

I myself am one of those who believe that many, if not most, of the guesses as to China's population in recent years have been too high. . . . On the basis of study and observations made with this definite purpose in mind, I am convinced that we in the West are likely to hold exaggerated notions of both the density and the size of China's population. We have been too much influenced in our notions of China's ability to support population by widely circulated descriptions of the intensity of her agriculture and by oft-repeated statements regarding the "limitless" riches of the country.

* * *

I am, however, disposed to accept Dr. Willcox's 350 million for the Empire as the figure for China Proper and to add about 50 million for the remainder of the Empire (including Manchoukuo), but I would want to hyphenate these figures and *guess* that China's population is somewhere between 325-75 million and that the Empire's population is 375-425 million. These figures seem to me as good as we can hope to arrive at until more reliable data are available. The simple fact is

[From *Population and Peace in the Pacific,* University of Chicago Press, Chicago, 1946. Pp. 177-183, 188-190, 197-198, 207-210, 215-217. Used by permission.]

that we do not know what China's population is within very large limits and that any figure used may well be in error by many millions. . . .

* * *

But I would like to emphasize the fact that the argument advanced in this book is not affected, whether China has a population of 350 million, or 400 million, or even of 450 million or more. The population is huge in any event, and, in making calculations for illustrative purposes, the round figures of 350 million for China Proper and 400 million for the Empire will be used. Should these figures turn out to be much too small, when China actually comes to count heads, the argument will only be strengthened.

BIRTH AND DEATH RATES

Of more importance to our purposes than the exact size of China's population, or even than precise birth rates and death rates, is a judgment as to the reasonable limits of her potential rate of growth. A variety of evidence is available on this point, and, although none of it is satisfactory, it is not altogether useless in trying to get a general view of the population situation in China and in evaluating future growth in broad terms.

* * *

. . . It seems reasonably certain that the birth rate in China is not under 40, and my *belief* is that it will average at least as high as that recorded in Formosa (45.6) and possibly even higher. The data on the death rate are even less consistent than those on the birth rate but seem to justify the statement that the death rate probably seldom falls below 35 and then only under conditions quite exceptional in China, such as in a small area where there is some health work or in a "good" year when the harvest is abundant and epidemic disease is mild. Furthermore, the death rate in China is highly variable from year to year and from place to place. . . . This violent fluctuation, much more violent than the fluctuation in birth rates, is probably characteristic of all

populations which, like that of China, have practically no health service and live close to the subsistence level even in "good" years.

* * *

CONDITIONS DETERMINING CHINA'S POPULATION GROWTH

The conditions that make for a low death rate everywhere have been referred to as "favorable living conditions." Among any people of high birth rate, population growth becomes more rapid as the level of living rises, because this quickly reduces the death rate. . . . With this in mind, I have done my best to find out whether the Chinese level of living had been improving over the last three or four decades. Since definite data are entirely lacking, I was forced to resort to personal inquiry while in the country. In pursuing these inquiries, I did not find anyone—either a foreigner who had lived long in China or an older native, either one who had traveled much or one who had remained at home—who would unhesitatingly say that the living conditions of any significant portion of the people he knew had changed appreciably within his memory. I also made a special point of inquiring about sanitary conditions, health service, and food supply, all of which would be likely to affect the death rate. I was unable to get anyone to say that living conditions, and in particular sanitary conditions, had improved during the last four or five decades for any but a tiny fraction of the people he knew, although I was frequently told that the well-to-do portion of the Chinese population in the treaty ports (not the more crowded population of the typically native quarters) was better off as regards sanitation.

On the other hand, many older persons believed that living conditions had considerably deteriorated during this period, especially since the fall of the Manchus and the complete breakdown of civil order in many regions. When due allowance was made for the tendency of older people to deplore present evils, it seemed to me that the only reasonable conclusion permitted by these inquiries was that there had been no significant improvement in living conditions, in sanitary practice, or in civil stability among the great mass of the Chinese people in recent decades. If this conclusion is correct, there is no reason to believe that there has been any appreciable decline in the death rate in recent decades which would have resulted in a growth of population comparable to that taking place in many other parts of the East.

POSSIBLE FUTURE GROWTH

Whatever the population is, whatever the birth and death rate, it is of far greater importance from the standpoint of our discussion here to understand the potentialities of population growth in China and the conditions under which these potentialities may become actual. The basic point for our argument is the simple statement which no one will dispute—that China has a huge population, almost certainly not less than 350 million and possibly in excess of 450 million. A second statement which no one at all familiar with living conditions in China will doubt is that the possibility of growth for several decades to come will be measured by the extent of the control achieved over the death rate, since the birth rate will remain high and will vary within rather narrow limits. The rate of growth for some decades to come might, therefore, easily equal and might well exceed that of Europe after 1800, if a strong, unified China were in a position, now that the war is over, to improve public health, to establish irrigation projects, to extend the tilled area by mechanized farming in regions of light rainfall, to build railroads and roads, and to industrialize. All of these improvements are confidently expected to come rather quickly, both by many Chinese and by many foreigners. A natural increase of only 10 per 1,000 per year in a population of 350 million would mean an increase of over 36.5 million in a decade, while a natural increase of 15 per cent in a decade, such as prevailed in India (excluding Burma) during the decade 1931-41, would raise this to about 56 million. An increase of about 25 per 1,000 per year, such as now prevails among

the Chinese in Formosa, would raise the numerical increase to about 98 million.

It must not be forgotten that in China we are dealing with numbers so much greater than those in the West that we are likely to under-estimate potential future growth. For China to add to her numbers in a single decade as many people as there are in France, or in the United Kingdom, or even in Germany would not require a rate of increase greater than that which has prevailed in many parts of Europe for relatively long periods during the nineteenth century and significantly less than that in much of the New World during that time.

It is not fantastic to contemplate such a population growth in China in the light of what we have already found happening in the Japanese Empire and . . . the actual population growth in Southeast Asia during the last several decades. We must face the fact that China will almost certainly grow by 40-60 million in each decade as soon as a few relatively simple economic and political changes are made.

How long can China care for such increases in numbers? How is she to feed, clothe, and shelter such numbers, even at the present subsistence level, twenty or thirty years hence when the first easy economic gains have been achieved? How is she to provide the higher level of living which her leaders are now urging, and which the people themselves will one day demand, if toward the end of the century her population is growing 50-70 million in each decade?

* * *

AGRICULTURAL IMPROVEMENT AND POPULATION GROWTH

The great danger, from the standpoint of a Westerner interested in seeing China achieve a better level of living, is that improvements in Chinese agriculture will take place so slowly that they will only serve to increase the population without raising the level of living. This often does happen among the most poverty-stricken peoples. Any increase in food reduces the death rate and thus raises the rate of natural increase, and very quickly the food available per capita tends to decline to about what it was before the increase in production took place. This happens so imperceptibly, so automatically, that the people themselves generally do not realize it, and thus have no clear choice between better living with little or no increase in numbers and the same low level with larger numbers. The larger numbers come *naturally* with the lower death rate following some easing of the struggle for subsistence because the birth rate remains at its customary level.

This is the usual result when people live as the Chinese are now living and when they take no thought for the adjustment of their numbers to their means of livelihood. . . .

MIGRATION AND POPULATION GROWTH

Migration might also have a pronounced effect on China's population growth. . . .

If the Chinese had several Manchurias to which they could move freely and cheaply, securing land without cost or at a very low cost as in the settlement of the United States, then we might expect an almost immediate improvement in the level of living for both old and new communities. There can be no reasonable doubt that, under these conditions, the Chinese would expand rapidly into any new area to which they could gain ready access and where agricultural conditions were reasonably familiar. They have proved good pioneers in Manchuria and Mongolia, in the north, and in a number of places in the tropics. But it should be made clear that the amount of migration from China would have to be large and continuous for many years in order to establish a better level of living. It seems doubtful now that any such vast migration can be managed in time to prevent the population at home from increasing during the next three or four decades about as fast as improvements in agriculture can be introduced.

In arriving at this conclusion, the probable effects of industrialization on the level of living are not being overlooked. But the speed with which industrialization can effect improvements is often exaggerated by the nationals of industrially backward countries. Furthermore, they seem to attribute all the improvements in level of living in the West to industrialization, to overlook the fact that the West had an abundance of land for settlement at the same time that industrialization was proceeding rapidly. It remains to be seen whether any crowded people having a very low level of living and without a relative abundance of land at its disposal can improve its level of living except very slowly when forced to rely to a large extent on the growth of machine industry.

*   *   *

INADEQUACY OF CHINA'S MINERAL RESOURCES

One must conclude that China's industrial development over a long period will be heavily handicapped by the lack of many important minerals, particularly by her small resources of high-quality iron and copper, and hence that she will be forced to rely heavily on imports from abroad for many types of goods essential to further industrial development and to the improvement of standards of living. It does not follow from such a conclusion that, other conditions being favorable, China cannot go ahead rather rapidly in the immediate future in the development of certain industries, but it does mean that the development of other industries will be handicapped for a long time or even indefinitely.

*   *   *

THE NEED FOR GREATER PER CAPITA PRODUCTIVITY

There is only one sure way to satisfy the larger need of economic goods and services which are essential to better living in China, and that is to make man's labor more productive, although we should not ignore the fact that a more just division of product between landlord and tenant would be very beneficial to a large proportion of the peasants. Likewise the myriad other inequities of the Chinese social system if corrected would help many individuals. But in a country as poverty-stricken as China there cannot be enough of anything to insure decent living to the masses of the people until the productivity of labor is greatly increased. . . .

If the Chinese are to live better, there must be a larger per capita product to divide, and this can come only if the whole system of agriculture and industry is revolutionized to make the farmer's and industrial worker's labor more productive. Farms must be increased in size (at present there is only about .43 acre of tilled land per person) and consolidated into units large enough to permit the use of improved machinery and to employ the farmer a larger portion of the year; the farmer must also have access to the credit needed to stock and operate an efficient farm unit and on terms which do not make him the virtual slave of the moneylender; research into better crops and farm practices must be established, and a system for the dissemination of its results must be organized.

As long as the Chinese peasant can scarcely produce enough to keep body and soul together, even when he owns his land, there is little hope of better living from the improvement of the distribution of his present product. He must produce more for a given amount of labor and work a longer year. The same is true also of the weaver and the spinner and the blacksmith and the other workers at non-agricultural tasks. They must have better tools and machines and a more efficient organization before they can produce much beyond the bare necessities of life.

JOBS FOR DISPLACED FARMERS

Supposing that the productivity of the agricultural worker can be increased, what, then, is to become of the farmers displaced by the increase in the size of the farm, by the use of more machinery, and by the adoption of more efficient farm practices? Obviously there are only two things they can do; they must go into some kind of industrial or commercial occupation or move onto new land. It seems highly doubtful that a people depending on a rice culture to the extent that the Chinese do can ever reduce their agricultural population to the 20 per cent that is approached in the United States and Australia and still have an abundance of food. But in the light of the studies of Buck and in view of what has actually happened in Japan, it would not appear unlikely that the proportion of the population engaged in agriculture could be reduced from 80-85 per cent to 40-45 per cent, or even somewhat lower, and yet produce enough so that every person could have a more satisfactory diet, better clothes, and a better house than at present, while the community supported a fairly efficient health service.

Such a displacement of population can, of course, take place only if a considerable part of the people no longer needed on the land can be employed in making goods for the farmers and themselves. This means a relatively high degree of industrialization as compared with what now exists. In the course of time China will become increasingly industrialized, but this change cannot come rapidly, and it is not at all certain that it will result in increasing the per capita product available anything like as much as in the West during the past century. In other words, it appears very doubtful whether more productive jobs can be found during the next few decades for all the Chinese who must have such work if agricultural improvement goes forward with fair speed.

* * *

CHINA'S MALTHUSIAN DILEMMA

This race between increasing per capita productivity and population growth is the real Malthusian dilemma, and China is caught on its horns. China is now experiencing the high death rate consequent upon having more children born than can be provided for under the present conditions of production. Probably China can temporarily, and to a limited extent, reduce the hardships of life and hence her death rate by reorganizing her agriculture and by building up her industry; however, we should not expect too much in the near future from industry alone or from agriculture and industry combined in a country already having a dense population and where the birth rate approaches the physiological maximum. Chinese industry would have to expand at a much more rapid rate than is probable to offer any real relief to the mass of her people during the next few decades, while permanent relief can come only after the country has learned to control its birth rate. All desired improvement in manner of living can easily be nullified during the next few decades by the more rapid increase of population.

We must think of China as having a strong tendency to increase in numbers for the next several decades and discuss possibilities of improvement with this in mind.

*   *   *

INDUSTRIALIZATION AND THE LEVEL OF LIVING

In order to make consideration of this topic as realistic as possible, certain definite assumptions will be made. They are (a) that political unity and stability will be achieved shortly; (b) that the transportation system will be vigorously expanded by this government; (c) that industrialization will go forward rapidly, perhaps as rapidly as in Japan after 1905, probably by the government guaranty of foreign loans; (d) that agriculture will be extended and improved at a fairly rapid pace through active governmental assistance; and (e) that all these advances will continue for the next forty to fifty years. What will then be the living conditions in China? Of course, this question cannot be answered with assurance, but some enlightening considerations can be adduced.

The first measurable effect on population of such a development as assumed here will be an improvement in general health with a marked lowering of the death rate. The basis for this statement is what has happened in most of the West, in Japan, in India, and in other parts of South and East Asia. An increase of population of 10 per cent in each

decade would be a very conservative estimate of the increase likely to follow such improvements in living; it is more likely to reach 15 per cent. Just to make easy figuring we will use 400 million as the population of the Chinese Empire, including Manchoukuo.

Assuming a 10 per cent increase in each decade, a population of 400 million in 1940 would become about 585 million in 1980. At a rate of increase of 15 per cent in a decade (which is approximately that of India for the years 1931-41 and less than the rate of the Philippines), China would have approximately 700 million by 1980. Fantastic! Perhaps, but this growth is taking place elsewhere in Asia, and a small measure of the favorable conditions assumed above are just the conditions which are bringing it about.

I have said "favorable conditions assumed," but most Chinese who talk about these matters would say that I have underestimated their resources and have made too much of both the economic and the psychological difficulties in the way of agricultural and industrial development. If this is so, then the probable increase in population is also underrated, because if there is faster improvement in the level of living than assumed, there will also be a greater drop in the death rate. Let us not forget that the Japanese figures for the Chinese in Formosa show a rate of increase not of 10 per cent in a decade, nor even of 15 per cent, but of about *25 per cent,* and that as yet there is no sign of any decrease in the birth rate, while the death rate is still falling.

Can the increase in per capita productivity go on fast enough during the next forty to fifty years to care for such an increase in numbers at a substantially higher level of living? The answer must be "No!" Therefore, it will not be any kindness to help China improve her agriculture and develop her industry merely to find that by the end of the century she has twice her present population existing at the level of living now prevailing. From the standpoint both of the welfare of the Chinese people and of our own position in the future when China has a greatly increased population and enough industry to make her a formidable military power, help to China in modernizing her economy *should be made contingent on the willingness of the Chinese leaders to show their people the need for voluntary control of population growth.*

There is not room in the world for the numbers that will naturally come if we teach all the "backward" industrial peoples how to reduce their death rates but do not at the same time show them the necessity of reducing their birth rates and how this can be done. Even with the most earnest efforts to teach these peoples how to control births they will grow rapidly once modern sanitation supported by a more productive industry and agriculture helps them to reduce their death rates. This is inevitable. Consequently, we must consider not only all possible means which can be made available for the care of this inevitable increase—the improvement of agriculture, the expansion of industry and emigration—but also the means of acquainting them with the control of their birth rates.

Making a Living

>>>

A peasant society is rooted in the soil. One of the reasons for the survival and continuity of the peasant society is the close affiliation its members have with the land. The man-land relationship is basic. As a first step in understanding the Chinese peasant's economy, we must understand his attitude toward his land. This affords us an insight into the system of property and ownership; into the methods used in tilling the land and raising livestock, and into his need for supplementing agricultural pursuits with related occupations. In this discussion of the peasant economy we also relate the individual farm to the outside world by asking where the surplus crops are sold, where needed supplies are purchased, where farm credit, as well as professional advice about ways of improving production, can be obtained. Since the factors associated with the level of living have been discussed in Selection 3 and will be alluded to in several selections to follow, no attempt will be made here to deal systematically with food, clothing, shelter, and health practices. Throughout the whole unit there are references to cooperatives and other formal organizations which fulfill economic needs for the villagers. These, too, should be regarded as a part of the economy.

A good introduction to the importance of land ownership is the brief discussion included by Hsiao-T'ung Fei in his study of a village on the Yangtze Plain, eighty miles west of Shanghai. Throughout most of China a peasant who owns even a little land can consider himself a landowner and can hold his head high, although his status within the landowning group rises as he obtains more land and shows the other qualities which his fellow villagers admire.

As has been pointed out already, the three societies described in this volume all serve to exemplify the profound and rapid sociocultural changes going on in the world today. In no aspect of a people's life is such change more easily seen than in the ways in which they make their living—the economic activities basic to all other phases of life. It will be pointed out, particularly in Selection 19, that industrialization and the modernizing of farming methods are affecting China profoundly; but first we shall consider the older but persistent attitudes of the farmers of China.

• 6 • Land as a Social Value

HSIAO-T'UNG FEI

. . . The primary function of land is to yield a food supply. But land is not only a means for producing food.

The productivity of land fluctuates according to the amount of attention and labor devoted to it. Furthermore, it is only partially controllable. There are unexpected risks. Thus land acquires its individuality through its variability in reacting to human expectation. Fear, anxiety, expectation, comfort, and love complicate the relation between man and land. People can never be certain what will come from the land. Land provides the means for self assertion, for conquering the unknown and for the pleasures of accomplishment.

Although the productivity of the land can be only partially controlled, this partial control supplies an empirical measurement of workmanship. Honour, ambition, devotion, social approval are all thus linked up with the land. The villagers judge a person as good or bad according to his industry in working on the land. A badly weeded farm, for instance, will give a bad reputation to the owner. The incentive to work is thus deeper than the fear of hunger.

The relative inexhaustibility of the land gives the people a relative security. Although there are bad years, the land never disillusions the people completely, since hope for plenty in the future always remains and is not infrequently realized. If we take the other kinds of productive work, we shall see that the risks involved in them are much greater. The sense of security is expressed in the following statement made to me by one of the villagers:

Land is there. You can see it every day. Robbers cannot take it away. Thieves cannot steal it. Men die but land remains.

The incentive to hold land is directly related to the sense of security. The farmer says, "The best thing to give to one's son is land. It is living property. Money will be used up but land never."

It is true that there are many ways of getting food. But the people will not exchange their land for other means, even if more productive. They do take up other occupations, such as the silk industry and fishing, but agriculture remains the principal occupation in the village.

The deeper we analyse the situation, the more it appears, not only that land in general has a particular value to the people, but that the property inherited by a Chia [the extended family] has for it a particular value. Land is transmitted according to fixed rules. People inherit their land from their fathers. The sentiment originating in the kinship relation and reinforced by ancestor worship is manifested also in this personal attachment to the particular plots of land. Religious belief in the importance of the continuity of descendants finds its concrete expression in the continuous holding of land. To sell a piece of land inherited from one's father offends the ethical sense. "No good son will do that. It is against filial piety." This comment sums up the traditional outlook.

Personal familiarity with a particular piece of land as the result of continuous work on it is also a cause of personal attachment to the land. It is very common for people to work on the same piece of land from early adulthood to death. To say that their land is an integral part of their personality is scarcely an exaggeration.

The non-economic value of the land complicates the transactions in land. Although land has its non-economic value, it does not

[From *Peasant Life in China: a Field Study of Country Life in the Yangtze Valley*, by Hsiao-T'ung Fei. Reprinted by permission of the Oxford University Press, Inc., New York, 1946. Pp. 181-183.]

in any sense lose its economic value. The sentimental and ethical reactions to the selling of the land do not rule out completely the possibility of land transactions. People sometimes need money urgently. Economic strain compels them to treat the land as an economic commodity. But I found no case of alienation except under real pressure.

If land is of such importance, we can reasonably ask, "Who owns the land?" The next selection indicates that more of the peasants in the wheat area (North China) own their farms than do those in the rice area to the South. This account of farm tenancy has been prepared by a special committee of American and Chinese experts who made a detailed study of the agricultural needs of China, particularly from the standpoint of what the Nationalist government could do to improve the situation. Already in North China at the time of this study, in 1946, the Communist government claimed that it was doing away with tenancy, that landlords were a thing of the past, and that the peasants themselves could own all the land. We shall understand these "agrarian reforms" better once we learn the background facts on land ownership. We shall be interested, later in this book, in comparing the tenancy problem in the Cotton South of our own country with that in China.

• 7 • Farm Tenancy in China

Tenancy is frequently referred to as a major agricultural problem in China. More than a quarter of a century ago, Sun Yat-sen set forth the principle that the man who operates the land should own it. This teaching has given emphasis to the importance of tenancy problems.

Many people, however, hold wrong impressions of tenancy in China, because they are not fully informed of the facts. There are many areas in which practically all the land is owned by farm operators. At the other extreme are many all-tenant communities in which the land is owned by many landlords, and still other areas where a single landlord owns a very large amount of the land. For all China, the best information available indicates that about 30 per cent of the land is rented. Tenancy varies widely in different Provinces and in different type-of-farming areas. In wheat regions, as a whole,

probably less than 15 per cent of the land is rented, compared with about 40 to 50 per cent in some of the heaviest rice-producing areas.

Tenancy should be viewed, also, from the standpoint of the proportion of farmers who rent part, or all, of the land they operate. Many farmers, known as part owners, own some land and rent additional land. They are in a much more secure position than that of tenants. Various sample studies indicate that for all China owner operators constitute approximately half of all farmers, and, of the remainder, part owners probably outnumber tenants. The situation is similar to that of some other countries, although the data for China will bear further analysis because of family custom.

A larger proportion of farmers in China own some land and rent additional land than in most other countries. One reason for

[From *Report of the China-United States Agricultural Mission*, Report No. 2, Office of Foreign Agricultural Relations, U. S. Department of Agriculture, Washington, D.C., May, 1947. Pp. 53-57.]

this is that, when small farms are inherited and the land divided between two or more sons, the one who remains on the farm may rent and operate his brother's share. As he accumulates savings, he may buy and gradually pay for the land of other heirs.

Sometimes heirs offer their small tracts for sale, and unrelated tenants, who, through their thrift, have saved some capital, purchase them. In this way, many tenants start on their way to land ownership while still renting part of the land they operate. Many tenants might have become part owners or full owners but for the fact that credit available to them was at such high interest rates they could not afford to use it for land purchase.

Many tenants do not desire to own land. They realize that they can advantageously invest their limited capital in operating equipment and farm more land than they would be able to own. Until they are well established financially, the sharing of risks with the landlord in various forms of share renting is a distinct advantage for tenants. Some landlords who are overburdened with debt incurred in buying land have poorer living conditions than many good tenants.

A landlord may be of service to a tenant by furnishing him capital and management and by acting as a buffer between the tenant and the state in paying taxes and attending to property rights. Tenants having little or no education need such assistance until they become able to assume these responsibilities for themselves. Making a man the owner of the farm he operates does not in itself insure his success.

A large part of the rented land in China is leased from landlords who own a small amount of land. Frequently a farmer who owns all the land he operates rents out a few mow [a mow is about one-sixth of an acre], possibly to a relative, while still operating the rest of his own land. Other owners, with opportunity to devote their time to business, rent their farms to others to operate.

Some landlords have acquired their land through their own thrift as farmers. Many such owners, reaching advanced years, render a service to society by affording wise guidance to young and inexperienced tenants. Many landlords are in a position to assist the tenant in obtaining the necessary farming supplies on better terms than he could obtain them himself. Unfortunately, some tenants do not have the necessary ability to handle their own business responsibilities, although some of them, perhaps, could be educated to these responsibilities.

Many farmers are tenants on large tracts of land held by landlords or by corporations and rented to many tenants. These tenants have practically no chance to attain ownership. Reclamation areas which require large amounts of development capital become rented land. In some areas large landholdings have been acquired by war lords. When severe famines occur, owners often sell their land to obtain food. The purchasers, usually local people having surplus capital, then rent to the seller or to other farmers.

Landlords frequently acquire land through the foreclosure of mortgages. Oftentimes a borrower must give up his property because of price changes, purchasing land at too high a price, drought, flood, or other misfortunes. The creditor will then rent it either to the debtor or to another farmer.

While some landlords give real aid to their tenants, others may exploit their tenants. The dense population in China and the competition for the privilege of operating the land enable owners to take unfair advantage of their tenants. Also, the large population and its concentration in agriculture have so reduced the size of farms, in many instances, that the division of the crop between the landlord and the tenant does not leave enough for the tenant to maintain a desirable level of living. In addition to requiring his tenants to pay a large portion of their crops as rent, a landlord sometimes requires his tenants to borrow their necessary credit from him at excessive interest rates, to sell their products to him, and to give him labor service, or other benefits. Instances were found of landlords renting their land to the highest bidder.

Also, some landlords require their tenants to pay rent before they have produced a crop. This is a real hardship to those who must borrow money at high interest rates to pay their rent in advance.

Many landlords, especially absentee landlords, pay too little attention to their property. Too frequently an owner rents land to one man who sublets it to tenants at excessive rentals. Managers for owners often extort excessive rents, even though the rental is not all paid to the landlord. Not many years ago tenants who were unable to pay their rent were, in some instances, put in prison, or were made virtual serfs of the landlord. Such malpractices and lack of personal supervision on the part of many landlords put tenancy as a system in disrepute.

FORMS OF TENANCY

Methods of renting land in China vary greatly within the same community but more especially between regions. In Kiangsu Province, for example, in one area most of the tenants pay the current value of a definite amount of rice, whereas in another area of the same Province 80 percent of all tenants pay a share of the crop actually produced.

In North China there are localities in which over 90 percent of the tenants are share renters. Where there is great risk from flood, or drought, tenants prefer share rent. Absentee landlords generally prefer cash rent because of less risk in collections, whereas local landlords often prefer renting their land in terms of produce.

China has a form of permanent tenancy that is limited to certain areas. In it the ownership of the land is divided between the soil itself and the surface rights. It may be described as follows: (a) "The landlord owns the soil" and pays the taxes, and (b) "The tenant owns the surface or the use of the land." The landlord who owns the soil cannot expel the tenant who owns the right to use it, unless unpaid rent reaches an amount in excess of the "value of the right to use the surface of the land" or the landlord purchases "the tenant's right to the surface of the land."

Although limited in extent, this is regarded as a good form of tenancy, since the interest of the tenant in conserving the land does not differ from that of the landlord.

Over one-half the tenancy in China is on a cash basis consisting of: (1) Payments of definite amounts of money, or (2) the market price of a definite amount of crop, or (3) payment of a fixed amount of produce delivered to the landlord.

Share renting, which makes up most of the remaining tenancy, is widespread in China and shows many variations. At Hsinghwa, Kiangsu, for example, several forms of share renting are found which indicate an attempt to adjust land rentals to the productivity of the soil and other factors, as follows: (1) Half-and-half, with most landlords furnishing land, buildings, and seed. Some of them also furnish some fertilizers or work animals, and some require the tenant to repay the seed and part of the cost of fertilizers at harvest. (2) A share of the grain and straw, which varies with the grade of land and kind of crops, with the landlord furnishing land, windmill, irrigation pump, one-half the seed and fertilizer, and one-half the labor of irrigating or draining in dry or wet years. Variations in such sharing of the income from the land are: (a) One-half the grain and straw from wheat and rice land, (b) two-fifths the grain and straw from rice land only, and (c) three-tenths the grain and straw from poor land.

Another form of renting is the "estimated half-and-half," usually associated with absentee ownership, where the yield is estimated before harvest and the rental fixed on this estimate. There is a little "cropper" renting, which is of minor importance, in poorer, or undeveloped, areas, where the landlord furnishes everything except labor and routine management.

MEANS OF SOLVING THE TENANCY PROBLEM

There are two ways of approaching the problems incident to tenancy. First, many of the evils of tenancy may be corrected by introducing better farm-leasing practices; and, second, tenants may be financed in the purchase of land through the development of farm-land credit facilities. Emphasis apparently should be placed on making it possible for tenants to acquire landownership if they are competent and desire to own their own farms. Others will do better as tenants under proper conditions of leasing and supervision. Either approach will succeed only insofar as wise procedures are devised. Likewise, any marked improvement in tenancy must have Government support. . . .

* * *

The problem of tenancy in China is similar in principle to that in many other countries. All major countries have faced this problem and out of their experiences has come much valuable information. It is clearly evident that tenancy in itself is not necessarily bad. But, if tenancy is to be considered a good form of land management, arrangements between the landlord and tenant should provide for: (1) A system of farming which will produce large yields and, at the same time, will maintain the productivity of the soil; (2) an equitable division of income between the landlord and tenant based upon their relative contributions; and (3) the removal of the master-servant relationship between the landlord and the tenant. Many instances may be found in China, as in other countries, where these provisions are reasonably met, and others where they are not.

There is probably no more authoritative voice on Chinese agriculture than that of J. Lossing Buck, who, during his long teaching career at the University of Nanking, conducted many studies of actual farm conditions. In order to round out our information on agriculture already obtained from Selections 6 and 7, we turn now to an analysis of Chinese agriculture by Dr. Buck. The village description of Taitou in Selection 17 presents a close-up of the farmer in action, but Dr. Buck provides the broad background for China as a whole, even including such topics as the marketing of crops and livestock, problems of mechanization, and a criticism of the collective farm, which is a part of the program in Red China today.

• 8 • Some Basic Agricultural Problems of China
JOHN LOSSING BUCK

I. INCREASING PRODUCTION

Improved Use of Land . . . The best use of land in China is very different from its use in other countries such as the United States of America, chiefly because of a very great difference in population density. Thus, in China greater attention is given to food producing crops for direct human consumption than to pasture and forage for animal consumption. Land which could not be cultivated in the United States is planted for crops in China where farm labor is more plentiful and must eke out an existence. For instance, certain hillsides are terraced at great labor expense, which, if in the United States, would be used only for pasture or forests, or left to the elements. Absence of adequate and cheap transportation in China prevents proper use of land and intensifies her problem of most capable use of land. Mountainsides better fitted for forests grow corn on slopes so steep that the

[From *Secretariat Paper No. 1*, Tenth Conference of the Institute of Pacific Relations, Stratford-on-Avon, England, September, 1947. Pp. 3, 5-13, 16-18, 20-21, 23-24, 49-53, 58-62. Used by permission.]

tassel of one plant is on the level with the roots of the plant above it.

Farmers, over the centuries, have made their own classification of land. They have decided what land is good for crops, for pasture and for forests or for fuel production. Their decisions, however, have been conditioned by factors other than the most capable use of land.

Tradition may prevent farmers putting some land into better alternative uses. Hill lands in parts of South China may remain in pasture and fuel production because of a prevailing custom that such land is free for all villagers to use for pasture or for gathering of fuel. Under such circumstances, no one farmer could stake out a claim and begin farming a plot in an area governed by these traditions. In other areas land best suited for pasture or forests is often cultivated with resultant large losses from soil erosion. Pressure of population and small farms often force farmers to use land in this way.

*　　*　　*

In China, the emphasis on food crops has created an unbalanced production between animals and crops. A great source of feed from oil cakes in China is lost by using them directly for fertilizers, rather than for feed. Crop by-products of straw, stalks and chaff, some of which would supply fodder, supply most of the fuel of the country. A substitute fuel would release a portion of these by-products for fodder. The use of oil cakes for feed and crop by-products for fodder should make possible a greater production of animals, which in turn would probably increase the fertility of farms. Moreover, integration of the economy of the range lands in the North and West with agricultural China is still undeveloped. It awaits cheaper and adequate transportation facilities. When the two economies are developed and interrelated, production of range lands will increase and exchange of products between the two regions should flourish to the advantage of both areas.

A better balance between forest, pasture and crop is also advisable. Some land is being cropped which should be in pasture or forest. Other land is producing grass and bushes cut annually for fuel. Large areas of mountainous land suitable for forests are burned each year for various reasons, the most common being to supply potash to rice paddy fields from water running off the burned slopes. Some of this mountainous land should be in forests to produce lumber and firewood and to insure a water supply for lower agricultural lands; other portions could be used for pasture which together with feed in the form of oil cakes and fodder from crop by-products would provide for the increased animal population already mentioned.

Not only is there an undue attention to crops as compared with animal production, but also to field crops versus horticultural crops. Fruits are considered a luxury and are not a normal part of the diet. Their nutritional value is not recognized. It is correct to describe the Chinese farmer as the best versed in grain production, but not a good fruit grower, although there may be exceptions where this generalization would not be true. Farmers in North China claim they do not grow more vegetables for home use for two reasons. First, because vegetable growing is a specialized business and they do not know how to grow vegetables. Secondly, that land in vegetables reduces area in wheat which is urgently needed for food. Here again is a complete ignorance of the value of vegetables in the diet. Increased production of fruits and vegetables with up-to-date methods would improve nutrition and still supply quantities of food required.

*　　*　　*

Multiple cropping is a feature of farming in China. Nearly one-half of the agricultural area of China produces two crops a year. Greater expansion of multiple cropping is possible, especially if more fertilizer is available at reasonable prices. Development of irrigation and drainage will also extend areas of multiple cropping.

The use of water resources for fish and aquatic crops is developed in China to a far greater extent than in most countries. The application of science in production of such crops would increase their output. Moreover, new areas might be utilized for these types of farming.

The amount of uncultivated land in China that might be brought into economic cultivation is often greatly exaggerated. Most of the good lands have been settled. Moreover, cultivation has extended to marginal areas which later had to be abandoned or where farmers are eking out a miserable existence. Most uncultivated hill lands in South China and Southwest China are badly eroded and a large portion cannot be brought under profitable cultivation until cheap fertilizer becomes available and soil and water conservation control methods are properly utilized.

*　　*　　*

Level of living in China is limited by the production per farm worker. It is not more than one-fourteenth of that for an American farmer. . . . At present there is a large oversupply of labor on farms for the greater part of the year. Development of local and city industries, irrigation, drainage and conservation projects, improvement of roads and canals for transportation, as well as an increase in professional services, will increase employment. Thus the man left on the land will become more productive in that he will have more working days and productivity per man will increase. Improved tools of production and processing makes it possible for one man to accomplish more work in the optimum time period for such work. With the help of such tools one farmer can produce as much as several farmers did before. Nothing could be more unfortunate than to overlook the welfare of the farmer in relation to land use. Land is only one factor which, when properly used by man, can give a satisfactory source of livelihood.

*　　*　　*

Increasing Rates of Production . . . One of the most important ways of increasing crop yields in China is through the control of water. Too much or too little water is proba-

bly the greatest factor limiting production. Irrigation needs to be extended to lands not now irrigated. Many areas already irrigated require an additional supply of water, either from the main irrigation system or by better equipment to pump water from the available supply. Water needs to be conserved where it falls, or drained off in a way to prevent erosion. There are large areas in South China where sheet erosion has washed away most of the top soil on hill lands. In the loessial areas of Northwest China, gully erosion has seriously reduced the area in farm lands. Conservation of water by forests in mountains is also required to supply a more constant quantity of water to the lower farm lands.

*　　*　　*

The second most important method by which yields can be increased, is by the use of more fertilizers (both organic and chemical). In general, farmers in China report insufficient fertilizers and insufficient credit to purchase additional fertilizers. . . .

Farm manures could be increased somewhat by greater use of crop by-products for fodder instead of for fuel, providing a fuel substitute could be found. Green manure crops are common in certain parts of China, and can be advantageously extended elsewhere. Bone meal is another possible source of fertilizer. Before the war Japan used to import large quantities of bones from North China, but China herself needs this source of phosphorus. There are also parts of China where better care of farm manures would increase the available fertility. Night soil [human excreta] is generally used, but its sanitary use from a health standpoint is a major problem.

Perhaps the third most important method of increasing yields of crops and of preventing losses of stored products is the control of insects and diseases. It is estimated that the rice borer alone produces an annual loss of 10 percent of the rice crop. Insects and diseases of crops in China are numerous, and if they can be economically controlled, yields can be materially increased.

*　　*　　*

Improved varieties of crops and nursery stock would definitely increase yields. Even simple mass selection would be an improvement over the present methods where fields are often found with mixed varieties of crops. Better varieties can be had through plant breeding which already has an important place in the agricultural improvement work of the Central Government. . . .

Better cultural methods will also increase yields to some extent. Some crops, like cotton and fruit trees, are spaced too closely. Scientific pruning of fruit trees would increase yields. Improved tools would make possible better tillage and timeliness in farm operations, in addition to increasing the output per worker.

Production per animal, as well as quality of product, may be increased profitably by the use of better breeds and strains. Only a limited amount of scientific breeding of livestock has been done in China and the best Government effort in this direction has been with swine.

* * *

Proper feeding and care is also a prerequisite to greater production. Insufficient feeding is conspicuous in the Northwest range areas where more winter feed, supplemental to the range, is imperative if large losses are to be prevented. Controllable diseases, like rinderpest, cause tremendous losses of stock, including large number of work animals, which in turn affects crop production. The Central Government has undertaken some rinderpest control work, but it is limited in amount compared with the need. Control of diseases, pests and parasites through immunization, better nutrition, sanitation and buildings would be another economical and practical method of increasing animal products. For work animals improved equipment such as harness and vehicles will increase output. The use of modern shearing equipment is one example of how equipment will do a better job and improve the quality and increase the quantity of the product.

* * *

Improving Agricultural Engineering Practices. Farm tools, machinery and equipment are used in order to do farm work better, more cheaply, more easily and more quickly, and to do work that cannot be done with human muscular effort. The extent to which the farmer should use equipment depends chiefly upon whether or not its use increases profits. Its use increases the area that can be cultivated by one farmer and increases per capita production.

The Chinese, to a large degree, have adapted their farm implements to suit their conditions, but improvements are both possible and desirable. The average farm has 26 important pieces of equipment. There are at least 60,000,000 farms, and the essential equipment totals 1,680,000,000 pieces. The average value of this equipment is about US $2.50 per acre, or approximately one-third of the value of farm machinery per acre in the United States.

Cast and wrought iron and wood are the chief materials used in manufacture. The Chinese used a plow with an iron share and mouldboard some 2000 years before Newbold, about 150 years ago, invented his cast iron plow in the United States and farmers were afraid to use it for fear the iron would poison the soil and make the weeds grow.

Although China designed her implements many centuries ago, she has not made many improvements. For instance, it is estimated that a better metal in the hoe to keep the edge sharp and to decrease the amount of sharpening necessary would decrease the labor of hoeing by 15-20 percent.

Present manufacture of agricultural implements is chiefly by artisan families. Small foundries are used for castings, blacksmith shops for wrought iron parts, and carpentry for wooden parts.

Modern techniques should produce better implements at the same cost or, if at higher cost, with enough improvement to enable the farmer to pay for the higher-priced implements because of the decreased labor cost in using them and/or because of increased production.

* * *

Modern Machinery. Computations have

been made for farm conditions near Nanking to compare (1) cost of plowing with a water buffalo and with a tractor, and (2) the cost of threshing with a flail and with a threshing machine. Based on these data, tractor plowing is over twice as expensive as water buffalo plowing. If plowing with a tractor prepares soil better and yields are increased then the rates of the increased yields minus the extra cost of the additional labor for handling larger yields should be subtracted from the estimated cost of tractor plowing.

The threshing machine has a better chance of success than the tractor even though the machine is used only fifteen days a year. Cost data on the small machine used at the University of Nanking show that it can thresh as cheaply as the flail and at the same time turn out a clean product. . . . But, as with so many machines, a difficulty arises in that the straw, which is much used for thatching, is not kept straight and stiff as with a flail. In South China, roads are also needed to move the thresher from one place to another. The threshing machine, however, saves labor at a time when needed for other work. The combine which cuts and threshes in one operation might be more economical than the thresher since it would also save labor needed in cutting with a sickle and in preventing some of the present losses of grain in harvesting.

The combustion engine is an example of a machine successfully and increasingly used in the lower Yangtze valley for irrigation and sometimes for drainage purposes. The water requirements for rice are so great that for many regions where water is not near the field level, human power is not enough and it is too expensive.

The extent to which modern farm machinery can be used depends not only upon its cost but also upon the farm layout. If the fields are too small or too irregular or paths too narrow, machines cannot be used to advantage. With consolidation of holdings, larger fields are possible. Recently, in the United States, machinery has been made in smaller sizes, and, if it can be produced cheaply enough, some of it may be practical for use in China.

In China, machine methods at present are not as important as in the United States because labor in China is cheaper and more plentiful. When China develops her industry, transportation and professions, farm people will leave the farm for these occupations. At that time, farm labor will decrease, will be more expensive, and farmers will have to use more labor saving machines and can afford to do so. The manufacture of machines in China with cheap labor and local materials should make such machines cheaper than imported ones. If so, farmers could use more machines than at present.

Certain types of small machinery and improved implements should be used but large machinery appears impractical for general use in China at present. If farms were made large enough for large machines, many farmers would be thrown out of work, unless other occupations are created, such as manufacturing, transportation and professions. Another disadvantage of power machinery is that fuel oil must be bought and it is very expensive in China. A cheap source of fuel will hasten mechanization. Still another disadvantage of machinery is delay in work caused by its breaking. On the other hand, farmers should be quick to use machinery when it will give them a greater net income.

Farmers should not use power machinery only because it is considered "modern." Farmers cannot afford to gain "face" by using machines if this means increasing expenses greater than the saving in labor costs. By doing this, the farmer will soon lose his farm.

The principle to remember is that labor is plentiful in China. The chief need for machinery is (1) to do work that man cannot do, (2) to do work that can be done more cheaply by machinery, (3) to do work more quickly, and (4) to do it sufficiently better to pay for the cost.

Some people think that any great immediate improvement in Chinese Agriculture depends upon use of large machinery. Such an idea is a mistake. China has a large number of farmers in comparison with the amount of land, and often, labor is cheaper than capital for investment in machines. Use of machinery on most farms in China would increase national production only slightly, or not at all. Large-scale farming with machinery would mean a complete change in the size of farms and in their management. Large-scale farming has so many disadvantages that the cost of production is usually greater than on family-sized farms. Only when China develops her industry, transportation and professions, will machinery become more profitable. Such a change will take place slowly. This change has begun, and as it develops there will be an increasing labor shortage for some farm operations and a need for labor-saving implements and machinery. Machinery makes possible a large production per capita. A high production per capita increases the farmer's income and raises his standard of living. In a country of dense population, other than farm work must be found to employ farmers who are thrown out of work by the use of machines. It is doubtful if thickly populated countries can use as much farm machinery profitably as can thinly populated countries.

* * *

Farm structures in China are largely built from local materials. Walls of buildings are constructed from bricks burnt locally, from adobe bricks made by farmers from earth in their fields, or by tamped adobe walls. Roofs are usually of tile or thatch, of wheat or rice straw. Roof sheeting in South China is usually made of rush mats, while in large portions of North China *kaoliang* [grain sorghum] stalks are used for that purpose. Thus the improvement of farm buildings insofar as materials are concerned must be based on an economical source of materials. There is opportunity for improvement in construction of these buildings, especially from the standpoint of sanitation. In many places the interiors of walls could be plastered over to make a smooth wall and reduce the collection of dust. Perhaps one of the biggest improvements needed is to eliminate earth floors in favor of a floor which provides against dampness and is easily cleaned.

The present method of storing grain is economical from standpoint of materials used, but it appears that losses may be too great. Careful study of the storage problem and of buildings and equipment for storage is essential for preventing losses. Present structures for irrigation, drainage, soil and water conservation and rural roads consist chiefly of stone set in a mixture of earth, sand and lime. Generally, it would appear that the increased use of structures in connection with control of water is essential, but economical materials are necessary.

Transportation and communication in country districts are greatly limited during wet seasons by improperly constructed roads, which often are ditches rather than roads. There is plentiful labor in country districts which could be utilized for properly constructed earth roads, and in many places it would be economical to surface roads.

Processing of farm products for markets is in a primitive stage and could be greatly improved. Ginning of cotton, baling of cotton, processing and grading tea, and oil pressing, offer opportunities for application of more efficient methods of processing. Also there is need for introducing preservation of food on farms and in rural communities, such as canning, drying and other processes.

* * *

II. ORGANIZATION OF MARKETING AND CREDIT MARKETING

Modern methods of marketing in China have advanced slowly. Standardization and grading of export products like tung-oil, raw silk, bristles and tea have been in operation for about a score of years. Also, there are a few good examples of cooperative marketing of cotton, tobacco and oranges developed before and during the war in Central and West China. However, most products are known only by the locality where they are produced. There is no other grading or standardization. Markets are not well organized, and primary markets are chiefly buyer's markets. Grain markets, usually called *hong,* are limited in number in any one locality and through custom have exclusive rights, either to buy and sell grain, or to act as a kind of commission firm where buyer and seller meet. The *hong* adjusts disputes and has a measurer who usually measures in the interests of the buyer of large quantities rather than impartially. Units of weights and measures vary throughout the country and even within the *hsien* [or district].

False measures or cheating in measuring is common. The standard system of weights and measures is not enforced except in larger cities. Adulteration by small merchants is a common practice. Produce exchange markets in the modern sense do not exist. The miller, or the silk reeler for instance, must send their own buyers to the country, or purchase products through a middleman, who in turn has made his purchase in the country districts. Warehousing in the modern sense is limited chiefly to silk cocoons. Losses from improper storage, packaging, handling and transit facilities are excessive. Middlemen are so numerous that only a few have an economic sized unit of business which keeps costs of operation at a reasonable figure.

* * *

Modern methods of marketing are particularly important for China in relation to agricultural export products and in relation to competitive agricultural import products. China cannot hope to supply world markets unless she adopts improved marketing practices. . . .

The adoption of better marketing practices is essential to meet competition of import products. Before World War II, millers in Shanghai imported wheat not because there were no available supplies within China, but because it was easier to send a cable to Australia, Canada or United States for a definite grade of wheat, supply a letter of credit and in due time the wheat of the quality ordered arrived. On the other hand, if the miller purchased wheat within China, it required

sending a purchaser to the purchasing areas, buying of small lots of varying qualities, collecting them together, often storing in the open until they could be loaded, and then having the shipment accompanied by the miller's agents to the mill. Such wheat often contained dirt and stones from the threshing floor and required special machinery for cleaning it. Under such conditions, it is practically impossible for the Chinese farmer to compete with other countries in supplying processors at port cities with agricultural products such as wheat or cotton.

Credit. The credit problem of China is misunderstood in regard to present sources of credit for farmers. The prevailing high interest rates are usually discussed in terms of usury practices by creditors. Popular discussion of credit usually gives less attention to uses of credit than to its sources or to interest rates. Several careful sample studies have been made of the situation over sufficiently large areas to indicate the position. One of the surprising results of these investigations is that on an average for each locality studied, the landlord supplies not more than one to four percent of the total credit extended to farmers. Friends and relatives of the borrowing farmers extend the larger share of credit from any single source, and this varies from 39 to 83 percent of total credit. More recently credit cooperatives have been organized and for the years 1940-41 a survey of 216 farms and 11 *hsien* of Szechwan show that 48 percent of the credit was obtained from cooperatives. During the war there was considerable extension of cooperative credit by the Chinese Government, but for China as a whole, the percentage of such credit is only a small fraction of total credit obtained by farmers.

A study of 15,000 farms in 22 provinces indicates only 6 percent of the credit was supplied by merchants, or shops operated by merchants. Mortgaging of land is infrequent and amounts to only one percent of the credit received by farmers. Although there may be isolated instances of large proportions of credit granted by landlords or merchants, at supposedly usurious rates, these instances do not portray the true picture for China as a whole. In the study of 15,000 farms it was found that interest rates charged by landlords averaged 30 percent, whereas friends and relatives charged 25 to 28 percent, and there was a locality where the family clans charged 42 percent. The rate charged by Farmers' Bank of China to farmers' cooperatives was the lowest—12.1 percent. Interest rates in China are high because of risk, the small amounts of each individual loan and the scarcity of loan funds. The problem, therefore, is not one of complaining about the high interest rate already charged but rather one of finding ways to tap and organize investment credit and devise an efficient system of extending credit to farmers. Improved methods of extending credit to the Chinese farmers was first begun by the International Famine Relief Committee of Peking, about 1921. Later, private banks became interested and entered the field of farm credit. About 1942 the Farmers' Bank of China took over all government extension of credit to farmers and other government banks discontinued credit to the farmers. The war also caused the private banks to discontinue farm credit.

* * *

Organization of Farmers. Organization of farmers to cooperate together for their common welfare is a more difficult task in China, as elsewhere, than is technical agricultural improvement. Farmers can obtain cheaper credit if they organize into groups and apply for one loan for the whole group. Products can be marketed at a lower marketing cost if farmers pool their products and ship them in one lot. Likewise, they can purchase supplies cheaper when buying in larger quantities. Many irrigation projects cannot be successful unless farms are organized into irrigation and drainage districts for administering the problems connected with irrigating or draining their lands. Organization for soil conservation may also be necessary.

If farmers are to receive the benefits of agricultural research, they can do so more easily and more quickly by organizing into groups through which agricultural extension agents of a government extension system can pass on improved practices.

Some organization of farmers has taken place in China. The Bureau of Social Affairs reports the existence of 77,890 cooperatives at the end of June 1945 as partly or solely engaged in agriculture. By the end of 1945 there were 8336 Farmers Associations of which 660 were *hsien* [district] Farmers Associations and 7676 were *hsiang* (township) Farmers Associations. The Farmers Associations are groups of farmers who organize to promote their own welfare, especially in agricultural production, and they often sponsor separate organizations of credit or marketing cooperatives. From this development of the cooperatives and farmers associations one may expect in the future a rapid increase in organization of farmers for economic activities.

* * *

III. IMPROVING LAND ADMINISTRATION

Land Measurement and Registration. China, like many countries, does not have a complete land survey of privately owned and public lands. The present Land Administration Office, by means of ground surveys in cooperation with *hsien,* have completed surveys of about 600 *hsien.* Samples of these surveys indicate that possibly as much as one-third of the cultivated area of China is not recorded in the Land Office files of the *hsien* land deed offices. Consequently, statistics of cultivated land area in China are far below the actual amount. Moreover, such land is not paying land taxes and thus creates great inequalities in taxation.

Proper registration of title deeds is dependent upon accurately measured land showing its location on a map. Land appraisal for various purposes, including that of extension of land credit, requires maps and records of land by ownership. The first prerequisite for consolidation of holdings in any community is measurement of the land by ownership. Holdings cannot be expropriated and owners equitably remunerated, unless the extent, location and ownership of such land is known and recorded. Land settlement and division of land to be settled has as its first requirement a land survey. When land is properly measured and mapped, classification of land for its most capable use and land use planning for irrigation, drainage, soil conservation and selection of enterprises becomes possible.

Land Taxation. The land tax is the principal source of revenue for *hsien* governments and more recently it is an important source of revenue for provincial governments. During the latter years of the war it was collected by the National Ministry of Finance and remitted in part to *hsien* and provincial governments. After V-J Day collection reverted again to the *hsien*. Classification and appraisal of farm land for taxation purposes varies throughout China. Quality of land rather than the farm as a unit is the actual assumed basis for determining rates. However, rates may be determined by landlords with political influence.

*   *   *

Consolidation of Holdings. The problem of consolidation of holdings concerns an existing situation where the number of parcels per farm vary from 1.1 to 5.9 plots and average 5.6 parcels per farm. Each parcel has one or more fields and the average number of fields is 11.6 per farm. This fragmentation of land favored by inheritance customs that provide for division of land among sons, presents a situation requiring careful organization for its amelioration. There are certain advantages and many disadvantages of fragmentation in China. The chief advantage, as given by Chinese farmers, is that the system prevents some farmers from having all good land and others all inferior land, or land adapted only to one kind of crop. For instance, in many parts of the great plains area of North China it would be a great disadvantage for a farmer to have only "lake land."

Another similar example is in East Central China in sections where there are both hills and valleys. Here a farmer desires some land in both places, for the hill land supplies him with fuel (from grass and bushes and in some places firewood) and green manure (from grass) for rice fields. The advantages mentioned in these two instances could be kept in any re-adjustment of the field system, however, and a farm planned to include both kinds of land in one piece; only if this were impossible would it be necessary to have two plots of land in one farm.

Irrigation is another matter to be considered in the re-arrangement of fields. In the *hsiens* of Wuchin (Changchow) and Tanyang of Kiangsu Province, it is a custom for farmers to cooperate by rotating wheat followed by rice in one section of contiguous fields and barley in association with soybeans in another. This facilitates irrigation since the irrigated fields are contiguous each year even though they may belong to a score of farmers. This advantage could undoubtedly be conserved even if the farms were re-arranged in one piece merely by continuing the same kind of cooperation.

Farmers in Kiangning *hsien,* Kiangsu, maintain that by having scattered pieces of land some escape the ravages of locusts. That risk from insects, flood, or drought is lessened must be admitted, but this risk might be covered by insurance and the farmer at the same time could receive the benefits of having the land in one piece.

The advantages of having in one area all the land farmed by one family, therefore, while of utmost importance, need be only briefly mentioned. Boundary lines would thus be reduced in number and extent, saving land and diminishing boundary disputes; larger fields would be possible and time saved in making trips to fields. Further, if land were all in one piece, barriers, such as fences, hedges, or ditches, could be erected to obtain privacy and prevent trespassing, thieving and gleaning. The control of irrigation and drainage water would be more easy; for instance, fields are now so scattered that often it is not economical for a farmer to dig a well for a small plot of ground and it is not always easy for several farmers to cooperate in using the same well. Control of pests, such as rodents, insects, and diseases, would also be less difficult. The advantages of having land in one piece so outweigh disadvantages that it seems economically advisable to undertake re-arrangement of fields in China.

In any consolidation program it may be necessary to give attention to certain advantages of fragmentation in a country of small farms by consolidating farms to only two or three parcels rather than one parcel.

* * *

IV. DEVELOPING TRANSPORTATION, COMMUNICATION AND INDUSTRIES

Transportation and Communication. Agriculture, like other aspects of national economy, is dependent upon well developed systems of transportation and communication. China's waterways and her long coast make it possible to move large quantities of goods by boats, small and large, but shipping facilities need to be increased and modernized. Railroads, although inadequate, have made rail shipments possible on two North and South and two East and West railways, and on other shorter lines.

* * *

The Post Office is remarkably efficient and its service reaches almost every village of the county seat. Likewise all towns, from a county seat upwards, are connected by telegraph.

Modern highways extend 126,000 miles, connecting most of the provincial capitals. Truck transportation is expensive because fuel oil must be imported and transported to the interior. In the summer of 1946, civilian airplanes totalled 60.

Transportation costs are high in China both by traditional methods and even by modern transport in comparison with many other countries. Studies . . . show pre-war costs by traditional methods in terms of U.S. dollars per ton mile to be: carrying with a pole, $0.48; motor truck, $0.33; pack horse $0.30; pack

donkey $0.24; wheelbarrow $0.20; pack mule $0.17; animal drawn cart $0.13; junk $0.12; rail $0.027; and steamboat $0.024.

Most Provincial capitals have their telephone systems but only a few cities have the dial system. Long distance telephone communication is limited and is in early stages of development.

Modernization, additional equipment and extension of services is required for both telephone and telegraph communication. Radio service has developed slowly partly because of the war and partly because of restrictions on receiver sets, restrictions imposed because of the internal political situation.

The bulk of agricultural products are transported by the high cost traditional methods and one can visualize the effect a complete development of modern transport and communication would have on agriculture as well as the entire economic life of the nation.

Large Scale Water Control Projects. No country has greater large-scale water control problems related to agriculture, production of power and navigation than has China. The immensity of the task of water control in the Yellow River watershed almost surpasses one's imagination. It is of course, both an engineering and agricultural problem. The watershed is hilly and mountainous west of the North China plains and has a large percentage of cultivated but easily erodible loess soil. The unusually high silt content of the Yellow River is caused by washing of soil from the farm lands in its middle and upper watershed. The very highest elevation could grow forests, but the bulk of the area is not suited to forests. The problem, therefore, is one of soil and water control on the watershed insofar as it is practical and a problem of engineering for control of floods and for use of the river water for irrigation in the plains of North China, development of power and navigation. Other important water control projects of less magnitude are for the Yangtze River, the Hwia River and others. The occasional severe Yangtze River floods may be impossible to prevent economically. The 1931 Yangtze Flood destroyed crops and animals to the value of US $442,800 (the purchasing power of the US $ in 1931 was very high indeed), and the previous similar flood occurred about sixty years before the 1931 flood. These losses do not include losses of bridges and other rural community structures. Whether or not engineers, agriculturists and foresters could devise economic means of preventing such infrequent disasters is an open question. Two feet of rainfall within two weeks over the whole Yangtze watershed, as occurred in 1931, is a tremendous amount of water to control, especially when such a large portion of the area is already under water for rice culture.

*   *   *

Processing Agricultural Products. Improved processing methods for agricultural products is a crying need in China. Modern methods of milling wheat flour, small power driven rice mills and canning of fruits, vegetables and meats have been successfully introduced. A simple treadle cotton gin, originated by the Japanese, has been increasingly used and is superior to the native hand roller gin. These introductions have proven the advantage of improved processing methods by mechanical power. Modern methods of processing save immense quantities of labor, produce quality products in large volume and, therefore, readily pay for the investment.

Food. Processing of food in China is an old industry, chiefly in the artisan stage. Its forms have been, and still are, (1) the drying of fruits, vegetables (including sweet potatoes and persimmons), poultry, meat and fish; (2) the smoking of meats; (3) the pickling of vegetables; (4) the milling of cereals; (5) the extraction of vegetable oils from soybeans, sesame, rapeseed, peanuts, sunflower seeds and tea seeds (camelia); (6) the conversion of soybean into bean curd with its by-products of milk and a high protein wafer; (7) the preservation of eggs in quick-lime which cooks the eggs and hermetically seals them; (8) the making of condiments and sauces; (9) the manufacture of syrups and sugar from barley as well as sugar cane; and (10) re-

cently, the canning of fruits, vegetables and meats.

The least developed process appears to be the milling of grains into forms other than flour. Modern flour mills are operating successfully in China with a concentration at port cities like Shanghai and Tientsin, but also with scattered mills in the interior, usually near large cities. Rice milling is largely by primitive methods, but small mechanical polishers are increasingly used. Freezing and dehydration are new methods still to be introduced, although a few foreign-operated factories have used these methods for exporting products from China to other countries. Refrigeration is a modern innovation and has been limited to the big port cities. No refrigeration has ever been available for products in transit within China.

The quantity of raw materials to be processed is very great. China's total food production exceeds that of the United States, partly because most of the production is used directly as food rather than first as feed for animals. Ninety-eight percent of the food energy (calories) of the rural population is derived from the vegetable kingdom, chiefly cereals and other seed products.

Although China has been processing food for the last 2,000 years, forms of processed products (with the exception of wheat flour and polished rice) are only a fraction of those in the United States, and quality and purity are also greatly inferior.

China grows nearly all the crops found in the United States, and produces several additional crops. Some of these would find a good export market in the United States; among them are the delicious fresh fruit, the lichee, bamboo shoots, and dried persimmons which should be even more popular than dried figs.

*   *   *

There are all kinds of possibilities, such as (1) extraction and refining of oils of many kinds produced in large quantities in China; (2) grain milling; (3) the processing of grains for porridges; (4) improvements in grading for standard quality, packaging, storage, warehousing and shipping of foods; (5) meat, poultry, egg and fish processing and packing; (6) fruit and vegetable storage and preservation by canning, freezing and dehydration.

Fibers. Cotton, silk, ramie, jute, wool, hemp, bristles, flax and camel hair are among the fibers produced in China.

Of these fibers, cotton is produced in the largest quantity. China is a land of cotton garments. Cotton is used for cloth, for padded garments and for padding bed quilts. China's climate is favorable for cotton production and she can produce all her requirements. Modern cotton textile mills have been operated successfully in China for years by Chinese owners as well as by foreign firms. China can be self-sufficient in her cotton industry, but erection of a large number of additional mills will be required.

Silk produced by silkworms fed with mulberry leaves is an important industry for domestic and foreign demand of silk. However, to maintain and increase her market for silk, greater attention must be given to rearing silkworms producing high quality cocoons, to baking of cocoons to kill the chrysalis and to improved reeling methods. Hand weavers and a few modern silk fabricating mills produce fine quality silks. Three thousand weavers of silk cloth at Tanyang, Kiangsu, have organized into cooperatives and produce such a fine quality of silk that they are able to compete in the Shanghai markets with machine-made cloth. It may be practical for China to develop a raw silk cloth export business, leaving the fabrication to importers of such cloth. The silk industry provides a large amount of labor and China should make every effort to supply a large portion of the world's silk market.

Ramie grows well in Central China and is used chiefly as cloth for summer dresses. Modern methods of decorticating and degumming might develop this industry to several times its present size.

Jute grown in North China and hemp in Central China are the chief fibers for string and rope. It is possible that modern methods of processing would be more efficient and would enable a greater production at lower costs.

Flax is grown in the high elevations of the Northwest, but the plant is an inferior variety. Production of fine linens in China appears possible and if embroidered by hand, such linens should supply a lucrative export and reduce import of linen for embroidery and re-export.

Carpet wool is an important export from the Northwest but the Chinese could increase their rug production, supply themselves with more labor and create larger quantities for foreign exchange. Scouring plants for wool should be installed at interior points.

Bristles are exported and a modern processing factory was set up in Chungking during the war. It appears that demand for bristles will continue for certain types of brushes.

Camel hair production can probably be increased to meet foreign demands and improved processing may aid such production.

Hides and Skins. Modern methods of tanning are beginning to be used in small factories in China, but the industry is in its initial stages. Use of leather for western types of shoes and other leather products is increasing. Since China produces large quantities of hides and skins (her density of animal population is as great as that of the United States) the tanning industry will undoubtedly be one of the big developments.

Special Products. Processing of tea for quality grades in large quantities is the only way by which China can increase her tea trade. Modern methods are in use in Formosa and should be adopted on the mainland.

Tung-oil has been one of China's chief exports and its grading in recent years has met foreign market requirements. However, the possibility of improving present methods of extraction requires attention in relation to production. The China-United States Agricultural Mission report advises production of tung-oil in concentrated areas and to give the tung-oil tree even greater cultural care than other horticultural crops. Concentration of its production might enable economical use of modern expellers.

Timber production in China is large and transportation of it is chiefly by floating down streams and rivers. There are still a few virgin forests, but they are not easily accessible. Large supplies of timber are also imported for use in coastal and river ports. It is probable that the use of modern sawmill equipment would be economical.

The handicraft industry for export as well as for domestic trade can be developed on a large scale. Most of the raw products would be from the farm or forest and a few are imported. China has the skills but has not yet organized the industry.

* * *

V. REQUIREMENTS FOR ACHIEVEMENT IN AGRICULTURE

. . . One of the fundamental questions to which attention must be given is the relation of population growth to resources. In most discussions about increasing production in China, the question is usually raised whether or not population will increase at the same rate, and therefore, negate the efforts toward increased production. There is reason to believe that parallel with efforts to increase production, other factors will be at work tending to decrease birth rates. Indeed there would be great danger if efforts were one-sided and confined only to increasing production. However, in China with the existing efforts to increase production there are other agencies at work promoting education, better health and higher standards of living. Moreover, there is an increasing social demand for a higher level of living. Thirty years ago most of the young men in high school were married; today the high school boys who are married are exceptions. The development of education will shorten the period of marriage and, therefore, decrease birth rates. It may be assumed that as China develops production, these offsetting factors to a population increase will also operate and create an adjustment between increased production and a population increase. It would be advisable, however, to establish an educational program on the importance of quality of population rather than numbers. [Compare this point of view with that in Selection 5.]

The success of any agricultural program is also dependent upon the type of trained personnel. The amount of trained personnel in China is entirely too small to adequately care for the immense agricultural problems in China. Until there is general education throughout the country, there is no possibility of sufficiently trained agricultural personnel becoming available. Such personnel, to be effective, must have had farm experience and understanding of farmers' viewpoints and ways of thinking and working. In addition to this, the agricultural teacher, research worker and extension agent must have a "spirit of service." The importance of these two qualifications for agricultural workers has been fully demonstrated in the United States and without the education of farm boys trained in the "spirit of service," agriculture in the United States would not have attained its present development.

One of the difficulties in China has been that many officials and the general public have not recognized the importance of agriculture in the national economy. In recent thinking, a great deal of emphasis has been placed on industrial development without much reference to agriculture. There appears to be a lack of understanding of how modern science can assist national economy through agriculture. Moreover, the attitude is altogether too prevalent that the farmer is chiefly a person to pay taxes and fight the wars. The present attitude of looking down on the farmer can often be noticed when a person from the scholar, merchant or official class talks to the farmer in a condescending way. Many agricultural students take the same attitude and, because they are not from the farms themselves, do not even know how to enter into conversation with a farmer and maintain his interest and respect.

* * *

. . . The family-farm system of agricultural production is the most practical of all methods for China and will probably continue. Attempts at collective and state farming, modelled after the Russian system, will undoubtedly be made but sudden universal application of collective or state farming is not to be expected. Those who advocate it are in the minority and do not understand the farm management problem involved. The physical factors such as topography, crops and climate are much more varied in China and create production problems quite different from those in Russia.

The advantages claimed for collective or state farming are (1) large size of business; (2) greater mechanization; and (3) full use of technical knowledge.

As to size of business, a farm can be too large as well as too small to be an economical unit. The advantages of size for purchasing supplies, selling products and obtaining credit can be had by farmers on family-sized farms by organizing into cooperatives. Thus the advantage of size can be obtained without its disadvantages of increasing the costs of production.

Not only is the size of farm an element in the future economic development of agriculture but also the extent of mechanization of farming. Some argue that there is no hope for Chinese agriculture without mechanization. As a rule mechanization does not increase production per unit of land. Essentially all that mechanization does is to save labor, to do work more quickly and to make farm work less irksome. It increases production per man but, in a country over-supplied with labor, alternative work must be found before the farmer can afford to pay for advantages of the machine. Labor-saving equipment and machinery will be practical for two purposes; first, to perform work man cannot now do, and second, to take the place of labor drawn from the farm for new developments in industry and professions.

As to use of up-to-date technical knowledge in production, a good agricultural extension system demonstrating improved practices to the farmers may not achieve application of new methods as quickly as in

a complete system of collective farming, but there would be less chance of failures. Managers of collective farms with authority over farm practices in large areas are subject to the making of mistakes which may affect production more adversely than could possibly happen under the family-farm system.

Would-be-reformers often accept the faulty thinking that collective farming or state farming increases the farm area per capita. If all China were collectivized tomorrow the land area per person would still be the same as it is today. To date, no scientific evidence has yet been presented showing that collectivized farms or state farms are the best economic units of agricultural production. On the other hand, there is considerable evidence that the family-farm is the best economic and social unit of organizations for farming. True, for certain types of farming where the work is routine, large units may produce as efficiently as the family-farm; but these are exceptions rather than the rule. One has yet to hear of any farm management specialist advocating collective or state farming. Even in China there are numerous examples of attempts at large-scale farming but to date not one successful large-scale farm.

Under the influence and pressure of reformers, so-called "cooperative farms," collective farms and state farms will be tried in limited areas. It is best that such experiments should be made to avoid a country-wide innovation which would undoubtedly increase costs of production and, hence, costs of food for the consumer. Small experiments will demonstrate success or failure. If they are a failure, the reformers will have to give in. If successful, the method can be applied on a larger scale. The experiments may be costly but it seems to be the only way to resolve present-day contentions.

China is, and must remain, an agricultural country in spite of all possible industrialization. Her resources, according to all present information, are scarcely enough for her own industrialization, although she may have surpluses for export of tin, tungsten, antimony and mercury. At best, she cannot expect to reduce her farm population to less than 50 percent of her total population. This has a different meaning than it would appear to have. At the present time one-fifth of the farmer's income is from sources other than the farm, partly from home industries. With industrialization in China the opportunity for farmers in home industries and local small scale industries will probably increase. The development in China will be one of farmers going into industry for part-time employment, whereas in the United States one sees the industrial worker going into farming as an adjunct to his industrial employment.

China in being an agricultural country can still be a strong country. It has enough resources to make possible a reasonable national defense. It does not have sufficient resources to permit export of finished products from heavy industries. Plastics with its raw material from agriculture may be of considerable aid to industry. Export of some mineral products, some agricultural products and more particularly of handcraft articles which combine raw materials and labor should be sufficient to pay for the imports required for a modest industrial development, especially if long term credits are extended to China. In the past, agricultural products have constituted China's chief export. Among these products were wood-oil, tin, silk, soybeans and soybean oil cake, bristles, sesame, intestines, hides and skins, meat, poultry, and its products and drugs. Most of these items can still maintain an important place in China's trade, but China cannot expect to pay for her industrialization by export of agricultural products alone.

Most of the discussion about industrialization in China is misleading and it is probable that not one person in a hundred understands its meaning or import. China's chief concern should be with increasing production per capita. This may be done with her present resources in the fields of both agriculture and industry. There is a tremendous surplus of labor on the farms, which could be used to develop irrigation and drainage projects; to improve land and water transportation; to develop water power, to better land use with proper control of soil and water; to proceed with re-afforestation of mountains; to manufacture farm supplies; to produce improved seeds, nursery stock and improved animals; to process agricultural products for marketing and for consumption; to manufacture improved types of consumer goods; and to develop heavy industry. Utilization of this large resource could be accomplished by a "labor" tax for those who have no money and a money tax for those with wealth. The projects would result in increased production per capita and greater efficiency in production and transportation, and would benefit the taxpayer. In other words, full utilization of labor and capital resources as well as the natural resources within the country would bring about increased production per capita, and therefore a higher standard of living.

Throughout China the peasants support themselves with supplementary occupations. The village on the Yangtze Plain described by Dr. Fei (Selections 6 and 14) specializes in the silk industry; in other regions there are other ways of increasing income. The following selection tells of maintenance practices in South China—in Phenix Village, not far from the port city of Swatow. Daniel H. Kulp described this village in 1925, and his study has become something of a classic in the field. There were 650 people in Phenix at the time of the study. Note that peasant villages are never completely self-subsistent; although each family tries to meet its own needs as much as possible, it must still turn to others for required products and services. The market town, where a farmer can sell his surplus produce and then buy needed articles, plays a very important part in the peasant economy (see Selection 8). Many of the simpler needs, however, can be supplied by specialists in his own village or even within his larger kinship group

• 9 • *Maintenance Practices in a South China Village*

DANIEL H. KULP, II

Farming is the basic industry of the region. It is not the extensive type found north of the Yangtse River, but intensive gardening, with the hoe as the chief implement. Orchards and gardens surround the village; they are particularly large on the north, and east across the Phenix River. On the south and west there are mainly gardens with a few groves of trees producing fruit and nuts.

The floods always threaten the farmer. Many times the waters will sweep the yams and peanuts from his gardens, but do not harm the trees. For this reason, the people have turned primarily to the development of orchards, thus saving themselves from starvation and ruin. There is not a single farmer in "Gwei Ho" dependent solely upon gardening for his subsistence.

The principal product of the district is oranges. Other products of major importance are, exclusive of rice and grains of other kinds, olives, bananas, persimmons, guava, plums, bamboo. These all grow above ground and are staple products. Cultivated to a less degree are sugar cane, pears, longan, loquat, walnuts, pomelo, lichi, pibaws, yams, peanuts, potatoes, peas, beans of various kinds, and berries of different types. . . .

During the seasons of harvest of the various fruits, especially of plums, pears, pibaws and berries—the perishables—the Chaochow and Swatow markets are glutted and the price drops very low. Cooperative canneries should be opened throughout the region. Then the products could be marketed gradually and the people could secure better incomes from their labors without increased effort.

VILLAGE WEALTH

In general, it can be said that the economic life of the people is one of "deficit." The frequent floods keep them from wealth, as has already been noted. The men depend upon their orchards, which develops in the farmers a tendency to "wait." They get what they can from gardening but count it as extra to their income from fruits. Though they have little to spare, yet they are far from starvation.

There is no doubt that scientific cultivation would raise the income of these people. They do not understand how to improve their crops. Their bananas are small and thin; their plums are bitter; their peanuts are dwarfed. Only the persimmons approach perfection. They should, through farm-demonstration work, learn to select seeds, graft, spray and cleanse the trees. They have ample time to cultivate in these ways. Only ignorance keeps them from producing fine crops, for the soil is deep and fertile alluvial deposit.

An occasional member of Phenix Village has amassed enough wealth to set up in a business venture but few have been successful. The dream of fortune has led many a young man to seek it in foreign lands. Those who are successful there send home regularly of their incomes. For the region as a whole, according to the consular reports for Swatow, during the year 1911 some three million emigrants in foreign parts remitted to their homes twenty-one million dollars.

Once in a while a fortunate villager returns home with wealth and foreign wife, trailing a flock of queerly-dressed children. It is thus

[From *Country Life in South China: The Sociology of Familism* . . . , Volume I—*Phenix Village, Kwantung, China,* Teachers College, Columbia University, New York, 1925. Pp. 84-101.]

quite natural that a father blesses a departing
son. In his emigrant kin he finds an additional
source of income. But the sons of luck are few.
The majority of the emigrants from Phenix
Village come back with empty hands, but
richer through sad experience, or else in distant lands complete their journey to "West
Heaven."

Some of the Phenix Village men have only
migrated as far as Chaochow or Swatow
where they are engaged in business. The
young men are clerks in stores or banks and
the older ones are partners in stores or banks.
That one of the heads of the families is contemplating industrial enterprise is shown by
his request to the writer for information on
the cost of a machine to manufacture shoe
nails. From these persons money is sent to
their closest kin in Phenix Village.

In addition to their products and their
emigrated kin, the third source of income for
the families of Phenix Village is the ancestral
property. This is established in the following
manner: a man of wealth sets aside a part of
his property which is not to be divided among
his children after his death. This provision
guarantees that his descendants, no matter
how poor they may become, will have the
means of offering sacrifice to his own departed
spirit, supplying him with food, money and
other things that mean happiness in the other
world as they do in this. Such property is considered as belonging to the ancestor even
though dead and not as owned by the group.
It must be clearly distinguished from other
property which may be owned by a familist-
group. The income from it is known as the
"ancestral fund." Since it is usually more than
what is needed to carry on ancestral worship,
the living descendants take turns in providing
the things required according to custom for
the sacrificial ceremonies and the feast that
follows for the representative descendants of
the ancestor worship. Whatever surplus exists,
goes to that person who managed the ancestral property during the year in order to carry
on ancestral worship. Inasmuch as some incomes from these ancestral properties are very
large, the surpluses are objects of interest. In

fact, they may be the only hope for some of
the poverty-stricken families. But they further
increase the incomes of the wealthy, for the
rich are not therefore deprived of their privilege in administering the ancestral estate, providing for ancestral worship, and sharing in
the surplus, according to the customary principles of rotation of responsibility.

OCCUPATIONS

The types of occupations by which the people maintain themselves are not numerous.
Nevertheless, it is very difficult to determine
the exact number of people who follow each
type. Most of them pursue several different
occupations at different times, according to
their needs and opportunities.

Except for agriculture and some handicrafts, there is no special training for the work
they do. They try one thing one day and leave
it the next without any real loss to anyone.
Sometimes they engage in pursuits not at all
for commercial purposes, simply out of convenience or for their own needs. Such might
be making bamboo-ware,—baskets, etc.,—cutting wood, fishing, raising geese and ducks,
gathering fruit. They sell the products of such
efforts when they need money or when there
is a surplus over the home necessities.

A general division of labor between men
and women is to be found in Phenix Village.
The men attend to business matters and do
most of the field work; the women carry on
the home industries. Practically all the village
wives, rich or poor, engage in the spinning
and weaving of flax into cloth for their own
use. The whirr of the spinning wheel . . .
and the click of the loom are heard in every
part of the village. The servants and slave
girls may today sew, sweep, cook, cut wood,
or spin, but tomorrow they may be hulling
rice or drying it in the courtyard. . . . It is
thus impossible to classify the people according to occupations.

Moreover, there are cooperative industrial
undertakings, such as sugar-manufacture or
boat-sailing of a temporary or irregular nature. For example, a student who had been
studying in Swatow owned a piece of land

which was being cultivated by one of his neighbors. It happened that one year he grew sugar cane on it. At the same time the fields all round stood deep with cane. When it was ripe for harvest all the farmers interested in the making of sugar gathered together and formed a cooperative society. It was not necessary for all to join so long as a number of people sufficient to launch the scheme was secured. In this case the student, through his ownership of the land, joined the corporation. Hands were hired to assist the farmers who knew most about sugar-making; implements and tools, such as mill-stones, knives, pans, and so on were purchased and rented. An office was built and the ovens constructed near the village temple by the side of the river.

This cooperative society lasted for several years and then went out of existence. Later another similar undertaking was organized but most of those engaged in the first enterprise refused to join the new movement. They gave as their reasons for refusing that the soil of their farms was not suited to sugar-cane or that they found it more profitable to dispose of their crop of cane as stalk cane. The broken mill-stones and the oven holes are still clearly visible; they are the remains of a cooperative enterprise that disappeared the moment the trend of practical interest was against it.

*   *   *

[The occupational distribution of Phenix Village is as follows, the principal occupations being marked with an asterisk:

Agricultural: *farmer, *gardener.
Industrial: *weaver (cotton, flax), woodcutter, carpenter, *fisherman, dyer, varnisher, cook, butcher, broom maker, boatman, silversmith, *bamboo-worker, beancurd maker (now stopped), livestock raiser, herb gatherer, sugar maker, mason, painter of pottery, tailor, hunter.
Professional: *merchant, *fruit dealer, teacher, official, preacher (Christian, now left), doctor, priest, servant, *clerk or salesman, tax collector, fortune teller, gambler, landholder, middleman.

Miscellaneous: emigrant, beggar, nibbler, parasitic idler.]

Some explanation of these occupations may serve to illuminate the manner in which the people carry on their economic activities. Of the two occupations listed under "agricultural," gardening is predominant. By "farmer" is meant all those whose greatest income derives from farming grains and cereals; by "gardener" is meant those who depend upon the cultivation of fruits and vegetables for their income. The farmer is, in most cases, somewhat of a gardener too, but the latter occupation is for him incidental.

Among the industrial and professional occupations butchering, fishing, woodcutting, sugar-making, hunting, landholding, and serving as a middleman are those which are carried on incidentally and intermittently by men. Similarly the women, in addition to their routine duties of the household, cooking, caring for the children, sewing, cleaning and so on, engage in broom-making, the manufacture of hemp twine, basketry, spinning, weaving cloth, raising geese, gathering herbs, and so on.

The prevalence of broom-making rests upon the practical needs of the housewives. They gather the wire grass from the hills, make up thirty to forty brooms in a day, take them to Chaochow where they sell them for an average of one cent apiece and so add to the family income. This extra day needed for marketing their products deters them from constant pursuit of the industry. The village leaders would do well to establish an agency for the cooperative marketing and merchandising of all home products. Such a facility would relieve the housewife of the trouble and yet put into her hands the income of her labors. It would make possible improvements in products, an increase in the number and kinds of products and the expansion of the markets.

Bamboo is very common and is used in a great variety of ways. The shoots of the young trees of certain species are dug up as soon as they break through the ground and are sold for food. One kind, known as the "incense frame" bamboo, is not edible and is allowed to grow to maturity. This is cut down and sold in bulk for the manufacture of incense frames. One hundred *catties,* about one hundred and thirty pounds, sell for thirty to fifty cents, local currency. This type of bamboo is used in the manufacture of baskets, furniture, drying frames, sun shades, beams and pillars in huts, string, rope, fishing tackle, and so on almost *ad infinitum.*

The gathering of medicinal herbs is also an occupation based upon the needs of the home. People regularly scour the nooks and crannies of the hills and mountains in search of the wild plants reputed to possess curative properties. Surplus quantities are disposed of at something of a profit. The dangers of the wild beasts, the toil of climbing the hills in the scorching sun, discourage the hunting for "green grass" as a permanent occupation.

There are practically as many wholesale fruit dealers as general merchants. The former buy the fruits before the harvest is even ripe; sometimes, when the trees are only in bloom. On the basis of the quality and abundance of the blossoms, the dealers estimate the probable quantity and quality of the crop and higgle with the gardener until a price per picul of harvested fruit is agreed upon. After the bargain has been struck the original owner is no longer responsible for the crop. Cultivation and care of the trees is then turned over to the fruit speculators, usually a joint stock concern because of the labor and finance involved— who then are burdened with the warnings of sun and rain. The realization of the profits is undertaken with all seriousness, for not infrequently the speculators have borrowed their capital at a heavy rate of interest—ten to twenty per cent. Some have in this way become rich in ten years. Others on account of bad weather conditions, sluggish markets, or poor judgments in striking prices, lose their money and their property. These unfortunate ones then help to swell the stream of emigration.

On the other hand, the fruit dealers may, when the fruit is ripe or nearly ripe for harvest, dispose of the fruit on the tree by selling out to traders who have greater capital. Thus the orchards may be bought up by a few dealers who then are in a position to maintain monopoly control of the local products. When the weather is favorable and the competition between these "big stomach" speculators is not so keen that they lose their heads and gamble blindly, they are quite successful. But the weather is a very uncertain factor: floods, typhoons, heavy fogs injure the plums; frost is fatal to the orange and the banana crops. Under unfortunate weather conditions, in the case of a single transfer of rights in crops, the original owner would have to take a discount upon the stipulated price. But when the crop is sold a second time or becomes the basis of "wildcat" speculation, the gardener is absolved from any such obligation.

The gamblers listed refer to those who keep houses especially for gambling and opium smoking and make a living thereby. Their shops are located just on the northern end of the business section of the village. Being responsible for the good conduct of their patrons, they are men of physical strength, members of strong "branches" of the familist group. They always stand ready, with the assistance of men who have specialized in boxing, to quell disorder or prevent outside interference. Among these the village parasites are found. They pander to everyone in the gambling house and beg gifts from the winners.

THE VILLAGE MARKET

Those who carry on single and clearly distinguishable occupations are the shopkeepers and clerks. Of the twenty-one open shops in the business section only five are run by merchants who are members of the Phenix Village familist-group. The others are rented by people from outside who have come in to do business with Phenix Village.

These shops serve not only the people of Phenix Village but also those of nearby villages who need business service. An inspection of [the diagram] reveals the general types of goods handled. What the people do not supply for themselves they purchase. To meet these

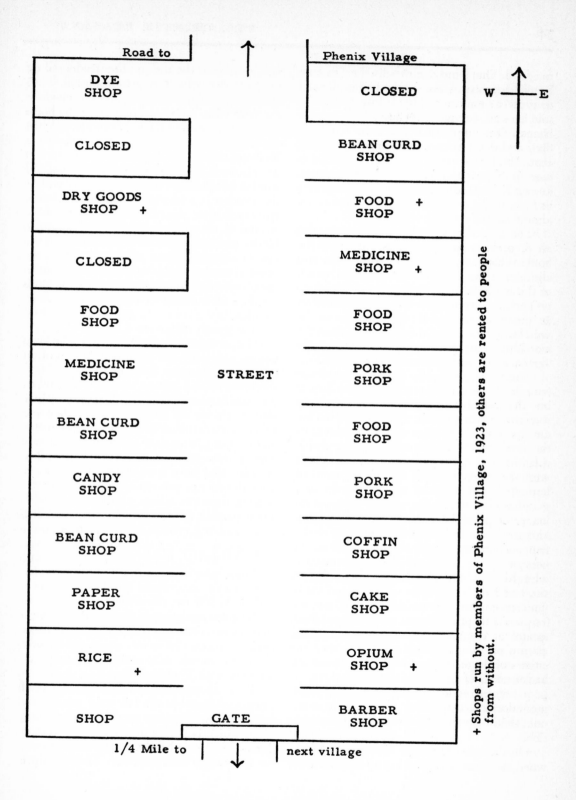

Road to   ↑   Phenix Village

W ——●—— E

DYE SHOP | **CLOSED**

CLOSED | **BEAN CURD SHOP**

DRY GOODS SHOP + | **FOOD SHOP** +

CLOSED | **MEDICINE SHOP** +

FOOD SHOP | **FOOD SHOP**

MEDICINE SHOP | **STREET** | **PORK SHOP**

BEAN CURD SHOP | **FOOD SHOP**

CANDY SHOP | **PORK SHOP**

BEAN CURD SHOP | **COFFIN SHOP**

PAPER SHOP | **CAKE SHOP**

RICE + | **OPIUM SHOP** +

SHOP | **GATE** | **BARBER SHOP**

1/4 Mile to   ↓   next village

+ Shops run by members of Phenix Village, 1923, others are rented to people from without.

needs the shops provide the distributive service. They procure the goods and offer them for sale. It is significant that competition works out here as everywhere. The more important shops have competitors. There are four food shops, two meat shops, two medicine shops, three bean curd shops, two rice shops under one merchant. Over half the shops are devoted to the sale of food of some kind or other. Adding to the above the candy shop and the cake shop, thirteen out of twenty-one deal in food. The others comprise the paper shop, dry-goods shop, coffin shop—the coffins are made and sold in this shop, sometimes to order—and the distinctly service shops, such as barber, opium, and dye shops.

The shops are an indication of the shortages of home production. They represent specialized services which the village community needs filled but which are not readily met by the ordinary maintenance practices. There are thus three areas of economic production and service by which this community maintains its physical life: (1) The home and fields; (2) the village market; (3) Chaochow. The more unusual needs that are not provided for in the shops of the village market are met in Chaochow where the range is great because of high specialization possible in urban communities. This kind of need is incidental.

The successful establishment and maintenance of these shops in a village as small as this correlates with the change in family economy. There are a number of people in the village who no longer follow either farming or gardening. These folk must purchase their food and other products as they need them. Such people are the merchants and clerks, the officials and professionals generally, and the boatmen. The service and professional people patronize most regularly the market; the others occasionally buy there to meet the unusual needs of familist economy.

Complete independence of familist economy does not exist either for any part of the village kin-group or for the village as a whole. This market mediates goods between the local producers and the village consumers of ordinary and occasional products and between the city producers and the rural consumers of extraordinary and incidental products.

The meat shops sell pork almost exclusively and some dried fish. The only meat the home produces is from chickens or geese, but the people find it more profitable to sell these and buy bits of pork as they need it.

The food shops sell vegetables, oil, and the like. This provides village families with a wider range of selection of foods for their diets than would be possible were they compelled by the inconvenience of markets to depend solely upon their own products. They grow a limited number of vegetables; other gardeners grow other kinds, and a monotonous diet is thus broken up by buying the different kinds of vegetables put on the market from other gardens.

The work of women is so varied, so important, and so interesting that it is worthy of special and extended treatment. It is possible here only to note its chief phases.

There is no evidence that children are exploited although they are engaged in incidental occupations. Thus they watch the geese, carry water, and assist in the simpler operations about the home. In general the children seem to have too much time for idling. The boys are freer than the girls because the women's duties provide more opportunities for work for girls than men's provide occupation for boys. The boys, and sometimes the girls too, do assist in picking berries or fruit and in watching crops. But they do not seem to be forced to engage in arduous field labor with the men.

THE WORK OF WOMEN

The women are engaged primarily in the home work of cooking of food. In the larger homes . . . the kitchens contain the regular large Chinese stoves. These are made of brick, with two pans placed over two fire boxes, quite small and fed with fuel through small openings in the front. The pans are covered with wooden covers; one pan is for cooking rice—which is always steamed—and the other for vegetables and meat.

Frequently, however, the housewives prefer the simple "wind-stove" or *feng-lo* to the large stoves. These are placed in the passageway convenient to the kitchen but outside of it in order to keep the smoke and fumes out of the room in which the people usually eat. These little stoves require less work to handle and are very economical. By burning charcoal in them they are very much cleaner than the large stoves that require ordinary stick-wood and underbrush as fuel. No coal is used for cooking.

Other regular duties are the making of the beds, care of the rooms, sweeping and dusting. When these are attended to, the housewife embroiders or sews for the family. Or she may spin, or weave, make twine, starch it and sun it, make baskets, or prepare rice for cooking. The latter takes much time and falls entirely within the women's sphere of labor and attention.

Quantities of rice are carried on the shoulders in buckets and spread out in the sun to dry. Several times during the day one of the women, probably a servant or slave girl who does the hard work in the wealthier families, will walk through the rice turning it over and over with her bare feet. The winnowing machine is carried into the court, the rice swept together and winnowed. Then it is kept in bags until it is carried out and hulled by pounding. Again it is winnowed, and when needed, is washed in water carried from the well or from the river, and steamed.

Drying fruits or seeds, beans and the like occupies the attention of the housewife also. These they take from the shells, spread out on broad drying baskets in the sun, and keep turning them over from time to time until ready for storage. They are bagged and placed in one of the corners of the second story.

There are no conveniences of a modern kind in any of these rural homes even of the best. Women must carry the water; take care of the candles or oil lights—to-day generally of Standard Oil manufacture—and carry them from place to place as needed. The furniture is heavy, especially in the older and wealthier families, and therefore difficult to move about.

And yet life is simple. It does not take long to prepare food for four or five people. A pot of rice, a few vegetables and a bit of meat. Commonly they use in all about sixteen different kinds of vegetables and five kinds of meat, fresh, salt or dried. The latter includes only beef, pork, goose, duck and chicken, and fish.

The women of the poorer families are always busy either in the routine work of preparing food, caring for the home or children, or carrying on some form of domestic industry. But the women of the wealthier families find time heavy on their hands. They occupy themselves with the lighter work of sewing and embroidery.

The intellectual life of the women of all classes is hemmed in by such rural isolation and domestic drudgeries growing out of crude household arrangements. The installation of radio receiving sets could be afforded by at least half the homes of Phenix Village and would greatly relieve the monotony of the wealthier homes and the drudgery of the poorer. A simple village cooperative lighting system could be installed at relatively low cost. These are the only practical improvements that ought to be installed as soon as possible in Phenix Village. Many others could be suggested, but they could not be worked out nor would they be accepted on account of the expense involved.

THE MIDDLEMAN

In addition to the foregoing types of work there should be added three more. Middlemen are very important functionaries in village life. They are necessary because of attitudes of avoidance that prevail among the villagers whenever any situation has possibilities of embarrassment or strain between the people involved. The desire to avoid "losing face" which is the popular phrase for avoiding the feeling of inferiority—or stated positively, the wish for dominance—leads them to deal through intermediaries in land transactions, quarrels, betrothal and marriage, and the determination of prices for products, chickens, pigs, crops and so forth. The women and some farmers use the middleman for their important transactions of the latter sort. The middlemen secure commissions on such work and in the case of land transactions manipulate for "fat" commissions.

This is not a distinct occupation in itself but rather a functional relationship assumed and discharged as occasion offers. In time certain people get the reputation of success through their patience and cleverness. Going back and forth among people in the village and outside, learning confidential matters in connection with the "deals" they put through, they are reservoirs of news and information, which they frequently turn to profit. They are in a sense the village newspaper and feed village conversation with matter for gossip.

BEGGARS

Then there are the nibblers and beggars. The former hang around the streets and food shops and maintain themselves by snatching bits of food whenever the opportunity arises.

The beggars are usually those physically handicapped by heredity or disease, and are thrown upon the mercy of their fellows for maintenance. Their plaintive wail is always most oppressing. Here is a song of the blind:

> *Oh . . . . !*
> *Teacher, matron and maid,*
> *Do good and help us!*
> *Save us blind children,*
> *Poor blind children!*
> *Parentless children!*
> *Grandfather is sick,*

> *Homeless, poor people, are we!*
> *O . . . . h!*
> *Save us! Oh, save us, rich people!*

Only the heart turned into stone by greed can refuse aid to these abject creatures that nauseate the sensitive with their filth and rags, as they pound their heads upon the flagstones of the street until the blood flows down their sightless eyes.

In the economy of Phenix Village, the beggar in his own way performs a social function as definitely as the farmer, the teacher, the fruit dealer or the gambler. The devout Buddhist hopes to gain "West Heaven," but charity and alms are the fundamental means, enjoined by the priests, of gaining that happiness. The beggar provides the object upon which the faithful may bestow his alms and pity and thus add to his credit in heaven. This is the basis of the kindly feeling that people take in beggars, loathsome as they may be.

In conclusion, the distinctive occupations of the village are agricultural,—farming and gardening, and mercantile. The mercantilists constitute a group larger than the agriculturists: almost one-tenth of the entire village population is engaged in the distribution function.

Exclusive of the types of vocations of the emigrants and the ordinary duties of the housewives, there are in all thirty-nine definite forms of maintenance activities to be found in Phenix Village, comprising productive, service, or parasitic functions.

Social Organization: Familism

>>>

A peasant society is strongly familistic. By now it should be strikingly clear that the family is the basic economic unit in peasant China, as it is in most rural societies. Even in the United States, where farm people make up only 15.6 percent of the total population, the ideal seems to be the family-sized farm, which can be taken care of by the members of the family and can provide them with an adequate level of living. But there the comparison with China ends, for our society is not *familistic.** We tend to stress individualism and to devote segments of our lives to many activities which have little to do with family-centered values. Therefore, as we read about the Chinese family, we must be prepared to notice its all-pervading influence as a pattern of association. The various selections will show the characteristics of the husband-wife, parent-child, in-law, and sibling and cousin relationships, and also follow the processes of socialization and social control through the daily routine.

· 10 · Familism the Foundation of Chinese Social Organization
CHENG CH'ENG-K'UN

Long before the collapse of the Manchu Monarchy in 1911, the social organization in China was founded on a large family system. This system exercised such a powerful influence that it completely dominated the thoughts and actions of the Chinese people. It taught

[From "Familism the Foundation of Chinese Social Organization," *Social Forces,* Vol. 23, No. 1, Baltimore, 1944. Pp. 50-59. Used by permission.]

* *Familism.* A social system wherein all behavior, all standards, ideals, attitudes and values arise from, center in, or aim at the welfare of those bound together by the blood nexus fundamentally. The family is therein the basis for reference, the criterion for all judgments. Whatever is good for the family, however that good is conceived, is approved and developed; whatever is inimical to the interests of the family, however they are formulated, is taboo and prohibited (Kulp, *Country Life in South China,* page xxix).

them the necessity of cooperation, courtesy, patience, and self-control in family relationship. It bred in them a sense of filial obligation toward their parents and respect for their elders. It inculcated in their minds the supreme importance of working for the honor and glorification of the family name. It caused them "to sweep snow in front of their own door, and not to bother about the frost on the roof of their neighbors." It aroused in them family consciousness and not national consciousness, and made them eager to fight for the protection of the graveyards of their ancestors and reluctant to shoulder arms in defense of their country. No satisfactory understanding of China and her present titanic problems of adjustment can be attained without an analysis of the deep-rooted influence of this system of social organization from which the Chinese people are emerging. . . .

How did this large family system come to play such a vital part in the organization of the Chinese nation? It all started more than four thousand years ago when that country was still largely wild and unexplored. There were impenetrable jungles, ravaging floods, and ferocious animals. The people were mostly nomads without fixed habitations and without uniform codes of conduct. [This traditional "history" is somewhat oversimplified.] At that time the advantages of farming had just come to the attention of the government. Emperor Shun recognized that the cooperation demanded in settled agriculture could be achieved only through standardization of human relationships. As a measure of insuring success in this new form of economic enterprise, he, therefore, laid down "Wu Tien" or "the five canons" for the purpose of regulating the relations between sovereign and subject, father and son, elder and younger brothers, husband and wife, and between friends. Of these five canons, three were directly connected with the family, and of the three, filial piety or devotion to and respect for one's parents was the most rigidly and widely applied.

*　　*　　*

After more than ten centuries of application, filial piety became firmly entrenched in the social order of China. It was upheld by law and sanctioned by philosophers. In Book II of the epoch-making document, *The Constitution of Chow,* supposedly written by the famous Duke of Chow somewhere around the 11th century B.C., it is stipulated that filial piety is the first of the six proper modes of conduct to be taught to the people and that the punishment of the unfilial is the first of the eight laws of punishment. In *Hsiao Ching* or *Classic of Filial Piety,* which is assigned to Confucius and one of his outstanding disciples, Tseng Ts'an, it is also stipulated that there are three thousand offenses against which the five punishments are directed, and none of them is greater than being unfilial.

THREE PRINCIPLES OF FAMILISM

Filial Piety. What was filial piety as applied by the Chinese people? In a country like China where "society" as an idea of human organization did not exist and where nationalism was never greatly developed because of her rarely challenged position, filial piety acquired a great variety of applications. Most of these applications were made and maintained as a result of the approbative evaluations of Confucius, Mencius, and other philosophers of their times. Filial obedience has been recognized the world over as an important virtue of man. But, in China, it was carried to the extreme. Chinese children were not allowed to talk back to their parents, to ignore their commands or thwart their wishes. They were discouraged from criticizing the acts of their father and mother even if these acts were heinous and wicked. Confucius once said: "A man may gently remonstrate with his parents. But if he sees that he has failed to change their opinion, he should maintain an attitude of deference and not oppose them."

Obedience was not the only application of filial piety in China. The Chinese people also served their parents with great devotion and respect. They honored them and supported them and would not do anything which was disgraceful to them. They believed that while parents were alive, a good son should not wander too far afield. They considered a man filial if he followed the footsteps of his parents and did not deviate from their ways. . . . They maintained that the highest achievement of true filial piety was to serve, by means of sacrificial offerings, "those now dead as if they were living." . . .

Furthermore, a filial son in China would take very good care of himself because his body was given to him by his parents. Also he should not show such attachment to his wife and children as to neglect "the nourishment of his parents." Above all, he should have offspring to carry on the name of his family. Once, in his discussion of the last mentioned subject, Mencius enumerated three things which were unfilial, namely: to be without posterity, to encourage parents in unrighteousness, and to desist from giving them succour in their poverty and old age. Of the three, in the opinion of the philosopher, to be without posterity was the most unfilial.

In this great variety of applications, filial piety constituted the first principle of familism in the social organization of China. Many Chinese rulers in history encouraged it by their own examples and, practically all of them, by giving awards of one kind or another to those who had been unusually devoted to their parents. Even alien rulers like the Manchus considered its preservation and promotion of paramount significance to their regime. In 1670 Emperor K'ang Hsi issued an edict of sixteen moral maxims, the first of which enjoins the people to pay great attention to filial piety in order to give due weight to human relationship. After his death, his son and successor, Yung Cheng, caused these maxims to be enlarged and improved, and in 1724 the new emperor decreed that they be read to the people on the first and the fifteenth of each month in every city and town throughout the empire. The decree was in force all the way down to the end of the nineteenth century.

Devotion of Younger Brother to Elder Brother. The second principle of familism was the devotedness of the younger brother to his elder brother. In his oft-quoted "Announcement" to his nephew, the Duke of Chow considered those who were unfilial and unbrotherly more detestable than robbers and murderers. He said: "Those who commit crimes like robbing, stealing, practicing villainy and treason and those who kill men or violently assault them to take their property are to be abhorred by all. But how much more detestable are the unfilial and unbrotherly . . . and the younger brother who does not think of the manifest will of Heaven and refuses to respect his elder brother." Mencius, in discussing the same subject, regarded filial and brotherly affections as laws of nature. . . . The importance attached to love and respect for one's elder brother among the Chinese people may be gathered from the fact that in the past nothing could be a better testimony of virtue than for a man to be spoken of by his relatives and friends as a "dutiful son" and "good brother."

Attitude of Wife toward Husband and Parents-in-Law. The third principle of familism was the proper attitude of a wife to her husband and her parents-in-law. In China when a woman was married she went to live with her husband in the family of his folks. She was expected to serve him, obey his orders, and not to thwart his wishes. It would be in contradiction to the mores for her to leave him under almost any circumstances. The Chinese people conceived of husband as heaven and wife as the earth and, to them, it was against reason for a married woman to change her feeling of duty toward her mate.

* * *

More important than the attitude of a woman to her husband was her attitude to her parents-in-law. In China the position of a woman in the family of her husband was extremely difficult. She was supposed to serve her parents-in-law with all human care, courtesy, and respect. According to customary practices handed down from legendary time, at the first crowing of the cock, the daughter-in-law should arise and dress and tidy herself. Then she should go to her parents-in-law and inquire about their health, bring in the basin for them to wash, prepare their breakfast and serve it to them with good cheer. She should maintain the same degree of alertness throughout the day and execute their orders promptly, efficiently, and willingly. Furthermore, she should observe all the rules of decorum in their presence and should neither spit, cough, sneeze, yawn, nor stretch herself, nor lean against anything, nor look askance. These and many other duties used to require as long as three months of instruction before a woman was adequately prepared to enter the house of her husband as wife and daughter-in-law.

UNIQUE FEATURES OF FAMILISM

Complexity. The universal application of these basic principles of familism in the agricultural economy of China facilitated and furthered the development of her large family system. This system had many unique features which made it so vastly different from the system that prevailed in the west. What were these unique features? In the first place, the Chinese family was a highly complex institution when viewed from the standpoint of size. In China it was not uncommon to find thirty or forty relatives living in the same household. [Dr. F. L. K. Hsu reminds us that the large family ideal was achieved mostly among the wealthier families, and that the actual mean or average size of all families is about 5.2 persons, or even less. Just the same, the ideal itself has proven an important social force. For further information see table prepared by Lewis S. C. Smythe as quoted by E. W. Burgess and Harvey J. Locke, *The Family: From Institution to Companionship,* American Book Company, New York, 1945, p. 42.] These relatives usually included husband and wife and their children, the parents and the grandparents of the husband, his brothers, sisters, cousins, and his brothers' wives. As the children grew up

and married, the size of the family increased by the natural process of propagation. To the Chinese people who knew little better than the agricultural mode of life their ancestors had developed, the size of the family meant its economic power. And it was on this basis that they considered it the acme of good fortune to have "five generations under one roof."

The complexity of the Chinese family was greatly intensified by the concubinage system. This system was in existence for more than four thousand years. The legendary sovereigns of China including Huang Ti or The Yellow Emperor and Emperors Yao and Shun all practiced polygyny. In the early part of the Chow Dynasty (1122-255 B.C.) it was a custom for the sovereign to have six grades of spouses representing an aggregate number of one hundred and twenty-six. At the end of the dynasty the custom was changed and the number of spouses of a man depended upon his social status. . . . Among the masses monogamy was the rule. This change in custom continued until the Ch'ing Dynasty (1644-1912) when wealthy farmers and merchants also took concubines. Between 1912 and 1931 many of the ignorant and irresponsible warlords exploited the system to satisfy their lust for sensual pleasure. . . .

The development of concubinage in China was a natural social phenomenon. However evil the system might seem from the modern point of view, its existence was traditionally considered indispensable among the Chinese people. To them, nothing could be more disastrous than for a family to have no male offspring to carry on its name. Therefore, a man was justified to take a concubine or concubines if his wife failed to give birth to a son. This justification was so widely accepted that throughout the ages all government regulations of the system were carefully qualified so that those who did not have male offspring would not be unduly affected. . . . [In the description of Taitou Village (Selection 17) note how uncommon concubinage actually is among the farm people.]

In such a complex family organization, all

its members were assigned to their proper positions for the purpose of facilitating the maintenance of domestic harmony. These members included both relatives from a direct line like parents and their children and grandchildren, and those from collateral lines like aunts, uncles, nieces, nephews, cousins, and other more distant relatives. Attached to their respective positions were their respective rights and duties. These rights and duties changed with the change of status of the individual. In the case of a male member, his status was determined by age in conformity with the long-established Chinese social practice. In the case of a female member, her status was determined not only by her age, but also by her ability to help increase the male population of the family. In her relationship with men, a woman's status changed in the following order: Before marriage, she followed and obeyed her father and elder brothers; when she married, she followed and obeyed her husband; and after her husband's death, she followed her sons.

Authority. The second feature was the way by which the family was controlled as one functioning unit. Theoretically, the father was vested with absolute authority consistent with the superior status customarily assigned to men in China. But in actual practice, there was a division of labor between the sexes. While the father occupied himself mainly with the duties of earning a livelihood for the family and upholding its honor, the mother was the center of Chinese domestic life. She generally decided when and where her children should begin their schooling. She arranged the matters concerning their betrothals. She managed the business of the household and directed all the punctilious social relations with kith and kin. She attended to the ceremonies with regard to births, marriages, and deaths, and saw to it that the relationships among the various members of her family were satisfactorily maintained. In reality she held a very exalted position among her children as was amply demonstrated not only by the respect they paid to her when she was living, but also by the mourning rituals they observed after her death. According to Chinese tradition, both father and mother were placed in the same category for first degree mourning except when the father survived the mother. In the latter case, the explanation was that "There are not two suns in the sky, nor two sovereigns in a country, nor two rulers in a state, nor two highest authorities in a family. Only one person rules the family (at a time), hence, while the father is alive, the mourning of the second degree is worn for the mother."

To strengthen the power of parental control in the Chinese family, a system of mourning was developed. This system was conceived on the basis of kinship and included five degrees. The first degree was observed for father, mother, husband and husband's parents and extended over a period of three years (actually from 25 to 27 months). . . . Of these five degrees of mourning, the first was generally considered "the highest expression of grief" and "the richest exhibition of feeling of affection and respect." Tsai Wo, a disciple of Confucius, once argued against the three-year mourning and insisted that one year was sufficient. When he went out, Confucius said: "This indicates Tsai Wo's want of virtue." In the opinion of the Master, the three-year mourning was the essence of propriety since "It is not until a son is three years old that he is allowed to leave the arms of his parents."

From this elaborate system of mourning emerged the cult of ancestor-worship to further strengthen the power of parental control in the Chinese family. This cult conceives the idea that the departed spirits of the ancestors are still hovering somewhere in the neighborhood looking after the welfare of their descendants. In order to keep these departed spirits from losing their sense of justice, the living must continue to demonstrate their respect for the dead. One way of demonstrating such respect was to follow the footsteps of the ancestors and keep to the path of virtue. Evidences of this line of thinking can be found throughout the massive history of China. As early as the fourteenth century B.C. when P'an Keng, the seventeenth ruler of the Shang Dynasty (1766-1154 B.C.) was preparing to move his capital to a better location, his people were unwilling to go with him. Thereupon he made an epochal declaration in which he justified his preparation in these terms: "My present undertaking to move the capital is to give repose and stability to the state. . . . Were I to err in my government . . . my ancestors would send down great punishment for my crime."

Another way of demonstrating respect for one's ancestors was the establishment of places where sacrificial offerings could be made to them after their death. In an ordinary family, the central hall was reserved mainly for this purpose. If the family split up as usually happened in three or four generations, several related families might have a common ancestral temple. In an official family the number of ancestral temples depended upon its status and influence. . . .

In these ancestral halls or temples the Chinese people offered seasonal and anniversary sacrifices to their departed ancestors. During the day of sacrifice the filial son was expected to be deeply engrossed in thinking of his parents. In entering the hall or temple he would seem to see them in the places where their *Ling Wei* or spirit-tablets were set up. On leaving it he would seem to be arrested by hearing the sounds of their movements. . . .

Family Solidarity. The third feature was the solidarity of the family. Centralization of domestic control in the hands of the parents and deification of them after their death were in themselves forces contributing to solidarity. But a more powerful force was the process of conditioning by which the corporate unity of the home was maintained. This process operated for the accomplishment of two chief objectives, namely: collective responsibility in behavior and mutual aid in livelihood. On the one hand children in China were taught that, whatever work they undertook, they must do it with the thought of glorifying the spirits of their ancestors and bringing honor to the family and not to disgrace their good names. In addition, the Chinese government system was such that the administrative authorities found it convenient to hold the family collectively responsible for the conduct of its members. In cases like treason against the State, the crime of one member might cause the death of the whole family irrespective of sex or age. Brought up in these forms of conditioning, the Chinese people naturally learned to think twice before they acted.

On the other hand, children in China were early impressed with the idea that security of the individual in the family lay in mutual aid among its members. They took nourishment of their parents and aged relatives as their first duties in life. They loved their brothers to the same degree as they loved their own "hands and feet." Sometimes a brother would travel thousands of miles across the sea and go through considerable privation to redeem the honor of a bankrupt brother. Oftentimes a successful man would willingly share his wealth with his relatives and use his influence to improve their economic status. The legendary Emperor Shun had a half brother named Hsiang. For many years Hsiang had cherished the desire to kill Shun. When the latter ascended the throne, he raised Hsiang to the rank of a prince. . . .

Feeling of Continuity. The fourth feature was the presence of a feeling of continuity in the family. To the Chinese people life was an unending process of succession. One generation died, another came up to take its place and the institutional functions of the family continued. . . .

In the writings of Tiehtze (a hitherto unidentified scholar who was alleged to have lived in the third century B.C.) there is a parable which also illustrates the influence of this feeling of "social immortality." According to the parable, there once lived in North China an old man of about ninety years of age. This old man had been living in a house facing the Tai Hang Mountain all his life. He was tired of climbing up and down the mountain whenever he went out. So he gathered his family one day and said to them: "Let us set to work and move this mountain so that we may have a level path leading straight to Central China." The family agreed. Thereupon the old man led three of his children and grandchildren and began to chip the rocks and scrape the earth and carry them in baskets to Po Hai, hundreds of miles away. An orphan boy of the widow next door who had just shed his milk teeth trod along with them and came home only once a year. These activities created periodical commotion in the neighborhood. A friend laughed at the old man saying: "What a fool you are! With all the strength and years left to you, you can't even scratch the surface of the mountain, let alone the rocks and earth." The old man drew a deep sigh and said: "It's only your mind that is not made up; when it is made up, nothing can stop it. You are of less use than the widow's son. When I die, there will be my children to carry on the work, and the children will have grandchildren, and the grandchildren will again have children, and the children will again have children, and the children will again have grandchildren. So my children and grandchildren are endless, while the mountain cannot grow bigger in size. Why shouldn't it be leveled some day?" The friend could not make any reply. Now the Snake Spirit overheard the conversation and went to speak to God. God had pity on the old man's sincerity and ordered the mountain to be removed.

THE FAMILY AS AN INDEPENDENT SOCIAL UNIT

Circumscribed in this kind of organization, the Chinese large family existed very much as an independent social unit. It was self-contained, self-disciplined, self-perpetuating, and self-sufficient. It fulfilled almost all the functions of an organized society and made the feeling of attachment to it strong and irresistible. Economically, it represented the most radical form of socialistic cooperation. Within its four walls all members worked and lived together. They all did what they could and took what they needed. They were all partners in the same productive enterprise. In their various positions, they were all employers, employees, middlemen, and holders of property. Between them there were no essential differences in social condition. They

shared wealth and prestige as well as poverty and degradation.

The operation of this form of socialistic cooperation depended on the subordination of desire for personal profit to the desire for virtue, the significance of which is repeatedly emphasized in Chinese classical literature. Once Mencius went to see King Hui of L'aing. The king asked if the philosopher had come with counsels to profit his kingdom. Mencius replied: "Why must Your Majesty use the word 'profit'? . . . If Your Majesty ask, 'What is to be done to profit my kingdom?' the great officers will ask, 'What is to be done to profit our families?' and the petty officers and the common people will ask, 'What is to be done to profit our persons?' Superiors and inferiors will then struggle against one another for profit and the kingdom will be in danger."

*   *   *

Judicially, the Chinese people believed and practiced the ancient saying that . . . "Disgraceful affairs of the family are not to be made known outside." They kept domestic conflicts very much to themselves. Disrespectfulness to parents, parents-in-law and elders in general, unfaithfulness to husband, disloyalty to elder brothers, and violation of marriage customs were usually hushed up and adjustments made by the parents or, in more serious cases, by the family council which was composed of the elders of the household. When conflicts involved two or more families, the matters were customarily submitted to and settled by the elders of the village which, in reality, was "the family raised to a higher exponent." These village elders, together with the local gentry who were schooled in law and history, formed an unofficial tribunal in which most of the civil disputes and petty criminal offenses were liquidated. That was why in spite of the fact that China possessed a minutely organized and dynastically revised system of law, her rulers never found it necessary to set up a separate law-enforcing machinery. The Chinese district magistrate was invested with judicial function, but at the same time, he was the warden of local prisons, the overseer of public roads, the registrar of land, the collector of taxes, the superintendent of education, and the commissioner of police.

Socially, members of the Chinese family were all insured against the many misfortunes of life. Whether the person affected was an orphan, a widow, a blind, a crippled, or a decrepit old man, he or she was taken as a charge of the family. It would be a gross disgrace to the names of the ancestors if any of these unfortunate relatives was allowed to wander about without assistance and care. This was especially true when applied to parents. Confucius once said that a man should serve his father as he would expect his own son to serve him. . . . Living in such a state of interdependence, the Chinese people never felt the need for organized relief outside the home circle. In fact, until the arrival of missionaries from Europe and America, there was no public philanthropic institution of any permanence within the confines of the Chinese nation.

Education was an important function of the family in China. There, scholars ranked first among the . . . four classes of the people and scholarship was always the basis on which government appointments were made. Nothing would do greater honor to the names of the ancestors than to have scholars and officials in the family. Hence, Chinese parents were generally enthusiastic about giving their intelligent sons every opportunity for education. In well-to-do families, private tutors were hired into the households to prepare the youths for civil examinations which were held periodically by the district, the provincial and the national authorities. In ordinary families, sons were sent to public schools or schools organized and supported by the villagers themselves. A good example of such parental enthusiasm was set by the mother of Mencius.

According to classical records, Mencius lost his father at the early age of three. His mother, a poor woman, was determined to bring him up right. At first the family was located near a cemetery and the little boy amused himself with mimicking the wailing scenes which he saw at the burial ground. This horrified the mother and she caused the family to be moved to another location near the market-place. But the change was not much of an improvement for the boy took to playing the part of a salesman, vaunting his wares and pretending to be bargaining with customers. So finally the family was moved to a house close by a public school. There the attention of the boy was attracted to the various exercises of politeness which the pupils were taught and which he tried to imitate. "This," the wise woman said with satisfaction, "is the proper place for my son."

As Mencius grew up, his mother worked hard and made all sacrifices in order that he could be sent to school. But the boy was not very diligent in his studies. One day when he returned home, his mother looked up from the web which she was weaving, and asked how he was getting along. With an air of indifference, he answered that he was doing well enough. Angry and disappointed, she took a knife and slashed through the web. The boy was very much alarmed and asked why she did that. The mother gave him a lecture and explained that her cutting the web was like his neglecting his studies. The lecture had its proper effect and Mencius went to work. In the end, he became one of the outstanding philosophers of all time.

Religious ceremonies constituted another important function of the family in China. Besides worshipping their departed ancestors, the ancient Chinese people worshipped "the spirits of the famous hills, the great streams . . . the land and grain" and made offerings to cats and tigers because they devoured rats and wild boars which destroyed crops in the field. But as a result of the introduction of Buddhism [see the brief explanation of Buddhism which follows this selection] into the country during the first century A.D., the form and content of their worship underwent considerable changes. In their rites of burial and mourning the changes were particularly deep-rooted. As late as the second decade of the present century, the Chinese people were still observing the rites of propitiating the dead which aimed at appeasing the hungry ghosts in "Hell" and keeping them from attacking the dead and at invoking the "Compassionate Spirit" so that the dead would be reborn in the "Paradise in the West," the Buddhist concept of "Heaven." Despite the influence of Buddhism religious ceremonies remained essentially a function of the Chinese family.

Like everything else in China, recreation bore the imprint of family influence. The Chinese people arranged and conducted their birthday and wedding ceremonies and annual festivities mainly on the basis of kinship. They dined, wined, drank tea and enjoyed theatrical performances together. Yet they never developed any "community spirit" or feeling of "civic consciousness." They were family-minded and not social-minded. None of the sports which they indulged in called for team-work. All their national games were organized in and for the family and the emphasis of these games was necessarily restricted to personal competition. "Kicking the shuttle-cock" and boxing were very popular with Chinese youths, but both were devised to cultivate the skill and improve the physique of the individual player. Even in card games like mahjong, each person played for himself.

Viewed as a social system, the large family in China worked with considerable effectiveness in a settled agricultural economy. Started from the legendary Emperors Yao and Shun, it stood well the test of forty centuries. It was encouraged in the belief that a nation of cultivated persons and properly regulated families should make a good nation. This belief emphasized the cultivation of the right mental attitude of the individual in human relationship as the most fundamental social function. Confucius regarded it as the key to the establishment of a state of peace and tranquility which he called "the highest excellence." He said: "Trees have their roots and their branches. Affairs have their ends and their beginnings. . . . In ancient time, those who wished to bring about enlightenment to the world, first ordered well their own states. Wishing to order well their states, they first regulated their own families. Wishing to reg-ulate their families, they first cultivated their persons. Wishing to cultivate their persons, they first rectified their hearts. . . ."

Chinese Social Norms. To facilitate the cultivation of the right mental attitude, Confucius developed a system of philosophy which included the three ethical principles of righteousness, benevolence, and propriety. In his opinion, righteousness aimed at the regulation of one's passions and involved constant examination and correction of one's own thoughts and actions. Benevolence aimed at attaining that plane of humanity on which one was able to do to others what one wished to be done to oneself. Propriety was a process of social education by which the people were taught to know that to be righteous and benevolent, "the father should be affectionate, the son should be filial, the elder brother should be kindly, the younger brother should be devoted, the husband should be loving, the wife should be submissive, the aged should be gracious, the young should be reverent, the friend should be sincere . . . " This process of social education operated to inculcate into the minds of the people from early childhood a proper understanding of their respective social positions together with their various relationships and duties.

As long as the neighboring countries were friendly and peaceful, there was nothing fundamentally wrong in this type of organization. But times have changed and neighbors have grown strong and aggressive. China can no longer exist as a nation of more or less independent families loosely held together by a government which has traditionally exercised a minimum degree of administrative control. Neither can she cling tenaciously to her age-old agrarian economy. She must effect a radical reorganization of her people so that they can develop the bounteous resources of their country to meet the challenge of the time. The program of this reorganization must include as its essential features the liquidation of the large family and the reorientation of the mental attitude of the Chinese people from family-mindedness to national consciousness.

So far, the large family system in China is rapidly being liquidated. The disruptive forces created by industrialization, urbanization, governmental actions in the nature of economic, social, and political reform, civil wars and external conflicts during the last hundred years have all combined to hasten this process of liquidation. But the break-up of the system has not been accompanied by a corresponding rapidity in the reorientation of the mental attitude of the Chinese people. In spite of the introduction of modern education, the influence of four thousand years of familistic tradition is still predominant in practically all phases of their national life. Without a comprehensive knowledge of the development and extent of this influence, it would be difficult to understand the titanic problems which are confronting China in her efforts to adjust herself to the modern world.

Earlier selections have already provided sidelights on the religious life of the Chinese peasant and its connection with the family. To tie together all this miscellaneous information we should first examine standard definitions* of Buddhism, Taoism, and Confucianism and then turn to an article which examines the Chinese religion from the standpoint of daily behavior.

Buddhism. The religion based upon the doctrine originally taught by Gautama Buddha [who lived in India in the sixth to fifth centuries B.C.]. The Great Enlightenment consisted in a perception of the causes of suffering and of the way of salvation from suffering. Buddhism teaches that *Nirvana,* release from liability to suffering, from mortality, is the highest goal attainable, now or hereafter. All beings, gods or men alike, are in need of such salvation. Buddha denied the special virtue of caste, ritualism, and asceticism, and insisted upon the necessity of pity, kindliness, and patience for salvation. Buddhism has developed and still embraces many sects. Buddhism spread through central, eastern, and southeastern Asia, and to Ceylon but is practically extinct in India proper.

Confucianism. The philosophical system of Confucius and his disciples, the basis of much of Chinese ethics, education, statecraft, and religion. Filial piety, benevolence, justice, propriety, intelligence, and fidelity are cardinal virtues. [Confucius lived in China in the sixth to fifth centuries B.C. Mencius was a later Confucian philosopher.]

Taoism. A religion and philosophy of China. Its traditional founder was Lao-Tse, sixth century B.C. Its greatest classic, the *Tao Te Ching,* teaches conformity to the Tao ["The Way"] and simplicity of social and political organization. Taoism is a liberal religion in contrast to the conservative absolutism of Confucianism. Later, the system largely degenerated into magic. Both magical and philosophical Taoism still survive.

* Adapted from Webster's *New International Dictionary.*

• 11 • Chinese Religion and Ancestor Worship

FRANCIS L. K. HSU

The so-called "Three Religions" are: Buddhism, Taoism, and Confucianism. Considerable amounts of ink have been spilled over the question whether Confucianism is a religion or not. Such arguments are irrelevant, for religion in China does not follow the pattern of interreligious exclusiveness of the West; there is no sharp dividing line as between Christians and Mohammedans, or even between Presbyterians and Baptists. Theological formulations may be argued by a few learned monks or priests but the average man has no interest in such things.

CHINESE RELIGION IN ACTION

The first thing that impresses one on entering a Chinese village or market town is the size and number of the temples. This is particularly true in South and Southwest China. The temples are usually built of bricks, in contrast to the family houses which have earthen walls and thatched roofs. The temples are brightly colored, whereas ordinary houses are gray or brown.

The temples are dedicated to a variety of gods, as the Dragon God or the Goddess of Mercy, or they may be dedicated to dignitaries of the community who were deified after death. In market towns, and particularly in district cities there are usually three other kinds of temples: to the God of Wealth, to Confucius, and to the district patron god, who is equivalent in the spiritual hierarchy to the district magistrate in the political one. Several others may also be found, including temples to the Goddess of Measles and to San Kuan (literally three gods—heaven, earth, and man). In some villages there is one to the Sun God, and in the towns and cities there are frequently temples to the God of Agriculture, or the God of War, or to Lu Chu, the most important Taoist god.

Most of the temples, however, house more than one God. Usually they are sacred to a number of gods or goddesses who are from what would be, judged by Western standards, different religions. Consider, for example, a modest temple of the patron of a town in Southwest China. The main altar is dedicated to the patron god, who in this case has the appearance of a warrior. The two side altars are occupied, respectively, by the Goddess of Measles and of Mercy. In front of the main altar are some tablets and images dedicated to the third son of the Dragon God and some lesser spirits. This is by no means atypical. There is one temple in this region which houses Confucius, Laotze (Founder of Taoism), and Buddha. This mixture is seen everywhere in China and indicates that the idea of monotheism is alien to the Chinese.

Identical patterns prevail in ritualistic observance as well as in the concrete arrangements of the temple. To quote from one of my notebooks:

Today saw old Mrs. Y with two grandsons and three granddaughters in the Pan Chu Temple. Offerings are made to every god (that is, every image) in the whole temple, both inside and outside the main hall. Even the dragons winding around the two main pillars of the main entrance received a share of the "food and money."

The old lady first burns paper money in front of the three main shrines. There are four gods occupying these shrines. As the paper burns she kneels down to koutou [kneel and strike the forehead on the ground, whence derives English "kowtow"] fifty times to each of the four gods.

[From *Most of the World: The Peoples of Africa, Latin America, and the East Today,* Ralph Linton, *ed.,* Columbia University Press, New York, 1949. Pp. 775-781. Used by permission.]

When these gestures of homage are over, she takes some of the food offered at the main shrines and puts it in a tray. She takes this tray and offers it in front of every other image in the temple one by one. In front of each image the procedure is as follows: She offers the tray by lifting it up with both hands to a position over her head. She lays it on the table. She burns some paper money. She kneels to koutou eight or more times. She prays only to the first four gods as she kneels to koutou.

The old lady on this occasion went to express gratitude and to report to the local patron god on the third day after the birth of a grandson; but she wanted to make sure that all gods, whether directly concerned or not, would be pleased, so that the child would grow up well. The yearly cycle of offerings to the gods observed in the same community reflects a similar attitude. Altogether thirty-four days of ritual observances are recorded for the community throughout the year. These include the birthdays of thirty different gods and one occasion on which all gods are worshipped.

During any emergency, such as an epidemic, drought, earthquake, or even after Japanese air raids, prayer meetings take place at which numerous gods and spirits are invoked. At one of these meetings, one scripture contained 608 gods with specific titles, including Jesus Christ and Mohammed, who are called sages and are subordinate to the Jade Emperor, the supreme ruler of heaven. Then the scripture goes on as follows:

In addition to the above the following gods are hereby invoked: Gods of ten directions; all fairies and sages; all fairy warriors and soldiers; ten extreme god kings; gods of sun, moon and nine principal stars; three officers and four sages; the stars of five directions; gods guarding four heavenly gates; thirty-six thunder gods guarding the entire heaven; twenty-eight principal stars of the Zodiac; gods for subjugating evil ghosts; god king of flying heaven; great long life Buddha; gods of Tien Kan and

Ti Tze; great sages of Trigrams and Nine Stars; secondary officials of five directions; secondary officials of ten directions; gate gods and kitchen gods; godly generals in charge of year, month, day and hour; gods and spirits in charge of four seas, nine rivers, five mountains, four corners; of hills, woods, all rivers and lakes, wells and springs, ditches and creeks, twelve river sources; every and all gods; Cheng Hwangs and their inferiors; local patron gods; minor local officials; gods of roads and bridges; of trees and lumber; spiritual officers and soldiers under the command of priests; all spirits in charge of protecting the taboos, commands, scriptures and the right way of religion.

THE SPIRIT WORLD

The Chinese believe strongly in an after life; in their conception, the spirits of the dead are closely bound to earth and interested in human affairs. The spirit world is divided into three parts: first, the Upper Heaven, ruled over by an Emperor with an extensive hierarchy of gods beneath him; second, the Western Heaven, where Buddha is the supreme ruler, also with a large group of high gods all of whom are subordinate to the ruler of the Upper Heaven (the exact relationship of the Upper and Western Heavens is never clearly expressed); and third, the Lower Spirit World where the spirits of the dead enter and are processed according to their record on earth. A ruler with ten judges working under him goes over the records. Those who have led good lives are rewarded with titles, leisure, and comfort. Exemplary characters may become gods in the Upper or Western Heavens or may be reincarnated into another existence on earth in which they attain honor and luxury. The wicked are punished by severe tortures, such as being sawed in half or boiled in oil. They may be banished permanently into hell, or reincarnated into another life beset with poverty and degradation, or they may be reincarnated as worms or rats or other lowly animals.

In broad outline this concept is not far

different from that held by Western society, but the spirit world and the world of humans is more closely allied in China than in the West. The Emperor of China was known as the Son of Heaven and many heroes of history and legend are considered to be gods reincarnated. New gods are continually being created and many return to earth in reincarnation. The emperor, as son of Heaven, has power over both humans and spirits. Even high bureaucrats, by virtue of the power vested in them by the emperor or because they are gods incarnate, have power over the lesser spirits.

Most important in this link between heaven and earth is the belief that spiritual reward or punishment may come in one's lifetime as well as after death, or may be visited upon one's children. Thus death by lightning, sudden and violent illnesses, as cholera, and serious accidents are generally regarded as punishments originating from the spirit world. For this reason the most important measure against epidemics and accidents is the prayer meeting, in which hired priests invoke the mercy of the superior deities who are presumed to have ordered the disasters as punishment against the community. Conversely, wealth and good fortune are usually held to be rewards originating from the spirit world in payment for good deeds performed by the recipient or his ancestors.

Thus the spirit world and the human world are counterparts of one another. The spirit world is based upon and functional to the existence of the world of humans, and the human world is in turn supervised and guided by the spirit world. They exchange personnel. They endorse the same virtues and condemn similar evils; they express mutual approval or disapproval. In the popular mind the spiritual hierarchy is a part of the social order just as much as the bureaucratic and political hierarchy is. That is why it is irrelevant or even erroneous to speak of different religions in China. To the Chinese there is only a spiritual order which stands as firm as the social order. As there is no question of a community living under two social orders, so it is inconceivable that there should be two

spiritual orders. If two religions are both true, they must find their place in the existing hierarchy. A creed for which this adjustment cannot be made is destined to be disregarded or forgotten.

ANCESTOR WORSHIP

The basic religion of China is ancestor worship, but, here again, it is a mistake to regard the cult as a separate religion, for it is part of the larger, all-inclusive structure. The ancestors have gone through the life-death routine of all human beings; that is, they have died and been processed by the Lower Spirit World. They may have been so good that they were received directly into one of the Heavens. Also they may have been reincarnated. If they were evildoers they may have been doomed to eternal punishment; but ancestors, in so far as their descendants are concerned, are different from all other human beings. To their descendants, ancestors are all great men and women with a glorious past and an exalted status. One may believe that someone else's ancestors are in hell, or reincarnated in some base animal form, but no true descendant believes that such a thing could happen to his own ancestors.

To understand this cult one must take cognizance of the family organization and the father-son identification. Between the father and the son there is not only a complete community of interest, but complete social identification. The son not only inherits all his father possesses but he is judged by his father's achievements. Conversely, the father not only has complete rights over his son's wealth but, when the son has reached maturity, the father is evaluated by his son's abilities. When we realize that a particular father and son are but a link in the infinity of many generations in any given family line, we see how the father-son identification becomes the foundation for the religious cult of ancestor worship.

The basic assumptions of the cult are threefold. First, the living owe everything to the departed ancestors, who are, therefore, regarded as persons of great magnitude. Since death only puts the relationship on a somewhat different level, and since the dead have the same needs as the living (namely, food, money, housing, and so on) it is necessary for the descendants to provide for them as if they were alive. Secondly, while the ancestors have already made their imprint on the fate of the descendants, their actions in the spirit world continue to affect the living. Conversely, the actions of the living descendants have bearing on the spirits of the ancestors. Thirdly, the interest of the ancestors is confined to their own descendants, particularly lineal ones. They concern themselves not only with ceremonial occasions—weddings, division of the family, birth of sons—but also take action in emergencies, as when a deserving descendant is about to be flunked by the chief reader in an imperial examination. On ceremonial occasions the presence of the ancestors is recognized by offerings of incense and food. But on occasions of emergency, the ancestors intervene in the form of apparitions.

Thus the ancestral cult shows the same close interrelation between spirit world and human world and the same close correlation between religious structure and social organization. As the family is the foundation of the wider society, so ancestor worship forms the link between the individual and the supernatural.

Familism involves more than common production of economic necessities by family members and more than religion based on reverence for ancestors. It also is closely related to festivals and merrymaking. As we shall see in the following selection, the Chinese peasants have fun as families even more than they do as individuals separately pursuing their own particular recreational tastes.

• 12 • Festivals
T. F. WEI

In a country so densely populated as China, the struggle for existence is naturally too keen to make much allowance for recreation and merry-making. Holidays therefore assume special significance, as to the toiling masses of China Sundays and Saturday half-holidays are practically unknown.

Fortunately, the monotonous life of the hard-working Chinese is not without a break. Including the Autumn Festival, there are no less than six "Big Festivals" in a year on which people of every walk of life lay aside their work and take their leisure either for ancestor worship, religious ceremony, or feastings and amusements. Three festivals of the six are known as *Ying Chieh* or Ghostly Festivals as they are dedicated to the dead, particularly the ancestors, for whom the Chinese people, irrespective of rank or religion, always hold the most intense feeling of gratitude and reverence: (1) The *Ch'ing Ming* (or "Pure Brightness"); (2) the *Shang Yuan* (the 15th of the 7th moon) and the *Shih Yueh Chao* (the 1st of the 10th moon). The other three festivals being occasions of great rejoicing and celebration are known as *Yang Chieh* or Festivals of the Living: (1) The *Tuan Wu* (or Dragon Boat Festival); (2) The *Chung Chui* (or Mid-Autumn Festival) and (3) The New Year. The latter are also debt settlement days; while socially, presents and calls are exchanged among relatives for days ahead. . . . All the people go in for various amusements and games and even the ladies are permitted to make merry tumult among themselves.

The first "Big Festival" of the year, *Ch'ing*

[From "Chinese Festivals," *The China Journal*, Vol. 34, No. 3, Shanghai, 1941. Pp. 106-110. Used by permission.]

Ming, falls on either April 5 or 6 in the Solar Calendar. In fact it constitutes one of the so-called 24 "joints and breaths of the year." Space does not allow a full explanation of these "joints and breaths," but sufficient to say here that they serve as a very accurate sub-division of the season on which the Chinese farmers so implicitly rely for sowing, planting and harvesting.

. . . It is but natural that with the arrival of the true spring of the year an agricultural people like the Chinese invoke the blessing of their ancestors by offering them the first fruits of the harvest newly sown and by refurnishing the mounds and the enclosures in which they may lie. In order to do honour to the spirits of the departed, the usual obeisance, such as the burning of incense-sticks and paper money, is performed before their tumuli. Those who find themselves far away from their native homes at the festival time, or so very occupied that a personal visit to the family burial-ground is impossible, will send a deputy and themselves perform certain rites in the house in which they happen to be. . . .

Excepting those recently bereaved, one sees no sign of grief or mourning in the people wending their way through the country-side, early in the morning of *Ch'ing Ming,* to pay respect to the dead. Although here and there a woman in white "keens" (weeps sorely) over the new grave of her husband or father, the majority who go "to worship at the hill" are clad in clean clothes and assume rather a holiday air as befits those who are on their way to take part in a pleasant picnic.

In fact, besides the solemn duties connected with them, the *Ch'ing Ming* visits to the country-side are looked upon as the first real excursions of the year. School children are especially jubilant when led on an outing on the "Spring Holidays," which always include the *Ch'ing Ming,* although the latter being one of the lunar festivals no longer receives the official recognition of the school authorities.

Western friends of China sometimes wonder why among the many grave-offerings of the Chinese no flowers are found. The reason may be a psychological one, but one story has it that in ancient days the offering of flowers to the dead was an exclusive privilege reserved to members of the royal family and therefore denied to commoners. The only plant that is in display everywhere at *Ch'ing Ming* is the willow. Not only does one see the willow branches stuck in grave-mounds, sprigs of it are also hung under the eaves of the houses. . . .

Next comes the *Tuan Wu* or Dragon Boat Festival which always falls on the fifth day of the fifth moon. . . .

To Western people, the *Tuan Wu* is better known as the Dragon Boat Festival. Dragon boat races are also held in the name of Chu Yuan [a great statesman-poet, fourth century B.C., who drowned himself in protest because an obstinate Prince refused to adopt his reforms], but the honour is supposed to extend to all of those drowned after him. Strikingly resembling dragons, these huge boats are gracefully slim but measure some 90 feet in length. They have high sterns with long steering-paddles rising many feet above the gunwales, while the prows are skillfully carved like a dragon's head with open mouth and cruel fangs and the long body between gaily painted to represent scales. No sooner is the starting signal given than the hundreds of paddles of the racing boats, each kept to time by a coxswain with a bright waving banner, send the slim dragons at top speed through the waters. The great exertion of muscular strength, the howling cymbals, the clashing of gongs, the life-like movements of the dragons' heads controlled by means of ropes and, at last, the thundering cheers of the spectators for the winner—all form part of the regatta.

According to the Chinese tradition, the fifth moon is regarded as the most poisonous month of the year when the Five Venomous Animals appear: The Snake, the Scorpion, the Lizard, the Toad and the Centipede. Because of all the evil influences being rampant during the month, the Chinese people have invented a long list of charms and talismans to combat them. On the *Tuan Wu* day, special care is taken to keep off devils and all malevolent creatures, visible or invisible. In addition to hanging out pieces of green, called the calamus, cut in the shape of two-edged swords, and antemisia on their gate-posts, the old folks will insist that every one in the household drink a concoction of sulphur and cinnabar dissolved in wine, as a further guarantee against the undesirables. Mothers never forget to write, by using the wet dissolved sulphur as ink, the character *Wang,* meaning king, on her baby's face, as this ideograph resembles the wrinkle on the forehead of a tiger, the terror of all spirits. Five-coloured threads are tied to the wrists of youngsters to insure them long life and happiness.

The Third "Big Festival," *Chung Yuan,* falls in the middle of the seventh moon or the "Moon of Hungry Ghosts." Being the second *Ying Chieh* of the year, this All Souls' Day is also dedicated to the dead, but it is essentially different from the *Ch'ing Ming* in the fact that the beneficiaries this time are the unhappy spirits who no longer have human descendants to offer them timely sacrifices. It is thought that these hungry ghosts should not be long neglected, otherwise they are likely to meddle maliciously with human affairs. With the introduction of Buddhism into China, the festival, which is traceable to remote antiquity, has become identified with the Buddhist ceremony of the *Yu Lan P'en Hui* commemorating the month during which the souls are released from hell and permitted to wander about to enjoy the worldy hospitality. At the *Yu Lan P'en Hui,* Buddhist priests hold masses everywhere for lonely souls, or such spirits as have suffered injustice or met violent death in their lifetime. . . .

As the service is drawing to a close, preparation is well under way for the start of a grotesque pageantry through the street. The procession is led by the giant figure of *Kwei Wang,* or King of the Devils, with the paper effigies of different ghosts, impersonating the drowned, the hanged and the poisoned, etc. closely following. Taking part also are the paper imitations of houses, cars, furniture and

money. Lastly come the priests continuously chanting the invocation "O mi to Fo"—"Buddha Amida."

The ceremony ends at an open space and always with a bonfire. Everything including the half-consumed incense-sticks must burn so that the ghosts may be able to take them away to the other world. . . .

Exactly one month after the All Souls' Day arrives the Mid-Autumn Festival. This second Festival of the Living may be more appropriately called the Moon Festival as all the myths told of the Festival, carried down to our own days by the flowing stream of tradition, are associated with this luminary. In contrast with the light and heat, symbolic of the Sun, the Moon, typifying softness and cold, early came to be regarded by most peoples of the world as a feminine deity.

* * *

Speaking of the celebration of the Festival itself, the moon cakes are the distinctive offerings of the Feast. Just when the moon sails into the high heavens, the service begins. On the altar, plates are set out filled with moon cakes and round fruits like apples, peaches and grapes—all symbolising the full moon. In the province of Kiangsu, an elaborately made "Incense-measure" called *Hsiang Tou* is also offered. The "Measure" is embellished with a paper *Pai-Lou,* symbolising the Moon Palace, which rises from the centre around a pillar of incense-sticks. The tip of this pillar is burned early in the morning, and throughout the day it slowly smoulders till, by midnight, the whole structure is burned when the religious rites proper to the Moon Festival come to an end. . . .

Now coming to the social pleasures, the feast is usually started in the evening and lasts to midnight—the hour when the moon is at the zenith of her brilliance. . . .

The first of the 10th moon or *Shih Yueh Chao* is the last of the three Festivals of the Dead and decidedly the least celebrated of all the "Big Festivals." Visits are again paid to the ancestors' graves, and the way of offering sacrifices including food, burning incense and candles and paper money, is the same as seen at the *Ch'ing Ming.* Now that the autumn harvest is gathered, opportunity is taken of the comparative leisure of the men to inspect lonely grave-yards and provide coffins and grave-sites for the poor. Among the families recently bereaved, the ceremony known as "burning the clothes" is observed. Paper imitations of warm garments and other household necessities are packed into parcels with paper money and carefully addressed to the ghosts for whom they are intended. In rich families, paper figures of man-servants and maid-servants and imitations of almost all the luxuries of life, e.g., automobiles and houses, etc., are burned together with the other offerings so that the worshippers feel confident that the ghosts receive all the comforts of this world.

By far the greatest, longest, happiest and noisiest of all the Chinese festivals is the New Year. As much preparation is required for the prolonged festivities to come with the New Year, the season normally starts with the 20th of the 12th moon, when a regular housecleaning takes place in every home. On the 23rd (or in South China the 24th) sacrifice to *Tsao Chun,* the "Kitchen God" is offered as he is leaving that night to report on the behavior of each family during the past year to the Jade Emperor of *Yü Wang.* . . . Prior to his departure, food-offerings are presented. A special sweet candy made of sticky rice is served in the hope that with this his lips will be stuck close so that he will not talk too freely or make unfavourable report against the household whose hospitality he should appreciate. After his feast *Tsao Chün's* portrait is carried to the court-yard, either in a miniature sedan chair or on a paper horse. Facing the flames of burning candles and incense-sticks, the image is set alight and sent off skyward to the "Precious-Throne" of the Jade Emperor.

About a week after comes the last day of the year, the greatest paying and settling day

among the Chinese. The custom requires that any one who is in debt must by now liquidate the outstanding accounts with his creditors. His failure to do so is considered a matter of great disgrace. However, if he sees no way of paying up, he hides till the New Year morning when he is immune, at least during the New Year holidays, from the bothering of his creditors. But a vigilant creditor will search for him with a lantern till the small hours in the New Year morning, for by a polite fiction, the light indicates that it is still dark, therefore, still yesterday, so that the debt may yet be collected without violating the New Year, when monetary dealings are tabooed.

On the New Year Eve the busiest souls on earth are the housewives. They must be responsible for the preparation of scores of dishes and seasonings to satisfy the appetites of both Gods and guests. . . .

When the hour arrives for the offering of sacrifices to the ancestors and Gods, the master of the household, on behalf of his dependents, *ko't'ou* before the altar and ancestral tablets to express his deep gratitude for all the blessings they have so graciously bestowed upon the family during the past year.

After the religious rites are completed, the New Year Eve supper is served to which all members of the family must try their best to attend. Presently, salvos of fire-crackers announce the arrival of New Year and the noise will continue till the dawn of the next morning.

The first day of the year is usually spent at home. The streets are practically deserted and shops tightly shut. It is a day of purely family re-union. After the first day, people begin to make a series of calls on their blood relations and intimate friends. . . .

Feastings, games and amusements complete the picture of the New Year celebrations, which usually last from 4 to 5 days in the cities but much longer in the country districts.

Even after one knows the statuses of family members and the roles each member plays in given situations, the picture is incomplete until one understands the motivational processes of socialization and social control and how these are tied in with differences in status. A good systematic treatment of these matters is afforded by Francis L. K. Hsu, whose book *Under the Ancestors' Shadow* provides one of the subtlest interpretations of Chinese family life. He also indicates the importance of competition as a type of interaction in personality development. Dr. Hsu, a professor of anthropology at Northwestern University, brings to bear upon the analyses of Chinese life the refined skills and techniques developed by social science. The village he describes is in the Province of Yunnan, near Toli, in southwest China, and is a day's journey on foot from the Burma Road.

• 13 • Personality Development in West Town
FRANCIS L. K. HSU

AUTHORITY AND COMPETITION

The two outstanding factors in the culture of West Town which appear to have the most bearing on the development of personality are authority and competition.

In all cultures infants are more or less supervised and fed by adults. Therefore we may say that all infants are subject to some authority. But the extent and intensity of the authority, as well as the manner in which this authority is exercised, vary widely. In West Town the mother, or on occasion some other female relative, closely supervises every movement of the infant and freely feeds it whenever it so demands. The father has practically nothing to do with the infant's early care but his role as a disciplinarian becomes more important as the infant grows older.

The father's authority over male and female children functions differently. With the son the disciplinary relationship is direct; discipline over his daughter is applied by his wife, acting as his agent. Should the mother lose control of her daughter or if a serious offense such as adultery is committed, the father will lose no time in taking direct disciplinary measures.

The thing which distinguishes West Town authority from that in many other cultures is, however, that, although it is intense and inclusive, it is far from being a one-sided command-submission pattern. In fact the obligations between the father and son are so mutual, and the power so counterbalanced that the father-son relationship is best described by the term identification. For paternal authority does not originate from the living parents alone, but springs from and is couched in the names of numerous forebears reaching back many generations and reinforced by the utterances and achievements of these glorified personages. The paternal authority does not stop when the younger person has come of age, but is continued as long as the father is alive. The father, while alive, acts as the ancestors' agent. Upon death he has merely become one of the ancestors whose influence remains the most potent factor to control the younger man's life. Then the younger man takes the father's place in the great family continuum.

Thus the son is under ancestral authority; but so is his father. The son is not free to act; neither is his father. Furthermore, while the son is dependent upon his father, the father is also dependent upon his son. The pattern of father-son identification makes them dependent upon one another not only materially but also socially and after death.

[From *Under the Ancestors' Shadow: Chinese Culture and Personality*, Columbia University Press, New York, 1948. Pp. 257-276. Used by permission.]

In this way the thing of primary importance in shaping personality is the ancestral authority. The more reliance upon this authority the individual shows, the better adjusted he becomes throughout life. This authority over him and prearrangement for him run through every aspect of his life and work, including his marriage and means of livelihood. At every turn the individual is confined within this prearranged framework.

Far from being opposed to the drive for competition the pattern of father-son identification actually encourages it. For every individual can add weight and content to this ancestral authority by his achievements. The drive for competition expresses itself not only in the acquisition of wealth but also in ceremonialism, ancestral honor, display of socially approved virtues and power, and various ways of insuring successes in general. Competition operates not only between different clans and different lineages within the same clan but also among different households within the same lineage and different members within the same household. It is largely responsible for the absence of a strong clan organization. Thus, while theoretically all members of a clan derive benefits from a "good" common graveyard, when it comes to burying one's own parents, competition narrows down to a struggle for the best location within the best graveyard.

If we look, however, at the objects of these competitive efforts, we find that they all come within the framework closely defined by parental authority and ancestral tradition. As long as ambition functions within this framework, the individual has every encouragement to get ahead of everyone else. The fortunate are those who are on the right side of the barrier; the unfortunate are those who are not. At this point there is an apparent paradox. Those who fail to do well reflect upon the conduct of their ancestors, and their ancestors share the disgrace of their failing to do well. The ancestors so affected may be those of the entire clan or the more immediate ones of a single lineage. From the point of view of the stranger, the poverty or the misery of certain families reflects upon the ancestors

of their entire clan. From the point of view of a clan member, it may merely refer to the immediate forebears of the particular lineage.

Those who have not done well under the ancestors' shadow are unfortunate, but those who are outside the shadow, namely, those in the penumbra, are in much worse circumstances. Everything depends upon whether one is within the shadow or outside, and the insecurity which threatens these unfortunates in West Town culture is much greater than in contemporary American culture. They are entirely at the mercy of the favors or disfavors of the people who act as substitutes for the relatives whose absence causes him or her to be in the penumbra. This insecurity increases the incentives to competitive efforts to get ahead.

These two patterns of behavior, authority and competition, are clearly reflected in West Town religion. I have shown the existence of an elaborate spiritual hierarchy and the place of ancestral spirits within this hierarchy. I have pointed out that this wider hierarchy corresponds to the machinery of government and that the hierarchy of ancestral spirits corresponds to the family and the kinship organization.

Under the jurisdiction of this spiritual hierarchy, highly and the lowly situated spirits are subject to the worldly patterns of submission to authority and competition. There are distinctions between the more fortunate spirits and those less fortunate according to the traditionally defined framework, and there are also unmistakable signs of struggle for personal salvation along the traditionally circumscribed ladder of ascendance. The spirit who had more virtues while alive and the one whose descendants have burned more paper money or performed more elaborate and numerous scripture-reading services for him will have a much better fate than others.

THE BASIC PERSONALITY CONFIGURATION

What is the effect of these cultural forces on the basic personality norm? As far as the overt behavior is concerned, the first outstanding quality is an explicitly submissive attitude toward authority. For the growing West Towner there are very few choices and very few uncertainties. All routes are, so to speak, barred except one, that which follows the foot-steps of his father, his father's father, and the whole line of his more remote ancestors. Along the established path, life is agreeable; all other trails lead to misery and self-destruction. The West Towner tends to be keenly aware of the necessity for orthodoxy. He tends to be apprehensive of any departure from the beaten path.

Within the socially approved framework and under the impetus to glorify his ancestors the individual exhibits a strong drive toward success. This is the second outstanding quality in the basic personality. Nothing would be farther from the truth than to characterize West Towners as being fatalistic. Fate and fatalism they talk about, but believe in only when such a belief happens to be convenient. The average West Towner is no more fatalistic than the early American who prayed to God and kept his powder dry. To the early American, God was a consolation. To the West Towner, fate serves the same function and is a good mechanism to tide over any frustration caused by failure. Furthermore, the West Towner, as do all Chinese, distinguishes between "lifelong fate" and "periodic fate." The former is the fate of the individual during his entire lifetime. The latter is his fate during a particular period of time, for the individual may now run into a "favorable periodic fate," and again into an "unfavorable periodic fate." When all signs point to an unfavorable periodic fate, one must be careful to avoid making important transactions or decisions, for a favorable periodic fate will come along later.

In general, the average West Towner, far from being confined by such ideas, will do everything in his power to solve his problems and improve his social and economic position at any time. Even when he has been told by the diviner that according to his lifelong fate he is doomed and even when he has already experienced many reverses, he will still try to do something about it, such as, perhaps, propitiating other gods or performing traditional good deeds. The most striking examples are found in connection with illness which threatens life. As long as the patient is still breathing and the family can finance the projects, no effort is spared and no stone is left unturned by way of finding a cure for the unfortunate person. Various kinds of doctors, various types of spiritualists, and all kinds of gods will be resorted to. But finally, when all efforts have failed and the patient has died, then, and then only, do the family members believe that "medicine can cure diseases, but cannot cure fate."

This is why we must conclude that in spite of his concern with rituals, gods, and other-worldly existence, the West Towner's orientation in life is essentially a worldly and positive one. For him the world of spirits is but a necessary supplement to the world of the living.

This untiring struggle expresses itself, however, within the definite limits of tradition. Both the lines of progress taken and the final objectives desired are well confined within this framework. Money is one objective for any male West Towner. Yet even if it is possible to make money by running a laundry in the community, he will not do it, for laundry work is woman's work and therefore below his dignity. Success in business enterprise is one of the objectives. If the fortune of the family has gone from bad to worse, the family head, although he will not turn a deaf ear to sensible advice on management, will have the sites of his ancestral homestead and graveyard checked by a geomancer. When the question of the next burial comes up within his household, he may even abandon the old site in favor of a more "advantageous" one.

Everyone wants prestige. The West Towner will try to acquire it not only by the acquisition of wealth and power, but also by generous contributions to local prayer meetings, elaborate funerals and other ceremonial displays, building huge but unused family homes, extensive and showy graveyards, and the exhibition of ancestral honors.

The two qualities just analyzed, submission to authority and competition for a superior place in life, lay the foundation of West Town basic personality configuration. Instead of conflicting with each other, they reënforce and merge into each other. As a matter of fact, the starting point of competition is the household. Brothers, instead of trying to get ahead by independent paths, tend to begin by competing for their father's favor.

In view of this groundwork, certain behavior characteristics become intelligible. The first of these characteristics is the preference for anonymity. The average West Towner wants to compete with other West Towners, achieve success, and show that he has something which the others do not have, but he does not want to prove that it is he as a person with a particular name and better creative ability who is winning the contest. He would much prefer to emphasize the fact that the merit really belongs to his parents and ancestors or is occasioned by fate, either of the life-long type or of the periodic type. To show that he personally has something which the others have not would be embarrassing to the latter; to pass the merit on to his parents or to his ancestors and fate would not be so embarrassing, because this would assume that his good fortune is something which is evidently beyond the control of the less fortunate.

By the same token, if the average West Towner has to punish or be hostile to someone else he prefers to couch the punishment or the act of hostility in terms of the culprit's offense against ancestors, sex morals, filial piety, or other good customs of the land. This preference motivates all behavior. In refusing to grant a request, a man will give as an excuse not that he cannot grant it, but that his employer does not allow it. The reason he gives for turning down an offer will be, not that he does not like the offer, but that his parents will not let him accept it.

The second characteristic is seemingly a contradiction of the first, the flare for success. It may seem impossible that people who are so much confined within a framework of tradition and who prefer to "pass the buck"

behind the protective wall of the ancestral shadow should be capable of excesses of any sort. Nevertheless, there are many observable excesses in the community. They occur not only in ceremonialism, such as exhibitionistic funerals and weddings, not only in the elaboration of family homes, graveyards, and clan temples, not only in the trouble taken to display honors earned by relatives in the remote past, but often in oppression, cruelty, and lack of calculated economy.

It is not hard to reconcile this trait with the meticulous attitude of submission to authority and conformity to form. Two factors are operative in this connection. The first is excessive parental tutelage, which tends to prevent the growth of economic foresight. This factor is above all responsible for the upper-class West Towners' habits of excessive spending and taking life too easy. The average child in American culture gets used to the idea of having some cash of his or her own very early in life. He is given a periodic allowance, and he has to make ends meet. The West Town child has no such experience. He spends what he can get out of his father, and when cash is short, all he has to do is to go again to the same person. In this way the authority of the father over his children is made firmer than ever. The same infantile attitude is continued in the West Towner's adulthood. A fixed budget seems out of the question because there are so many competitive social obligations which he must fulfill. Everybody tries to be a little more showy in the conventional sense than others, and in due course, his means will be no longer sufficient to meet his ends. When he no longer has a loving father magically to rescue him from his financial difficulties, he will go to someone else, according to custom; for the ends, which have the backing of authority and tradition, cannot be changed, and the ends justify any means. This is at the root of extravagance and official corruption.

However, there are two customs in West Town culture which appear, at least theoretically, to compensate for the lack of economic foresight. One is the custom of family division under the same roof, and the other is the importance of trading.

In a situation in which most members of most families assist in or carry on trading procedures or enterprises an appreciation of monetary values and the ability for rational calculation tend to be sharpened. The youngsters may not be fully aware of all the difficulties which their parents encountered in their struggles, but they are not likely to be entirely out of touch with reality. They may be competent to maintain whatever success their forebears have achieved in life.

The custom of family division under the same roof may exert a greater influence upon the formation of the personality. Without this custom the youngsters would have little opportunity for economic independence or any family responsibility. The emphasis on the big-family ideal tends to delay the partial emergence of the young from the over-all protection of the old. However, the true weight of trading with regard to this partial emergence of the young in West Town culture remains to be ascertained by further investigation. At this point it should be remembered that trading is not engaged in by sons of the rich and that the good effects of family division under the same roof may be nullified by the omnipresent shadow of ancestors.

The second factor bearing on customs which seem excessive is the psychological effect of displacement. In practice this may be implied in several types of oppression and cruelty, such as the cruelty which may be imposed on a slave girl, or on some unfortunate woman who has eloped, but got caught, or on those who are in the penumbra, or on those who have no present tie with any kinship group.

Its overt manifestation is as follows. The son has to submit to his father's authority regardless of his own wishes. He must do the same with reference to all those to whom he stands in a similar authority-submission relationship. He has no complaints against the arrangement as such, because his turn will come later, when others will have to submit to his authority.

A woman has to submit to the authority of her father, husband, mother-in-law, and, after the death of her husband, even her sons. She merely waits for her chance to "take it out on" her daughter or daughters-in-law or on the men or women who are not related to her, but happen to be in her way. In West Town it is uncommon to find two men fighting each other with their fists, but it is not at all uncommon to observe women tearing each other's hair and rolling on the ground, one on top of the other. To observe a husband beating his wife or even an older brother punishing his younger sister would make one conclude that women of West Town are unquestionably submissive and that because of their helpless attitude and behavior under such circumstances they deserve sympathy. But given the opportunity to be roused by an outsider, whether the latter be a man or a woman, the same "helpless" woman will fight most valiantly and to the end. There is no mystery about this phenomenon; it is simply that energy may be so released that could not escape in other ways. The higher incidence of fighting among women is probably explainable by their greater submission to authority. The man who gets a chance to hit an unfortunate girl who has eloped is responding to a similar psychological stimulus. The severity of the cruelty inflicted on such women merely testifies to the intensity of the suppressed wishes which have not found any regular outlet.

The third behavior characteristic closely follows the other two. This is the inability to create or to enter a new and untried path. The individual encounters comparatively little insecurity in life, but neither is he encouraged to make any plans of his own. He does not have to grope for his future, but he is also not equipped to meet new situations. He will certainly possess no means for seriously challenging the existing scheme of things. If and when the existing scheme of things has broken down, he will merely try to build up a new series of schemes in strict accord with the forms and principles defined and delimited by the recognized authority. Within the framework of tradition the individual behaves and works with the greatest of ease; outside the framework the individual is at a loss and puzzled at every turn. Within the framework the individual will manifest benevolence, kindliness, and generosity or excess cruelty, harshness, and cold-bloodedness, according to circumstances. Outside the framework the individual merely becomes bewildered, panicky, and frantically eager to get back into the framework. In other words, within the framework it is comparatively easy for the individual to adjust; outside, the same individual will be hardly capable of adjustment. The individual will see the necessity of alms for the poor and donations for prayer meetings against cholera epidemics. He will recognize the importance of contributions for the establishment of schools and a hospital as long as they can be calculated to increase his spiritual welfare and social prestige. But he is not likely to see that they are needed in terms of a higher percentage of literacy and an improved state of communal health; therefore his very act of charity may nullify its good effects.

Within the framework the individual is fortunate, lucky, and secure; outside, he becomes unfortunate, suffers, and is miserable and insecure. Since the individual has been trained to depend upon this framework for his every movement, it is obvious that only the eccentric will even dream of trying to question or improve it. This fact has been responsible for the misleading observation that China is a country of the golden mean. As seen from the above analysis, this principle has little to do with West Town behavior.

STATUS PERSONALITY CONFIGURATION

Thus far, the behavior characteristics emphasized are those of the basic personality configuration and are stated, except in a few instances, as they apply to the male. What are the characteristics of the status personality configurations? To answer this question it is necessary to give, first of all, a résumé of the statuses recognized in the community.

There are six general categories of paired statuses: (1) upper generation versus lower generation; (2) male versus female; (3) older versus younger; (4) rich versus poor; (5) high bureaucrats versus low bureaucrats; and (6) bureaucrats or literati versus commoners and illiterates. Needless to say, any one individual usually occupies several of these statuses at any given time. For example, a person may be male, upper generation, older, rich, a bureaucrat at the same time just as another may be male, lower generation, old, poor, and illiterate.

Let us examine the characteristics of these groups, which must for present purposes be combined into three broad groups. Generation must be seen together with age. The former usually, though not invariably, coincides with the latter, for there is usually an age difference between two individuals of different generations. The center of generation or age statuses is the father-son relationship. The relative positions of other individuals of different generations or age levels are more or less varied versions of this relationship. Generation and age are practically synonymous with authority and submission. That is, with relation to each other, an individual of the upper generation is older and is authoritative, and the person of the lower generation is younger and is submissive. The one commands; the other obeys. At any given point of time the individual of the upper generation or older in years than another has a higher social worth than the younger. Whether it is true or not, such an individual is regarded as being wiser and better acquainted with life than the other.

Most active Americans dread the idea of retirement. The height of the American male's career is in his early middle age. From that point, he starts to slow down, and his worth becomes less and less, until he comes to a point when he understands or is made to understand that he is completely out of the running. For the American female the turning point comes somewhat sooner.

This is not the case with West Towners. . . . The kinship structure is such that the worth of the individual is commensurate with his or her age or generation. Except for those in the penumbra, the individual is in a continuous process of transition through which he or she reaches increasingly greater security, prestige, and value. The son in West Town culture can surpass his father by making more money and attaining higher degrees and offices than the older man. But the father-son tie identifies his achievements with those of his father, and the usages with regard to generation and age enable his father to outrank him at all times.

From the point of view of personality formation such an arrangement must have significant consequences. Yet apart from the dominance-submission pattern there is little that we can point out as typifying the personality configuration of an individual of the upper generation or one of the lower, or of an older or a young person. This is not hard to explain. Any West Towner is likely to be on both generation levels at most given periods in his lifetime. Unlike his American brothers, who may live in isolated homes without parents or children, the West Towner usually resides among parents, uncles and aunts, sons and daughters-in-law, and other relatives of various generation levels. For this reason the personality of an individual of a certain generation level tends in the course of the lifetime of any West Towner to merge with that of individuals of other generations. The same picture is more or less true in respect to the differences between older and younger persons.

The really important status personality difference occurs (1) between male and female on the one hand, and (2) between the rich or highly placed and the poor or lowly situated on the other [the latter being a combination of categories (4), (5), and (6) given at the beginning of this section].

As far as can be observed, the cultural patterns of submission to authority and encouragement for competition apply to the male as well as to the female. Like the male, the female has to submit to the authority of parents, ancestors, and tradition, but unlike the male she must also submit to the authority of her husband and certain other related males. Like the male, the female freely exhibits a desire for competition, but unlike the male she often competes for a different set of objects. Her competitors may be her husband's concubines or his brother's wives. Her objects may be success in business ventures or the fostering of good behavior in her children. As may be expected, her life is circumscribed by the household environment, and her opportunities in the struggle for a better place in life are much more limited than those of her husband. For example, for the man success or failure in marriage is a matter of fate in the periodic sense; but to his wife, it is a matter of lifelong fate. The husband can transcend fate and look forward to a better period in his life when he may be married to someone better suited to him; his wife has to resign herself passively and accept the unhappiness as one of life's inevitables. What is more, while it is possible as time goes on, for the younger ones to become older, for the sons to become fathers, and, at least theoretically, for the poorer to become richer, there are no means which will enable females to become males.

The result is a female personality configuration which exhibits two distinguishing marks. First, the female is much more limited by fate than the male. For the male, fate is but a temporary retreat; for the female, it is often a permanent shelter. That is partly why West Town women appear to be so much more devoted to religious worship and other spiritual matters than are their husbands and sons. The second distinguishing mark of the personality norm is rather its lack of any sharp distinction from that of the male. In Western Europe and America the ideal type of woman, in the minds of the upper class at least, may be summarized as a graceful ministering angel. She will be personal in her views, kindly, likely to faint at the sight of blood, completely devoted to her love object, and protected in every way. The personality difference between her and her husband or sons is qualitative rather than quantitative.

This is not so in the female personality configuration of West Town, where there is no idea that women have finer sensibilities than men or possess qualities which will magically heal men's wounds. . . . The female in West Town is expected to exhibit about the same general personality characteristics as the male. She differs from the male only in the same sense that a person of one generation of social status differs from someone in another generation or social status. They differ to a certain extent in work and very much in prestige. They also differ in the physiological sense, which makes women ritually unclean. The female is likely to burst into tears or be unreasonable in the same way that petty men or children may be. But these are about the only differences that West Towners recognize in the personalities of the two sexes. If a rough comparison is helpful, we may say that in terms of personality females are regarded as immature males who will never grow up.

The differences in personality configuration between the rich and the poor, or between the "top dog" and the "under dog," are more drastic in nature. They have their roots in the entire family and social organization.

To understand these differences, it will be necessary briefly to review once again the objects and methods of education. The objects of the education of the rich and of the poor . . . are different in several respects. Their training with regard to a livelihood differs almost completely. The common elements in the activities of the rich are superiority and dominance; both are significantly lacking in those of the poor. The training in social adequacy is similar in both status groups, with the exception of objectives of competition. The activities of the poor are calculated to achieve some degree of financial security. For the rich security is taken for granted, and their activities are aimed at attaining greater power, prestige, and ancestral glory. Therefore, the basic orientation of the poor in competition is economy, while that of the rich is conspicuous waste.

Significant though these differences are, they are not as important as some factors in the methods of education. Apart from the fact that boys emulate their fathers, and girls their mothers, there is no basic sex difference in the technique of education. This is also true of the rich and the poor. The techniques of education are, universally, (1) direct participation (observation, imitation, and conscious instruction) and (2) a system of reward and punishment. There is no sphere of adult life, except that of sex, from which the male child is entirely excluded. In fact, the latter is encouraged to enter adult life as early as he can.

The result is that sons of the West Town rich are as rich and as powerful as their fathers. Sons of the poor are as poor and insignificant as their fathers. The father-son identification and the big-family ideal require that there shall be complete community of interests between the old and the young. Whatever the father has, the sons share, and vice versa, without qualification. Children are, therefore, encouraged to be frugal and hardworking if their parents happen to be poor and to lead the life of wasteful parasites if their parents happen to be wealthy. In fact, the wealthy parents consciously or unconsciously consider their children's leisure and comfort as partly indicative of their own social prestige. The psychological mechanism underlying father-son identification is thus not unlike that which exists between the husband and the wife in Euro-American culture so graphically pointed out by Thorstein Veblen. (*The Theory of the Leisure Class,* New York, 1899.) It is in the light of these considerations that an apparent contradiction in West Town culture may be understood. We may ask, why is it that while in general West Town children are subject to strict authority, they are nevertheless free from restraint with regard to food habits?

The answer is twofold: first, West Town parents have little obsession over their children's diet as a matter of principle, but the children's freedom may be drastically curtailed as a result of practical necessity. Wealthy children can overeat, but poor children often must tighten their belts. Even the mother's milk may be drastically reduced by malnutrition. From this angle it is obvious that a large number of West Town children are forced to grow up under food restrictions regardless of parental intentions.

Much more significant, I think, is a second point. West Town parents do not merely refrain from imposing restrictions on their children's feeding habits. Those who have no cause to worry about food take great pleasure in seeing their young ones eat freely. The same is true regarding the spending of money.

Thus, hard as I tried, I did not find that frugality and industry were valued intrinsically; they were but necessary evils under pressure of adverse circumstances.

In most societies, including those of Europe and America, the objectives of the rich and of the poor are different. Take contemporary United States as an example. Most wealthy American industrialists and business men do not care about their ancestral glory, but many of them work for prestige, fame, and power, while the poor merely struggle for their very existence. However, their methods of training their children for life are a far cry from those employed by West Towners. The primary difference lies in the fact that West Towners emphasize direct participation and encourage their children to share in adult life on a full scale, but the Americans, while not excluding direct participation, expect their children to develop under the limitations of childhood and to share in adult life only gradually. Sons of American millionaires have much more limited resources at their disposal than do the sons of wealthy Chinese parents. The absence of the father-son identification and the big-family ideal make most American youngsters realize early that they will have to work for what they want. Sons of West Town rich, on the other hand, tend to have the entire resources of their fathers at their disposal. In fact, the wealthy father feels very proud to be able to say that his son does not have to work at all. If the youngster is in trouble, the older man will do whatever he can to help the young ne'er-do-well. He will usually back the latter up, regardless of the issues involved, to the limit of his ability.

I have no doubt that there are wealthy American parents who give their sons "soft" jobs in their own establishments and pamper them, but there seem to be more that require their sons to go through a strict course of discipline, regardless of their social status.

For this reason sons of the wealthy and the powerful in West Town tend to have wealth and power go to their heads early in life. The degenerating effect of wealth and power on the young is given full play. When the youngsters do not voluntarily react to their surroundings in that way, the people in their environment tend to give them preference because of their fathers' wealth and power and influence their thinking accordingly. Wealth and power, even in the hands of adults who prospered by hard and honest work and have feelings of justice and humanity, if unchecked will be detrimental in the long run. How much more dangerous will they be in the hands of youngsters who have never worked for a single day and who firmly believe that whatever they desire in life will be forthcoming to them simply for the asking or the taking?

Thus, through the same cultural patterns of a strong father-son tie and the big-family ideal, both of which are integrated under the ancestor's shadow, two different personality configurations are formed. The poor sons share their parents' hard-working habits and receive the training of honest, hard-working men. The rich sons share their parents' power and glamor and begin life in the firm belief that they are destined to command, rule, control, and be supplied with a permanent bed of roses.

Little wonder that the status personality configuration of the poor and the lowly differs strikingly from that among the rich or the highborn. These differences tend to become more pronounced in the younger members of a family one or two generations after its rise to power. The personality configuration of the former status group tends to be submissive, careful, rational, frugal, realistic, industrious, and sincere. The personality configuration of the latter status group tends to be vain, unsympathetic, licentious, impulsive, unrealistic, extravagant, carefree, insincere, and to lack economic and common sense.

Certain qualifications must be attached to this categorization. First, it is extremely difficult to ascertain the exact dividing line between the two status personality configurations, because it is impossible to ascertain the exact line at which West Towners may be divided into rich and poor, or the highly placed and the lowly. There are observable a polarization of behavior at the extremes and numerous intermediate grades. Secondly, it is not asserted that *every* individual who is definitely placed in one or the other group invariably possesses the general personality configuration of his particular status group. A few individuals whose social and economic stations place them without doubt in one status group nevertheless exhibit the general personality characteristics of the other group. Thirdly, the poor and the lowly exhibit the personality characteristics of their status group, not with any great sense of pride, but because of necessity. As soon as they prosper, their sons or at latest their grandsons, will tend to exhibit the personality traits of the other status group, and no one will then have any desire to tell the youngsters to do otherwise.

This difference in personality configuration between the two status groups explains, it seems to me, in large part, why family fortunes tend to rise and fall within a period of two or three generations. The hard-working children of poor parents may not succeed in causing their family fortune to rise at once, but there is at least such a possibility. The easygoing children of rich parents may not bring about their family's immediate downfall, but their parasitic life will probably be the beginning of a downward trend.

It is possible that the customs of general trading and of family division under the same roof may have exerted some beneficial influences on the personality configuration of the status group of the rich, so that it will at least be plausible to expect that the fortunes of West Town big families will hold out longer than elsewhere in China. However, as far as my investigation is concerned, I have discovered no definite evidence for such optimism. Of the four highest-ranking families, only the sons of one show that they will at least be able to maintain the status quo if not to improve matters. The sons of two others show signs of the usual weaknesses. The fourth family does not yet present any consistent picture. Outside of these families, I can point to several loafers whose forebears only one or two generations ago were great names in the community.

Social Organization:
Village Life

A peasant society is usually village-centered. The village and the market town tend to make up the peasant's social universe. Wars or famines may uproot him temporarily, or even permanently prevent his return home, but always within him there is the sense of attachment for his own village. As long as he considers himself a peasant, the village is his normal social world. Those who, because of higher education or for other reasons, turn their backs on their peasant origin find it necessary to leave the village and dwell in towns and cities, where there is greater possibility of mobility up the social scale. But individuals such as these frequently have a poignant nostalgia for the village of their youth.

What is there about the village that takes such a hold on its people? Peasant villages are usually muddy in winter, dusty in summer; sanitary conveniences are minimal; work is at times laborious; social control is so strong that an individual can exercise only a limited freedom in his behavior. And yet villages survive as a major locality association for most of mankind. Perhaps it is simply habit; or perhaps Baker Brownell, a philosopher at Northwestern University, has, in his writings, put his finger on an important point. He maintains that in the small community one knows one's neighbors as whole personalities, one is familiar with the totality of the roles that they play, in contrast to the segmental acquaintanceship among people in urbanized areas.

As we have already noted, the family is the first major pillar of peasant life; the community is the second. Many villages in China are family villages in that they are inhabited by members of a single clan, who are interrelated. Many others are made up of people from two, three, or more clans. When the youngsters—or the elders, for that matter—leave the household, self-contained as it tends to be, they find a broader panorama of events in the village square. Commerce is carried on there; the village temple receives frequent visitors; the agents of the local government perform their duties near by; and any local gentry stop in at the tea house. The square also may be the setting for the dramas staged by itinerant actors, although the outskirts of town may be the preferred location.

The preceding paragraphs apply to many villages in other parts of the world besides China. An old English village, described in Selection 60, fits the description neatly. In contrast, the villages of the United States vary considerably from their Old World prototypes, as may be seen in Selection 45.

A good introduction to basic features of village life on the Yangtze Plain is found in Hsiao-T'ung Fei's book, from which we quote in Selection 6. Notice the role of the neighborhood as well as that of local government, both of them interesting patterns of association.

• 14 • A Village on the Yangtze Plain
HSIAO-T'UNG FEI

For various social functions, households are associated together to form larger local groups. These groups do not form a hierarchical series but superimpose on each other. The village, being an aggregate of households in a compact residential area, separated from other similar units by a considerable distance, sets a limitation on the direct extension of territorial ties for various functions. It marks a common boundary for those intimate territorial groups. It synthesizes various social functions and also takes up special functions that cannot be fulfilled by smaller units—all these are performed through the village government by the village headmen.

Village heads are always accessible, because they are known to every villager, and a stranger will be received by them immediately. The visitor will be impressed by their heavy burden of work. They help the people to read and to write letters and other documents, to make the calculations required in the local credit system, to manage marriage ceremonies, to arbitrate in social disputes and to look after public property. They are responsible for the system of self-defence, for the management of public funds, and for the transmission and

execution of administrative orders from the higher government. They take an active part in introducing beneficial measures such as industrial reform into the village.

There are two village heads at the present time. The following note gives a short sketch of them.

Mr. Chen is an old man, nearly sixty. He received his order of scholarship—Hsiu Ts'ai —under the late imperial examination system which was abolished at the end of the last dynasty. He had failed to proceed further in his scholastic career and was invited to become a family tutor in the town. At the beginning of the Republic, he came back to the village to start a private school and remained as the only schoolmaster in the village, for more than ten years. From that time on he has assumed the leadership in the village under various formal titles according to the ever-changing administrative system. In 1926, he initiated the silk reform programme with the support of the Provincial Sericultural School and started the experimental station in the village. In 1932, he was formally responsible for the establishment of the co-operative silk factory. He then gave up his job as a school-

[From *Peasant Life in China: A Field Study of Country Life in the Yangtze Valley*, by Hsiao-T'ung Fei. Reprinted by permission of the Oxford University Press, Inc., New York, 1946. Pp. 106-116.]

master and became manager of the factory. When the new administrative system, Pao Chea, was introduced, he found work with the government was not suited to his taste and thus retired from the office, but nevertheless he has remained the *de facto* head of the village, and is still responsible for community affairs.

The other head is Mr. Chou. He is younger, being about forty years of age. He was educated by family tutors but was too late to take the imperial examination. Without scholastic interest he was content to be a simple peasant with his brother. Being literate and honest, he was picked by the reform agent of the silk industry as an assistant. He has from that time on secured the confidence both of the reformers and of the people and gradually shared with Chen leadership in public affairs in the village. When the Pao Chea system was introduced he was, on the recommendation of Chen, formally elected and actually appointed the head of the Hsiang which includes the village.

Headmanship in the village is not hereditary. Chou's father is engaged in the tile trade and his elder brother is still working on the farm. His son is in the town and is not likely to succeed him in the future. There is no kinship relation between Chen and Chou.

Although both Chen and Chou are well-to-do persons, neither is considered the richest person in the village. The richest person is, I believe, a man named Wang, who lives in obscurity and is without any outstanding prestige. It is true that a child of a poor family has less chance of attaining the position since headmanship has no direct economic reward and requires rather long and expensive preparation (to attain the necessary standard of literacy), but wealth alone does not give power or prestige.

Even legal status is not essential for the headmanship. Chen is still the senior head in the village, but he has no position in the formal administrative system. Elder persons tend to avoid the trouble of dealing with the higher government. The basis of the headmanship lies in public recognition and support in the leadership in community affairs, and in being the representative of the community against the outside world. Chen started his career as a schoolmaster and Chou as an assistant in the silk factory. Their service and ability have given them authority and prestige. In the village there are few who are literate and still less who are at the same time willing to take up the responsibility without economic reward. Young men of ambition are not satisfied with the position: it is considered by the two middle school graduates I met in the village as sterile and hopeless. Thus the range for the selection of village heads is not very large.

Although they have no direct economic reward, they enjoy prestige and presents from the persons who have received services from them. For example, they are respected by the people, and can call the generation senior to them, except their own near kin, by their personal names without adding any relationship terms. This cannot be done by an ordinary person. Their leading position in the village also helps them to hold privileged jobs such as schoolmaster and manager of the silk factory.

Headmanship is not connected with any privileged "class." Even seniority in age is not an essential qualification, as is shown in Chou's case. But the sex disqualification has not yet been entirely overcome; women are excluded from public affairs. Only recently women have acquired the same position as men in the silk co-operative society, and a woman teacher has been appointed at the school; but the latter has very little influence in the community except among boys and girls.

As mentioned, the village as such has no legal status because side by side with the functional territorial groups there is an administrative system imposed on the village organization. These two systems, which I have termed *de facto* and *de jure* respectively, do not coincide with each other. In this section, I shall describe the *de jure* system and compare it with the *de facto* system to show the discrepancies.

The new administrative system is called Pao Chea. The term Pao Chea is an old one. The government recently had the idea of reviving an old administrative system which had been proposed by an administrative reformer in the Sung Dynasty (960-1276). How far this old system had actually existed is another question, but for this village it is entirely new. The head of the village explained that the arrangement for the new system had only recently been completed, and it had never within living memory been in existence. He added that the villagers had been summoned by the town head and told to arrange their houses in a manner prescribed by the district government. This had been done. To study this Pao Chea system, therefore, it is nceessary to go back to the statute book to see what is the intention and what principle the government followed in its organization.

On June 5th, 1929, the National Government in Nanking promulgated the Law Governing the Organization of the District, based on the principle of local self-government of the late Dr. Sun Yat-sen. According to the law, each district (Hsien) must be divided into several Chu and each Chu into twenty to fifty Hsiang (in rural areas) and Chen (in urban areas). In the rural areas, villages with more than 100 households would be taken as a Hsiang and those with less than this number would be combined with other villages to form a Hsiang. In urban areas, towns with more than that number would be taken as a Chen, and those with less would combine with other villages to form a Hsiang. The Hsiang is again subdivided into Lu (twenty-five households) and Lin (five households). All these units were to be self-governing through their elected headmen and councils. The functions of these local governments are listed in the law as follows: Census taking, population registration, land survey, public works, education, self-defence, physical training, public health, water regulation, forest preservation, industrial and commercial improvement, food storage and regulation, protection and prohibition of plantation and fishery, cooperative organization, improve-

ment of customs, public belief, public enterprise, financial control, etc.

These functions are not altogether new to the local community, most of them having been carried out by various traditional *de facto* groups. The law created new territorial groups with the purpose of facilitating the self-governing administrative functions. But, in fact, there is the danger that it will actually hamper the normal functioning of the *de facto* groups. Thus in the Second National Administrative Conference in 1931 the rigidity in the size of the units was severely criticized. Consequently, an amending bill was introduced in the Legislative Yuen.

While the bill was still in the stage of discussion, another system was instituted which affected the local government. In August, 1932, the Headquarters of the Punitive Campaign Against the Communists, in Central China issued a decree organizing the people in the area of military operation (Hopei, Honan, and Anhwei) into uniform self-defensive units under the system of Pao Chea. According to this system, each ten households (Hu) form a Chea and each ten Chea a Pao. The intention of this organization was stated in the decree to be "to organize the people in the devastated area in a more effective way and secure an accurate census in order to increase the power of local self-defence against the communists and to enable the army to discharge its function more efficiently." This system was introduced mainly for military purposes. Unless the population could be accurately registered, it was very difficult to prevent the communists from mixing with non-communists in the disturbed areas. To counter the active propaganda of the communists the army introduced the system of mutual responsibility of the individuals in the same Chea and Pao, so that they could act as a check one upon the other.

In 1933, the spread of communist influence drew Fukien into the military area. In Fukien the provincial government had already started the organization of the local self-governing system according to the Law of 1929. The provincial government was ordered by the

Headquarters to suspend the local self-governing system and to substitute for it the Pao Chea system. In their conflict between the Law and the Decree, the provincial government submitted to the central government; and the Central Political Council decided to absorb the Pao Chea system in the self-governing system. The Law of 1929 was superseded by a series of laws of 1935. These two systems were compromised in the following six points: (1) the uniform units of Pao and Chea were substituted for the old units Lu and Lin, and the units Chu, Hsiang, and Chen were to be on the same level: in other words, the original status of Chu as an intermediary unit between district and Hsiang or Chen was abolished; (2) before the completion of the Tutelage period, the method of indirect election was to be substituted for direct election according to the Pao Chea system; (3) a census was to be taken in the process of arranging the households in the Pao Chea system; (4) military training in the Pao Chea system was to be extended into a more general civil training; (5) the system of mutual responsibility was to be applied only in cases of emergency; and (6) the Pao Chea system was to take up the function of self-government, but local modifications were to be allowed to suit particular conditions.

Obviously, the compromise has not solved the fundamental problem, that is, how far the *ad hoc* self-defensive units with their uniform size could undertake the general administrative functions listed in the Law of 1929. The real issue was not the legal conflict between the law and the decree but whether the traditional functions that have been carried out in the *de facto* territorial groups could be taken over by the arbitrarily created Pao Chea. Since the old units Lin and Lu, of a less rigid kind, had proved to be impracticable it did not seem that a more rigid system was likely to function any better. The effectiveness of the Pao Chea system in self-defence in cases of emergency also did not assure its suitability as a system for administrative self-government. It could indeed be argued that in the process of political integration in China

it was desirable to substitute for the heterogenous traditional structure a rational and uniform structure. But it remains to be considered whether such a substitution was necessary and how much it will cost to enforce. Since this new system was only introduced less than a year before my visit to the village, it is too early to draw any conclusions. But an analysis of the working of the system against the background of the traditional structure will obviously throw light on the general problem, and will at least help to stress the importance of this issue in the future administrative policy.

The Pao Chea, as instituted in this village with allowance for local modifications, does not strictly accord with the numerical prescription of the law. The village with its 360 households is divided geographically into four Pao. . . . The houses in the village are built along both sides of the streams and are thus distributed in four *yu*. The houses in the same *yu* are grouped into one Pao. According to their positions, counting from east to west and from south to north, the houses are arranged in order, approximately ten in number, to form the units of Chea. These four Pao are combined with another seven Pao in neighbouring villages into one Hsiang, which is called after the name of the village Kaihsienkung Hsiang. Pao and Chea are known by numbers. The four Pao in the village are numbered from eight to eleven. A further discrepancy between practice and law is that the Chu in the old law is still preserved as an intermediary unit between the district and Hsiang, and roughly corresponds to the functional unit of the marketing area of the town . . . : This village can be defined in terms of the administrative system as:

Kiangsu (province)
Wukiang (district)
Chen tse (Chu)
Kaihsienkung (Hsiang)
No. 8-11 (Pao)

To examine the nature of the Hsiang, we must inquire into the problem of inter-village relations. Is there any special bond between the villages that are grouped into the same Hsiang? What is the functional group that corresponds to this administrative unit? Economically, villages in this region, as I shall show later, are independent of each other. Every village has its own agent boat which serves as the buying and selling agent of the villagers in the town market. A village, however large it may be, does not form a sub-marketing centre among its neighbouring villages. In other words, the town as the centre of the marketing area is able, owing to the ease of water transport and the institution of the agent boats, to collect from and distribute to its tributary villages without any need for intermediate stoppage of the movement of the goods. Within the area, there are several dozens of villages dependent on the town but independent of each other. These villages, which are occupied in similar work and produce similar goods, find little need for trade with one another. Thus the unit of Hsiang, standing between the marketing area and the village, has no economic basis. The same is true from the point of view of kinship relations. Although inter-village marriage is popular, there is no sign that those villages included in the same Hsiang are preferred to those outside.

Linguistically the name Kaihsienkung in daily speech refers strictly to the village alone. It seems ridiculous to the local people to say that the neighbouring village is a part of Kaihsienkung. Their obstinacy in this is not unreasonable. The change means a great deal to the people. Some people told me, "If the neighbouring villages are part of Kaihsienkung, then the lake that belongs to Kaihsienkung people will be shared by the people of the neighbouring villages. But of course this cannot be permitted."

At present the increasing prestige and the economic function of the silk reform movement, and the administrative status of the head of the Hsiang, which both have their head offices in this village, have drawn together the villages around it. I noticed that people from other villages, not limited to those of the same Hsiang, visited the village more frequently than formerly to order silkworm eggs, to supply cocoons for the factory, and to settle inter-village disputes. But in the last analysis, the head of the Hsiang, Chou, did not work in his legal capacity, but mostly through his own personal influence as the assistant manager of the silk factory, and he did not make any important steps without getting into touch with the *de facto* heads of the village concerned.

Of course, given time and increasing experience of the new administrative functions, there is no reason to say that the new unit will remain on paper for ever.

The unit of Pao, however, is different. To divide the village according to the boundary of streams is not likely to be successful. It is assumed in this case that the stream is a dividing line for social activities. This assumption is not true. As shown, boats are active on the water, and bridges are built to connect those separated pieces of land. They are means, not obstacles, of communication.

Lastly, we come to the Chea. Among the functional groupings, we have seen that there is a type of group called *shanlin,* the neighbourhood, which consists of ten households. But it does not correspond with the Chea. Chea is a fixed local segment while *shanlin* is a chain of overlapping units; each house taking its location as the centre of reference. The segmentation of Chea is very artificial and contradictory to the idea of the people.

Nevertheless, it will be interesting to study the problem in a future investigation to see how far planned social change can be started from the social structure including the form of the group, formal rules of behaviour, and formal system of thought; such attempts are evidently becoming more and more popular in a situation where state uniformity is desired.

The village theater, which has a strong hold upon the Chinese people, is being used effectively today by the Chinese Communist government to indoctrinate the people with the new ideology. How and why this is being done will be much clearer after the following account by Arthur H. Smith, whose book on village life in China has been a standard reference since its publication in 1899. Most of his statements still hold true today.

· 15 · The Village Theater
ARTHUR H. SMITH

That the Chinese are extravagantly fond of theatrical representations, is well known to all who live in China. The Chinese trace the origin of the stage to the times of the Emperor Ming Huang, of the T'ang Dynasty (died 762) who, under an alias, is supposed to be worshipped as the god of play-actors. It is a popular saying that if the players neglect to do homage to this patron, they will altogether fail in their representations, whatever these may be.

With the history of the Chinese stage, we have in this connection no concern. According to the Chinese themselves, it has degenerated from its ancient function of a censor in morals, and has become merely a device for the amusement of the people. It is a remarkable circumstance that while the Chinese as a people are extravagantly fond of theatrical exhibitions of all sorts, the profession of play-actor is one of the few which debars from the privileges of the literary examinations. The reason for this anomaly is said to be the degradation of the theatre by pandering to vitiated or licentious tastes. To what extent the plays ordinarily acted are of this sort, it is impossible for a foreigner to decide. The truth seems to be that the general (theoretical) contempt for the stage and its actors in China, is a product of the moral teachings of Confucianism, which uncompromisingly condemn the perversion of the right uses of dramatic representation. But while this (theoretical) view is the one which is constantly met, it is

like many other Confucian doctrines, chiefly remarkable for the unanimity with which it is disregarded in practice.

In what we have to say of Chinese theatres, we must disclaim any knowledge of them at first hand, that is to say, by listening to acted plays. There are several obstacles to the acquisition of such knowledge by this method, even were other difficulties lacking. Most Chinese plays are laid out upon so extravagant a scale, as regards time, that they may be spread over many hours, or possibly several days. The most indefatigable European could not listen to the entire performance of any one of them, without becoming utterly exhausted. The dialect in which the actors speak is so different from the spoken language, that it is hard to form an idea of what they are saying. The tone adopted is that shrill falsetto, which is not only fatiguing to an Occidental hearer, but almost of necessity unintelligible.

When to these embarrassments are added the excruciating music, the discomfort attending the dense crowds, and the universal confusion which is an invariable concomitant of a Chinese theatre, it is not strange that these representations have for Westerners very few attractions, after the first glance has satisfied curiosity. This indifference on our part is almost unintelligible to the Chinese. That a foreign traveller, who is told of a theatre in full blast at the town at which he expects to spend the night, should feel no joy, but should deliberately push on so as to avoid spending

[From *Village Life in China: a Study in Sociology,* Fleming H. Revell, New York, 1899. Pp. 54-69. Used by permission.]

the night at that place—this is to the Chinese profoundly incomprehensible.

Except in a few large cities, the Chinese have no theatres in our sense of the term, provided with seats and enclosed by walls and roof. The stage is a very simple affair, and is entirely open to inspection. Sometimes it is built like a temple with an open front. But by far the larger part of the rural representations of theatrical companies take place on a temporary scaffolding which is put up for the purpose the night before the plays begin, and is taken down the moment the last play closes. The players resemble their ancient Grecian prototypes in that they are a migratory band, going wherever they are able to find an engagement.

The stage equipments, like the stage itself, are of the simplest order, the spectator being required to supply by his imagination most of those adjuncts in the way of scenery, which in our days, are carried to such perfection in the theatres of the West. There is no division of a play into separate acts or scenes, and what cannot be inferred from the dress, or the pantomime of the actors, they must expressly tell to the audience, as for example who they are, what they have been doing, and the like. The orchestra is an indispensable accompaniment of a theatrical representation, and not only bursts into every interval of the acting, but also clangs with ferocity at such stirring scenes as a battle attack, or to add energy to any ordinary event.

*   *   *

The village theatrical company owes its existence to some rich man, who selects this as a form of investment. As all the available land in the greater portion of China is wholly out of the market, it is not easy for one who has more money than he can conveniently use to decide what to do with it. If he should go into the theatrical business, it is not necessarily with the expectation that the money will yield him a large return, but in order to provide a popular amusement for a great number of people, and at the same time re-

ceive a larger or smaller interest on the amount invested.

The person whose capital is used in the costumes, which are the main part of the outfit of a Chinese theatre, is called the "Master of the chest." The whole outfit may be leased of him by an association of persons, who pay a fixed sum for the use of the costumes, which must be kept in good condition. In a first-class theatre, these costumes are very costly, and include what are called "dragon robes," and "python robes," each with double sets of inner garments, of fine quality, and handsomely embroidered. Of these there are at least two suits, five suits of armour, and numberless other articles of clothing, such as trousers, skirts, boots, buskins, etc. Another "chest" contains the accoutrements of the players, as swords, spears, and the like, made of gilded wood.

The value of all these various equipments, in a well-furnished theatre, is said to be fully $5,000, and in those of the cheaper sorts, two-thirds or half as much. Each of the three "chests" in which the stage accoutrements are stored, is in charge of three men, who are responsible for the security and the care of the contents of the cases.

The players are divided into classes which are called by different names, the members of each class receiving pay according to the dignity of their position. There are, for example, two individuals, one civil and one military, who represent high-class historical characters . . . . Another class . . . represent personages . . . . In addition to these are persons of less importance, who represent ladies, officials' wives, young girls, or others. After these come what may be called clowns, who are termed "flowery-faced," . . . subdivided into first, second and third. These represent the bad characters . . . down to the lowest class who take the most despised and hateful parts of all. In addition to these main characters, there is a considerable force detailed as soldiers, servants, messengers, or to personify boatmen, innkeepers, and the like. The rear is brought up with a large staff of cooks, water-carriers, etc., whose duty it is to provide for the material comfort of the players in their vagrant life.

Aside from the regular theatrical companies one frequently meets with companies of amateurs who have inherited the art of giving performances on a small scale called "a little theatre." They are young farmers who delight in the change and excitement of stage life, and who after the crops are harvested are open to engagements until the spring work begins. There may be only fifteen or twenty in the band, but the terms are low, and the food furnished them much better than they would have had at home, and when the season is over they may be able to divide a snug little sum to each performer.

The manager, or lessee of the theatrical equipment . . . engages the players for a term of about ten months, beginning early in the spring, and ending before the close of the year. The whole company may number between fifty and a hundred men, and the best actors may be engaged for sums ranging from the equivalent of a hundred dollars for the most skilled, down to a few tens of dollars for the inferior actors, their food in each case being furnished. It is thus easy to see that the expense of maintaining a theatre is a vast drain upon the resources of the lessee, and presupposes a constant succession of profitable engagements, which is a presupposition not infrequently at a great remove from the facts of experience.

The lessee of the theatre supplies himself with the material for the development of actors, by taking children on contract, or apprenticeship, for a fixed period (often three years) according to a written agreement. At the end of their apprenticeship, these pupils are at liberty to engage in any company which they may elect, for whatever they can get, but during their term of indenture, their time belongs to the man who has leased them of their parents. The motive for such a contract on the part of the parents, is to secure a support for the children. Sometimes children run away from home and make engagements on their own account, attracted by the supposed freedom of the player's life.

The amount which each child receives during the time of his apprenticeship, is the merest pittance, and it is said that in three months at most he can learn all that it is necessary for him to know. A large part of his duties will be to strut about on the stage, and mouth more or less unintelligible sentences in a grandiloquent tone. If the number of plays in which he appears is large, the tax upon the memory may be considerable, but Chinese children can learn by rote with amazing facility, and constant practice must in a short time fix in his memory everything which the young actor requires to remember.

*   *   *

It is one of the contradictions which abound in the Chinese social life, that while play-actors are theoretically held in very light esteem, the representation of a play is considered as a great honour to the person on whose behalf it is furnished. Instances have occurred in China, in which such a representation has been offered by the Chinese to foreigners, as an expression of gratitude for help received in time of famine. The motives in such cases, however, were probably very mixed, being composed largely of a desire on the part of the proposers to gratify their own tastes, while at the same time paying off in a public manner a technical debt of gratitude.

To suggest under such circumstances that the money which would have been absorbed in the expenses of the theatre, should rather be appropriated to the purposes of some public benefit, such as a free-school, would not commend itself to one Chinese in a thousand. Only a limited number of scholars could receive the benefit of a free-school, whereas a theatre is emphatically for everybody. Moreover, a theatre is demonstrative and obtrusively thrusts itself upon the attention of the general public in a manner which to the Oriental is exceedingly precious, while to set up a free-school would be "to wear a fine garment in the dark," when no one would know the difference.

The occasion for the performance of a play is sometimes a vow, which may have been made by an individual in time of sickness, the theatricals to be the expression of gratitude for recovery. In the case of an entire village, it is often the returning of thanks to some divinity for a good harvest, or for a timely rain. A quarrel between individuals is frequently composed by the adjudication of "peace-talkers" that one of the parties shall give a theatrical exhibition by way of a fine, in the benefits of which the whole community may thus partake. In view of the well-known propensities of the Chinese, it is not strange that this method of adjusting disputes is very popular. We have known it to be adopted by a District Magistrate in settling a lawsuit between two villages, and such cases are probably not uncommon.

Sometimes there is no better reason for holding a theatre than that a sum of public money has accumulated, which there is no other way to spend. A foreigner could easily propose fifty purposes to which the funds could be appropriated to much better advantage, but to the Chinese these suggestions always appear untimely, not to say preposterous.

* * *

It is a common proverb that the country villager who witnesses a theatre, sees only a great hubbub, a generalisation strictly within the truth. It is upon this ignorance of the villager that the theatrical manager presumes when he furnishes an inferior representation, instead of the one for which his contract calls. But if the villager ascertains the fraud, consisting either in deficiency of players or inferior acting, he rises in democratic majesty, and "fines" the company an extra day or two, or even three days, of playing as a penalty, and from this decision it would be vain to appeal.

The individual who communicates with the village which hires the theatrical company, and who receives the money, is called the program bearer (*"pao-tan-ti"*). The scorn in which theatrical folk are supposed to be held, appears to be reserved for this one individual alone. He makes arrangements for the conveyance of all the trunks containing the equipment from the previous place of playing, to the next one, and especially for the transportation of the staging.

In inland regions, where it is necessary to use animals, it requires a great many carts to move about so much lumber, which must be done with great expedition in order not to waste a day, at a time when engagements are numerous; and, even to a Chinese, time is precious, because the food and pay of so many persons have to be taken into the account. The carts for this hauling are provided by the village which is to enjoy the exhibition, being often selected by lot. Sometimes, however, a small tax is levied on all the land in the village, and the carts are hired.

The day previous to a theatre in any village is a busy one. Great quantities of mats are provided, and in a short time some barren spot on the outskirts of the hamlet begins to assume the appearance of an impromptu settlement; for aside from the theatre itself, great numbers of small mat-sheds are put up to be used for cook-shops, tea-shops, gambling-booths, and the like. During the day, even if the village is but a small one, the appearance is that of the scene of a very large fair.

In the larger towns, where fairs are held at more or less regular intervals, it is usual, as already mentioned, to begin them with a theatrical exhibition, on the first day of which hardly any business will be done, the attendants being mainly occupied in gazing at or listening to the play. In such cases the attendants can frequently be safely estimated at more than 10,000 persons. In large fairs there is generally a performance every day as long as the fair holds, an arrangement which is found to be very remunerative from a financial point of view in attracting attendance, and therefore customers.

From a social point of view, the most interesting aspect of Chinese village theatricals is the impression which is produced upon the people as a whole. This impression may be feebly likened to that which is made upon children in Western lands, by the immediate imminence of Christmas, or in the United States by the advent of a Fourth of July. To theatrical holidays in China every other mundane interest must give way.

As soon as it is certain that a particular village is to have a theatre, the whole surrounding country is thrown into a quiver of excitement. Visits by young married women to their mothers' homes, always occasions to both mothers and daughters of special importance, are for a long time beforehand arranged with sole reference to the coming great event. All the schools in all the neighbouring villages expect at such times a holiday during the whole continuance of the theatricals. Should the teacher be so obstinate as to refuse it (which would never be the case, as he himself wishes to see the play) that circumstance would make no difference, for he would find himself wholly deserted by all his pupils.

It is not only brides who take advantage of this occasion to visit their relatives, but in general it may be said that when a village gives a theatrical representation, it must count upon being visited, during the continuance of the same, by every man, woman and child who is related to any inhabitant of the village and who can possibly be present. Every Chinese family has a perfect swarm of relatives of all degrees, and the time of a theatrical performance is an excellent opportunity to look in upon one's friends. Whether these friends and relatives have been invited or not, will make no difference. In the case of ordinary villagers, the visitors would come even if they knew for certain that they were not wanted.

It has frequently been remarked that hospitality as such cannot be said to be a characteristic Chinese virtue, although there is at all times such a parade of it. But whatever one's feelings may be, it is necessary to keep up the pretence of overflowing hospitality, so that whoever comes to the yard must be pressed to stay to a meal and to spend the night, however anxious the host may be to get rid of him. On ordinary occasions, guests will not stay without such an amount of urging as may suffice to show that the invitation is *bona fide,* but during the continuance of a theatre it often makes very little difference how lacking the host may be in cordiality, the guests will probably decide to stay, as the play *must be seen.*

It is by no means an uncommon thing to find that in a village which has engaged a theatrical troupe, every family is overrun with such visitors, to such a degree that there is not space enough for them to lie down at night, so that they are forced to spend it in sitting up and talking, which may be easily conceived to be an excellent preparation for the fatiguing duties of the morrow. As a theatre seldom lasts less than three days, and sometimes more than four, it can be imagined what a tax is laid upon the village which is overrun. When it is considered that every married woman who returns to her home, as well as every woman who visits any relative, always brings all of her young children, and that the latter consider it their privilege to scramble for all that they can get of whatever is to be had in the way of food, it is obvious that the poor housekeeper is subjected to a tremendous strain, to which the severest exigencies of Western life afford very few analogies.

The cost of feeding such an army of visitors is a very serious one, and to the thrifty Chinese it seems hard that fuel which would ordinarily last his family for six months, must be burnt up in a week, to "roast" water, and cook food for people whom he never invited, and most of whom he never wished to see. It is a moderate estimate that the expense of entertainment is ten times the cost of the theatre itself, realizing the familiar saying that it is not the horse which costs but the saddle.

The vast horde of persons who are attracted to the village which has a theatre, has among its numbers many disreputable characters, against whom it is necessary for the villagers to be constantly upon their guard. For this reason, as well as on account of the necessity for being on hand to look after the swarms of guests, the people of the village have little or no opportunity to see the play themselves. Guests and thieves occupy all their time! Eternal vigilance is the price at which one's property is to be protected, and the more one has to lose, the less he will be able to enjoy himself, until the danger is over. It is a common observation that, after a theatrical performance, there is not likely to be a single chicken left in a village. To prevent them from being stolen by the expert chicken-thieves, the villagers must dispose of their fowls in advance.

Such being the conditions under which the Chinese village theatre is held, it is surprising that so great a number of theatrical troupes contrive to make a living—such as it is—out of so precarious an occupation, which is likely to fail altogether during years of famine or flood (never few in number), and also during the whole of each period of imperial mourning, when actors are often reduced to extreme misery. One reason for their passionate attachment to the theatre, must be found in the fact that for the Chinese people there are very few available amusements, and for the mass of the country people there is literally nothing to which they can look forward as a public recreation, except a few feast days (often only two or three in the year), the large fairs with accompanying theatricals, or theatricals without fairs.

It is evident that a form of exhibition which is so much valued by the Chinese, may become an important agency in inflaming the minds of the people. This is at times undoubtedly the case. Many instances have come to the knowledge of foreigners, in which theatricals representing the Tientsin massacre or some similar event, have been acted in the interior of China. In some cases this is doubtless done with the connivance of the magistrates, and it is easy to see that the effect upon the minds of the people must be very unfavourable, if it is held to be desirable to maintain among the Chinese respect for foreigners.

In China, as in other lands, it is easy for theatrical representations to deal with current events which have a general interest. In a certain case of warfare involving two different Counties, as to the right to make a bank to prevent inundation, several lives were lost and a formidable lawsuit resulted. The occurrences were of such a dramatic character that they were woven into a play, which was very popular at a little distance from the scene of the original occurrence.

The representation of historical events, by Chinese theatres, may be said to be one of the greatest obstacles to the acquisition of historical knowledge by the people. Few persons read histories, while every one hears plays, and while the history is forgotten because it is dull, the play is remembered because it is amusing. Theatricals, it is scarcely necessary to remark, do not deal with historical events from the standpoint of accuracy, but from that of adaptation to dramatic effect. The result is the greatest confusion in the minds of the common people, both as to what has really happened in the past, and as to when it took place, and for all practical purposes, fact and fiction are indistinguishable.

Among the most popular Chinese plays, are those which deal with everyday life, in its practical forms. Cheap and badly printed books, in the forms of tracts, containing the substance of these plays, are everywhere sold in great numbers, and aid in familiarizing the people with the plots.

Our notice of the Chinese drama may fitly conclude with a synopsis of one of these librettos, which contains a play of general celebrity, to which references are constantly made in popular speech. It is said to have been composed by a native of Shan-hsi, and is designed as a satire upon the condition of society in which, as so often in China at the present day, it is almost impossible for a teacher, theoretically the most honoured of beings, to keep himself from starvation.

It is a current proverb that in the province of Shan-tung, the number of those who wish to teach school is in excess of those who can read! The scene of this play is therefore appropriately laid in the land of the sages Confucius and Mencius, and in a district within the jurisdiction of the Capital, Chi-nan Fu.

The characters are only two in number, a teacher called Ho Hsien-sheng who is out of employment, and reduced to extreme distress, and a patron named Li, who wishes to engage a master for his boys, aged nine and eleven. The teacher's remarks are mixed with extensive quotations from the Classics, as is the manner of Chinese schoolmasters, who wish to convey an impression of their great learning. He affirms that his success in instruction is such that he will guarantee that his pupils shall reach the first degree of *hsiu-tsai,* or Bachelor, in three years, the second of *chu-jen,* or Master, in six, and attain to the eminence of *chin-shih,* or Doctor, in twelve.

The teacher begins by a poetical lament that he had lost his place as a teacher, and that a scholar so situated is far worse off than a handicraftsman, who, he says, has always enough to eat. After this, the teacher comes on the stage, crying out like a peddler, "Teach School! Teach School!" Upon this Li comes forward, suggests that a man who offers to teach probably knows at least how to read, and explains that he feels the need of some one in the family who can decipher the tax bills, etc., but that he really cannot afford the expense of a teacher for his children.

He explains that his boys are dull, that the food of the teacher—the bill of fare of which he details—will be poor and coarse. There will be only two meals a day, to save expense, and at night there will be no fire. The coverlet is a torn dogskin, no mat on the bed, only a little straw, and no pillow. The salary is to be but 8,000 cash a year, but this is subject to a discount, 800 counting for 1,000. The teacher is never to leave the schoolyard while school is in session.

The school will be held in a temple, hitherto occupied by nuns. These will be removed to a side room, and the teacher will be required to strike the bell, sweep out the building, and perform the other necessary services on the first and fifteenth of each month, and these duties must be executed with punctilious care. He is also cautioned not to allow his morals to be contaminated by the nuns whose reputation is so proverbially bad. None of his salary will be paid in advance, and a *pro rata* deduction will be made for every day of absence. During the summer rains the teacher must carry the children to school upon his back, that they may not spoil their clothes and make their mother trouble. Whenever school has been dismissed, the teacher is to carry water, work on the threshing floor, take care of the children, grind in the mill, and do all and everything which may be required of him. To all the foregoing conditions, the teacher cheerfully assents, and declares himself ready to sign an agreement upon these terms for the period of ten years!

Perhaps the most instructive aspect of Chinese theatricals, is that which takes account of them as *indices* to the theory of life which they best express, a theory in which most Chinese are firm, albeit unconscious, believers. It is a popular saying that "The whole world is only a stage-play; why then should men take life as real?" It is in strict accordance with this view, that the Chinese frequently appear as if psychologically incapable of discriminating between practical realities which are known to be such, and theoretical "realities" which, if matters are pushed to extremities, are admitted to be fictitious.

The spectacular theory of life is never for a moment lost sight of in China, and it demands a tribute which is freely, unconsciously, continually, and universally paid. It is upon this theory that a large proportion of Chinese revelling is based, the real meaning being, "You have wronged me, but I am not afraid of you, and I call upon all men to witness that I defy you." It is this theory upon which are grounded nine-tenths of the acts which the Chinese describe as being done "to save face," that is, to put the actor right with the spectators, and to prove to them that he is able to play his part and that he knows well what that part is. Never, surely, was it more true of any land than of China, that

"All the world's a stage,
And all the men and women merely players."

Chinese villages have formal organizations too. These are purposely created to meet specific needs and must be included in any study of the major patterns of association of Chinese peasant life. Although there are regional differences, Daniel H. Kulp's description of such associations in South China gives a fairly representative picture. You will recall that his study was the basis for Selection 9.

• 16 • Village Associations
DANIEL H. KULP, II

In addition to the familist groupings, Phenix Village contains a number of social groups of an artificial or intentional character. The basis of membership in them is similarity of attitudes with reference to the objectives or values commonly recognized by the members. People are born into familist groupings but they choose to join these associations. The members constantly shift and change so that the composition of the groups is not permanently fixed.

They are all formed to meet a clearly recognized need, which may be present and temporary or in the nature of a future contingency. In the latter case the association develops an organization that provides sufficient continuity to keep it going until its functions have been completed. In one way or another, the groups function for protection, economic gain, and recreation. The means used may be thought of as mutual aid devices. In practically all of them sociability appears quite definitely during their meetings and assemblies.

The six different associations in Phenix Village are the Mutual Aid Club, the Parent Burial Association, the Society for the Manufacture of Sugar, the Irrigation Club, the Boxing Club, and the Music Club. In each case the purpose of the association is clearly suggested by the name.

THE MUTUAL AID CLUB

The Mutual Aid Club is usually of a very temporary nature. It lasts until each member gets his money returned in cash and feasts, when it dissolves automatically without ceremony. It arises out of the needs of the poor people on the one hand and the refusal of the rich families to give loans without sufficient securities, on the other. When a number of poor villagers find themselves in similar circumstances of financial need, they turn to each other for help.

The method of providing this aid has been worked out into a practicable mutual aid device. For example, a certain man needs fifty dollars, presumably for some worthy purpose. He goes to those in the village who are most friendly toward him and who are in similar situations of need and asks them to join his "club." He explains his need, the amount of money he wishes to raise, suggests the amount each should pay, which in turn determines the number of people who may be allowed to join.

In this instance, when he has found ten persons who are willing to pay him five dollars each, he has the money he needs. Perhaps a few weeks or a month later, he invites them all to a feast, which costs him about five dollars. This is his first repayment on the instalment plan. The organizer does not pay back in cash but in the feasts which he provides at a cost equal to the amount paid to him by each member. Usually about one month intervenes between each festive occasion. In a club of ten persons in addition to the organizer, it takes ten months until the

[From *Country Life in South China: The Sociology of Familism . . .* , Vol. I, *Phenix Village, Kwantung, China,* Teachers College, Columbia University, New York, 1925. Pp. 189-215. Used by permission.]

club ceases to exist. The organizer thus secures with interest, for the first month, fifty dollars, after which he has five dollars less each month until the tenth month when the loan is repaid.

At the first feast each member casts dice once and the one who throws the highest score is paid five dollars by every member of the club except the organizer. . . .

At the following feasts the procedure is repeated until each has been paid his forty-five dollars. Thus each man pays in fifty dollars, gets out forty-five in cash . . . does the organizer a favor . . . enjoys the feast with the food, the companionship and conviviality.

*   *   *

THE PARENT BURIAL ASSOCIATION

The Parent Burial Association partakes of this same characteristic of economic assistance. Its purpose is fundamentally benevolent. In the past it has flourished among the poorer families. In recent times, however, even the rich families have found it worth while to join these associations. It is difficult for them by ordinary procedure, to find help during the period of mourning. At present there are two of these associations in Phenix Village.

What is the need and what is the situation that give rise to this form of voluntary grouping? It has already been mentioned that over half the people of Phenix Village are dependent upon the other half in varying degrees. Poverty and death are haunting spectres of the poor. They roam through the village and inspire fear that is not physical but social.

It is not that the villager fears death; his belief in Fate relieves him of that worry. But to think of his parent drawing near to the time of departure without adequate funds for proper rites and burial,—this is a real fear. To fail in the provision of rites, feasts, coffin, and funeral would be conduct the most unfilial and condemned by social opinion. The family would be disgraced and the prestige of the village lowered in the estimation of the regional community, so far as gossip would extend on the matter.

Every one, rich or poor, must die; the son knows that the needs arising out of the parent's death are inevitable. Foresight is required of the poor that the material means of the social requirements may not be lacking when the time comes. Such are the attitudes of the poor toward a familist crisis created by the death of a parent.

That it is not death itself that primarily inspires the fear is further attested to by the fact that the rich families also need such associations. They have money and ordinarily are able to employ what help they need. They can finance the material needs of burial ceremonies. With them, as with the poor, the real fear is a fear of inability to meet the required demands of a parent's death as prescribed by community tradition. With them, in contrast to the poor, the need is not for finances but for hands to help in the performance of the humble but necessary duties of laying out the corpse, mourning, and so on. The rich suffer but one need; the poor face two.

The crisis that exists for rich and poor alike arises out of the superstitious attitudes of uneducated people toward touching or handling a dead body. The revulsion against it is deep-seated. The villagers consider a dead body unclean and likely to bring a curse upon those who come into close contact with it. Quite naturally, few seek and all avoid as much as possible the giving of such assistance. So strong is this attitude of avoidance that often not even money can buy for the rich the assistance they need at such times. That is why, in order not to fail in their traditional duties, they too join the burial associations.

Not only are people needed to handle the corpse and the coffin, but also to assist in the mourning rites. Wailers are needed to exhibit to the countryside the deep grief suffered through the departure of the respected parent. The more wailers, the greater the filial piety and, consequently, the greater the prestige the family achieves. This wailing is not a desirable occupation and villagers avoid it as much as possible. Rich and poor both find it difficult to secure mourners. Here the avoidance attitude is secondary to that regarding the corpse. Sometimes the attitude is even transferred to members of the natural-family which has lost someone by death. People simply prefer to stay away from homes where there are dead bodies.

Some societal device is clearly necessary in order to guarantee the performance of the death duties, the burial rites and ceremonies. The avoidance attitudes must be either neutralized or supplemented; otherwise the social and religious needs of the death-crisis cannot be met. The Parent Burial Association, by creating voluntary bonds of responsibility prior to the appearance of the specific and undesirable duties, represents familist technic of adjustment and resolution of the crisis of death.

* * *

THE SUGAR MANUFACTURING ASSOCIATION

Another type of grouping is the Sugar Manufacturing Association. The people form this society to make sugar but even here one finds the religious and social features. When the organization is established they have religious worship in the interests of the success of the undertaking; from time to time they conduct religious worship so that the good spirits may continue to favor them; when they dissolve the organization after the completion of the sugar-making, they conduct worship in gratitude for successful enterprising.

The social nature of this society is even more prominent than the religious. The members work together in a cooperative way; the success of one is the success of all. This interdependence forms a nexus of effort and thought that makes for close group unity. When the day's work is finished, they meet in their common room, built especially for the work of this association, eat, drink, chat and rest.

The general relationship among the members is very democratic, for each member feels himself on an equal footing with every other in responsibility and in participation in the benefits of the association. There is also a desire to deal honestly with one another so that the enterprise may not be wrecked nor the investments of time and money lost.

Finally, each is supposed to work zealously so that the financial gains from the undertaking may be as large as possible. Products are thus turned out cheaply and with the maximum elimination of waste and duplicate effort. The incapacity of the individual to conduct such manufacture alone because of the capital needed is compensated for by collectivity.

* * *

THE IRRIGATION COOPERATIVE SOCIETY

Another organization of similar type and function is the Irrigation Cooperative Society. This association arises directly out of maintenance practices and needs due to unfavorable climatic conditions. Successful cultivation of rice becomes impossible when droughts set in, for the paddy fields, instead of being flooded, suffer desiccation. The ordinary practice is to dig small holes at the corner of the fields for the collection of water which is then pumped into the fields as they dry up. But when continued lack of precipitation has forced the farmers to use all of the water from these holes, they are compelled to secure water from Phenix River.

Under such unusual and difficult exigencies, the farmer finds himself unable to cope with the crisis. He turns to others for help. Many others in similar situations readily join together and form a cooperative society for the irrigation of their rice fields and so save them from turning yellow before the crop is ripe. Each member pledges himself upon joining the association to cooperate in every way possible with the others, by contributing labor for the enterprise according to the extent of land to be irrigated. Where lands are too extensive to provide this labor through personal effort, the arrangement involves the employment of hands or the payment in kind or cash to other members of the society who may make up a deficiency in labor. Both men and women are found in these organizations. They divide themselves into shifts to work the irrigation pumps and so send a continuous stream of water into the fields.

* * *

THE BOXING CLUB

Still another type is the Boxing Club. Some villager who has a slight knowledge of Chinese boxing suggests to a number of young men that a fund be raised to secure the services of an instructor and to rent a place for the "school of self-defense"! An entrance fee is proposed and, when on that basis enough money is collected to launch the school, an itinerant boxing instructor is employed and a suitable place rented. Usually the classes are held in an old school building or temple where the open paved court serves as an open-air gymnasium.

The instruction is given at night when the young men have most leisure. After a few lessons in a series of body movements designed to dispose of an opponent, the pupil is initiated into the mysteries of thrusting, parrying, slashing, and warding with a variety of weapons popular in ancient warfare in China.

At first the movements are learned by mass imitation of the instructor; later they are perfected through practice with a sparring partner to develop experience, confidence and precision. When the sparring begins, and especially when the classes convene while the teacher is instructing in a neighboring village, some of the hardier members "get rough" and troubles arise. Each develops a drive for conquest rather than finesse and precision until the organization comes to a more or less sad ending.

* * *

THE MUSIC CLUB

Finally, there is the Music Club. It too is an association designed to meet a specific need, and dissolves when the need is met. It rests upon a broad basis of community appreciation of music, for the people commonly find recreation and wholesome enjoyment in it; wherever people gather to spend their leisure time music is provided either by professionals as wandering minstrels or by themselves. The taste for music is a product of the local theatricals which are presented on the stages set up before the temple doors.

Once a year the village turns out for a religious procession, for the success of which there must be attractive music. To provide this music, the young people of the village are canvassed, a group is selected to form a band for the New Year's procession. These people are formed into a school similar to that of the Boxing Club. Money is raised by subscription among the villagers who are rich or interested, in order to supply the instruments and employ a teacher in instrumental music and theatrical singing. This instructor may receive a very high salary, and for the two or three weeks he teaches he is treated as a highly honored guest of the village.

He must teach the children how to handle the musical instruments, such as the gong, the drum, the cymbals, the trumpet, the flute and the violin and banjo, and to chant and sing the songs popularized by the stage.

The pupils are young children of a musical bent, for they can most quickly learn how to handle the instruments and sing the theatrical songs. The high falsetto notes of these songs can best be reached by immature voices. For two or three weeks these children receive instruction day and night. Then the instructor moves on to another village but the band goes on practicing until the religious procession is held. When that great annual event is passed, the club disbands, the members return to their major interests, and the children, to school.

* * *

All these associations are really cooperative societies organized to pay the expenses either by cash, by labor, or by kind, of carrying on the activities of the members. The economic nexus runs like a red thread through a string of beads, binding practically all the groups into a fundamental unity of function and purpose.

A fitting addition to the preceding discussion of Chinese rural life is a detailed description of a single village. At this point it is well to review the elementary conceptual scheme around which this book is organized:

1. Society consists of social relationships.

2. Each relationship is made up of people occupying statuses and playing roles appropriate to those statuses in a given situation.

3. When we classify the statuses we arrive at a number of patterns of association which we have been describing in considerable detail: the family and kinship system, the locality groupings of neighborhood and community, the economy (as a set of farmers, middlemen, creditors, landlords, tenants, and consumers), the local government, religion, theatricals, and specific purposive organizations.

4. When we classify the roles we get a glimpse into the types of interaction involving competition and conflict, cooperation and accommodation. In some of the selections, also, we paid particular attention to the motivational processes of socialization and social control. The account of Taitou Village, which follows, will add considerably to our information on this score.

5. *Social values,* inherited and thus traditional, carry tremendous weight and help the Chinese peasant rank the various statuses in terms of importance and prestige. We have noted that the scholar and the landowner rate high, the actor and the soldier low. We have seen the relative standing within the family of father and mother, younger brother and older brother, and we shall gain further insight into the status differences among family groups within a village.

6. Another mentifact, or cultural trait of much significance, is the *norm,* which specifies limits of variations allowed in the carrying out of the roles. This gives us a key to the matter of "losing face," so important in the East; it also means that human behavior is predictable to the extent that individuals have been socialized to observe the norms in the performance of their roles.

7. Any society exists only if it possesses a sufficient degree of integration. There must be a correspondence between norms and values, statuses and roles. Patterns of association and processes combine to make up social systems.

Therefore, as we turn to Taitou and its extended treatment, we shall consider it as a small social system—a collection of people interacting with one another in differing ways according to the social relationships existing among them. We shall note the ways in which the integration of daily life is maintained, how the rough edges are worn away; and also the threats to integration in the form of forces coming in from outside. The village studies used thus far include the one by Hsu, in Southwest China (Selection 13), the one by Kulp, in South China (Selections 9 and 16), and the one by Fei, on the Yangtze Plain (Selections 6 and 14). Taitou is located on the Shantung Peninsula in North China. Martin C. Yang, the author, is a well-trained social scientist who has brought objectivity and an analytical approach to the study of the village which he once knew well and which he revisited in later years. From our reading thus far we should be able, to some degree, to distinguish features of Taitou life which seem to be local and regional, as well as to identify those characteristics which seem to hold true for peasant China as a whole.

For convenience in locating the topics treated, the following page references will be useful:

• 17 • A Village of Shantung Province
MARTIN C. YANG

PREFACE

The village of Taitou has been selected as the object of . . . [this] study because the writer was born and reared there, and lived there until he entered high school. Until recent years, he has returned to the village at least once each year, the periods of his visits varying from five days to several months. He has maintained his contacts with his relatives in Taitou and has kept himself informed about the daily life and significant happenings in the village. Therefore, this study is a record of facts which have been personally seen, heard, and experienced.

*   *   *

1. THE VILLAGE SITE

The village of Taitou is located on a stretch of level land ringed with mountains on the southwestern shore of Kiachow Bay.

Directly across the bay to the east is a small peninsula, on the southern end of which is the city of Tsingtao. This city, which has grown up in recent decades, now provides Shantung and its neighboring provinces with means of access to the outside world. It is a center of commerce, industry, and transportation, and thus plays an important role in the growing trade between rural China and the manufacturing centers in distant parts of the world.

This region is one of the oldest agricultural areas in China. Its people are almost all farmers who cultivate their own land and live in compact villages. There are about twenty villages and a rural town. The town is Hsinanchen—the only marketing center for the region. Taitou is about two thirds of a mile south of Hsinanchen, with which it is connected by a new highway.

*   *   *

[From A Chinese Village: Taitou, Shantung Province, Columbia University Press, New York, 1945. Pp. ix, 1-2, 4, 6-7, 9, 11-17, 23-28, 30-34, 38, 40-43, 45-48, 50-63, 65-68, 73-76, 79-84, 86-90, 103-117, 119, 123-124, 126-129, 132-135, 137-138, 140-145, 147-158, 160-161, 163, 165-170, 174-181, 183-188, 190-191, 193-194, 198-200, 228, 230, 233-235, 238-242. Used by permission.]

The climate of the area is good because of the proximity of the sea and mountains.

* * *

The village site can be divided roughly into two parts: the residential area and the immediate outskirts. The former is situated on the north bank of the Taitou River. Here the one main street follows the bowlike curve of the river, with narrower roads branching from it in both directions. A number of small lanes and paths, all running northward, connect with the main street. Most of the residences are located north of the street. The local people call the lanes and paths *hu-tung,* and, if the villagers of a certain *hu-tung* are members of a certain clan, then the name of the clan is added to the *hu-tung's* name. . . .

The central section of the main street is quite spacious. To the south it opens on the river and affords a view of the open country. On the levees built by some of the wealthier families along the riverbank grow rows of willow trees. This part of the main street is something of a social center or public square for the village. In the summer, the villagers sit on the stones or on the levees under the trees and talk through the hot afternoons. In winter, the old people relax against the walls in the warm sunshine and watch the children at play in the square. Men weaving baskets or knitting straw rain coats or perhaps working on farm tools work out here rather than in their narrow and smoke-filled homes. Some portions of this open space are the private property of different families, who often use their part as an open stable for their animals during the day and also as a place to keep manure and earth before it is removed to the field.

All the better houses are in the central part of the residential area. *Hu-tung* divide the area into four main divisions according to the four clans in the village. The first part, which is almost eight-tenths of the whole area and includes almost all the good houses, is occupied by the P'an clan, the largest in the village. The second is occupied by the Ch'en clan, the third by the Yangs, and the fourth by the Lius . . . The families of each clan cluster together in one section forming a nucleus out from which the clan's territory extends. A few isolated families of each clan have settled among families of other clans or live outside the main residential area . . . Generally, the older and wealthier families occupy the main parts of the residential area, whereas the poorer or smaller families spread in the outlying areas. In the main residential area are the village school, the Christian church, the two oil-pressing shops, and a small foundry. The village school does not have its own building, but occupies one or two rooms of a family house. The Christian church, which was built more than twenty-five years ago, is a good building, the only finer one being the new home of the P'an family.

Immediately beyond the residential area lie the vegetable gardens and the threshing grounds. . . .

Beyond the gardens lie the graveyards of the four clans. There is no general cemetery; each clan buries its dead on land which is believed to be favorable to the future generations of the clan. When the clan becomes large and several branches split off, each branch chooses its own ground for burial. . . .

The southern side of the residential area is quite beautiful in summer. Along both sides of the river there are several stretches of wooded swamps. Not long ago, when the countryside was peaceful and when the P'an families were in their prosperous period, the village was admired by travelers who approached it from the south. Before one reached the edge of the river one could hardly see the village because of a thick green wall of trees. But as the traveler went on, suddenly the village burst into view before him, and in the next instant he was walking before the watching eyes of the villagers and could see the farmers hoeing in the vegetable garden or working on the threshing grounds, women washing their clothes on the river dikes while children played around them, people sitting and working under the tall willow trees, and also the big oxen and mules standing on the river bank. Unfortunately, a great part of that is gone. During the last ten years the P'an family [have] declined rapidly. The woods have been cut, broken river levees have not been repaired, and the tall willow trees are almost gone, as are the oxen and mules. . . .

2. THE PEOPLE

It is hard to say just how large the population of the village is . . . Each family must post on the top of the front door a card bearing the name, age, sex, kinship status, and occupation of the family members. However, access to this means of counting is impossible, so our estimate must be made on the basis of the size of an average family and the approximate number of families in the villages. . . .

According to the present writer's impression, a family in Taitou . . . [would] average . . . six persons, including parents, children, and grandchildren.

The number of families in the village is also difficult to estimate. More than ten years ago it was generally believed to be about a hundred but there is no doubt that the number has increased in the last decade. Many large families have broken into three or four separate units. None has moved, but a few may have died out. It seems safe to say that there are now about 120 families in the village. If we take these two estimates, then the number of the village's population should be about 720 people.

*   *   *

The death rate among children is high, about two out of every six or seven born. The villagers, for the most part, accept this as a matter of course. If a family loses more children, three out of five for example, the neighbors feel that something must be wrong; either the wife has brought bad luck on the family, or the ancestors have committed actions destructive to God and against human principles. If, on the other hand, all the children in a family live to grow up, the mother and the family are considered very fortunate and unusual. The death rate is highest among children under the age of three; it tapers off decidedly between the ages of five to ten. When a young baby dies, the body is not deeply buried and is easily dug up by wild dogs or wolves. When an old woman asks the name of a neighbor's child and is told that the child is ten years old, she will say, "Good, the child is out of the reach of dogs!" —meaning that the danger of death is past.

The average life span of adults is about sixty to seventy years. Women die earlier than men. This may be because they bear children, work hard, and usually have a diet which is inferior to that of men. When a man of sixty or over is too ill to leave his bed for more than several days at a time, the whole family take it very seriously. But if he is under sixty, they are less concerned since the possibility of death is much less. When a person under forty dies, the death is regarded as very unusual and great grief is shown by both relatives and neighbors. When a person under sixty dies, the death is still considered unusual, but there is less grief because the deceased has grown-up children to continue the family line and to care for the infirm. If the deceased is over sixty, the death is taken as a matter of course, and only close relatives grieve. In case a person lives longer than seventy or eighty years, his death is a relief to relatives and friends. This is especially true if the family is poor and the young people are not filial. Death may also be a happiness because the deceased had lived long and had enjoyed a good life; it is good for him to die before he becomes too old to be liked by the younger generations.

The marriage system in this community as in all other Chinese communities is patri-local—the woman goes to her husband's home. This is the chief form of population displacement; emigration and immigration are rare.

*   *   *

On the whole the population of Taitou is stable. Families rarely leave the village. Individuals move about and many of the young people go to the larger towns to work, but they maintain close ties with their relatives at home and usually come back to the village, eventually to settle down. Any population change in Taitou is more apt to be a result of changing birth or death rates than of shifting population.

3. AGRICULTURE

In this area, as in all other parts of the country, the cultivated land has for long been elaborately partitioned into very small fragments. A farmer, or a family, does not own one but a number of plots, and these are generally scattered in a number of localities. Homes are not on the cultivated land but are in the village. To get to his farm a farmer has to go to several different places, some of them quite distant. Each field belongs to a different owner and each owner must have some way of reaching his field, so there are numerous roads or paths crossing the land. In the summer, or during the growing seasons, the land resembles many small strips of different colors lying side by side.

Even within the environs of a single village, there is a wide range in the value of the soil. The extreme fragmentation prevents ownership of all the land of a given quality by one or a few families and thereby reduces the possibility of complete crop failure for any one family. Since different land is more or less suited to different crops, a family which has land in several places can grow various kinds of food, will always get some return from its land, and, being, therefore, self-sufficient, has less need to trade. In former times the fields must have been larger. Since a father's holdings are equally divided among all his sons, there is an endless process of division and redivision. Another factor which increases the parceling is the numerous small transactions in buying and selling land. Families buy small bits of land from their neighbors, but seldom whole fields. It is impossible to recombine these fragments, for that would require owners of two or three fields to relinquish them at one time to one person. A family does not sell land unless it absolutely has to, so that the possibility of several families having to sell at once would be extremely rare.

The size of the fields varies greatly. The smallest may be only one-tenth of a *mow* [a *mow* is about one-sixth of an acre], while the largest may be as much as five *mow* or more. Fields in the hills and valleys and in the water [flooded] land are usually small, while those in the level land are large. In the hilly places many tiny fields are terraced on the slopes and bottoms. Sometimes these are just little corners—a plot as large as a *mow* is rare among them. The water land has always been greatly treasured by the villagers, and each small piece is worth a great deal. It has been divided into many plots so that each of the well-to-do families can have one.

* * *

... About ten years ago there were two or three families each of whom had as much as eighty to ninety *mow* [about 13 to 15 acres] and five or six families who had from fifty to sixty *mow* [about 9 to 10 acres]. In the last decade all these families have either broken into small units, or else been forced to sell their land because of losses inflicted by bandits or because of the extravagance of their children. At present, perhaps no family has a holding greater than forty *mow*.

The main crops are wheat, millet, barley, soybeans, corn, sweet potatoes, and peanuts. A variety of vegetables are grown in the gardens: cabbage, turnip, onions, garlic ... radishes, cucumbers, spinach, several kinds of string beans, squashes, peas, and melons. There are also many kinds of fruit but none of them in quantity. While there are no orchards, one or two fruit trees may be seen on the edges of most of the vegetable gardens.

A great part of the land is good for growing sweet potatoes and peanuts, and the yield in these crops is abundant. Because most of the families own only a very limited quantity of land, they have to grow the crops which are most suited to the soil and which offer the best prospects of a good yield. From June to October, sweet potatoes, peanuts, and soybeans occupy almost 50 to 60 percent of the crop land. Next in importance is millet, to which 30 percent is given, leaving only 10 percent for other crops and vegetables. From November to June of the following year, part of the land is devoted to winter wheat and winter barley and part of it is left fallow. Families with larger holdings grow more wheat, millet, and soybeans, while the poorer ones have to raise more sweet potatoes and peanuts. Wheat takes a longer time to grow and requires more fertilizer, and the yield is not high, but wheat flour is regarded as one of the best foods. Wealthy families like it and can afford to grow it. It is also a good cash crop. Sweet potatoes grow well in hilly and sandy soil and do not require much fertilizer, which is an advantage. They are a much more dependable crop, both in quantity and nutritive value, than wheat. Therefore, a family without much land has to grow more *mow* of sweet potatoes than other crops. Since peanuts grow well in soil that is not suitable for wheat, they are the main cash crop of the poorer families. Soybeans are important as a cash crop and also for home consumption; all families grow them in large quantities. Millet is also generally grown and is the most important staple for local consumption.

All but a few families have vegetable gardens. Some vegetables are grown in the open fields. Each family grows from one tenth to one half of a *mow* of turnips. String beans and peas are planted between the rows of the crops or at the edges of the field. A few families also raise water and honey melons. On the water land wet rice is grown. The year's harvest of this crop is not of any significance in the village's whole economy, but it is interesting to note that it gives the village some rice culture which is rare for this area.

* * *

Farm implements are generally simple. Those of importance are the plow, two kinds of harrows, a weeding hoe and a digging hoe, wooden and iron rakes, wooden and iron shovels, a harvesting sickle, and different kinds of forks. For threshing, the stone roller and the flail are important. The wheelbarrow

is most used, for the mule-cart is not seen in this part of the country. This is perhaps because the land is hilly and most of the roads are merely narrow paths. . . .

With the exception of a few crude baskets, the villagers do not make their own tools because they can buy all they need at the special country fairs, held twice a year in the market town. Some of the tools are made in neighboring villages where materials are locally available; others are made in distant places and imported by dealers. Before the harvesting or plowing season, itinerant blacksmiths come to the village to repair or reinforce the metal tools or the steel parts. . . .

For fertilizing the fields, both human and animal dung are carefully gathered and preserved. At a corner of the front court or in the backyard a pit and an adjacent pigpen are enclosed by walls or fences which open on the court. The pit is used as a privy and into it are gathered all the manure and other refuse from the barn or from outside; even the ashes from the kitchen are carefully preserved here. When the pit is full, the contents are removed to an open space set aside for the purpose and are covered with a layer of mud. In the pit the mixture has already undergone fermentation and here the process continues. According to the local farmer's experience, raw manure is not good; the fermented mixture is the best fertilizer he knows. When the sowing season arrives, the pile is broken down and the mixture is dried in the sun. It is then made into powder and transported to the fields as needed.

A second important fertilizer is soybean cakes. After the oil has been extracted from the beans, the residue is made into cakes which are used both as animal feed and fertilizer. As fertilizer, the cakes are always mixed with the compost, not only because the farmer cannot afford to use soybean cakes alone, but because the local people believe that the mixture is more effective.

* * *

Green manure is very rarely seen. This is partly due to the lack of mineral fuel. Instead of coal and gas, tree branches and leaves, stalks and wheat and other crops are used as fuel. Although the area is almost surrounded by mountains, wood is still too expensive to be burned as fuel. Consequently, every bit of vegetation that cannot be used for other purposes is carefully gathered and preserved to feed the kitchen stoves. The main sources of animal feed are the stalks of millet, the vines of peanuts and sweet potatoes, and many kinds of grass. In addition, the houses are all thatched with straw, except for a few that have been recently built with tile roofs. The farmer does not consider it economic to use green manure, since there are so many other uses for vegetation. Wheat stalks, for instance, are used for cooking. The ashes are taken out from the stove and mixed with animal manure to fertilize the field. Thus, the stalks serve two purposes: cooking and fertilizing.

* * *

Oxen, mules, and donkeys are the customary farm animals. The donkey is the cheapest . . . A family owning less than ten *mow* cannot afford any animal and must either work without one or cooperate with a more fortunate neighbor by exchanging labor for the use of his animal.

Oxen are chiefly used for plowing and sowing, and seldom for pulling wheelbarrows or drawing the millstones. After plowing or sowing an ox remains in the barn, under the shade of the willow trees, or in the sunshine near a wall. Mules are used more frequently— for transporting harvested crops from the field to the threshing ground, pulling the millstones when the donkey is too tired, or for riding to other villages on visits.

Practically every family has a donkey. They are used for every kind of transportation and in many ways in domestic work. Housewives of the village do not often touch the ox, and never try to handle a mule, but they can control donkeys like pets. The absence of a donkey would not only hinder the small farmer in his field, but his wife at home as well.

Although agriculture is the main means of livelihood, many subsidiary occupations supplement income in the slack periods of the farm work. For example, a little foundry was established by two brothers of the P'an family in Taitou. . . . There is also a woodworking shop where one carpenter and an apprentice make furniture parts, plain doors and windows, and a number of simple farm implements. In addition to filling villagers' orders they produce goods to be sold in the market town. . . .

There are three or four cloth weavers. One of them once bought an improved loom and opened a workshop. There he worked for himself and sold his products in the market town or in other villages. Unfortunately, he had to stop because he was short of capital and also because he could not work steadily at it. All the other weavers have only old looms and their rate of production is very low. Recently they have been forced to compete with factory-made cloth which comes in to the country in daily increasing quantities. Young people prefer the fine cloth whenever they can afford it, though the old people still believe that homespun is much better—they say it lasts longer and is better-suited to rough farm work. . . .

A few years ago three families owned oil-pressing shops. In the winter and spring they pressed oil from the locally raised peanuts and soybeans. One of them also opened a shop for making the baskets used as containers for shipping oil to Tsingtao. It was a profitable business and for some time supplied work for ten or more people; but, recently, due to bandit raids and heavy taxes, all the shops have been closed. . . .

There are five or six masons who build houses for the villagers and for people of neighboring villages. Some of them also work periodically in Tsingtao. Their earnings are as good as the carpenters' and several families whose sons are masons have attained a better standing in the community.

It is interesting to note that all these craftsmen are members of poor families. Some have bettered the family status, others have kept their relatives from starvation. Only the oil-pressing shops were owned by members of wealthy families. But we see that nonetheless very few are engaged in industry. What the local people value most is land: big land holdings and a prosperous farm are to them the real signs of prosperity and this is why no rural industry has ever developed into a business of any significance. Necessity is the only incentive, or at least it is the main one, for taking up any means of livelihood other than farming.

* * *

There are two kinds of hired farm laborers, the yearly or permanent, and the daily or temporary, laborer. . . . A yearly laborer is not necessarily one who works throughout the entire year. Usually his term of employment runs from the sixteenth day of the first month on the lunar calendar up to the first day of the tenth month. Daily laborers are hired chiefly in the busy seasons, when sowing, hoeing, and harvesting have to be done. Families who have yearly laborers may also hire daily laborers for a few days to get the work done on time. During this period a group of able-bodied men carrying hoes or sickles and wearing straw raincoats and rain hats wait every morning at a corner of the main street in the market town to be hired. This is called locally the "market of laborers." Any farm family who needs help sends someone there to hire a man.

* * *

Relations between the family members and the hired laborers are generally congenial. Change in economic status is frequent, so that in the same generation a family who has been hiring laborers may come to the point of hiring their own members out to others. On the other hand, a number of families who were poor may become relatively well-to-do. Since mobility of this kind is great, one family cannot feel superior or inferior to another. Moreover, most of the hired men come from families who own land, though it may be but a small piece, and as long as a family owns even an inch of land they consider themselves on

a par with their fellow villagers . . . Workers and owners all follow the same occupation and work together in the fields. All these factors tend to minimize distinctions between wage-earners and employers. But recently the situation has been changing. More disputes rise; laborers demand higher wages and better meals. The employers try voluntarily or involuntarily, to meet these demands, but they complain that it is very difficult to handle hired laborers in these days. . . . The situation as a whole is unfortunate because the rising price of labor is not due to a natural shortage but to social and political chaos. Since the outbreak of civil war, with the attendant increase in banditry and local upheaval, many young people have abandoned the old tradition and have become restless. Some have joined the bandits, others have entered the militia employed by ambitious local chieftains, and others have simply disappeared.

4. STANDARD OF LIVING

The population of Taitou can be divided roughly into four classes on the basis of food consumption. At the lowest level is the group for whom sweet potatoes are the main item of diet; next are those who have a combination of sweet potatoes and millet; third, those who eat millet and wheat; and at the top, those who eat mainly wheat. All classes eat garden vegetables in large quantity when these are available. The first two groups rarely have animal products of any kind; the last two have them only occasionally.

Among the poor, sweet potatoes are eaten at every meal every day throughout the year. From harvest time until the spring of the following year, they eat fresh sweet potatoes; when these are gone, they eat stored dry slices. These are boiled, or ground into meal which is mixed with other flour to make bread or noodles. Supplementing the potatoes are, first, a kind of gruel made of barley flour and peanut powder; second, a kind of hash made of chopped turnips and soybean juice; and third, one or two kinds of pickles. Occasionally some kind of bread is served.

During the busy season food is more plentiful. Steamed millet or millet bread takes the place of sweet-potato slices, and green vegetables cooked with fat are added to the diet. On a poor family's table, meat, fresh fish, or eggs are seen only on special occasions, when guests are entertained, or for the New Year celebration. Soybean oil, peanut oil, are used in cooking, and in richer households, pork fat. A poor woman tastes sugar only when she delivers a child.

. . . Food consumption varies with the season.

* * *

When sweet potatoes and peanuts are harvested, the busiest time of the year, the diet of a well-to-do family is better than at any time except during the New Year celebration or at special feasts. The food is both plentiful and varied—more pork and beef, more wheat flour, and cabbages are added to the menu. Everybody is well fed, even the beggars look healthy. But as soon as the fields and threshing grounds are cleared up and the hired laborers gone, the diet is again restricted until the coming of the New Year season.

* * *

Because wheat flour is the preferred food, a number of social practices center around it. When a marriage is arranged, for example, the most important gift presented by the boy's family is a number of big steamed rolls made of pure wheat flour, each weighing two catties (about three pounds). On top of the roll is pasted the Chinese word "happiness," cut from a piece of red paper. The girl's family distributes some of the rolls to relatives, friends, and neighbors, thus formally announcing the engagement, and returns the rest to the boy's family to be distributed among their relatives and friends.

* * *

A group of poor villagers speaking of a Christian preacher, a school-teacher, or a businessman from the market town, will say: "He is a man who eats wheat flour every day, why should he not have a smooth face!"

When a person has a run of good luck, his fellow villagers might say: "Just as meat is always served with wheat flour rolls." A successful man is compared by the villagers to winter wheat, which is superior to other cereals because it survives the severest winter weather. So a person who has achieved success and fortune through hardship and self-denial is compared to wheat and admired by all who know him.

* * *

The houses of Taitou can be classified roughly into three types. Those of the wealthiest group are built of stone, burned bricks, lime, and a good grade of wood and roofing material. A stone foundation is laid underground and rises aboveground about six inches. Upon this foundation are built the walls. The lower part of the walls, about four feet high, is built of stone blocks. The blocks used on the front wall are well cut in squares or oblongs; for the back wall irregularly shaped stones are used. Above the lower part is a layer of burned brick. From here on, the wall is constructed of small stones or beaten earth with a layer of lime plastered on the outside. This is topped with an arched wooden roof covered with thatch. The inner side of the wall is set with small, unpolished stones.

The houses of the average income group are constructed in the same way except that the materials used are inferior . . . The houses of the poor are small, made of inferior materials, and not regularly shaped. They are simply huts. . . .

The main house, or the north house, called the *cheng wu,* is usually composed of three to five rooms, while the house on the left or right side of the court generally contains two or three rooms. The width of a main house in the wealthy first group may measure about twelve feet; the length varies greatly. The floors in all kinds of houses are of beaten earth. The walls are papered. The windows are pasted over with thin white paper (sometimes oiled), which usually admits sufficient light and sunshine. The rooms are crowded by the big brick beds and wooden beds, the tables, bureaus, cabinets, and numerous personal belongings. As the kitchen is connected with the bedrooms and the stoves are attached to the tunnels inside the brick beds, the house is kept warm in the winter, but in the summer it sometimes becomes insufferably hot. Temporary kitchens may then be built in the court or in an empty house.

In the house of a well-to-do family one or two rooms are specially furnished and kept for guests. An average family, however, uses the parents' bedroom as a guest room. Guests are almost always relatives so that there is no embarrassment on either side. The parents' bedroom also serves as the dining room for the whole family and their guests in the winter. The large brick bed is covered with a thick layer of straw above which a neat, smooth mat of stripped skins of kaoliang [grain sorghum] stalks is laid. During the winter when the nights are long and it is cold outside, the family usually gathers in the parents' bedroom to work or talk. Neighbors also come and sit on the same bed. Thus, the parents' bedroom is really the center of family life.

A married son and his young wife live in the room across from the kitchen. The door of this room is always kept closed, for the interior should not be seen by the father or by any man who is not of the family. The grown-up daughters always live in the room back of the parents' room so that no one can enter it except by first passing through the parents' room. When male guests or male neighbors are present, the daughters of the house must leave their room beforehand or remain there quietly until the guests or neighbors have gone. . . .

The earth floor of the houses is always dusty, and when it is swept the dust flies about the room. Sometimes water is used to moisten the floor before sweeping, and though this helps, it is not enough. Under the tables, under the wooden beds and bureaus, odds and ends accumulate and heavy layers of dust form. Mothers let their infant children urinate or soil the floor. Because the rooms are crowded, there is not enough fresh air. A pottery bucket is placed in every bedroom for night use. In the winter, when all the windows are carefully pasted over with paper and the doors closed, the air is very foul, especially in the morning. Only when the weather is fine and the doors can be left open is the odor somewhat dissipated.

* * *

The farmer's work garments are made mainly of cotton. Silk trousers are worn by quite a few villagers in the summer, but this silk is raised locally and spun at home and is a coarse but very lasting material. In July and August a number of middle-aged wives of the well-to-do families wear linen jackets when working. A number of villagers also possess fur coats or jackets and wear them when they go to the market town or when no manual work has to be done. Wool is used only in winter shoes, winter caps, and winter bed sheets. A few well-to-do families have woolen clothes but do not wear them very often and never for work.

* * *

A farmer may have two or three suits of work garments. Cotton-padded jackets and trousers are worn in cold weather. In the spring and autumn the farmer wears a lined jacket and the cotton padding is removed from the trousers. For the summer he has two or three coats and several pairs of trousers. These coats are worn in the winter as underwear, and the same trousers are again padded with cotton. . . .

Everyone has one or two suits of dress clothes. . . . For the New Year celebration, weddings, or formal visiting, the better dress garments are worn. For ordinary occasions, work garments newly washed and pressed are worn. A man's ceremonial dress garment consists of a long gown and a jacket made of fine cloth. A woman's is a skirt and jacket made of fine cloth or silk. Ordinarily a woman wears only a pair of trousers and a jacket, and no skirt. A woman's jacket, whether it is a dress or a work garment must be five inches below her hips and must hang loosely, for if she wears short, tight jackets she will be sharply criticized and suspected of wanting to attract men.

Color is important. Girls, young women, and brides are allowed to wear bright colors— red, pink, purple, or green; the accepted color for grown-up men and middle-aged women is blue. No man under thirty should wear white shirts, and no man under fifty, white trousers. For middle-aged people, cotton-padded trousers may be white, but cotton-padded jackets must not be. Dress garments are usually colored. The long gown is always blue and the jacket black. A woman never wears white unless she is in deep mourning. Men's shoes and caps are always black. Women's shoes are red, pink, or green when they are young, but black when they have passed middle age. Women do not wear hats.

*   *   *

5. THE COMPONENTS OF A FAMILY

A Chinese family, especially in rural China, is far more than a group of related individuals. In Taitou, as well as in other villages, it is a complex organization of family members, family property, domestic animals, family reputations, family traditions, and family gods. It can be said that the family extends to the as yet unborn generations and to the long-deceased ones. The living traditionally believe that their ancestors' spirits, whether in the ancestral graves or in Heaven, are with them and are keeping watchful eyes upon them at all times. A family's fortune or misfortune is largely controlled by spirits of the ancestors. When the spirits are pleased, the family will receive blessings; but when they have been antagonized, disaster inevitably comes. They must be invited to participate in all special occasions, such as festivals, weddings, and births, and homage must be paid to them at their graves, in the ancestral halls, or before the ceremonial tables of the family. This sense of kinship is strongest at the New Year Festival, a time when the living feel their ancestors to be actually with them.

A great part of the household activities is regulated by the invisible power of the ancestors. A Chinese family, or an individual, does many things which are primarily designed to please the ancestral spirits. One studies hard, for example, to advance in the official scale in order to glorify one's ancestors; on the other hand, one does not want to be a beggar, a thief, or a prostitute, because that would bring disgrace to them. The belief in the unbroken continuity of the family is manifest in the behavior of the descendants and the bond between the generations is never broken. It is a well-known fact that the Chinese always make great efforts to protect their ancestors' graveyards, ancestral halls, and the ceremonial tables, because these things represent their ancestors' spirits, and, as such, are a real and living part of the family.

The importance of the future generations can be seen by the anxiety of the parents to see their sons married, and to accumulate property for their children. With this in mind they work hard and live thriftily so that they can save some capital for the prospective children. They feel guilty when unusually good food is eaten or extra money is spent, not because they cannot afford these things, but because they want to have something to leave to their descendants. A family may have enough houses for all its members to live in, but they keep on buying and building new ones and acquiring land for the future generations. On New Year's Eve, or on other special occasions, family members not only invite their ancestors but also observe rites to symbolize the birth of additional children. Just as the authority of the dead figures in the decisions of the living, the rights of the unborn determine the composition and well-being of the families of which they will become part.

Land is the most important form of property, for it belongs to all the generations. It means much more than a piece of earth on which crops are cultivated; it is the very foundation of the family. Without land a family can never be settled and the family members will never have a sense of security. People and land are the two pillars of the Chinese farm family. When we say a family is broken, we mean that the family's land is gone. Thus, land becomes a part of the life of the farmer and his family, and they have a very deep sense of attachment to it; their land is no less dear to them than are their children. In the village a family's status depends very much on the amount of land owned, for this indicates to others how much the family cares for its past and future obligations and how faithfully these are observed. Land ownership also gives the farm family independent personality, spiritual inspiration, and a feeling of freedom.

* * *

Domestic animals are an important part of the farm life. In Taitou, these are chiefly oxen, mules, donkeys, dogs, cats, pigs, and chickens. The first four are considered as part of the family and are accorded special treatment. The farmer is most attached to his ox. The feeling is so strong that he may feel worse about the loss of his ox than he would about the death of his infant child, for the loss of the animal endangers the life of the whole family. The slaughter of oxen is condemned by all. There is no law or social custom to forbid the professional butchering of oxen, it is true, but everybody looks down upon anyone who practices it. People believe that no one could become rich in such a business, that the soul of a butcher will be condemned eternally to hell, and that his offspring, if he has any at all, will always be poor and weak. A farmer usually keeps his cow or ox as long as possible. If one day, for some reason, he is forced to sell his animal, there is great sadness in the family. When the farmer turns his animal over to the buyer and sees it being led away, he may shed tears. For one or two days at least the family will maintain silence at the dinner table and the situation will not be relieved until a new cow is purchased.

* * *

The quality of the ox also reflects the social status of a family. By noting the size of the ox tied to a tree before the front door, one can estimate about how may *mow* of land the family owns and to what class it belongs in the village. For this reason, a large and well-fed ox is always a source of great pride to its owner, and will be tied, for all to see, to the front door or at a place where people walk or gather. During the summer days many fine oxen can be seen standing under the big willow trees along the river bank at the southern end of the village, which is the favorite gathering place of the villagers. Recently, most of them have been either hidden in backyards or sold, because of the threat of bandits and the decline of the well-to-do families.

* * *

The intangible components of a family are also important, and the most highly regarded of these is reputation. A family wants to be admired and talked about by people of a neighborhood or of a considerable territory. This is a great source of pride to families of the middle and upper classes who are generally much concerned with what people think of them. There are five ways of achieving reputation, and the first of these is to have members in ranking official positions. If one of the family, for example, is a county magistrate, villagers and others will refer to the family as the *Hsien-chang chia,* or the magistrate's family, and will show great respect to its members. As the official position rises, the family's fame climbs with it.

Scholastic fame comes from having a member in the family who has passed the academic examinations. In the old days, if one of the family passed the first Imperial Examination, the family was known as a *hsiou-ts'ai chia.* Although a *hsiou-ts'ai* was not important, nevertheless on special occasions the family was distinguished by the title from plain farmers. . . .

Since most of the villagers believe that farming is the most dependable and desirable means of livelihood, a family is proud of having plenty of land and many sons who are eagerly cultivating the land. A family which is devoted to agriculture, and has also some scholastic attainment, is the ideal family in the countryside, and usually referred to as a family of farm and study.

*   *   *

Family fame is also built on wealth. If a family is rich, it will be known over a wide area.

*   *   *

Wealth alone cannot build up family fame. A family may be known as a wealthy one, but not necessarily as one worthy of respect. Two additional factors are needed: first, some distinctive and gracious feature which sets it apart from its neighbors; and, second, a certain degree of socialization which makes it a pleasant topic for discussion. . . .

Conspicuous virtue also enhances a family's reputation. A family may become well known because it has an unusually filial son or an especially good daughter-in-law, or because all its members are so good that the big household has been able to hang together for four or more generations. Filial piety and feminine loyalty are the two most treasured virtues. . . .

A family known as a good neighbor has amicable relations with most of the people in the village. If they are pleasant, mild mannered, and honest, they will be well liked, even if they are not distinguished in other ways. Such people always give way to others. Thus, all the villagers like to do business with them and will speak well of them at social gatherings. There are several families with such a reputation in Taitou. The Yang family is one of them and then there is a P'an family which has four sons, the first son being the teacher of the village school. . . .

Family reputation is a basic social value. Not many families have been able to achieve it, nor can it be maintained forever, or even, usually, for as long as a century.

*   *   *

6. INTRAFAMILIAL RELATIONSHIPS

A young wife must . . . keep from showing that she loves her husband. The general attitude is that a decent wife should love her husband, but must not let her love spoil his career or make him neglect his duty to his family. A good wife stays at her work with her mother-in-law or sisters-in-law during the day, and at night she must wait until all the family members have retired before she can go to her room and be with her husband. . . .

A newly married wife cannot but feel lonesome and strange, because she is really in a strange home with strange people. The sudden separation from her mother, the stern face of her mother-in-law, the pretended dignity of the father-in-law, and above all, her sudden introduction to the continuous housework, all make her feel that she is completely at the mercy of these people. Since she cannot go back to her mother, the only one from whom she can seek protection is her husband. She will generally respond with great warmth and gratitude if she is well received by him. . . .

The partners of an unsuccessful marriage are in an unhappy plight. Divorce is out of the question: they must make the best of it. Outwardly they seem no different from any other couple. They will not quarrel openly; the husband will not beat his wife; she does her work dutifully. However, it is easy to note that the loved wife is active, cheerful, and energetic, while the unhappy wife is listless and slow in her work. . . .

However, if an initially unhappy marriage survives at all, if the hopelessness and sorrow and burden of work do not break down the unhappy wife, the relationship between the couple improves with time. A woman who survives these hardships without committing suicide or breaking down becomes a heroine in the eyes of her relatives. She has proved that she has patience, far-sightedness, and unusual wisdom and kindness. As the couple grow older and their children reach maturity, their feelings toward each other mellow. . . .

In privacy, romantic love decreases, while the feeling of companionship grows stronger. In their bedroom the wife will tell her husband what has happened in the household during the day and what she thinks about their problems. She will also talk to him about their children. The husband tells her about the crops in the field, the work of his brothers and the hired laborers, and so on. Because of his consciousness of being a man, a filial son, a good brother, and a dignified husband, he is supposed not to listen to, or at least not to believe, his wife's complaints about other household members. In spite of this he frequently accepts her statements, and secretly acts on her suggestions and advice on other matters.

As the husband and wife mature, they come to have their own home and undivided authority over their children. The companionship ripens and is no longer kept secret but becomes the foundation of the newly independent family. . . .

When a couple reaches the age of fifty or sixty, the wife generally becomes the dominant person in the household. She is now the mother-in-law of one, two, or even four daughters-in-law. She is the grandmother of a long line of children and is also the overseer of a large household. The middle-aged sons have almost invariably developed strong attachment to their mother but not to their father. The father's authority in the fields, now that he does not work there, is considerably lessened. He has lost his role in business transactions because he is too old to take the farm products to the market town and deal directly with the dealers. To a certain extent, his importance in relations with the neighbors is diminished, because people find that he is no longer the real authority and that his position as family head is more nominal than real, although he is still respected by all the household.

*   *   *

The relationship between father and child has none of the warmth and freedom existing between mother and child. The father's attitude is dignified, even remote; his authority is unquestioned and he expects submissiveness from his sons. Although in a farm family some informalities are permitted—as, joking in the presence of one's parents, taking a place of equal importance to that occupied by one's father, not rising when the father approaches—yet the father and son relationship is far from free or intimate. . . .

The relationship between mother and son, on the other hand, is comparatively close. Although a boy who reaches the age of ten is dependent entirely upon his father's authority and teaching, this does not interfere entirely with his intimacy with his mother. Because of the lack of female companions and the meager possibilities for recreation, a young man spends much time talking to his mother during his formative years. . . . In her turn, the mother may tell him what she and his father think of him. A son at this time has no one, except his mother, to whom he can tell his thoughts freely, and this provides an unshakable foundation for the long-lasting mother-son relationship.

The affection between mother and son is threatened when the son marries. If the mother is selfish or narrow-minded, as many mothers are, she will become jealous of the young wife. Not a few of the difficulties between mother-in-law and daughter-in-law are unconsciously based on such jealousy. A common saying has it that "A son is lost when he is married."

*   *   *

When a girl is born, she is cared for by her mother in much the same way a boy is. The father maintains his usual attitude of indifference. When the next baby is born, the three- or four-year-old girl has a place of her own or is temporarily taken care of by her grandmother rather than sharing her father's side of the bed as a boy does. When she is six or older, she gradually starts helping her mother to look after the younger sister or brother. By the time she is thirteen, she begins to learn to sew, cook, spin, and many other things. By fifteen, she is indispensable to her mother. Mother and daughter develop an intimate relation, and the father and daughter become more distant. He may have a genuine affection for his daughter, especially if the latter conforms to the prevailing standard of a good girl, but the affection between them must be restrained. His knowledge of his daughter is gleaned indirectly through her mother. Generally, a daughter's marriage is arranged by her mother and only the mother can ask the girl's opinion in the matter. The father is consulted, of course. After the arrangement is made, the mother supervises everything the girl makes for her wedding and also persuades the father to be generous with the dowry. At the wedding both mother and daughter feel sad, which brings them even closer together than they were before. For two or three days before the ceremony, mother and daughter lie awake talking all night. The mother tells her daughter everything she knows about marriage, except the sexual details, and instructs her in the ways in which a bride should behave. Needless to say, the impending separation is difficult for both. When the girl has gone, her mother tries to learn whether or not she has been satisfactorily received by her husband and if she is kindly treated by the senior members of the household. If all goes well, the daughter appears happy when she pays her first visit home and the mother is happy too, but if the situation is not a good one, the daughter will cry at her mother's feet and the mother suffers unspeakably.

* * *

Relations between mother-in-law and daughter-in-law are sometimes strained, sometimes harmonious, but always less intimate than those of a daughter and her own mother. A daughter-in-law's obligations to her mother-in-law and to her husband are similar, but there are many points of friction inherent in the situation between the two women.

* * *

There are not a few mothers who are soft-hearted and far-sighted enough to see the importance of cooperation amongst the family members to the well-being of the large household. There are also not a few daughters who have been brought up in homes where broad-mindedness, obedience toward the senior generation, tolerance, filial piety, diligence, frugality, sincerity, and faithfulness have been the objectives in the training of the children. When such a mother and daughter come to live together, they will treat each other with consideration.

* * *

During boyhood, brothers are playmates and are on more or less equal terms. Fights between them are not frowned upon. Later, the elder brother is expected to be friendly to his younger brother, but there is some restraint in the situation. The younger one is expected to respect the elder. Before they marry, or when only the eldest has married, they continue to get along well with each other. They work together in the field or at home under their father's direction, and though there may be rivalry or even occasional clashes there is also cooperation, mutual help, and mutual confidence. . . .

In the early years of life, a girl is usually dominated by her brother in play or disagreements. This is due partly to the fact of male priority in a Chinese family. . . . When a boy is twelve or fifteen years old, he begins to feel that it is his duty to protect his sister, even if she is older than he. A Chinese girl over twelve years is not allowed to associate with any boy other than her own brother or her father's brothers' sons. Since her desire for male company grows stronger as she gets older, she eagerly accepts her brother's company and protection. Unmarried brother and sister have a free and intimate relationship. . . . A sister may act as a go-between for her brother and a girl he is interested in. He may confide to her his as yet unrevealed ambitions and he may ask her to speak for him to their mother.

* * *

Relations between the wives of brothers may be harmonious but are frequently marred by rivalry. The wives form a team under the direction of their mother-in-law. They help each other by looking after each other's children, by lending each other small articles— a needle, a roll of thread, a piece of cloth, or a little money. They can generally agree as to the order of work, so as to leave time for each to visit her parents. A family with such daughters-in-law will be cited as a model and be praised by all the villagers. Unfortunately, such cases are rather rare. In many large households the rivalry outweighs the harmony, for the wives compete for the favor of the mother-in-law. One may feel that the mother-in-law favors another, and quarrels arise. The antagonism will be accentuated if children carry tales against one another. The fathers are brought into it, first to complain, then to resent, and finally to fight each other.

* * *

The adjustments necessary between the members of a large family are delicate ones and it is only when they can be made with a minimum of friction that a large household can hold together. Jealousies and disagreements between certain members will throw the entire organization out of balance, and, if no immediate remedy is found for the situation, the household may break up. It is the most important duty of the head of a household to keep these relationships functioning smoothly. The task would be impossible, even for a family head of great tact and skill, were it not that so many traditions, rituals, and social sanctions operate as controls in the situation.

There are two basic relationships: that between parents and children (with the emphasis, of course, upon the sons), and that between a son and his wife. Theoretically, these two should be complementary. In practice, however, they are antagonistic to one another. It is true that when parents find a wife for their son they hope that the couple will be compatible and are pleased on the wedding day to receive such congratulations as "Harmony in one hundred years"; "A heavenly sanctioned union"; "Sincerity and love between husband and wife." However, the parents are displeased when the young couple are too devoted to each other, for this menaces the relationship between parents and son, especially that between mother and

son. . . . Marriage is not primarily for the happiness of the husband and wife alone, but also for the parents—to help in their work, to wait upon them, to satisfy their desire for grandchildren while they are living, and to continue their "incense and fire" when they die.

Whether a large family can be held together or not depends very much on the congeniality of the married brothers, which, in turn, depends largely upon their wives. If the wives are on good terms, the brothers are very likely to be on good terms too—most conflicts between them are caused by their wives. There are numerous folk tales and proverbs which warn against this sort of discord. However, it is hard for any man to ignore his wife's complaints. He may be able to do so at first, but not after five or six years of marriage.

7. THE FAMILY AS A PRIMARY ECONOMIC GROUP

Continuing the family line is the main concern of a Chinese farmer, but it is easier to produce progeny than to bring them up. When a man marries, his parents and the spirits of his ancestors are made happy at the thought of the new generation, but the man himself, if he is old enough, feels that a great burden has been put on his shoulders. He is no longer a "free" man but one who has to work for his wife's and his future children's livelihood. His parents also know that the hope of having progeny requires facing the important problems of how to feed, clothe, shelter, and educate the children, and that this problem can only be solved by working hard and living frugally. . . .

The old parents share the responsibility, and though they can no longer work as hard as they did, they save as much as they can of what they have. The parents of many families live more frugally than their children, for they are constantly anxious lest their children face poverty or starvation.

A young wife works harder than anybody else in the family and she lives more thriftily.

She does not speak of it, but to her nothing is more important than the security of the family. Her most important role is to see that her husband lives cheerfully and works well, and she advises him on the management of the farm. Further, she must see that her children are properly trained to do their share toward building up the family economy.

* * *

All three generations have a common interest in the family's economic security. It is a source of happiness to all: when it is imperiled, all feel the disaster. This is obvious to anyone who sees a family at a time when their important crops are threatened by drought or flood. Not only the older generation manifest great concern, but the young too share the anxiety. If, on the other hand, the harvest of the year is especially abundant and there is a good possibility of having some savings at the year's end, then everybody, old and young, is happy. When a piece of land is bought, even if it be a very small piece, it occasions happiness in the heart of every member of the family. In such a year the family's New Year Festival will be celebrated with great cheer and color.

A farm family is a unit unto itself in production. The family members produce collectively and they produce for the family as a whole, not for any individual member. This holds true for everything.

The work, in the field, on the threshing ground, in the vegetable garden, and at home, is divided among persons according to experience and physical ability. For example, the father is assigned to plant the sweet potato vines, since he is the experienced one. He knows which is the upper end and which the bottom end of the vines and can put them in the right positions. He knows how deep the vines should be planted and also the proper distance between every two plants. Others may also know these things but as yet cannot put them into practice as efficiently. The elder son is asked to carry water from a distant place because he is the strongest in the family. The younger brother and sister are put to pouring water into the small holes because this does not require much experience or strength. Finally, the work of covering the vines and of accumulating earth to support the young plants needs some experience but not much physical strength, and that is why the mother and the elder sister are assigned to these tasks.

We must bear in mind that this organization is not elaborately planned beforehand, but happens very naturally. When the family arrives at the field, the members simply begin their proper tasks; neither the father nor the mother has to give any orders. Needless to say there is flexibility in the arrangement. When there is enough water for a while, the elder son may pick up his father's work for practice. At another time the second son may ask permission to carry water for at least one trip in order to show that he, also, is strong. Or, the elder daughter may insist that she exchange positions with her younger sister on the pretext that the latter should learn a grown-up's work.

* * *

In an old-fashioned family, the kind which predominates in Taitou, everyone works or produces for the family as a whole, be he a farmer, a mason, a cloth weaver, a merchant or what not. It goes without saying that those who work on the family's farm work for the whole family. Any earnings made in special trades also belong to the family. If someone keeps a part of his wages, he will be condemned by the family head and suspected by all the other members of the family as being untrustworthy. A merchant who has to do his business outside may spend what he has made for his living expenses and according to his own judgment, but he must turn over all the rest and report what he has spent to the family head. If some of his expenses are found to have been unnecessary, he will be questioned about them in detail. Only when satisfactory reasons are given will his account be closed. If he is already middle-aged and has a prominent position, he may have more freedom in spending his money and the family head may not restrict him too much. But even so, he must know the limits of his freedom and must give the family the lion's share, or the others will complain and the unity of the family will be threatened. When a son goes to work on another family's farm as a hired laborer, his wages are given directly to his father or to his family. He may ask his father to give him a few dollars from his wages, or he may keep or spend the small money given to him by his employer for attending an opera or the local fair, but he is not working for himself but for the family of which he is a member.

*   *   *

The daughters are given a dowry at the time of their marriage, to which they add any money they may have earned and saved while in their parents' home. The young wife can either invest this sum in small home industries or lend it at interest to fellow villagers. When the sum is sufficient, she can buy land with it and this land will belong to the small family unit including herself, her husband and children, and not to the large family of her husband. Her husband's family may cultivate her land and get the harvest. Sometimes the wife may lend her money to the large family, in which case the family would pay it back with interest. . . .

Wives often think of how many *mow* of land and how many *gien* of house each unit will have when the family has separated. They are happy when a piece of land is added to the common property but their happiness is different from the joy of the primary family group. It is not only shallow but each of the wives secretly wishes that the land will become the property of her own group. She may think that the piece of land is largely the result of her own husband's effort and feel it is unfair to make it common property and have it divided equally among the brothers. She may persuade her husband to accumulate personal property by hiding a part of his earnings, if he has any, or by grabbing from the family's income.

*   *   *

The continuity of a family line depends not only on having generation follow generation, but also upon the uninterrupted transmission of the family's common property. Thus, inheritance becomes an important matter in a Chinese family. As we have noted, to the Chinese mind, a family is not merely a group of related people, but also the land, the houses, the livestock, and the family reputation. A prosperous family is one which is increasing in members and in property. In a declining family both are disappearing. This idea is indicated in the common saying "family property depleted and members perished." For this reason, when a dying father realizes that he has no property left, he feels guilty toward his ancestors and ashamed before his offspring, because he has only half accomplished the continuity of the family line. This is not only because property is the most dependable insurance for the next generation, but also because the family is an economic unit, so that family property is one of the primary interests which hold them together. As long as the property is intact the family exists. When the property is sold, the individual members may still remain, but the family is gone. . . . Parents who leave nothing to their children will either be blamed for a long time after or be forgotten immediately. Parents who added something to the property, or who restored the original fortune of a family, are inscribed on the family record. They are celebrated by their descendants, and are talked about with pride as long as the family exists.

In this part of the country inheritance is patrilineal, though daughters in some cases have a certain share. Sons have exclusive and definite claims on what the father has left.

*   *   *

The principle of division of land and houses is that an equal share goes to each son. If the division takes place while the parents are still alive, they may prefer to keep a larger share than is given to any of the sons. Whether or not they succeed depends upon their ability to exercise their authority, the opinion of the witnesses, the attitude of the sons, and the size of the total property. Daughters, if unmarried, have a certain amount of money put aside for their dowries. Unmarried sons also have an extra amount for future marriage expenses. Indebtedness is shared equally by the different parties. . . . An important feature is that the youngest son, although not expressly favored, in reality has certain advantages. The mother, or the parents usually choose to live with him, sometimes because he needs further tutelage and protection. In such instances, the parents invariably specify in the contract of division that after their death, their property must be given to the son who has served them. In this way, a further share of the inheritance is given the youngest son. But if the parent or parents live independently after the division of the property, their share will be redivided equally among the sons after their death.

*   *   *

In discussing inheritance we must not neglect the seeming contradiction between the desire of keeping a family's property intact and the desire for more progeny. Once a Western friend told the writer that since the Chinese inheritance system is to divide the family's property equally among the sons he could not understand why Chinese parents want so many sons. Though apparently a reasonable observation, this is not the way Chinese see it. When a son is born even to a poor family, he is not looked upon as someone who will further divide the family's land, but as one who will add to it. When a second son is born, the parents do not worry that their small piece of land will be divided into two parts. Instead, they begin to hope that when their sons are grown up, one will be a hired laborer, another a mason, and they will earn not only their own living but add fifty dollars or so to the family every year. In two or three years, they can buy one more *mow* of land with their savings. Thus, when the parents are old, they will be better off than they now are. This expectation increases with

each son born. A son, unlike a daughter, is always looked upon as an economic asset.

*   *   *

8. THE FAMILY AS A PRIMARY CEREMONIAL GROUP

In the families of Taitou, as in families of other places, there are numerous occasions in the year on which ceremonies are held for dead ancestors, for celebrating good harvests, for worshiping the divinity, or for driving off evil spirits. It is a rule that only family members, or persons of the same family line within a certain number of generations, are allowed to participate. A ceremonial celebration, in fact, is one of the clearest indications of the family's exclusiveness, its conception of itself as a separate entity.

Of the ceremonies observed, those for lamenting and ushering a deceased parent into the long rest and those celebrating the dead ancestors are the most important. The death of a parent, especially of an old one, is taken very seriously. . . .

When a parent dies, all projected affairs are automatically suspended and signs of happiness hidden away. No wedding or rejoicing feast can be conducted during the mourning period; and all things colored red, pink, or purple are put away or covered over with white, blue, or black material. Thus, the most obvious sign of heavy mourning is white; white paper pasted on doors and windows and the wearing of white garments and shoes by the mourners.

*   *   *

Immediately after the body is placed in the coffin, animal sacrifices are made. Offerings, mostly of food, are brought to the family. After the coffin is sealed, it is kept in the house for a period usually of from one to three months, though some wealthy families have been known to keep the coffin at home for nearly a year. This period varies according to the economic and social position of the family. The richer the family, the more elaborate the decoration of the coffin and the length of its retention. While the coffin remains in the house, vegetable dishes are frequently placed before it and incense sticks, candles, paper money, and images are ceremonially offered. Money and foodstuffs are presented to the family to help defray the expenses of the funeral, which otherwise might seriously deplete their resources.

* * *

The funeral of a large family always forms a considerable parade. Before the procession starts, the monk of the local Buddhist temple recites a prayer or reads a selection from a classic. When he finishes the chanting, the coffin is immediately moved out of the house. At this moment, all the near kin of the deceased wail loudly and sadly. The coffin is put on a heavy bier which is covered with a red cloth embroidered with dragons. Then the funeral procession begins. Heading it are neighborhood boys or men carrying banners, on which characters are written in praise of the good conduct of the dead. Next comes the brass band playing the mourning music. Then come the paper house, the paper trunks, the paper servants, and many other paper articles which are supposed to be used by the deceased in the other world. Following these is the coffin carrier, and after the carrier is the mourning group with the sons first, then the daughters, then the daughters-in-law, and finally the grandchildren. The procession proceeds very slowly and sacrifices may be offered by important friends on the way. Friends or distant relatives who come to lament may also participate in the funeral but they walk in front of the coffin. When the parade is out of the village, the women mourners leave it and return home, but the sons and grandsons follow the coffin to the grave. When the procession reaches the grave, another sacrifice is made before the coffin, which is then put into the grave while each of the mourners drops a handful or a spadeful of earth upon it. After this, they all take off their mourning garments and go home.

* * *

After the parents are dead and buried, the descendants try to remember them, to remember their good deeds and words, their glory, and achievements. They are reluctant to believe their parents are gone and rather pretend that they are still living and still with them. Parents' deeds and words still control their children's behavior. It is easy to remember one's parents the first few years after they have died, but it is hard to do so forever. For this reason, the ancient worthies devised and developed an enormous body of ceremonies and a number of feasts by which the forgotten parents remain fresh in their descendants' minds. These ceremonies and feasts are observed by all families as a matter of course. Whether or not a family really wants to remember its dead ancestors, the ceremonies are practiced and the feasts celebrated. This ceremonial practice is called by Westerners "ancestor worship." In a strict sense, this is a mistake, because the Chinese do not worship their ancestors in the way that gods are worshiped. The Chinese do have the vague idea that their dead parents are with them in an invisible form, but this is a result of consciously trying to keep the memory alive. It should not be interpreted in a religious way; it is a consecration, but in the sense of an unbroken continuity.

* * *

9. MARRIAGE

The Chinese believe that their lives are continued in the lives of their children and that, so long as generation succeeds generation, the predecessors are perpetuated. The maintenance of family continuity is one's greatest responsibility to one's ancestors, for failure to produce offspring means not only the end of the family line but the death of all the ancestors as well. Mencius has said: "There are three things that are unfilial, and to have no children is the greatest of these." The illiterate farmers may not be familiar with the literature, but they are fully aware of their duty in keeping the family tree alive.

The assumption of the responsibilities attendant upon having a wife and anticipating children is the mark of adulthood. An unmarried man of twenty-five is regarded as a boy, whereas a youth of twenty, who is married, is considered a man.

* * *

The sons of a wealthy family are married off as a matter of course. In a poor family, however, marriage of sons is an economic problem. Poor parents like to have a number of sons because grown sons are a great asset, but securing wives for them presents difficulties because marriage demands the means to support the additions to the family. But it is also a source of great shame to the parents, especially to the mother, to have a number of grown-up unmarried sons. This will be the subject of gossip and though the boys may not worry about it, their parents will feel greatly humiliated and the situation must be remedied before they can walk on the street with their heads erect.

Let us assume that the family works hard and begins to buy land. They accumulate some surplus and pay their debts. The mother will certainly not hesitate to inform her neighbors of the improvement and simultaneously lets her wish for a daughter-in-law be known. At first, the women of the neighborhood may ridicule her, but as the family's economic condition grows better and better, some of the matchmakers will change their attitude and start suggesting girls. Of course, the mother will not risk her chances by making the standard too high, and a match is soon arranged. Great news! Everybody in the neighborhood is surprised, and in no time the whole village is informed. Street corner conversations change.

"So, that woman will also have a daughter-in-law."

"Can you imagine, that poor family can also marry their sons."

"Why, it is a decent family. Both old and young work hard and honestly. I cannot see why their sons should not be married."

"Yes, Uncle Sheng is right, if a boy like that cannot marry, I don't see which one of us would deserve a wife."

"Poor family? Who said they were poor? Have not they bought land every year and had their houses repaired? It doesn't matter how much land you have, all that matters is whether a family is rising or declining. I would rather marry my daughter to a plain but growing family than to one which is going down."

After the marriage, the family's social status is raised and, when the daughter-in-law has been seen by all the neighbors, many congratulations are heard from the very women who had made fun of the mother's ambition.

"Well, well, I said you were a lady of great fortune. Just see what a wonderful daughter-in-law you have! Your son really deserves such a beautiful one. By the way, is your second son already engaged? If not, I should like by all means to tell my sister to give you her daughter. As I have said time and again, I don't see where we can find as decent a family as yours."

"Ah, ya-ya, isn't that the Second Aunt? I've just heard that you've married a wonderful daughter-in-law. I have always said that a family like yours should have had a daughter-in-law long ago. But just because your standard is so high that very few girls would suit your sons, so it has been delayed. But any way you got what you wanted. You must be very happy, indeed. Your fate is really a lady's. We are proud of being your neighbors. We should like to come and see your beautiful one. Please do drop in to see us when you are not too busy."

* * *

Marriages are arranged by the parents, more specifically by the mother.

* * *

Generally, the selection of a daughter-in-law is simpler than that of a son-in-law. The economic condition of the family is more important than the boy's personal qualities, provided he has no particular physical or mental defects, but in the girl's case her family is not subjected to the same scrutiny. The chief requisites for a daughter-in-law are physical health to insure progeny, efficiency in domestic work, a good reputation—which means that the girl is not known for love affairs or disobedience to parents—and, lastly, freedom from physical or mental defects. . . . Frequently the girl's family is of poorer social and economic status than the boy's. The prevailing opinion is that one should not select a daughter-in-law from a family that is much more prosperous than one's own, otherwise the bride may compare the new household unfavorably with the home she has left, complain about the deprivations, and feel superior to the other daughters-in-law.

In choosing a family for one's daughter the situation is reversed. The parents' first consideration is the economic condition of the family—how much land and how many houses the family owns. The girl's mother finds out how many sons the family has and calculates how much each one of the brothers will have when the property is finally divided. It makes a great difference when one compares a family that has twenty *mow* of land but only one son, with one that has thirty *mow* but three sons. If the economic condition is satisfactory, the mother will take the boy's personal qualifications into consideration, but will not make too much fuss about this. . . .

When the two families are satisfied, a formal letter is sent by the boy's family in which the engagement of the girl to the boy is requested. This is accompanied by presents to the girl's parents . . . The girl receives jewelry, dress material, money, and other articles useful to a bride, the amount and quality varying according to the economic condition of the boy's family.

*   *   *

About a half year to three or five years elapses before the wedding. Children of rich families are usually engaged when they are very young and the period may last three years or more, but if a family is poor and it is hard for a son to find a wife, so that he is not young when he is engaged, the wedding takes place immediately after the engagement, with only enough intervening time for the girl to make her wedding dresses.

The wedding outfit includes a number of jackets, shirts, trousers, gowns, underwear, shoes, and bedding. A girl should have at least twelve suits for winter weather and twelve suits for warm weather. All of them should be made of either silk or fine cloth. About ten or twelve pieces of bedding are prepared. All this takes time and the wedding of a well-to-do girl requires a very long period for preparation. In addition, things like trunks, suitcases, boxes, bureaus, cabinets, and toilet articles must be either bought or made. Of course the boy's family supplies some of these things, but the girl's parents must do their best if they do not want themselves and their daughter shamed. . . .

In this period of waiting, the members of the two families are not supposed to see each other often, and even avoid each other except for necessary meetings. In spite of this pattern they remain extremely attentive to each other's affairs. Because the engagement is not as final as marriage, it is not immutable. Although no decent family likes to see the engagement broken, nevertheless, such cases have happened and, if the two families are intimate with each other, a broken engagement will be the occasion of great embarrassment for all. The meeting of the engaged boy and girl before marriage is definitely improper. The boy is not allowed to visit the girl's family and it remains impossible for him to see his fiancee, unless she is seriously ill. Since all but a few of the engagements are between families of different villages or communities, any meeting of the two parties is difficult at best.

*   *   *

On the morning of the wedding day, the boy's family sends a decorated bridal chair borne by four able-bodied men to the girl's home. . . . When the chair arrives at the girl's home, the bride, who has been waiting for it, is immediately carried into the chair by one of her elder brothers or by an uncle, while the mother weeps and the father stands silent. The bride wears a formal wedding dress or bridal robe of red or deep pink and her face is covered with a piece of red satin. The bridal chair is closed with a curtain so that nobody can see her on the road. Two brothers, close cousins, or perhaps her uncle, accompany her. On the road, the bridal procession proceeds slowly so that the bride will not get seasick, and also so that the enormous and extravagant dowry can be seen and admired by the people in the villages on the way. Meanwhile, the groom, attired in formal wedding gown of blue and jacket of black, waits in the wedding room.

When the bride arrives at the bridegroom's front door, two elderly women come out to meet her, while the men take care of the dowry and welcome the guests who have accompanied the bride. The women's duty is to transport the small boxes in which the bride's toilet articles are contained from the bridal chair to the *hsi-fang* [the room in which the couple will live], and then to take the bride to the place where the wedding ceremony will be performed. This is usually the front court of the home, if the weather is good. In the center of the court is set a table on which are offerings to the gods of Heaven and Earth, a pair of red candles and three sticks of incense. The bride and groom stand side by side in front of the table and pay homage to the gods. Then, facing each other, the bride bows to the bridegroom and he returns the gesture. . . . In the house both the bride and groom make ritual homage to the ancestors, if the family is orthodox enough —otherwise, the ceremony performed in the court is assumed to have been shared by the ancestors. In the *hsi-fang,* the bride is seated on a wooden bed, while the groom takes his place on the brick bed. He is asked to take the red cloth off the bride's head. This is a very important moment to both bride and groom because they are to see each other face to face for the first time. The bride is fed with food which has been brought with her from her home and this is shared by the groom and his parents. After this, the bride is led

to pay her respects to her parents-in-law and the groom accompanies her. When they return to their own room both of them will sit on the brick bed and the formal dresses are taken off. The young members of the family and of the neighborhood can now come to see the bride and look at the dowry. The bride is expected to sit on the bed quietly without speaking. The bridegroom also sits there looking very much embarrassed.

The whole family is busy entertaining guests. The two people who have accompanied the bride are the most honored guests and are entertained by senior members of the clan or village leaders, or by the schoolteacher. The feast is the best that the family can afford.

* * *

On the evening of the wedding day, the room of the bride and groom is well illuminated with candles and lamps. The room is fully packed with young relatives and intimate friends, who have come to make fun of the bride and groom. Sometimes joking gets out of bounds, but usually it takes the form of jibes at the expense of the groom. . . . After they have all gone, though it may be midnight or still later, the bride and groom perform the last ceremony of the wedding before they retire. This is called toasting each other for the union. A small tray with a bottle of wine and two dishes of vegetables is brought to the room. The door is closed and the couple are alone. They are supposed to drink the wine and eat the food, but in most cases they are unable to do more than pretend to drink and eat after the day's mental and physical strain. Only after this ceremony are the two really united and the titles of husband and wife assumed.

The three things which sanction the marriage are the bridal chair which brings the bride, the parade from the bride's home to that of her husband, and the ritual homage to the gods of Heaven and Earth and to the ancestors of the husband's family. It is well known that in rural China marriage is not recognized through a formal contract signed by the two parties, although the *mei-chi,* marriage-requesting-letter, has been written by the boy's parents and consented to by the girl's. It is not registered in any kind of civil agency. The bridal chair has for long been socially recognized as the only proper vehicle for carrying the bride to her husband. If she is brought in anything else, she will not be regarded as a proper wife and will perhaps have a shameful position in the family and in the eyes of the relatives.

* * *

In other parts of the country, marriages between girls of fifteen and boys of seventeen years old have been reported, but in Taitou the average age is about twenty years. No bride under seventeen, or groom under nineteen, is known. The sons of poor families marry even later.

* * *

Marriage is absolutely monogamous, though until recently the possession of two women by one man simultaneously was not illegal. A few years ago, a man of a neighboring village became rich and after he came home to settle down he married a concubine on the ground that his first wife, who was then forty-five, had failed to bear a child. This was frowned upon generally, though it was permitted by the old civil law. . . .

Marriage in Taitou, as well as in most parts of China, is patrilocal and patrilineal. The woman is taken to the husband's family and his clan name is added to hers. Although four different clans are represented in Taitou, marriage between a boy and girl of the same village is discouraged, and no case of intravillage marriage is known to this writer. Some villages are all of one clan and, in such cases, village exogamy is necessary. Another possible reason for the absence of intravillage marriage may be that families related by marriage do not like to live near each other. The engaged couple would be likely to see each other and be tempted into a love affair. Families related by marriage should always be reserved with each other and if they lived in the same village, they would see or visit each other

very often. Families in the same village can also very easily become involved in the same village or neighborhood controversies. It would be extremely embarrassing for affinal relatives to find themselves on opposite sides in such a dispute. On the whole, intravillage relations are more intimate than is considered proper for affinal relatives.

* * *

In the last thirty or forty years, there has been only one case of divorce. The wife had become pregnant before her marriage. After she was married, she stayed only a few days at her husband's home. When she was paying her formal visit to her mother after marriage, she refused to return to her husband and took refuge with her lover. Neither her family nor her husband's could find her, so her husband could do nothing except to announce a divorce. . . .

This attitude has changed in the last ten or fifteen years, although the change has not as yet been felt in Taitou. Divorces in farm families have been reported in increasing numbers. Most of these recent divorces are results of discrepancy in education. Many young sons and young daughters of well-to-do families now go to the new schools. After graduation, they find jobs in the cities and do not return to farm villages. Away from home, modern boys meet modern girls. They fall in love and want to marry, even though many of them already have wives in their farm homes. In these cases divorce is the only solution. These young men are beyond the ties of the old communities and the family rules cannot reach them; the new government has legalized divorce and the families are financially able to support the wives at home, so that no great difficulty arises. In such cases the young men simply dictate a divorce to their ignorant and old-fashioned wives and then marry and establish new homes in the cities, relinquishing their right to inherit their share of land. . . . Even when the divorce is illegal, as it sometimes is, the family does not take action. The rural people still regard this kind of affair as their own business and would feel it a great shame or embarrassment if the case were brought to public view or dealt with in court. Second, the divorced wives are ignorant of any legal procedure and afraid of strangers. They are heartbroken, to be sure, but they also realize that there is no use in fighting— their husbands are already lost to them.

* * *

No social inequality between men and women is so apparent as the discrimination in the matter of remarriage. When a man's wife dies, he is perfectly free to marry again, and he can marry a virgin. The ceremonies, the congratulations, the parade, the happiness of his relatives, occur just as at his first marriage. The dead wife is forgotten altogether, unless she left a child. A widow, however, must not remarry. If she is the wife of a family of status, or if she has a child, especially if the child is a son, she is supposed to remain in widowhood for the rest of her life. Public opinion is that a decent woman should be the wife of only one man.

* * *

Sexual relations without formal marriage are morally forbidden. Adultery between persons of the same clan or family is severely condemned. The male suffers permanent loss of social and family position. The woman, if unmarried, will probably commit suicide, for she has lost her chance of being properly married. If a young man has an affair with a girl of a different clan, his punishment may be light—sometimes no more than the laughter of the villagers; but the girl will suffer. There are three or four families in the village whose social standing is so low that the villagers do not think of them in comparison with other families. Sexual immorality in these families is taken for granted and nobody cares unless in some way it shames the community as a whole.

* * *

10. CHILD TRAINING

When a child is about to be born, all the men, unmarried girls, and children are sent away, or, if the house has many rooms, they may merely be banished to some of the empty rooms and told to keep quiet. . . . The necessary articles for the confinement are made ready in the mother's room and the midwife is called. She is usually one of the old women of the neighborhood whose only qualification is the fact that she has delivered other babies; she may also be a witch doctor, and this is considered an added recommendation. . . .

After the child is delivered, its mouth is "opened" with a few drops of water, a ceremonial feeding which is called *kai kou*. . . . The child is wrapped in pieces of cloth and allowed to nurse at the mother's breast.

The third day after the birth is . . . ceremonially celebrated. The child is bathed and clothed in its first garment, a little jacket made of a single piece of red cloth. He is then presented to his grandparents. The family has a feast on this day, but not an elaborate one. . . . Food is also distributed to neighbors and clan members so that they may share the family's joy in the newborn child. Upper-class families take this occasion to thank their ancestors for the birth of the child and to pray for the safety of the new life. Congratulations and gifts from neighbors and clan members are received. Neighboring families usually offer glutinous millet, twenty or thirty eggs, and some brown sugar, since these foods are thought to be the most nourishing for the mother. The gifts come in a fine basket covered with a piece of red cloth and are presented by the mother of the donor's family. She sees the child when presenting her family's gift and praises it and the mother. All gifts must be recorded or at least the givers' names must be remembered, so that similar congratulatory offerings may be made on the birth of a child in the donor's family. These reciprocal presentations go on for many generations.

Also on the third day the baby is given its small name by the head of the family. If there are no grandparents, this duty falls upon the baby's parents. Generally a male child's small name directly or indirectly refers to the family's prosperity or continuity. This is because a boy is expected to be a breadwinner and one who will bring fortune to the family. These expectations create great joy when a boy is born and a high value is placed upon the child. Both the celebration of the birth and an appropriate name reflect the parents' wishes for his health, longevity, and expected talents. Names like *Hsi* (joy) and *Lo* (happiness) indicate the parents' feelings on the occasion. Words like *Pao* (precious), *Kwei* (highness), *Kin* (gold), *Ku* (jade) are often used as names. If the parents feel that the child is a token of the coming of good fortune to the family, they will name him *Fu* (fortune), *Jui-hsiang* (blessing), *Fa* (prosperity), or *P'ing-an* (peace). They may also choose from among words like *Ch'in* (diligent), *Hsiao* (filial piety), *Shun* (obedience), *Hsueh* (learning), *Ts'ung* (intelligent), *Ch'ang* (strong), *Hu* (tiger), to express their hopes for his being blessed with special gifts.

* * *

The birth of a child, especially a boy, is tremendously important to a mother. When the young wife finds that she is pregnant, her thoughts, her interests, her activities, in short her whole personality begins to change. She thinks more and more of the coming of the child and asks her sisters-in-law to tell her what kind of child it will be. She is most interested in ascertaining its sex. She fears the birth pains, but she also looks forward to the honor which will be given to her as the mother of a child.

* * *

After the birth of the child, the mother is in constant attendance and generally wants very little assistance. She feeds him at her breast (later he will have liquid and soft foods) day and night. She changes his wet clothes and washes him frequently. She is the only one who attends the child in case of sickness, and it is she who worries most if the illness is serious. The young father shows no interest in his child; on the contrary, he is angry if it disturbs him by crying at night. Occasionally a father hates the very existence

of his child. He will not touch it for any reason. He is embarrassed when a relative asks him about it, and to be seen actually holding the baby is a disgrace. He believes that he has helped in "making" the child, and that this in itself was shameful to him. He won't do anything to help because he believes that baby-tending is entirely a woman's job.

When the child is three or four years old, he stays close to his mother most of the time. . . . One always sees a young wife with her child playing beside her as she washes her clothes on the river bank, grinds grain on a street corner, or works in the vegetable garden or on the threshing ground.

* * *

At the age of six or seven, a boy will either be sent to the village school, if the family is well-to-do, or be taken to the farm. If he goes to school, his duties at home will be light— sweeping the courtyard or carrying food to the field. During the harvesting seasons, he learns by trying to work within sight of his father. . . .

Boys and girls under ten years may play together but from that time until they are fifteen, they may play together only in groups and remain in places where they can easily be seen by adults. Girls over fifteen are not allowed to talk privately with boys of their own age. Conversation between adolescent boys and girls in the same neighborhood or between cousins is permitted if others are present but bodily contact is strictly forbidden. They may joke with each other, but strictly without reference to sex. Grown-up boys and girls of different neighborhoods do not see each other often and consequently do not talk much. A grown-up girl should not do any favor directly or privately for any young man who is not a member of her family, except with the knowledge and assistance of an adult.

* * *

A father should not only keep his hands off a married son but also should refrain from scolding him. When a son is married, he is supposed to be an adult, and the former discipline no longer applies to him. If the son does not behave properly, then his father must talk over any matters that seem to require correction with his family members, including the son's wife, when they are sitting together after supper.

* * *

11. THE RISE AND FALL OF A FAMILY

A farm family's rise is largely accomplished by the buying of land, its fall occasioned by the emergencies that force the sale of land. It is interesting to note that no family in our village has been able to hold the same amount of land for as long as three or four generations. Usually a family works hard and lives frugally until they can begin to buy land. Members of the second generation continue in the same pattern so that more land is added to the family holdings and it becomes well-to-do. Those of the third generation merely enjoy themselves, spending much but earning little. No new land is bought and gradually it becomes necessary to begin to sell. In the fourth generation more land is sold until ultimately the family sinks into poverty. This cycle takes even less than a hundred years to run its course. The extravagant members die out, and their children begin again to accumulate property. Having suffered, and being fully acquainted with want, they realize the necessity of hard work and self-denial to repair the family fortune. By this time the original big family is gone and in its place there are several small, poor families. Some of these begin to buy land. Thus the same cycle is started again.

. . . Because the cycle of change is common to all, no family regards another as significantly different from itself, and each family takes pride in its own possessions. The emphasis is, therefore, not on quantitative comparison at any given time, and the inequality of income does not seriously threaten the sense of village solidarity.

Since the rise and fall of the various families is constantly in process, land transactions are also continually going on. Every winter sees the transference of some pieces of land from the jurisdiction of one family to another. The amount of money needed for buying one *mow* of crop land varies according to the quality and location of the land. Each year the price may be different. When a family needs a fairly large amount of money urgently, they usually get it together by mortgaging some of their land. The family which has the money and wants to lend it gives some to the needy family and receives the right of using the land for a certain length of time, with full rights to whatever it produces during that period. A written certificate is issued by the landowner to the money lender, for perhaps three years or longer, and the land cannot be redeemed before the stipulated time has expired. No mortgages are foreclosed. The time may be indefinitely extended, for the money lender can use the land until his money is repaid. The land tax is paid under the name of the owner but it is in fact paid by the person using the land. A family that has to secure money by mortgaging land will feel sad on the New Year and ashamed to walk on the street. The family which has authority to use the land will feel happy, their happiness second only to what it would have been had they actually bought a piece of land.

* * *

The direction in which a family is tending can also be seen in its position in the clan, and the general strength, or lack of it, of clan consciousness among its members. When a family has developed into a number of separate households, most of which live in proximity and maintain close relations with each other, it is called a clan. A clan is a group of families connected not only through kinship but also, and more importantly, by means of mutual obligations and privileges. Each family, as well as each individual in it, has duties to perform for the benefit of the others and at the same time has the right to benefit by their efforts. The bond that holds these families together is informal but powerful. Authority is vested not in a particular family or individual but in the group as a whole. The manipulation of this force is the basic function of the clan. When the clan's influence is far-reaching, it indicates that the clan as a whole is strong and has good morale. A clan is the extension of the family and therefore when a clan is prosperous, the families in it are strong; when it is decadent, its families are probably approaching poverty and disruption. A well-functioning clan is really an indication that most of the basic families of that group are developing, not declining.

A clan provides its members with a sense of social orientation and acts as a transitional grouping between the family and the village, uniting them in some ways and bringing them into conflict in others. In South China many fairly large villages are composed entirely of families belonging to one clan. There are villages composed of only one clan in North China also, but for the most part villages contain two, three or four clans.

*   *   *

In the past the clan had numerous functions. Until very recently there was in China no kind of public social security for the provision of the needy. The clan took care of its members and was supposed to provide for the destitute. Religious organizations or private philanthropy might serve this function in the cities and the market towns, but in the villages the clan was the most important agency. Indeed, one of its chief duties was to see that none of the members should starve or suffer.

*   *   *

Diverse functions of the clan include supporting a school, maintaining a hall for ancestor worship and for disciplining the unfilial or misbehaving members, keeping a clan book and teaching young members the clan's history including the good deeds of their ancestors, and collecting funds to support a brilliant but poor clan member in obtaining

advanced education. The P'an clan had a school in Taitou. The schoolhouse changed locations frequently, but the teacher was always a member of the P'an clan. It was established primarily for P'an children, but children of other clans were also allowed to attend. Because some members of the other clans felt that their children were not treated like the P'an children, the Ch'en and Yang families established a bi-clan school where children of the Lius and P'ans were also received. Recently the P'an clan school has been recognized by the county government as a public school and is now subsidized by public funds. The bi-clan school has changed into the present Christian school, under a council composed of members of the Yang and Ch'en families, its pupils are for the most part children of these two clans.

So far none of the clans of our village has built an ancestral hall. It seems that the villagers do not have much interest in the elaborate ceremonies of ancestor worship. . . . In other villages, however, one frequently sees the ancestral halls of a large clan. It serves rather as a symbol of a clan's unity than as a functioning institution. Clan consciousness is not active in everyday life, but it can be refreshed when the members see or enter the ancestral hall. On the New Year Festival and other similar occasions the members are summoned to the hall, where they go through some of the ceremonies, listen to the preaching and lectures of the leaders, and discuss clan affairs. This revives the feeling of unity among the kinsmen, and consequently the association of the clan's families becomes stronger than before.

*   *   *

In Taitou no clan has actually given financial support to any of their young members for education, though they have taken interest in similar cases. A member of the Yang clan, for example, had a very good reputation as a student when he was in the market-town school. He was praised by the teachers, the community leaders of the whole market-town area, and also by the senior members of the

P'an clan, so that great hope was aroused among all the people of the clan. . . .

. . . The interest is not based solely on an interest in the development of the young man but primarily on the prospective benefits that will accrue to the clan if he turns out to be a success. In the past, the Imperial Examinations were so important that a person who passed even the first one was qualified for some sort of Imperial Honor and was certain to secure a position, albeit a minor one, in the government. The honor and the benefits accruing therefrom were shared by the whole clan. After the establishment of the Republic, the old system was abolished. The number of students in the country has increased greatly and graduation from primary or high schools has become an ordinary event. Even graduation from a university no longer assures one of a government post. These changes have no doubt greatly disappointed the orthodox, both in the country and in the cities, who no longer see the point of expensive training and long years in school. They may continue to send their children to school because the latter insist upon going, but they certainly have lost interest in helping their poor relations go to college.

* * *

The new social trend helps to break the clan's control over individual members. In the last fifteen or twenty years most young people have learned to disobey their families and the seniors of their clans. They depend more and more on themselves and show less and less trust in the older generation. The political chaos and the general social disorder have helped to disrupt the old unquestioning reliance upon traditional ways of living. Moreover, under the new system the households of a village are organized into numerous small units. Families and individuals are directly under the authority of the leaders of these units, a fact which has contributed markedly to the decline of the influence of the clan.

12. VILLAGE ORGANIZATION

From a survey of the surrounding crop land one receives a strong impression of the unity of the village. The fields belonging to village families lie side by side in a circle around the cluster of houses. Although the area overlaps at many points, the boundary line is quite recognizable and there is never any doubt as to which village any piece of land belongs to.

Village solidarity can be seen in many things. Methods of cultivating crops, of threshing, storing, or preparing foodstuffs, of cooking or preparing feasts for the New Year celebration are exactly the same for every family within a single village. In a neighboring village, even though the activities are the same, there will be slight variations in technique. One often hears farm laborers who hire out to different villages tell each other that this village's food is superior (or inferior) to that village's.

Organizations in the village can be roughly divided into three categories: those which cover the whole village, those limited to a single neighborhood, and those based on family associations.

The first village-wide organization is the village defense program, in which every family is required to take part. . . . Wealthy families are expected to equip themselves with rifles, pistols, old-fashioned tube-guns, and the necessary ammunition; other families need to have only a rifle and ammunition. Families that cannot afford to buy rifles are asked to contribute other materials useful in defense. . . . The able-bodied men of all the families are registered and organized into a number of teams. The recruiting system is based on the family unit, each family supplying one grown-up son for duty each night.

Two defense lines were built around the village, the outer one consisting of removable mines—iron tubes filled with powder and scrap iron and connected by wire. The villagers knew where they were and how to pass through the line safely, but a stranger could not enter the village without being trapped by the wires which exploded the mines. The defenses were removed in the daytime for the safety of the villagers. The second line, built within the limits of the village, consisted of a number of fortifications, lane gates, and gun placements on the backyard walls. At night, the young men were assigned, first, to lay the explosive mines and wires for the outer line, and then to patrol the streets, lanes, and strategic points. . . . The village had not been attacked since the organization of the defense. It was rumored that bandits feared to come near it. . . .

The village school, though it had been built by the P'an clan and was mainly supported by them, was attended by boys from the entire village. Until the establishment of the Christian school, this was the only general educational establishment in the village. Girls were not sent to school but trained in the domestic arts at home by their mothers. . . . The school council was made up of the heads of families and this cooperation in managing and supporting the school brought families together. . . .

The villagers regard education as a means by which a family can raise its position. Children are taught to read names, to understand the content of land deeds, and to recognize the different kinds of paper money orders so that they will not be cheated in business transactions. The sons not needed for farm work are trained for a career, for business or a trade. Calligraphy, account keeping, the use of the abacus, and the learning of the terms for farm products, farm implements, domestic utensils and manufactured commodities also held an important place in the curriculum, and there were some who regarded the school as the place where one learned good manners and absorbed the teachings of the ancient worthies.

In the past, most boys were not in the least interested in their schoolwork. The school itself was a one-room affair with a dirt floor. . . . The tables, benches, and stools were brought by the pupils from their homes. Boys ranging in age from six to twenty years were herded together in one room. The teachers' quarters were partitioned off from the schoolroom and here the teacher sat all day, except when he had calls to make, went to the market town, or was invited out to entertain a guest or to write documents for a village family. At school, his chief function was to maintain order.

* * *

Thirty years ago, the first modern school was established in Hsinanchen by the county government. . . . The school in Taitou was also modernized to a certain extent. In these new schools life was interesting to the pupils and, as a result, the attitude toward going to school changed. The textbooks were fascinating; they were written in the contemporary idioms familiar to the pupils and were beautifully illustrated. Above all, they contained interesting stories about children's daily life, which were entirely comprehensible and opened new vistas to the young minds. The arithmetic was new and interesting. Learning the symbols of numbers and new methods of counting was most fascinating. The chalk, the blackboard, the clay stick and the clay plate were all delightful things which had never been seen before. In the old school, singing had been absolutely forbidden, but now the young teachers cheerfully taught the boys to sing as part of the curriculum. They sang the songs of the coming and going of the swallows, the joy of study, of patriots, and of the flowers and the stars. The boys also learned the symbols of music. Few had any musical talent, but they liked to sing and imitated the teacher with great gusto. Physical education was a regular part of the school day. This was most exciting. In the old days they were punished for making noise or for having fun, now they were taught and led by the teachers in exercises and games. They also had some military instruction. . . .

Another village-wide organization is the collective protection of crops. A crop-watcher is hired by the village every year. His duty is to see that the crops are not damaged by animals nor stolen by thieves. He receives a yearly wage and while he is on duty is supplied with meals by families who have more land than the average. . . .

Punishment of theft is a common concern

of the village. Petty theft is dealt with summarily. Sometimes a boy or girl of a poor family may steal some heads of the millet crop, or some string beans, or other crops. If the culprit is caught on the spot by the owner of the field, he may be scolded and forced to give up what he has stolen, or he may get a beating. . . . An adult thief is merely shamed and derided if the theft is a minor one.

* * *

Burglary, however, is regarded as a crime. When a home is robbed at night, the owner may use weapons to defend his property, and if the burglar is killed no action will be taken against the man who kills him. If the thief is caught he will either be punished according to village custom or sent to the county government. A man who steals a considerable quantity of the crops, or who breaks open the doors of homes to steal grain, animals, or other useful things at night, is considered a criminal; he is fined or punished by the local leaders according to the local regulations, and though he loses his social position, he may continue to live in the village and eventually redeem his reputation. Those who break into houses to steal money, threatening the family with weapons, are unforgivable criminals and must be taken before the government authorities if they are caught. . . .

Social control is a village-wide affair; its chief instrument is public opinion. For the kind of behavior that is approved by most of the villagers, a person is everywhere honored and praised. Disapproval, therefore, is a powerful check. For instance, though the villagers do not interfere with or harm a promiscuous woman, they sever their relations with her family and ignore the greetings of any of its members. Social isolation is a terrible punishment. Only the three or four families whose social position is so low that they are in a sense immune from public opinion are indifferent to disapproval and fear only physical punishment.

* * *

Close neighborhood associations in many cases supersede the village feeling or the clan consciousness. A family of the P'an clan, for example, may have closer relations with some Yang families than with their own clansmen, simply because the Yangs live in the same neighborhood. Frequent contact in daily life brings families together, and consequently the whole village is divided into a number of neighborhoods, or *hu-tung,* which have no reference to the clan. There are nine neighborhoods within the village limits. . . .

People living near by recognize certain social obligations to each other. When there is a marriage, the bridegroom's family distributes steamed rolls made of wheat flour among the neighbors to announce the wedding and extends an invitation to the party. In return, the neighbors offer presents, mostly of food needed for the occasion. . . . In case of a funeral, the neighbors help to build the tomb. They may carry the coffin, or take care of the domestic work while the relatives of the deceased are mourning. This aid is offered voluntarily. . . .

. . . In time of emergency, such as fire, theft, or sudden illness, neighbors are far more helpful than relatives or friends who live at a distance. A common saying runs: "Distant relatives are not as dependable as near-by neighbors."

. . . When a person needs money to pay debts incurred by gambling, opium-smoking, or drinking, he can borrow the sum from his neighbors, but the rate of interest will be exceedingly high and a contract is drawn up. Two men of good credit are required as guarantors and a certain amount of land or a house is demanded as security. These loans extend for short periods and if the payment is postponed twice, the creditor is permitted to cultivate the land of the debtor. This indicates how difficult it is for a person or a family without a good reputation to borrow any money. . . .

Women of neighboring families gather before their front doors to talk and gossip. Especially in the summertime, when the men are eating at home, the women come out to have a breath of fresh air under the trees. A spontaneous and informal group is formed and the talk ranges from discussion of the daily work to gossip about the marriage of a family at the other end of the village. This continues until the men come out and it is the women's turn to eat. After dinner when the weather is hot and the people don't feel like working, the men and boys go to sleep or play on the main street, on the river bank, or in the groves. The old women go to their bedrooms to take a nap. But the young women and little girls come out again to sit under the trees or in their doorways, bringing with them some piece of work. All of them are members of the same *hu-tung*. They sit about for one or two hours, then return to their homes and resume their important work—sewing, mending, ironing, embroidering, and the like. The men and boys go to the fields.

*   *   *

Because of the need for children's labor in the field and at home and also because there is no surplus money for frivolity, recreation for children is not encouraged and almost no toys are provided for them. Children of the same neighborhood, however, play group games which require little equipment. One of these is *Ta-wa,* a game played with two teams, which requires only some small stones.

*   *   *

Ts'ang-more, a girl's game, is somewhat like blindman's buff.

*   *   *

Another game played by boys is *Ti-Chien-tze*. A group of older boys or young men play with a shuttlecock made by tying some poultry feathers on a coin. This *Chien-tze* is thrown up in the air, and the players try to keep it from touching the ground, kicking or butting it but not touching it with their hands. The game is popular in winter since it is very active and helps the boys to keep warm.

*   *   *

It is easy to draw a checkerboard on the ground and to use stones as checkers. For this reason, checkers is a very popular game in the summer. Younger girls and boys play quietly under the trees on the riverbank with a number of others sitting beside as on-lookers. Sometimes the players get into a serious argument and the spectators take sides with them. While the cows are grazing, the boys sit down and play the game, sometimes letting their animals wander far away over the fields. In the winter a group of young people may gather to learn Chinese boxing or to sing songs in the houses where social gatherings usually take place. During the New Year Festival some active young people may also organize country dramas.

13. VILLAGE CONFLICTS

In addition to the clan and neighborhood organizations, there are other kinds of intravillage groupings. Families of similar social and economic status, families which support a certain school, and the families which have become Christianized all tend to divide off into special groups.

Families of the same neighborhood may not be as close as families of different neighborhoods, because of status differences. Two or three Liu families, for example, live in the neighborhood where most of the Yang families live. The Lius are very poor and do not have much to do with the Yangs because they feel inferior to them, and the Yangs do not make overtures to them, either. But another Liu family, which has recently become prosperous, has gradually become intimate with the Yangs. Their children were asked to attend the Christian school. The mother of another Liu family had tried desperately to achieve these social relations without success. To this end, she sent one of her two sons to the Christian school, but failed in her purpose because her husband and sons had a bad reputation in the village.

. . . Formerly, the ten or twelve wealthy families of the village had more intimate relations with each other than they had with their neighbors. There was also a group of middle-class families. Their association was not strong but recognizable. The poor families also constituted an informal group. In the past decades, distinctions based upon wealth have broken up because of the decline of the rich families and the general disruption caused by the war. In general, this kind of stratification is rather superficial, for, as we have seen, the status of a family may change in a few generations. The shifting certainly counteracts the building up of permanent social classes. Another point to be mentioned is that a family with wealth but no culture is usually the most isolated; the rich cultured farmers look down upon it, and yet it does not want to associate with the poor people. Thus, wealth alone does not give a family high position in the community.

*   *   *

The introduction of Christianity brought about new groupings of families. Ten or twelve families belong to the Protestant church, and five or six families belong to the Catholic church. The Protestant families include the Yangs and Ch'ens and, formerly, also one of the P'an families. The Catholic group is composed of four or five P'an families and two of the Ch'ens. Because Christianity is a new religion and is contradictory in some ways to the traditions and customs of the local society, the two groups of families which identified themselves with this belief are sharply differentiated from other families. This differentiation caused a kind of "we-group" consciousness in each of the two groups. The dozen Yang and Ch'en families have maintained closer relations than would have been likely under other circumstances. The several P'an families which belong to the Catholic church are poor and of very low social status, and are considered by their kinsmen as a group of outcasts. As a result, they have developed a feeling of unity among themselves. Both the Protestant and the Catholic groups regard themselves as "chosen people," thinking that they belong to Heaven while the rest of the villagers are sinners, or people of this world. The preachers of the churches have taught their members to dis-

tinguish themselves from the other people. Needless to say, this has tremendously widened the gap between the Christian groups and the rest of the families in the village. But the distinction does not stop here. Protestant-Catholic antagonism has split the two Christian groups. All the non-Christian families practice ancestor worship. They have the Kitchen God in their kitchens, burn incense sticks and kow-tow in the shrine of the God of Earth on the New Year Festival, and patronize the Buddhist temple in the district. For these reasons, we may consider them as another religious group, though they are by no means organized.

*   *   *

The Christian groups and the other villagers came into difficulty over the question of sharing expenses for practicing opera in the village. The opera was a most important amusement and it was an annual occasion. All the families contributed to it according to their means, except the Christian groups who refused to pay their share. They held that the opera was a kind of thanksgiving to the Dragon God and therefore contradictory to Christianity, and Christians could not give money to it; but that did not prevent the Christian families and their relatives from attending the performance and enjoying the entertainment as much as anyone else. This greatly annoyed the other villagers and the Christian groups were regarded as no longer properly belonging to the village. The villagers' resentment grew when they were told that the Christians were protected by foreign power.

This was not the only friction that occurred between the Christian groups and the other villagers. The Christians were taught that they were God's chosen people, that they no longer belonged to this world but to God's world, and that they must organize themselves into one body against all who were not Christians, and who, therefore, were "sinners." The poor Christians, who felt that they had been oppressed or ill-treated by the wealthy people, wanted to avenge themselves and to express their feeling of injustice. The ambitious members assumed that they were as good as, or even superior to, those who held leadership in the village, the village gentry. They considered it an injustice that they did not have the opportunities to demonstrate their leadership. Besides, the Christians had the attitude that the non-Christians were pitiful because they resisted the "true God" and were, therefore, committing the sin of worshiping false gods. On their side, the non-Christian villagers regarded both the Protestant and the Catholic groups as mean people—people who refused to pay homage to their ancestors, who betrayed their countrymen but made friends with foreigners. Since both sides had prejudices like these, conflicts could hardly be avoided. It was only after people had had time to become more familiar with the religion, and the excitement at the strange things had abated, that the hostile attitude of the non-Christians was lessened. The reconciliation was also attributed to the enlightenment of many of the Christians. In recent years, many well-trained leaders grew up among the Chinese Christians who understand Christianity much better than their predecessors, the first converts, did. These men take a liberal attitude and cooperate in many collective activities with other groups, and refrain from condemning other beliefs.

A conflict between school factions also made village history. Years ago, an ambitious and self-made scholar of a Ch'en family wanted to become a schoolteacher. He fostered the idea among the families of the Yang, Ch'en, and Liu clans that their children were not treated as well as the P'ans by the teacher in the P'an clan's school. Since all three clans felt subordinate to the P'an clan, indignation was not difficult to arouse. In addition, a number of families of the Ch'en and Yang clans had accepted Christianity, and this new religious belief had brought the families into close relationship. The scholar vigorously advocated the establishment of a new school for their own children so that they could be independent of the P'an school. He finally succeeded, and a second school was opened in the house of a Yang family. All the pupils were boys of the Ch'en and Yang clans. The teacher of the "orthodox" school and important members of the P'an clan resented this new move. Rumors were spread by them about the Ch'en teacher, attacking his scholarship, and also warning the minor clans that they could expect retaliation in one form or another. The Yangs and Ch'ens called a meeting at which they resolved to uphold their rights and support their teacher in every way. The antagonism between this group and the P'an clan lasted for several years.

* * *

Clan feuds were a not uncommon source of village conflict. Such a feud existed between some families of the P'an and the Ch'en clans. In the course of it, a Ch'en family was attacked one night by gangsters whose faces were either painted or covered by masks. The family and their relatives all suspected some of the P'ans, but since they could not produce any evidence for their suspicions, the P'ans pronounced the accusation a great insult. Although the case did not develop into a serious clan fight, the bad feeling between the two clans was heightened.

* * *

Through many generations the Chinese village gentry have learned an interesting way to end certain kinds of village conflicts. This is to do nothing about it. When two lower-class families get into a dispute, the mothers scold each other on the street, their husbands may have a fist fight, and then it all suddenly stops. The next day their children play together as usual, the adults may not speak to each other for ten days or more, but they conduct their own business as usual and gradually forget the matter. Disturbances of this kind are usually ignored by the village leaders. . . .

. . . Pacification has been for long the measure usually employed to end important village disputes. Usually this is done through the good offices of the village leaders, but when the gentry or the chief clans are involved, the ordinary village leaders do not have sufficient prestige to intervene. In these cases, leaders from other villages are called in. These may be no more capable than the local leaders, but because they are from a different village their presence means more to the conflicting parties, and, therefore, they have a greater "face." Many disputes are thus settled by outside intervention.

The general procedure is as follows: First, the invited or self-appointed village leaders come to the involved parties to find out the real issues at stake, and also to collect opinions from other villagers concerning the background of the matter. Then they evaluate the case according to their past experience and propose a solution. In bringing the two parties to accept the proposal, the peacemakers have to go back and forth until the opponents are willing to meet halfway. Then a formal party is held either in the village or in the market town, to which are invited the mediators, the village leaders, clan heads, and the heads of the two disputing families. The main feature of such a party is a feast. While it is in progress, the talk may concern anything except the conflict. The expenses of the feast will either be equally shared by the disputing parties or borne entirely by one of them. If the controversy is settled in a form of "negotiated peace," that is, if both parties admit their mistakes, the expenses will be equally shared. If the settlement reached shows that only one party was at fault, the expenses are paid by the guilty family. . . .

Generally, when the two conflicting parties both belong to the middle or upper class, no compensation is paid when the settlement is made. Receiving money or other material compensation from a losing opponent causes great shame. The victory lies in the general opinion of the public that one is right and the opponent is wrong. When this is won, any damages suffered can be overlooked. The important thing is that your opponent has to admit that he has been wrong, and this is very hard for a man of equal status to do. A feast provides the ideal situation for such an enforced acknowledgment. Overtly the feast is given to the mediators, actually it is an admission of defeat. The person who pays for it apologizes by this means.

Very few—perhaps none—of the disputes in this village have been solved by a lawsuit. . . . Villagers forced into a legal case must go to the county seat and hire lawyers, and the ensuing costs are prohibitive for any of the farm families. Nine out of ten families who have sought recourse to the law have had to sacrifice a great part of their small property. Countless stories and proverbs have discouraged farmers from referring their cases to the government. Private mediation has been and is now the most important legal mechanism in rural districts throughout the country. Social justice has been in the past much more important than legal power in protecting the weak against violence of any sort. It is a fact that no matter how small or weak a family may be, if its members behave fairly to the other villagers, both the strong and the lawless will either help it or leave it alone. If it is unreasonably attacked, the attacker would sooner or later be discovered and the whole village would punish him. . . .

Since a number of village conflicts are caused by hurting somebody's "face," it is necessary to discuss the losing or gaining of "face." "Face" is a literal translation of the Chinese character *lien* or *mien*. Although *lien* or *mien* means just what the English word face does, the Chinese expression *tiou lien* (losing face) or *yao mien-tze* (wishing a face) has nothing to do with face in our usual understanding of the term. It does not mean a certain expression on, or the physical appearance of, the face, such as implied by "a funny face" or "a sad face." When we say in Chinese that one loses face, we mean that he loses prestige, he has been insulted or has been made to feel embarrassment before a group. When we say that a man wants a face, we mean that he wants to be given honor, prestige, praise, flattery, or concession, whether or not these are merited. Face is really a personal psychological satisfaction, a social esteem accorded by others.

Perhaps this can be better understood by

analyzing the factors involved in losing or gaining face. The first factor is the status of social or other equality between the persons involved. For instance, if a village dignitary asks another to make a social call with him or to grant some other favor and is refused, he will feel that he has lost face. If, on the other hand, a peasant is similarly refused by one of his own rank, he will not have this feeling. . . .

The second factor is the inequality between the social status of the two persons. When a boxer is defeated by an opponent as strong as he is, he will feel sorry but will not lose face. But if the victor is known to be inferior to him, then he will consider his defeat a great loss of face. . . . However, this principle cannot be extended indefinitely. It would not be true to say that the lower the opponent's status, the greater the loss of face. If the insulting person is only a plain peasant or one who has been considered ignorant or mean, a cultured man does not lose face at all, because people will say that the trouble is caused by the peasant's ignorance and is not the other's fault, and if the latter remains impervious to the taunt, he will win great praise from the villagers for being too great to quarrel with a mean person, or so kind that he can forgive another's ignorance. . . .

A third factor is the presence of a witness. In fact, the question of losing or not losing face is based on anticipation of the effect upon a third person or party. If the indignity has not been witnessed or is certain to remain unknown to anyone else, then bitterness may be roused but not the sense of losing face. . . . But the effectiveness of the presence or knowledge of a third party varies with the degree of intimacy between the third party and the persons involved.

Thus, social relationship is a fourth factor. If the third person is intimate with one or both of the opposing parties, the defeated or insulted party does not feel that he has lost face, or at least the feeling will be negligible. But if the third person is not an intimate, the situation is quite different. In the family, for instance, there is no problem of losing or gaining face in relations between husband and wife, parents and children, or between siblings, but there is such a problem between the in-laws. The problem becomes more serious when the social distance extends outside the family to the neighborhood, to the village, and even beyond. Beyond a certain distance, however, this factor becomes ineffective. When a man lives in a completely strange society there is no problem of face, no matter what kind of mistakes he may make, because nobody knows him. . . .

A fifth factor is social value or social sanction. One may commit different and numerous mistakes, but not all of them entail loss of face. In a society where agriculture is the main occupation, one loses face if his farm is not cared for. People pay much attention to filial piety and ancestor reverence, and a family loses face if its members do not hold together as long as their parents are alive or do not conduct a proper funeral for them when they die. . . .

The consciousness of one's own social prestige is a sixth factor. The more conscious one is of his status, the stronger is his fear of losing face. For instance, a liberal or free-minded village gentry would not be particularly disturbed if a junior villager should unwittingly offend him. But if he were highly conventional or orthodox, he would be outraged and if the offender did not apologize immediately it would become a serious case. . . .

Thus, age becomes a seventh factor in the problem of face. Young people have not as yet acquired much social prestige and therefore do not have much face to lose. On the other hand, old people frequently do not feel loss of face. They can easily be excused (and they always excuse themselves) on the ground that they are old, and besides, experience has made them too mature to be easily embarrassed. Only the middle-aged people, who are very careful to safeguard their social prestige, are serious about losing or gaining face. Lastly, a person's sensibility is also a factor. A situation that makes one person lose face leaves another unhurt. It is very easy to hurt a sensitive person's feelings and if the slight occurs in the presence of a third person he is certain to feel that he has lost face.

*   *   *

14. VILLAGE LEADERS

. . . After the establishment of the Republic, the *Chu-Hsiang-Lu-Lin* system was installed. The rural district was organized into units, and each unit had its own leaders and councils. The *Chu-chang* was the highest official leader of the rural district; the *hsiang-chang* was [the village head] . . . and the other two officers, the *lu-chang* and the *lin-chang,* were subordinates of the *hsiang-chang* and generally acted as his assistants. All the officers were elected locally and were supposed to act on behalf of the villagers.

In spite of these changes, the official leaders in Taitou are still essentially of the old category and function in the old manner. A middle-aged man of the P'an clan now serves as the official head of the village. Older people still call him *chwang-chang,* while the young villagers who like to pick up new terms address him as *hsiang-chang.* He takes charge of all public affairs and acts on behalf of the villagers in dealing with the government or with other villages. This man has been in office about ten years. Before him, the *chwang-chang* was his father, and before that, it was a man of the Ch'en clan.

*   *   *

At the beginning of every year a meeting is held to elect a *hsiang-chang,* his chief assistant, and other subordinate officers. Those who attend are the senior members of the families. Every family may be represented by at least one member, though a number of families do not send anyone. . . .

The election is conducted very informally. There is no ballot casting, no hand raising, and no campaign for candidates. The meeting is held in the village school or in some other customary meeting place. When several members of each clan have arrived, the person who presides over the meeting will stand up and say, "Uncles and brothers, now we are all here to discuss the public affairs of our village. As you all know, our *Chwang-chang,* Uncle P'an Chi, has served us very well in the past year. He has worked hard and honestly to pacify disputes, to defend our village, to help families which have been involved in unfortunate controversies, to represent our interests in dealing with the government, and so on. As you also know, to be a public servant in these days is really a headache. Road building, military training for civilians, land surveys, school establishment, village defense, and what not, are all troublesome duties. . . . Uncle P'an Chi has recently said that he feels his age, that he is too tired to bear the heavy burden any longer, and would like to be relieved. I want to know whether we should let Uncle P'an Chi retire and elect another person to be our *Chwang-chang,* or should we ask him to continue. Since this is a matter of importance to our whole village, you are requested to express your ideas and let us know what your opinions are."

This opening address is followed by a moment of silence. Then one of the electors, usually a partially recognized village leader, will say, "Since, as Uncle Heng Li has just said, Uncle P'an Chi has served us well in the past, I cannot see why we should let him retire. I myself, and, I believe, many other fellow villagers, really appreciate Uncle P'an Chi's service, and I do not see any other person among us that is better for the office than he."

"Brother Heng Chun is right," says another representative, who is spinning his home-raised silk on a small spindle and has his long, thin tobacco pipe in his mouth. "We must ask Uncle P'an Chi to continue as our *Chwang-chang.* He has the ability and the experience. Who else can deal with those tricky government servants as he can? I know I couldn't."

. . . When several others have been asked and given an assenting answer, the election is decided, and the village's *chwang-chang* is again in office.

Other officers, such as the *lin-chang, lu-chang* or *chia-chang,* are elected at the same meeting, but in a still less dignified manner. Every villager knows that no upper-class person wants to be elected to any of these offices and knows also that in each neighborhood there are two or three persons who would not refuse to serve. They simply tell one of these persons in each *hu-tung* that he is elected as the *lu-chang* of the neighborhood. The *chwang-chang* chooses one or two assistants, generally the persons who have already been his aides in the past.

The election is a relatively simple matter since there is no competition for office. On the whole, it may be said that the majority of villagers do not wish to serve in any official capacity and are glad to find among their number an individual who is eager to do so. This is sometimes enough to assure the election, for there are very few such aspiring persons.

The late P'an Chi was considered a successful *chwang-chang* in Taitou, and he may be taken as the type of person who generally became an official leader. He was a man of leisure. He had no farm business to occupy his time, nor was he a craftsman who had to work day and night when business was good. He was the head of a family of three grown sons who were capable of working the family's small holdings of land, so his help in the fields was not needed. He was a man who did not balk at petty deception when the situation warranted it, and he often admitted openly that, for the benefit of the village and for his personal profit, he had to play tricks every so often. He said that not all villagers were honest people and that not all honest villagers would see that some of the means by which the *chwang-chang* received compensation for his services were reasonable. In order to cope with those who were not honest and with those who were honest but unreasonable, subterfuge was necessary.

*   *   *

Once such a person is elected, the probability is that he will remain in office for a long time. Some villagers may not be satisfied

with him, but as long as he does not make serious mistakes they will not bother to elect someone else. If he himself really wants to retire, he informs the important villagers of his intention, so that the chairman of the election will make a different kind of opening address and the villagers will not reelect him. If he has done something inexcusable, then either he himself would not have face to hold office any longer or the influential laymen leaders would suggest his dismissal. In this case, the chairman of the meeting would also hint that a new *chwang-chang* should be elected and the villagers would follow the cue. The result of the election is therefore to some extent prearranged and the meeting is a routine matter. The real authority lies in the hands of the laymen leaders. Most villagers understand this and do not attribute too much importance to the office of *chwang-chang*.

The most important duty of the official leaders is dealing with the local or county government on behalf of the villagers. When a government order arrives, the local authority summons the *chwang-chang* of all villages in the district to the market town, where they are informed of their duty. The local *chwang-chang* returns to his village, sees the important laymen first, and discusses with them the way in which the order will be carried out. Then a tentative plan is drawn up. After this has been done, the *chwang-chang* calls a meeting of his assistants and all the other village officers, including representatives of some families of each clan, at which the government order and the tentative plan are presented. After some discussion, the final details for recruiting labor, sharing expenses, and planning the schedule of work are roughly formulated. Then the assistants and other subordinate officers inform all the families of what they are to do. In case some of the villagers complain about the plan or attempt to evade their responsibilities, the *chwang-chang* or his chief assistant will rebuke them on the main street or at a public gathering—provided they are not persons of importance.

*   *   *

Finally we see that the *chwang-chang* is often the chairman of the few significant village meetings that take place, such as discussions on how to participate in the government's rural reconstruction programs, or the organization of village defense, and so on. We also see that the *chwang-chang* is often asked to be present at the time of the separation of a family. His presence is not actually required in such an instance, but if the brothers have no important relatives or clan head he is the most suitable person to act as a witness to the proceedings.

* * *

The *chwang-chang* and his chief assistant receive compensation for their services in money or in entertainment and gifts. Formerly, the *chwang-chang* and other officers were not paid. Expenses were paid out of the public funds and the officers made a commission which took the place of a regular salary. If the actual expenses were ten dollars, for example, they would collect twelve and keep the difference for themselves. No villager ever bothered to make a fuss about this as long as the amounts were small.

* * *

In each village there are a number of persons who are in a sense leaders though they hold no official position. Their influence in public affairs or in the community life may be much greater than that of the official leaders, but it may not be evident. They are known essentially as respected laymen. The most notable of these are the village elders, those who have performed special services for the village as a whole, and the schoolteachers. . . .

In a Chinese village a *tsu-chang,* or head of a clan, has some influence over a designated group of families, but his influence is only recognized by the clan and operates within its limits. He is usually an older member but sometimes may be the person who is the wealthiest family head in that particular community, for his wealth allows him to do things others cannot afford. A neighborhood leader is someone who can influence the five or ten families in his *hu-tung,* or small lane, by virtue of his personality or intelligence or general reliability.

* * *

There were several other types among the village gentry. One was the gentleman, distinguished by his handsome figure, neat dress, high spirits, good manners, humorous conversation and endless leisure. He was in sharp contrast to the other type of leisured villager who was aggressive, dominating, and inordinately fond of public hearings. Years ago these two types were well exemplified by the heads of two wealthy P'an families. One of them was admired and liked by all the villagers; the other was admired but was not liked because he often showed himself to be stingy in his dealings with hired laborers. These men were not ambitious to be leaders, but they exerted their leadership nonetheless, for it was forced upon them by the position they held in the eyes of the villagers. They were necessarily public figures. This was especially true of the more popular of the two. Because of his mild, impartial, and unassuming manner, he was sought after to mediate disputes that arose between families. He was known in the entire market-town area for his skill in arbitration.

Another man, also the head of a large and wealthy P'an family, was of enormous build, active, voluble, and given to fierce gesturing. He was not a learned man, but had bought a military degree from the Manchu government. He was very ambitious but had failed to win a position in the government and this was a constant source of chagrin to him. He dominated all village affairs and insisted in having a voice in all administrative problems of the entire market-town area. On the whole, the village leaders and some of the local gentry made concessions to him and did not resist his attempts at leadership.

* * *

The laymen leaders remain in the background, but their role is so important that without their advice and support the *chwang-chang* and his assistant are unable to accomplish anything. The village gentry are also heads of the chief clans or families. If they object to a program, or even if they merely take a negative attitude, the administration faces an impasse. Laymen leaders do not, as a rule, deal with the government authorities directly. Sometimes the district leader or the county government invites them to a conference to hear their opinions regarding a certain case; not infrequently their advice influences government policy. In the old days there were various ways of determining public opinion in the countryside, but as a rule public opinion was created not by the small farmers but by the rural gentry and clan heads.

* * *

Traditionally, the magistrate or his secretaries paid respect to the village gentry, schoolteachers, and the large clan heads, but would assume an air of superiority toward the official leaders. No villager of social rank or much self-esteem wanted to be an official, for he would lose face in dealing with those who outranked him in authority but not in social status. Besides, no one wanted to be at the beck and call of the government or to have to take orders. A Chinese country gentleman or a rural scholar might welcome a post in the district, provincial, or central government, but would nevertheless hate to bow to a lesser man. For this reason, village officials have generally been recruited from the poorer families; they are men who do not care overmuch for reputation or social status or who are exceedingly interested in the profits to be made. Naturally this has kept the offices low in the eyes of the people, who have never felt called upon to respect those who hold them. . . .

. . . The old type of *chwang-chang* does not fit the new requirements, and trained people are replacing him. This has had its effect on the old pattern of subordination to the laymen leaders, who observe this change with a good deal of resentment. The old assurance of their status is gone and in the present insecurity lies the core of much of their antagonism to the new government. They are necessarily the "conservative" element of the population. Their criticism of the government is not specifically directed at policies or the plans for improving the rural areas, but rather at those appointed to carry out these changes.

* * *

The teacher of the village school has been traditionally a person who occupied simultaneously several statuses. He was the schoolteacher, head of the P'an clan, a member of the village gentry, and a local scholar. The present teacher is no exception; he is an important layman leader, although he is too young to be his clan's head. The teacher of the Christian school has always been an outsider, so his leadership has not, as a rule, been widely recognized. One of these teachers, however, was a very influential person because he possessed the attributes of a real Chinese gentleman. In addition to his specialized training he was able to paint landscapes, write poems, carve wood and stones, conduct conversations, and appreciate natural beauties. He could also smoke like a gentleman and sip tea like an old scholar. He behaved very conventionally before women and old people, but was humorous when he talked with a group of young farmers. As a result he got acquainted with most of the younger villagers and all the old people spoke well of him. He taught in the school for six or seven years, during which time he exerted a significant influence on the cultural opinions and activities of the village.

* * *

15. INTERVILLAGE RELATIONS

Taitou is closely related to Hsinanchen, the market town and connecting link between the various villages which surround it. The limits of the market-town area are set by the communication and transportation facilities and by the natural physical barriers of the region. There are points at which it may overlap that of another market town, and there are also some "neutral zones" between these areas, but, on the whole, although there is no clear-cut line of demarcation, each market town has a definite and recognizable area, and looks upon the people of certain villages as its primary customers; in turn, it is regarded by the villagers as their town.

Hsinanchen is much larger than any of the villages in its area, and has many good buildings, both commercial and residential. The important streets and avenues all meet at the center of the town to form a public square. The business section has broad streets lined with shops, drugstores, restaurants, and inns. At the northeastern end of the town is the Confucian temple and the new primary school. On the outskirts are the village-type houses of the farming families.

Since Hsinanchen serves more than twenty villages, it has a considerable volume of business. The five or six drugstores sell, in addition to drugs, sugar, oil, spices, and other things. There are also several blacksmith and silversmith shops, three or four bakeries, two hardware shops, one bookstore, two large wine-making establishments, two carpenter shops, three or four small inns and several restaurants. These shops are open all week but are busiest on regular market days. The owners and clerks came originally from the villages where their families still live, and customers patronize those from their own village. Shops are patronized by the same families for generations; farmers go to them because their fathers and their grandfathers went there.

Most of the trade still takes place on the six regular market days, which occur on the first, fifth, tenth, fifteenth, twentieth, twenty-fifth, and thirtieth day of every month. . . . On market days the business life of the town is in full swing. On the evening before the market opens, the professional itinerant traders begin to pour in with their wares; early in the morning come the village butchers with their dressed hogs; the country merchants with their bags of wheat flour, cans of petroleum, bales of spun cotton yarn; and the carpenters with their homemade furniture and farm implements. Later come the traders who deal in dried foodstuffs, fish and seafood, fruits, pottery, chinaware, and scores of other merchandise. Then the farmers begin streaming in from the surrounding villages with their loads of grains, beans, fresh vegetables and fruits, animal feed, and firewood. Some also drive in livestock which they hope to sell or exchange. Later come the people who have nothing to sell but only want to buy. Some member from almost every household in the village is in the town on market day. In the morning every road leading to the town is crowded with people. Very few women go to market, with the exception of some old women from poor families who carry eggs, or chickens, or baskets of seafood for sale or some of their handiwork which they hope to exchange for a little money.

All the available space in the town is crowded with booths, counters, and platforms heaped with merchandise. Traders dealing in similar commodities occupy the same section, thus forming more or less specialized markets. The livestock market and the fuel market are located outside the town on the riverbank. People crowd the streets, shouting, bargaining, greeting friends, yelling, and swearing. The excitement reaches its peak at noon and then begins to decline. Soon the roads are filled once more with homeward-bound villagers, but the marketing continues until late afternoon. . . .

* * *

The market town provides opportunities for farmers from different villages to meet one another, and is in fact one of the few places where they can meet. Chinese farmers always have friends and relatives in other villages and these meetings in the market take the place of visits, which would be more expensive. When the farmers return home they report to the whole family what they have seen and heard and, in this way, people are kept informed about one another.

Most of the leaders in a Chinese rural community have leisure time, which they are apt to spend in the wine shops or the teahouses in the market town. They talk or argue in the stores on current affairs or historical events and discuss community problems. Many community programs, good and bad, come out of such informal gatherings and many problems have been solved, wisely or not, in these discussions. A score of villages are linked together or separated in conflict whenever their leaders take measures to avoid each other in the market town.

* * *

In general, every large market town is crossed by a main road on which persons from the outside world travel. They bring news from distant places. In the town there are telephone and telegraph offices. The post office brings mail into the town to be distributed to the villages. Commercial agents from the county seat or other large cities bring information from their headquarters, which travels to the villages immediately. Teahouses and wine shops generate rumors which are widely spread. There is an old saying that statesmen should listen to the talk in these hidden corners. Public opinion and social attitudes take form in them and there are numerous historical tales of Chinese officials who visited them in disguise in order to discover what the common man was saying about current affairs. It is well known that the farmer does not have much to say at home but is a good talker whenever he finds himself in the market town and sits with his fellow villagers in the teahouse.

* * *

Since commercialization and industrialization have gradually penetrated the countryside, the farmer becomes increasingly dependent upon goods not produced by himself. He produces only the primary foodstuffs on his farm and in his vegetable garden, and everything else must be bought from the market town or other cities. This means that he depends more and more on the market town, that its stores play an increasingly important role in the rural economy, and that its trade service is becoming an essential factor in organizing the local community. It also means that the village and the outside world are becoming more interdependent through the agencies of the local market town, the market towns in the outlying areas, and the growing contact with Tsingtao.

* * *

Economic relations with Tsingtao are on the increase, both in trade and in the employment of villagers. Every year large quantities of farm products are sold to Tsingtao either directly by the farmers themselves or through the grain dealers and vegetable merchants. The farmer's inclination for growing special crops and raising certain livestock for the market in Tsingtao is becoming more obvious day by day. The increased acreage for growing soybeans, wheat, certain vegetables and fruits, and the increased amount of poultry and hogs is all due to the new market. In return, Tsingtao supplies the farmers with an ever-increasing amount of manufactured goods. In every rural market town one can see huge quantities of factory-made wheat flour, cotton yarn or cloth, cans of petroleum, boxes of matches, soybean cakes for animal feed, and hundreds of other articles. The self-sufficient economy of the village as well as of other villages has become an historical fact [rather than a present-day fact]. . . .

Sociocultural Change

>>>

China today is important not only for what is happening to it as a massive, strategic area of land and a huge population aggregate; it is important because it is a case study in (1) the effect of Western industrialization and other culture traits upon a peasant society, and (2) the more recent effects of a Communist-dominated government upon a property-conscious peasantry. Two matters of such scope cannot be covered adequately in the space available here, but they at least can be touched upon so as to make us aware of the issues involved. The social scientist would consider that these issues are chiefly those having to do with changes in social relationships (social change) and modifications in traditional ways of doing things (cultural change).

One of the major changes underway in China before World War II was the rise of an industrial group, small in numbers but great in power. This moneyed, urban-centered group of financiers, manufacturers, and international merchants was threatening the position of the landowning gentry, a class which in the past had provided the scholars, who in turn became bureaucrats and managed governmental affairs. With this shift in power for the nation as a whole, the status of the peasantry required re-examination. The following selection not only provides a keen insight into the social structure of old China, tying in the clan with the gentry, but shows the new forces underway even before the coming of the Communists.

• 18 • Peasantry and Gentry
HSIAO-T'UNG FEI

The gentry differ from the aristocracy in the West in that the former do not form a political party with the responsibility of running a government. Never in the history of China have the Chinese gentry organized their own government. As a class, they never

[From "Peasantry and Gentry: An Interpretation of Chinese Social Structure and Its Changes," *American Journal of Sociology*, Vol. 52, No. 1, Chicago, 1946. Pp. 1-16. Used by permission.]

reject any monarch who is able to seize the power and who recognizes the right of land-owners. They will enter any government with the purpose of protecting their own kin and local people from the encroachment of the absolute power, but not for the sake of political power itself. They have no sense of political responsibility. They do not even want to remain in their official position for long, and certainly they abhor public duty. I do not think that it is only a matter of pretentiousness that the ideal gentleman is the one who enjoys himself among the people but not in the court. A large bulk of poetry reveals the psychology of retirement of the officials and is popular and typical. The happiest moment of a successful official is when he retires to his own country with high honors. Honor and prestige which the official gentry seek at any price have practical values. They mean security to his own clan and to the people of his locality. In fact, even when he is holding an office in the government, he is at the same time working as a representative of his kin and relatives. The latter function is indeed his main job, but, in order to realize it, he has to take the former. Toward his public position he assumes a negative attitude. He is ready to resign whenever his record and influence are well established and can perform his function as protector of his people without a public office. The gentry as a class are outside the government. They take official positions individually. They are moved by social but not by political responsibility. This is why we should not rank them as aristocracy.

It may also be important to point out here that, owing to their pivotal position in the power structure, the gentry have through long history acquired a set of codes of professional ethics. They preach the doctrine of order: every one should behave according to and be satisfied by the position one occupies in the social structure. The task of Confucius was to set down for each social status its canon of correct behavior. The gentry's interest is not in possessing political power but in maintaining order irrespective of who the monarch is. They will serve him as long as he behaves as a benevolent ruler, but if he becomes despotic and suppresses the peasants too hard, the gentry will exert their pressure against him. On the other hand, if the peasants revolt against the ruler, and disturb the social order, they will fight on the side of the monarch. This is their social responsibility. Being a privileged class themselves, they are never revolutionary. Order and security are their sole interests.

. . . A peasant who works on the land is bound to the land as a peasant. Therefore, we may ask how the gentry emerges. Of course, we must admit that, since there is no social barrier preventing a peasant from entering into the gentry if he can afford to lead a leisurely life, there will be those hard-working peasants who strive to rise from the bottom. But it will take them several generations to climb up the social ladder, each generation promoting itself a little. Despite thrift and endurance, this is not only a long but also a haphazard way, because in the rural community misfortunes of all kinds are not uncommon. . . . It will be most rare for a family to keep up its morale for several generations and to have no misfortune strike at them in the meantime.

Another factor which prevents a hard-working and well-to-do peasant family from rising is the high pressure of population. . . . The birth rate is as high as that of the poor peasants and the death rate is comparatively low owing to their better living standard. Such a family grows fast. If it cannot expand its estate at the same rate, its standard of living will sink in the next generation. It already requires fairly strenuous efforts for a peasant family to maintain its footing, but the hope of rising into the leisure class is slight.

It is quite natural that the common tendency among the peasants is not to rise on the social ladder but rather to sink toward the bottom. A petty owner may become a tenant when he sells his land as misfortune befalls him. He may further sink from a tenant to a landless farm laborer. He may in the end die disgracefully or disappear from the village. These outcasts are desperate. They have nothing to lose but their life of drudgery. They leave the village and plunge themselves into banditry or smuggling, or join the army, or seek employment as servants in big gentry houses. These are economically nonproductive jobs, but it is only by taking up such jobs, in addition to good luck, that the outcasts from the rural society can hope to obtain wealth quickly. Of course, hundreds and thousands of such fortune-seekers die in despair and are forgotten by the world. But, once loosened from the soil, they have freed themselves from the bond of the land. They are the dissatisfied class and thus revolutionary in nature. When the ruling class is strong, they are suppressed. Only a few reach their aim through various kinds of more or less unlawful ways. But if the ruling class is degenerate and weak, they are the uprising group aiming at power. In Chinese history there are several instances where new dynasties were inaugurated by such desperate outcasts.

In peacetime the few successful upstarts when they have obtained wealth will buy land and insinuate themselves into the leisure class. They are looked down upon and looked at with a prejudiced eye by the gentry. Only gradually and especially by means of affinal alliance, are they admitted into the upper layer of the social structure. Not until one of the family members enters into the scholar group and into officialdom is their position in the gentry consolidated.

The gentry are maintained economically by owning land and politically by occupying a position in officialdom. As a landowning class they have the leisure to learn classical literature which is the professional requirement of an official. For nearly a thousand years the monarch has offered regular examinations to recruit officials from the literati. Only a few low classes are excluded from the right to take part in such examinations. Theoretically men from the peasantry are free to enter into the competition. And there are notable cases in which a son of a poor peasant learned the classics on the back of his buffalo while he was working in the field and attained high honor in the examination. But, after all, these are exceptions, for otherwise such stories would not be circulated like legends. It is true that in China there is no such social class system as the caste system, but it is another question as to whether the Chinese class system possesses high mobility. I have no statistical information to prove the case, but from studies on existing rural communities it is clear that a child from a peasant family engaged in farm work has little chance of receiving a high school education. I cannot help being cautious in accepting the popular belief that in the good old days everyone had a chance to become an official through equitable examination. The mobility between peasantry and gentry has been rather limited. It is needless to add that the existence of the belief among the peasants in the possibility of promotion to the gentry is important because it gives an incentive and eventually stabilizes the structure at large.

Conversely we may ask how frequently the members of the gentry return to peasantry. As far as my own knowledge goes, I cannot find a single case where a good-for-nothing gentleman picks up farming again. It seems impossible that the gentry should return to the farm. Manual labor is highly deplored in the current ideology in China, even today. The gentry are especially conscious of it. A long gown that signifies leisure is the emblem of honor and prestige and is the last thing a gentleman will cast away. It is worth more than one's life. I had an uncle who became destitute by his fortieth year. He lived in a bare room and was penniless. But he carried on his life as usual in the tearooms and wore his long gowns until his death. The scene of his death was most pathetic. He lingered on at his last moment and was unwilling to close his eyes, as a cousin of my clan put it who visited him on his deathbed. He was worrying that he would not die as a gentleman, dressed in silk and buried in a coffin of good quality. My cousin comforted him by showing him all that he was going to have when he ceased to breathe. He smiled and then passed away in satisfaction. This incident presents in full the inner psychology of the gentry. The question will then arise as to how he could afford to live up to the standard of a gentleman. The answer is that he was helped by his clan members. The clan is a system of mutual security. When I was young, I frequently witnessed the visits of my clan uncles to my home. They were poor, but they talked and laughed without mentioning any financial need. When they left us, my grandmother used to give them a handsome amount of money as a present. My grandmother was not rich then. I knew very well that she had sent a maid to the pawnshop from our back door in order to get enough money to aid our clan members who were in distress. The same spirit leads an official to offer jobs to his clan members regardless of their ability. The sense of responsibility for mutual aid and collective security among the clan members is stronger than the sense of duty as an official of the government.

* * *

Posed on the peak of the social pyramid, the gentry possess prestige and privilege. Prestige and privilege attract the daring and the aggressive individuals from the classes below. The new recruits revitalize the gentry, but, when they are assimilated, they become pacified and neutralized. The energy that may cause upheavals is channeled into the petty mobility in the social structure and is finally eliminated in the pattern of leisurely life. The gentry class is in fact a safety valve in social changes. Conservatism becomes the rule of Chinese society, and China as a culture is singular in the history of human kind in its stability and perpetuation.

Traditional China has not passed. It is present, although in many respects it has been covered by modifications and by novelties. This is why I have consistently used the present tense in the above description. Let no one think that what I have described is only a page of dead history. The essential

pattern of the social structure is functioning as ever. That it is changing, I am sure. But the new order will . . . be born from the old through the gradual change of the habitual way of living of the millions. . . . The above analysis is a preparation for our further discussion on the changing aspect of the Chinese social structure.

It seems that traditional China achieved a certain equilibrium from which ensued stability. This equilibrium was upset when China came in contact with the Western powers, with their industrial supremacy. Modernization is imposed on the Chinese by the machine age, and China is forced to enter the world community. Hence the change in the Chinese social structure.

. . . Modern industry gives the West a power unprecedented in history over agrarian communities. Unlike an age of agriculture when people can live harmlessly alone, the industrial age is an age of expansion, a lure to a world community. Seeking raw material and markets, the industrial nations will not let the Eastern Hemisphere alone. To be sure, trade is for mutual benefit, and industry is the best cure for the poverty of the East. But to the Westerner it is still a mystery why the Chinese of the past generation were so stubborn in refusing to let in Western industrial influences. And it certainly seems regrettable that China should be opened by force. Many friends in the West still wonder, too, why the Chinese should be so reluctant in receiving the salvation of their souls by Christianity and of their life by machine. Had this been all due to cultural inertia, the reaction would have faded away when the salvation showed its proofs. To say that the Chinese were prejudiced against new creeds of religion and new ways of production as such is without historical foundation. Buddhism was new to China when it was first introduced, but it was soon incorporated into Chinese religious beliefs and became deeply rooted among the peasants. New crops like the potato and tobacco spread without meeting resistance. To me, the unhappy history of the first period of contact between the

East and the West is mainly caused by social factors which can be seen in the perspective I have outlined above.

When the Industrial Revolution started in Europe, it was the middle class who took the lead. Medieval feudalism was receding. But in China at the time of the contact with the West, the middle class was the conservative gentry. The ideal of the gentry is to enjoy leisure under the protection of officialdom. Production is the occupation of the peasants and is considered low. The initiative of the gentry in economic pursuits has long been suppressed. Industrialism is not like Buddhism. When Buddhism made its first appearance, it caught the spirit of the gentleman of leisure. It fitted neatly into the tradition of retirement. Therefore, it was able to recruit from that class a number of talents who spread the creed in China. But modern industrialism, on the contrary, runs counter to the traditional spirit of the gentry. The value of practical knowledge is slighted by them. They learn literature because it signifies leisure and delicacy and because it leads to officialdom. The abhorrence of manual work is strong even among the students of modern universities. Chinese engineers prefer making designs to handling machines. The social gulf between those who use the mind and those who use the hand is still present in modern factories in China and has created serious problems in labor administration. How could industrialism find an easy entrance into China?

The crisis created by the intrusion of Western industrial influences, since the Chinese government failed to resist the powerful intruding force, did not call forth the immediate and effective adjustment of the gentry. They failed because the crisis did not present itself as a direct threat to them. Their interest was in rent-collecting. As long as the peasants were able to pay their rent, the gentry had nothing to worry them. It would have needed foresight to see that Western industrial influences, if not adjusted to the rural conditions in China, would lead eventually to the bankruptcy of the peasants and affect the economic basis of the gentry. But the gentry lacked foresight. Having no strong sense of political responsibility, they were naturally even less sensitive to the fact that China's political sovereignty was dwindling. They had little impulse to meet Western industrialism squarely and none to re-examine their own position in the destiny of China. The leading social class thus failed to live up to their social and cultural responsibility. The government at that time was in the hands of an alien monarch. The Manchu imperial house was degenerating. They certainly felt the danger of foreign intrusion, but the caliber of the ruling class was weak. They resorted to the primitive method of counteraction, such as the Boxers' Rising. The antiforeign policy of the government furthered the aloofness of the gentry, who were submissive in nature.

The rapid intrusion of the Western powers, mainly motivated by commercial interests, on the one hand, and the ineptitude of the Chinese government and the leading class, on the other, resulted in a peculiar adjustment in the first phase of contact between the East and the West. It was characterized by the creation of a special zone of foreign settlement which was later developed into the so-called treaty ports. Treaty ports were created for the benefit of Western traders. To protect them, Western laws were allowed to apply in those cases in which Western interests were involved. Order in the ports was maintained by a specially organized government either in the hands of the consuls or in the hands of the representatives of the foreign residents. The Chinese government had no voice in the rule of the special zone. In such zones a type of cosmopolitan community developed. A brief analysis of the nature of such a cosmopolitan community will help us understand the main trend in the change of Chinese social structure during the last hundred years.

Cultures come in contact with each other through their agents. In the treaty ports different elements of the Western peoples and the Chinese are gathered. Among the westerners, traders are predominant. Their inter-

est is in making profit. They are not concerned with the wider spheres of social welfare and international good-will which bear
no immediate commercial benefit and engen-
der no community security. No efforts have
been made on the part of the Western traders
to improve the incongruous relation with the
people among whom they are living. On the
contrary, affected by their superiority complex, they make deplorable discriminations
against the Chinese. These make a respectable Chinese uncomfortable. Humiliation prevents harmonious association. Therefore to
such ports a special type of Chinese was attracted. They are known as *compradors*. I
possess no sufficient data on the family background of those who form the first line of
contact with Western traders, but I strongly
suspect that those "secondhand foreigners"
were, at least for the early period, recruited
from the outcasts of the traditional structure
who had lost their positions and sought their
fortune through illegal means. Treaty ports
are open to them. If they find regular employment in the community, such as servants or
interpreters in a foreign concern, they gradually become compradors or first-boys; if
they fail, they form gangs. They live in, and
take advantage of, the margin of cultural contact. They are half-caste in culture, bilingual
in speech, and morally unstable. They are unscrupulous, pecuniary, individualistic, and agnostic, not only in religion but in cultural
values. Treaty ports are ultraurban. They are
a land where the acquisition of wealth is the
sole motive, devoid of tradition and culture.
It is unfortunate that the East and the West
should meet on such a ground.

To the towns in the interior come foreign
missionaries. As individuals they are decent
people. But they carry, in one hand, the enthusiasm to convert the heathens who are
not conscious of their sins themselves and, in
the other hand, the privilege of political protection given to the nationals of the Western
powers. Religious salvation attracts few because the ordinary Chinese feels no need for
a new creed, but the political protection
shines in the eyes of those who need extra

shelter for their illegal pursuits. Before the
light of God has penetrated into the souls of
the Chinese social outcasts, they have already
done a lot in the name of God, who will
never approve of their deeds. The antagonism
against foreign missions that was aroused at
the early period and resulted in open conflicts
and wars between China and the Western
powers came not from the ill feeling of the
Chinese people against foreign missionaries
but from their hatred toward the "second-
hand foreigners" who had turned God into
the devil.

However, as the influences from the West,
both political and economical, grow in China,
the special group of Chinese, nursed in the
treaty ports and in the churches in the interior, gathers importance. Regardless of the
type of their character, they occupy a strategic
position in China's transition. They are the
first few who know foreign languages and
the ways to deal with Western people. As
their children grow up, they give them modern education and send them abroad to attend
Western universities. From this group a new
class is formed. They are engaged in professional jobs; at first mainly dependent on foreign sponsors and later on their own feet.
But, being reared in a cosmopolitan community, they are fundamentally hybrids. In
them are manifest the comprador characteristic of social irresponsibility. It is this class
that dominates the first phase of Chinese
social and political changes.

Western industrial influence does not stop
at the treaty ports. It works its way far into
the interior. As I have mentioned above, the
bulk of Chinese manufacturing industry is
widely scattered in the homesteads of the
peasants. The peasants work on their simple
looms in their spare time. They have to take
up jobs like that because the farm is too small
to support them. But handicraft is far less
efficient than machine work. Native products
cannot compete with the manufactured goods
from Western factories. The quality of native
products is poor and the cost high. Gradually
the native workers lose their jobs. The cheap
but good cloth made in factories, for instance,

penetrates deep into the remotest villages. This means that thousands of looms in the peasants' homes must stop working. The decline of native industry owing to the invasion of Western industrialism further impoverishes the already poor peasants. Rural depression forces the peasants to sell their land, and more and more peasants sink into tenancy. This is not the end. Tenants have to pay rent to the owners. This means an increase in the peasants' burden. In the area near the modern cities in the coastal provinces, where Western industrial influence is most strong, more than 80 per cent of the peasants are already tenants. The annual drain on rural produce in terms of rent payment is terrific. Many peasants leave their land and become landless laborers. They crowd into the treaty ports to be factory workers or gangsters. Those who remain in the villages linger on, hard pressed under the exacting taxes, rents, and interest. They are desperate.

Rural depression at last threatens the privileges of the gentry. They begin to disintegrate. Those who cling to the traditional privileges have to resort to stronger political backing. They become the spearhead of the oppressors of the peasant movement. They exert pressure on the government to maintain their privilege. However, being an intellectual class, a part of them, the second generation of the old landed gentry, after receiving modern education, take up professional jobs and earn their living independent of land.

Here we find another front of contact between the East and the West. This front is different from that found in the treaty ports. It is mainly cultural. Early in the last period of the imperial dynasty, a new form of gentry had the opportunity to go abroad, mainly on government missions or scholarships, and, unlike the compradors, grew interested in Western civilization. They were educated in academic centers, mostly in England. They translated the works of Adam Smith, Herbert Spencer, Montesquieu, J. S. Mill, and others into classical Chinese (which, I believe, are still the best translations of Western classical works in Chinese). They tried to dig into the source of Western civilization and to introduce the best of the West to China. But it is a slow process, and much slower than the aping of the irresponsible and superficial commercial spirit of the foreign traders in the treaty ports. Slow as it is, it moves on gradually. The new gentry started the movement of the Chinese renaissance. It was a movement for vernacular literature, scientific research, democracy, and modern morality. This movement was a combined effort of the returned students and students in Chinese colleges. Most of them were the children of the landed gentry.

However, the new gentry share with the old the same traditional spirit in their lack of active political responsibility. They frequently voiced their disapproval of the government politics but rarely attempted to assume government responsibilities by taking up political power themselves. The central power, since the downfall of the Manchu Dynasty, has been held by the war lords and by the treaty-port group. The rising of a soldier into imperial power is an old story. In the traditional structure, when a ruler is degenerate and abuses his unbounded power, he will encroach on the peaceful life of the people. The peasant will suffer most. Many of them will become bandits and begin to revolt. Inefficient government will not be able to check the uprising. A new ruler will appear. In the same way, war lords appeared in the early years of the Republic. Most of them were of peasant origin and many started their career as outlaws. The treaty-port group rose from the same background and took a similar way. The difference is that they were settled in the protection of the cosmopolitan community and attained their power not through military strength but through financial strength. They lusted for power, and, living under foreign traders, they soon realized that the opportunity enjoyed by foreign traders could be theirs if they could get into power. With these matured compradors are the gangsters who form an integral part of the treaty-port group. They are well organized and disciplined in their gang spirit.

They are daring and unscrupulous. The instability of the Chinese political situation gives those power-thirsty elements the opportunity to seize power. Indeed, I am not trying to minimize the importance of other groups of the Chinese people in the political struggle. Successive revolutions were prepared mostly by the new professional gentry and carried through by the peasants and workers; but, owing to the lack of political responsibility in the gentry and the backwardness of the peasants, power repeatedly slipped into the hands of the war lords and the treaty-port group.

The economic decline of the land interest on the one hand, and the rising of a new politically conscious treaty-port group, on the other, undermined the importance of the gentry in the social structure of China.

By now the reader will be familiar enough with China to appreciate the point of view of the authors of the next article. Although they recognize the need for "industrialization" in some form, they argue that it must be accomplished in conformity with the already existing social and economic structure. A mere transferral of European or American industrial patterns would hardly help the millions of Chinese villagers who need to supplement their inadequate farm incomes. In China, as elsewhere, every aspect of a people's life is closely interrelated with every other aspect, so that planning any such momentous change as industrialization must proceed from a firm and comprehensive knowledge of the country and the people. Fei and Chang are Chinese sociologists who have devoted their lives to the systematic development of such knowledge; consequently they write with both insight and authority.

• 19 • Agriculture and Industrialization
HSIAO-TUNG FEI AND CHIH-I CHANG

INDUSTRY AND COMMERCE IN RURAL ECONOMY

... Rural industry has two bases: one the necessity for finding employment on the part of the farmers, and the other the striving for profit on the part of the rich. The second type of rural industry emerges when a large amount of capital is needed to set up mills and factories. As technology develops, capital becomes more important than labor in the process of production. Mills and factories cannot be established in small huts and carried on by poor peasants who have nothing but labor to sell. Moreover, such industry, organized on a capitalistic basis, finds its limits in interior China, where transportation is difficult and markets restricted. When the margin of expansion is reached, the profits gained cannot be invested in the same enterprise. This capital then goes back to the land again and begins to concentrate land in the hands of big owners.

Most of the rural industry in traditional China is developed from a local supply of raw material and is only a process of refining agricultural products. But in those places where communication is improved and raw material can be brought in from outside through commerce, new forms of industry are growing up. . . .

Because of the fact that the poor peasants

[From *Earthbound China: a Study of Rural Economy in Yunnan,* Routledge and Kegan Paul, London, 1948. Pp. 299-312. Used by permission.]

are barred from sharing the profits of industry and commerce organized on a capitalistic basis, the development of industry and commerce brings them disastrous consequences. It is interesting to note that, where commerce is developed in China, tenancy follows suit and that, in the area where commerce is underdeveloped, we find more occupying owners. In Yunnan the exchange of goods among villagers takes place largely in periodic markets, temporary gatherings in which producers and consumers meet. In this system of exchange the profits from trade are diffused throughout the general population. There is only a limited scope for the commercial activities of the middleman. Here the tenant is in the minority. In northern China, where the periodic marketing system is common, a similar situation in regard to land is found. But in the coastal regions, like the Yangtse and Canton deltas, where from 80 to 90 per cent of the farmers are tenants, big towns, where middlemen sell produce in stores, are in existence.

A more significant fact in the development of commerce in the rural areas is that it prepares the way for the intrusion of foreign goods, which are gradually wiping out traditional industry. As the latter disappears, the peasants lose a source of income and are the more impoverished. The chances of losing their land are increased. Contact with Western industry is the most important factor in the present agrarian situation in China. Let us examine the process more closely.

We may begin with the basketmaking in Yits'un [a small village of southwestern China]. The basketmaker uses his own material, works by himself, and sells by himself. He gets a sum in return which includes the value of the raw material, wage, transportation fee, and selling profit. In Yuts'un [another small village of the same region], in the former days, the work of the weavers was similar to that of the Yits'un basketmakers. They grew the cotton, made the dye, spun the cotton thread, wove it into clothes, and sold it to the buyers. But as a result of the development of commerce, they now receive cotton thread from, and return the woven piece goods to, the shops. The money received amounts to wages only. They have lost their position as producers of raw material, spinners, and sellers. Thus the profits derived from this product are shared with a number of other persons. If the techniques of production were to be improved, the total profits might be increased; and if these profits were distributed equally among the participators in the process, the weavers might gain an even larger return than by carrying on the entire process by themselves alone with primitive techniques. But this is not true. The lion's share of profit goes to those who supply the capital. The poor weavers have no power in bargaining. They have to accept any terms, since they must take up some subsidiary work, as dictated by their agricultural situation. The amount allotted to the weaver is, at the present time, insufficient to maintain bare existence. Even so, the weavers have no choice but to continue to work; otherwise they will lose more through total unemployment.

In the case of the Yuts'un weaving industry, we can already see that the development of modern industry and commerce has wiped out certain occupations of the Chinese villagers. In this case, the villagers have given up spinning entirely because the thread made from the local process is costly and lower in quality than that made in Lancashire and Manchester. Very soon even the cotton piece goods woven in Yuts'un will lose its market when, with the improvement in transportation, the machine-woven clothes from modern industrial centers flow into the interior. The same situation is seen even more clearly in Kiangts'un, where the native silk industry is declining rapidly in the face of the competition of the better silk made by machine in Japan and of the rayon industry in America.

Now let us once more remind the reader of two fundamental facts in Chinese rural economy: the first is that traditional Chinese industry is diffused among villages, and the second is that the farmers depend on it for subsistence. The industrial revolution in the West at last threatens the peasants in the Chinese villages in their capacity as industrialists. It is a hopeless struggle for the unorganized mass of petty owner-workers. However skillful they may be, they are fighting a losing battle against the machine. But they must keep on fighting, because otherwise they cannot live. The result is that China is gradually being reduced to an agrarian country, pure and simple; and an agrarian China is inevitably a starved China.

The desperation of this situation is felt by every household where income is declining. Any stroke of misfortune will force the peasant owner to sell his land. We have emphasized the fact that Chinese peasants do not sell their land for profit but only when they are in real distress. In the interior, where Western industrial and commercial influences are less strong and the traditional order is still maintained, the system of mutual help and fortitude with regard to material adversity helps to tide them over their financial crises. So long as they can find any other means to get out of their financial difficulties, they will hold onto their land. As a result, the rate at which land is becoming concentrated in the hands of a few is slow. Even in Yuts'un, in the last twelve years, only about 65 *mow* of land has left the hands of the villagers. It would take seventy years under the present rate to attain the status of Kiangts'un, where nearly half of the land is in the hands of absentee landlords. But when rural industrial workers face a direct attack from Western machine industry, it appears to take only a short period to sink most of the petty owners to the status of tenant. This is the reason, we believe, why at present in the coastal provinces a very high percentage of tenancy is found. Of course, the hypothesis which we are stating will require further research before its full validity is established. But the present study clearly supports this conclusion.

* * *

DEVELOPMENT OF CO-OPERATIVE RURAL INDUSTRY AS A SOLUTION TO THE LAND PROBLEM

Since a definition of a social situation is a preliminary step toward action, if the agrarian situation is defined in technological terms only, the actions followed will be limited to technological improvements. It is essential, however, for us to recognize that the situation is much more complicated. We do not deny the importance of technological improvement, but we must also understand its limitations. The present study—far from conclusive—at least indicates that the Chinese treatment of rural economic problems merely as problems of agriculture is one-sided. We should like to emphasize our conclusion that the land problem is aggravated by the problem of rural industry. If we are correct, then the ultimate solution of the land problem is closely allied to the problem of Chinese industrialism.

In the matter of technological improvements, enough attention is already being paid by experts in that field. Marked success in the improvement of crops and of soil and insect control has been attained where scientific knowledge has been applied. We need discuss this side of the question no further. However, with regard to problems such as the mechanization of farm tools and the enlargement of the size of farms—problems in which the social situation is generally involved —no effective reforms have been achieved. It is unfair to blame the government on that score. Policies for reform are not lacking; but when they are applied, difficulties arise which make ineffective all efforts. The crux of the matter is that, unless we can stop the constant decline in the standard of living of the peasant by increasing his income considerably, every measure adopted will be one of temporary relief rather than cure. An increase in agricultural productivity, for instance, is helpful, indeed; but, by employing all scientific means available, it is estimated that the possible increase can be only about 20 per cent above present productivity. Such an increase is dwarfed in comparison with the rapid decline in price of rural industrial products, such as silk, for example.

Again, take the measure for the equalization of holdings. It is indeed essential, in view of the present unequal distribution of land. But we must remember that, if the government were to pass measures entirely re-allotting all available land to the peasants, the size of a farm would still be under 5 acres, this figure including much which is uncultivable. In Yunnan the maximum size, not including mountainous country, would be about 1 acre. One acre of farm land, even with all possible scientific improvement of crops, gives a yield permitting a standard of living no better than the average at present. This policy, if it can be carried out, will make for an equitable distribution but will not effect great improvement in the economic status of the average villager.

There are two ways to enlarge the size of farms: one is the extension of land under cultivation, and the other is reduction in population. Manchuria and northwestern China may offer some relief for land hunger; but how much population can be moved to these parts is still unknown, and the prospect of extension is uncertain. Reduction in population has been the most common solution to the Chinese agrarian situation throughout her history. Periods of prosperity are usually followed by periods of disturbance, in which large numbers of people are wiped out by civil war and famine. Such catastrophes, of course, must not be allowed to occur again. With an improvement in public health, even if measures for decreasing the birth rate are introduced simultaneously, there will not be a quick reduction in population. Therefore, a practical solution cannot be sought along that line either.

The remaining alternative is to move the agricultural population out into other occupations. This certainly sounds like a promising solution. We are told that in 1870 the percentage of rural population in the United States was as high as 73.8, but by 1930 it was reduced to 43.8. American experience shows definitely the possibility of a reduction of rural population by the development of industry in urban centers. However, these figures do not hold any real promise for China. Stated realistically, we may say that, even if China can achieve as rapid an industrial development as the United States did in the last sixty years, we can only reduce by 30 per cent the population in the rural areas, giving a possibility of enlarging our individual farms less than ½ acre per owner.

It seems unreasonable to hope that in the near future the Chinese peasant can live entirely on agriculture. This does not mean that China is born to be poor forever. Her economic potentiality is large, in view of her abundance of manpower and resources. It means only that we must not hope that agriculture alone will save China and give a higher standard of living to the people. If we recognize this fact, the way open to us is one similar to that which has been employed for centuries—the supplementing of agriculture with diffused industry.

We must make our position very clear in this connection. We are not concerned here with the ideal type of industry or the most efficient industrial organization but with a practical type of industry . . . that will fit into the situation of the masses of the peasantry, a situation which is constantly deteriorating. It is perhaps important to bear in mind that, given the opportunity, China will inevitably be industrialized; but whether or not this new industrialization will be beneficial to the peasants is the problem. The answer depends upon the form taken by this new industry. If it develops according to the pattern of European and American industry of the last few centuries—that is, if it is concentrated in urban areas and in the hands of a few capitalists—it will only aggravate the distress of the rural population, because it will take away from the village all its homestead industries and thus further decrease the income of the peasants. This process has already been taking place during the last few decades. The further industrialization of China in this way would simply mean that the wealth concentrated in industry will be in the hands not merely of foreign but also of Chinese industrialists—a difference which will not alter the economic condition of the peasants. It is true that the government might tax the industrial profits of the Chinese industrialist for the benefit of the peasants. But this, again, is merely an alleviation. What we are seeking is rather a way to avoid the evil in the first place.

It should also be pointed out, at this point, that, if the mass of peasants cannot share in the profits of industry but only suffer from its effects in decreasing their livelihood, the growth of newly developing industry in China will be checked by a shrinkage of its markets. An all-round planning of industry should consider not only how much can be produced and how much profit can be gained but also how much can be sold. The impoverished masses, though too weak to challenge the power and privileges of the industrialists, will block the way simply by their inability to buy industrial goods. Therefore, for the success of industrial development in any form, we should try to work out a solution to these problems in terms of its ability to lift the standard of living of the common people, among whom the peasant is by far the most numerous. From this point of view, we can then lay down the principle that the future form of China's industrial organization must be such that the peasants can share in its profit in order to raise their standard of living, since agriculture alone is unable to do so. In order to achieve this, some part of industry must be decentralized and established in villages or in centers near villages, so that the profits of the industry can be widely distributed among the peasants.

To return to the traditional principle of supplementing the family income of the peasants by industry does not mean to retain the old industrial technology. To argue for retention of traditional industrial practices in the village is impractical. The handicraft technology must be improved by introducing machinery. What we should retain is the fundamental principle underlying the traditional form of this industry—that of a diffused industry suited to the agrarian situation in China. For, in the immediate future, it does not seem likely that conditions in the rural areas will be radically altered. The traditional principle is a practical solution to the problem gained through years of experience. Let us not be blind to the teachings of the past. However the question which now arises is whether it is possible to have technological improvement under the traditional principle of diffused industry.

Historically, it is true that the industrial revolution was achieved through the concentration of machine equipment and of population. The improvement in technology has been, so far, largely parallel with the development of urban centers. However, this was mainly due to the employment of steam power at the first stage of industrial development. When electric power was introduced, the trend toward concentration of industry changed. Charles Abrams said:

The use of steam power was the first major step in the development of a modern system, and it made for concentration of manufacturing operation within a small area, since it could be generated economically only in large plants and could be transmitted only by belt or shaft, and then only over short distances. Factories and related activities were thus confined to a relatively compact center, from which the manufactured products were transported to the more distant markets now made accessible by steam transportation.

But with the development of electric power which can be transmitted economically over relatively long distances, a counter trend became discernible. The pattern now broadened out, and a network of smaller plants spread over a larger area, replacing, to some extent, the huge establishments of Victorian days. The barriers of distance dwindled with the perfection of communication devices and the sweeping improvements in transportation technique, so that the ever widening influence of the city came gradually to embrace huge metropolitan areas, in which purely local matters became less and less important.

It is, therefore, clear that decentralization of manufacturing plants is not a regression in industrial development but a general tendency in modern industry. Ought China, as a late-comer in the modern industrial world, start with the old pattern and only later move to reorganize? The economic history of the West is a warning against such a policy. The cost involved in such reorganization is great and explains why the decentralized pattern, although it has been proved to be more economical, is slow in being adopted in the West. Large investments in old-style industrial plants prevent a quick adjustment to new technological advances. China thus may have an advantage in starting from the industrial front instead of from the rear. Therefore, it appears that the decentralized industrial pattern is to be recommended, in view both of the traditional background and of modern technology.

. . . However, mere decentralization of industry is not sufficient. . . . It is . . . essential to widen the industrial opportunities of the masses. This consideration makes us advocate the principle of the co-operative in economic organization. The co-operative movement in China is already developing rapidly. Both the government and private individuals have been active in promoting it. There is no need for us to stress again the merit of this system, which appears to be the form of modern industry best adapted to China. However, the success of small-scale rural co-operative factories depends as much upon their external relations with other similar factories and with the markets as upon their internal organization. . . . A large organization, which will co-ordinate the small manufacturing units, is necessary for the new rural industry of China.

Given a co-ordinating organization, manufacturing centers scattered through the villages can work on machine parts or on a specific part in a manufacturing process. They can pool together their products, to be assembled later in a central plant. Thus the advantage of large-scale production is preserved while the concentration of population in urban centers is done away with. For the central co-ordinating management we will look to the government for aid.

A decentralized pattern for China's new industry is suggested mainly in order to improve the people's livelihood. We have shown the necessity for industrial employment in the village and the possibility of introducing modern technology into such an organization. But, at the end of our discussion, we must point out that such industry must be confined to the manufacturing of consumers' goods. For heavy industry a concentrated plant is necessary. Therefore, another problem arises. What kind of industry, heavy or light, should be emphasized in China in the immediate years after the war? If we concentrate our efforts on heavy industry first, as Russia did after World War I, it seems that there will be no alternative but to follow the Western pattern. Moreover, if development of transportation lags behind, manufacturing industries will naturally be located near heavy industries. The result will be a rapid concentration in urban centers and the deterioration of the rural areas as pictured above. Thus the sequence in which the various types of industry develop will determine their location.

We can offer no choice as to this sequence because it depends upon another factor, which is not settled at present—that is, the international order. In China there is today an unprecedented enthusiasm for industrialization. This is due to the plain fact that we have suffered so much in this war because of our industrial backwardness. That enemy planes have been able to fly over our cities and villages and drop their bombs at will without any opposition has been a profoundly painful experience. To protect our wives and children, it is natural that we should feel that we must have our own planes and tanks. If

there are no international guaranties of security, every sane Chinese will be willing to go
to any length in order to prevent a recurrence
of such disasters in the future. In other words,
if the postwar world is again to be governed
by power alone, China will have no alternative but to give first place to heavy industry
and armaments. It is needless to add that such
tactics will be disastrous to China as well as
to the world. Defense industries are costly,
and the capital thus invested does not profit
the investor. Since the standard of living in
China is already on a bare subsistence level,
any further decline will mean starvation and
death. If the international order is such that
the Chinese government, in view of the national safety, must prepare for another war—
or at least must arm, to maintain an effective
neutrality in the coming world struggle for
power—it will be obliged to adopt extremely
strong measures in order to squeeze the last
pennies from the people. This, in turn, will
inevitably block the development of democratic institutions in China. Let our friends
in the West who are worrying about political
trends in the East keep in mind the fact that
China has been ever ready to trust international tribunals and that the ideal of T'ien
Hsia, the global community, is deeply rooted
in her tradition. It is for the coming world
order to prove that such an ideal can be realized and to offer guaranties of security and
prosperity to all peace-loving peoples. China
cannot achieve this by herself alone.

*   *   *

Let us recognize that we are now at a
crossroads. The fate of innocent Chinese
peasants is in the hands of those who will
decide the pattern of China's industry in the
future. No one nation can decide the issue,
however; the choice of what sort of a world
we are to live in must come with the wide
co-operation of the citizens of the world,
whose opinion will ultimately decide the case.

Industrialization and the growth of commerce have not been the only sources of
social change in China. The new education, stemming largely from a Western orientation,
has had a profound effect, as the following selection will show.

• 20 • *Education*
GERALD F. WINFIELD

Perhaps nowhere in the world is learning
more revered than in China, yet there are
few places where a larger percentage of the
population is without formal education. While
almost everyone is trained in some skill or
another, whether it be farming or a trade, in
no other equally large population is the general level of modern knowledge so low.

In the broad sense of the word "education"
it cannot be said that a ricksha man is "uneducated" if he possesses a vast and ready
knowledge of his own culture and folklore,
can sing the most famous parts of his great
operas or repeat long and pertinent passages
from the equivalent of Shakespeare or Schil-
ler even if he can't read and write. Yet
this type of cultural information is common
throughout China.

Education in this broad sense penetrates
deep into the life of the Chinese people. The
entire culture of the country is based firmly
on the writings of the sages who lived five
hundred years before Christ and who recorded the knowledge of the previous three
thousand years and gave to it the prestige and
historical influence it still possesses. The great-

est and most influential of these sages was Confucius, a teacher on whose work was built the more than 2,000-year-old Chinese educational philosophy and content.

The focus of Chinese education was the system of imperial civil service examinations, first established more than two thousand years ago by the Western Han dynasty. It was a system which inspired the commendatory writings of many of the first European visitors to China and which indirectly influenced the pattern of our own civil service. During the time of Addison and Steele, several English writers mentioned the desirability of the Chinese system whereby any citizen might attain high public office by means of knowledge alone.

These examinations, which continued from the year 165 B.C. until they were abolished by imperial edict in 1905, exerted a profound influence not only on education but on the whole social system. Any person who felt himself qualified might take the lowest grade of examination given each year in the local hsien magistrate's *yamen*. If successful, the candidate possessing the equivalent of a primary school education was eligible for the provincial examinations and for appointment to one of the lower ranking positions of government. If the candidate then passed the provincial examination, he assumed a more advanced title and was eligible for the national and highest examination as well as for more responsible government positions. Those successful at the highest examinations became full-fledged scholars and, when appointed, sacrosanct officials, who, under the prevailing family system, raised not only themselves but their entire clan to an enviable social position. Because all examinations were literary in content, Chinese education is literary by tradition, and Chinese officialdom down through the centuries has been composed of the literati.

Since official posts carried with them social prestige and opportunities to accumulate wealth, it was not long until education, wealth, and official position became practically synonymous and the perquisites of a relatively small group. The scholar who had passed an official examination had special immunity before the law. He could not be given corporal punishment, and his person must be respected and kept inviolate. The scholar, with this special position, frequently became the spokesman of the poor and the oppressed of his community. Over and over again it was the scholar who restored integrity to Chinese government after periods of corruption and venality. Even today, nearly fifty years after the abolition of the old-style examinations, the student and scholarly groups in China enjoy a very special position in the community. It is for this reason that student movements play such an important part in China's modern political history, just as they have in centuries past.

Down the generations families have risen to or lost their foothold in this educated class. They have risen because of the ability of a brilliant son, for it has always been possible for a lad with exceptional ability and with an opportunity to study to obtain official position. Many poor families have made great sacrifices to educate their most capable sons because they have known that by success in his scholarly pursuits he could elevate the fortune of the whole clan in a single generation.

The flaw in this system has always been the problem of the opportunity to study, since the type of learning necessary can be acquired only by many years of effort. Even the most brilliant cannot master the complicated and difficult Chinese language and literature in odd moments. The student must have his entire time free from the demands of other work, and he must have both books and teachers. While some poor families in every generation have succeeded in providing these conditions for their sons, most of those who obtained the opportunity to study came from the wealthier families who could afford the books, teachers, and living costs of sons who spent their days at study. In many cases the father and grandfather were the first instructors. Consequently a large proportion of educated officialdom came from already scholarly families.

The old-style education, preparing for the examinations, was entirely classical and literary and was dominated by the elements of Confucian morality (a precept somewhat analogous to the contents of McGuffey's Readers used in American schools since 1836, except that the Chinese classics comprised the sum and total of Chinese education). Dr. Arthur H. Smith, in writing of the limitations of Chinese classics as educational texts, commented in his *Village Life in China:*

> Regarded as the sole text books for a great nation they [the classics] are fatally defective. They are too desultory, and too limited in their range. Epigrammatic moral maxims, scraps of biography, nodules of a sort of political economy, bits of history, rules of etiquette, and a great variety of other subjects, are commingled without plan, symmetry, or progress of thought. The chief defects are the triviality of many of the subjects, the limitation in range, and the inadequacy of treatment.

Nevertheless, the Chinese classics were advanced at the time of their origin, and the system of examinations and officialdom based upon them remained unique until the French Revolution led to a similar civil service system in 1791, exactly 1,956 years after its Chinese origin.

For the successful scholars, education began early in life. It was not uncommon for a child of two or three to begin recognizing characters, and at four or five to study with his father or grandfather, if he was fortunate enough to belong to an educated family. At eight or nine the neophyte began to work with a hired tutor or to attend a small private tutorial school maintained by a retired local scholar or someone who preferred teaching to government service. Almost from the first day of study the child began with the classics, reading the abstruse and profound ideas of Confucius and the other sages, ideas made even more difficult by the highly condensed form of literary writing developed in complicated ideographs. Although the child had little conception of the meaning of the sentences memorized, he was required to hammer away day after day, pounding the classics into his nervous system until he could *pei* them word for word without error. To pei, or "to back," is to turn the back to the teacher and repeat in a high singsong voice the memorized but little understood words of the classic texts.

It was from this historic method of "backing" that the Chinese practice of studying aloud came into being—a system which never fails to arouse the curiosity and interest of foreign visitors, although it is sometimes employed in the teaching of foreign languages in American schools. The practice, still prevalent, is even used in modern Chinese schools. It was brought home to me almost daily by the high singsong voice of my cook's little boy as he sat out of doors repeating in a shrill meaningless monotone, *"Che shih woti fangtze. Woti fangtze shih wo chuti ti fang. . ."*—"This is my house. My house is where I live. . ." and so on through an interesting little modern reader which was certainly not intended to be read in a high monotone.

This classical method of preparation for the imperial examinations produced many thousands of brilliant scholars through the years of China's long history. Among them were men who initiated and maintained numerous periods of great prosperity and cultural achievement, who produced a huge mass of literature and philosophy, and who developed the Chinese language as a medium of expressing and recording rich contributions to human thinking and experience.

On the other hand, the old classical education saddled China with two persistent curses. It has laid the curse of ignorance on the masses, and it has laid the curse of the scholar on the educated.

The curse of ignorance exists because the language structure, the nature, and the teaching methods of classical learning are much too difficult for the average person to grasp in a short time, with the result that the knowledge of the average peasant in China today is severely limited. Most of them spend their entire lives within walking distance of the house in which they were born. Most of them have never seen a map and cannot conceive of anything alien to their immediate experience. One day, for example, a group of Hopei peasant boys who had been conscripted into the Chinese army at the end of the war was watching the loading of a four-motored transport plane bound for Shanghai. I sauntered up to them and opened a conversation.

"It's a big plane, isn't it?" I said.

"You speak Chinese!" they exclaimed. "Where will this plane go?"

"We are going to Shanghai," I replied.

"How long will it take you to go there?" one of the boys asked.

"Between four and five hours."

"Shanghai is in that direction, isn't it?" another asked, pointing in the general direction of the Himalayas.

"No, Shanghai is straight south," corrected another, "and it's more than a thousand li away, too." (A *li* is a third of a mile.)

"Shanghai is off to the southeast in that direction," I said, pointing, "and it is more than two thousand five hundred li from here in a straight line."

These boys had all heard of Shanghai. They knew it was somewhere to the south, but they had no clear idea of how far or precisely where, even though residents of North China are exact about directions in their own areas. Within a few minutes the peasant boys had eagerly accepted my invitation to help load baggage so they might see the inside of the plane.

The same lack of geographical knowledge, coupled with complete ignorance of distance and speed of flight, was the cause of one abortive expedition made by young Chinese recruits who had been flown into India for basic training. After a few days of talking the matter over, several homesick boys went AWOL and started to walk home, following a dusty road eastward across the plains of Central India, still so far from the great mountain ranges separating China from India that they could not see them. After they were

intercepted by trucks and returned to camp, they were questioned by officers.

"We were just walking home," explained a spokesman. "We were homesick."

"But don't you know it is too far to walk?"

"It can't be very far," was the reply, "for it only took a few hours to come here from Kunming."

Scores of times, on trains, at country markets, and in villages, I have been engaged in conversations that ran about like this:

"Sir, what is your honorable country?"

"I come from America."

"Does it rain in your country?"

"Yes, it rains in my country. In some parts it is very wet, but in others it is dry. The amount of rain that falls varies from place to place in my country just as it does in China."

"Is it hot in your country?"

"My country is very large, just as China is, so it is hot in the south and cold in the north just as it is here."

"Do you have wheat in your country?"

"Yes, we grow a great deal of wheat."

"Do you have millet in your country?" "Do you have cows in your country?" "What do you make your houses of?" "Are there mules in your country?" And so on endlessly for as long as I would continue to answer. A monstrous ignorance and a mighty curiosity.

Most Chinese peasants are anything but stupid. Their knowledge of their own folklore and folk history is extensive, although it is frequently far from being historically accurate. Usually the history the country person knows has been learned at the opera, and he is frequently unable to say whether a certain character is a real person who lived at a definite time or merely the creation of a dramatist. This confusion is the more frequent because so many of the characters of Chinese drama are patterned after actual people of history.

The curse of the scholar, which lies equally heavily on the educated of China, may be summed up in the proverb: "The scholar can neither shoulder a carrying pole nor lift a basket."

All China accepts the fact that an educated man does not work with his hands. He is considered to be so far above the need for physical effort that nothing would cause him to lose face more completely than to descend to its level. It might be added that the long years of mental labor necessary to master Chinese learning usually undermine the physique of scholars to such an extent that they are unfit for bodily efforts (N. B. the statistics on tuberculosis among students). Because this tradition is held by those who work, as well as by the scholars themselves, many young scientists and engineers returning to China with advanced foreign training, eager to do great things for their country, have their initiative extinguished by community condemnation whenever they engage in shop or laboratory work.

These two great curses of Chinese knowledge, the curse of ignorance and the curse of the scholar, are slowly but surely diminishing. Literacy and the knowledge of things, of people, and of events are slowly spreading. The young men and women of modern China are gradually breaking away from the restrictions imposed on the scholar class.

What of China's education today? If the ability to read a simple book and to write a simple letter is taken as a definition of literacy, what proportion of the Chinese population is literate? I recently put this question to Miss K. S. Kao, lately in charge of the division of Social Education in the Shanghai Municipal Bureau of Education. "We estimate," she said, "that about forty per cent of the people of the city of Shanghai can read and write. Since Shanghai is the largest and most modern city in China we think that our literacy rate is considerably higher than that of the nation as a whole. However, we must be deeply concerned about the sixty per cent of our citizens who cannot read and write."

Peiping education authorities estimate that between 30 and 40 per cent of their population can read and write. Buck found that only a little over 15 per cent of the rural population above seven years of age could pass even the lowest test of literacy. In spite of public education efforts carried on since 1905, 75 or 80 per cent of those over seven years of age are illiterate, although more than a hundred million people can read and write. The largest daily newspaper in China has a circulation of over 100,000, but most newspapers are limited to circulations of less than 10,000.

The possibility of a literate population in China did not exist before the literary revolution that began about thirty years ago. Before that time, only the highly telegraphic classical style of writing was employed, using single literary characters to express key ideas in each sentence, a system of writing so condensed that it is almost unintelligible when read aloud. In order to understand literature at all, the reader had to see the characters, and, worse, he had to recognize many rare characters expressing ideas never used in everyday speech.

The literary revolution came when Dr. Hu Shih, graduate of Cornell and Columbia, and later ambassador to the United States, together with a group of young colleagues began to write with the same word order that is used in speaking. When this was done the number of necessary characters was greatly reduced and, fitted together into conversational sentences, became easier to learn and use. After years of controversy and continued use it was gradually accepted that to write as one speaks is good literary form. Now, while many scholars still use the literary form, most popular works are written in the spoken language or in what is known as "modern Chinese," in reality a cross between the literary form and the pure spoken language form.

As the literary revolution gained ground, the "Thousand Character" movement was initiated by Dr. Y. C. James Yen. A graduate of both Yale and Princeton, he began mass education work among the Chinese labor corps in France during World War I in order that their members might be able to write home and read simple newspapers. His movement, providing a sort of basic Chinese using only thirteen hundred characters, is the foundation for the mass education movement that has long since spread far beyond the organization he first formed.

So successful were Dr. Yen's methods, that the Ministry of Education adopted mass education principles and is conducting classes for adults in the Central People's Schools and the *pao* schools. In each *pao,* a group of one hundred rural families organized for political, educational, and defense purposes, the Ministry of Education intends to organize one school, with large Central People's Schools in the more populous market towns and cities. Between 1928 and 1943, almost fifty million adults were reported as having made progress toward literacy in these two types of schools and in other special adult classes. In addition, courses were broadened to include instruction in citizenship and some technical knowledge.

One of the remarkable achievements of the Chinese during World War II was the steady growth of literacy education for adults in spite of immense handicaps imposed by war. In 1936-1937, the last year of comparative peace, more than three million adults received instruction in reading and writing. In 1942-1943, during the height of the war, over nine million in unoccupied China received such instruction.

It may be inferred from this and other chapters that World War II, which began as the fifth Sino-Japanese War, had an extraordinary effect on education in China and a direct bearing on the rise in the level of literacy. The calculated attempts of the Japanese to destroy educational institutions which were imparting morale, knowledge, and skill for the building of a stronger China, exemplified, for instance by the systematic blasting of every last vestige of Tientsin's Nankai University, had the unexpected effect of sowing dragon seed. The ultimate effects, when viewed from the safe distance of history, were to unify the Chinese, to give impetus to the development of kuo-yü (Mandarin) as a common spoken language, to create a stronger and more general desire for education, to acquaint large numbers of remote people with modern ideas of health and education, and to create a more general awareness of and interest in the ultimate purpose of government.

Much was gained merely by the shifting of populations, distributing new ideas and materials, breeding modern attitudes and methods. Thousands of foreigners trekked through the most remote reaches of China, and thousands of Chinese were introduced to new and better ways of living through periods of military or industrial training in India and the United States. Among the most important causes of the broadening of thought was the overland exodus of seventy-seven colleges and universities from the enemy-occupied coast toward the hills of free China. Carrying with them almost fanatical devotion to education, they left behind, when they returned in 1946 and 1947 to their former campuses, not only a new appreciation for education itself and for better ways of living and thinking but also a new series of educational institutions spawned in areas which would have remained long untouched if left to normal educational development.

Literacy in China is extremely low, but there is no doubt that World War II reduced ignorance, even as World War I gave birth to the Mass Education Movement that has made this improvement possible. But what of the general education system?

China's system of modern education may be said to date from the edict of September 1, 1905, which abolished the imperial civil service examinations. Continual loss of wars and territories had suggested to the occupants of the Dragon Throne that something more than classics, humanities, discipline, and contemplation was needed in Chinese education, and that additional educational facilities were necessary. Prior to that time, education was largely private, and girls usually were not considered worth educating. By 1905 there were a number of Chinese who had studied abroad who helped prod the Dragon Throne out of its traditional and antiquated conservatism, and who further influenced the trend of educational organization, curricula, and methods. To assist them there existed a nucleus of foreign mission schools and colleges exemplary of modern education already adapted to Chinese needs.

It may be observed here that in 1932 a group of European-trained educators representing the League of Nations was invited by the Chinese government to inspect the budding Chinese system of education. Among many valuable suggestions, the commission reported that the whole system was much too American. The honorable members were right.

Although the system itself dates from 1905, modern education in China goes back nearly one hundred years more to 1807 when Robert Morrison, an American Protestant missionary, arrived in South China.

The arrival of Morrison to set up a school in South China, at a time when students had to be paid to attend or recruited from an ample supply of street waifs, marked more than the beginning of a long exodus of Chinese students for study abroad. The first such student, one who originally had been coaxed to attend the Morrison school, was Yung Wing. Actually there were two others, but one of these suffered from homesickness and returned to China with all convenient speed; the other was sponsored by a Scotsman who insisted that he study in Scotland. Yung Wing not only finished his formal education at Yale College, but he returned to China as the first native proponent of modern education in China and of study abroad.

In the one hundred years that followed Morrison's arrival, literally hundreds of hospitals and schools were established in China by American private interests, and millions of American citizens acquired a very real interest in Chinese health and education. The oldest of China's modern universities, founded by American missionaries in 1864 with a student body of eight, later developed into Cheeloo University of Tsinan, Shantung province. Gradually fifteen foreign-supported colleges and universities developed. Fu Jen University at Peiping and Aurora University at Shanghai were Roman Catholic institutions, partially sponsored by American funds but staffed by Chinese and Europeans. The other thirteen

were developed as Protestant ventures in international co-operation, with a large percentage of support and manpower coming from the United States. Two of them, Ginling and Hwa Nan, were the first colleges for Chinese women. Some of the thirteen institutions were chartered under the Regents of the State of New York, and all have held consistently high practical standards, equal to the best in the United States. From these American-supported institutions have come many of the men and women who now hold posts in China's educational system and in governmental and private agencies of primary importance.

In addition, the United States Government has recognized the importance of education in the establishment and maintenance of a modern, democratic China. The last empress of China, Tz'u-hsi, a recalcitrant observer of modern encroachment on her traditional domains, making a last powerful endeavor, in 1900, to drive the hated Westerners into the sea, lost to a combined army representing many nations with interests and nationals in China and was assessed an ample indemnity. When the United States Government had settled private claims for damages sustained during the Boxer Rebellion, more than $12 million remained. In 1908, during the administration of Theodore Roosevelt, the United States took the initiative in returning the surplus funds to China to be used for educational purposes (followed by Austria, Belgium, France, Germany, Great Britain, and the Netherlands, all of whom had considerably lesser claims).

With these funds, Tsing Hua College was founded in 1912 at Peking. Enjoying the nickname "Indemnity College," it later became Tsing Hua University. The purpose of this institution was to train men for further study abroad, a privilege which was extended later to successful competitors from other Chinese universities. Until inflation drastically reduced invested funds in and after 1945, each year several hundred Chinese pursued graduate study in the United States under this arrangement. In 1924, the American government having returned more indemnity funds, the Chinese and American committee (ten Chinese, five Americans) established the China Foundation for the Promotion of Education and Culture. The China Foundation in turn founded and supported scientific research institutes and libraries in China, fostered graduate research abroad, and was responsible for the founding in 1926 of the China Institute in America at New York. Since the suspension of the indemnity payments by the Chinese government at the end of 1938, both the China Foundation and the Tsing Hua Foundation have been maintained largely by dwindling endowments and other sporadic, inadequate income.

When the new national government had begun to build the educational system of China under the republic, Professor Paul Monroe of Columbia University was called in as adviser on education. His influence was both direct and indirect, since many Chinese who were sent to study at Columbia Teachers College under pragmatist John Dewey returned imbued with modern American methods of education.

In 1921-1922 a group of American educators under the direction of Professor Ernest Burton of the University of Chicago visited China, studied Chinese educational organization and needs in conjunction with a group of Chinese educators, and issued a report containing suggestions to the Ministry of Education.

When World War II prevented free movement between China and the rest of the world from 1942 to 1945, the United States channeled into China by air a constant flow of educational material, ranging from instructions for the maintenance of typewriters to vaccines and scientific journals. In addition, many American experts in agriculture, engineering, and public health went to China during the war years at the request of the Chinese government. Released for such work by American commercial and industrial organizations, universities, and even by the armed forces and American governmental agencies, their salaries were paid or supple-

mented by these agencies or by the government. At the same time over five hundred Chinese students stranded in the United States for four years were permitted to continue or complete their education with American government support. Private sources also rallied to the needs of stranded Chinese students, with many state and private institutions providing scholarships and fellowships ranging from a single endowment to free tuition for all Chinese. Among other commercial benefactors, the International Harvester Company established a half million dollar program in agricultural engineering, bringing students from China for study and maintaining chairs in the subject at two Chinese universities.

Although probably the largest number of Chinese to study abroad until World War II were Japanese-educated and many have studied in Europe, Americans have done a great deal directly and indirectly to shape the education of China. The report issued by the League of Nations commission was quite correct in its charge. During the years when the Chinese government was setting the pattern for an education system, American-trained Chinese and American-operated institutions in China provided a ready-made pattern on the spot.

In spite of all her efforts to develop primary education China still has no free compulsory education, as Westerners understand that term. Not more than 30 per cent of the children of primary school age are in school. To remedy this situation the Ministry of Education intends to set up a four-year course of study in its pao country schools and a six-year course in its Central People's Schools. Just before the last Sino-Japanese War, there were in all China 320,000 primary schools with a reported total enrollment of over 18 million. In 1942-1943 there were 258,000 primary schools in unoccupied China alone, with a reported enrollment of over 17,500,000.

The war years also saw an expansion of secondary schools, called middle schools in China. In 1936-1937 there were 3,264 middle schools registered with the Ministry of Education with a reported total of 627,246 students. By 1942-1943, in spite of war, in unoccupied China alone, and not including the "more advanced areas," there were 3,455 registered middle schools with a reported enrollment of 1,101,087. Normal schools and vocational schools at the middle school level are included in the total.

In spite of the amazing educational efforts that brought about unprecedented expansion during the war years, the quality of education declined. The hasty moving of schools resulted in heavy losses of books, materials, and equipment. Living, teaching, and health conditions deteriorated in crowded wartime quarters. Many British and American teachers were forced out of China, impairing the quality of English teaching, an effect almost immediately discernible among graduate students arriving for further study in the United States after the war. A further aggravation has been the lack of good textbooks even though efforts were made to produce enough texts with the limited supply of fourth-rate paper available in unoccupied China.

Middle schools in Japanese-occupied territory also had difficulties, although books were more plentiful and better made. English studies were reduced to the number of hours required in Japanese schools; Japanese language was added to the curricula; and textbook contents were modified, especially in regard to civics, history, and social studies generally. Students in occupied China, always aware of and active in national crises, continued to go to school, but developed a resistance to learning. Since it was patriotic to avoid learning the Japanese language, students competed for the lowest grades. However, the resistance to learning conscientiously developed over a period of eight years eventually backfired. Postwar teachers found that these students had difficulty in learning when they wanted to.

Postwar graduates from all middle schools far outnumbered prewar graduates but are much less well prepared to enter college or even to hold employment.

Although middle school education, even during the war years, has been largely conventional, there have been some significant attempts at experimentation. One of the most successful and interesting of these experiments was inaugurated by Dr. Tao Heng-chih, a returned student who obtained his progressive ideas of education from the University of Illinois and from John Dewey at Columbia and applied them at *Yu Tsai* school, or the "school for talent." Most of the students in this unusual school are orphans, and all are of exceptional ability. The aim of the school is to provide a broad, socially centered education, with emphasis on fine arts, including music, dancing, and drama, while supplying training in science and shopwork. Its philosophy decrees that children learn to use their hands in conjunction with their brains and to associate dignity with labor. Perhaps the most significant feature of the school, however, is its emphasis on service to the community. The late Dr. Tao was the originator of the "little teacher" movement by which school children go out to teach other children and adults. The Yu Tsai school practices this doctrine with great success.

Another significant experiment in education is conducted by the Chinese Industrial Co-operative Movement in the Baillie schools. These schools are basically technical schools, but of a strikingly new type. Since their purpose is to train effective community leaders as well as to provide technicians for the industrial co-operatives, the curriculum is flexible, permitting development according to the aptitude of the individual. Each of the several Baillie schools consists of a small group of instructors and a number of boys selected from among the sons of members of the industrial co-operatives, plus some orphans, all living together as a common work and study group with emphasis on the management of their own affairs by the students. Into these schools come flea-ridden young boys with little education and limited opportunities, and out of them go clean young men who have learned how to live and work in a group, who know a great deal about the world, even though their information is necessarily secondhand, and who have the capacity to develop into effective leaders.

A third type of experiment has been the expansion of conventional types of technical middle schools modeled after Western technical high schools. They are experimental only in the sense that they are relatively new to the Chinese educational system. Some of the best have been developed in southeastern China. None is well equipped, nor do they provide as thorough or varied a training as they should, but their future development can provide a badly needed group of skilled technicians.

Higher education in China more than doubled in volume during and in spite of the war, although it too has had to accept lowered standards. When the last imperial dynasty was overthrown in 1911, the college scene was drab indeed, with a few Chinese colleges enrolling only a few thousand students. By 1936-1937, in all China, 108 colleges, universities, and technical schools of college grade were registered with the Ministry of Education. In the academic year of 1936-1937, 41,922 college students were enrolled and 9,154 were graduated. In 1944-1945 there were 145 institutions of higher learning in unoccupied China alone, with 73,669 students enrolled and 10,514 graduating. The rehabilitation of institutions after the war has brought the total number of colleges and universities to 182 and the total number of students enrolled to approximately 110,000. These figures do not include the twenty-seven research institutes and graduate schools above college grade.

With the rate of college graduations exceeding 10,000 a year the total number of college-trained people in China is still probably not more than 250,000, including those who have studied abroad. This total number, which includes a number of people retired from private life or approaching retirement age, is less than half the number graduating from college *each year* in the United States.

The supply of modern trained leadership that China now possesses is totally inadequate to modernize her society. The scarcity of medical and health personnel is an example. In 1943-1944 there were 8,329 students graduated from academic colleges and universities as distinct from technical colleges. If all these students were to enter medical training, and if all were to graduate, it would require thirteen years to supply the number of doctors China needs.

Similarly, China has only about 10,000 engineers of all types in her brain barrel. In America, during World War II, 202,400 people, highly trained in the engineering fields, were registered by the National Roster of Scientific and Specialized Personnel, a ratio of one engineer to each 650 of our population. In order to equal this ratio, China would have to train 778,461 engineers.

From top to bottom, China's education structure is far too small to provide the level of literacy and technical development she urgently needs.

It was the realization that China needed modern technology that resulted in the decree of 1905, which removed the classical examinations. The general shift from humanities to technology has not diminished since that time.

Most Chinese colleges and universities provide what might be called a liberal arts course. However, specialization starts not only with a first-year separation of arts from science courses, but also includes a further division into departments from the very beginning. A student taking an entrance examination for the freshman arts curriculum must state whether he wishes to enter the Chinese Language and Literature Department, the Economics Department, the Sociology Department, or some other department, the subjects required and the subjects elected being determined by his choice of department. The tendency has been toward too early and too thorough specialization. For example, the required curriculum in biology a few years ago was so concentrated in biological subjects that students majoring in biology had more courses in the field during their undergraduate years than I had taken after completing my Sc.D. in biology in the United States.

This overspecialization is now in the process of being modified.

Even with its weaknesses and lack of balance, the curriculum of the modern Chinese university is a far cry from the scholarly studies of years gone by—and many times more useful.

What of the quality of the average Chinese college student? How does he compare with the average American student?

Students in China, like students anywhere, range from the very brilliant to the relatively stupid. On the average their intellectual abilities match those of students in any American college of high academic standing. In terms of application to work and effort to learn, they average considerably better than American students. American teachers who have taught both Americans and Chinese rate the Chinese as a group somewhat better students than the Americans, and those who have studied in the United States have made consistently better records than any other national group. They are influenced by the long tradition of extreme diligence and discipline imposed by the difficulties of the old classical education and held as the proper qualities of a scholar. In addition they are impelled to great effort by the realization that they are members of a small and highly privileged group with opportunities rare and enviable in China. The paucity of college-trained men in China in relation to a plethora of manpower caused the Chinese government to request that students refrain from active participation in the last Sino-Japanese War. Their potential value as leaders was considered far in excess of their actual value as officers and soldiers.

The change, within forty years, from an educational system that was a veneer of highly refined, almost superficial, philosophical contemplation, possessed of no more than a few institutions of college grade into a network of comparatively modern public schools and colleges numbering at least 510,000 units and bringing some degree of enlightenment to at least 75,000,000 common people, is a stride worthy of historical note. There remains, however, a herculean and expensive task to bring China to the educational level of a modern nation.

Lewis S. C. Smythe, in the personalized article which follows, re-emphasizes the part played by Western education in the changes within China. He also has astute observations to make regarding the coming to power of the Communist regime, which he observed at first hand, and he indicates signs of present dissatisfaction among peasant groups with some of the measures now being carried out.

• 21 • Recent Social Changes in China
LEWIS S. C. SMYTHE

CHANGES IN FAMILY LIFE

When I first went to China in the fall of 1928 the students in my class on The Family were debating very hotly two issues: (1) Should sons and daughters have the right to choose their own mates for marriage? Up till about that time the parents had chosen the mates for their sons and daughters. (2) Should girls be treated equally with boys, or women equally with men, in society? By the time that the Sino-Japanese War ended in

[This article was prepared especially for this book by Dr. Smythe, a trained sociologist, who is now Professor of Christian Community at the College of the Bible, Lexington, Kentucky.]

1945 these two questions had been answered in the affirmative among educated groups in the cities. But in country districts, which include over 80 per cent of the population, and among worker groups the old order still prevailed for most members of these groups. The Provisional Code of the Nationalist Republic of China, dated 1931, had granted equality in family matters to women, had granted free choice of mates to sons and daughters on reaching the legal age of 20, and had outlawed the old system of concubinage. But family matters were still handled by families and clans and not according to a Nationalist law book.

When the Chinese Communists took over the government on the mainland of China, many Chinese expected them to "destroy the family" in a manner similar to the Soviet attack on the family in the early years of the Russian Revolution. But contrary to expectations, they were content to legalize the long-standing revolt of the educated groups against the domination of their elders, and especially of the older men. The Marriage Law of the People's Republic of China, promulgated by the Central People's Government on May 1, 1950, was based on the following general principles:

> The arbitrary and compulsory feudal marriage system, which is based on the superiority of man over woman and which ignores the children's interests, is abolished.
> The New Democratic marriage system which is based on free choice of partners, on monogamy, on equal rights for both sexes, and on protection of the lawful interests of women and children, shall be put into effect.
> Polygamy, concubinage, child betrothal, interference with the remarriage of widows and the exaction of money or gifts in connection with marriage shall be prohibited.
> (From an English translation provided the author by Dr. Theodore H. E. Chen, Division of Asiatic Studies, University of Southern California.)

Before I left China in February, 1951, the Communists were having some difficulty in putting this new marriage law into effect in an area where they probably least expected it. The chief difference between their law and that of the Nationalist Government of 1931 was that, instead of specifying every detail, they left many matters to be decided by the local authorities. But they did specify that a man must be 20 years of age and a woman 18 years of age before marrying. In Shantung when their cadres [trained Communist party workers] went into rural districts to educate the people in the new marriage law, they found that some girls under 18 had been married after the law was promulgated. The cadres said the marriages would have to be annulled. But the local people said, in effect, "Not on your life; our girls were decently married." There were also murmurs against treating women as equal to men and against allowing young people to choose their own mates.

The only thing in the Chinese Communist marriage law that would be questioned by Americans is its provision for divorce by mutual consent. Since about 90 per cent of American divorce cases are not contested, it looks as though we do in fact what the Chinese Communists legalize but are not able to carry out in fact.

When it comes to the question of what is the cause of these changes in the family life of China, the experts disagree. The latest study, that by Marion J. Levy, attributes it to the effect of industrialization. But as indicated above, I found that the change began in the educated classes and those groups of Chinese that had either studied in Western countries or had had considerable contact with Western ideas. However, LaPiere and Wang beat me to the documentation of this idea in an article in the *American Journal of Sociology* in 1931. When Olga Lang was studying the Chinese family in China in the early 1930's she found that worker groups had in fact the basis for equality of women but in tradition and practice did not make effective their equality. The Communist marriage law was codified by a group of intellectual and professional revolutionaries and not by either the workers or peasants of China! And it is based on Western practice, even while they are criticizing the West!

CHANGES IN ATTITUDES TOWARD "PROGRESS"

In the spring of 1946 a Chinese colleague and I were studying a market town near Chengtu, Szechwan, where most of the land was owned by two large Taoist monasteries. In order to get some historical perspective, we interviewed the leading abbot and asked him what was the most fundamental change that had occurred in the area during the Sino-Japanese War; that is, during the previous 10 years. He startled us by saying: "Before the war these local people were mainly interested in local law suits. Now they are mainly interested in progress." Further inquiry found that it was what we call "material progress," new bus lines, etc., but it also included Western-style education from elementary school up through college and university. The great movements of population during the recent Sino-Japanese War had brought new roads, auto trucks, busses, airplanes (for freight, passengers, and bombs), radio, radio-telephone, more newspapers with more world news; students, intellectuals, missionaries, Christians from East China and more Westerners including G.I.'s; new economic organization in the form of rural credit, consumer, and industrial cooperatives, modern banking; and numerous effects of Western and modern products too numerous to mention. These streams of new and modernizing influences flowed by plane to the larger cities, by trucks and busses to market towns, by wheelbarrow and ricksha from there to the villages. But the total ferment was tremendous.

LAND REFORMS

And yet in the midst of all this ferment, one very fundamental situation in West China remained unchanged; the ownership and control of agricultural land. The only change that occurred was that Nationalist generals got control of more land during inflation than the previous local war lords. But this only strengthened and entrenched the old system. When the Nationalist Army first introduced a modern method of training its soldiers in Szechwan, they included a scientific, balanced diet. To their surprise the boys from the peasant households got fatter and stronger on army fare than they had in their homes where most of the crop had gone to the landlord. General Stillwell and others in India demonstrated that these peasant lads, taken straight from the farms, could learn to handle modern tanks more quickly than anybody had dreamed. On their little farms the only power, besides human power, had been oxen and water buffalo. They were glad to risk the high flight over the Hump without oxygen masks in order to secure the better uniforms and food in India.

Sun Yat-sen, known as the "Father of the Chinese Republic" (established by the Revolution of 1911), in his book *The Three People's Principles* (The People's Livelihood, Nationalism, and Democracy), 1924, had set the pattern for the Nationalist Revolution of 1926. He preached a principle of land reform for China: "The cultivator shall own the land he cultivates." The Nationalist Party Congress in 1928 adopted this principle but when the Chinese Communists were threatening the Yangtze Valley in 1948, twenty years later, nothing had been done about it. Meanwhile, the Chinese Communists who had been allied with the Nationalists before 1927, had set up a small area of their own in southern Kiangsi province but were driven out of there by the Nationalist armies in 1934 and made the "Long March" to Shensi province in northwest China. There from 1934 to the end of the Sino-Japanese War in August, 1945, they had experimented with a program that would suit the Chinese peasants. Sun Yat-sen's principle was adopted and put into operation. After the Chinese Communists had conquered all the mainland of China by the end of 1949, they set about carrying out land reform in all parts of their realm. The procedure was to send a group of "experts" into an area smaller than a county and survey the whole situation. Any recalcitrant landlords that did not see the light of the new day were eliminated by various means. Then the land was divided to each family according to the number of mouths. As Hsiao-t'ung Fei pointed out in *Earthbound China,* this did not change the *average* size of land holding, 3.5 acres, but it did level up the land holding of the poorer peasants and gave land to some of the landless proletariat commonly found in many parts of China. Theoretically the landlords received equal treatment. But the Chinese Communists knew the prestige and the social and political power of former landlords in local areas. Consequently, they often put the landlord under a form of house arrest, took all his crops and animals, and then fed his family with a rice dole from month to month. But it was not only the large landlord that was dissatisfied. Anyone that had had more than the average of three and one-half acres of land, felt that he had lost by the deal. Because of the costly military program, the Peiping (Communist) government had to continue high taxes on farmers. The first year in many areas they took a hundred per cent of the rice crop. Consequently, many farmers said, "We received paper deeds for land that we were already cultivating as tenants and lost all our rice crop!" In some instances they turned down improved seed because they said if they used it their land would be given a higher productive rating and their tax rate would be higher.

Life magazine for December 31, 1951, had a very interesting account of how the Chinese Communists had studied an area in northwest China where land reform had been carried out five years before. They found that some peasants had sold their land for marriages and other expenses; while other peasants had bought land and become rich. The Communists said that they would have to concentrate on eliminating "the peasants' bad self-generated tendencies." A strange conclusion for a party that proclaims the ideology that people's ideas are but the reflection of their economic condition. The complete summary of results of this survey is worth quoting because it shows so many sidelights on Chinese village life today as well as attitudes of the Chinese Communists:

The surveyors reported that the peasants were eating more now, that literacy had increased notably among both children and adults, that the keeping of diaries (which the police like) had become "a mass movement," that village hygiene has improved, that "sexual promiscuity has been reduced 74%," that men beat their wives less frequently and that "drowning of girl babies has stopped." But the old class distinctions have been re-emerging. The investigators were surprised to find that 96 peasant families had sold land to pay for wedding and funeral expenses, an affront to the new social order. About 20% of the peasants had become poor again; an equal percentage "obviously wealthy." This was blamed on the fact that 99 family heads had increased their land holdings, causing prices to rise. They had even begun lending money to less fortunate peasants at the usurious rate of 60% per annum. Peking newspapers discussed the survey tellingly. "Our problem," said the Peking *People's Daily,* "is to find out how to sweep away the decadent dirt from people's consciousness. We must pay close attention to the thought transformation of peasants. We cannot let the peasants' bad self-generated tendencies go unguided."

Actually, the Chinese Communists have not been satisfied with a purely economic sort of Marxism. From the very beginning they have put a great deal of emphasis upon thought transformation, what we call "indoctrination," of the people, from the ignorant peasant to the most educated intellectual, in both city and country. Before I left China "brain washing" was so common that servant women or peasant women walking along the road could be heard to ask each other, "Have you had your mind changed yet?"

CHANGES IN DRESS

A lighter side of wars and revolutions is the "uniform" various groups wear. The first Revolution, in 1911, compelled most Chinese men to have their queues cut off. The Nationalist Revolution in 1926 made most of the educated and urban girls bob their hair. Later the Nationalist officials affected Western-style clothes, well-polished leather shoes, a felt hat, and invariably a cane with a big curved handle. When the Communists came in, they made very simple clothes the order of the day. Later everyone, men and women alike, was supposed to wear a cotton cap, padded trousers and jacket of a dull gray color. But at first only the so-called "progressives," that is, those who sympathized with the new regime or were opportunists and wanted to get a job, wore the garb of the new order. People would discuss a man and say, "He must have joined them because he wears the outfit." But some of those who put on the "uniform" earliest said, "You have to pretend in order to live now," "Not all that glitters is gold," and "Not all who wear the uniform accept the doctrine."

One high school principal told me that shortly after the 1926 Revolution, he saw the foreign-style cap of the first boy who dared to wear one to school kicked around the school yard. All the other boys wore the old-style Chinese dome cap with a button on top. About 1946 the same principal told me that he had seen the last Chinese button cap kicked around the school yard! When I first went to China the men college students wore long silk gowns with flowing sleeves, satin slippers, and either those dome buttoned hats or no hat. Just before the Communists came, both high school and college students were wearing khaki western-style trousers, shirts with no tie and sleeves rolled up, and leather or tennis shoes. Under the Nationalists the Chinese girls wore permanent waves, but shortly before I left I saw Chinese girls in barber shops having their hair cut Communist-style with

long straight bobs, and getting as much enjoyment out of it as they had out of the permanents! The "uniform," including hair-do and cap, provides an easily recognizable symbol of those who want to appear like-minded, just as the bobby-soxers do in America.

CHANGES IN RECREATION AND FESTIVALS

In the old Chinese villages very few of the people could read. So the historical events and novels were repeated over and over in story form by story tellers in the teashops—from which teashops, women of class were excluded, regardless of the type of story. They had to get their stories through gossip. But all could attend the village drama performed on an open air stage with the crowd on the village common. Audio-visual experts in the Nationalist era in China capitalized on this practice by simply putting up a screen and showing movies out of doors to vast crowds. The Chinese Communists brought the new ideas, including caricaturing Nationalist foibles and evils, to the peasants and city workers by all forms of drama and dances. On April 1, 1949, Communist sympathizers organized a parade of college students in Nanking and taught them to dance the "Yang-ko," a dance they probably copied from the tribespeople of west China on their long march. A group of boys dance back and forth to a group of girls. *Life* magazine showed pictures of it being danced in the streets of Shanghai when that city fell to the Communists in May, 1949. But a year later in Nanking when our students were preparing for the May Day parade, they were told that the "Yang-ko" was forbidden because it was "too primitive for China." However, school groups were encouraged to use the "Yao-ku," or back drum. It is a pity that Chinese boys have not had a drum for about 9,000 years! It looked at one time as though the long, barrel-shaped, red drum would be the most lasting symbol of the Communist order. But before I left, the families had begun to frown on their children using the drums unless the family accepted the new ideology. Another "uniform"! So Chinese boys whose families do not accept Communist ideology will have to wait for the toys they crave until their parents go through the long process of becoming politically reliable as shown by their shirts, clothes, hair-dos, and caps. Thus it is that fashions, fads, ideologies, forms of industrial organization, military procedures, and many other things change in human life according to psycho-social laws and the shifting panorama provides zest to the life of all and grist for the sociologist's mill.

Festivals have been treated in very much the same way as uniforms. The Nationalists started out to modernize China by making the Chinese coolie wear a shirt in hot weather and abolishing all the old festival practices which they labelled "superstitious." The "foreign New Year" (i. e., January 1st) was given great favor and much celebration while college students were made to attend school all day of the old China New Year (geared to the moon, like our Easter, usually occurring around February 1st). When the Chinese Communists came in they reversed this and put great emphasis upon the old festivals to appeal to the peasants and workers but modernized the Nationalists' practice of counting years from the first revolution, 1911, and used the system of counting years in a "scientific way," from the birth of Christ!

REGIONALISM

The Nationalists fought any attempt to recognize old regions in China. They feared sectionalism which troubled the United States so much in the Nineteenth Century. But since China, with its inadequate transportation system, is too large to govern easily from one center, the Chinese Communists changed this and installed seven regional governments including several provinces in each region. Manchuria, formerly with three provinces, was one of the first so organized. It gave rise to the idea that Manchuria was going to be separated from the rest of China. The intervention of the Peiping Government in the

struggle in Korea probably ended that danger, if there ever was one, because it has brought about another big mass migration of soldiers from what used to be called "China Proper" to Manchuria and campaigns are put on all over the country to buy Russian equipment for Chinese so-called "volunteers" going to Korea by way of Manchuria.

CHANGES STILL IN STORE

What the next cycle of change will be a sociologist cannot tell even though he would like to become a modern prophet and be able to predict. Before I left China a year ago, Chinese wags were saying, "The Nationalists deteriorated in twenty years; will the Communists last that long?" Or, "The Communists are so much more efficient than the Nationalists that they ought to be able to bring about their own deterioration in less time." Revolutionaries have worked too hard for their victory to give up easily. And the Chinese Communists have a peculiar faculty when not succeeding in one way of trying another. It is a new phenomenon in the rather indifferent China of the Nineteenth Century, but it is well to remember that other countries have changed greatly too in the past century.

We have confined this discussion to indigenous changes in China, although some of them resulted from imported ideas. Even the Japanese invasion of China, 1937-1945, brought only slight changes. In 1946 when we got back to Nanking, we were surprised to find that very few things remained of Japanese culture. Most of their illegitimate babies had been suffocated at birth by their Chinese mothers. Their beer halls, opium dens, and Geisha girls had vanished. All that was left in Nanking was the addition of a door to control the draft on the "flower-pot" stove—literally a large earthen flower pot with a grate in it used as a table stove. A few Chinese had inherited Japanese dogs, and the Chinese army had a few Japanese horses. Everything else had "Gone With The Wind." But the Nationalist government in Chungking had copied some of the police control methods of the Japanese! They copied the Japanese in requiring every Chinese, as well as foreigners, to have a "Peaceful Citizen's Pass." When the Communists came in they not only took over the system but used the Nationalist passes more than a year! Since then the Chinese Communist government has done everything in its power to strengthen its control over the Chinese people on China's mainland. How many of their changes will remain after a few years, only a prophet can foretell!

Conclusion

In preceding selections, we have seen that the Chinese peasant is still bound to the land, even though often he does not own the land that he tills so laboriously. The population of China is enormous, but relatively few of its people live in cities. The peasants of China most commonly live in villages, which are made up of closely knit family units. For purposes of mutual aid and defense and for the observance of public ceremonies the families of a village work together. But it is expected that an individual will find most of his security against life's misfortunes, will make his living, and will find most of his joys and satisfactions within the confines of his own family group rather than as a member of some larger social unit.

The last selections have shown us the Chinese peasant trying to adjust to new forces which are sweeping the world. He is giving up subsistence farming for the more risky commercial farming in the expectation of greater returns. The local industries on which many villagers have depended for an important part of their livelihood are being destroyed by the penetration of industrial products from the cities. New ideas and ambitions are replacing those that have for centuries been passed from parents to children in a firm and unbroken tradition. China, like the rest of the world, is caught up in violent and sometimes uncontrollable changes.

The Chinese Communists called upon the Chinese peasant to participate both in mass movements and in the army engaged in fighting the United Nations. But still he and his family at home suffer very much the same fate that their ancestors have borne for centuries: they are invited to "participate" in producing food, clothing, and babies; in carrying out the government's mass organization either for public works or for propaganda purposes; and in fighting the Communists' battles for them. But again they find to their sorrow that it is "participation without representation." The directing ideas and the program are all decided in the "emperor's courts" in Peking. A new "mandarinate," which is more powerful than the old one, has penetrated the whole country and night and day watches every villager to see that he does what he has been ordered to do by the same old Peking. But in order to evoke greater effort from more peasants than ever before, these new masters have had to use methods that are slowly but surely arousing the minds of the peasants. Participation in mass movements and in foreign wars is changing their sons so that they will never again be content to settle down in the old village and follow the plow. In time, they too will demand, "No participation and no taxation without representation."

The heavy hand of the centuries bears down on the modern Chinese peasant. China has long seen an oft-repeated cycle which is well described by Olga Lang in *Chinese Family and Society* (p. 7, New Haven, 1946):

> The peasants supported the state and the ruling class with a part of the product of their labor. This was delivered in the form of taxes rather than of rent paid to the landlord. But the system of private landed property which prevailed under the empire led unavoidably to the accumulation of lands in the hands of the landlords who were powerful enough to refuse to pay taxes to the central government. This resulted in the weakening of the state, in agrarian crises, many peasant rebellions, dynastic changes, and foreign invasions and conquests. The long history of China abounds in such dramatic events.
>
> A new dynasty usually began by redistributing the land among the peasants, thus solving the agrarian crisis and strengthening the state machine. But the fundamental social structure with all its weaknesses remained, and soon a new crisis arose.

In other words, as the landlords grew stronger, the government grew weaker. Then, when a strong government was formed and was able to collect its share—or more than its share—of the surplus created by peasant labor, the landlords lost much of their power, if not their lives. But what about the peasant? He was as badly off under one system as the other: he gave the surplus either to the landlord as rent or to the government as taxes. Thus far, the Chinese Communists have simply carried out a strong-government phase of this cycle.

J. H. Boeke (*American Journal of Sociology*, 1952) has compared three attempts to improve the lot of the people of southeast Asia. He points out that both redivision of the land and the Western method of setting up large industries will fail to lift the level of living of the poverty-stricken masses. Boeke urges, instead, helping the Asian peoples to work out democratically their own solutions not only of the land problem but also of agricultural and industrial cooperative programs, educational and cultural development, and governmental reforms. For this a knowledge of the social traits of the people and of the processes of social change will be indispensable.

THE COTTON SOUTH

The old Cotton South depended, in an economic sense, on an enormous production of a single crop which was in great demand in the world market. Means of production were relatively inefficient, especially the use of a vast, unskilled labor force—first Negro slaves and then free Negroes (*top*). Today, not only is cotton growing moving westward, to states where cotton can be grown under irrigation, but the mechanical cotton picker (*bottom*) is working a revolution in the states making up the Cotton South. A tremendous labor force is being released for other occupations—and for migration to other parts of the United States.

The development of industry in the South has been so rapid and so extensive that many Southerners are themselves not completely aware of the change. In the chemical industries, development has been particularly rapid. *Top:* Part of the installations at Decatur, Ala., for the manufacture of Acrilan, one of the new synthetic fibers. Such plants find the South suitable because of the mild climate, the availability of labor, and, in many instances, the accessibility of raw materials. The textile industry (*bottom,* a mill in North Carolina), began its shift to the South somewhat earlier, but for the same reasons.

A greater contrast could hardly be found in any region than is reflected in these two pictures. *Above:* The country store, operated by a white storekeeper, serves as one of the few meeting places for the Negroes of the community. As a social center it obviously leaves much to be desired; it represents the wretched conditions under which a large part of the people of the South pass their lives. *Below:* A mansion built before the Civil War is reminiscent of the South of "magnolias and moonlight," the life of a few aristocrats, never shared by either the slaves or the "poor whites."

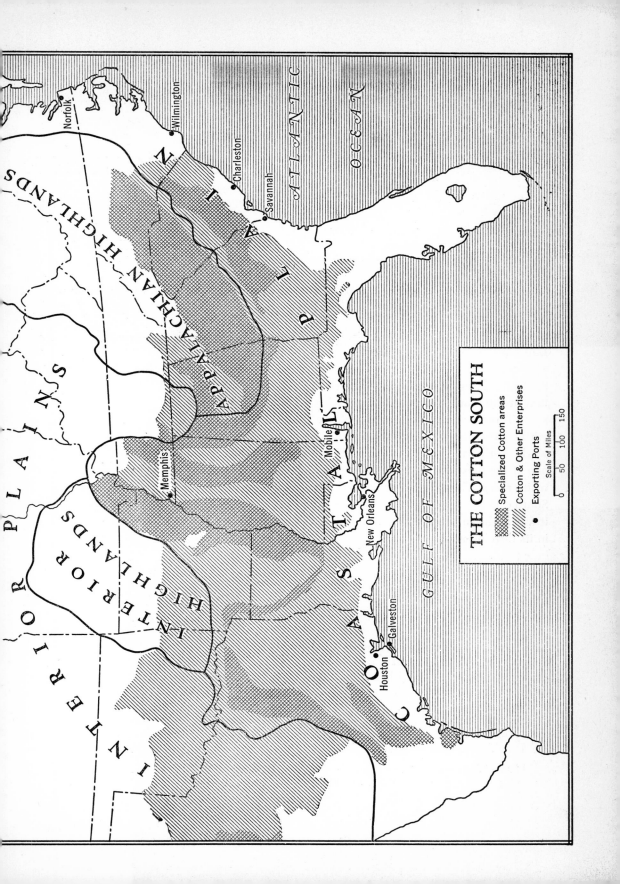

THE COTTON SOUTH

Specialized Cotton areas

Cotton & Other Enterprises

● Exporting Ports

Scale of Miles

0   50   100   150

ATLANTIC OCEAN

GULF OF MEXICO

PLAIN

APPALACHIAN HIGHLANDS

INTERIOR HIGHLANDS

INTERIOR PLAINS

COASTAL

Norfolk

Wilmington

Charleston

Savannah

Memphis

Mobile

New Orleans

Galveston

Houston

Introduction

»»

Life in the Cotton South presents some interesting contrasts to the Chinese peasant way of life. Both regions are agricultural, to be sure, but from its early settlement the Cotton South has stressed cash crops rather than self-subsistent farming. Furthermore, the tradition of the plantation system has strongly influenced Southern life and thought.

Too often we think of the plantation South as an isolated historical development, without realizing that it resembles a type of society still dominant in several areas of the world; furthermore, it is well to remember that the plantation system has in the past been one of the most usual media through which colored races have come into contact with the white races. The careful reader will notice that in a few details the plantation of the Old South differed from typical modern plantations, described below. In part, this was because it was in the subtropics rather than the tropics and, in part, because of historical differences in its development.

• 22 • The Plantation System
GEORGE McC. McBRIDE

The term plantation was originally used to designate a plot of ground set with plants; during the period of British colonization of the West Indies and North America it came to denote a group of settlers or even the political unit constructed by such a group. Thus the colony of Rhode Island was long known as the Providence Plantations, the colonies in the West Indies as the Caribbean Plantations. . . . As overseas possessions came to be called colonies the term plantation was restricted to the large scale agricultural units in the warmer climates. It is commonly applied moreover only to a property producing a single crop or possibly two crops grown primarily for export. Plantations accordingly are

[From "Plantation," *Encyclopaedia of the Social Sciences,* Vol. 12, Macmillan, New York, 1937. Pp. 148-153. Used by permission.]

a form of great landed estate, usually in colonial or semicolonial countries, which raise such tropical or semitropical products as cotton, sugar, rubber, coffee, tea, rice, pineapples and bananas, with a laboring class kept in economic if not political servitude.

Plantations are essentially tropical institutions; they are not found in regions where winters are cold or where altitude results in year round temperatures too low for the typical plantation crops. Only in location, however, is the plantation tropical: the owners and managers are mostly from the middle latitudes, the laborers alone being from the warm lands to which its crops belong. It represents therefore an invasion of the tropics prompted by the growing desire among nontropical peoples for the objects (mainly edible, but including two important industrial raw materials, cotton and rubber) which only the warmer lands can furnish. Plantations are intimately bound up with colonial and imperialist conquest and exploitation.

[This pattern of exploitation is giving way, in many parts of the world, to attempts at improvement of technically underdeveloped areas. Ellsworth Huntington describes this in optimistic—and rather ethnocentric—terms in *Principles of Human Geography* (6th ed., p. 480) as follows:

On the best and most profitable plantations the employees are obliged to live in better houses and take better care of health and sanitation than tropical people ever thought of before. Drains are dug, stagnant pools are filled, and other measures taken to get rid of mosquitoes and other disease-bearing insects. Machinery is introduced, and the natives are taught to use it. At first they are rarely competent for any but the simplest tasks. Little by little, however, they acquire skill and industry. Preference is given to those who work regularly, keep their huts neat, obey health regulations, and show evidence of willingness and ability to learn the more complicated methods of the white man. Incentives to progress include the desire to imitate the white man

as well as to purchase some of the luxuries displayed in company stores.]

PLANTATIONS IN THE SOUTHERN STATES

In the British North American colonies the plantations of the south at first depended upon growing tobacco, but precedence was soon yielded to cotton. While these plantations were bound up with the colonial system, they lost their colonial character after the War of Independence and never acquired an imperialist character; but their general economic and labor relations bear striking similarity to those of plantations in colonial and semicolonial countries. Originally the plantations relied for labor upon free or indentured white laborers; but their persistence and expansion were made possible by Negro slavery, without which the plantations could not have developed as they did notwithstanding favorable climatic conditions. The planters, a small group owning millions of slaves, became a sectional ruling class, dominating the economics and politics of the southern states until their power was broken by the Civil War. The abolition of slavery imposed new relations between master and man. Many of the plantations ceased to exist; others, however, adjusted themselves to the changed conditions and operated with Negro tenants, croppers or cash renters; while still others employed their former slaves at a nominal wage or under a system of peonage. In all these cases the laborers were still in a semiservile state. Moreover, while the plantation was usually divided into tracts or parcels of land, instead of being cultivated as a whole by gangs of laborers under direct control of an overseer, it did not lose its distinguishing feature of unified supervision over the choice of crop, the methods of cultivation and the marketing of the yield. In this form the plantation continues to exist in the American south, where it is the characteristic agricultural type.

There are few plantations in the United States north of the Mason and Dixon's line; in climatic rather than in political terms, almost none are found far enough north to have fewer than two hundred days of frostless season. The usual plantation crops, if raised beyond this frost line, are grown on small holdings or with independent laborers. Westward, too, of such a line which passes through northwest Oklahoma and cuts off the western third of Texas the plantation is practically unknown; it is supplanted by the cattle ranch or the irrigation farm, reappearing only, and then in small numbers and in a modified form, upon the delta of the Colorado River and in the mild climate of California. While plantations are thus limited almost entirely to the southern states, none is found in the hill country or in the less fertile areas, where agriculture is carried on in other forms. The plantations are restricted to the regions where soil is best and where land is level or nearly level. . . .

PLANTATIONS IN OTHER REGIONS

Plantations in the West Indies developed sugar as their principal crop. In Cuba, Porto Rico and several of the other islands of the Lesser Antilles the plantation is still the customary unit of production for this commodity. Tobacco figures, although not as prominently. . . . It was as sugar estates that these islands first became of value to the British, the French, the Dutch and to a lesser degree to the Spaniards. Throughout their history the plantations have played a conspicuous part and planters have largely dominated in all affairs. In Jamaica during the seventeenth and eighteenth centuries most of the cultivated land was in this form; much the same was true in the Barbados and other British islands. Many of the plantations disappeared with the rise in the price of slaves, the numerous Negro insurrections and finally the abolition of slavery, but many still survive. In Cuba most of the sugar growing, which makes that island the foremost producer in the world, is carried on under the plantation system with hired labor but under conditions that leave little economic independence to the laborer. Many of the sugar plantations are owned by American capital, which dominates the sugar industry as a whole.

* * *

South America's agricultural holdings, despite their large extent, belong, like those of Mexico and Central America, mainly to the hacienda [mixed farming] class. In a few regions, however, agriculture is of the plantation type. The coffee estates of Brazil and Colombia constitute the bulk of this kind of property, although in the latter country much of the coffee grown is on small holdings. In Brazil the coffee *fazendas,* as distinguished from the many small farms which also grow this plant and from the great estates given over to stock raising or mixed farming, are definitely in the plantation class. Most of the coffee exported from the country is the product of these large properties, where thousands of acres are devoted to a single crop and where the land is worked by low class labor and owned and administered in huge units. . . .

In the British and Portuguese possessions of tropical east and west Africa there are many large plantations owned by Europeans and worked under their supervision by native laborers; the chief crops are cotton, sugar, maize, tobacco and coconuts. Cotton is grown also upon enormous plantations in . . . the Sudan and in other sections along the Nile. American tire interests have for some time contemplated the development of huge rubber plantations in Liberia. . . .

The plantations of the Hawaiian Islands are devoted to two principal export crops, sugar and pineapples. Their combined acreage constitutes probably 50 per cent of all the improved land on the islands. Ownership and management are in the hands of Americans, while Asiatic labor is used generally. Plantations are maintained in a few other islands of the Pacific, native labor being employed to cultivate such crops as coconuts, sugar and rice.

The plantation is the typical unit for the raising of export products in India, Indo-China, the Straits Settlements and the Dutch East Indies. It is devoted mainly to rubber, sugar, tea, coffee, tobacco, rice and coconuts, which are for the most part produced on large holdings, real plantations in the strict meaning of the word.

* * *

The plantation has come into far greater prominence within the last half century. This development has been made possible by the improvement in ocean transportation, including refrigeration and ventilation systems, which permit the shipping of products to the distant regions where large industrial populations are concentrated. The demand for automobile tires has fostered the growth of rubber cultivation. In recent decades the extension of plantations has far outstripped older types of agriculture, including the one-family farm. Most of the plantations in such regions as the Straits Settlements, the Caribbean coasts of Central and South America, and Brazil date from the beginning of the twentieth century. If the demand for tropical products continues to increase, it is probable that the plantation system will be still more widely extended.

* * *

SOCIAL TRAITS OF THE PLANTATION SYSTEM

A plantation society develops a character of its own. The native order is usually disrupted seriously, as families or members of families are uprooted and moved into a new environment, under new superiors who know little of the hereditary customs and institutions of their laborers. In this new setting people of diverse customs must adjust their ways to the habits of their fellows. Such a mingling was strikingly apparent in the slave communities of the southern United States, where Negroes from several parts of Africa were assembled without regard to the differences among them and where the elements of several diverse primitive cultures were further modified by the white civilization into which they had been introduced. The planters' culture too suffered a modification, its

language, customs, art, music, literature and even its religion being affected by the slaves. Much the same situation existed in the plantations of Brazil and the West Indies. Something of this social amalgamation is in process in Malaya, where Indian, Javanese and Chinese laborers meet under supervision of Anglo-Saxon, Japanese or Chinese planters, and in Hawaii, where Hawaiian, European and Asiatic cultures mingle.

At the same time the plantation exerts a conspicuous influence in its introduction of new tools, machinery, systems of wages, fashions in clothing, standards of living, notions of sanitation, types of organization, methods of work, sometimes educational institutions and ideas and not infrequently religious beliefs and practices. The effect of these changes is extended beyond the bounds of the plantation and helps to mold the general social order of the district. . . .

A further consequence, and one which seems inherent in the system, is the stratification of society. Upon the plantation and in a plantation society there is a sharp differentiation between the upper class, represented by the owners and the higher (particularly the white) agents of the plantation, and the laboring class. As the line of cleavage between the upper and lower classes is at least partly racial as well as economic, it becomes firmly fixed and individuals seldom pass from one to the other. This division runs through all phases of life, economic, social and political. The laborer may be completely free and still considered of a lower order. The higher foreign employees may be of low social origin in their native land, yet on the plantation they belong distinctly to the upper class. . . . Where such a class division becomes typical of the agricultural population, it inevitably characterizes most if not all of the spheres of life, since the planters generally dominate all circles of society. These differences are emphasized by their introduction into industrial and commercial enterprises, where employees are drawn largely from the rural laboring class and where the lowest foreign employee lords it over the native workers. The aristocracy, mainly agrarian, is sharply separated from the servile class of workers.

In such a social order there is little room for a middle class. The plantation largely markets its own crops; it procures supplies, directly or indirectly, for its entire population; hence the trader class is small and usually dependent upon the estate. Economic groups outside of the plantations are also decidedly limited. The professional class is not numerous. Most of the population bears some relation to the plantation and falls into one or the other of the categories into which its people are divided. Furthermore the plantation tends, precisely as in the old plantation system of the southern United States, to prevent the development of a middle class farming population, in that it crowds out the small agricultural holding. This process was particularly conspicuous in the British West Indies, where the planters made success for the small farmer virtually impossible. The consequent stratification of society results in political oligarchy. In many regions where the plantation regime is established the laborers are imported from other sections and have no more share in governmental affairs than if they were slaves. Such is the status of the laborers from India, China and the Dutch East Indies employed on the plantations of the Middle East, of many laborers on the banana plantations of Central America and on numerous plantations in Africa. Even where the laborer is a native of the region in which he works, he generally has no legal part in the government or, if accorded such rights by law, he has little opportunity of exercising his privileges. The political situation in the southern United States, in Cuba, Java and Malaya, is characteristic of a society built upon a plantation regime.

The political oligarchy of a plantation country is intimately tied up with foreign interests. Where the country is independent the connection is economic and financial, with an indirect political character. The political connection becomes direct where the plantation country occupies a colonial or semicolonial status, as is usually the case. From the beginning the plantation has been a colonizing force, a means of occupying new lands effectively and of initiating their development.

The author of the preceding selection may be considered unduly critical of the plantation system, but his remarks are based on careful study of the situation in all parts of the world. Some of the less attractive features of the system arise because the plantation is often the scene of rapid social change, resulting from the sudden exposure of a simple society to a highly elaborate commercial or industrial society. In southeast Asia, for example, such exposure for only a few generations has helped precipitate violent movements for political and economic independence.

Certain aspects of the plantation system which McBride has mentioned briefly will be the subject of more detailed treatment in the following pages. The people of the Cotton South were colonists, although here the workers as well as the masters came from distant lands. The habitat will be considered, including the semi-tropical features favorable to the plantation system. Besides the economic details of the plantation, we shall note its social effects, which resulted in the extreme social stratification of the Old South. Finally, in order to emphasize the varied aspects and complexities of social change, the Old South will be contrasted with the New South.

The People

>>

The Cotton South, like every other part of the United States, is inhabited by people of extremely diverse origins. The three major racial groups of mankind are represented: Mongoloid, Negroid, and Caucasian. The Indians are Mongoloids who originally reached the New World from Asia. They have now been greatly reduced in numbers and crowded into a few small sections of their former homeland, where many of them have intermarried with Negroes and whites.

The Negroes make up 29 percent of the population of the deep South and somewhat less in the upper South. Constant migration to the North has made the net increase in numbers of the Negroes less than that of the whites, although both groups have maintained a higher birth rate than the rest of the nation. The ancestors of the South's Negro population were brought as slaves from Africa, most of them from the West Coast or the areas adjacent to it. They were sold into slavery by the Negro rulers of the West African kingdoms or were captured and sold by traders from outside. The Negroes brought to the New World did not have either tribal unity or a common language. People from the same locality and even of the same family were purposely separated to prevent their ganging together against the slave holders. Thus very little of Negro African culture was preserved by this population element. There are few genetically pure Negroes in the United States today, since whites and Negroes have mated ever since the introduction of the Negroes. People with any discernible Negroid characteristics have been classified socially as Negroes, even when they are virtually pure white in physical inheritance. Many people of partly Negro ancestry but of Caucasian appearance pass into the white population every year, usually moving to a new area, where their background is not known.

The white population in the South is predominantly descended from European immigrants of the colonial period—English, Scotch, Irish, and German. Few representatives of later migrations from central, southern, and eastern Europe have settled in the area. For this reason, and also because it has remained chiefly rural in economy, the South has retained many ways of life, attitudes, and even patterns of speech which were once common to the United States as a whole but which have been weakened outside the South by the introduction of new cultural strains and by urbanization.

Since the Civil War there has been a steady flow of whites and Negroes to the northern and western United States. This flow was greatly accelerated during the two World Wars, when people of both races sought jobs in the North. Much of western Oklahoma, New Mexico, and Arizona was populated, when these states were still territories, by white Southerners seeking new land and opportunities. The trend westward has continued, with Negroes joining in the move in the last decade, attracted by new developments in both agriculture and industry. However, the growing industrialization of the South is putting a partial halt to this emigration and is even bringing newcomers into the South from other parts of the nation.

Migration to the North, particularly to the cities, has been more constant on the part of the Negro population of the deep South than the white, and even in depression periods the Negro has kept up his search for better opportunities in jobs, schooling, and social position. Many immigrants to the North have undoubtedly been disappointed by finding many of the same attitudes and restrictions that they had hoped to leave behind.

• 23 • People as a Southern Resource
RUPERT B. VANCE, JOHN E. IVEY, JR., AND MARJORIE N. BOND

. . . Anyone who wants to understand the South and the South's place in the nation asks first about the people. Who are the people, and where did they come from? Where do they live? Is there anything about them which is a little different from people in other regions? How well are they using Southern resources?

WHO THE PEOPLE ARE

The South is rich in human wealth. It has a great many people. In 1940 a Census of the United States was taken, and heads were counted all over the country. The nation then had about 132,000,000 people. A few more than 37,000,000 of them were in the South.

Indians are still living in some parts of the South. Oklahoma has more than 60,000. North Carolina has over 20,000. Others are scattered throughout the rest of the region—

one or two hundred in some states, one or two thousand in a few others. Altogether the South has about 95,000 Indians. These are all that remain of the people who first lived here.

The Red Men were not able to hold on to their country, but they left their mark on the land and in the waters of the South. More than half the Southern states have names that come directly or indirectly from the Indians: Kentucky, Tennessee, Alabama, Mississippi, Arkansas, Oklahoma, and Texas. Every state shows traces of its Indian past. Look on a map and you will find the Rappahannock River in Virginia; Currituck Sound, off North Carolina; Saluda in South Carolina; the Chattahoochee River in Georgia; Lake Okeechobee in Florida; Catawba in Kentucky; Chattanooga in Tennessee; Talladega in Alabama; Pelahatchee in Mississippi; the Ouachita Mountains in Arkansas; Tioga in

[From *Exploring the South*, University of North Carolina Press, Chapel Hill, 1949. Pp. 35-45. Used by permission.]

Louisiana; Chickasha in Oklahoma; Comanche in Texas. There are many other examples.

The South had almost 10,000,000 Negroes in 1940. They live in every Southern state, but most of them—about 8,000,000—are in the Southeast. Negroes make up more than a third of the population in Georgia, Alabama, and Louisiana. Over two-fifths of the population in South Carolina and about half the population in Mississippi are Negroes.

In 1940 the white people in the South numbered close to 28,000,000. Texas has more than five million—a larger number than any of the other Southern states. Kentucky, North Carolina, Tennessee, Georgia, Oklahoma, and Virginia each has over two million white people. The other Southern states each has over a million.

Most Southerners are descendants of the people who were already living here before 1800. The Negroes are descendants of freemen and of slaves from Africa. The whites are descendants of the early colonists who came from the British Isles and a few countries on the continent of Europe.

Englishmen were the first to find places for themselves in the new world. Their earliest colony, on the coast of North Carolina, disappeared, but a later settlement in Virginia held its ground. From Virginia the English spread south, where they were joined by Scotsmen. Some of the Scots came straight from their native country. Some lived for a while in Ireland before they reached America. Because of this they are often called Scotch-Irish.

Germans moved to the Southern colonies from Pennsylvania, bumping along in wagons over the rough wilderness roads. Irishmen found their way to various settlements along our coast. French families made new homes in the Carolinas and Louisiana. Those who came to Louisiana from France generally settled in the larger communities, especially New Orleans. Other Frenchmen moved south from a part of Canada which was then called Acadia. These Acadian French, who were rural people, chose the Louisiana back-country.

Few newcomers came to the United States for a number of years after the American Revolution. About the year 1820 people started migrating from Europe again. In the beginning this immigration was gradual, like the trickle of a small stream high up in the mountains. After 1880 immigration increased. From 1900 to 1920 it flowed over the states of the north and into the west like a river in flood.

The South was generally left untouched by this flood of new Americans. Few foreigners have come to our region since 1800. From time to time people move here from other parts of our nation. But most Southerners are descendants of the families who first settled along the coast and then spread toward the south and the west.

WHERE THEY LIVE

People in the South have plenty of room. Within the borders marking the Southern region lie more than a million square miles of land. This is more than a third of the nation's area. On this land are less than a third of the nation's people.

The census shows that more than two-thirds of the people in the region live in the country. Most of them are families who depend on farming for a living. Some of them are people who are not farmers. They are in villages which are not classed as towns because they have less than 2500 people. Or they are gathered around the edges outside the limits of towns and cities where they work.

Less than one-third of the Southern people live in towns or cities. Even this urban part of our population is never very far from the country, for the South has no really big cities. The largest in the region are New Orleans, Houston, Louisville, Atlanta, and Dallas, and not one of these is among the ten largest cities in the nation. This means that all Southerners, in town or country or city, live close to the land.

Resources for farming and resources for manufacturing are like magnets drawing the population to them. People live where they can make a living. Those who work in industry settle close to the factories. Those who farm for a living are spread out over the parts of the South where the land and the climate are suitable for agriculture.

A belt of good soils and plentiful rain curves irregularly through the Shenandoah Valley, the Piedmont, and the Coastal Plain. It rounds the southern tip of the Appalachian Mountains and joins another belt lying between the mountains and the Mississippi. Then it crosses the river into eastern Texas and Oklahoma. Within these belts are most of the Southerners who depend on farming for a living. Many people are crowded onto the land, and the farms are often small.

The Southern population is largest near our industrial centers. Workers cluster around the coal fields of Virginia and Kentucky, the iron ore deposits near Birmingham, Alabama. They settle down in the Piedmont section of Virginia or the Carolinas and get jobs in the factories making textiles or furniture or cigarettes. They live near Atlanta's processing plants and transportation outlets. They move to oil fields and refineries in Texas or Oklahoma or Louisiana. They go to the great port cities of New Orleans or Houston or Norfolk.

Away from the industrial centers and the main agricultural areas the South has fewer people. Population thins out wherever the chances for work are small. This means that not many Southerners are living on the tidewater land close to the coast, in the Everglades of Florida, on the heavily wooded slopes of the mountains, or on the hot dry land in central and western Texas and western Oklahoma.

ARE SOUTHERN PEOPLE DIFFERENT?

Are people in the South different from those in other regions? Travellers who come here and write about their impressions of the South seem to think so. They often say that Southerners are friendlier than people in other parts of the country. Some of these visitors think that we are slower and less energetic, more easygoing. We seem to enjoy life more than other people.

Many Southerners think that they can see differences between the people in one region and another. Listen to the men sitting around in the neighborhood store while they talk about fishing or politics or crops or people. Eventually they start talking about the South. They sometimes say they could never live anywhere else because people in other parts of the country are so different. . . .

The differences that visitors see and Southerners sometimes talk about are impossible to prove. After all, they are only matters of opinion. However, specialists studying the South have found a number of ways in which people in our region really differ from those in other parts of the country. . . . In the first place, our families are larger than those in other regions. Southern people, especially people living in the country, have a great many children. This means, of course, that the South has more children to take care of than any other region. . . .

We have a great many children in the South, but only a small proportion of our population is made up of working men and women of middle age. What happens to all the children we rear? Why have they not grown up into a large group of workers? The fact is this: when Southern children grow up, many of them move away. They go to some other part of the country, hoping for a chance to earn a better living than they might if they stayed at home. . . .

*   *   *

White Southerners take part in this moving if the change means work or perhaps better pay. If there is a depression and jobs are scarce, not so many leave. Southerners working in other parts of the country are among those who lose their jobs. When they have no way of making a living, some of them come back home to hunt for work or scratch a living out of the soil.

In good times and in hard times Negroes are leaving the Southern states. They too are looking for better jobs, better pay, greater opportunity. Few of them ever come back, even in a depression. As a result, the Negro population is increasing faster in some other parts of the country than it is in some of the Southern states.

In 1900, for example, South Carolina had 780,000 Negroes, and in 1940 it had 815,000. After forty years the number had increased by only 35,000. In 1900 New York City had 60,000 Negroes. In 1940 it had 478,000—almost eight times the number in 1900. The industrial cities of the Northeast and the Middle States all now have a large Negro population.

Demographers, or students of population, are not only concerned with the numbers and composition of the people they study—that is, with *quantity;* they also investigate the *quality* of the people from the standpoint of health, education, and the possession of basic occupational skills. In the selection that follows, H. C. Brearley, of George Peabody College, who has been aptly termed by Allen Tate as one of the most objective students of Southern life, analyzes the question "Are Southerners really lazy?" In doing so, he suggests that climate and other habitat factors influence Southern behavior *indirectly* rather than *directly,* that health and nutritional levels are low, and that other cultural considerations must be taken into account.

• 24 • Are Southerners Really Lazy?

H. C. BREARLEY

Among friends and enemies, early and late, the Southerner has been condemned for his "laziness." Back in 1728, William Byrd of Virginia was highly critical of "the slothfulness of the people" of one of the South's many sandy ridges, "where plenty and warm sun confirm them in their disposition to laziness." In 1862, according to an eminent historian, General Robert E. Lee was much disturbed by the inertia of the Southern soldiers whom he was trying to lead in building the fortifications of Richmond. And in 1947, a professor at a Southern university openly defended the thesis, "In the South a man's social status depends upon the amount of hard work he does *not* do."

Surely in these, and in innumerable other criticisms, there must be a modicum of truth. Superficially at least, the Southerner seems to be a person who, to put it mildly, lacks the initiative and persistence of his Yankee rivals. Is the Southerner's inactivity the result of some inborn deficiency—some taint of the blood? Has a malevolent fate predestined him to a life of sloth and indolence?

Most Southerners vehemently deny the charge of "laziness," but they rarely completely convince themselves or others. One Southern state has even changed its motto from "Here we rest" to "We dare defend our right." This alters the emphasis from "the lazy South" to "the fighting South," but it does little to explain the far from mysterious bases of these accusations of slothfulness.

The only explanation that is at all acceptable to the Southerner is the placing of the blame squarely upon the immutable providence that gave the region its climate. "The hot weather, you know," is, in fact, one of the South's top defenses against criticism. (As such, it ranks with poverty, the Civil War and Reconstruction, and the presence of the Negro.) The climatic theory is stated thus by Ellsworth Huntington of Yale University, "In the South we find less energy, less vitality, less education, and fewer men who rise to

[From "Are Southerners Really Lazy?" *The American Scholar,* Vol. 18, No. 1, New York, 1949. Pp. 68-75. Reprinted by permission of the United Chapters of Phi Beta Kappa.]

eminence than in the North, not because Southerners are in any way innately inferior to Northerners but apparently because of the adverse climate."

This comforting doctrine does not, however, bear close examination. In Huntington's own *Civilization and Climate,* from which the quotation is taken, he states that about 63 degrees Fahrenheit is the best temperature for industrial and other manual work. Yet he ignores the fact that much of the South has mean annual temperatures around 63 degrees Fahrenheit, and if averages are deceptive—as they sometimes are—the effects of the South's hot summers cannot be assumed to extend throughout the year. And many visitors from the energetic North give generous praise to the South's briskly cool winters and equable spring and autumn seasons. Moreover, it is possible that the human organism is quite as depleted of energy by its efforts to maintain its normal temperature of 98.6 degrees during the bitter Northern winters as it is enervated by the opposite struggle during the hot days of Southern summers. The Michigan farmer, hovering over his stove after each painful sortie to the barn to care for his cattle, is perhaps merely the obverse picture of the Carolina share-cropper dozing upon his tiny porch during the "long noon" of an August day.

Admitting the South's disagreeable summer climate does not necessarily lead to the conclusion that efficiency must thereby be markedly decreased. Careful studies, especially by the New York State Committee on Ventilation, indicate that high temperature and humidity and little movement of air have much less effect upon *true* efficiency than upon *felt* efficiency. However unpleasant may be the effects of hot, damp and stuffy air, they seem to have little measurable influence upon output, provided the worker really concentrates upon his task. If these conclusions are not in error, the Southerner could, even during the hottest and stickiest days of summer, make good records in both quality and quantity of work, provided he could learn to ignore his feelings of discomfort, fatigue and inefficiency.

The conclusion seems inescapable that the direct physiological effects of the South's hot summers upon the year's round of activity level of its people must be small indeed. This does not deny the probability that the *indirect* effects of climate may have far-reaching consequences. The climate certainly does affect other parts of the natural environment, such as the incidence of parasites, that in turn may greatly influence the Southerner's energy. Similarly, climatic conditions may combine with cultural factors—for example, in the development of the plantation—to establish attitudes unfavorable to hard work. But the emphasis upon the direct bodily effects of the Southern climate itself is doubtless a satisfying rationalization that leads toward fatalism and the neglect of more reprehensible, but at the same time more remediable, explanations.

Ill health ranks easily among the more significant of these basic reasons for the South's low activity level. A sick man is a tired man, and a half-sick one certainly seems to be "lazy." In 1938 the National Emergency Council reported, "The low-income belt of the South is a belt of sickness, misery and unnecessary death. Its large proportion of low-income citizens are more subject to disease than the people of any similar area" in the United States. The same story is told by the rejections for military service during World War II. Up to June 1, 1944, every Southern state was in the lowest third of percentages of draftees certified as suitable for duty in the armed services. Other data on military rejections give the same tragic report that the South is a region of ill health and physical defect. These conditions do not, of course, arise from any innate weakness, but from ignorance of preventive measures, inadequate medical services, and the inability to purchase proper food and care.

The South also has at least two major parasitic diseases that sap the energy of its people. A decade ago the area was estimated to have 2,000,000 cases of malaria each year.

Relatively few deaths result from this source, but the malaria victim may suffer for years, or even a lifetime, from the loss of physical vigor resulting from the destruction of his red blood corpuscles and the injury to his liver and spleen.

Possibly just as significant as malaria is the presence of intestinal parasites, especially the hookworm that has been aptly called "the germ of laziness." These parasites literally rob the sufferer of much of the benefit of the food that he eats, and condemn him to a state of chronic fatigue. Anyone who has observed at first hand the enervating inroads of malaria and intestinal parasites upon human vitality will not hesitate to hold them responsible for much of the South's apparent "laziness."

But ill health may not be as significant as is malnutrition in the making of the Southerner's "laziness." Studies of the effect of underfeeding upon volunteer conscientious objectors reveal that activity levels fall rapidly when the intake of food is decreased. Similarly, the half-starved prisoners of World War II have given graphic reports of the hopelessness and helplessness of inanition, of the "dhobi stare" upon faces stupefied by long-continued hunger in Japanese concentration camps.

Semi-starvation in the South is not dramatic, but it is chronic and long continued from generation to generation. For example, Youmans and his associates at Vanderbilt Medical School found that in a comparatively well-to-do middle Tennessee county 14.3 per cent of the whites and 42.1 per cent of the Negroes obtained less than the 1250 calories of food supposed to be the minimum daily requirement for each person. [According to figures published by the Food and Agriculture Organization of the United Nations, the country with the lowest national caloric average is Algeria with 1421 calories (1948-1949). The United States average in 1948-1949 was over 3100.] The primary reason for this deficiency of food, which is probably typical of much of the South, is not ignorance but unmitigated poverty. Like other groups, Southerners have some indefensible food practices and prejudices, but in general they wish tasty and nutritious foods quite as much as do non-Southerners. In fact, the "Southern cooking" of the upper classes is justly acclaimed. But according to statistics of income, membership in the upper classes is necessarily quite limited. In general, the South's per capita annual income is only about 60 per cent of the nation's average. Even in 1947, a relatively prosperous year for agricultural areas, every one of . . . fifteen Southern states had per capita incomes in the lowest third of the entire country. Yet the per capita dollar cost of an adequate diet is approximately the same below the Ohio as it is north of it. The Southerner does not obtain his food at lower prices—he merely goes hungry, or exists upon a cheaper and generally less nutritious diet.

The deficiency of the B vitamins in the diet of Southerners is especially significant. This group of vitamins seem to be necessary for a normal activity level, yet it is often notably lacking upon Southern tables. The poor man in Dixie frequently has to content himself with his "three-M diet"— meat, molasses and meal. The meat, however, is usually salt pork—"fat back," that provides calories but little of the vitamins of fresh lean meat. The molasses, or its equivalent in sugar or corn syrup, is also low or lacking in B vitamins. The meal is usually bolted or degerminated corn meal, from which the vitamins of the whole grain have been largely removed.

If the Southern family is fortunate enough to be above the poverty level, the food may be more wholesome, yet still not adequate. The corn meal of the poor man may be replaced by white flour for hot biscuits, or by boiled polished rice, but both of these cereals reach the table with but a small part of their vitamin-rich natural content. Vegetables, especially the leafy ones, are traditionally cooked by long periods of boiling, perhaps with "a pinch of soda" that effectively neutralizes the vitamin C content. Difficulties of refrigeration, and traditional prejudice against the use of fresh pork during the summer months, also prevent an adequate intake of foods rich in B vitamins. As a consequence of these factors, middle and upper class Southerners are unfortunately often not as free from malnutrition as are similar groups in other regions of the United States.

In summer the need for the B vitamins, especially for thiamin, is markedly increased, according to studies by Clarence A. Mills and others. For example, Mills has found that white rats kept in a room at 90 degrees Fahrenheit required twice as much thiamin for healthy development as did a control group in a 68 degree temperature. The hot-room rats on a thiamin deficient diet were "too lazy" to seek a supply of better food nearby, even when the cage doors were left open. By his Panama studies Mills has also found evidence that lean meat and eggs produced in tropical climates are much less rich in thiamin than are similar foods imported from the temperate zones.

These investigations have a double significance for the Southerner, since they show that his need for thiamin greatly increases during the summer months, when his intake of this vital food element is at a low level, largely because of the inadequate supply of fresh lean meat. And even if he produces his own meat or buys it locally, apparently he may be purchasing a product that is somewhat deficient in the very food element that he himself so urgently needs. Other research studies also indicate that food raised on poor or eroded lands, prevalent in the South, is very likely to be short in nutritional value.

The South's lack of an adequate diet is tragically illustrated by the fact that 90 per cent of the nation's deaths from pellagra occur in the thirteen Southern states. Pellagra is a disease resulting primarily from a deficieny of one of the B vitamins, niacin, also known as nicotinic acid. Although only about one thousand Southerners die of pellagra each year, this fact does not begin to indicate the extent of this deficiency disease, since it is estimated that only about one-sixth of the pellagra cases ever consult a physician, and that many thousands of medically unrecognized "near pellagra" victims are to be found among the South's millions of underfed people.

To infer, however, that ill health and hunger are the sole explanations of the low activity level of many Southerners would be a great oversimplification. Other factors may be less dramatic or measurable, but they nevertheless enter into the pattern of life under analysis.

Slavery, for example, resulted in the discrediting of hard manual labor by either whites or blacks, and helped put the Southern gentleman of leisure at the top of the social pyramid. Even today "working like a Negro" is a term of reproach, just as "Kaffir work" has, for similar reasons, the same connotation among the whites of South Africa.

In the North and West, the European immigrant and his children are easily among the most vigorous and energetic workers. But since the Revolution, the South has received few immigrants except those unwillingly brought from Africa. Moreover, the conservative South exports many of her most ambitious "go-getters." Those left behind are more likely to be satisfied with things as they are.

Much of Southern farming, especially the cultivation of cotton and of cigarette tobacco, is really only a six- or seven-months task. This has permitted many rural Southerners to cherish the long winter vacation and the midsummer "lay-by time." The relative absence of dairying and poultry and livestock raising has also enabled the Southern rural worker to enjoy much hunting, fishing and plain or fancy loafing, and has made him accustomed to more leisure than even wealthy non-Southerners normally find it possible to attain.

In America, as elsewhere, the rural pattern of life is slower-paced than that of city-dwellers. This slower reaction does not, however, indicate any innate inferiority or inherent laziness. It is merely the result of a less stimulating environment, relatively free from the now-or-never decisions of the man of the city. And the South, it should be remembered, is the most rural region in the United

States, and even its larger cities are greatly affected by rural ways and attitudes. A significant part of the South's leisurely manner of living is, accordingly, rural rather than Southern. Even in energetic New England, some farmers are markedly deliberate in speech and action. Yet no one assumes this slowness to be an unmistakable evidence either of laziness or of moral degeneracy.

Another element in the South's alleged laziness is primarily a difference in life values. The true Southerner, white or colored, is not concerned with mere activity for activity's sake. He wishes to sip the joys of life, rather than to down them at one gulp. Often his motto is "don't hurry through life or you'll pass by more than you catch up with." Perhaps some of this attitude is a rationalization for a low level of activity, but a part of it is a reflection of a philosophy of life that emphasizes the present rather than the future. In Southern cities this leisurely tempo of life is now becoming but a memory—the crowds in Atlanta and Birmingham scurry along with set faces in much the same unhappy way as they do in New York or Pittsburgh. But over the South as a whole, the people still believe in taking time to enjoy themselves.

The South has suffered much at the hands of the local-color school of writers—native, Northern and European. These writers, with the most honorable of avowed intentions, have so misrepresented the South that Southerners sometimes hardly recognize themselves in literature. The hard-working yeoman farmer is ignored, but the shiftless "poor whites" become the heroes of Tobacco Roads. The self-respecting Negro artisan is crowded out of the pages of books by the more picturesque but atypical migratory singer of "blues." An occasional planter sits upon his veranda and drinks a mint julep, but for every one of these there are thousands of farmers who literally earn their bread in the sweat of their faces.

"O'nery" folk are not confined to the South. "Poor white trash" can be found in the Midwest, and ne'er-do-wells live in every Northern city. Even if the South has more than its proportionate share of the lazy and incompetent, this is no reason to condemn all Southerners indiscriminately. The many thousands who work with vigor and initiative should not be made to suffer from a hasty and inaccurate generalization.

One favorable aspect of the whole situation is that the principal conditions that have brought about these accusations of wholesale laziness are at least remediable, although not without much expense and cooperative effort. In the first place, the development of inexpensive air conditioning may soon give many Southerners the equivalent of a more invigorating summer climate. The enervating effects of even hard labor in the hot sun can be at least partially counteracted by a night's rest in a cooled bedroom. In the South, as in other warm regions, summer cooling may some day become as common as winter heating in the temperate zones.

But the South does not need mechanical refrigeration as much as it needs: (1) larger incomes for its numerous underprivileged groups; (2) more adequate medical care of all types; (3) a varied and nutritious diet for everyone; and (4) a realistic understanding both at home and elsewhere of the conditions and attitudes that have been erroneously interpreted as laziness.

In recent years, moreover, many of the situations that have fostered the South's reputation for laziness have shown significant improvement. The ravages of malaria and hookworm are being markedly decreased. Growing industrial development, more soil conservation, and higher prices for farm products have resulted in some relative increase in income. These larger incomes, the free lunch programs in the schools, and the emphasis upon home gardens and "the seven basic foods," are slowly but surely bettering dietary practices. Hard work more often receives recognition. Possibly the day is not far distant when "these lazy Southerners" will be recognized as an inaccurate stereotype that has gone with the music and the magnolias of the South that almost never was.

The Habitat

>>>

Many geographical details of the region which a group occupies have a profound effect on the way in which its people live. In the next two selections the rich natural endowment of the Cotton South will be briefly summarized, as well as some of the serious limitations that nature has placed on man's use of this endowment. Then, the geographic limits of the Cotton South will be more precisely defined and its meaning distinguished from such terms as the South, and the Cotton States.

• 25 • Nature's Legacy to the South
ALMON E. PARKINS

. . . Man's discovery of the economic possibilities of the Southern environment, as known today, is a matter of several centuries of hard work on the part of hundreds of "explorers." History records the explorations of Ponce de Leon on the Florida coast, of de Narvaez, De Soto, and La Salle in the Gulf region, the sad experiences of Raleigh's colonists in Albemarle Sound [Roanoke Sound], John Smith's exploration of Chesapeake Bay, Governor Spotswood's *de luxe* expedition to the crest of the Blue Ridge; but the annals of only a few of the hundreds of trappers and traders who traversed valleys, passes, and plains of the vast interior have ever been told.

They brought back information that stimulated the cupidity of thousands and sent westward wave after wave of land seekers that continued for two centuries or more until the agricultural lands of every section of the South were taken up. These pioneer trappers and farmers picked up practical information concerning the lands, the vegetation, and the climate of the Southern environment. But the definite scientific information regarding the topography, the geology, mineralogy, soils, and climate that we now possess is largely the work of scientists of the last half century.

*   *   *

[From *The South, its Economic-Geographic Development*, John Wiley, New York, 1938. Pp. 23-29, 35-36, 37-39, 41-54, 56-58. Used by permission.]

THE LANDS

Two mountain and plateau areas—the Southern Appalachian Highlands and the Ozark-Ouachita area—break the monotony of plains land that spreads from the Potomac to the Rio Grande. Fully three-fourths of the area of the South has elevations less than 1,000 feet above sea level.

The only formidable topographic barrier to the free movement of man and goods is the Cumberland-Allegheny Front, the eastern scarp of the Cumberland-Allegheny plateaus. From the Potomac southward to northeastern Alabama this 800- to 1,000-foot wall (above the Great Valley at its eastern base) has only a few breaks that open westward to the lowlands of the Mississippi basin. The westward-moving pioneers in the South used, for the most part, only one break, the Cumberland Gap, and through this, between 1790 and 1830, streamed more than 100,000 people in search of the rich farming lands of the Transappalachian region.

The Mississippi, though serving in the past as the South's greatest artery of commerce, drawing to the main stream the commerce of the wide-spreading areas, has always restricted the free east-west movement of commerce and people by land. Wide, marshy, pestilential flood plains, a broad strip of water, and valleys filled with unconsolidated mud and sand so deep and soft that finding a substantial footing for heavy bridge piers is difficult have greatly retarded the number of crossing places. In the days of westward movement there were only two important crossing places: one near St. Louis, the other at Natchez. . . . Until the last few years the only bridges across this mighty river between the mouth of the Ohio and the Gulf were at Memphis.

*   *   *

The Coastal Plain. The largest of the physiographic regions is the Coastal Plain, divided into the Atlantic and the Gulf plains. Its area is about 255,000 square miles, larger than France, Belgium, and the Netherlands combined, and nearly a third of the total area of the South. It includes parts of Maryland, Virginia, Kentucky, Arkansas, Oklahoma, and Texas, and the whole of Florida, Mississippi, and Louisiana. . . .

The Coastal Plain is the flattest of the plains lands of the South. It is highest along the inner border, and here rather conspicuous hills are to be found in some states. The outer border is half sea and half land. Shelving sandy barrier beaches topped by sand dunes behind which are lagoons, marshes, and wet flatwoods are the features . . . along most of the coasts of the South from the ocean's edge inland. The width of this low outer tidal border varies greatly. It is widest in eastern North Carolina . . . extending 50 to 70 miles inland from the ocean. Tidewater lagoons and bays along the Atlantic farther south and likewise along the Gulf extend 20 to 30 or more miles inland. Marshes and flatwoods occur still farther to the interior. . . .

Between the low outer marshy, tidal portion of the Coastal Plain and the inner dissected section is the broad flat Middle Coastal Plain, well drained yet flat enough to reduce surface erosion to the minimum. Before the coming of white men this portion of the Coastal Plain bore the best of the longleaf pine forests. It was, and still is, the section most used for agriculture.

The outer belt of the Coastal Plain, except here and there where truck gardens and seaports dominate the landscape, remains much the domain of nature. Several generations of lumbermen in the seventeenth, eighteenth, and nineteenth centuries battled with nature, at times almost obliterating the forest trees with axe, saw, and fire, but each time the trees have come back, though the last generation shows terrible scars of battle. Today much of the cut-over land of the Coastal Plain is in this outer belt. It may become the most active pulpwood-producing area of our country.

Most of the harbors of the South are the drowned mouths of the Coastal Plain rivers, and though they are shallow and subject to silting man finds it is easy to deepen them and excavate new channels. Baltimore and

Richmond are at the inner edge of the Plain at its meeting with the Piedmont, but . . . all the other large ports are at or near the outer border of the Plain [such as Savannah, Mobile, New Orleans, Galveston, Houston].

The inner border of the Coastal Plain from central Alabama northeastward is the Fall Line, an "imaginary" line connecting the row of rapids of the rivers that flow across both Piedmont and Coastal Plain. From central Alabama to the Rio Grande a fall line is scarcely discernible. The lower rapids of the Tennessee near Muscle Shoals and the hard rock in the Arkansas River at Little Rock are comparable to the Fall Line rapids, but elsewhere the inner boundary of the Coastal Plain is not sharp. . . .

The Piedmont Plateau. West of the Atlantic Coastal Plain is the Piedmont Plateau, extending from central Alabama northeastward beyond the northern border of the South, on into Pennsylvania. Though called a plateau it is really a plain, a plain of denudation, with only a few hills (monadnocks) rising above the otherwise gently rolling surface. . . . The Piedmont is higher, drier, and healthier than the Coastal Plain. Its flat surface like that of the Coastal Plain in no way erects barriers to man's movements.

*   *   *

The Central Lowlands or Plains, broad and flat and extensive, cover most of Oklahoma and extend southward into Texas. Only a small part of this vast physiographic province is in the South. There are some interruptions in the continuity of the plains—low mountains or rocky ridges.

*   *   *

THE USEFUL MINERALS

The Coastal Plain . . . is young, geologically. The mineral materials forming it are of marine origin derived from animals or are land material that has been deposited in the borders of the sea and worked over on the shores by waves and currents. No metallic minerals occur except bog iron ore that accumulated or was assembled in boggy areas after the Coastal Plain was formed. Sands, gravel, and shell marl are widely distributed. Clay is less abundant. Fuller's earth [used in filtering] and diatomaceous earth [used as a fine abrasive] are fairly common. Limestone is confined mostly to Florida and near-by portions of Georgia and Alabama.

*   *   *

For some unexplainable cause the petroleum and gas deposits of the Coastal Plain, so far discovered, with one exception, are in the West Gulf Coastal Plain. Salt and sulphur are likewise confined to the West Gulf Plain. The Coastal Plain also has peat and lignite deposits. . . . As long as bituminous coal is available at low prices the lignite deposits will remain mostly unworked.

. . . Gold and silver have been found in the Southern Appalachians but for the most part not in paying quantities sufficient to develop a mining industry. Copper is mined in several localities in North Carolina and southwestern Virginia. . . . Other mineral deposits . . . are mica, feldspar, kaolin (weathered feldspar), soapstone, talc, and magnetite. Granite of excellent quality is taken from many quarries in the mountains and hills of the Piedmont. . . .

THE CLIMATE AND WEATHER

The location of the South, (1) between 25° N and 39° N latitude, (2) in the southern edge of the belt of the Westerlies, and (3) in the southeastern portion of the continent with the sea on the east and the south, and the low relief of the land determine the characteristics of its climate and weather.

The Seasons. Owing to its comparatively low latitude, the South has a high sun during the year as compared to the North. The length of the growing season is longer than in the North, and the length of the day in winter and in summer does not vary so markedly. The median growing season for the Lower South is 240 days and for the Upper South 180 to 210 days, except in the plateau and mountain sections. The growing season for more than half of the South is long enough for two harvests of some crops, and in the Lower South for three. This also means that the hot season is longer. If we assume that a monthly average of 68° and above is *hot* and below 32° is *cold,* the length of the hot season and of the cold season at selected places is as follows:

	Hot	*Cold*
St. Paul, Minnesota	2 months	4 or 5 months
St. Louis	4	1
Montgomery.	5	0
New Orleans.	7	0
Miami	12	0

A high sun is a hot sun. The evaporation of water from the ground and the transpiration from plants are high in most of the South. Much more water is needed for crops in general than in the North, and droughts are more frequent and disastrous. But, surprisingly, the maximum temperature in the summer is, as a rule, little above that of more northerly localities. A comparison of the absolute maximum (the highest temperature ever recorded), up to December 31, 1929, at a few cities is interesting: Atlanta 102°, Montgomery 107°, Louisville 107°, Little Rock 108° . . . , Nashville 106°, Omaha 110°, St. Paul 104° . . . , St. Louis 107°. The summers of the South differ from those in the North in the greater length of the hot spells and their more frequent occurrence. The reverse is of course true of the winter in the two sections. Cold spells are short and infrequent in the South.

. . . The flatness of the Mississippi Basin permits the free movement of the winds whether from the south or from the north. South winds tend to cool off as they move northward, and north winds warm up as they move southward. The Gulf and Atlantic winds tend to give coastal lands for one hundred or more miles inland cooler temperatures than those at localities farther north. The hottest section of the South in the summer is the northern half of the Gulf Coast States.

The Appalachian Highlands are barriers to the movement of winds to only a slight degree, but the ridges do affect the distribution of rainfall. The regions of heaviest rainfall are near the coast and on the east-facing slopes of the ridges of the Southern Appalachian Highlands.

. . . The South is largely in the Hot Summer [av. 68° or higher] and Cool Winter [av. 32°-60°] Region. Only a small part of the Appalachian Highlands has Hot Summer and Cold Winter [av. 32° or lower] temperatures, and only the Gulf Coastal lands and Florida have Hot Summer and Mild Winter [av. 50°-68°] temperatures. This latter temperature region is often known as the Subtropical. The one to the north may be called the Warm Temperate.

Rainfall. . . . About three-fourths of the South has more than 30 inches of rainfall on the average during the year. This we may call the humid portion. Most of the remainder of the South may well be called subhumid, grading into semiarid. The east-facing slope of the Blue Ridge has the heaviest rainfall in the Southern States, one station recording more than 80 inches.

* * *

Rain water may be stored in the ground for weeks and months and in the deep porous soils of the High Plains of Texas for a year or two, yet in most parts of the Southern States, with much of the surface in slope and a high summer sun, it is but a matter of a few rainless days before the vegetation with superficial root systems begins to hang out a distress sign. . . . A drought as defined by the Weather Bureau is a 30-day period (consecutive) in which the precipitation during any day is below one-tenth of an inch. . . . Low flat lands suffer less from droughts than hilly lands. A drought of 60 days or more results in a leaf fall in deciduous trees, such as happened in 1925, particularly on slopes. From 15 to 20 per cent (or more) of the forest trees in the drought area were killed. The writer is firmly convinced that *dry spells* (mostly less than 30 days' duration) *are the most widespread and destructive of all weather phenomena to agricultural operators in the South.*

* * *

Cold Weather. "Cold spells" or "cold waves" form a second weather phenomenon that affects agricultural operators adversely. The greatest damage is felt in the Lower South where such weather is considered abnormal. In the northern part of the South freezing temperatures are normal experiences from early December to early March, though at any time during this period there may be several days in succession of springlike weather. The severest "cold spells" in the winter come in the rear of well-developed elliptical lows that pass slowly eastward across the Gulf States, provided there is to the northwest of this low a well-developed, slowly moving high. Under such conditions great volumes of cold, clear, dry, biting blasts move southward down the flat Mississippi Basin plains to the Gulf Coast and Florida.

* * *

Hurricanes and Tornadoes. A third type of destructive weather phenomenon in the South is the tropical hurricane. Its fury is felt mostly along the Atlantic and Gulf coasts, especially in lower Florida. The newspapers in recent years have so fully described the paths and the destruction wrought that further comments are not necessary here. Some data on the frequency and period of occurrence may be of value. In the 38 years between 1887 and 1925, records show that a total of 240 hurricanes struck or came near our southeastern coasts. . . . Only a few of these 240 were destructive. . . .

Tornadoes, similar in some respect to tropical hurricanes except that they develop on land and cover a much narrower and shorter path, are characteristic of the interior of the Mississippi Basin from the Gulf States to Wisconsin and Michigan. They may be thought of as concentrated hurricanes. The velocity of the wind in the hurricane rarely reaches more than 100 to 125 miles an hour, but in the tornado it may be 300 to 500. Tornadoes are associated with thunderstorms but are distinguished from thunderstorms by their funnel shape. The area of the base of the funnel covers much less than a mile, some not more than a quarter mile. A single tornado may travel a hundred or hundreds of miles before working itself out. Rarely is a path of destruction continuous for this distance, but the tornado may come down to the surface of the earth and leave a record of its presence at only a half dozen places. . . .

Sunshine. Has the expression the "Sunny South" any scientific evidence? The following data for a few selected cities (selected at random) will answer the question:

PERCENTAGE OF POSSIBLE SUNSHINE FOR YEAR

Cities in the South		*Cities in the North*	
New Orleans	58	Buffalo	49
Montgomery	62	St. Paul	56
Vicksburg	64	St. Louis	59
Miami	67	Des Moines	61
Ft. Worth	71	Huron	63

For some non-Southern readers it may not be amiss to be reminded that one does not step into Florida and Gulf climate as soon as one crosses Mason and Dixon's line or the Ohio River. Under normal weather conditions it gets warmer in both summer and winter the farther south one goes, yet every year Nashville, for example, may have colder weather than Illinois in winter and cooler temperatures in the summer, for several days in succession. The summers are not so enjoyable in the middle South as in the middle North; but the winters in the middle North are not as enjoyable as those in the middle South.

* * *

THE ORIGINAL PLANT LIFE

. . . Although for the most part most of the original vegetation is gone, enough of the original is left here and there for us to know the species that composed it perfectly.

* * *

From eastern Texas eastward, the natural

plant life on the drier portions of the outer and on the middle Coastal Plain sections is pine—longleaf, loblolly, and slash. In this belt the rainfall varies from 30 to 60 inches or more, everywhere sufficient, except in years of drought, for a luxuriant growth of trees. This belt lies almost wholly on the Coastal Plain. The loose, porous soil permits rapid drainage except on the flat lands near the streams. . . . This forest region lies mainly in the Hot Summer and Cool Winter belt of temperatures with the southern edge in the Hot and Mild belt. Conifers the world over, as a rule, dominate in regions of cold winters and moderate summers. The presence of coniferous vegetation in such temperatures as here prevail is probably to be attributed to the dominance of soil (edaphic) conditions over climate. The pine . . . finds little difficulty in getting a foothold in land badly eroded or denuded of its humus by burning—a factor of great moment in the reforestation of cut-over lands.

Bordering this pine belt on the north is a transition belt in which deciduous trees, largely oak, and pines compete; yet the competition is not strong. The pines occupy the sandier and better-drained lands; the oak the more fertile tracts on the gentle slopes and flats. In the long run, were the natural forces and tendencies not disturbed, much of the pine would likely be replaced by the oak or other deciduous trees owing to changes in the humus and life conditions of the soil. . . . Oak-pine vegetation dominates on the Piedmont but it also appears on the Coastal Plain of the Chesapeake Bay region, on the Cumberland Plateau in Alabama, the dry sandy and loessal lands in Mississippi, and the dry, hilly, sandy lands (primitive or young soil) in Louisiana and Arkansas.

The deciduous or hardwood belt covers the Upper South and extends far to the southwest into Texas. East of the Mississippi the variety of species is largely chestnut, chestnut oak, and Carolina poplar. On the higher mountain slopes species of more northern climes are numerous, even those of Canada. West of the Alluvial Valley of the Mississippi,

the oak takes precedence among the trees, an adaptation, no doubt . . . to the drier conditions.

*   *   *

An east to west plant profile in North Carolina would begin with the formations of dune and barrier beach, followed by those of the coastal marsh and flatwoods, the drier belts of the Coastal Plain, the Piedmont, and the mountains. . . .

A north-south profile from the Gulf to the Ohio through Alabama and across Tennessee and Kentucky would show types very similar to those in the Carolina profile, except that the high-altitude, and therefore high-latitude types, are absent. There is nothing comparable to the Black Belt of Alabama in North Carolina.

The Black Belt of Alabama is generally referred to as a prairie region. Mohr, who studied it in the nineties of the last century, writes regarding the original vegetation, "The term 'prairie region' refers less to the timberless tracts, which originally formed a small fraction of its area, than to the black, calcareous, highly fertile soil of these uplands, which being rich in humus as a result of the reaction of its calcareous constituents upon vegetable matter, closely resembles the equally productive soil of the western treeless prairies."

*   *   *

THE ORIGINAL ANIMAL LIFE

The bison and elk roamed the forest tracts of the Upper South until the middle of the eighteenth century in Virginia, and the early part of the nineteenth in the transmontane sections of the Mississippi Basin. It is only during the last six or seven decades that the bison has become extinct as a free animal in western Texas. Beaver in small numbers in the sluggish streams of the Appalachian Highlands are within the recollection of our older mountaineers. Bears, wild cats, pumas, wolves, and the lynx have been seen in the sections remote from civilized man's habitations within the present generation. Foxes are common, so also are the general varieties of deer. Among the game birds are the turkey, mallard duck, wild goose, partridge, and quail and the prairie chicken in the west. These are fairly common. The opossum, rabbit, and squirrel have furnished a limited amount of food since the earliest occupancy of the lands.

A beginning is now being made in the restocking of some of the national forests and parks in the South with selected types which civilization either drove westward or destroyed. Most of the states have or are providing state parks, state forests, or game preserves. The National Government maintains several forests in the South.

*   *   *

THE SOILS

Soil has come to be considered an evolving thing. It is more than just dirt, mineral matter with a little humus. The soil body is, in its maturity (when completely developed), the result of a long series of complex changes, the particular type of development and quality of soil being affected by the natural environment. A soil in its evolution starts as a mass of disintegrated rock. This parent soil material is further weathered. Water moving through it shifts soluble mineral matter and colloidal bodies, even the finer mineral particles. Chemical changes of many sorts take place. Leaching goes on where the rainfall is sufficient to give a downward movement of the water. Capillary water brings materials from the lower to the upper horizons. Microscopic and ultramicroscopic organisms come to make the evolving soil their home and become an integral part of it. They multiply rapidly under certain conditions and are destroyed under adverse ones. A cubic inch of soil may contain many tens of millions. Besides these microscopic forms of life there are many sorts of beetles and worms. The earthworm contributes much to the soil-making process. It opens up channels in the ground from a few inches to five feet long, and Darwin found that its excreta—castings—annually formed a layer of a fifth of an inch thick. In the course of thirty years, he discovered, earthworms had converted a stony field in England into a meadow. The remains of all forms of ground burrowers produce organic matter and gases in the soil. The plant cover makes its contribution. The roots shift soluble minerals from the soil to the leaves and stems which later are added to the topsoil. Some roots harbor nitrogen-making bacteria. Thus the solum [soil] is a busy place, a workshop, in which are produced, directly or indirectly, the essentials for all land life, the soil. The raw material is the parent soil material. The processes that the raw material undergoes depend upon the temperature, rainfall, topography, and many other conditions. It takes hundreds of years, no doubt, to make a mature or completely developed soil. The best topographic environment is gently sloping land with the soil porous enough to permit freedom of movement of air and moisture. Poorly drained lands, lands subject to sheet wash and gullying or too frequent deposition as in river valleys, do not develop a mature soil.

There are two major soil groups in the south—one group is sometimes referred to as the lime-accumulating soils, in which moisture rising to the surface and evaporating leaves carbonates, such as lime, in the soil. These lime-accumulating soils are found on the western margin of the Cotton Belt, where the rainfall is so light that the lime accumulation is not washed away. These soils are therefore naturally fertile and are very valuable, since commercial fertilizers are needed far less. In this soil the western part of the Cotton Belt has a considerable advantage over the eastern part.

The other group of soils, prevailing over the eastern part of the Cotton Belt from the

Mississippi Valley eastward, are non-lime-accumulating, because heavier rainfall leaches the lime from the surface. In order to maintain soil fertility an expensive program of fertilizing has to be provided.

The extensive plains, fertile soils, forests, and wild game of the South were largely untouched before 1800. To the Indians this South was a highly desirable habitat. Their simple life found abundant satisfaction in the immediate environment, and nature was not disturbed. Their agriculture, based on corn, beans, and squash, was mainly confined to the rich river bottoms. The vast forested areas were hunted continuously but never to the point of serious depletion of the game. The Indians occupied or used the entire South, but their total number probably never rose above 200,000 for the whole region from the Rio Grande to the Ohio and Potomac.

All of this changed drastically with the intensive exploitation of the area by the white man. The result is a very different type of economic wealth for a vastly larger number of people as well as a different habitat. The creation of a wealthy class from cotton promoted contacts with the entire world in providing for their wants, and nature was often disregarded for the creation and maintenance of this financially exclusive group. But the evils of exploitation pressed hard upon the bulk of the natives. Worn-out lands or lands naturally unfit for cotton production constituted the only space available for many people too poor for any other way of independent life. The bulk of the common people were dependent upon the owners of lands profitably producing cotton. They could not rise above the wages or goods paid for the menial and manual tasks associated with cotton. In this state they were highly vulnerable to habitat handicaps. The mud of winter rendered most of the people immobile and restricted such public functions as education and health; the work required by cotton limited or excluded education and recreation. Disease and insects plagued or ravaged man, beast, and plant with little control.

Paved roads, improved farm equipment and methods, and the control of diseases and insects are throwing into sharp focus such promising aspects of the habitat of the South as its large area, its vast extent of lowland plains above flood level, its accessibility through streams, its extensive coast line and direct overland routes, its temperate climate, its productive soil, and its abundant and varied natural resources. Indeed, many think that no other area in the world exceeds the South in terms of promise.

But some of the greatest problems confronting the South arise in large part from the changes in habitat wrought by man in the era of exploitation. These are described below.

• 26 • Man's Natural Enemies
ALMON E. PARKINS

INSECTS

Space will permit only a brief discussion of a few of the pests known in the South.

The boll weevil is a Mexican pest that first entered southern Texas in 1892. By 1922 it had spread over the entire Cotton Belt. In 1921 it was estimated that this one pest reduced the prospective total yield of cotton for the United States 31 to 34 per cent. The loss for Georgia was estimated at 45 per cent, and that for Oklahoma at 41 per cent. The boll weevil, however, has little affected the total crop of cotton. Since it is known that the yield per acre will be less, to maintain the normal cotton crop, the acreage must necessarily be increased and the cost of production is increased.

The cattle tick which carries the germ of the Texas cattle fever has been known in North America since Colonial days, probably having been introduced along with Spanish cattle into Mexico, Texas, and Florida. . . . It is only in recent decades that a thorough study of the disease has been made and a method for the eradication of the tick devised, namely, dipping the animals in a vat of insecticide. In 1906 there were 985 quarantined counties in the South in the infested area. By 1934 the number that had been released was 914 [leaving only 71 quarantined]. . . . Where the tick has been eliminated a surprising improvement and development in the cattle industry have usually resulted. Packing plants have been introduced in many sections, so also have creameries, condenseries, and ice-cream plants.

The Mediterranean fruit fly has been the South's most recent insect scare. Early in 1929 this pest was found well established in central Florida in the citrus-fruit sections. . . . Upon a careful survey it was found to be in 980 localities scattered over 20 counties, or about

8,000,000 acres in all. This area produced 67 per cent of the citrus fruit of Florida in 1928, and 76 per cent of the three years' average. Utter ruin to the citrus-fruit industry of Florida was the prospect unless the fly could be exterminated. . . . Both state and nation began the work of eradication. Many millions of dollars were appropriated. The active measures used won the day for man. This is the first instance in America of an insect pest being entirely destroyed over a large area within a few months.

Owing to the hot moist weather that prevails over a large area, the South is open to ravages by subtropical, tropical, and warm-weather diseases such as yellow fever, cholera, and malaria. . . . Malaria, known to our early settlers as ague, is the most persistent and widespread of the warm-weather and warm-climate diseases. It is more prevalent in the marshy sections, and since marshes are widespread and cover large sections of the South, the malaria districts total an immense area. . . . But every Southern state has taken active measures against this disease, and in spite of the poverty and ignorance with which health authorities have had to contend—malaria, ignorance, and poverty are concomitant phenomena—surprising results have been attained.

*   *   *

SOIL EROSION

Studies conducted throughout some twenty years have shown that the Savannah River, which drains the adjacent parts of Georgia and South Carolina, is carrying 135 carloads (50 tons each) of soil (mantle rock) daily to the Atlantic Ocean—more than 2,500,000 tons of suspended material annually. Similar investigations of the Mississippi give the stupendous figure of 340,500,000 tons of suspended rock material being deposited in the Gulf each

[From *The South, its Economic-Geographic Development,* John Wiley, New York, 1938. Pp. 67-75, 77-79, 81-83, 85-88. Used by permission.]

year. In terms of train loads (of 40 cars, each carrying 50 tons), 466 trains would need to leave the mouth of the Mississippi daily to return this immense amount of rock debris to its original home. According to a report of the United States Bureau of Chemistry and Soils several years ago, Fairfield County, South Carolina, in the Piedmont, had lost 90,000 acres of productive land by gullying. In Stewart County, Georgia, the inner part of the Coastal Plain, 70,000 acres have been made practically useless for agriculture by excessive erosion. In western Tennessee 300,000 acres are reported as having been destroyed. These instances are typical of a process that is going on over a large part of the South.

Erosion, even the sheet wash that is scarcely noticeable, is responsible for much soil depletion, unprofitable farming, tax delinquency, and farm abandonment. The total loss for the country at large, it is estimated by competent Federal Government experts, amounts to $400,000,000 a year. Fully 100,000 acres of productive land are destroyed each year, and in addition a much larger area is being hopelessly impaired. About 50,000,000 acres have been essentially destroyed in the United States, an area equivalent to nearly 625,000 farms of 80 acres each; another 50,000,000 acres are in almost as bad condition. The total loss already is at least $10,000,000,000. More than a third of this—the area of the South is about one-third of the total of the country—should be assigned to the South, for nowhere else in the United States are the conditions quite so favorable for loss by soil erosion. Man, if he intends to build a permanent civilization in the South, must awaken to a realization of the ultimate effects of the slow but relentless destruction of his most valuable of all resources. The vast stores of iron ore, coal, oil, gas, sulphur, and salt, and the power of the thousand streams that roll onward down the slopes to the ocean, can amount to little if the productive power of the soil is impaired. *Soil is a resource that belongs to the public, present and future. Permitting its destruction should be considered a crime!*

*   *   *

There are two phases of soil erosion: surface or sheet wash and gullying. There is hardly an area in the South, outside the flat lands near the coast and in the river flood plains, that is not suffering from excessive loss of topsoil, and many parts have had hitherto productive lands rendered worthless by gullying. Gullying is most active in the loessal districts of Kentucky, Tennessee, and Mississippi, on many of the slopes of the plateaus, the Great Valley, and the Piedmont, and in the inner hilly sections of the Coastal Plain. In Georgia the writer has seen scores of gullies in the Coastal Plain 50 or more feet deep that are the product of 50 years or less of unchecked erosion.

*   *   *

Soil erosion—wash and gullying—is active in the South because:

1. During only a few weeks each year, even in the Upper South, is the ground frozen. In middle Tennessee it is a rare winter that the ground is frozen for more than a week or so at a time. Southward the winters are even more open. Erosion, therefore, goes on almost unimpeded twelve months in a year. In the Lake States, by contrast, the ground remains frozen most winters to depths of two or three feet from November to early, even late, March.

2. The staple crops, as cotton and corn, leave the surface of the soil uncovered during the off season, unless the farmer grows winter oats, rye, or wheat, and even these leave much opportunity for erosion. More grass is needed in the rotation schemes in the South. At present the millions of acres of weeds, though a despoiler of the appearance of the cultural landscape, serve to check erosion and therefore are not an unmitigated evil.

3. Most of the land is in slope, that is, it has a mature topography and much of the topsoil is of a sort that washes and gullies readily—a light porous upper soil on a denser subsoil.

4. Lastly, because of the cheapness of the land and the prevalence of tenancy (on a large number of farms it is shiftlessness and ig-

norance), little is done to prevent surface wash and check gullying in its incipient stages.

* * *

Soil wash and gullying *can be prevented*. Such waste of land is practically unheard of in Europe. For forty centuries lands have been cultivated in China and Japan and are better today than 4,000 years ago, partly because soil erosion is not permitted. If the South is more susceptible to such processes of land deterioration, *and it is,* the farmers of the South should adjust themselves more than they have hitherto done to the adverse natural conditions and redouble their effort to prevent such losses. Many thousands of acres of slopes now tilled should be reforested. The prevention of soil wash and gullying is an economic burden; but unless the problem is faced squarely, nature in the end will dominate and man will lose out.

* * *

WET AND OVERFLOW LANDS

The total area of wet and overflow lands in the South is about 65,000,000 acres. . . . About 50,000,000 acres of this is potential crop land, but not necessarily economically possible of reclamation at present.

The Atlantic and Gulf Coastal Plain and the Alluvial Valley of the Mississippi . . . have almost the entire acreage of wet lands in the South. In the South Atlantic and Gulf States all estuaries, bays, and sounds, and most of the alluvial lands of the rivers below the Fall Line are bordered by salt-water and fresh-water marshes. The strips of marshes along the rivers are five to ten or more miles in width. Some of the streams draining the flat alluvial lands bear the title swamps, not rivers. . . . Alabama has a large area of wet lands, mainly along its rivers in the Coastal Plain. One of the largest wet areas in the South is the Mississippi Alluvial Valley from Cairo to the Gulf. Almost the entire areas of the St. Francis Basin, the Yazoo delta, the Tensas and Atchafalaya basins, all highly

productive sections of the Southern States, will need millions of dollars spent on levees, drainage ditches, and pumping plants to fit them for agriculture.

* * *

FLOODS AND FLOOD CONTROL OF THE MISSISSIPPI

Floods are perfectly normal phenomena, for most rivers. Southern rivers certainly are no exception. The Southern river that has received the most attention in this country because of its destructive floods is the Mississippi. Nearly every year it has a period or periods of high water, but it is only occasionally that the height of its flood waters becomes excessive. During such times a large area of the flood plain, with its agricultural lands and buildings, cities, and traffic lines, is covered by water, and the usual trend of business affairs is interrupted. Yet these unusual floods are normal, for small floods and large floods must have been the regular order in the life history of the Mississippi for hundreds of thousands of years. . . .

One of De Soto's men wrote an account of a Mississippi River flood that occurred in 1543. "Then God Our Lord," his report runs, "hindered the work with a mighty flood of the great river, which at that time [about the eighth or tenth of March] began to come down with an enormous increase of water, which in the beginning overflowed the wide level ground between the river and the cliffs. Soon it began to flow over the fields in an immense flood, and as the land was level, without hills, there was nothing to stop the inundation." . . .

. . . The destructiveness of the flood waters is ever increasing, not necessarily because the floods are higher, although they probably are; but because the number of people that take chances in areas subject to inundation is increasing, and more and more property is being accumulated. No statistical data are available for determining whether the floods of late decades are higher than those of the earlier decades of the historic periods. It seems very clear, however, that though floods are natural happenings man has in various ways ... in his modification of the natural environment, particularly in the removal of the forests, added a few inches, if not feet, to the "peak" height of the flood waters.

Experiments at Spur, Texas, and at an experimental station on the Piedmont, show that grass cover reduces the run-off materially. ... Forest cover is equally if not more effective. We know that dense mesophytic woods, like the broad-leaved hardwood forests of central United States, are damp and cool, that many forest springs dry up when forests are removed, and that small streams from cleared lands do not have the uniformity of flow that is characteristic of streams from forested tracts. All this would lead us to believe that forests do regulate stream flow to a material degree. ...

The levee system of the Mississippi was devised in the beginning to protect the lowlands from flood; later it was constructed chiefly to improve navigation of the Mississippi. The first levees, thrown up in 1717 by Le Blond de la Tour, were to protect New Orleans. By 1828 the levees were continuous almost to the Red River, 190 miles, except where bluffs bordered the channel, and for 65 miles below New Orleans. Congressional action in 1849-1850, which turned over to the several states unsold swamp lands within their borders to be sold and the funds devoted to flood protection, was a great stimulus to levee building. The people of Louisiana about the middle of the last century, becoming alarmed lest the building of levees along the Mississippi above the northern boundary should greatly endanger life and property on the vast area of alluvial lands within the state, complained to the Federal Government through their representatives in Congress. A careful survey of the whole scheme of flood control and improvements to navigation along the Mississippi was decided on by Congress, the work to be done by army engineers. Andrew A. Humphreys was put in charge, and after

ten years of field observations he rendered his report. This report, published by the War Department in 1874, has been the chief guide for much of the work done on the river since. Humphreys and his co-workers contended that the bottom lands about the Red River, before levees were constructed, did not function as reservoirs during high flood stages; that reservoirs in the headwaters of the tributaries would have little effect on restraining floods; that straightening the course of the river by making cut-offs artificially would be dangerous; that there were no suitable sites for distributaries to be developed artificially; and, finally, that a levee system properly constructed would, when completed, protect the alluvial lands adequately, against all floods. And so the work of extending the levee system went on.

*   *   *

Spillways ... through which or by which flood waters can reach natural distributaries and be carried away to the Gulf as the water was carried before man interfered, are a second feature worked out for flood control. ... In portions of the Alluvial Valley the original condition is approached, and yet the work of man is preserved, to some degree at least, by providing a series of overflow basins enclosed by levees. ... Such of the basins as are subject to frequent overflow will be devoted to the growing of forests or to such crops as may mature quickly. The building of homes in the basins most subject to overflow should not be permitted. The construction of reservoirs at the headwaters of the tributaries, though of benefit in many floods, cannot be relied upon to function at all times, for often the heavy rains that cause floods do not fall at the headwaters as previously stated.

*   *   *

That the present works will handle *all* future floods no one, of course, can assert, for every now and then nature does the unexpected. The flood of 1937, that brought such appalling disaster to the Ohio Valley, was handled with ease by the Mississippi works after the flood waters had passed the Tiptonville meander some fifty miles downstream from Cairo. But would the task have been so easy if the "unprecedented" rains had continued to fall instead of ceasing as they did shortly after the crest of the flood had passed Louisville and Paducah? . . .

The preceding discussion has dealt with the habitat problems of the South as a whole, consisting of thirteen states, including on the north Virginia, Kentucky, and Arkansas, and on the west Oklahoma and Texas. Now we shall turn to a more limited area, the *Cotton South.*

Some parts of the South have never raised cotton in significant amounts and are thus excluded from our discussion. Also, some states now raising cotton in quantity, particularly California and Arizona, are not part of the South. The *Cotton South,* as the term is used in this book, refers primarily to the older cotton-producing areas of Georgia, Louisiana, Arkansas, North Carolina, South Carolina, Alabama, and Mississippi. Many of the selections will cover a wider scope, but their focus will be upon these particular states and the way of life which their people developed.

In addition to their many similarities in people and habitat, the states of the Cotton South form a relatively unified section of the country because they share a common historical background. Although some of these states were still wilderness when others were important colonies, they grew to resemble one another in the nineteenth century, particularly in their dependence on slavery and the plantation system. Finally, they were united politically in the Confederacy during one of the most protracted and devastating wars of modern times. After sharing the humiliation of defeat, they continued to be drawn closely together as a consciously "different" social and economic region by their common economic and social problems. Thus, as in other societies we are studying, small diversities are overlaid by a unity of background and traditions from the past and by shared ways of living and meeting the problems of the present.

· 27 · The Cotton South
J. R. SCHWENDEMAN

The Cotton South can most simply be defined as the area of the production of cotton. J. Russell Smith says, "One single commodity binds together one-sixth of the United States into a single human-use region appropriately called the Cotton Belt. Within this region Cotton is King since for over a century it has been the economic life-blood of a people."

Certain portions of the Cotton South of tradition no longer emphasize cotton, and should not be considered as a portion of the modern Cotton South. Among such portions are the following: most of the outer portion of the Atlantic Coastal Plain; the northern portion of the Piedmont Plateau, i.e., north of northern North Carolina; the industrial area about Birmingham, which is a part of the Appalachian Highlands; the Black Belt of Alabama, now agriculturally diversified; the Atlantic-Gulf Coast, with autumnal rains and poor drainage; and the mouth of the Rio Grande, with greater emphasis upon truck-gardening.

Within the modern Cotton South certain

areas specialize on cotton: the Inner Atlantic Coastal Plain; the southern Piedmont; the Northern Alabama area associated with the Tennessee River; the Mississippi Bottom; the Black Waxy (Black Earth) area of Texas; the coastal plain of Southern Texas; and the High Plains (Red Prairies of Texas-Oklahoma). These six areas account for a great part of the cotton land shown in Table 1.

TABLE 1.—PERCENTAGE OF CROP LAND HAR-
VESTED DEVOTED TO COTTON IN COTTON
BELT (1944)

State	Percent
Mississippi	35.4
Arkansas	29.5
South Carolina	24.7
Texas	24.0
Louisiana	23.3
Alabama	22.3
Georgia	16.4
North Carolina	11.7
Tennessee	11.2
Oklahoma	10.5
Missouri	3.1
Florida	1.4
Virginia	0.7
Kentucky	0.2

Outside the South three states in the West are growing cotton by irrigation—New Mexico, Arizona and California. About ½ million acres were used for cotton in 1944 and it is increasing.

Total acreage in 1944 was about 19 million acres of which 18.5 million was grown in the states tabulated above. Of this latter figure only about ½ million acres are grown in the states of Florida, Virginia, Kentucky and Missouri. The Cotton Belt economy falls mainly within the states of North Carolina, South Carolina, Georgia, Tennessee, Alabama, Mississippi, Arkansas, Louisiana, Oklahoma, and Texas, each of which devoted from 10 per cent to roughly 30 per cent of its crop land to cotton. As recently as 1929 the South gave *half* of its crop land to cotton, the total being over 43 million acres. However, the decline in production was not proportional to the decline in acreage—from 14.6 million bales in 1929 to 11.5 million bales in 1944.

The basing of the area of the Cotton South Habitat on cotton is because it is the most important cash crop of the area. Also, the Cotton South has at times, produced more cotton than all the rest of the world combined. Thus, in many ways, it is the dominating influence in the life of the area. While man can extend the production of cotton into bordering areas by using modern techniques of plant selection, its traditional area of production falls within natural limits which influence its growth and profitable production. These natural limits are then operative in keeping the production where it is and thus are considered the natural boundaries of the habitat.

• 28 • The Natural Limits of the Cotton South
CLARENCE F. JONES AND GORDON D. DARKENWALD

... The cotton belt includes regions in which the value of cotton is greater than that of any other crop. Boundaries of the cotton belt are determined by climate, topography, and soil. The northern boundary follows closely the 210-day frost-free area, which enjoys a mean summer temperature of 77° F. Since the ad-

vent of the boll weevil, there has been a tendency to push this line farther north because cold winters kill many hibernating weevils. In western Texas, because of lower precipitation and more frequent below-freezing temperatures, the boll weevil is much less of a menace. The western boundary of the

[From *Economic Geography*, Macmillan, New York, 1941. Pp. 206-209. Used by permission.]

cotton belt is about at the 20-inch annual-rain-fall line, but 20 inches is sufficient only where soils and the seasonal distribution of the rain-fall are favorable. The southern boundary is approximately at the 10-inch autumn-rainfall line. Heavy rains in the fall damage the lint and interfere with picking, while heat and moisture combined in this southern section greatly aid the development of the boll weevil. However, these coastal lowlands are well suited to rice culture in southern Louisiana and Texas, to cane growing in the Mississippi Delta, and to fruit and vegetable farming in sandy areas of other sections. The eastern boundary of the cotton belt is in general the border between the outer and inner coastal plains. The outer coastal plain has much swampy land, infertile, sandy soil, and an ex-cessive autumn rainfall of from 10 to 13 inches, all of which tend to restrict cotton culture.

The concentration of cotton culture in a few large areas within the cotton belt results chiefly from favorable relief and soil condi-tions.

In the old cotton regions of the inner coastal plain and piedmont gently sloping or rolling lands provide good drainage. The yellow sandy loam of the inner coastal plain is low in fertility, and the brownish red clays and sandy loams of the piedmont are only slightly more fertile. Both are low in humus, but friable and easily worked. The soils of these areas were utilized first because these areas were settled first. As long as cheap land was readily available, planters would aban-don fields as soon as yields declined and clear new fields with cheap labor during the winter. This cotton economy, once firmly established, was difficult to abandon. The development of textile manufacturing in the southern Ap-palachians provided a near-by market for cotton from piedmont and coastal plains. The application of much fertilizer has maintained cotton farming in these old areas, and, owing

to methods of tillage and fertilization, cotton yields are higher here than the average for the entire cotton belt.

Rich alluvial soils of the Tennessee, Mis-sissippi, Arkansas, and Red River valleys, have been responsible for a concentration of cotton production on level bottom lands and adjacent rolling interstream areas, where yields are usually high without the use of fertilizer. Soil material brought down from moist regions of the upper Tennessee River does not contain the large amount of plant food found in the fluvial deposits of the other three rivers whose upper portions flow through the dry fertile regions of the prairies and Great Plains or the rich glaciated regions of the corn belt. The Mississippi Valley region, from southern Illi-nois to central Louisiana, has the highest yield and produces the longest fiber of the cotton belt. In this region two soil belts, dark silt loams on the flood plains and brown silt loams of adjacent loess plains and hills, are especially fertile. This region, however, has its disad-vantages in that the Mississippi goes on fre-quent rampages, causing great loss of property and life. However, each flood leaves behind a rich layer of silt, some of which, when dry, is picked up by the winds and deposited on near-by lands.

The best cotton soils of Texas are in the grasslands of the central and western parts. Those of the central portion are reddish brown to black, deep, high in humus and calcium carbonate, and easily worked. Both undulating land and flatland respond to ma-chine culture and are not subject to excessive erosion or leaching. The soil of western Texas is dark brown, friable, and high in humus and lime. In these grasslands a smaller rain-fall with greater variability and somewhat more extensive methods of farming result in a lower average yield per acre than that in the more humid regions. On the other hand, the drier conditions are hard on the boll weevil.

The Old South, 1850–1860

»»

The general theme of this book is social change—particularly the kind of change that results when the twin processes of industrialization and urbanization begin to bring about a new social landscape. The South, as much as any area in the country, is now caught in the current of this change; furthermore, it has been studied more intensively than any other large section, with the result that changes can be interpreted against a background of facts. But if we are to study the changing South we must have some idea of what it once was like and recognize the forces that have led to the passing of an old order. How was life in the Old South? What traditional characteristics still leave their impress? Why are Southerners considered different, a point touched upon in Selections 23, 24, and 44?

Obviously, in a book of this sort it is impossible to present a detailed account of the history of the South, interesting though that would be. Instead, the selections that follow present a panorama of what the Old South was like in a single decade, 1850-1860, a period which most historians agree is the basis for most of the traditional concepts about the South which persist to our day. Once the reader is familiar with this period he will have a bench mark against which to look at changes following the Civil War and the other wars of later years.

In the eight selections that follow, notice how the people made their living, their methods of transportation, and their types of dwelling, food, and dress. What was the nature of their family life, their religion, their local government? What were the social distinctions among the whites: the planter, the yeoman, and the "poor white"? Then, too, what was the relationship between the Negroes and whites, institutionalized as it was in slavery? What public issues attracted attention and led to the psychological conditioning of the "Southern mind"?

We can get something of the flavor of life in the Old South if we follow Frederick Law Olmsted on a short part of his rather extended journey during 1853-1854. We join him as he travels through South Carolina, Georgia, and Alabama, describing some of the countryside and chance events, a visit to a plantation, a church service, stopovers in Savannah, Columbus, Montgomery, and Mobile, with intermediate transportation provided by rail, stagecoach, and river steamer. Throughout this account you will note the reaction of a Northerner, who was a trained observer, to a wide range of Southern attitudes. Olmsted was a nationally known landscape architect who helped plan Central Park in New York City and the Capitol grounds in Washington, D. C.

• 29 • A Journey in the Seaboard Slave States
FREDERICK L. OLMSTED

TRAVEL IN SOUTH CAROLINA

... The character of the scenery was novel to me, the surface very flat, the soil a fine-grained, silvery white sand, shaded by a continuous forest of large pines, which had shed their lower branches, so that we could see from the coach-top, to the distance of a quarter of a mile, everything upon the ground. In the swamps, which were frequent and extensive, and on their borders, the pines gave place to cypresses, with great pedestal trunks, and protuberant roots, throwing up an awkward dwarf progeny of shrub cypress, and curious bulbous-like stumps, called "cypress-knees." Mingled with these were a few of our common deciduous trees, the white-shafted sycamore, the gray beech, and the shrubby blackjack oak, with broad leaves, brown and dead, yet glossy, and reflecting the sunbeams. Somewhat rarely, the red cedar, and, more frequently than any other except the cypress, the beautiful holly. Added to these, there was often a thick undergrowth of evergreen shrubs. Vines and creepers of various kinds grew to the tops of the tallest trees, and dangled beneath and between their branches, in intricate network. The *Tillandsia* hung in festoons, sometimes several feet in length, and often completely clothed the trunks, and every branch of the trees in the low ground. It is like a fringe of tangled hair, of a light gray pearly color, and sometimes produces exquisite effects when slightly veiling the dark green, purple and scarlet of the cedar, and the holly with their berries. The mistletoe also grew in large vivid, green tufts, on the ends of the branches of the oldest and largest trees. A small, fine and wiry, dead grass, hardly perceptible, even in the most open ground, from the coach-top, was the only sign of herbage. Large black buzzards were constantly in sight, sailing slowly, high above the tree-tops. Flocks of larks, quails, and robins were common, as were also doves, swiftly flying in small companies. The red-headed woodpecker could at any time be heard hammering the old tree-trunks, and would sometimes show himself, after his rat-tat, cocking his head archly, and listening to hear if the worm moved under the bark. The drivers told me that they had, on previous days, as they went over the road, seen deer, turkeys, and wild hogs.

At every tenth mile, or thereabout, we changed horses; and, generally, were allowed half an hour, to stroll in the neighborhood of the stable—the agent observing that we could reach the end of the staging some hours before the cars should leave to take us farther; and, as there were no good accommodations for sleeping there, we would pass the time quite as pleasantly on the road. We dined at "Marion County House," a pleasant little village

[From *A Journey in the Seaboard Slave States in the Years 1853-54, with Remarks on Their Economy*, Vol. 2, G. P. Putnam's Sons, New York, 1904. Pp. 7-13, 37-69, 82-93, 188-194, 203-205, 207-218, 220-224. Used by permission.]

(and the only village we saw during the day), with a fine pine-grove, a broad street, a court-house, a church or two, a school-house, and a dozen or twenty dwellings. Towards night, we crossed the Great Pedee of the maps, the *Big* Pedee of the natives, in a flat-boat. A large quantity of cotton, in bales, was upon the bank, ready for loading into a steamboat—when one should arrive—for Charleston.

The country was very thinly peopled; lone houses often being several miles apart. The large majority of the dwellings were of logs, and even those of the white people were often without glass windows. In the better class of cabins, the roof is usually built with a curve, so as to project eight or ten feet beyond the log-wall; and a part of this space, exterior to the logs, is inclosed with boards, making an additional small room—the remainder forms an open porch. The whole cabin is often elevated on four corner-posts, two or three feet from the ground, so that the air may circulate under it. The fire-place is built at the end of the house, of sticks and clay, and the chimney is carried up outside, and often detached from the log-walls; but the roof is extended at the gable, until in a line with its outer side. The porch has a railing in front, and a wide shelf at the end, on which a bucket of water, a gourd, and hand-basin, are usually placed. There are chairs, or benches, in the porch, and you often see women sitting at work in it, as in Germany.

The logs are usually hewn but little; and, of course, as they are laid up, there will be wide interstices between them—which are increased by subsequent shrinking. These, very commonly, are not "chinked," or filled up in any way; nor is the wall lined on the inside. Through the chinks, as you pass along the road, you may often see all that is going on in the house; and, at night, the light of the fire shines brightly out on all sides.

Cabins, of this class, would almost always be flanked by two or three negro-huts. The cabins of the poorest class of whites were of a meaner sort—being mere square pens of logs, roofed over, provided with a chimney, and usually with a shed of boards, supported by rough posts, before the door.

Occasionally, where the silvery sand was darkened by a considerable intermixture of mould, there would be a large plantation, with negro-quarters, and a cotton-press and gin-house. We passed half a dozen of these, perhaps, during the day. Where the owners resided in them, they would have comfortable-looking residences, not unlike the better class of New England farm-houses. On the largest one, however, there was no residence for the owner, at all, only a small cottage, or white-washed cabin, for the overseer. It was a very large plantation, and all the buildings were substantial and commodious, except the negro-cabins, which were the smallest I had seen—I thought not more than twelve feet square, interiorly. They stood in two rows, with a wide street between them. They were built of logs, with no windows—no openings at all, except the doorway, with a chimney of sticks and mud; with no trees about them, no porches, or shades, of any kind. Except for the chimney—the purpose of which I should not readily have guessed—if I had seen one of them in New England, I should have con-jectured that it had been built for a powder-house, or perhaps an ice-house—never for an animal to sleep in.

We stopped, for some time, on this planta-tion, near where some thirty men and women were at work, repairing the road. The women were in majority, and were engaged at exactly the same labor as the men; driving the carts, loading them with dirt, and dumping them upon the road; cutting down trees, and draw-ing wood by hand, to lay across the miry places; hoeing, and shovelling.

They were dressed in coarse gray gowns, generally very much burned, and very dirty; which, for greater convenience of working in the mud, were reefed up with a cord drawn tightly around the body, a little above the hips —the spare amount of skirt bagging out be-tween this and the waist-proper. On their legs were loose leggins, or pieces of blanket or bagging wrapped about, and lashed with thongs; and they wore very heavy shoes. Most of them had handkerchiefs, only, tied around their heads, some wore men's caps, or old slouched hats, and several were bare-headed.

The overseer rode about among them, on a horse, carrying in his hands a raw-hide whip, constantly directing and encouraging them; but, as my companion and I, both, several times noticed, as often as he visited one end of the line of operations, the hands at the other end would discontinue their labor, until he turned to ride towards them again. . . .

At length, the overseer dismounted from his horse, and, giving him to a boy to take to the stables, got upon the coach, and rode with us several miles. From the conversation I had with him, as well as from what I saw of his conduct in the field, I judged that he was an uncommonly fit man for his duties; at least ordinarily amiable in disposition, and not passionate; but deliberate, watchful, and efficient. I thought he would be not only a good economist, but a firm and considerate officer or master.

*   *   *

A VISIT TO A PLANTATION

. . . Nowhere in the world could a man, with a sound body and a quiet conscience live more pleasantly, at least, as a guest, it seems to me, than here where I am. I was awakened this morning by a servant making a fire for me to dress by. Opening the window, I found a clear, brisk air, but without frost—the mercury standing at 35° F. There was not a sign of winter, except that a few cypress trees, hung with seed, attached to pretty pendulous tassels, were leafless. A grove which surrounded the house was all in dark verdure; there were green oranges on trees nearer the window; the buds were swelling on a jessamine-vine, and a number of camelia-japonicas were in full bloom; one of them, at least seven feet high, and a large, compact shrub, must have had several hundred blossoms on it. Sparrows were chirping, doves cooing, and a mocking-bird whistling loudly. I walked to the stable, and saw the clean and neatly-dressed negroes grooming thoroughbred horses. They pawed

the ground, and tossed their heads, and drew deep inspirations, and danced as they were led out in exuberance of animal spirits, and I felt as they did. We drove ten miles to church, in the forenoon, with the carriage-top thrown back, and with our overcoats laid aside; nevertheless, when we returned, and came into the house, we found a crackling wood fire, in the old-fashioned fire-place, as comfortable as it was cheerful. Two lads, the sons of my host, had returned the night before from a "marooning party," with a boat-load of venison, wild fowl and fish, and at dinner this evening there were delicacies which are not to be had in perfection, it is said, anywhere else than on a rice-plantation. The woods and waters around us abound, not only with game, but with most interesting subjects of observation to the naturalist and the artist. Everything encourages cheerfulness, and invites to healthful life.

Now to think how people are baking in their oven-houses at home, or waddling out in the deep snow or mud, or across the frozen ruts, wrapped up to a Falstaffian rotundity in flannels and furs, one can but wonder that those who have means stay there, any more than these stay here in summer; and that my host would no more think of doing than the wild-goose.

But I must tell how I got here, and what I saw by the way.

A narrow belt of cleared land—"vacant lots"—only separated the town from the pine-forest—that great broad forest which extends uninterruptedly, and is merely dotted with a few small corn and cotton-fields, from Delaware to Louisiana.

Having some doubt about the road, I asked a direction of a man on horseback, who overtook and was passing me. In reply, he said it was a very straight road, and we should go in company, for a mile or two. He inquired if I was a stranger; and, when he heard that I was from the North, and now first visiting the South, he remarked that there was "no better place for me to go to than that for which I was bound. Mr. X. was a very fine man—rich, got a splendid plantation, lived well, had plenty of company always, and there were a number of other show plantations near his. He reckoned I would visit some of them."

I asked what he called "show plantations." "Plantations belonging to rich people," he said, "where they had everything fixed up nice. There were several places that had that name; their owners always went out and lived on them part of the year, and then they kept a kind of open house, and were always ready to receive company. He reckoned I might go and stay a month around on them kind of places on —— river, and it would not cost me a cent. They always had a great many Northerners going to see them, those gentlemen had. Almost every Northerner, that came here, was invited right out, to visit some of them, and, in summer, a good many of them went to the North themselves."

During the forenoon, my road continued broad and straight, and I was told that it was the chief outlet and thoroughfare of a very extensive agricultural district. There was very little land in cultivation within sight of the road, however; not a mile of it fenced, in twenty, and the only houses were log-cabins. The soil varied from a coarse, clean, yellow sand, to a dark, brown, sandy loam. There were indications that most of the land had, at some time, been under cultivation—had been worn out, and deserted.

Long teams of mules, driven by negroes, toiled slowly towards the town, with loads of rice, or cotton. A stage-coach, with six horses to hasten it through the heavy road, covered me, as it passed, with dust; and, once or twice, I met a stylish carriage (not the old Virginia "family chariot, with its six well-conditioned grays," but its descendant in fashion), with fashionably-clad gentlemen and ladies, and primly-liveried negro-servants; but much the greatest traffic of the road was done by small one-horse carts, driven by white men, or women.

These carts, all but their wheels, which come from the North, look as if they were made by their owners, in the woods, with no better tools than axes and jack-knives. Very little iron is used in their construction; the different parts being held together by wooden pins, and lashings of hide. The harness is made chiefly by ropes and undressed hide; but there is always a high-peaked riding-saddle, in which the driver prefers to sit, rather than on his cart. Once, I met a woman riding in this way, with a load of children in the cart behind her. From the axle-tree, often hung a gourd, or an iron kettle. One man carried a rifle on his pommel. Sometimes, these carts would contain a single bale of cotton, more commonly, an assorted cargo of maize, sweet potatoes, poultry, game, hides, and peltry, with, always, some bundles of corn-leaves, to be fed to the horse. Women and children were often passengers, or travelled on foot, in company with the carts, which were usually furnished with a low tilt. Many of them, I found, had been two or three days on the road, bringing down a little crop to market; whole families coming with it, to get reclothed with the proceeds.

The men with the carts were generally slight, with high cheekbones and sunken eyes, and were of less than the usual stature of the Anglo-Saxon race. They were dressed in long-skirted homespun coats, wore slouched hats, and heavy boots, outside their trowsers. As they met me, they usually bowed, and often offered a remark upon the weather, or the roads, in a bold, but not uncourteous manner—showing themselves to be, at least, in one respect, better off than the majority of European peasants, whose educated servility of character rarely fails to manifest itself, when they meet a well-dressed stranger.

The household markets of most of the Southern towns seem to be mainly supplied by the poor country people, who, driving in in this style, bring all sorts of produce to exchange for such small stores and articles of apparel as they must needs obtain from the shops. Sometimes, owing to the great extent of the back country from which the supplies are gathered, they are offered in great abundance and variety; at other times, from the want of regular market-men, there will be a scarcity, and prices will be very high.

A stranger cannot but express surprise and amusement at the appearance and manners of these country traffickers in the market-place. The "wild Irish" hardly differ more from the English gentry, than these rustics from the better class of planters and towns-people, with whom the traveller more commonly comes in contact. Their language, even, is almost incomprehensible, and seems exceedingly droll, to a Northern man. I have found it quite impossible to report it.

I shall not soon forget the figure of a little old white woman, wearing a man's hat, smoking a pipe, driving a little black bull with reins; sitting, herself, bolt upright, upon the axle-tree of a little truck, on which she was returning from market. I was riding with a gentleman of the town at the time, and, as she bowed to him with an expression of ineffable self-satisfaction, I asked if he knew her. He had known her for twenty years, he said, and until lately she had always come into town about once a week, on foot, bringing fowls, eggs, potatoes, or herbs, for sale, in a basket. The bull she had probably picked up astray, when a calf, and reared and broken it herself; and the cart and harness she had made herself; but he did not think anybody in the land felt richer than she did now, or prouder of her establishment.

In the afternoon, I left the main road, and, towards night, reached a much more cultivated district. The forest of pines still extended uninterruptedly on one side of the way, but on the other was a continued succession of very large fields, of rich, dark soil— evidently reclaimed swamp-land—which had been cultivated the previous year, in Sea Island cotton, or maize. Beyond them, a flat surface of still lower land, with a silver thread of water curling through it, extended, Holland-like, to the horizon. Usually at as great a distance as a quarter of a mile from the road, and from a half mile to a mile apart, were the residences of the planters—large white houses, with groves of evergreen trees about them; and between these and the road were little villages of slave-cabins.

My directions not having been sufficiently explicit, I rode in, by a private lane, to one of these. It consisted of some thirty neatly-white-washed cottages, with a broad avenue, planted with pride-of-China trees, between them.

The cottages were framed buildings, boarded on the outside, with shingle roofs and brick chimneys; they stood fifty feet apart, with gardens and pig-yards, enclosed by palings, between them. At one, which was evidently the "sick-house," or hospital, there were several negroes, of both sexes, wrapped in blankets, and reclining on the door-steps or on the ground, basking in the sunshine. Some of them looked ill, but all were chatting and laughing as I rode up to make an inquiry. I learned that it was not the plantation I was intending to visit, and received direction, as usual, so indistinct and incorrect that it led me wrong.

At another plantation which I soon afterwards reached, I found the "settlement" arranged in the same way, the cabins only being of a slightly different form. In the middle of one row was a well-house, and opposite it, on the other row, was a mill-house, with stones, at which the negroes grind their corn. It is a kind of pestle and mortar; and I was informed afterwards that the negroes prefer to take their allowance of corn and crack it for themselves, rather than to receive meal, because they think the mill-ground meal does not make as sweet bread.

At the head of the settlement, in a garden looking down the street, was an overseer's house, and here the road divided, running each way at right angles; on one side to barns and a landing on the river, on the other toward the mansion of the proprietor. A negro boy opened the gate of the latter, and I entered.

On either side, at fifty feet distant, were rows of old live-oak trees, their branches and twigs slightly hung with a delicate fringe of gray moss, and their dark, shining, green foliage meeting and intermingling naturally but densely overhead. The sunlight streamed through and played aslant the lustrous leaves, and fluttering, pendulous moss; the arch was low and broad; the trunks were huge and gnarled, and there was a heavy groining of strong, rough, knotty branches. I stopped my horse and held my breath; for I have hardly in all my life seen anything so impressively grand and beautiful. . . .

Alas! no angels; only little black babies, toddling about with an older child or two to watch them, occupied the aisle. At the upper end was the owner's mansion, with a circular court-yard around it, and an irregular plantation of great trees; one of the oaks, as I afterwards learned, seven feet in diameter of trunk, and covering with its branches a circle of one hundred and twenty feet in diameter. As I approached it, a smart servant came out to take my horse. I obtained from him a direction to the residence of the gentleman I was searching for, and rode away, glad that I had stumbled into so charming a place.

After riding a few miles farther I reached my destination.

Mr. X. has two plantations on the river, besides a large tract of poor pine forest land, extending some miles back upon the upland, and reaching above the malarious region. In the upper part of this pine land is a house, occupied by his overseer during the malarious season, when it is dangerous for any but negroes to remain during the night in the vicinity of the swamps or rice-fields. Even those few who have been born in the region, and have grown up subject to the malaria, are generally weakly and short-lived. The negroes do not enjoy as good health on rice plantations as elsewhere; and the greater difficulty with which their lives are preserved, through infancy especially, shows that the subtle poison of the miasma is not innocuous to them; but Mr. X. boasts a steady increase of his negro stock of five per cent. per annum, which is better than is averaged on the plantations of the interior.

* * *

The plantation which contains Mr. X.'s winter residence, has but a small extent of rice-land, the greater part of it being reclaimed upland swamp soil, suitable for the culture of Sea Island cotton, which, at the present market, might be grown upon it with profit. But, as his force of slaves has ordinarily been more profitably engaged in the rice-fields, all this has been for many years "turned out," and is now overgrown with pines. The other plantation contains over five hundred acres of rice-land, fitted for irrigation; the remainder is unusually fertile, reclaimed upland swamp, and some hundred acres of it are cultivated for maize and Sea Island cotton.

There is a "negro settlement" on each; but both plantations, although a mile or two apart, are worked together as one, under one overseer—the hands being drafted from one to another as their labor is required. Somewhat over seven hundred acres are at the present time under the plough in the two plantations: the whole number of negroes is two hundred, and they are reckoned to be equal about one hundred prime hands—an unusual strength for that number of all classes. The overseer lives, in winter, near the settlement of the larger plantation, Mr. X. near that of the smaller.

It is an old family estate, inherited by Mr. X.'s wife, who, with her children, were born and brought up upon it in close intimacy with the negroes, a large proportion of whom were also included in her inheritance, or have been since born upon the estate. Mr. X. himself is a New England farmer's son, and has been a successful merchant and manufacturer. He is also a religious man, without the dementifying bigotry of self-important humility, so frequently implied by that appellation to a New Englander, but generous, composed and cheerful in disposition, as well as conscientious.

The patriarchal institution could be seen here under its most favorable aspects; not only from the ties of long family association, common traditions, common memories, and, if ever, common interests, between the slaves and their rulers, but, also, from the practical talent for organization and administration, gained among the rugged fields, the complicated looms, and the exact and comprehensive counting-houses of New England, which directs the labor.

The house-servants are more intelligent, understand and perform their duties better, and are more appropriately dressed than any I have seen before. The labor required of them is light, and they are treated with much more consideration for their health and comfort than is usually given to that of free domestics. They live in brick cabins, adjoining the house and stables, and one of these, into which I have looked, is neatly and comfortably furnished. Several of the house-servants, as is usual, are mulattoes, and good-looking. The mulattoes are generally preferred for indoor occupations. Slaves brought up to house-work dread to be employed at field-labor; and those accustomed to the comparatively unconstrained life of the negro-settlement detest the close control and careful movements required of the house-servants. It is a punishment for a lazy field-hand, to employ him in menial duties at the house, as it is to set a sneaking sailor to do the work of a cabin-servant; and it is equally a punishment to a neglectful house-servant, to banish him to the field-gangs. All the household economy is, of course, carried on in a style appropriate to a wealthy gentleman's residence—not more so, nor less so, that I observe, than in an establishment of similar grade at the North.

It is a custom with Mr. X., when on the estate, to look each day at all the work going on, inspect the buildings, boats, embankments and sluice-ways, and examine the sick. Yesterday I accompanied him in one of these daily rounds.

After a ride of several miles through the woods, in the rear of the plantations, we came to his largest negro-settlement. There was a street, or common, two hundred feet wide, on which the cabins of the negroes fronted. Each cabin was a frame building, the walls boarded and whitewashed on the outside, lathed and plastered within, the roof shingled; forty-two feet long, twenty-one feet wide, divided into two family tenements, each twenty-one by twenty-one; each tenement divided into three rooms—one, the common house-

hold apartment, twenty-one by ten; each of the others (bed-rooms), ten by ten. There was a brick fire-place in the middle of the long side of each living room, the chimneys rising in one, in the middle of the roof. Besides these rooms, each tenement had a cock-loft, entered by steps from the household room. Each tenement is occupied, on an average, by five persons. There were in them closets, with locks and keys, and a varying quantity of rude furniture. Each cabin stood two hundred feet from the next, and the street in front of them being two hundred feet wide, they were just that distance apart each way. The people were nearly all absent at work, and had locked their outer doors, taking the keys with them. Each cabin has a front and back door, and each room a window, closed by a wooden shutter, swinging outward, on hinges. Between each tenement and the next house, is a small piece of ground, inclosed with palings, in which are coops of fowl, with chickens, hovels for nests, and for sows with pig. There were a great many fowls in the street. The negroes' swine are allowed to run in the woods, each owner having his own distinguished by a peculiar mark. In the rear of the yards were gardens—a half-acre to each family. Internally the cabins appeared dirty and disordered, which was rather a pleasant indication that their home-life was not much interfered with, though I found certain police regulations were enforced.

The cabin nearest the overseer's house was used as a nursery. Having driven up to this, Mr. X. inquired first of an old nurse how the children were; whether there had been any births since his last visit; spoke to two convalescent young mothers, that were lounging on the floor of the portico, with the children, and then asked if there were any sick people.

"Nobody, oney dat boy Sam, sar."

"What Sam is that?"

"Dat little Sam, sar; Tom's Sue's Sam, sar."

"What's the matter with him?"

"Don' 'spec dere's noting much de matter wid him now, sar. He came in Sa'dy, complainin' he had de stomach-ache, an' I gin him some ile, sar; 'spec he mus' be well, dis time, but he din go out dis mornin'."

"Well, I'll see to him."

Mr. X. went to Tom's Sue's cabin, looked at the boy, and, concluding that he was well, though he lay abed, and pretended to cry with pain, ordered him to go out to work. Then, meeting the overseer, who was just riding away, on some business off the plantation, he remained some time in conversation with him, while I occupied myself in making a sketch of the nursery and the street of the settlement in my note-book. On the verandah and the steps of the nursery, there were twenty-seven children, most of them infants, that had been left there by their mothers, while they were working their tasks in the fields. They probably make a visit to them once or twice during the day, to nurse them, and receive them to take to their cabins, or where they like, when they have finished their tasks—generally in the middle of the afternoon. The older children were fed with porridge, by the general nurse. A number of girls, eight or ten years old, were occupied in holding and tending the youngest infants. Those a little older—the crawlers—were in the pen, and those big enough to toddle were playing on the steps, or before the house. Some of these, with two or three bigger ones, were singing and dancing about a fire that they had made on the ground. They were not at all disturbed or interrupted in their amusement by the presence of their owner and myself. At twelve years of age, the children are first put to regular field-work; until then no labor is required of them, except, perhaps, occasionally, they are charged with some light kind of duty, such as frightening birds from corn. When first sent to the field, one-quarter of an able-bodied hand's day's work is ordinarily allotted to them, as their task.

But very few of the babies were in arms; such as were not, generally lay on the floor, rolling about, or sat still, sucking their thumbs. The nurse was a kind-looking old negro woman, with, no doubt, philoprogenitiveness well developed; but she paid very little atten-

tion to them, only sometimes chiding the older ones for laughing or singing too loud. I watched for half an hour, and in all that time not a baby of them began to cry; nor have I ever heard one, at two or three other plantation-nurseries which I have visited. . . .

From the settlement, we drove to the "mill"—not a flouring mill, though I believe there is a run of stones in it—but a monster barn, with more extensive and better machinery for threshing and storing rice, driven by a steam-engine, than I have ever seen used for grain on any farm in Europe or America before. Adjoining the mill-house were shops and sheds, in which blacksmiths, carpenters, and other mechanics—all slaves, belonging to Mr. X.—were at work. He called my attention to the excellence of their workmanship, and said that they exercised as much ingenuity and skill as the ordinary mechanics that he was used to employ in New England. He pointed out to me some carpenter's work, a part of which had been executed by a New England mechanic, and a part by one of his own hands, which indicated that the latter was much the better workman.

I was gratified by this, for I had been so often told, in Virginia, by gentlemen, anxious to convince me that the negro was incapable of being educated or improved to a condition in which it would be safe to trust him with himself—that no negro-mechanic could ever be taught, or induced to work carefully or nicely—that I had begun to believe it might be so.

We were attended through the mill-house by a respectable-looking, orderly, and gentlemanly-mannered mulatto, who was called, by his master, "the watchman." His duties, however, as they were described to me, were those of a steward, or intendant. He carried, by a strap at his waist, a very large number of keys, and had charge of all the stores of provisions, tools, and materials of the plantations, as well as of all their produce, before it was shipped to market. He weighed and measured out all the rations of the slaves and the cattle; superintended the mechanics, and himself made and repaired, as was necessary, all the machinery, including the steam-engine.

In all these departments, his authority was superior to that of the overseer. The overseer received his private allowance of family provisions from him, as did also the head-servant at the mansion, who was his brother. His responsibility was much greater than that of the overseer; and Mr. X. said, he would trust him with much more than he would any overseer he had ever known.

*   *   *

[Olmsted here goes into an interesting description of how the slaves were worked on this plantation. This is omitted here, since Selection 31 is devoted to that topic.]

After passing through tool-rooms, corn-rooms, mule-stables, store-rooms, and a large garden, in which vegetables to be distributed among the negroes, as well as for the family, are grown, we walked to the riceland.

*   *   *

A CHURCH SERVICE

A majority of the public houses of worship at the South are small, rude structures of logs, or rough boards, built by the united labor or contributions of the people of a large neighborhood or district of country, and are used as places of assembly for all public purposes. Few of them have any regular clergymen, but preachers of different denominations go from one to another, sometimes in a defined rotation, or "circuit," so that they may be expected at each of their stations at regular intervals. A late report of the Southern Aid Society states that hardly one-fifth of the preachers are regularly educated for their business, and that "you would starve a host of them if you debarred them from seeking additional support for their families by worldly occupation." In one presbytery of the Presbyterian Church, which is, perhaps, the richest, and includes the most educated body of people of all the Southern churches, there are twenty-one ministers whose wages are not over two hundred and fifty dollars each. The proportion of ministers, of all sorts, to

people, is estimated at one to thirteen hundred. (In the Free States it is estimated at one to nine hundred.) . . .

The two largest denominations of Christians at the South are the Methodists and Baptists—the last having a numerical superiority. There are some subdivisions of each, and of the Baptists especially, the nature of which I do not understand. Two grand divisions of the Baptists are known as the Hard Shells and the Soft Shells. There is an intense rivalry and jealousy among these various sects and subsects, and the controversy between them is carried on with a bitterness and persistence exceeding anything which I have known at the North, and in a manner which curiously indicates how the terms "Christianity," "piety," etc., are misapplied to partisanship, and conditions of the imagination.

*   *   *

The religious service which I am about to describe, was held in a less than usually rude meeting-house, the boards by which it was inclosed being planed, the windows glazed, and the seats for the white people provided with backs. It stood in a small clearing of the woods, and there was no habitation within two miles of it. When I reached it with my friends, the services had already commenced. Fastened to trees, in a circle about the house, there were many saddled horses and mules, and a few attached to cars or wagons. There were two smouldering camp-fires, around which sat circles of negroes and white boys, roasting potatoes in the ashes.

In the house were some fifty white people, generally dressed in homespun, and of the class called "crackers," though I was told that some of them owned a good many negroes, and were by no means so poor as their appearance indicated. About one-third of the house, at the end opposite the desk, was covered by a gallery or cock-loft, under and in which, distinctly separated from the whites, was a dense body of negroes; the men on one side, the women on another. The whites were seated promiscuously in the body of the house. The negroes present outnumbered the whites, but the exercises at this time seemed to have no reference to them; there were many more waiting about the doors outside, and they were expecting to enjoy a meeting to themselves, after the whites had left the house. They were generally neatly dressed, more so than the majority of the whites present, but in a distinctly plantation or slave style. A few of them wore somewhat expensive articles, evidently of their own selection and purchase, but I observed, with some surprise, that not one of the women had a bonnet upon her head, all wearing handkerchiefs, generally of gay patterns, and becomingly arranged. I inquired if this was entirely a matter of taste, and was told that it, no doubt, was generally so, though the masters would not probably allow them to wear bonnets, if they should be disposed to, and should purchase them themselves, as it would be thought presuming. In the towns, the colored women often, but not generally, wear bonnets.

During all the exercises, people of both classes were frequently going out and coming in; the women had brought their babies with them, and these made much disturbance. A negro girl would sometimes come forward to take a child out; perhaps the child would prefer not to be taken out and would make loud and angry objections; it would then be fed. Several were allowed to crawl about the floor, carrying handfuls of corn-bread and roast potatoes about with them; one had a fancy to enter the pulpit; which it succeeded in climbing into three times, and was as often taken away, in spite of loud and tearful expostulations, by its father. Dogs were not excluded; and outside, the doors and windows all being open, there was much neighing and braying, unused as were the mules and horses to see so many of their kind assembled.

The preliminary devotional exercises—a Scripture reading, singing, and painfully irreverential and meaningless harangues nominally addressed to the Deity, but really to the audience—being concluded, the sermon was begun with the reading of a text, with which, however, it had, so far as I could discover, no

further association. Without often being violent in his manner, the speaker nearly all the time cried aloud at the utmost stretch of his voice, as if calling to some one a long distance off; as his discourse was extemporaneous, however, he sometimes returned with curious effect to his natural conversational tone; and as he was gifted with a strong imagination, and possessed of a good deal of dramatic power, he kept the attention of the people very well. There was no argument upon any point that the congregation were likely to have much difference of opinion upon, nor any special connection between one sentence and another; yet there was a constant, sly, sectarian skirmishing, and a frequently recurring cannonade upon French infidelity and socialism, and several crushing charges upon Fourier, the Pope of Rome, Tom Paine, Voltaire, "Roosu," and Jo Smith. The audience were frequently reminded that the preacher did not want their attention, for any purpose of his own; but that he demanded a respectful hearing as "the Ambassador of Christ." He had the habit of frequently repeating a phrase, or of bringing forward the same idea in a slightly different form, a great many times.

* * *

At the end of the sermon he stepped down from the pulpit, and, crossing the house towards the negroes, said, quietly, as he walked, "I take great interest in the poor blacks; and this evening I am going to hold a meeting specially for you." With this, he turned back, and without re-entering the pulpit, but strolling up and down before it, read a hymn, at the conclusion of which, he laid his book down, and speaking for a moment, with natural emphasis, said:

"I don't want to create a tumultuous scene, now;—that isn't my intention. I don't want to make an excitement—that ain't what I want,—but I feel that there's some here that I may never see again, ah! and, as I may never have another opportunity, I feel it my duty as an Ambassador of Jesus Christ, ah! before I go———." By this time he had returned to the high key and whining yell. Exactly what he felt it his duty to do, I did not understand; but evidently to employ some more powerful agency of awakening, than arguments and appeals to the understanding; and, before I could conjecture, in the least, of what sort this was to be, while he was yet speaking calmly, deprecating excitement, my attention was attracted to several men, who had previously appeared sleepy and indifferent, but who now suddenly began to sigh, raise their heads, and *shed tears*— some standing up, so that they might be observed in doing this by the whole congregation—the tears running down their noses without any interruption. The speaker, presently, was crying aloud, with a mournful, distressed, beseeching shriek, as if he was himself suffering torture. . . . "Oh, any of you wives that has got an unconverted husband, that won't go along with you to eternal glory, but is set upon being separated from you, oh! and taking up his bed in hell—Oh! I call upon you, if you love him, now to come out here and jine us in praying for him. Oh, if there's a husband here, whose wife is still in the bond of iniquity," etc., through a long category.

It was immediately evident that a large part of the audience understood his wish to be the reverse of what he had declared, and considered themselves called upon to assist him; and it was astonishing to see with what readiness the faces of those who, up to the moment he gave the signal, had appeared drowsy and stupid, were made to express agonizing excitement, sighing, groaning, and weeping. Rising in their seats and walking up to the pulpit, they grasped each other's hands agonizingly, and remained, some kneeling, others standing, with their faces towards the remainder of the assembly. There was great confusion and tumult, and the poor children, evidently impressed by the terrified tone of the howling preacher, with the expectation of some immediately impending calamity, shrieked, and ran hither and thither, till negro girls came forward, laughing at the imposition, and carried them out.

At length, when some twenty had gathered around the preacher, and it became evident that no more could be drawn out, he stopped a moment for breath, and then repeated a verse of a hymn, which being sung, he again commenced to cry aloud, calling now upon all the unconverted, who were *willing* to be saved, to kneel. A few did so, and another verse was sung, followed by another more fervent exhortation. So it went on; at each verse his entreaties, warnings, and threats, and the responsive groans, sobs, and ejaculations of his coterie grew louder and stronger. Those who refused to kneel, were addressed as standing on the brink of the infernal pit, into which a diabolical divinity was momentarily on the point of satisfying the necessities of his character by hurling them off.

All this time about a dozen of the audience remained standing, many were kneeling, and the larger part had taken their seats—all having risen at the commencement of the singing. Those who continued standing were mainly wild-looking young fellows, who glanced with smiles at one another, as if they needed encouragement to brazen it out. A few young women were evidently fearfully excited, and perceptibly trembled, but for some reason dared not kneel, or compromise, by sitting. . . .

The last verse of the hymn was sung. A comparatively quiet and sober repetition of Scripture phrases, strung together heterogeneously and without meaning, in the form of prayer, followed, a benediction was pronounced, and in five minutes all the people were out of the door, with no trace of the previous excitement left, but most of the men talking eagerly of the price of cotton, and negroes, and other news.

The negroes kept their place during all of the tumult; there may have been a sympathetic groan or exclamation uttered by one or two of them, but generally they expressed only the interest of curiosity in the proceedings, such as Europeans might at a performance of the dancing dervishes, an Indian pow-wow, or an exhibition of "psychological" or "spiritual" phenomena, making it very evident that the emotion of the performers was optionally engaged in, as an appropriate part of divine service. There was generally a self-satisfied smile upon their faces; and I have no doubt they felt that they could do it with a good deal more energy and abandon, if they were called upon. I did not wish to detain my companion to witness how they succeeded, when their turn came; and I can only judge from the fact that those I saw the next morning were so hoarse that they could scarcely speak, that the religious exercises they most enjoy are rather hard upon the lungs, whatever their effect may be upon the soul.

FROM SAVANNAH TO MOBILE

I left Savannah for the West, by the Macon road; the train started punctually to a second, at its advertised time; the speed was not great, but regular, and less time was lost unnecessarily, at way-stations, than usually on our Northern roads.

I have travelled more than five hundred miles on the Georgia roads, and I am glad to say that all of them seemed to be exceedingly well managed. The speed upon them is not generally more than from fifteen to twenty miles an hour; but it is made, as advertised, with considerable punctuality. The roads are admirably engineered and constructed, and their equipment will compare favorably with that of any other roads on the continent. There are now very nearly, if not quite, one thousand miles of railroad in the State, and more building. The Savannah and Macon line—the first built—was commenced in 1834. The increased commerce of the city of Savannah, which followed its completion, stimulated many other railroad enterprises, not only within the State, but elsewhere at the South, particularly in South Carolina. Many of these were rashly pushed forward by men of no experience, and but little commercial judgment; the roads were injudiciously laid out, and have been badly managed, and, of course, have occasioned disastrous losses. The Savannah and Macon road has, however, been very successful. The receipts are now over $1,000,000 annually; the road is well stocked, is out of debt, and its business is constantly increasing; the stock is above par, and the stockholders are receiving eight per cent. dividends, with a handsome surplus on hand. It has always been, in a great degree, under the management of Northern men—was engineered, and is still worked chiefly by Northern men, and a large amount of its stock is owned at the North. I am told that most of the mechanics, and of the successful merchants and tradesmen of Savannah came originally from the North, or are the sons of Northern men.

Partly by rail and partly by rapid stage-coaching (the coaches, horses, and drivers again from the North), I crossed the State in about twenty-four hours. The railroad has since been completed from Savannah to Montgomery, in Alabama, and it is being extended slowly towards the Mississippi; of course, with the expectation that it will eventually reach the Pacific, and thus make Savannah "the gate to the commerce of the world." Ship-masters will hope that, when either it or its rival in South Carolina has secured that honor, they will succeed, better than they yet have done, in removing the bars, physical and legal, by which commerce is now annoyed in its endeavors to serve them.

At Columbus, I spent several days. It is the largest manufacturing town, south of Richmond, in the Slave States. It is situated at the falls, the head of steamboat navigation of the Chattahooche, the western boundary of Georgia. The water-power is sufficient to drive two hundred thousand spindles, with a proportionate number of looms. There are, at present, probably from fifteen to twenty thousand spindles running. The operatives in the cotton mills are said to be mainly "Cracker girls" (poor whites from the country), who earn, in good times, by piece-work, from $8 to $12 a month. There are, besides the cotton mills, one woollen mill, one paper mill, a foundry, a cotton-gin factory, a machine shop, etc. The laborers in all these are mainly whites, and they are in such a condition that, if temporarily thrown out of employment, great numbers of them are at once reduced to a state of destitution, and are dependent upon credit or charity for their daily food. Public entertainments were being held at the time of my visit, the profits to be applied to the relief of operatives in mills which had been stopped by the effects of a late flood of the river. Yet it is boasted constantly that Slavery is a perfect safeguard against such distress.

I had seen in no place, since I left Washington, so much gambling, intoxication, and cruel treatment of servants in public, as in Columbus. This possibly was accidental; but I must caution persons, travelling for health or pleasure, to avoid stopping in the town. The hotel in which I lodged was disgustingly dirty; the table revolting; the waiters stupid, inattentive, and annoying. It was the stage-house; but I was informed that the other public-house was no better. There are very good inns at Macon, and at Montgomery, Alabama; and it will be best for an invalid proceeding from Savannah westward, if possible, not to spend a night between these towns.

I should add that I met with much courtesy from strangers, and saw as much real hospitality of disposition among the people near Columbus, as anywhere else in the South. I was much gratified by a visit to the garden of Mr. Peabody, a horticulturist, who has succeeded wonderfully in cultivating strawberries upon a poor, sandy soil, in a climate of great heat and dryness, by a thin mulching of leaves.

A day's journey took me from Columbus, through a hilly wilderness, with a few dreary villages, and many isolated cotton farms, with comfortless habitations for black and white upon them, to Montgomery, the capital of Alabama.

Montgomery is a prosperous town, with very pleasant suburbs, and a remarkably enterprising population, among which there is a considerable proportion of Northern and foreign-born business men and mechanics.

I spent a week here very pleasantly, and then left for Mobile, on the steamboat *Fashion,* a clean and well-ordered boat, with polite and obliging officers. We were two days and a half making the passage, the boat stopping at almost every bluff and landing to take on cotton, until she had a freight of nineteen hundred bales, which was built up on the guards, seven or eight tiers in height, until it reached the hurricane deck. The boat was thus brought so deep that her guards were in the water, and the ripple of the river constantly washed over them. There are two hundred landings on the Alabama river, and three hundred on the Bigby (Tombeckbee of the geographers), at which the boats advertise to call, if required, for passengers or freight. This, of course, makes the passage exceedingly tedious.

The principal town at which we landed was Selma, a thriving and pleasant place, situated upon the most perfectly level natural plain I ever saw. In one corner of the town, while rambling on shore, I came upon a tall, ill-proportioned, broken-windowed brick barrack; it had no grounds about it, was close upon the highway, was in every way dirty, neglected, and forlorn in expression. I inquired what it was, and was informed, the "Young Ladies' College." There were a number of pretty private gardens in the town, in which I noticed several evergreen oaks, the first I had seen since leaving Savannah.

At Claiborne, another considerable village upon the river, we landed, at nine o'clock on a Sunday night. It is situated, upon a bluff, a hundred and fifty feet high, with a nearly perpendicular bank, upon the river. The boat came to the shore at the foot of a plank slide-way, down which cotton was sent to it, from a warehouse at the top.

There was something truly Western in the direct, reckless way in which the boat was loaded. A strong gang-plank being placed at right angles to the slide-way, a bale of cotton was let slide from the top, and, coming down with fearful velocity, on striking the gang-plank, it would rebound up and out on to the boat, against a barricade of bales previously arranged to receive it. The moment it struck this barricade, it would be dashed at by two or three men, and jerked out of the way, and others would roll it to its place for the voyage, on the tiers aft. The mate, standing near the bottom of the slide, as soon as the men had removed one bale to what he thought a safe distance, would shout to those aloft, and down would come another. Not unfrequently, a bale would not strike fairly on its end, and would rebound off, diagonally, overboard; or would be thrown up with such force as to go over the barricade, breaking stanchions and railings, and scattering the passengers on the berth deck. Negro hands were sent to the top of the bank, to roll the bales to the side, and Irishmen were kept below to remove them, and stow them. On asking the mate (with some surmisings) the reason of this arrangement, he said:

"The niggers are worth too much to be risked here; if the Paddies are knocked overboard, or get their backs broke, nobody loses anything!"

The boat being detained the greater part of the night, and the bounding bales making too much noise to allow me to sleep, I ascended the bank by a flight of two hundred steps, placed by the side of the slide-way, and took a walk in the village. In the principal street, I came upon a group of seven negroes, talking in lively, pleasant tones: presently, one of them commenced to sing, and in a few moments all the others joined in, taking different parts, singing with great skill and taste— better than I ever heard a group of young men in a Northern village, without previous arrangement, but much as I have heard a strolling party of young soldiers, or a company of students, or apprentices, in the streets of a German town, at night. After concluding the song, which was of a sentimental character, and probably had been learned at a concert or theatre, in the village, they continued in conversation, till one of them began to whistle: in a few moments all joined in, taking several different parts, as before, and making a peculiarly plaintive music. Soon after this, they walked all together, singing, and talking soberly, by turns, slowly away.

*   *   *

There were about one hundred passengers on the *Fashion,* besides a number of poor people and negroes on the lower deck. They were, generally, cotton planters, going to Mobile on business, or emigrants bound to Texas or Arkansas. They were usually well dressed, but were a rough, coarse style of people, drinking a great deal and most of the time under a little alcoholic excitement. Not sociable, except when the topics of cotton, land, and negroes, were started; interested, however, in talk about theatres and the turf; very profane; often showing the handles of concealed weapons about their persons, but not quarrelsome, avoiding disputes and altercations, and respectful to one another in forms of words; very ill-informed, except on plantation business; their language very ungrammatical, idiomatic, and extravagant. Their grand characteristics—simplicity of motive, vague, shallow, and purely objective habits of thought; spontaneity and truthfulness of utterance, and bold, self-reliant movement.

With all their individual independence, I soon could perceive a very great homogeneousness of character, by which they were distinguishable from any other people with whom I had before been thrown in contact; and I began to study it with interest, as the Anglo-Saxon development of the Southwest.

I found that, more than any people I have ever seen, they were unrateable by dress, taste, forms, and expenditures. I was perplexed by finding, apparently united in the same individual, the self-possession and confidence of the well-equipped gentleman, and the coarseness and low tastes of the uncivilized boor— frankness and reserve, recklessness and self-restraint, extravagance and penuriousness.

There was one man, who "lived, when he was to home," he told me, "in the Red River Country," in the northeastern part of Texas, having emigrated thither from Alabama, some years before. He was a tall, thin, awkward person, and wore a suit of clothes (probably bought "ready-made") which would have better suited a short, fat figure. Under his waistcoat he carried a large knife, with the hilt generally protruding at the breast. He had been with his family to his former home, to do a little business, and visit his relatives, and was now returning to his plantation. His wife was a pale and harassed looking woman; and he scarce ever paid her the smallest attention, not even sitting near her at the public table. Of his children, however, he seemed very fond; and they had a negro servant in attendance upon them, whom he was constantly scolding and threatening. Having been from home for six weeks, his impatience to return was very great, and was constantly aggravated by the frequent and long-continued stoppages of the boat. "Time's money, time's money!" he would be constantly saying, while we were taking on cotton, "time's worth more'n money to me now; a hundred per cent. more, 'cause I left my niggers all alone, not a dam white man within four mile on 'em."

I asked how many negroes he had.

"I've got twenty on 'em to home, and thar they ar! and thar they ar! and thar ain't a dam soul of a white fellow within four mile on 'em."

*   *   *

There were three young negroes, carried by another Texan, on the deck, outside the cabin. I don't know why they were not allowed to be with the other emigrant slaves, on the lower deck, unless the owner was afraid of their trying to get away, and had no handcuffs small enough for them. They were boys; the oldest twelve or fourteen years old, the youngest not more than seven. They had evidently been bought lately by their present owner, and probably had just been taken from their parents. They lay on the deck and slept, with no bed but the passengers' luggage, and no cover but a single blanket for each. Early one morning, after a very stormy night, when they must have suffered much from the driving rain and cold, I saw their owner with a glass of spirits, giving each a few swallows from it. The older ones smacked their lips, and said, "Tank 'ou, massa"; but the little one could n't drink it, and cried aloud, when he was forced to. The older ones were very playful and quarrelsome, and continually teasing the younger, who seemed very sad, or homesick and sulky. He would get very angry at their mischievous fun, and sometimes strike them. He would then be driven into a corner, where he would lie on his back, and kick at them in a perfect frenzy of anger and grief. The two boys would continue to laugh at him, and frequently the passengers would stand about, and be amused by it. Once, when they had plagued him in this way for some time, he jumped up on to the cotton bales, and made as if he would have plunged overboard. One of the older boys caught him by the ankle, and held him till his master came and hauled him in, and gave him a severe flogging with a rope's end. A number of passengers collected about them, and I heard several say, "That's what he wants." Red River said to me, "I've been a watchin' that ar boy, and I see what's the matter with him; he's got the devil in him right bad, and he'll hev to take a right many of them warmin's before it be got out."

The crew of the boat, as I have intimated, was composed partly of Irishmen, and partly of negroes; the latter were slaves, and were hired of their owners at $40 a month—the same wages paid to the Irishmen. A dollar of their wages was given to the negroes themselves, for each Sunday they were on the passage. So far as convenient, they were kept at work separate from the white hands; they were also messed separately. On Sunday I observed them dining in a group, on the cotton bales. The food, which was given to them in tubs, from the kitchen was various and abundant, consisting of bean porridge, bacon, corn bread, ship's biscuit, potatoes, duff (pudding), and gravy. There was only one knife used, among ten of them; the bacon was cut and torn into shares; splinters of the bone and of firewood were used for forks; the porridge was passed from one to another, and drunk out of the tub; but though excessively dirty and beast-like in their appearance and manners, they were good-natured and jocose as usual.

"Heah! you Bill," said one to another, who

was on a higher tier of cotton, "pass down de dessart. You! up dar on de hill; de dessart! Augh! don't you know what de dessart be? De duff, you fool."

"Does any of de gemmen want some o' dese potatum?" asked another; and no answer being given, he turned the tub full of potatoes overboard, without any hesitation. It was evident he had never had to think on one day how he should be able to live the next.

Whenever we landed at night or on Sunday, for wood or cotton, many negroes would come on board from the neighboring plantations, to sell eggs to the steward.

Sunday was observed by the discontinuance of public gambling in the cabin, and in no other way. At midnight gambling was resumed, and during the whole passage was never at any other time discontinued, night or day, so far as I saw. There were three men that seemed to be professional sharpers, and who probably played into each other's hands. One young man lost all the money he had with him—several hundred dollars

Mobile, in its central, business part, is very compactly built, dirty, and noisy, with little elegance, or evidence of taste or public spirit, in its people. A small, central, open square—the only public ground that I saw—was used as a horse and hog pasture, and clothes drying-yard. Out of the busier quarter, there is a good deal of the appearance of a thriving New England village—almost all the dwelling houses having plots of ground enclosed around them, planted with trees and shrubs. The finest trees are the magnolia and live oak; and the most valuable shrub is the Cherokee rose, which is much used for hedges and screens. It is evergreen, and its leaves are glossy and beautiful at all seasons, and in March it blooms profusely. There is an abundance, also, of the Cape jessamine. It is as beautiful as a camelia; and, when in blossom, scents the whole air with a most delicate and delicious fragrance. At a market garden, near the town which I visited, I found most of the best Northern and Belgian pears fruiting well and apparently healthy, and well suited in climate, on quince-stocks. Figs are abundant,

and bananas and oranges are said to be grown with some care, and slight winter protection.

The Battle House, kept by Boston men, with Irish servants, I found an excellent hotel; but with higher charges than I had ever paid before. Prices, generally, in Mobile, range very high. There are large numbers of foreign merchants in the population; but a great deficiency of tradesmen and mechanics. . . .

The great abundance of the best timber for the purpose, in the United States, growing in the vicinity of the town, has lately induced some persons to attempt ship building at Mobile. The mechanics employed are mainly from the North.

The great business of the town is the transfer of cotton, from the producer to the manufacturer, from the wagon and the steamboat to the sea-going ship. Like all the other cotton ports, Mobile labors under the disadvantage of a shallow harbor. At the wharves, there were only a few small craft and steamboats. All large sea-going vessels lie some thirty miles below, and their freights are transshipped in lighters.

There appears to be a good deal of wealth and luxury, as well as senseless extravagance, in the town. English merchants affect the character of the society, considerably; some very favorably—some, very much otherwise. Many of them own slaves, and, probably, all employ them; but Slavery seems to be of more value to them in the amusement it affords, than in any other way.

*　　*　　*

The steamboat by which I made the passage along the north shore of the Mexican Gulf to New Orleans, was New York built and owned by a New Yorker; and the Northern usage of selling passage tickets, to be returned on leaving the boat, was retained upon it. I was sitting near a group of Texans and emigrating planters, when a waiter passed along, crying the usual request, that passengers who had not obtained tickets, would call at the captain's office for that purpose. "What's that? What's that?" they shouted; "What did he mean? What is it?" "Why, it's a dun," said one. "Damned if't ain't," continued one and another; "he is dunnin' on us, sure," and some started from the seats, as if they thought it insulting. "Well, it's the first time I ever was dunned by a nigger, I'll swar," said one. This seemed to place it in a humorous aspect; and, after a hearty laugh, they resumed their discussion of the advantages offered to emigrants in different parts of Texas, and elsewhere.

A party of very fashionably-dressed and gay, vulgar people, were placed near me at the dinner-table; opposite, a stout, strong, rough and grim-looking Texan, and his quiet, amiable wife. There was an unusual number of passengers, and consequently a great deficiency of waiters, and the only one in our vicinity had been entirely engaged with the fashionable party; their plates had all been changed, and he had opened two or three bottles of wine for them, without paying any regard to the rest of us. At length the Texan, who had been holding a plate ready to hand to the waiter, and following his motions for a long time, with an eye full of hunger and disgust, as he was again dashing off to execute an order, shouted, with a voice loud enough to be heard the length of the boat, while he looked defiantly at the small, moustached person opposite, who had given the order, *"Boy!"* "Sir," said the negro, turning at once. "Give us something to eat here! damned if I——" "Hush," said his wife, clapping her hand on his mouth. "Well, if——" "Hush, my dear, hush," said his wife, again putting her hand across his mouth, but joining in the universal smile. The fashionable people did not call upon the waiter again till we all had got "something to eat."

THE RAPID GROWTH

The territorial Government of Alabama was established in 1816, and in 1818 she was admitted as a State into the Union. In 1820, her population was 128,000; in 1850, it had increased to 772,000; the increase of the previous ten years having been 30 per cent. (that of South Carolina was 5 per cent.; of Georgia, 31; Mississippi, 60; Michigan, 87; Wisconsin, 890). A large part of Alabama has yet a striking frontier character. Even from the State-house, in the fine and promising town of Montgomery, the eye falls in every direction upon a dense forest, boundless as the sea, and producing in the mind the same solemn sensation. Towns which are frequently referred to as important points in the stages of your journey, you are surprised to find when you reach them, consist of not more than three or four cabins, a tavern or grocery, a blacksmith's shop, and a stable.

A stranger once meeting a coach in which I was riding, asked the driver whether it would be prudent for him to pass through one of these places, that we had just come from; he had heard that there were more than fifty cases of small-pox in the town. "There ain't fifty people in the town, nor within ten mile on't," answered the driver, who was a Northerner. The best of the country roads are but little better than open passages for strong vehicles through the woods, made by cutting away the trees.

The greater number of planters own from ten to twenty slaves only, though plantations on which from fifty to a hundred are employed are not uncommon, especially on the rich alluvial soils of the southern part of the State. Many of the largest and most productive plantations are extremely unhealthy in summer, and their owners seldom reside upon them, except temporarily. Several of the larger towns, like Montgomery, remarkable in the midst of the wilderness which surrounds them, for the neatness and tasteful character of the houses and gardens which they contain, are, in a considerable degree, made up of the residences of gentlemen who own large plantations in the hotter and less healthful parts of the State. Many of these have been educated in the older States, and with minds enlarged and liberalized by travel, they form, with their families, cultivated and attractive society.

Much the larger proportion of the planters of the State live in log houses, some of them very neat and comfortable, but frequently rude in construction, not *chinked,* with windows unglazed, and wanting in many of the commonest conveniences possessed by the poorest class of Northern farmers and laborers of the older States. Many of those who live in this way, possess considerable numbers of slaves, and are every year buying more. Their early frontier life seems to have destroyed all capacity to enjoy many of the usual luxuries of civilized life.

Notwithstanding the youth of the State, there is a constant and extensive emigration from it, as well as immigration to it. Large planters, as their stock increases, are always anxious to enlarge the area of their land, and will often pay a high price for that of any poor neighbor, who, embarrassed by debt, can be tempted to move on. There is a rapid tendency in Alabama, as in the older Slave States, to the enlargement of plantations. The poorer class are steadily driven to occupy poor land, or move forward on to the frontier.

In an address before the Chunnenuggee Horticultural Society, by Hon. C. C. Clay, Jr., reported by the author in De Bow's *Review,* December, 1855, I find the following passage. I need not add a word to it to show how the political experiment of old Virginia, the Carolinas, and Georgia, is being repeated to the same cursed result in young Alabama. The author, it is fair to say, is devoted to the sustentation of Slavery, and would not, for the world, be suspected of favoring any scheme for arresting this havoc of wealth, further than by chemical science:

I can show you, with sorrow, in the older portions of Alabama, and in my native county of Madison, the sad memorials of the artless and exhausting culture of cotton. Our small planters, after taking the cream off their lands, unable to restore them by rest, manures, or otherwise, are going further west and south, in search of other virgin lands, which they may and will despoil and impoverish in like manner. Our wealthier planters, with greater means and no more skill, are buying out their poorer neighbors, extending their plantations and adding to their slave force. The wealthy few, who are able to live on smaller profits, and to give their blasted fields some rest, are thus pushing off the many, who are merely independent.

Of the twenty millions of dollars annually realized from the sales of the cotton crop of Alabama, nearly all not expended in supporting the producers is reinvested in land and negroes. Thus the white population has decreased, and the slave increased, almost *pari passu* in several counties of our State. In 1825, Madison cast about 3000 votes; now she cannot cast exceeding 2300. In traversing that county one will discover numerous farm-houses, once the abode of industrious and intelligent freemen, now occupied by slaves, or tenantless, deserted, and dilapidated; he will observe fields, once fertile, now unfenced, abandoned, and covered with those evil harbingers—fox-tail and broom-sedge; he will see the moss growing on the mouldering walls of once thrifty villages; and will find 'one only master grasps the whole domain' that once furnished happy homes for a dozen white families. Indeed, a country in its infancy, where fifty years ago scarce a forest tree had been felled by the axe of the pioneer, is already exhibiting the painful signs of senility and decay apparent in Virginia and the Carolinas; the freshness of its agricultural glory is gone; the vigor of its youth is extinct, and the spirit of desolation seems brooding over it.

The selection above necessarily omits Olmsted's references to other Southern states which he visited. His stay in Louisiana, for example, proved a rich experience. His visit to Texas and his inland travels are described in *A Journey Through Texas* and *A Journey in the Back Country,* works which many readers may want to consult.

But Olmsted, like many travelers of his day, has been criticized for thinking of the

Southern people as made up of either planters or else "poor whites," or "crackers." The author of the next selection questions how the Confederacy could have fought so costly a war for so long a period if these two classes were the only ones in the South. He found by research that in reality there was a third important group, the yeomanry, who were landowning, self-respecting, substantial citizens and who gave the South its stability.

• 30 • The Southern Whites
A. N. J. DEN HOLLANDER

The conception of the ante-bellum South current especially among non-southerners presents us with a dual picture of the white society of that romantic region. On the one hand is the southern planter, an aristocratic "colonel" in a soft felt hat with a mint julep in his hand and a darkey hovering deferentially in the background. On the other hand is the "poor-white," a densely ignorant, morally degraded, lawless being, despised alike by planter and slave. He lives in a dilapidated log cabin and ekes out a wretched existence by the half-hearted cultivation of a few corn rows, by hunting squirrels in the pine woods, and by fishing for catfish around the cypress stumps of sluggish streams. There is something wrong with him, something inferior, possibly, in his blood. He eats clay; he goes barefoot and has the "ground itch"; his lips, beard, and chin are yellow with tobacco juice; and he often has a little "blind tiger" on hand to drink or to sell.

Indeed, some such planters and some such "poor-whites" were present in the ante-bellum South, but neither made up the bulk of the population. White farmers, who held only a few slaves if any at all, made up an independent yeoman group of primary importance numerically. In the popular conception this group has too often been either overlooked altogether or, what practically amounts to the same thing, confused with the "poor-whites." American historians and other writers of high repute could be cited as evidence that not only

the uncritically minded conceived of all the non-slave-holding whites of the old South as a large class of men conforming to the "poor-white" pattern and constituting a distinct social menace.

But any picture of the South as it was in ante-bellum days must portray not the two classes of aristocratic slaveholders and shiftless "poor-whites," but a more complex civilization in which (1) the slaveholders themselves were made up of, first, a small group of wealthy planters owning slaves in large numbers—roughly the gentry—and second, a much larger middle class of smaller planters, substantial farmers, professional men, and tradesmen; and in which (2) the classes below the slaveholding level were not simply "poor-white," but were first, and in greater numbers, yeomen farmers, artisans, and mechanics, and second, and in much smaller numbers, the true "poor-whites"; indigent, shiftless, and generally inferior.

*   *   *

The number of planters in the ante-bellum South was really small. If a holding of twenty slaves of all ages entitled one to be called a planter, the members of the planter class comprised little more than three per cent of the white population of the slave states, one and one-third per cent in the border states, and four and three-fifths per cent in the cotton states. In 1860 only 2,291 planters held a hundred or more slaves each. More than seventy-

[From "The Tradition of 'Poor Whites,' " in *Culture in the South*, edited by W. T. Couch, University of North Carolina Press, Chapel Hill, 1934. Pp. 403-406, 409-417, 422. Used by permission.]

three per cent of the slaveholders held fewer than ten slaves. Few farms contained more than five hundred acres. In the whole South such farms comprised not quite three per cent of all the farms containing more than three acres of improved land; not quite two per cent in the border states and not quite three and a half per cent in the cotton states. On the other hand, non-slaveholders constituted more than three-fourths of the southern white population: four-fifths in the border states and more than two-thirds in the cotton states.

As has been already said, it is a false assumption that the majority of this three-fourths of the white population conformed to the popular picture of the "poor-white." In recent decades historians of southern antecedents have repeatedly stressed the fact that the old South was not so aristocratic as it is often supposed to have been, that social divisions were not sharp, and that the majority of the people were essentially not unlike those in other parts of the Union and certainly were not hopelessly inferior. Yet little has been done to give an accurate account of the humbler folk, to analyze and evaluate the conditions which surrounded them and influenced their lives. The obstacles to giving such an account cannot be gainsaid. These people were poorly educated, if literate at all, and lived isolated, simple lives; the records they left are few and of small historical value. To the upper classes they were not nearly so important as the slaves, about whom much can be learned from the writings of their masters, who considered their less fortunate neighbors, with the exception only of the overseers, of too little consequence for more than brief mention. Economically, socially, and politically the lower classes were of less importance in the life of the section than in the northern states. To a larger extent than is desirable, therefore, casual remarks and observations of travellers have to be utilized in reconstructing this particular phase of the old South. These sources neither exist in abundance nor can they be used without great caution.

Generally, of those who lived on the farms and did not own slaves—or owned only a few —three types may be discerned.

(1). In the Appalachian mountains, excepting the broader valleys where more prosperous people dwelled, lived the mountaineers, descendants of pioneers who did not complete their westward march. The pioneers had settled in the valleys; their kind and others who came later occupied the areas more difficult of access, spread into the higher valleys, and the narrow coves, there to live in great isolation in the "land of do-without"—a term indicative of destitution indeed. There is no reason to believe that these people were in any sense of low quality or in any way originally different from those who crossed the mountains and settled the Mississippi basin. In particular there seems no ground for the assumption that the Appalachians have been predominantly peopled with such by-products of the developing plantation belts as recently liberated servants or small farmers who were pushed aside in the competition for land. The mountainous *milieu* was principally responsible for the peculiar mode of life which prevailed in the highlands and still prevails with little change in the less accessible parts of the region.

(2). Outside the mountains yeomen farmers made up the majority of the rural white population. Some owned a few slaves and worked alongside them in the fields. Others obtained help from a single Negro. But most of them earned their living exclusively by the toil of their own hands and those of the members of the family. These farmers, though most numerous outside the staple-producing areas, could be found almost anywhere; they were not absent from the black belts. In the upper piedmont, in eastern Tennessee and Mississippi, and along the western and northern borders of the slave states, they were by far the dominant type. In the pine barrens thrifty and sturdy farmers numbered many thousands. They did not make up, of course, a perfectly homogeneous group. Differences in the fertility of the soil, ease of transportation, length of settlement, personal qualities, luck, health, and wealth were reflected in their modes of living. To many a "good liver" the farm gave a comfortable existence and a few luxuries, but at the other end of the scale were a larger number of country dwellers whose well-being was at a lower level than can be called plain. Generally the yeoman farmer and his sons had to work from sun-up to sun-down at a great variety of tasks, and the toils of his wife and daughters are reflected in the homely adage that "woman's work is never done." These people had little to do with money, produced most of what they consumed, usually owned land, stock, and implements, had as a class no debts, were little influenced by fluctuation in staple prices and were socially as well as economically independent. In general they lived on a level that was foreign to luxury and destitution alike. As a group they must be called poor, because their per capita property represented little value, but according to standards existing in the region they were not very badly off. The comparable classes in the free states, however, lived undoubtedly on a superior level. Many travellers, both European and American, commented on the crude log cabins, homespun garments, coarse and monotonous food, and the general lack of comfort among the farmers, as well as the small planters, in the slave states, and among the former dire poverty could be found without seeking. The available data point to a great variety of traits.

*   *   *

Crudeness of speech and manners was certainly no indication of meanness of mind any more than it was always an indication of real poverty or even lack of local prestige. The farmers were uneducated; many could not read, more could not write; they took a man's drink whenever there was fit occasion, which was often; they settled their arguments by physical means if they deemed it necessary; they did not work as hard or plan as consistently as their northern colleagues; they were somewhat careless in varying degrees; all were rustic and informal, many were uncouth; urban genteels devised nicknames for them; but as a class they were honest, proud,

and independent, had confidence in life, had desires and usually ambition, and in a measure were substantial. In their own eyes and those of others in the South they were respectable citizens. It cannot be assumed that the differences between these farmers and those in the North indicate the lack of any essential qualities by the former. Their physical and moral stamina were such as to stand a severe test in the Civil War. Nor were the attainments of the planters other than those which can be brought about by the inheritance or fortunate winning of property and the consequent advantages of education, refinement, the ownership of property, and the exercise of leadership. Their blood was the same as that of the farmers out of whose ranks all but few had emerged not so long ago. Many of those in the old South who rose to public positions of distinction were of humble origin indeed. The differences in style and culture between the rank and file of the planters—the majority of whom were not refined, cultured, elegant, or genteel—and the yeomanry have, furthermore, been exaggerated.

The complex causes of the general condition of the yeomanry cannot be given more than brief consideration here. The same influences which have held the whole South on a low level of economic development were also hostile to the prosperity of the non-slaveholding whites. The small farmers did not give as much attention as the planters to the production of staple crops for export. But the ideal toward which they strove was that of the planter. There was no other opportunity for profitable investment of capital, and, consequently with the exhaustion of fertility in the east, profits were re-invested in slaves and owners migrated westward in search of more fertile lands. To a certain extent, the presence of the Negro slave undoubtedly had placed a stigma on labor. A self-respecting owner might work in the fields beside his slave, or he might work with a hired slave; but generally, the white man drew the line at hiring himself out to work either in field or factory alongside the Negro. Thus, pre-occupation with the staple crop system, the existence of large areas of fertile lands waiting to be exploited, and the slave system, all combined prevented the development of an integrated agricultural and industrial economy. When capital migrated westward to new and fertile soils, the older regions were left with exhausted soils and without resources for immediate development. These abandoned regions then became stagnant and retained traits of the frontier which have persisted even to the present day.

The plantations developed in the regions suited for them, where soil and topography were favorable, but more especially where transportation was easy. They were in touch with the outside world. Some of the small farmers who, among others, had opened up such districts developed into planters; some of them sold out to engrossing neighbors and left, trekking westward or moving to regions like the upper piedmont, there to join those living already in a region where pressure was not brought to bear upon small holders; others, again, might drift to sterile stretches or to the pine barrens, there to sink to the "poor-white" level; and others, refusing to sell, remained as small farmers. At the end of the ante-bellum period this segregation of groups was fairly well completed. White labor played a minor role in the production of the staples; of the cotton crop it produced not more than fifteen per cent.

Although a number of farmers were in a position to raise crops for the market, as a whole they farmed to feed and clothe themselves with their own produce. When one considers the circumstances under which they found themselves, their small comfort has little that is mysterious. Living on isolated farmsteads, with means of communication rudimentary, public schools scarce and inadequate, in a purely rural environment far from markets, without a surplus to sell, working with a crude technique often on soils which were either not very productive or rapidly eroding and soon exhausted, with little opportunity to rise in the social scale, they necessarily resembled more a poor frontier people than a class of thriving New England

farmers. In considering their social position it has to be remembered that the chances for the yeoman and his children in an exclusively rural commonwealth, where large scale agricultural operations prevail, have never and nowhere been very good. For the rest, in making comparisons between the social mobility of the North and the South, sight should not be lost of the fact that in an almost completely rural civilization social capillarity always tends to be less than in an urbanized commercialized area where important steps toward industrialization have already been made. In contemplating the ante-bellum South one must resist the temptation to place slavery persistently in the center and see it as the direct cause of everything. Although Negro slavery and the plantation system were so intimately tied up with each other that it is of little practical value to make an ideological distinction as to the prime importance of either one of them, it may yet clarify thought to remember that the former was only incidental to the latter. It is not improbable that the general condition of the small farmers would have been materially the same had other sources of controllable labor been available for the large scale production of staples. Negro slavery, however, had some concomitants which made it militate still more against people of small means. Chief of these must have been the constant draining away of capital from developing regions by the continual capitalization of labor. Slavery was a clog in the progress of every district where it had established itself and limited in different ways the opportunities for the whites of little or no capital.

(3). The poorest of these farmers gradually merged into the bottom rank of southern rural white people, the listless and squalid dwellers to be found in many widely scattered localities, but chiefly in the sandy ridges of the plantation districts, the pine barrens of the coastal plains, of Florida, and of central and eastern Mississippi, and the sand hills along the fall line. Variously denominated as "sand hillers," "clay eaters," "crackers," and so on, they lived in shiftless poverty on what the half-hearted cultivation of a few acres, hunting and fishing could offer in the way of subsistence, while occasional stealthy bartering with slaves and stealing of cattle and hogs made them a nuisance to planters. Not all of them were squatters or tenants, but the possession of some barren tract made small difference. Travellers described their sickly and slovenly appearance, habitual drinking, tobacco chewing, utter ignorance, strange dialect, inert behavior, and such strange proclivities as clay-sucking, resin-chewing, and snuff-dipping—though the latter custom was not limited to the women of this class.

*   *   *

How numerous these people were cannot be ascertained in any definite way. Certainly they did not comprise the majority, or even a considerable part, of the non-slaveholding whites. In definite areas, however, they were too consistently present to warrant the statement that their number was negligible.

These people were not an exclusive product of ante-bellum development. At all times similar specimens could be found in the southern backwoods. The human material of every society is of divergent merits. That the southern populace contained an element with small capacities and ambition is not more surprising than that northern prisons and poor-houses were not empty. The difference in social environment accounts for the proportionately fewer inmates of southern penal and charitable institutions, and other differences between the sections can readily explain how this lower fringe in these parts assumed its peculiar form. On the southern frontier, as well as on other borders, there was an element satisfied with the minimum obtained without constant exertion. In the lower latitudes to live in such a manner is easier than in a severer climate, but circumstances peculiar to the South conspired in producing its particular type of rural "poor-white." The system of self-contained, slave-worked plantations, the sparsity of towns and manufactures, and the loosely organized economic life of this section limited the chances

of steady employment for those who had only their labor to offer. It must have made a start in life difficult for many who under other conditions might have played a minor role in organized production. This restriction of industrial opportunities may have contributed to the shiftlessness for which the "poor-whites" were known. The explanation of their characteristics, however, has chiefly to be sought in their undermined health. The descriptions of their outward appearance and uncommon predilections leave no doubt that as a class they were sufferers from chronic malaria and were in very many cases heavily infested with hookworm. The soil pollution around their cabins on loose sandy soils in the warm shade of southern piney woods made a dangerous *milieu* for those who walked barefoot. Hookworm was not diagnosed in these parts before the turn of the century; otherwise epsom salts and thymol might have done much towards the eradication of this disease. Now the "poor-whites" stood out in the eyes of contemporaries as examples of the persistent force of "ancestral degeneracy," as an illustration that Anglo-Saxon exploitation of this sub-tropical country was possible only through the management of tropical labor by a ruling white caste, or they were referred to as a standing reproach against slavery which, it was said, had the inevitable tendency not only to establish an aristocracy among the members of the ruling race by elevating a minority to wealth and culture, but also to push down the major portion to a depth of groveling baseness.

We have seen that in the ante-bellum South the non-slaveholders were not all of the "poor-white" class. The term "poor-white" has been, however, and still is, responsible for much poorly directed thinking about the South. The limits of the class of people to whom the ante-bellum South applied the term are not clearly laid down. In discriminating southern speech, it was not used to include all white persons who were poor. It was a term of contempt for the indolent hunter-fisher-farmers just described, certain other small farmers, the rude and ignorant cattle rangers of the piney woods, a small number of factory hands, teamsters, and boatmen, and a group of improvident, inefficient and unstable white laborers and poor loafers, but not for all white workmen, artisans, handicraftsmen, and mechanics of small means who, of less importance than in the North, were not absent. The "poor-whites" were those who were both poor and conspicuously lacking in the common social virtues and especially fell short of the standard in certain economic qualities. Laziness, carelessness, unreliability, lack of foresight and ambition, habitual failure and general incompetency characterized them. The term, though used in the South, was not by far so commonly used and certainly not so sweepingly applied as one might suppose on reading comments of northern or European origin.

There was a wide difference between the recognition of certain groups among the white population whose shortcomings on occasion might be signalized by this expression, and the inclusive stigmatization of the many millions of southern people who did not own slaves by the indiscriminate indication of the same undesirable characteristics. Yet this was already more or less current practice in non-southern quarters before the Civil War, and up to the present there has been a persistent inclination to apply the term to all southern whites who economically and socially rank below the middle class.

How did this confusion—or misconception—originate? How could such a radically wrong view gain credence in one part of a country concerning the state of society in another part within easy travelling distance?

The myth seems to have been started by ante-bellum travellers. Knowledge of other countries and of other parts of the same country was in those days incomparably more fragmentary and exceptional than at present. The world was still wide; tourists without special merits as observers or the knowledge necessary for correct interpretations wrote books which were published and read. The statements, and especially opinions, of travellers possessed an authority out of proportion

to their real significance. The attitude of readers was not nearly so critical as it is now. This was true of the accounts written by tourists in all parts of the world, but for the American slave states forces making the easy acceptance of travellers' notions doubly easy were at work.

Most visitors to the South were biased. So were the readers of their books who lived in the North or in Europe. Few of the former (especially after the 1830's, when the abolition movement was gathering force) were in sympathy with slavery.

Various circumstances favored the idea by outsiders that the non-slaveholding whites of the South stood out in pronounced contrast with the slaveholders. The southern planters formed an aristocratic element in democratic America; their country was accordingly conceived of as a strictly aristocratic, if not feudal, commonwealth. This suggested the three elements of noble planters, servile slaves, and socially dependent "poor-whites." The favorite analogies drawn between the plantations of the southern states and the latifundia of ancient Rome, between planters and patricians, and other comparisons made between the slave empire of the past and that of the present also suggested the presence of an element comparable to the plebeians of yore. Exposés by those who lack intimate and detailed knowledge are apt to follow general lines, and in reducing the impressions to writing, tendencies toward schematization also make themselves felt. Social contrasts always have possessed a tempting charm as an object of depiction. Slavery, furthermore, loomed so large in the discussion of everything southern that everything was viewed from that angle. Anti-slavery zealots were eager to point out as many evil consequences of the system as could with some plausibility be indicated. The doctrinaire thought and tone peculiar to political scientists and economists in the decades preceding the Civil War re-enforced this inclination. For them a certain institution was either good or bad. If bad, it was so absolutely, always, everywhere and in all directions; its consequences were uniformly harmful and manifest in everything. The view that slavery was detrimental not only to the Negroes but to the whole society in which it operated, that it made impossible the consummation of the democratic ideal on southern soil by degrading a great mass of white Americans to uselessness as citizens, offered possibilities as abolitionist propaganda. Certain aspects of rural life in the South helped. There were the slatternly, dirty, and indolent "sandhillers." No traveller who met them failed to describe them in vivid terms. This would have been done anyhow, because unusual and striking phenomena naturally invite mention, but existing prejudices made for biased and incorrect generalizations. Fanny Kemble, in a letter to a friend in the North, spoke of the pinelanders of the vicinage, who, indeed, were far from prepossessing, as "the most degraded race of human beings claiming an Anglo-Saxon origin that can be found on the face of the earth—filthy, lazy, ignorant, brutal, proud, penniless savages, without one of the nobler attributes which have been occasionally allied to the vices of savage nature." Their condition, she went on to generalize after a stay of short duration, was that of all the nonslaveholders of Georgia. "Labor being here the especial portion of slaves, it is thenceforth degraded, and considered unworthy of all but slaves. No white man, therefore, of any class puts his hands to work of any kind soever."

The itinerary most commonly followed by travellers brought them in contact with the lower piney woods people and "poor-whites" to be found in the neighborhood of plantations. On the other hand, regions like the upper piedmont, eastern Tennessee and eastern Mississippi, where a vigorous yeomanry lived, lay outside the tourist route. Besides the generally crude and poor aspect of the farmsteads, the tumbledown fences, ramshackle outhouses, razorback hogs rooting under the porches, and the coarse "hoecake" or "hog and hominy" of the common people impressed northerners as unfavorably as their ignorance, rough-and-ready easy-going manners, and willingness to be satisfied with little. Fred-

erick Law Olmsted wrote elaborately on this point [see Selection 29]. Visitors from across the Atlantic mostly came South after having glanced over New England and the middle states, and did not fail to notice the existing discrepancies which, indeed, were not flattering to the South. James Sterling, an English tourist, making remarks on the differences between the houses of rich planters and poor farmers, wrote in 1857: "There is not the same appearance of equally disseminated comfort. There are handsome dwellings here and there, and there are poor, mean-looking homesteads; but one misses the neat farm houses that dot the landscape of New England, and speak of comfort, equality, and intelligence." Some observers made careful and illuminating notes, sticking to details and avoiding facile statements of a too general nature. Others, not so modest, let their opinions shine through the lines they wrote and did not abstain from suggestions and explanations which obscured the facts. It was the custom among most travellers of that time in the South and elsewhere also, not to be content with describing what they saw, heard, and experienced, but to add their generalizations and interpretations. These were always amateurish, mostly biased, and too often misleading. They imposed their viewpoints without the necessary knowledge for criticism, and often their misinformation fitted neatly into the existing prejudices of their readers.

* * *

So the myth could grow. A few southern protests could not find a wide hearing. The civilized world read anti-slavery literature in which, in the later ante-bellum decades, the tripartite tableau of southern society is featured.

* * *

The expression "poor-white" has remained part of the stock vocabulary especially of those of non-southern extraction writing on the southern states. This term was originally used particularly by southerners themselves to denote a relatively small class of shiftless human beings, "poor," it is true, and designated "white" to differentiate them from the Negroes whose living standards were not very dissimilar from theirs. The term was early used in its derogatory—and therefore misapplied—sense, of all non-slaveholding white people in the South, by travellers to the South and by propagandists who sought to show the terrible influence of Negro slavery. As the years have passed those so denoted have become a class of much larger size, with more definite limits and special characteristics, and the expression itself has attained greater significance in northern and European nations than it ever possessed in the South. As such it has unfortunately come to embody for many non-southerners an entirely wrong conception of the plain people of the South before the Civil War as well as in later years. As can be expected, its effects are still noticeable. The fact that for a long time the standard histories of the United States have been written almost exclusively by New Englanders, that the northern point of view prevails throughout American historiography, must further be taken into account in tracing the "poor-white" fable.

So much, then, for the kinds of white people in the South. What about the Negroes? Not all of them were slaves, nor did all slaves live on large plantations. As a matter of fact, only 46,274 persons owned twenty or more slaves; of these, less than 2,300 persons owned as many as one hundred slaves, according to the census of 1860. Although Selection 29 from Olmsted has already presented some accounts of the smaller plantation, it is of interest to note a vivid picture from *Huckleberry Finn,* in which Mark Twain draws upon his memory of ante-bellum days and describes a small farm belonging to a slave-holding family living near the Mississippi River. We see it as described in the words of Huck himself:

> Phelps's was one of these little one-horse cotton plantations, and they all look alike. A rail fence round a two-acre yard; a stile made out of logs sawed off and up-ended in steps, like barrels of a different length, to climb over the fence with, and for the women to stand on when they are going to jump onto a horse; some sickly grass-patches in the big yard, but mostly it was bare and smooth, like an old hat with the nap rubbed off; big double log house for the white folks— hewed logs, with the chinks stopped up with mud or mortar, and these mud-stripes been whitewashed some time or another; round-log kitchen, with a big broad, open but roofed passage joining it to the house; log smokehouse back of the kitchen; three little log nigger cabins in a row t'other side the smokehouse; one little hut all by itself away down against the back fence, and some outbuildings down a piece the other side; ash-hopper and big kettle to bile soap in by the little hut; bench by the kitchen door, with bucket of water and a gourd; hound asleep there in the sun; more hounds asleep round about; about three shade trees away off in a corner; some currant bushes and gooseberry bushes in one place by the fence; outside of the fence a garden and a watermelon patch; then the cotton-fields begins, and after the fields the woods.

But for those Negroes who lived on the larger plantations there was a general pattern of life which U. B. Phillips has described in his classic book *Life and Labor in the Old South*. Some contemporary historians think that Phillips' Georgian heritage made him view plantation life too favorably, but the value of his work lies in the minute descriptions of specific plantations, although many of his generalizations are of interest also.

• 31 • Life in Thraldom
ULRICH B. PHILLIPS

The simplicity of the social structure on the plantations facilitated Negro adjustment, the master taking the place of the accustomed chief. And yet these black voyagers experienced a greater change by far than befell white immigrants. In their home lands they had lived naked, observed fetish, been bound by tribal law, and practiced primitive crafts. In America none of these things were of service or sanction. The Africans were thralls, wanted only for their brawn, required to take things as they found them and to do as they were told, coerced into self-obliterating humility, and encouraged to respond only to the teachings and preachings of their masters, and adapt themselves to the white men's ways.

In some cases transported talent embraced the new opportunity in extraordinary degree. A contemporary Spanish narrative of the English conquest of Jamaica in 1655 says of a slave captured while carrying an enemy message: "Although an Angola black, this negro was clever. He could read and write, knew the movable feasts, conjunctions, moon and tides, as well as though he had especially studied them; he was a good sugar-master, and could give an excellent account of himself when necessary." On the other hand some of the captives rebelled with violence against the new authority. Thus in Georgia in 1774 "six new Negro fellows and four wenches" killed their overseer, murdered his wife and ran amok in the neighborhood until overpowered. But in general, as always, the common middle course was passive acquiescence.

To make adaptation the more certain, it was argued that "no Negro should be bought old; such are always sullen and unteachable, and frequently put an end to their lives." And indeed planters who could afford an unproductive period were advised to select young children from the ships, "for their juvenile minds entertain no regrets for the loss of their connections. They acquire the English language with great ease, and improve daily in size, understanding and capacity for labour." The proportion of children in the cargoes was great enough to permit such a policy by those who might adopt it. But the fact that prices for imported Negroes, even after seasoning, ranged lower than for those to the American manner born is an evidence that the new habituation as a rule never completely superseded the old. Thanks, however, to plantation discipline and to the necessity of learning the master's language if merely to converse with fellow slaves of different linguistic stocks, African mental furnishings faded even among adult arrivals.

To the second and later generations folklore was transmitted, but for the sake of comprehension by the children an American Brer Rabbit replaced his jungle prototype. If lullabies were crooned in African phrase their memory soon lapsed, along with nearly all other African terms except a few personal names, Quash, Cuffee, Cudjoe and the like. And even these may have owed such perpetuation as they had to the persistence of the maritime slave trade which long continued to bring new Quashes and Cuffees from the mother country. In short, Foulahs and Fan-

[From *Life and Labor in the Old South*, Little, Brown, Boston, 1929. Pp. 194-217. Used by permission.]

tyns, Eboes and Angolas begat American plantation Negroes to whom a spear would be strange but a "languid hoe" familiar, the tomtom forgotten but the banjo inviting to the fingers and the thumb. Eventually it could be said that the Negroes had no memories of Africa as a home. Eventually, indeed, a Virginia freedman wrote after thirteen years of residence in Liberia, "I, being a Virginian," rejoice that "the good people of my old state are about to settle a colony on the coast of Africa"; and went on to say of himself and his compatriots, "there is some of us that would not be satisfied in no other colony while ever there was one called New Virginia." His very name, William Draper, is an index of his Anglo-Americanization; and a pride which he expresses that Virginia Negroes have been the founders and the chief rulers "of almost all the settlements" in Liberia proves him a true son of the Old Dominion, "the mother of states and of statesmen." But William Draper was an exceptional specimen. In the main the American Negroes ruled not even themselves. They were more or less contentedly slaves, with grievances from time to time but not ambition. With "hazy pasts and reckless futures," they lived in each moment as it flew, and left "Old Massa" to take such thought as the morrow might need.

* * * * *

The plantation force was a conscript army, living in barracks and on constant "fatigue." Husbands and wives were comrades in service under an authority as complete as the commanding personnel could wish. The master was captain and quartermaster combined, issuing orders and distributing rations. The overseer and the foreman, where there were such, were lieutenant and sergeant to see that orders were executed. The field hands were privates with no choice but to obey unless, like other seasoned soldiers, they could dodge the duties assigned.

But the plantation was also a homestead, isolated, permanent and peopled by a social group with a common interest in achieving and maintaining social order. Its regime was shaped by the customary human forces, interchange of ideas and coadaptation of conduct. The intermingling of white and black children in their pastimes was no more continuous or influential than the adult interplay of command and response, of protest and concession. In so far as harmony was attained—and in this the plantation mistress was a great if quiet factor—a common tradition was evolved embodying reciprocal patterns of conventional conduct.

The plantation was of course a factory, in which robust laborers were essential to profits. Its mere maintenance as a going concern required the proprietor to sustain the strength and safeguard the health of his operatives and of their children, who were also his, destined in time to take their parents' places. The basic food allowance came to be somewhat standardized at a quart of corn meal and half a pound of salt pork per day for each adult and proportionably for children, commuted or supplemented with sweet potatoes, field peas, sirup, rice, fruit and "garden sass" as locality and season might suggest. The clothing was coarse, and shoes were furnished only for winter. The housing was in huts of one or two rooms per family, commonly crude but weather-tight. Fuel was abundant. The sanitation of the clustered cabins was usually a matter of systematic attention; and medical service was at least commensurate with the groping science of the time and the sparse population of the country. Many of the larger plantations had central kitchens, day nurseries, infirmaries and physicians on contract for periodic visits. The aged and infirm must be cared for along with the young and able-bodied, to maintain the good will of their kinsmen among the workers, if for no other reason. Morale was no less needed than muscle if performance were to be kept above a barely tolerable minimum.

* * * * *

The plantation was a school. An intelligent master would consult his own interest by affording every talented slave special instruction and by inculcating into the commoner sort as much routine efficiency, regularity and responsibility as they would accept. Not only were many youths given training in the crafts, and many taught to read and write, even though the laws forbade it, but a goodly number of planters devised and applied plans to give their whole corps spontaneous incentive to relieve the need of detailed supervision. Thus John McDonogh near New Orleans instituted in 1825 an elaborate scheme of self-government and self-driving with a prospect of self-emancipation by his corps as a unit; and a plan of trial by a jury of his peers for any slave charged with a plantation offense was followed by Joseph and Jefferson Davis on "Hurricane" and "Briarfield" in Mississippi. The traveler Laincourt when visiting the Pringle plantation in the South Carolina lowlands in 1796 found its proprietor "in every respect a worthy man, amiable and communicative, and so happy that his equals are but seldom found. He is an excellent master to his Negroes, and asserts, against the opinion of many others, that the plantations of mild and indulgent masters thrive most and that the Negroes are most industrious and faithful. He is beloved by his slaves. The cultivated part of his plantation is in the best order, and the number of his slaves increases yearly by a tenth." A similar achievement was described to Frederika Bremer as that of Thomas Spalding of Sapelo on the Georgia coast, "a rich old gentleman who upon the beautiful island where he lives has allowed the palmettoes to grow in freedom, and the Negroes to live and work in freedom also, governed alone by the law of duty and love, and where all succeeds excellently." We share Miss Bremer's regret that she could not accept an invitation to visit this Elysium. We have, however, from the pen of William Faux a description of such an establishment in the Carolina uplands, that of the venerable Mr. Mickle, who said of his slaves: "They are all, old and young, true and faithful to my interests; they need no task-master, no overseer; they will do all and more than I expect them to do, and I can trust them

with untold gold. . . . I respect them as my children, and they look on me as their friend and father." And the traveler says: "This conversation induced me to view more attentively the faces of the adult slaves; and I was astonished at the free, easy, sober, intelligent and thoughtful impression which such an economy as Mr. Mickle's had indelibly made on their countenances."

The civilizing of the Negroes was not merely a consequence of definite schooling but a fruit of plantation life itself. The white household taught perhaps less by precept than by example. It had much the effect of a "social settlement" in a modern city slum, furnishing models of speech and conduct, along with advice on occasion, which the vicinage is invited to accept. The successes of Pringle, Spalding and Mickle, if correctly reported, were quite extraordinary. Most planters did not even attempt an emulation, for not one in a hundred could hope by his own genius and magnetism to break the grip of normal slave-plantation circumstance. The bulk of the black personnel was notoriously primitive, uncouth, improvident and inconstant, merely because they were Negroes of the time; and by their slave status they were relieved from the pressure of want and debarred from any full-force incentive of gain.

Many planters, however, sought to promote contentment, loyalty and zeal by gifts and rewards, and by sanctioning the keeping of poultry and pigs and the cultivation of little fields in off times with the privilege of selling any produce. In the cotton belt the growing of nankeen cotton was particularly encouraged, for its brownish color would betray any surreptitious addition from the master's own fields. Some indeed had definite bonus systems. A. H. Bernard of Virginia determined at the close of 1836 to replace his overseer with a slave foreman, and announced to his Negroes that in case of good service by the corps he would thereafter distribute premiums to the amount of what had been the overseer's wages. After six months' trial he wrote: "I can say for this experiment that never certainly in my life have I had so much work so well done nor with equal cheerfulness and satisfaction, not having had occasion to utter an angry word except to a little cattle minder." And in Louisiana sundry planters made it a Christmas practice to distribute among the heads of industrious families a sum amounting in aggregate to a dollar for each hogshead of sugar in the year's product.

But any copious resort to profit-sharing schemes was avoided at large as being likely to cost more than it would yield in increment to the planter's own crop. The generality of planters, it would seem, considered it hopeless to make their field hands into thorough workmen or full-fledged men, and contented themselves with very moderate achievement. Tiring of endless correction and unfruitful exhortation, they relied somewhat supinely upon authority with a tone of kindly patronage and a baffled acquiescence in slack service.

For example a French traveler in South Carolina at the middle of the nineteenth century reported his observations on the plantation of a German, "certainly the least cruel and tyrannical of men, ... who does not wish to beat his slaves. The ungrateful slaves work with great laziness and carelessness. When he entered a hut where the Negresses were cleaning cotton he was content to show them how badly it was done. ... The result of his remarks was a pout and a little grumbling." And there was no sequel except a plea from the planter for the visitor's commiseration.

It has been said by a critic of the twentieth century South: "In some ways the negro is shamefully mistreated—mistreated through leniency," which permits him as a tenant or employee to lean upon the whites in a continuous mental siesta and sponge upon them habitually, instead of requiring him to stand upon his own moral and economic legs. The same censure would apply as truly in any preceding generation. The slave plantation, like other schools, was conditioned by the nature and habituations of its teachers and pupils. Its instruction was inevitably slow; and the effect of its discipline was restricted by the fact that even its aptest pupils had no diploma in prospect which would send them forth to fend for themselves.

*   *   *   *   *

The plantation was a parish, or perhaps a chapel of ease. Some planters assumed the functions of lay readers when ordained ministers were not available, or joined the congregation even when Negro preachers preached. Bishop Leonidas Polk was chief chaplain on his own estate, and is said to have suffered none of his slaves to be other than Episcopalian; but the generality of masters gave full freedom as to church connection.

The legislature of Barbados, when urged by the governor in 1681 to promote the Christianization of slaves on that island, replied, "their savage brutishness renders them wholly incapable. Many have endeavoured it without success." But on the continent such sentiments had small echo; and as decades passed masters and churches concerned themselves increasingly in the premises. A black preacher might meet rebuke and even run a risk of being lynched if he harped too loudly upon the liberation of the Hebrews from Egyptian bondage; but a moderate supervision would prevent such indiscretions. The Sermon on the Mount would be harmless despite its suggestion of an earthly inheritance for the meek; the Decalogue was utterly sound; and "servants obey your masters," "render unto Caesar the things that are Caesar's," and "well done, thou good and faithful servant" were invaluable texts for homilies. The Methodists and Baptists were inclined to invite ecstasy from free and slave alike. Episcopalians and Presbyterians, and the Catholics likewise, deprecating exuberance, dealt rather in quiet precept than in fervid exhortation—with far smaller statistical results.

*   *   *   *   *

The plantation was a pageant and a variety show in alternation. The procession of plowmen at evening, slouched crosswise on their mules; the dance in the new sugarhouse, preceded by prayer; the bonfire in the quarter with contests in clogs, cakewalks and Charlestons whose fascinations were as yet undiscovered by the great world; the work songs in solo and refrain, with not too fast a rhythm; the baptizing in the creek, with lively demonstrations from the "sisters" as they came dripping out; the torchlight pursuit of 'possum and 'coon, with full-voiced halloo to baying houn' dawg and yelping cur; the rabbit hunt, the log-rolling, the house-raising, the husking bee, the quilting party, the wedding, the cock fight, the crap game, the children's play, all punctuated plantation life—and most of them were highly vocal. A funeral now and then of some prominent slave would bring festive sorrowing, or the death of a beloved master an outburst of emotion.

*   *   *   *   *

The plantation was a matrimonial bureau, something of a harem perhaps, a copious nursery, and a divorce court. John Brickell wrote of colonial North Carolina: "It frequently happens, when these women have no Children by the first Husband, after being a year or two cohabiting together, the Planters oblige them to take a second, third, fourth, fifth, or more Husbands or Bedfellows; a fruitful Woman amongst them being very much valued by the Planters, and a numerous Issue esteemed the greatest Riches in this Country." By running on to five or more husbands for a constantly barren woman Brickell discredits his own statement. Yet it may have had a kernel of truth, and it is quite possible that something of such a policy persisted throughout the generations. These things do not readily get into the records. I have myself heard a stalwart Negro express a humorous regret that he was free, for said he in substance: "If I had lived in slavery times my master would have given me half a dozen wives and taken care of all the children." This may perhaps voice a tradition among slave descendants, and the tradition may in turn derive from an actual sanction of polygamy by some of the masters. A planter doubtless described a practice not unique when he

said "that he interfered as little as possible with their domestic habits except in matters of police. 'We don't care what they do when their tasks are over—we lose sight of them till next day. Their morals and manners are in their own keeping. The men may have, for instance, as many wives as they please, so long as they do not quarrel about such matters.'" But another was surely no less representative when he instructed his overseer: "Marriages shall be performed in every instance of a nuptial contract, and the parties settled off to themselves without encumbering other houses to give discontent. No slave shall be allowed to cohabit with two or more wives or husbands at the same time; doing so shall subject them to a strict trial and severe punishment."

Life was without doubt monogamous in general; and some of the matings were by order, though the generality were pretty surely spontaneous. This item, written by an overseer to his employer, is typical of many: "Esaw and Biner has asked permission to Marry. I think it a good Match. What say you to it?" Here and there a man had what was called in slave circles a "broad wife," a wife belonging to another master and dwelling at a distance. Planters of course preferred their slaves to be mated at home.

In the number of their children the Negro woman rivaled the remarkable fecundity of their mistresses. One phenomenal slave mother bore forty-one children, mostly of course as twins; and the records of many others ran well above a dozen each. As a rule, perhaps, babies were even more welcome to slave women than to free; for childbearing brought lightened work during pregnancy and suckling, and a lack of ambition conspired with a freedom from economic anxiety to clear the path of maternal impulse.

Concubinage of Negro women to planters and their sons and overseers is evidenced by the census enumeration of mulattoes and by other data. It was flagrantly prevalent in the Creole section of Louisiana, and was at least sporadic from New England to Texas. The regime of slavery facilitated concubinage not merely by making black women subject to white men's wills but by promoting intimacy and weakening racial antipathy. The children, of whatever shade or paternity, were alike the property of the mother's owner and were nourished on the plantation. Not a few mulattoes, however, were manumitted by their fathers and vested with property.

Slave marriages, not being legal contracts, might be dissolved without recourse to public tribunals. Only the master's consent was required, and this was doubtless not hard to get. On one plantation systematic provision was made in the standing regulations: "When sufficient cause can be shewn on either side, a marriage may be annulled; but the offending party must be severely punished. Where both are in the wrong, both must be punished, and if they insist on separating must have a hundred lashes apiece. After such a separation, neither can marry again for three years." If such a system were in general effect in our time it would lessen the volume of divorce in American society. But it may be presumed that most plantation rules were not so stringent.

*   *   *   *   *

The home of a planter or of a well-to-do townsman was likely to be a "magnificent negro boarding-house," at which and from which an indefinite number of servants and their dependents and friends were fed. In town the tribe might increase to the point of embarrassment. A Savannah woman wrote: "My only reason for desiring a plantation at times is for my host of little and big people—few to be sure of the latter and quite too many of the former. The city, to my dear bought experience, is a bad place, though I have nothing to complain of with regard to the conduct of my people." The domestics were likely to consider themselves entitled to luxurious fare. The wife of a Congressman when visiting her home after two years' absence wrote: "I have been mobbed by my own house servants. . . . They agreed to come in a body and beg me to stay at home to keep my own house once more. . . . I asked my cook if she lacked anything on the plantation

at the Hermitage. 'Lack anything?' she said, 'I lack everything, what are corn meal, bacon, milk and molasses? Would that be all you wanted? Ain't I been living and eating exactly as you all these years? When I cook for you, didn't I have some of all? Dere now!' Then she doubled herself up laughing. They all shouted, 'Missis, we is crazy for you to stay home.'"

Each plantation had a hierarchy. Not only were the master and his family exalted to a degree beyond the reach of slave aspiration, but among the Negroes themselves there were pronounced gradations of rank, privilege and esteem. An absent master wrote: "I wish to be remembered to all the servants, distinguishing Andrew as the head man and Katy as the mother of the tribe. Not forgetting Charlotte as the head of the culinary department nor Marcus as the Tubal Cain of the community, hoping that they will continue to set a good example and that the young ones will walk in their footsteps." The foreman, the miller and the smith were men of position and pride. The butler, the maid and the children's nurse were in continuous contact with the white household, enjoying the best opportunity to acquire its manners along with its discarded clothing. The field hands were at the foot of the scale, with a minimum of white contact and privileged only to plod, so to say, as brethren to the ox.

At all times in the South as a whole perhaps half of the slaves were owned or hired in units of twenty or less, which were too small for the full plantation order, and perhaps half of this half were on mere farms or in town employment, rather as "help" than as a distinct laboring force. Many small planters' sons and virtually all the farmers in person worked alongside any field hands they might possess; and indoor tasks were parceled among the women and girls, white and black. As to severity of treatment, the travelers were likely to disagree. Schoepf and Stirling thought the farmers' slaves were in the better case, while Russell surmised the contrary. A Georgia physician found himself impelled to plead against over-incitement by small proprietors: "Men who own but few slaves and who share the labors of the field or workshop with them are very liable to deceive themselves by a specious process of reasoning. They say, 'I carry row for row with my negroes, and I put no more upon them than I take upon myself.' But the master who thus reasons is forgetful or ignorant of the great truth that the Negro's powers of endurance are really inferior to his; while in the case of the latter there is wanting those incentives to action that animate and actually strengthen the master."

However the case may have been as to relative severity on farms and plantations, there can be no doubt that the farmers' slaves of all sorts were likely to share somewhat intimately such lives as their masters led and to appropriate a considerable part of such culture as they possessed—to be more or less genteel with their gentility or crude with their crudity, to think similar thoughts and speak much the same language. On the other hand, the one instance of wide divergence in dialect between the whites and the Negroes prevailed in the single district in which the scheme of life was that of large plantations from the time when Africans were copiously imported. On the seaboard of South Carolina and Georgia most of the blacks (and they are very black) still speak Gullah, a dialect so distinct that unfamiliar visitors may barely understand it. And dialect, there as elsewhere, is an index to culture in general.

* * * * *

The life of slaves, whether in large groups or small, was not without grievous episodes. A planter's son wrote to his father upon a discovery of mislaid equipment: "The bridle and martingal which you whipped Amy so much for stealing was by some inattention of Robert's left in Mr. Clark's stable." Again, an overseer, exasperated by the sluggishness of his cook, set her to field work as discipline, only to have her demonstrate by dying that her protestations of illness had been true.

Grievances reinforced ennui to promote slacking, absence without leave, desertion and mutiny. The advertising columns of the newspapers bristled with notices of runaways; and no detailed plantation record which has come to my hand is without mention of them. As an extreme example, here is a summer's account by an overseer, or so much of it as can be deciphered: "August the 20 1844 Randle caught at Mr. Cathram brung home . . . [he had] left on the 12th July 1844 Lem runway on the 25 of July caught on the 2 of August by 1 of Mr Kings negroes Oscar runway on the 27 of August . . . George attempt to git away I coat him and put a ringe and chane on him under the neck Lem runway on the 21 of August September the 3 Beny Bill Elijah Ellie all gawne together and Carline runway on the 3 stayed out 2 days . . . Joe runway on the 11th September."

Certain slaves were persistent absconders, and the chronic discontent of others created special problems for their masters. Thus a citizen in the Shenandoah Valley declined to hire one of his slaves to the proprietors of an iron furnace because "the previous bad character of the fellow in connection with recent declarations of his has left no doubt on my mind but he would make an effort to reach the State of Ohio, and by being placed at your Works it would certainly facilitate his object. Was I to send him I am persuaded that he would render you no services, and it might be the means of losing the fellow entirely." On the other hand, a mistress in the same locality sought an employer for her woman slave because "Ann has become very impudent and should be hired to a strict master who can handle her." But a strict master carried no guarantee of success, as an Alabama news item will show. William Pearce had notified an erring slave that a flogging was to be given him after supper. In due time Pearce called the man, who came from the kitchen with a pretense of submission, "but so soon as he got in striking distance drew an axe which had been concealed, and split in twain the head of his master."

For steady success, indeed, experience taught that the master's authority "should be exercised in a firm but mild manner. He should even to a Negro unite in his deportment the *suaviter in modo* with the *fortiter in re*." This planter continued: "I never saw any degree of courtesy shown to a Negro (that is kept under good subjection) but was returned with usury. Cuffee is hard to outdo in politeness." Another planter accepted the challenge of this task yet more gallantly when urging the value of kindliness and praise: "Give me a high spirited and even a high tempered negro, full of pride, for easy and comfortable management. Your slow sulky negro, although he may have an even temper, is the devil to manage." But as to the female of the species: "The negro women are all harder to manage than the men." A third was almost driven from the planter's career, as he said, "by the great aversion which I have to the manner of cultivating our lands in Virginia by slaves. I feel myself utterly incompetent to the task of managing them properly. I never attempt to punish or to have one punished but I am sensible that I am violating the natural rights of a being who is as much entitled to the enjoyment of liberty as myself." A fourth, less troubled by scruples, was baffled by his problems: "The proper management and discipline of negroes subjects the man of care and feeling to more dilemmas perhaps than any other vocation he could follow. To keep a diary of their conduct, it would be a record nothing short of a series of violations of the laws of God and man. To moralize and induce the slave to assimilate with the master and his interest has been and is the great desideratum aimed at; but I am sorry to say I have long since desponded in the completion of the task." A fifth maintained a strong note of optimism: "The character of the negro is much underrated. It is like the plastic clay which may be moulded into agreeable or disagreeable figures according to the skill of the moulder. The man who storms at and curses his negroes and who tells them they are a parcel of infernal rascals, not to be trusted, will surely make them just what he calls them; and so far from loving such a master, they will hate him. Now if you be not suspicious, and induce them to think by slight trusts that they are not un-worthy of some confidence, you will make them honest, useful and affectionate creatures." A sixth, eschewing exalted thought and ignoring profundities, contented himself with being a cheery fellow and relied upon a single prod with a double prong. We may see this Georgian only through the eyes of his slaves. "They say when they cultivated poor lands in Warren County that he used to hurry them by saying 'hurra, boys, the land is poor—if you don't work hard you'll make nothing.' When he removed to better land on this side the river it was 'hurra, boys, you have got good land to work now, make haste.' "

* * * * *

By one means or another good will and affection were often evoked. When his crop was beset with grass and the work strenuous, a Mississippian wrote of his corps as being "true as steel." A Georgian after escaping shipwreck on his way to Congress in 1794 wrote: "I have ever since been thinking of an expression of old Qua's in Savannah a few days before I sailed. The rascal had the impudence to tell me to stay at home & not fret myself about Publick—'What Publick care for you, Massa? God! ye get drowned bye & bye, Qua tell you so, and what going come of de Family den?' " An Alabama preacher while defending slavery as divinely ordained said of the Negro: "He is of all races the most gentle and kind. The man, the most submissive; the woman, the most affectionate. What other slaves would love their masters better than themselves?" And a British traveler wrote from his observation of slaves and masters: "There is an hereditary regard and often attachment on both sides, more like that formerly existing between lords and their retainers in the old feudal times of Europe, than anything now to be found in America."

On some estates the whip was as regularly in evidence as the spur on a horseman's heel. That cruelties occurred is never to be denied. Mrs. Stowe exploited them in *Uncle Tom's Cabin* and validated her implications to her own satisfaction in its *Key*. Theodore D. Weld had already assembled a thousand more or less authentic instances of whippings and fetters, of croppings and brandings, of bloodhound pursuits and the break-up of families. Manuscript discoveries continue to swell the record. Here for example is a letter which lies before me in the slave's own writing:

Charlottesville, Oct. 8th, 1852

Dear Husband I write you a letter to let you know my distress my master has sold albert to a trader on Monday court day and myself and other child is for sale also and I want you to let [me] hear from you very soon before next cort if you can I don't know when I don't want you to wait till Christmas I want you to tell dr Hamelton and your master if either will buy me they can attend to it know and then I can go afterwards. I don't want a trader to get me they asked me if I had got any person to buy me and I told them no they took me to the court house too they never put me up a man buy the name of brady bought albert and is gone I don't know where they say he lives in Scottesville my things is in several places some is in staunton and if I should be sold I don't know what will become of them I don't expect to meet with the luck to get that way till I am quite heartsick nothing more I am and ever will be your kind wife Maria Perkins.

To Richard Perkins

We cannot brush away this woman's tears. But it is fair to show the smile of another when writing in mellow retrospect to her ex-master, years after their severance by emancipation:

Huntington, W. Virginia
Sunday, June 12, 1881.

My old boss i heard that you was still alive and i now take the opportunity to address you a fiew lines i am well and doing well and i hope you are the same i am your servant whom you raised from a child up Catherine Miller who married Henry Miller. i expect you have forgot me but i have not forgot you. i was glad to hear that you was still alive. i have wrote home several times to hear how all the old folks was but i never could find out so i thought i would write you and see if you could tell me. i wish you would send me mine and Mary Janes ages exactly. Mary jane has growed to be such a big girl i don't expect you know her. i would like to see and here you pray once more before I die. i must now come to a close answer right away and tell me every thing that you think will give me any satisfaction about home sweet home. i hope that you will always remember me in your prayers. please excuse short letter and bad writing.

Your old servant Catherine Miller.

* * * * *

Most of the travelers who sought evidence of asperity in the plantation realm found it as a rule not before their eyes but beyond the horizon. Charles Eliot Norton while at Charleston in 1855 wrote home to Boston: "The slaves do not go about looking unhappy, and are with difficulty, I fancy, persuaded to feel so. Whips and chains, oaths and brutality, are as common, for all that one sees, in the free as the slave states. We have come thus far, and might have gone ten times as far, I dare say, without seeing the first sign of Negro misery or white tyranny." Andrew P. Peabody wrote of the slaves of his host at Savannah: "They are well lodged and fed, and could have been worked no harder than was necessary for exercise and digestion." Louis F. Tasistro remarked of the slaves on a plantation at the old battle field below New Orleans: "To say that they are underworked and overfed, and far happier than the labourers of Great Britain would hardly convey a sufficiently clear notion of their actual condition. They put me much more in mind of a community of grown-up children, spoiled by too much kindness, than a body of dependants, much less a company of slaves." Frederika Bremer had virtually nothing but praise for the slave quarters which she visited or their savory food which she tasted. Welby, Fauz,

Lyell, Basil Hall, Marshall Hall, Robert Russell, William Russell, Olmsted and sundry others concur in their surprise at finding slavery unsevere, though some of them kept seeking evidence to the contrary without avail.

The surprise was justified, for tradition in the outer world ran squarely opposite. And the tradition was reasonable. Slavery had been erected as a crass exploitation, and the laws were as stringent as ever. No prophet in early times could have told that kindliness would grow as a flower from a soil so foul, that slaves would come to be cherished not only as property of high value but as loving if lowly friends. But this unexpected change occurred in so many cases as to make benignity somewhat a matter of course. To those habituated it became no longer surprising for a planter to say that no man deserved a Coromantee who would not treat him rather as a friend than as a slave; for another to give his "people" a holiday out of season because "the drouth seems to have afflicted them, and a play day may raise their spirits"; or for a third to give one of his hands an occasional week-end with a dollar or two each time to visit his wife in another county, and send two others away for some weeks at hot springs for the relief of their rheumatism.

The esteem in epitaphs, whether inscribed in diaries or on stone, was without doubt earned by their subjects and genuinely felt by their composers. One reads: "On the 14th [of May, 1821] Old Bina died, about 12 o'clock, full of days and entitled to the grateful thanks of the whole family. She was a country born slave [i.e., a native of America], and in my wife's family from birth, 75 years. She is now a free woman. Her virtues were numerous, and her vices such as arose from her station in life." A slab in a South Carolina churchyard is engraved: "Sacred to the memory of Bill, a strictly honest and faithful servant of Cleland Belin. Bill was often entrusted with the care of Produce and Merchandize to the value of many thousand dollars, without loss or damage. He died 7th October, 1854, in the 35th year of his age, an approved member of the Black Mingo Baptist Church. Well done, thou good and faithful servant. Enter thou into Joy of thy Lord." And on another Southern stone:

JOHN:
A FAITHFUL SERVANT
AND TRUE FRIEND:
KINDLY, AND CONSIDERATE:
LOYAL, AND AFFECTIONATE:
THE FAMILY HE SERVED
HONOURS HIM IN DEATH:
BUT IN LIFE, THEY GAVE HIM LOVE:
FOR HE WAS ONE OF THEM

For he was one of them indeed, and his name was well-nigh legion. Ancestral halls were fewer far than ancestral servitors, for a planter's migration would vacate the house but carry the personnel.

On the other hand slaves in large numbers were detached from their masters, whether by sale, by lease to employers or by hire to themselves. The personal equation was often a factor in such transactions. Some slaves were sold as punishment, for effect upon the morale of their fellows. On the other hand some whose sales were impelled by financial stress were commissioned by their masters to find buyers of their own choice; some purchases were prompted by a belief that the new management would prove more congenial and fruitful than the old; and still more transfers were made to unite in ownership couples who desired union in marriage.

In the hiring of slaves likewise the personal equation often bulked large, for the owner's desire for a maximum wage was modified by his concern for assured maintenance of physique and morale, and the lessee on his part wanted assurance from the slave of willing service or of acquiescence at least. The hiring of slaves to the slaves themselves was a grant of industrial freedom at a wage. It was an admission that the slave concerned could produce more in self-direction than when under routine control, a virtual admission that for him slavery had no industrial justification. In many cases it was a probationary period, ended by self-purchase with earnings accumulated above the wages he had currently paid his owner.

Slave hiring and self-hire were more characteristic of town than of country. Indeed urban conditions merely tolerated slavery, never promoted it. And urban slaveholders were not complete masters, for slavery in full form required a segregation to make the master in effect a magistrate. A townsman's human chattels could not be his subjects, for he had no domain for them to inhabit. When a slave ran an errand upon the street he came under the eye of public rather than private authority; and if he were embroiled by chance in altercation with another slave the two masters were likely to find themselves champions of opposing causes in court, or partisans even against the constables, with no power in themselves either to make or apply the law.

Town slaves in a sense rubbed elbows with every one, high and low, competed with free labor, white and black, and took tone more or less from all and sundry. The social hierarchy was more elaborate than on the plantations, the scheme of life more complex, and the variety wider in attainment and attitude. The obsequious grandiloquence of a barber contrasted with the caustic fluency of a fishwife. But even the city chain gang was likely to be melodious, for its members were Negroes at one or two removes from the plantation. All in all, the slave regime was a curious blend of force and concession, of arbitrary disposal by the master and self-direction by the slave, of tyranny and benevolence, of antipathy and affection.

The economy of the Old South, as has been indicated in several of the preceding selections, was predominantly agricultural. To understand it one should know how production of cotton, rice, and sugar was carried out both on the larger plantations and the small farms. And what happened to the cotton, the rice, and the sugar when it had been grown and harvested? Since these crops could not be used at home by those who had grown them, they were sold for cash, and this cash was used in the purchase of necessities for the rural people, most of whom were not self-subsistent to the same degree as the Chinese peasant.

The *cotton factor* was the agent who handled the sale of these agricultural commodities and in turn bought for the planters what they needed, ordering many articles from Europe for those with sophisticated tastes.

The following selection, by Alfred H. Stone, although written many years ago, is still one of the best descriptions not only of what the cotton factor did but also of the role he played in the colonial period in helping Europeans start plantations in the New World. This selection and the one which follows on industry give a general outline of the economy of the Old South.

• 32 • The Cotton Factor
ALFRED H. STONE

Like many other features of its ante-bellum agricultural economy, the factorage system was not of Southern origin. It had its beginning in the West Indies. It is hardly possible definitely to fix the date of the factor's emergence into the scheme of colonial staple

[From "The Cotton Factorage System of the Southern States," *American Historical Review*, Vol. 20, No. 3, New York, 1915. Pp. 557-565. Used by permission.]

agriculture. He followed the trading companies, merchant adventurers, and similar instruments of colonization. He was an important cog in effecting the transition from the group to the individualistic system of agriculture. He was to the individual planter what the chartered companies had been to the whole body of colonists, or to the colony itself as a distinct entity.

The factor was the home agent of the colonial planter. He was at once his merchant and banker. He bought the goods which the planter had to purchase at home, and sold for him the products returned in exchange. He became an important link in the chain which brought Europe, Africa, and America into commercial association. If an Englishman wished to embark his son in the business of sugar planting in Jamaica or Barbadoes, he could negotiate the entire transaction with a factor in Bristol or London. The latter could purchase the estate, arrange with the African Company for the necessary complement of slaves, supply the needed equipment of machinery, merchandise, and tools, and otherwise outfit the enterprise. He would furthermore engage to finance the venture from start to finish.

The factor's business thus brought him into close and confidential relationships with many classes of people; with those who were or sought to become planters; with those holding grants or patents of colonial lands, and desiring settlers or purchasers therefor; with those engaged in the African trade, whether as dealers in slaves, or as manufacturers of commodities to be sent to Africa for slave-trading purposes; with those who handled the manifold articles used in the plantation colonies; with those who purchased plantation products sent home in payment of the enormous obligations incurred in undertaking and prosecuting such ventures; with the shipping interests engaged in effecting these various exchanges of slaves and goods; with the financial sources which supplied the reservoirs of capital which were constantly tapped in behalf of the factor's clients.

Knowing something of the intricacies and ramifications, as well as the magnitude of the business, we do not need specific documentary assurance of the standing and influence of the head of such an establishment, long and successfully conducted.

The business was extremely hazardous. The profits sought were correspondingly large. The ultimate fate of the West Indian planter was usually bankruptcy. Even a tropical soil could not forever meet the demands which such a system taxed against it, plus the extravagance and waste which the system engendered. For every planter who made good the not uncommon boast that he would return with an income of ten thousand pounds, there were scores who wore out their lives and wrecked their bodies and minds, and transmitted to their sons the sole legacy of a hopelessly inextinguishable debt.

When the West Indian system had itself all but collapsed of its own dead weight, and was given its finishing blows by the abolition of slavery and the modification of tariffs, the British Parliament came to its relief with a government land loan ostensibly designed to aid the planters. I am willing to advance the opinion that it was the great English factorage houses who really engineered the deal, and who are almost its sole beneficiaries. Of the millions of pounds thus advanced by the government, practically all but a pittance remained in England, for the amortization of ancient debts which otherwise would never have been cancelled.

Like the plantation slavery system, the West Indian factorage system, with various modifications, was transferred to the Southern colonies of America. It seems to have been the very corner-stone of large-scale, staple, slave-labor agriculture. When the Revolution destroyed the business of English factors, their places were taken by enterprising men in the more important Southern commercial towns. Some of these had been exporting agents and correspondents of English houses. Others were attracted to the business by the promise of large returns, and because it was from the first recognized as an eminently respectable and honorable form of employment for capital and brains; and the social prejudice against trade did not obtain against it.

The importance of the Southern factorage system developed with the growth of the cotton industry. Indigo planting disappeared with the destruction of the English bounty system by the Revolution. Tobacco culture was confined to a more or less restricted area, and did not offer an inviting field for widespread and large-scale capitalistic enterprise. Rice, which took the place of indigo in South Carolina, became an important crop and had its own system of development, in which the factor played a considerable part. In Louisiana the sugar factor became as important a part in the commercial system, as it had been in that of the West Indies. But it was in cotton that the factorage system reached its greatest development, became most powerful, and flourished longest. Cotton was a crop ideally adapted to a capitalistic system of agriculture. It grew through a wide range of geographical area. Its non-perishable nature lent itself peculiarly to a system which required the concentration of its product at seaboard, at a time when transportation and warehouse facilities were poor, and rough handling, exposure, and long delays would have destroyed the value of any other agricultural commodity. It is therefore the cotton region which offers the student the largest promise of reward for investigation of the system and its effects and ramifications.

The functions of the Southern factor were the same as those of his English progenitor. But the Southern system had one feature not contained in the English. The business here developed relations between factor and client not possible with the West Indian oversea system. The relations between the cotton factor and planter were of the most intimate and confidential character, as close probably as was ever the case between business associates. The ties between them frequently were life-long and their relations were of a social and personal as well as business nature. How far this close personal association affected plan-

tation policy, it is not possible to say. But it is certain that the counsel and advice of the factor were frequently reflected in the planter's affairs. It was a relationship which often effected a close union of business interests and political, social and economic policies between a large and dominantly influential body throughout the cotton-producing South, and the men who were the leading and dominant figures in the business and financial life of Southern cities. It also raised to the nth power the definite and tangible value of the moral hazard in business. It is not too much to say that the great factorage houses of the South looked quite as much to the character of a customer as to the securities he had to offer. Millions of dollars have been advanced by Southern factors upon the mere personal word of the planter, with no formal security at all, and with only a memorandum to witness the amounts involved. A unique basis of agricultural credit was established, which must be taken into account in interpreting such documentary evidence as plantation and slave mortgages and other securities of record. Another manifestation of the personal equation was in the opportunities offered by the factorage system to men of little or no capital, usually of the overseer class, to embark in business for themselves. An overseer identified with the successful management of a plantation estate was often as well known to his employer's factor by reputation as the planter himself was personally. Such a one, who possessed the necessary initiative, had little difficulty in establishing a factorage connection on his own account. Many of the largest and most successful planters of the South were men who got their start in this way.

It is not to be supposed that there were no cases of conflicts of interest and of opposing policies between the planter and the factor classes. The business was of too great magnitude and its ramifications far too extensive for this not to have occurred. As in the case of the earlier English factors, it was a business of considerable hazard and it had to carry a corresponding burden. It has always been the misfortune of large-scale staple plantation enterprises—that is, those requiring large capital and a heavy labor equipment—that the vicissitudes to which they were subject tinctured them with something of both the nature and the spirit of games of chance. With the planter it has always been either a feast or a famine. In the very nature of things this chance had in some measure to be shared by the factor, and naturally the system developed a scale of charges which were correspondingly high. I do not know that there was much complaint at these charges. They were accepted as the price to be paid for a necessary accommodation. But when, as was often the case, a few years of adversity found the planter struggling under a burden of debt which was steadily increasing, it was natural that he should sometimes give utterance to the feeling that "in the fell clutch of circumstance" he was hopelessly harnessed to the factor's plow. On the other hand there were enough instances of abuse of confidence and credit on the planter's part; of the reckless squandering at Northern resorts and on European travel of funds furnished for purely business purposes; of neglect of their common interests, with resulting heavy losses to both, to make the factor feel that though his profits were many times greater than they were supposed to be, they would still be insufficient to balance the risks he ran. It was by no means a one-sided game.

We have seen that the factor furnished the planter with funds; that he acted as a commission merchant in the purchase of plantation supplies, and that he discharged the functions of an agent in selling the plantation product. What were the charges for these services, and what were the characteristic features of the system, which differentiated it from any other relation of principal and agent? And what were its general economic tendencies and effects? The interest rate varied with times, places, and conditions. It probably ranged between eight and twelve per cent. It was usually charged only as funds were actually drawn, though in some instances it was computed on the face of the loan, regardless of the average time of its actual use by the borrower. There was also in some cases a customary brokerage fee of from one half of one per cent to two and one half per cent added to the interest charge. To the price of the goods, wares, and merchandise purchased for the planter was added a commission which varied according to custom from two to ten per cent or more. The customary charge for selling the crop was a commission of two and one half per cent, but sometimes this was as high as four.

These were the only items of open profit to the factor in the transaction. But there were others which helped to make the business attractive, notwithstanding its hazards. In the early days cotton sales were effected through a broker who acted as a middleman between the factor and the resident agent of a foreign mill or merchant. To this broker was paid a commission of one half of one per cent, nominally borne by the mill agent. In practice and custom, however, one-half of this commission was paid by the factor and charged to the planter. This was supposed to be divided between the factor and the broker. The planter was taxed with various other charges, as freight, storage, insurance, drayage, weighing, sampling, mending, and repairing. These were returned on the account of sale to the planter at a uniform rate, fixed by custom or agreement, and were supposed to represent the actual amounts paid by the factor for the service rendered in behalf of the planter. As a matter of fact, custom early developed a system of rebates to the factor on practically all these charges. This seemed to be an inevitable incident of the control by the factor of large quantities of cotton to be warehoused, drayed, insured, compressed, and otherwise handled solely at his direction. Those who were engaged in such business at cotton ports naturally offered the factor the inducements of special rates and drawbacks in consideration of the heavy volume of business which he could divert to their hands.

The exaction of one of these exerted a particularly baneful influence upon the plantation system. This was the penalty commission feature of most advancing contracts between factors and planters, incident to the repayment of all loans in kind, rather than in money. The fundamental consideration inducing extensions of credit under the factorage system was not the matter of interest on the funds advanced. This, indeed, was the least of such inducements. The very foundation of the system was the medium which it offered for the control and manipulation of large volumes of a great staple commodity holding a recognized position of prime importance in the commercial world. The planter's note, backed by his contract with the factor, with the latter's endorsement, could be rediscounted with the factor's correspondents in any financial centre in this country or abroad. The tremendous stocks of cotton accumulated in the factorage cities of the South, warehoused, insured, and controlled by the factor, furnished him a basis of credit unequalled by any other form of security the South had to offer. It was practically as convertible as the best forms of commercial paper. If cotton was king, the cotton factor was the power behind the throne. We do not need any documents to tell us that the inevitable consequence was the elevation of the mere volume of business—the naked number of bales of cotton grown by the planter and controlled by the factor—to a position of importance out of all true and proper economic relation to what should have been the primary considerations of cost and profit to the producer. The penalty commission was a simple expedient for stimulating the production of more bales of cotton. It was a proviso coupled to the agreement for paying the customary commission on sales, under which the planter bound himself to pay to the factor a certain sum per bale, sometimes ranging as high as four dollars, for each and every bale by which his actual production fell short of the stipulated number of bales which he agreed to ship. This was in addition to the agreement to plant so many acres in cotton calculated to produce so many bales. Travelers and foreign observers of

Southern conditions were accustomed to comment on the South's devotion to cotton, to the neglect of the principle of proper diversification, so essential to a permanently prosperous and well-balanced system of agriculture, and to attribute the trouble to slavery. Such foundation as there was for this criticism was in large measure due to the influences which we have suggested. Cotton was the only cash crop. It was moreover the only crop which could be used as a basis of credit. Every planter who was in debt fondly dreamed of the year when through a combination of a bumper yield and a fair price he would be enabled to throw off his shackles. But the only avenue of escape was through this happy combination, and it was too seldom realized. Even when a planter did finally grow independent the impulse to enlarge his undertakings had become deep rooted and was apparently irresistible. There was a sort of atmospheric psychology in the situation which seemed to make a man forever dissatisfied with a stagnated sufficiency. He wanted more land and more slaves, which meant more cotton, and as more cotton was both a means and an end, the economic circle was thus easily established. But here again we have the personal equation. These men included in their ranks many who by inherent ability and force were as much captains of industry in their day and generation as were the cotton factors of the cities. Their activities simply found expression in expansion along lines normal to their period and environment, precisely as is the case in the industrial and financial world to-day. There need be no mystery about that phase of the matter.

In order to render absolute the factor's control of the entire crop, one of the cardinal features of the system was the requirement that every bale of cotton grown by the planter should be consigned to the factor. If the total crop were one thousand bales, and the first five hundred discharged the planter's debt, an exceedingly improbable supposition, the remaining five hundred bales must nevertheless go forward also. There were few, if any, agricultural lien laws in those days, but this requirement took their place. It also probably made their ultimate enactment less difficult, through common familiarity with the practical operation of their essential principle, which was a certain measure of control, by the financing agent, of the product grown through his assistance.

The broader economic effects of the factorage system would form in themselves alone an interesting and valuable field of inquiry. A primary incident was the concentration of Southern capital, and hence of its real wealth, in the few Southern cities which were its important factorage centres. Within the limitations of this paper, it would be useless to attempt even a casual consideration of this branch of the subject. But I am satisfied of the inaccuracy of the commonly accepted idea of ante-bellum Southern wealth as something naturally and essentially rural, as might be expected in a country whose sole business in popular estimation was that of agriculture.

One effect of the system was the retarding of the normal tendency toward the founding and developing of smaller urban communities, common even in an agricultural section. The factorage centres were enormous supply depots, from which were distributed to the interior South, through the factor in bulk, instead of through a local merchant by ordinary processes of retail trade, all the common necessities, comforts, and conveniences of daily life. And it is a mistake to assume that I am here dealing with ancient history. The system outlived by many years the ante-bellum era, and within my memory, in the case of my own family, all the staple articles of domestic and plantation use were bought through my father's factor in New Orleans, and shipped four hundred miles by river, and then hauled by wagons twenty-odd miles further into the interior.

When interior urban development at last took place, it was naturally patterned after that of the seaboard factorage centres. Prosperous and influential factorage houses grew up at what became important interior river points. Here we had a repetition on a smaller scale of the accumulation of cotton and the concentration of capital and wealth which were the rule at seaboard. But this was a step in the direction of the diffusion, not of the break-up, of the system. These interior houses were in the nature of tributaries to the larger streams.

The beginning of the end of the seaboard system did not come until some years after the Civil War. The two most potent instrumentalities in its final dissolution were the railroads and the land-mortgage companies. The development of railroads made it possible for cotton to be shipped direct from the field of its production to that of its foreign or domestic consumption, which in turn made possible a real interior market. The advent of land-mortgage companies made possible a refunding process whereby the whole, or a large part, of a planter's obligations could be financed on a basis of the land alone. His current business could then be transferred on the security of a crop lien and personal property to smaller interior merchants and factors, whose capital, though limited as compared with the old institutions, had become large enough to meet the necessities of the business after the loan companies had assumed a large part of the burden. The country merchant had frequently become a factor through natural gradations, and he was at hand to take care of the smaller business at first, and gradually to extend the field of his operations. Largely from his ranks was developed the country banker, who was an indispensable feature in the slow process of modifying and finally revolutionizing the ancient system. The country factor did business along the same general lines as his city prototype. But where he has taken over the factor's business at all, and this he has largely done, the country banker has practically abandoned the last vestige of the old system. He lends on the same security as the factor, but the business is on the same basis as any other commercial transaction. The railroad and the country merchant and factor, the country compress and the country bank, have been followed by the country buyer, who furnishes the last link in the chain between raw cotton production and consumption. The elimination of the entrepreneur has by no means been accomplished, but the industry has been relieved of a large part of the load which it carried for the greater portion of the first century of its existence. Even in the remote interior a planter can today gin the cotton which yesterday was in the field, and tomorrow receive a check for it from a buyer who will consign it from the planter's platform to its destination at Fall River, Bremen, or Liverpool. Within the span of my personal experience, I have seen the time when a similar transaction would require from two to six months for its consummation, with the intervention of a dozen different agencies of transportation and trade.

One of the chief accents in the South today is industrialization. Not only are Southern communities actively seeking Northern factories but they are also facing up to the profound changes that industry brings to their time-honored way of life. Every Southern state has the equivalent of a planning board or a development commission which is vigorously pushing industrialization within that state. To see such activities in historical perspective we turn to a passage from Dr. Clement Eaton's excellent *A History of the Old South,* which will round out the discussion of the ante-bellum economy. He makes reference to the *factors,* who have been the topic of the previous selection; he also shows how the textile industry, which has had such a phenomenal growth in the South, got its start before the Civil War.

• 33 • *The Progress of Southern Manufactures*
CLEMENT EATON

Manufacturing in the Southern states did not originate in the post-war "New South," when Henry W. Grady and his fellow editors publicized the expansion of cotton mills. Rather, the South had made an important progress in industry prior to 1860, which was interrupted by the Civil War and resumed in the decade of the 1880's. Southern manufacturing had slowly emerged from the handicraft stage of colonial days. During the eighteenth century and to a lesser extent in the ante-bellum period household industries were carried on by slaves, who were employed on the large plantations to weave cloth, to make bricks, staves, and barrels, to manufacture nails, to boil soap, to do blacksmith work, and even to make artistic furniture. Also in the back country frontier women were engaged in a variety of household industries, particularly the weaving of linsey-woolsey cloth, while their husbands developed into jacks-of-all-trades, making rude furniture, shoes, and agricultural equipment. As late as 1810, according to incomplete census returns, the Southern states were ahead of the rest of the country in the manufacture of homespun cloth and especially in the spinning of flax. In the Piedmont region there were numerous spinning frames in operation, but these rudimentary factories were not equipped with Arkwright machinery, such as had been introduced into New England. The movement of industrialization below the Mason and Dixon line was stimulated to some degree by the War of 1812, but to a much greater extent by the depression of agricultural staples in the period of 1839-1850.

The progress of manufactures below the

[From *A History of the Old South,* Macmillan, New York, 1949. Pp. 423-442. Used by permission.]

Mason and Dixon line was impeded by a number of psychological and physical handicaps. The agrarian ideal caused many Southerners of the ante-bellum period to hold prejudices against trade and manufacturing and to regard planting and politics as more honorable occupations. Southern capital was largely monopolized in buying more land and slaves. The accumulation of capital needed to start manufactures was retarded also by the indirect method of selling the Southern agricultural staples, which enabled Northern business men to exploit the South and which contributed largely to perpetuating the colonial status of that region. Lesser reasons for the industrial lag of the South were the necessity of supporting a relatively larger dependent population of children and old people than existed in the North, the avoidance of the South by European immigrant laborers, the aversion of yeomen farmers to give up the independence of the farm and become "mill hands," the belief that Negroes were not suited to the handling of machinery, and the argument that the rise of manufactures would weaken the slave system and the opposition in the South to the protective tariff. Consequently, in 1860 the South produced slightly less than 10 per cent of the manufactures of the United States (measured in terms of value).

The development of cotton mills in the ante-bellum South was socially more significant than the rise of any other industry, for it pointed the way to utilizing the labor of the poor whites in factories. The Southern states enjoyed at least three advantages in the early development of mills. They had excellent water power along the fall line, they could procure cheap white labor, and they could obtain clean, freshly-picked cotton, undamaged by shipping and exposure. The early Southern mills were small establishments engaged in spinning yarn. South Carolina was prominent in pioneering in the development of cotton mills. . . .

The most influential promoter of the textile industry of the ante-bellum South was William Gregg of Charleston, South Carolina.

Trained as a watchmaker and silversmith, Gregg became a successful jeweler in Charleston, thus obtaining the capital which he later invested in the cotton mill industry. His interest in this industry had been attracted when as a boy he had been associated with his uncle in an unsuccessful venture in cotton manufacturing in Georgia. As early as 1836 he acquired an interest in the Vaucluse Cotton Mill. His revolutionary role in the development of Southern cotton mills, however, began in 1844 as a result of a tour of New England which he made to observe the operation of the textile industry in that region. Upon his return, he wrote ten articles for the Charleston *Courier,* entitled "Essays on Domestic Industry," which were published in pamphlet form in 1845. In these essays he preached the new gospel of developing manufactures in the South by utilizing the great reservoir of poor white labor that had hitherto been largely neglected. He advocated confining slave labor to agriculture and to the reclamation of swamps. By bringing the poor whites into the factories, he maintained, not only would their labor be profitably employed, but their moral and social condition would be thereby improved. The Southern mills, he thought, should at first confine their efforts to the production of the coarser cotton goods and should import experienced Northern men to aid in starting the factories. He pointed out that by building cotton mills the South could prevent the emigration of its sons to the West. Furthermore, he did not demand tariff protection for these infant industries, primarily because they specialized in making yarn and the cheaper grades of cloth, which needed protection from New England rather than from foreign nations.

Gregg determined to build a model cotton factory to demonstrate the value of his ideas. In 1846 he constructed a remarkable cotton mill at Graniteville, South Carolina, not far from Augusta, Georgia. It was built of granite, "airy and commodious," the grounds landscaped and ornamented with shrubbery and flowers. To house the workers he erected eighty-five cottages in the Gothic style, also of granite, each cottage provided with a large garden. His mill people, he boasted, lived "under parental care," for they were not allowed to solace their arduous labor with alcohol, they were required by their leases to their cottages to send their children to school, and no children "of tender age," that is, under twelve years old, were worked in the factory. Thus Gregg started the first compulsory school system in the South. He was a benevolent despot, who caught truants from his school and punished them personally, but he also gave them picnics and lectures on politeness and thrift. He required that his employees should be moral and sober, and he prohibited such hedonistic practices as dancing in Graniteville. Gregg's paternalistic policy may have been influenced by the Lowell factory in Massachusetts, but it also carried over plantation traditions into industry and the mill village. Graniteville must have been a very thrifty and sober community, but a very dull place in which the sparks of freedom and individuality were smothered.

Graniteville Factory was operated by water power. The superintendent and overseers were Northern men, but the labor force was composed of three hundred "piney woods" folk. The operatives were chiefly women and children over twelve years of age, for the older people who came from the hill districts and pine barrens did not have the flexibility to make good mill hands. The employees worked twelve hours a day, the men receiving four to five dollars a week, the women three to four dollars per week. The mill cottages rented from sixteen to twenty-five dollars a year. These wages were very low, but they compared favorably with wages paid to mill workers in Massachusetts and to agricultural wages in the South. It was an era when respectable, church-going factory owners exploited human labor without recognizing any injustice in making large profits and giving their employees a pitiful share of the returns of their labor.

Although there were failures, the well-managed textile mills in the South during the decade of the 1850's paid good dividends. The Graniteville Mill in its early years paid a 7 per cent dividend and later as much as 18 per cent. Gregg pointed out that the Southern mills had the advantages over their Northern rivals in securing labor 20 per cent cheaper, cotton at one and one-half cents a pound cheaper, and the superiority of bright, freshly picked cotton over shipped cotton. The Southern mills, almost without exception, manufactured the cheaper grades of cloth, osnaburgs, "nigger cloth," sheeting, and yarn. Moreover, their market remained largely below the Mason and Dixon line.

In North Carolina the Battle family had a pioneer mill at Rocky Mount, but the most important cotton mill leader during the antebellum period was Edwin Michael Holt. . . . He gathered the capital for his adventurous enterprise of a cotton mill in his native state from his profits as a farmer, small merchant, distiller, sawmill owner, and miller. In 1837 he erected his mill on Great Alamance Creek in the North Carolina Piedmont, procuring his machinery from the North. With his slaves he made brick for the buildings and cut the timber for his water wheel. His first few years were devoted to spinning yarn, which he transported by wagon to the nearest town, Hillsboro, and to the more distant market of Fayetteville. A considerable amount of his yarn was sold in Philadelphia, Pennsylvania. In 1845 his manuscript diary records the installation of machinery for weaving cloth. He bought fresh, bright cotton for his mill in the near-by towns. Three years later the Holt Mill was paying 7 cents a pound for raw cotton and selling the finished products, yarn, for 15 cents per pound, and sheeting for 7½ cents a yard. In 1849 the mill was running twelve looms which were making sheeting "as good as you ever saw," and selling its goods as fast as they could be made.

But there were ups and downs in the precarious cotton mill business in the South, so that the following year his partner wrote that the factory was paying very poorly, since the cost of cotton was too high for the prices obtained for their cotton yarn and cloth. Furthermore, the water in the creek became at intervals so low that the mill had to stop running. In 1853 a French dyer came to Alamance County and was employed by Holt to teach his mill operatives the art of dyeing cloth. Thus the Holt Mill became the pioneer factory south of the Potomac River in introducing colored cotton cloth made by power looms—"the Alamance plaids." By 1861 the Holt Mill had increased from the original start of over five hundred spindles to twelve hundred spindles and ninety-six looms.

The human side of early textile manufacturing in the South is also illustrated by the records of the Holt Mill. The proprietor arrived at the factory early in the morning and left it after the hands had completed their day's work of twelve hours. He attended strictly to business, eschewing the pursuit of political office, training his sons to be cotton manufacturers with the mottoes: "Stick to business," and "Put your profits into your business." Very religious, he stopped the mill at times in order to permit the hands to attend camp meetings and religious revivals. He built tenement houses for them near the factory and sold them goods from his store. At least on one occasion there was a strike resulting from the overseer "being too tight" with them. Very low wages were paid, and the majority of the workers were women and children. Before his death in 1884 this hard-driving capitalist attained the greatest fortune owned by any individual in the state.

The growth of the cotton mill industry in the South was particularly rapid in the last decade of the ante-bellum period. Although the number of factories in 1860, one hundred fifty-nine in eleven Southern states, was exactly the same as reported by the census ten years before, and although there was an actual decrease of 137 in the number of hands reported, the value of the product of Southern mills had risen 43 per cent. On the eve of the Civil War these mills employed 9,906 hands, of whom approximately two-thirds were female, and the average annual wage was $145.41. The South at that time produced one-third of the national output of yarn. Nevertheless, the expansion of the textile industry in the ante-bellum South should not be exaggerated, for the value of cotton goods manufactured by New England in 1860 exceeded the value of the Southern output almost ten times, and the single town of Lowell, Massachusetts, had more spindles running than the whole South. The largest cotton manufacturing state in the land of Dixie at that time was Georgia, whose thirty-three mills were capitalized at $2,126,103 and employed 2,813 hands. Only three other states listed by the census as "Southern," Virginia, North Carolina, and Alabama, manufactured cotton goods exceeding the value of a million dollars. But Maryland, which was classified by the census officials with the Middle States, had twenty mills that produced nearly three million dollars' worth of cotton textiles.

Another Southern industry was based on the habit of chewing plug tobacco which in the America of the nineteenth century was widespread among all classes of society. President Andrew Jackson injured his frail health by chewing tobacco over a long period of years. The Mormon prophet, Joseph Smith, received a revelation from God against the use of tobacco by his followers after his wife, Emma, had protested vigorously against the practice of the visiting elders who spit on the cleanly swept floors of their house. Even the most eminent orators, statesmen, and preachers indulged in this minor vice, and there were Southern tobacco-chewers whose prowess in spitting accurately at the targets of distant spittoons resembled the unerring marksmanship of "Wild Bill" Hickok. Cigarettes were not manufactured in the South until after the Civil War, while cigars were made principally in the North. But the habit of chewing tobacco was responsible for the growth of an industry which ranked third in importance among the manufactures of the Old South. Only flour and lumber exceeded in value the finished product of tobacco within the Southern states. The tobacco factories, concentrated in Virginia and North Carolina, were chiefly plug tobacco establishments, 98 per cent of them being devoted to this manufacture and only 2 per cent to pipe tobacco.

The manufacture of tobacco below the Mason and Dixon line began as a home industry. The tobacco "twists" thus made were peddled in a horse and wagon through the lower South. In the decades of the 1830's small factories were established in Richmond, Petersburg, Lynchburg, Danville, and in Caswell County, North Carolina. Unlike the cotton industry, the tobacco factories employed slaves as their principal labor force. The larger factories in 1860 employed between fifty and one hundred and fifty slaves, principally men, of whom about half were owned by the factories and the others were hired at rates of from $100 to $200 annually, plus food and maintenance.

* * *

The tobacco manufactured in these Southern towns was sold chiefly to factors in New York and Philadelphia. Although some of this chewing tobacco was peddled in the South by wagons, the Southern merchants as a rule ordered their tobacco through New York and Philadelphia, a roundabout method of purchase which enhanced the profits of Northern business men. After the California gold rush, large quantities of Virginia tobacco were sent to the Pacific coast. The Northern factor received a commission of 5 to 7½ per cent of the sale price, and he granted to his customers a credit of eight months. The Panic of 1857 caused the Virginia and Carolina tobacco manufacturers to combine to remedy their grievances against the Northern factors. In December of that year a Tobacco Manufacturers' Convention, consisting of one hundred delegates, met in Richmond and resolved that all factors should limit their credits upon the sale of tobacco to four months and that the commission should not exceed 6½ per cent.

* * *

The growth of the tobacco industry in the upper South was phenomenal. By June, 1860, Virginia and North Carolina factories were producing 61 per cent of all plug, smoking, and snuff tobacco manufactured in the United States. Instead of shipping their raw tobacco abroad, as in former times, these states processed two-thirds of the tobacco grown within their boundaries. There had been a steady evolution from small factories to larger units so that in 1860 eighty-five factories, or almost one-fourth in the Virginia-Carolina area, employed fifty or more hands. Richmond, with its fifty-two factories, was by far the largest tobacco manufacturing city in the United States. The eleven Southern states produced a total of $14,612,442 worth of manufactured tobacco and employed 11,321 male and 2,300 female hands.

* * *

Prior to the founding of Birmingham, Alabama, in 1871, the iron center of the New South, Richmond was the most important iron-manufacturing city below the Mason and Dixon line. Here was located the Belle Isle Iron Works, founded in 1839, which manufactured nails that became famous throughout the land of Dixie. By 1856 this company, its name changed to the Old Dominion Nail Works, was producing over a thousand tons of nails a year. Richmond had the advantage of being located near a coal basin that furnished abundant supplies of cheap bituminous coal. Raw material for the iron-manufacturing industry was obtained from the charcoal-burning furnaces of the Valley of Virginia, which produced a superior grade of iron of great tensile strength. Indeed, the furnaces and forges of the Valley had from the early nineteenth century made bar iron for the numerous blacksmith shops of the South.

The greatest iron company of Richmond, and of the South, was the Tredegar Iron Works which was founded in 1837. The masterful personality behind the success of the Tredegar Works was Joseph Reid Anderson, a graduate of West Point Military Academy, who became sales agent of the company in 1841 and seven years later purchased the business for $125,000. The Tredegar Company secured contracts from the United States government to furnish cannon for the navy. By 1860 the company had sold thirteen hundred cannon to the Federal government. The company also manufactured shells, chain cable, rails and spikes for the expanding railroads, and steam machinery for the Louisiana sugar plantations. The market of this Richmond company was largely in the North, for Southerners were prejudiced against buying home-made iron products. The chief contribution of the company to Southern industrial development was the manufacture of over forty locomotives for Southern railroads. During the Civil War the Tredegar Works played a vital role in Confederate armament, one of the reasons for the stubborn defense of Richmond.

The iron industry of Virginia employed slave labor extensively. Half of the labor force of the Tredegar Company, for example, was slaves. Some of the slave hands were owned by the company, but most of them were hired at rates ranging from $100 a year in 1849 to $175 in 1860. These black laborers were taught the skills needed in the iron industry by trained white mechanics imported from the North. In 1847 this situation led to a strike by the white mechanics, who demanded that slaves should not be used in the skilled processes of puddling and rolling. Anderson replied that he would not relinquish his constitutional right to employ or discharge anyone at his pleasure and notified the strikers that they had discharged themselves. After this event he began more extensively to employ slaves, who made satisfactory employees. White mechanics, however, were reluctant to teach Negroes their acquired skills in the iron industry, for they feared that the Negroes would later usurp their jobs.

* * *

In 1860 the milling of flour and cornmeal still ranked at the top of Southern manufactures. A familiar and picturesque sight on the roads of the upper South was a boy like the young Henry Clay riding to the grist mill with a sack of wheat or corn to be ground into flour or cornmeal for the subsistence of the family. In the lower South much of the flour consumed was brought from the North-

west down the Mississippi River. Thousands of small grist mills all over the South served local needs, but the tendency was to concentrate commercial milling in a few urban centers such as Richmond and Baltimore. At Richmond were located the largest grain mills in the world, a single mill having the capacity of producing a thousand barrels of flour a day. Baltimore was also a great flour-milling city. From these two centers vast quantities of flour were exported to the lower South and to Brazil. According to the report of the Census Bureau of 1860 the value of flour and meal produced in the eleven Southern states which later joined the Confederacy, $37,996,470 yearly, was twice as great as the value of the next most important industry of that region, the sawmill or lumber business.

The processing of the forest resources of the South was a highly dispersed industry. Numerous small sawmills were scattered throughout the land of Dixie, operated by water power or steam engines, producing over nineteen and a half million dollars of wealth per year. Yellow pine lumber, live oak timber for ships, cypress shingles, staves for barrels, were cut from the illimitable virgin forests. Frequently lumbering was a by-product of clearing the land for the purpose of agriculture. The lumber industry in the South employed approximately sixteen thousand persons, the largest labor force engaged in any Southern manufacturing enterprise. There were also over four thousand persons employed in extracting turpentine from the long-leaf pines of the Carolinas and Georgia—a seven and a half million dollar business. In 1860 North Carolina still retained its colonial supremacy in the production of turpentine, furnishing 60 per cent of the turpentine produced in the United States. After the Civil War leadership in this field passed first to Georgia and later to Florida.

The Southern states also supported a variety of minor industries. In 1860 there were within eleven of the Southern states one female and 3,695 male blacksmiths. Three thousand workers were engaged in the leather industry, producing goods to the value of

$4,426,870. The carriage and buggy industry employed over four thousand men constructing vehicles worth nearly four million dollars. The making of steam engines absorbed the energies of 4,328 men, whose annual product was worth $5,624,375. Although the South imported huge supplies of shoes from Massachusetts, nearly four million dollars' worth of shoes were manufactured in the Southern states, representing an increase of approximately 90 per cent during the decade. In the Great Kanawha Valley and at Saltville in the Holston Valley of southwestern Virginia much salt was produced by boiling the brine of the salt springs. Of the 12,717,200 bushels of salt produced in the United States in 1859, Virginia's share was 2,076,513 bushels. The eminent Negro leader, Booker T. Washington, born in slavery, worked in the salt works of western Virginia as a boy. Although some cottonseed oil was produced in the South, there were only two small sugar refineries in the land of Dixie, employing a total labor force of thirty-eight persons.

Throughout the ante-bellum period the Southern states depended largely upon the North for the manufacture of agricultural implements.

*   *   *

In one branch of manufacture, the making of cotton gins, the South had a monopoly in 1860. Alabama was the leading state in the Union in the production of cotton gin machinery while Georgia came second. Daniel Pratt, a native of New Hampshire, was the most successful manufacturer of cotton gins below the Mason and Dixon line. He established a flourishing village at Prattville, Alabama, where in addition to his gin factory he built a cotton mill, a sawmill, and a grist mill. In 1851 he was employing two hundred hands and making annually six hundred gins of a superior quality.

*   *   *

A now forgotten industry which existed in the Old South was the mining of gold. The Federal government derived its entire gold supply for the coining of money between the years 1804-27, from the state of North Carolina. Until the discovery of this precious metal in California in 1848 the Southern states were the chief gold-producing region of the United States. . . .

From an economic point of view the South was never liberated from its colonial status. Although its manufactures were developing in a promising fashion during the last decade of the ante-bellum period, still the South remained largely rural. Two-thirds of all exports from the United States to Europe consisted of Southern agricultural products, rice, tobacco, sugar, and cotton. Nevertheless, much of the profit from the sale of these staples went into the pockets of Northern business men, through the cotton factorage system, the indirect trade with Europe via Northern ports, and the purchase of Northern manufactured goods. Thomas Prentice Kettell, editor of *Hunt's Merchants' Magazine,* attempted to show the various ways in which the South was exploited by the North in a book entitled *Southern Wealth and Northern Profits* (1860). He included in his bill of indictment Federal bounties to fisheries, customs duties, profits of Northern manufacturers on goods sold in the South, profits of importers of European goods, profits of factors, brokers, and commission men, interest charges on money loaned to Southerners, profits on the numerous Southern travelers who patronized Northern resorts, and the money sent northward by Yankee teachers and tutors in the South. He pointed out the folly of agitating the slavery question on the part of the North and thus driving out of the Union Southern customers who were so profitable to the North.

*   *   *

In order to liberate themselves from Northern exploitation, the Southerners considered various proposals: the establishment of direct trade with Europe, the development of Southern manufactures, the boycotting of Northern manufactures, the diversification of Southern agriculture, the building of railroads, and the reopening of the African slave trade. How much the growing sentiment of Southern nationalism contributed to the rise of manufactures below the Mason and Dixon line is impossible to measure. In an address entitled "The Industrial Regeneration of the South" (1852) the Honorable J. H. Lumpkin of Georgia urged his section to free themselves from dependence on the North by developing their own industries. "Will the South, the chivalrous South, remain longer in a condition of colonial servitude?" he asked. William Gregg, eight years later, appealed to provincial patriotism, especially to the devotion of Southern ladies, to patronize Southern manufactures, but he sadly observed the tendency of Southerners to prefer Northern goods. "Graniteville goods," he wrote, "are more popular in New York and Philadelphia than at home."

One of the most influential voices of the South which advocated Southern economic nationalism was *De Bow's Review of the Southern and Western States*. This periodical reflected the interests of the merchants, the planters, and the business men of the South. Its editor, James D. B. De Bow, was a South Carolinian, educated at the College of Charleston, who carried the South Carolina doctrines of Southern nationalism to New Orleans. Here he founded *De Bow's Review* in 1846. In this magazine he encouraged the development of Southern manufactures, direct trade with Europe, the building of railroads, the patronizing of Southern colleges and health resorts, and the organization of Southern commercial conventions. His *Review* also carried articles on the management and care of slaves, the diversification of crops, and improvements in the cultivation of cotton and sugar. In politics he sought to form an alliance between the South and the West, and after 1858 he acted with the Southern fire eaters. His magazine became quite prosperous, rivaling *Hunt's Merchants' Magazine* of the North, and it survived both the Civil War and Reconstruction.

De Bow was quite influential in the deliberations of the Southern Commercial Conventions that were held at intervals between 1837 and 1860 in the leading cities of the South. Such meetings of Southerners from all parts of the land of Dixie were compared by De Bow to the assembly of the Greeks at the ancient Olympic games, since both peoples thus developed a sense of unity and a realization of common aims and grievances. At these meetings many resolutions were passed and much oratory was expended but little was accomplished, except the engendering of ill feeling against the North.

* * *

Southerners felt keenly their dependence on the North for manufactured goods. It was often asserted that Southerners were rocked in a cradle manufactured in the North, dressed in Northern-made clothes, read Northern books and magazines, used Northern plows and agricultural instruments, sent their children to Northern colleges, and were buried in Northern coffins. Resentment over this economic vassalage to the Yankees was intensified by the rise of the abolition crusade and the attempt to exclude slavery from the territories. After John Brown's Raid in 1859 a strong demand arose to boycott Northern goods. The agitators for Southern nationalism beginning in 1850 proposed commercial non-intercourse with the North. Bills were introduced in state legislatures to levy a tax of 10 per cent on all Northern goods imported into the Southern states. Southern Rights Associations were formed to arouse the people not to patronize Northern resorts like Saratoga Springs or Newport, not to subscribe to Northern magazines or newspapers, nor employ Yankee teachers in Southern schools, nor send Southern youth to Northern colleges nor use Northern manufactures. Although the state governments failed to pass drastic laws to carry out such a policy, individuals of extreme Southern feelings did boycott Northern manufactures. The fire eater Edmund Ruffin wore a suit of Southern manufacture and Senator Mason of Virginia dramatized Southern nationalism by appearing in a home-spun suit in the national Senate. Lincoln ridiculed such displays by observing that the dignified

Senator from Virginia should have come into the Senate barefoot as well as wearing his home-spun suit. "If that's the plan," he remarked, "they should begin at the foundation, and adopt the well-known 'Georgia costume' of a shirt collar and a pair of spurs."

These various efforts to free the South from its colonial status represent an early form of economic planning. Many of the proposals of the ante-bellum "regional planners" and of the Southern Commercial Conventions were sound, but they could not be realized by paper resolutions or the facile dreams of orators. The South was rural, conservative, individualistic, and only by a slow process of education or by drastic economic pressures could Southern ways be radically changed. Furthermore, the South was more prosperous in the decade of 1850-60 than ever before, with cotton selling twice as high as in the preceding decade. If cotton and tobacco had declined disastrously in price at this time, discontent would have aided the reformers and "regional planners." One aspect of the agitation toward economic independence, however, was pernicious—the generation of a bitter anti-Northern feeling in the South. In calling attention to the problems of the South, the Southern Commercial Conventions and the extremists tended to weaken the bonds of the Union.

Although preceding selections have shed some light on the family life of the Old South, further comments seem necessary to point out the close relationship between the home and the economy, between the traditions and the bringing up of children, and between paternalism on the plantation and the acceptance of male supremacy. Arthur W. Calhoun, in his monumental study of the American family, has collected much information describing the South. The next selection is made up of excerpts from his work.

• 34 • Notes on Family Life in the Old South
ARTHUR W. CALHOUN

Courtship among the southern aristocrats was reminiscent of the age of chivalric gallantry. ... The girl ... grew up apart from the great world yet was not provincial. As a child she was self-possessed and able to entertain her mother's callers in proper fashion. She began to have beaux in girlhood and exacted a protracted devotion of her lovers. . . . Girls were kept and cherished in right romantic fashion. Extreme modesty was assiduously cultivated; self-help was not expected. . . . [One] writer says:

No set of girls in Christendom were watched with more vigilant eyes . . . in all ways more surely girdled about, as with a wall of fire, from the sensual temptations of society, at home and elsewhere, than the Southern young women of the more favored sort in these early days.

*   *   *

Page says that the Virginia girl was generally a coquette, often an outrageous flirt, not from heartlessness but as a normal expression of her life. "She played upon every chord of the heart. Perhaps it was because, when she grew up, the surrender was to be absolute. . . ."

There were runaway matches. Greensboro,

[From A Social History of the American Family from Colonial Times to the Present, Vol. 2, Barnes and Noble, New York, 1945. Pp. 311-355. Used by permission.]

North Carolina, served as a Gretna Green for Virginians. Excessive restriction upon sex acquaintance furthered such clandestine matches.

* * *

The Reverend J. D. Long wrote . . . :

Among a sparse population, where there are comparatively few social topics to enlist attention, many long winter evenings and summer days are spent in discussing the minutest incidents of a courtship. If a marriage is to come off, the bride's lace or her nightcap is a subject of criticism. Colored people take a deep interest in the marriage of their owners. Courtships are frequently conducted through them.

* * *

But it is particularly in the romanticism of the new southern literature that the woman of the old South shines as queen and saint, a being of rare social gifts and sensibility to exalted sentiments and embodying in her person the quintessence of all that was lovely in the civilization of an effulgent people. Modesty, refinement, and sweet gentility grace the memories of her that linger in the thoughts of her children. Her "highest ambition was to be president of home."

To some extent the status and functions of the middle and upper class women of the old South merited the encomiums that are bestowed. The southern women of the middle class were modest, virtuous, industrious housekeepers, devoted wives and mothers. They were frequently gullible, knowing little of the world, and aloof from public diversions. Having to look after the wants of the few slaves—the making of their garments and the like—the labors of these ladies were onerous. They lived "only to make home happy."

In general there could be no complaint of lack of domesticity in southern wives. Marriage prefaced a life-time of self-devotion; sprightly girls became sober, retired wives, bent on making home a man's delight, and devoted to family welfare; their husbands'

relatives and connections became their own. The married woman was not a figure in society; romance is built about the young girl; the social functions of the little cities consisted chiefly of balls and dances that brought the young of the two sexes together. After marriage women lived in plantation isolation; only the few that maintained town houses and spent part of the year in Richmond, Charleston, or New Orleans retained their social connections "and for them a staid and modified social life was deemed fitting. For them the dance was over. . . ."

* * *

The duties of a plantation mistress were often truly formidable. Many a plantation was a crude industrial plant comparable as to household comfort with a mining camp. On such estates many a lady lived. If slavery released the lady from manual drudgery, it overworked her in other ways; she was typically deficient in vitality, often nervous and sensitive, yet she often had to contend with an aggravated form of the servant problem, for slaveholders did not always manage to get rid of trying and unprofitable servants. Except perhaps a butler and a head housemaid the help was often idle, incompetent, and in need of constant supervision. . . . A southern lady of an old and wealthy family visiting in New York said: "Your two servants accomplish a great deal more, and do their work a great deal better than our twelve."

Every household operation had to be under scrutiny. Every consumable thing had to be kept locked up, hence the mistress carried a huge bunch of keys and doled out "on incessant requests" whatever was wanted for the household. Continually she was being called upon to attend to some want of one of her many dependents. The plantation nurse brought a list of the sick and the serious cases had to be visited. The wagons came with the carcass of a beef or sheep and the mistress saw to the cutting up. The makers of garments had to receive attention.

* * *

Unfortunately there was not much chance for a progressive movement among Southern women. A very interesting *Ladies' Magazine* begun at Savannah in 1819 was forced to suspend at the end of six months for lack of patronage. The lady of the archaic South left little written record. As in the North, woman received no worthy education. An actor remarked in 1842 upon the rarity of daughters of the far South among the vast number of women magazine writers. Gentlemen of the old regime in the South would say, "A woman's name should appear in print but twice— when she marries and when she dies." There was no economic opportunity for women outside the home. If there had been, social status would have debarred woman from acceptance of it.

* * *

Even the chastity of the Southern women (a monopolized excellence) was scarcely a virtue, but rather a matter of course. Men sedulously shielded their female perquisites of white blood. A young lady of South Carolina got a verdict of one thousand dollars against a man (of moderate means) for imputation of unchastity. Education and public opinion were strained to the preservation of the purity of free women, or rather of such as belonged to the master race. Somewhat of the spirit of the regnant male may be glimpsed in the remark of a Natchez gentleman about 1808: "The ladies in general are extremely delicate, which never fails to please, and excite the warmest sensations in the beholder. . . . Tho chaste as the virgin queen before the Gordian knot is tied, yet indulgent as the Cyprian goddess for ever after."

* * *

Death and widowhood in the old South complicated the problem of keeping intact the family name and dignity. . . . In old eastern Virginia it was not expected that a widow would remarry and usually she did not. It was almost a matter of course for a husband to make enjoyment of the estate conditional on non-marriage; the chief gospel was the preservation of family name and these restrictions were not considered cruel.

* * *

In so far as city life developed, the simplicity of the family life tended to disappear. At Richmond in 1800 "the higher circle consisted of the families of the neighboring planters, who left their estates to the management of overseers, and spent the larger part of the year in Richmond because of its social advantages." . . . The first tendency of the spirit of Revolutionary days was to do away with artificial social distinctions. Primogeniture was abolished in Virginia and Maryland; so that only by will could estates be maintained intact (as was in fact done in some notable cases for the sake of prestige). In Maryland, following the Revolution there was an open contempt for anything savoring of caste and nobility. "Coats of arms were destroyed and even erased from family silver in some cases, and all evidences of pride of lineage frowned down by the American patriots and their descendants, so that not to know one's grandmother was not rare."

After the Revolution, soil exhaustion in the older states and competition in tobacco reduced old families to poverty and oblivion. . . . By the early [eighteen] thirties at Charleston abolition of primogeniture had undermined old families. "Comparatively few of the old families now remain who are wealthy. . . . Therefore, the sons of the best men of the South are wisely placed in countinghouses in the great trading cities, or . . . bred to some useful calling." (But there were many showy idlers.) The South Carolina planter no longer inherited enough to send his sons to English universities. Division of property was killing patrician notions.

* * *

In spite, however, of all contrary tendencies, the family in the South was a much more potent institution than elsewhere in the republic. Old families held the day. In Kentucky, family feuds cost sundry lives. The eldest son of the old Virginia families was regarded as representative of the kin. In old east Virginia, family was a fetish. Estates were entailed to the limit of the law—one generation, and the heir commonly renewed religiously the entail. The tidewater owner of large estates would have been insulted by the idea of selling his home. The ancestral abode was the one spot on earth. . . .

Relationship was traced by Southerners to a remote degree. The bond of fellowship stretched to include all that were worthy, even tho they had removed to distant places. A post-bellum writer on North Carolina said: "In the many political canvasses which I have made, from East to West, I have never, to my best recollection, visited a county however distant, without being asked by some one about his kinsmen living in my county." It would be hard to overestimate the power of a great and strongly entrenched southern family connected with a dozen like families all holding a common point of view and action. Marriage and intermarriages and the tangle of consanguinity welded the slave power.

The Old South of the decade before the Civil War was as much as anything else a state of mind, not simply a vague idealization with little meaning but, as our next selection shows, a strong and living force for which the Confederate soldier was ready to die.

Out of what did this romantic legend of the South grow? The following selection, summarizing the changes in the South between 1819 and 1848, does much to answer this question.

• 35 • *The Affirmation of Southern Perfection*

CHARLES S. SYDNOR

How far the South had come toward sectionalism or nationalism by the late 1840's depends on the meaning ascribed to these words. But this much is clear. To the South's ancient economic and social distinctiveness there had been added, chiefly in the 1820's, something of a political platform. In the 1830's, regional self-consciousness and hostility toward the North became evident in many aspects of Southern thought and expression. By the late 1840's, there were those who desired a separate South.

While the relationship of the South to the nation was deteriorating and the power of the South in Congress was declining, changes were taking place within the region itself. Most noticeable, perhaps, was its southwest-ward expansion, engulfing the Indian lands of the lower South and sweeping across the Mississippi River into eastern Texas. The declining strength of the Southern states in Congress between the 1820's and the 1840's is measured by the loss of three seats by the South while the rest of the nation gained twenty-two seats. Within this same period the southwestward shift of Southern population caused the seaboard states to lose fifteen seats in the lower house of Congress while the rest of the South gained twelve seats.

Beyond the realm of statistical measurement, a more significant political shift had occurred. The strong and nationally respected leadership of Virginia in early years had vanished. By the 1840's, the leading Southern

[From *The Development of Southern Sectionalism, 1819-1848* (Vol. V of *A History of the South,* edited by W. H. Stephenson and E. Merton Coulter), Louisiana State University Press, Baton Rouge, 1948. Pp. 331-339. Used by permission.]

politicians were in the cotton states, and few of them had much influence outside the South. Much of the cotton South, stretching from South Carolina to Texas, was newly settled—a blend of the South and West—and most of it was in the vanguard of the democratic movement. On several counts, the cotton-kingdom politicians were too aggressive, and their viewpoint was too sectional, for the older and more conservative tobacco South.

Nonpolitical changes were also occurring in the region. Railroads and steamboats were introduced, a few factories were established, colleges increased in numbers, evangelical churches multiplied, significant literary developments occurred, and democracy made much progress. These were important, but the sum total of them all was probably less important than the relative changelessness of the South in a nation that was changing fast. The booming cities, the factories, the multiplying railroads, the expanding population, and the changing attitudes and viewpoints above Mason and Dixon's line account for tension between North and South far better than any changes that were taking place in the South.

The South of the 1840's, like the South of the previous century, was a land of farms and plantations, of few towns and of scattered population, of internal waterway transportation, and of a great export trade to foreign markets. Through all of this period Negro slavery continued. In the formation of the Union and in its early years, the South was accepted as a respectable part of the nation; by the 1840's it was regarded by many Northerners as an obstacle to American social and economic progress and as a moral pariah. The explanation of this change in attitude is to be found in part in the long series of conflicts between the diverging sections, and sectional divergence was due chiefly to those forces that were transforming the North. Because of this fact, the student of this period of Southern history must rely heavily on the student of Northern economic, social, and religious movements; for these were the forces that

remade the North and that in a large measure gave to the North a new and more critical attitude toward the South.

As the South declined in political power and as it experienced the growing force of the antislavery movement, the mind of the South was transmuted into something very different from what it had been a generation earlier. This mental change, in its various aspects, was one of the most notable developments in the South between 1819 and 1848.

To speak of the mind of the South implies, perhaps, a unity in the thinking of Southerners when, as a matter of fact, there was much diversity. They disagreed about the merits of the Whig and Democratic parties, about slavery, about the Union, and about a host of other subjects. But within the area of Southern thought and expression, certain traits and qualities had developed which if not universal in the region or even dominant were at least influential and significant.

* * *

. . . A great change had come over him [John C. Calhoun] and over many of his generation of Southerners. In the first place, he and they had lost faith in some of the fundamental premises of democracy. Perhaps they had never thoroughly believed that all men were created free and equal and that all had an inalienable right to liberty, but neither had they denied these tenets until the slavery controversy forced them to face the contradiction between slavery and the Declaration of Independence. Compelled to make a choice, they denied the accuracy and validity of the Revolutionary doctrines; and Jefferson, the personification of democratic idealism, they repudiated as a theoretical and dangerous visionary.

Going beyond theories, Calhoun's contemporaries pointed to evils in the actual operation of democratic government. They believed, and with good reason, that grave injuries had been done to the substantial interests of the South during the 1820's within the framework and through the procedures of democratic government. The conclusion was inescapable that a democracy could and often did oppress minorities within itself. Much thought was therefore given to devices for limiting and controlling self-government so as to protect smaller parts against the tyranny of the majority. The doctrine that the will of the majority ought always to be followed was utterly repudiated.

Inasmuch as the government to be held in check operated under a written constitution, the discussion turned into constitutional rather than philosophical channels. Champions of the South seldom began with the nature of man or with the good of man and society. Their arguments usually started with the written words of the fundamental document, and thence they proceeded by close reasoning and logical skill that was sometimes amazingly subtle. As one follows their mental operations he feels at times that he is watching intellectual giants struggling with very real and very profound problems of constitutional government, but at other times they seem to be no more than medieval scholastics working in an unreal world where little matters except logical technique.

The narrow but brilliant operation of the Southern mind on questions of government was accompanied by a restricted and abstract concept of humanity. Although the object of Southern political thought was to afford protection to the individual, far less attention was given to man than to checks and limitations on the machinery of government. It had not been so at an earlier period of Southern history. Jefferson and Madison knew, as Calhoun seems finally to have forgotten, that man is a creature of many parts, compounded of good as well as of bad, and that government must be fitted to man rather than man to government; they had tried to build democracy on such elements of goodness and wisdom as could be found in humanity. Calhoun, in contrast, limited himself to the task of devising a system of government that would hold in check the destructive tendencies of man. Yet, the last word must be said for Calhoun. The grim, narrow, pessimistic spirit that had come over him was not altogether and perhaps not mainly of his own

creation. The selfish and reckless tendencies in human nature which he was trying to place under legal and constitutional limitations were the forces that had in large measure placed his region on the defensive and made him the champion of a minority.

Along with its concern about problems of government, the mind of the South was becoming preoccupied with the problem of its own social organization. For a long time the South had possessed a distinctive social order, compounded of such elements as ruralism, the plantation system, Negro slavery, and a complex pattern of customs and conventions. To this way of life Southerners had conformed without much thought that they were odd persons living in a curious and different society. But by the 1830's the Southern mind was turned inward to a consideration of its own society. Among the forces that engendered this regional self-consciousness were Southern writers, like Kennedy and Simms and the school of local-color humorists, who described aspects of the Southern scene; foreign and Northern travelers who commented on distinctive Southern characteristics; and Northern opponents of slavery who extended their criticisms to include the whole fabric of Southern society. The bitter and extravagant antislavery attack was the major force in making Southerners aware that their region had a way of life that was far different from the rest of the United States, and the shock of the attack was aggravated because it came at a time when there was deep concern in the region over its failure to keep pace with the North and West in the march of progress.

The first response of Southerners to the vigorous onslaught was frequently one of startled amazement. . . . But defensive forces were soon rallied, and something of a plan of campaign began to emerge. It consisted in small measure of an attack upon the enemy's country, and this was aimed at the Northern characteristic that was most unlike the South, namely industrialism. One of the earliest American critiques of an industrial society, with emphasis on its exploitation of labor, was evolved in the South as a counter-attack against Northern critics of slavery.

But the master plan of the South in this war of words called for a defensive instead of an offensive war. It denied the validity of Northern criticisms, and it evolved into a remarkable apologia of virtually every aspect of the Southern way of life. Inasmuch as the attacking forces charged that Southern life was blighted throughout by slavery, Southern defenders rallied to this point. They claimed that slavery was good, that slavery had a beneficent influence upon Southern life, and that the South like ancient Greece had evolved a noble civilization because the institution of slavery was an integral part of it.

In 1835 Governor George McDuffie of South Carolina . . . affirmed that no human institution was "more manifestly consistent with the will of God," better designed to enhance the happiness of the Negro, or a firmer "corner stone of our republican edifice." The following year Senator James H. Hammond said: "It is no evil. On the contrary, I believe it to be the greatest of all the great blessings which a kind Providence bestowed upon our glorious region. . . . it has rendered our southern country proverbial for its wealth, its genius, and its manners." Somewhat later he claimed that slavery was responsible for the superiority of the moral code, the educational system, the religious beliefs and practices, and other attributes of Southern life. . . .

The effect of slavery upon the character of slaveholders was praised. It was claimed that many of the "highest, manliest and most admirable qualities in the Southern character have been preserved in their pristine strength, if not engendered by our peculiar social and domestic system." It set apart and gave a vigorous individuality to Southern men. Accustomed to commanding, they became leaders wherever they went, demonstrating their prowess in all acquisitions of national territory, and displaying their capacity for political leadership in the predominance of Southerners in the presidency of the United States.

It was also claimed that slavery was the only perfect and permanent foundation for democracy. Because of a servile population, citizens of the Southern states were said to be equal, and "Equality among its citizens is the corner-stone of a republic." Again, it was said that slavery, as it existed in the South, was the only safeguard against anarchy and aggressive skepticism, and that "the destruction of African slavery would be the destruction of republicanism." As proof of this remarkable claim, it was argued that under a system of universal suffrage all political power must eventually fall into the hands of men without education or property, and that property was the great conservative force in government.

In sharp contrast to current pessimism about the economic plight of the South, regional defenders boasted of the indispensable character of Southern staples in the commerce of the world and of the essential importance of the South as a market for the manufactured goods of the North. But their greatest claim to economic excellence was that slavery abolished the usual feud between capital and labor. Thus, the South could escape the discontentment and turbulence of the North because the Southern laborer was freed from the uncertainty and misery of the Northern laborer, especially in depression years.

From this point the argument sometimes moved into a sweeping defense of the social fabric of the South. The Southern laborer was said to be an integral part of the economic and social life of his region whereas his Northern counterpart floated loosely on the surface of society without belonging to it. Having so small a stake in society, the great body of Northern labor was "easily, on any occasion of excitement, formed into a mob—so easily swayed by artful and designing demagogues." The impermanent and granular quality of Northern society allowed its members to have much freedom but it gave them little security. In contrast, Southern society was stable because each person, rich and poor, black and white, was firmly rooted in a close-knit, organic social order.

. . . The champions of the Old South claimed that theirs was the ideal social order and the only permanently founded democracy, all because it had, with God's blessing, slavery. Surely, Southerners had come a long way from Jefferson and a long way out of reality. Fighting to defend their way of life they had taken refuge in a dream world, and they insisted that others accept their castle in the sky as an accurate description of conditions in the South.

The ancient Hebrews looked back to the Garden of Eden and the Greeks to a Golden Age. Early in the twentieth century, zealous and uncritical devotees of evolution looked into the distant future for the ideal society. The ante-bellum defenders of the South, rare among mortals, claimed that their own age was the golden age, and they claimed that its main foundation was Negro slavery.

It would be fruitless to point to fallacies in their reasoning and to the great contrast between the perfections they described and the imperfections that lay all about them. It would be impossible to guess how many Southerners agreed with these spokesmen in their extravagant claims and boastings about the perfect society of the Old South. It is enough to recognize that before the middle of the century there were some Southerners whose minds, under the impact of a long train of bitter criticism of their region and with a realization that the power of their opponents was growing, had turned into this curious psychopathic condition. And one thing else must be recognized. Even though the idealized portrait of the South was false, it was to be a strong and living force in the years ahead. In the long run, the vision of the perfect South was to supply a substantial element in the construction of the romantic legend about the Old South. In the nearer future, it was to give the Confederate soldier something to die for.

Politics in the Old South was an honored calling and a field of great interest. The next selection, although written at times in sweeping generalizations, gives an over-all account of how much power the Southern planters held and what the basis of that power was.

• 36 • *The Planter in Politics*
WILLIAM E. DODD

The political basis of the plantation system was the county court, and the county court of the South came from the banks of the James and the York rivers. In old Virginia a county court was composed of a group of justices of the peace meeting once a month to try petty cases of law. These justices were the grandees of their respective neighborhoods. They were vestrymen in the established church, owners of plantations, and lords of manors. Their wives were the ladies of the land and their daughters set the hearts of young blades aflame when they appeared in church. They were men of good common sense, familiar with the codes of Virginia and to a less degree acquainted with the precedents of English law courts. Everybody looked up to them; and they made themselves responsible in considerable measure for the good behavior of the countryside. What they thought was right was likely to become law.

Now when these bewigged and bepowdered gentlemen took their seats on the county bench, the wheels of justice in the old commonwealth of Virginia began to revolve. But aside from the ordinary business of courts, they sat in administrative sessions to appoint

[From "The Cotton Kingdom: a Chronicle of the Old South," by William E. Dodd, Vol. 27, *The Chronicles of America*, edited by Allen Johnson. Copyright Yale University Press, New Haven, 1920. Pp. 118-121, 146. Used by permission.]

sheriffs and road overseers and to order the building of bridges and schoolhouses. At informal meetings they determined which of their number ought to stand for election to the next assembly, passed upon the conduct of returning members of Congress, and as time went on learned to denounce the conduct of rascally Yankees. The government of Virginia during the first half of the nineteenth century rested securely upon the shoulders of the county justices of the peace.

In fact, these justices inherited their social position from honorable English ancestors who had sworn by the name of the King; or, if they were self-made men, they were duly recognized by the planter gentry as worthy of a place among them. The county bench was the source of many good things. Vacancies in the court were filled by the surviving judges; and all was done with such regard to precedent and after such deliberation that county courts seldom ran amuck. Through all the storms of the Revolution and the trials of the Jeffersonian period, these local organizations functioned smoothly and never for a moment lost their hold either upon the public or upon the course of events.

This was the model upon which South Carolina remade her judicial system when at the end of the Revolution she took into political partnership her great and growing up-country. The county courts of Georgia, Alabama, and Mississippi were but images of Virginia institutions planted upon a distant soil. Florida and Louisiana readjusted their French and Spanish procedure to fit the general model, though retaining the Napoleonic code. Texas took her system from Missouri, which in turn had taken hers from Virginia.

The justice of the peace was an institution of the lower South quite as much as of Virginia herself. To know this gentleman of the old school, this humane and good-natured autocrat, mildly proud of himself and keenly resentful of any criticism of his Latin or of his law, is to know the political life of the South as well as of the cotton kingdom, because every justice of the peace, save on the distant frontier, was a slaveholder or likely soon to become such, a conservative in politics and religion, and a member or prospective member of the Legislature.

The political power of the cotton kingdom therefore was firmly lodged in the hands of successful business men. There was never in America a more perfect oligarchy of business men than that which ruled in the time of Jefferson Davis and Alexander Stephens. Laws were made by the owners of plantations; the higher courts were established by their decrees; governors of States were of their choosing; and members of Congress were selected and maintained in office in accordance with their wishes. And, as we have already seen, they were the ruling members of all the churches. Truly nothing of importance could happen in the lower South without their consent. This fact gave to the South its unity of political purpose and that moderation of social change which men of wealth always prefer. Security of property, loyalty to church, and safety in education were the guarantees of the system. . . .

Lincoln was elected. The cotton States prepared to leave the Union. Their unique culture, their still powerful position in national politics, and their remarkable prosperity were all staked upon the event. They would form a State in which the laboring class should be the property of the capitalist; they would perfect a society in which every man should have a place and every man should keep his place. In the lower South there were to be slaves, farmers, and gentlemen. There would be no poverty; nor would there be any serious disagreement on the fundamentals of society, for sermons, speeches, books, and teaching in the colleges were all to defend the existing order and to look towards its perfecting. Society in the lower South was to be the realization unhindered of the social philosophy which began with the repudiation of the Declaration of Independence and ended with the explicit recognition of social inequality. There was then no doubt of final success, and there was little if any serious protest against the ideals that were to be realized.

The New South:

A Changing Economy

>>

The Old, or ante-bellum, South has been portrayed in considerable detail so that we can trace the changes between that era and those which have followed. In this book we do not discuss the Civil War, although it is readily to be recognized that all war—and particularly that war—brought with it great destruction of life and property and also wrought many social and economic changes.

The New South, as the next selection, written in 1921, reminds us, is not necessarily the contemporary South but that which began to take shape after the Civil War. There was no sharp break with the past but rather a turning toward the future by people who had formerly faced only the past.

• 37 • *The Background of the New South*
HOLLAND THOMPSON

The South of today is not the South of 1860 or even of 1865. There is a New South, though not perhaps in the sense usually understood, for no expression has been more often misused in superficial discussion. Men have written as if the phrase indicated a new land and a new civilization, utterly unlike anything that had existed before and involving a sharp break with the history and the traditions of the past. Nothing could be more untrue. Peoples do not in one generation or in two rid themselves entirely of charac-

[From "The New South: a Chronicle of Social and Industrial Evolution," by Holland Thompson, Vol. 42, *The Chronicles of America*, edited by Allen Johnson. Copyright Yale University Press, New Haven, 1921. Pp. 1-8. Used by permission.]

teristics which have been developing for centuries.

There is a New South, but it is a logical development from the Old South. The civilization of the South today has not been imposed from without but has been an evolution from within, though influenced by the policy of the National Government. The Civil War changed the whole organization of Southern society, it is true, but it did not modify its essential attributes, to quote the ablest of the carpetbaggers, Albion W. Tourgée. Reconstruction strengthened existing prejudices and created new bitterness, but the attempt failed to make of South Carolina another Massachusetts. The people resisted stubbornly, desperately, and in the end successfully, every attempt to impose upon them alien institutions.

The story of Reconstruction has been told elsewhere. A combination of two ideas—high-minded altruism and a vindictive desire to humiliate a proud people for partisan advantage—wrought mischief which has not been repaired in nearly half a century. It is to be doubted, however, whether Reconstruction actually changed in any essential point the beliefs of the South. Left to itself, the South would not, after the War, have given the vote to the negro. When left to itself still later, it took the ballot away. The South would not normally have accepted the negro as a social equal. The attempt to force the barrier between the races by legislation with the aid of bayonets failed. Without the taste of power during the Reconstruction period, the black South would not have demanded so much and the determination of the white South to dominate would not perhaps have been expressed so bitterly; but in any case the white South would have dominated.

Economic and industrial development was hindered by Reconstruction. Men of vision had seen before the War that the South must become more nearly self-sufficient; and the results of the conflict had emphasized this idea. The South believed, and believes yet, that it was defeated by the blockade and not by military force. According to this theory, the North won because the South could not manufacture goods for its needs, because it did not possess ships to bring in goods from abroad, and because it could not build a navy to defend its ports. Today it is clear that the South never had a chance to win, so long as the will to conquer was firm in the North. As soon as the War was over, the demand for greater industrial development made itself felt and gained in strength when Reconstruction came; but during that period the people had to devote all their energies to living day by day, hoping for strength to endure. When property was being confiscated under the forms of law, only to be squandered by irresponsible legislators, there was little incentive to remake the industrial system, and the ventures of the Reconstruction government into industrial affairs were not encouraging. Farm property in the South—and little was left except farm property after the War—depreciated in value enormously in the decade following 1860. Grimly, sullenly, the white man of the South fought again to secure domination, this time, however, of his own section only and not of the nation. When this had been achieved, a large portion of the population was overcome by that deadly apathy so often remarked by travelers who ventured to visit the land as they would have visited Africa. The white South wished only to be let alone.

During this apathetic period there was some talk of the natural resources of the South; but there was little attempt on the part of Southerners to utilize these resources. There was talk of interesting foreign capital, but little effective work was done to secure such capital. Many men feared the new problems which such development might bring in its train, while others, more numerous, were merely indifferent or lukewarm. Many of those who vaguely wished for a change did not know how to set about realizing their desires. The few men who really worked to stimulate a quicker economic life about 1880 had a thankless and apparently a hopeless task.

*   *   *

As the years passed, apathy began to disappear in some parts of the South. Wiser men recognized that the old had gone never to return. Men began to face the inevitable. Instead of brooding upon their grievances, they adjusted themselves, more or less successfully, to the new economic and social order, and by acting in harmony with it found that progress was not so impossible as they had supposed. White planters found that the net returns from their farms on which they themselves had labored were greater than when a larger force of negroes had been employed; shrewd men began to put their scanty savings together to take advantage of convenient water power. Securing the bare necessities of life was no longer a difficult problem for every one. Men began to find pleasure in activity rather than in mere passivity or obstruction.

Somehow, somewhere, sometime, a new hopefulness was born and this new spirit—evidence of new life—became embodied in "the New South." The expression is said to have been used first by General Adam Badeau when stationed in South Carolina, but the New South of which he spoke was not the New South as it is understood today. Many others have used the term loosely to signify any change in economic or social conditions which they had discovered. The first man to use the expression in a way which sent it vibrating through the whole nation was Henry W. Grady, the gifted editor of the *Atlanta Constitution*. In a speech made in 1886 by invitation of the New England Society of New York City, he took for his theme "the New South" and delivered an oration which, judged by its effects, had some of the marks of greatness. "The South," he said, "has nothing for which to apologize. She believes that the late struggle between the States was war and not rebellion, revolution and not conspiracy." He went on, however, to express the feeling that the outcome had been for the best, and painted a picture of the new spirit of the South, a trifle enthusiastic perhaps, but still recognizable.

Today a New South may be said to be everywhere apparent. The Old South still exists in nooks and corners of many States, it is true: there are communities, counties, groups of counties, which cling to the old ideas. In the hearts of thousands of men and women the Old South is enshrined, and there is no room for the new; but the South as a whole is a New South, marked by a spirit of hopefulness, a belief in the future, and a desire to take a fuller part in the life of the nation. . . .

In the rest of our study of the Cotton South, a variety of passages have been chosen to help you compare the Old South with the New. We shall not undertake to trace all of the subtleties of social change for even a single topic over the past six or seven decades; instead, we shall examine contrasting pictures which in themselves carry suggestions as to why the changes occurred. It is only by comparing the changes in Chinese peasant society with the changes in the Cotton South or in the English Midlands that we can begin to form some clear-cut ideas about the ways in which new ideas are introduced and become a part of any given society.

Social change focuses on changes in social relationships. An economy, for example, is made up of the relationships among people commonly engaged in what we call economic activities. The industrial system exists as people work together in the roles of capitalist, manager, and worker; the business system is a set of relationships between people who have goods or services to sell and those who are willing to buy. The words *banking, transportation,* and *utilities* remind us of money or credit, railroad trains, and power lines, but even these become a part of the economy as *people become associated together* for the purpose of supplying credit, transportation, or electricity.

When, therefore, we look for changes in the economy of the Old South, we try to discover what happened to the relationships between the planter and his labor force (or slaves), between the cotton factor and his landlord clients, between the few paternalistic industrialists and their workers.

In the four selections that follow, the emphasis is upon human relationships rather than upon commodities or material evidences of an economy, important as these tangible possessions are to any individual or nation. First, what occurred to the plantation system? Secondly, what merchandising arrangement took the place of the factor? Thirdly, what changes paved the way for the increased tempo of industrialization in the South today?

Selection 38, dealing with the social aspects of the plantation system, calls attention to the contrasts between 1860 and 1930. From time to time, reference is made to some intervening year, such as 1910. The author, T. J. Woofter, is a competent social scientist who is not only familiar with sound research methodology but has an intimate acquaintance with the Cotton South. An able corps of co-workers helped him sample in considerable detail the plantation life through the whole cotton region during the early 1930's. This was a time of economic depression, and the federal government was casting about for various rehabilitation programs. This study, *Landlord and Tenant on the Cotton Plantation,* was to provide much valuable information on which later policies were based.

• 38 • *Social Aspects of the Plantation System*
THOMAS J. WOOFTER, JR.

A plantation is defined for purposes of this study as a tract farmed by one owner or manager with five or more resident families. These may include the landlord, the laborers, share tenants, or renters. Except in the case of renters the landlord exercises close supervision over operators, and except in the case of wage laborers each family cultivates a separate piece of land. . . . In those parts of the South where fairly large operative units prevail, the plantation owners, through their control over large acreages of the best land and of large numbers of tenant and laborer families, still dominate the economic, political, and cultural life. Landlord-tenant relationships on the smaller units in such areas are patterned after those on the larger holdings.

*   *   *

In true plantation areas there is a high degree of concentration of land ownership, with a consequent high proportion of tenants among the farm operators. Such areas are further characterized by per capita incomes higher than those in other southern agricultural counties but lower than those in other farming sections of the Nation; small proportions of urban and village dwellers; scarcity of non-agricultural industries; large families; poor school facilities, especially for Negroes; and a highly mobile population, with families frequently on the move in search of better

[From *Landlord and Tenant on the Cotton Plantation,* Works Progress Administration, Division of Social Research, Washington, 1936. Pp. xix-xxiv, xxvii-xxix, xxxi, xxxiii, 9-11, 22, 31-33.]

conditions. These areas are utterly subject to King Cotton, booming when the King is prosperous and slumping when the King is sick. Aside from feed for livestock and a limited amount of produce for home consumption, practically no other crop is grown.

As land resources are now used, plantation labor conditions and population trends are largely determined by the pressure of population on these resources. Concentration on one crop—cotton—demands a large labor supply for only part of the year. Landlords prefer large families to meet the labor demands of the peak seasons, thus encouraging a high birth rate. This high rate of population increase in turn perpetuates the plantation system. Natural increase in southern rural areas, especially of the white population, has been more rapid than in other sections. The Negro birth rate is also high, but the high Negro death rate, particularly among infants, results in a lower natural rate of increase for Negroes than for whites. This surplus labor supply has reduced the bargaining power of the individual plantation tenant, making it increasingly difficult for him to free himself from the plantation system and become an independent farmer.

*   *   *

Wage labor replaced slave labor on plantations immediately after the Civil War, but share-cropping was soon introduced as a method of labor operations. Most of the plantations are now operated largely by share-croppers—virtually laborers who receive half of the crop in return for working the land. Wage labor continues on a few plantations. Others are operated by various types of tenants, some of whom provide work stock and tools and thus receive a larger share of the crop than the share-cropper and some of whom rent the land outright, paying rent in cash or produce. Often all classes of tenants are found on the same plantations. Of the plantations covered in this study, 71 per cent were operated by families of mixed tenure, while 16 per cent were operated by croppers,

4 per cent by wage hands, 3 per cent by other share tenants, and 6 per cent by renters.

Prior to 1910, when the acreage of improved land was expanding, wage laborers and tenants were sometimes able to improve their status through saving enough to buy work animals and implements, to rent land outright, or even to buy small tracts of land. In 1860, all Negro agricultural workers in the South were laborers. In 1930, only 29 per cent were laborers, 58 per cent were tenants, and 13 per cent were owners. The 58 per cent that were tenants included many share-croppers, whose status was essentially that of laborer.

As population pressure increased, whites began to compete with Negroes for places on the land as tenants and laborers. While the vast majority of white agricultural workers were owners in 1860, by 1930 over three-quarters of a million white families in the Southeast had joined the tenant or laborer class. The proportion of white ownership declined steadily with the increase in white tenancy. Whites now make up the majority of tenants in the Old South, as well as in other parts of the country, although nearly all of the plantations in this survey still had Negro tenants, 53 per cent operating exclusively with Negroes, 5 per cent exclusively with whites, and 42 per cent with both. It is evident, therefore, that white tenants are concentrated on the smaller holdings and Negro tenants on the larger.

*   *   *

The plantation system requires an abundance of skill, energy and knowledge on the part of the landlord if his operations are to be successful and his tenants are to make a profit. He must be able to plan and assign the crop acreage to the best advantage, handle financial operations, manage labor, animals, and implements, and supervise marketing and subsistence advances. On the very large plantations there is often the additional management of such supplementary enterprises as commissaries, gins, mills and shops. Usually the owner or landlord is also obligated to aid in the social and community affairs of his tenants. The large plantation owner or manager is assisted in executing these functions by managers, overseers and gang bosses. On small plantations all of these functions are performed by one man.

One of the landlord's major duties, and one upon which the success of his operation depends, is the expenditure of the plantation's working capital, in the purchase of seeds and fertilizer, in plantation upkeep, and in the apportionment of subsistence advances to the tenants for food and clothing. This practice of subsistence advances, to be repaid by the tenants when the crop is marketed, is one of the chief trouble spots for the landlord. The supervision of these advances determines the living standard of the share tenant.

The plantation system is bound up with the cash-crop system. Concentration on cotton increased from the Civil War until the boll weevil invasion soon after 1910. Since 1910 there has been a marked shift of the cotton acreage to the States of Texas and Oklahoma, the combined acreage in these States having increased 100 per cent from 1910 to 1930. In 1930, half the cotton acreage of the United States was concentrated in those two States. Cotton acreage had increased 40 per cent in Mississippi, Arkansas, and Louisiana, while the eastern plantation States, Alabama, Georgia, North Carolina, and South Carolina, had 5 per cent less acreage in cotton in 1930 than in 1910. This decrease was largely due to the disorganization caused by the boll weevil as it passed across the South. In some areas of the Southeast, financial distress became serious 25 years ago and the trend for the cotton producer has been downward for a long time, interrupted by only short periods of high prices. The depression since 1930, therefore, merely added to the effects of previous disasters. Weevil damage caused drastic acreage reduction for a few years, and as each State reduced its acreage, Texas and Oklahoma added to theirs. When weevil disorganization had passed and the Eastern Cotton Belt began to attain its former production, States west of the Mississippi continued to expand their acreage. As a result, the supply of cotton far exceeded the demand. Over-production reached a peak when the 1931 crop of 16 million bales was added to a carry-over of 10 million bales, at the same time that domestic and foreign demand was shrinking. As a result, the price fell to 6 cents a pound in 1932, causing heavy losses to all producers. Only the semi-self-sustaining farmer, or the planter with resources or good credit, could continue to operate.

. . . The average plantation family in this study was allotted 25 crop acres; croppers had an average of 20 crop acres; share tenants and renters had about 25 crop acres; and wage hands, about 45 crop acres per family.

Although spoken of as a one-crop system, the cropping arrangement of the Cotton South is really a two-crop system: cotton for cash, and corn for food and feed. Most plantations have as much acreage in corn as in cotton. Four per cent of the total expenditure of the plantations studied, however, was for feed which could easily have been grown on the plantations. Up to the inauguration of the cotton reduction program, the plantations of the South tended to be less and less self-supporting, in contrast with the practices of slave plantations which produced a large proportion of their subsistence needs.

*　　*　　*

Fuel and house rent are part of the tenant's perquisites but the houses furnished are among the poorest in the Nation. Unpainted four-room frame shacks predominate. Screening is the exception rather than the rule and sanitation is primitive. In a study of farm housing in the Southeast in 1934, it was found that wells furnished the source of water for over 80 per cent of both owner and tenant dwellings.

The low income for large families provides only a meager subsistence. About one-third of the net income is in the form of products raised for home consumption—a few chickens and eggs, home killed pork, syrup, corn meal, cowpeas, and sweet potatoes. These food items are usually available only in the late summer and fall.

During the months when crops are cultivated, the tenant uses another third of his income, at the rate of about $13 per month, for food—mostly flour, lard, and salt pork—and also for kerosene, medicine, and such clothing purchases as cannot be postponed till fall. Another third is spent for clothing and incidentals, usually soon after the fall "settlement." Thus, by winter, resources are exhausted and "slim rations" begin. Clothing, usually purchased once a year, is of the poorest quality. Often the children do not have sufficient warm clothing to go to school.

* * *

Few of the tenants in this study had gardens and only 55 per cent had cows. The effect of poor housing and meager diet was reflected in the health of the families studied. The lack of balance in diet is largely responsible for pellagra and the digestive disorders that are prevalent in the South. Lack of screening makes the control of malaria difficult.

MOBILITY

Tenants who have not succeeded in locating on good land or with a fair landlord are continually searching for better conditions, many moving from farm to farm each fall. Although they move often, they do not move far. Most of them remain in the county of their birth or locate in adjoining counties.

The rate of farm-to-farm mobility appears to be closely linked with tenure status. The higher the farmer climbs up the "agricultural ladder" the more stable he becomes.

Mobility within the farming occupation is also relatively common as farmers change from one tenure to another. In periods of prosperity, the tendency is to move up the agricultural ladder, while in years of unprofitable operation there is a tendency to shift down the ladder. Until 1910 there was a net movement upward. Since 1910 croppers have made little progress toward share tenancy, and there has been an actual decrease in the number of renters and owners.

A third type of mobility is the shift from the open country to town as the tenant periodically tries his luck at the sawmill, the cottonmill, or odd jobs.

The evidence indicates that Negro tenants are a more stable group with respect to residence than white tenants. This is probably accounted for, to a large extent, by the fact that there are relatively fewer opportunities for Negroes outside of agriculture and that Negro tenants are more easily satisfied than are white tenants.

The average number of years lived on each farm by white plantation families in this study was 4.8 years, and by Negro families, 6.1 years. White share-croppers lived on each farm for an average of 4.4 years, and Negro share-croppers for 5.6 years.

In a study of farmers in South Carolina in 1933, it was found that white tenants move about once every 4 years, and Negro tenants once every 5 or 6 years. White farm owners move about once in 11 years, and Negro owners once in 12 years.

* * *

THE AVERAGE COTTON PLANTATION

(Based on rounded averages for the 646 plantations)

The typical cotton plantation operated by 5 or more families in 1934 included a total of 907 acres, of which 385 were in crops, 63 idle, 162 in pasture, 214 in woods and 83 in waste land. Approximately 86 per cent of the 907 acres was owned by the operating landlord and 14 per cent was rented from other owners. Of the crop land harvested, 44 per cent was planted to cotton. On the typical plantation the wage hand cultivated 45 crop acres, the cropper 20, the other share tenant 26, and the renter 24.

The plantation had a total value of about $28,700 of which $21,700 was in land, $3,900 in buildings, $1,900 in animals, and $1,200 in implements. The average long term indebtedness was $11,700.

The typical plantation was occupied by 14 families, exclusive of the landlord's family, of which 3 were headed by wage hands, 8 by croppers, 2 by other share tenants, and 1 by a renter. Of these families, 2 were white and 12 were Negro The average family, the head of which was 41 years of age consisted of about four persons, of whom two to three were employable. The average number of years of residence on the 1934 farm was 8 years for all families, 7 for wage hands, 7 for croppers, 11 for other share tenants, and 13 for renters.

The typical plantation had a gross income of $9,500 in 1934 of which approximately $7,000 was obtained from sales of crops and livestock products, $900 from A.A.A. payments, $200 from land rented out, and $1,400 from home use production.

The net plantation income, after deducting expenses, was $6,000. The operator's net income averaged $2,600, leaving $3,400 to be divided among the tenants. If 6 per cent is allowed as the return on the landlord's investment, he received approximately $850 as his labor income, or $2 per crop acre.

Wage hands had a net income of $180, croppers $312, other share tenants $417, and renters $354. The average tenant family received a subsistence advance of $13 per month for 7 months.

*   *   *

TENANT CLASSES

The predominant social characteristic of plantation regions is the class-caste system which is built around the landlord-tenant relationship, for tenancy has become not only a method of making a living but also a way of living. [Review, in this connection, Selection 7, on farm tenancy in China.]

While the plantation proprietorship has continued since pre-Civil War days, merely shrinking somewhat in size, the methods of operation have undergone radical changes. The first of these was, of course, the shift from slave to free labor. The next was the shift from hired labor to half share-cropping, which began very soon after the Civil War. Operation by wage labor continued on those plantations whose owners could afford to finance such operations, but in most instances it was replaced by various forms of tenancy. Share-

cropping, in which the farm operator contributes only his labor and receives in return a share of the crop, has persisted, but other forms of tenancy have also emerged. The "third and fourth" arrangement is made with tenants who own their work stock. From them the landlord, instead of receiving half, receives a third of the cotton and a fourth of the corn. These tenants, together with other miscellaneous share tenants, are referred to as "other share tenants" throughout this study. Tenants of a still more independent type rent the land outright, receiving the whole proceeds of their crop minus a fixed rental which may be in cash or produce. These tenants are referred to as "renters" throughout this study.

*   *   *

Although share-cropping is predominant, all classes of tenants often mingle on the same plantation. Even though the landlord may prefer half share-cropping, he will often take a tenant on terms of third and fourth share or straight rent if he has a tract vacant, especially when production is expanding. Of the plantations covered in this investigation, 4 per cent were operated entirely by wage hands, 16 per cent were operated entirely by croppers, 3 per cent entirely by other share tenants, 6 per cent by renters, and 71 per cent were mixed in tenure. On the mixed places, however, croppers predominated.

Both white and Negro tenants were often employed on the same plantation. Of the plantations studied 53 per cent were operated entirely by Negro tenants, 5 per cent entirely by white tenants, and 42 per cent by both white and Negro tenants. In general, the percentages of Negroes in the plantation population in each area followed the percentage of Negroes in the rural population.

It must also be remembered that the relations between landlord and tenant are traditionally informal. Detailed agreements are not usually worked out and contracts are practically never written. Such records of advances and repayments as are kept are almost always in the hands of the landlord. This becomes a complicated account when debts from previous years are carried forward and added to current advances. This situation places the absolute control of relationships in the hands of the landlord and the fairness of settlements is largely dependent upon his sense of justice. The tenant's only recourse is to move, which of course does not adjust his past transactions but merely enables him to seek more satisfactory conditions.

Thus the prosperity of landlord and tenant are interwoven and mutually dependent upon three principal factors: (1) the productivity of the land, (2) the efficiency and energy of the landlord, and (3) the ability and energy of the tenant. There is evidence that these factors also interact on each other. In their efforts to farm more efficiently the most able landlords tend to get the most productive land. In their wanderings to better their condition the most able tenants eventually gravitate to the fairest landlords. Under these conditions there tends to be a multiplication of supermarginality with the best land, the most capable management, and the most efficient tenants at the top, and a multiplication of submarginality with the poorest land, the poorest managers, and the least able tenants at the bottom. . . .

It is the absentee landlord who, through ignorance, laxity of supervision, or cupidity, most often allows the "mining" of the land and the loss of the productive top soil through erosion. It is on the absentee-owned plantations that fences and buildings most frequently fall into disrepair. It is these plantations which are least stable in a crisis. Since the owners of these tracts are most often holding the land for speculative or sentimental reasons, they do not "back up" the credit of their tenants to the same extent as do resident landlords. Hence, when a break in prices or a disaster like the boll weevil occurs and credit from merchants and bankers becomes tight, the tenants on these places are the first to find themselves without resources and are often forced either to move to the city or to become laborers or croppers on the more stable farms.

* * *

NON-AGRICULTURAL ENTERPRISES

It is beyond the scope of this study to comment in detail on the non-agricultural enterprises of the larger plantations, such as gins, shops, mills, and commissaries. These are merely adjuncts to the production and marketing of the cash crop and as such are operated only by part of the plantations.

The commissary is one of the most criticized plantation features but may, if fairly administered, be of advantage to the tenant. Usually the commissary is introduced by the operator so that he, rather than the supply merchant, may control the expenditures for subsistence and keep these amounts within the limits of the tenant's ability to produce. The landlord also gets the advantage of wholesale prices with discounts if he is able to finance purchases in cash.

The advantage, or disadvantage, of this practice to the tenant depends entirely upon the extent to which the landlord passes the economies of wholesale buying on to the purchaser and the extent to which the landlord merely substitutes himself for the exploitative merchant. Many examples of both types could be produced. In the present study more than a fourth of the plantations had commissaries, 15 per cent having commissaries whose use by the tenants was compulsory and 11 per cent commissaries whose use was optional.

For performing these varied services, the average landlord makes little more than the cost would be of hiring managers and overseers to do them. Calculated on the basis of salaries paid in 1920 on large plantations, Brannen concluded that the cost of hiring supervision was $1.80 per acre on cotton plantations. According to the present study the landlord profit (after deducting interest on his capital) averaged only $2.01 per crop acre.

SOCIAL CONTRIBUTIONS

Having established and perpetuated a paternalistic relation to tenants and having taken the responsibility for close supervision not only of agricultural operations but also of family expenditures, the landlord is also often

called upon for services of a social nature, for
the large plantation is a social as well as an
economic organism and the matrix of a number of plantations often constitutes or dominates the larger unit of civil government in
the locality.

Among efficient landlords, tenant health is
one of the major considerations and doctors'
bills are paid by the landlord and charged
against the tenant crop. Those tenants who
have a landlord who will "stand for" their
bills are far more likely to get physicians'
services than are the general run of tenants.
On some plantations socialized medicine is
approximated. The landlord pays a flat rate
to a doctor who agrees to serve all the tenants
for a year, and this charge is distributed on a
per visit basis. On plantations where medical
contributions or advances are made by the
management these average about $40 per
plantation.

Landlords and managers are also expected
to "stand for" their tenants in minor legal
difficulties such as may grow out of gambling
games, altercations, and traffic infractions.
This function is, of course, not exercised indiscriminately. A good worker will, in all
probability, be "gotten off" and a drone left
in the hands of the law. In past decades, the
sheriff seldom went on large plantations,
minor discipline being one of the manager's
undisputed prerogatives. The broad leather
strap was the principal instrument of discipline. These practices of plantation discipline
have passed, but the landlord assumes responsibility for such tenants as are arrested for
minor offenses, especially during the busy
season. In the present study 11 per cent of the
landlords had, in the year 1934, acted as parole
sponsor for tenants and 21 per cent had paid
fines.

Use of plantation animals for social or
personal purposes is also one of the plantation
contributions. Three-fourths of the plantations studied allowed the use of their animals
for trips to town and on Sundays, but of these
more than one-fourth did not allow such use

as often as once a month. Thus, a large proportion of the tenants who did not own work
animals either had no means of transportation
or had such means available less than once a
month.

Landlords are also frequently expected to
contribute to plantation social life through
aid to churches, schools, and entertainments.
The present study revealed that direct contributions to schools were relatively small although the use of land for school buildings
was frequently permitted. Planters interviewed reported an average annual contribution to tenants' churches of approximately $13
and to tenants' entertainments of $6. In addi-
tion, it goes without saying that plantation
waters are open to tenants' fishing, and plantation rabbits and quail are theirs for the taking.
Usually the landlord's contribution of supplies
for entertainments such as fish fries, barbe-
cues, and dances is more substantial than his
cash contribution.

The contribution of the landlord to plantation efficiency may be summarized as that of
the pocketbook and brain. The contribution
of the tenant is largely that of supervised
brawn. Landlords vary widely in their capa-
bility of performing these functions efficiently.
Some prefer to stay in town rather than ride
over their land. Others work very energetically at their job, thereby contributing materially to their own fortune and to that of their
tenants. It is clear that the efficient landlord
is not only a capitalist, but also an agronomist,
a diplomat, a capable manager, and occasionally a veterinarian and social arbiter.

Tenants have traditionally depended on
landlords for services such as those described
in this chapter and any plan for replacing the
plantation organization with other forms of
tenure or small ownership must take into consideration the reality of the managerial function and the practical necessity for supervision
of a plantation. It must either provide a similar management until tenants outgrow its
need or, through intensive education, train
the tenants to perform these duties efficiently.

The selection just concluded shows that many of the features of the 1860 plantations persisted—particularly the paternalism and the provision by the landlord for most of his tenants' needs. Sharecropping was an adjustment to the abolition of slavery; concentration on a single cash crop, with corn as a supplementary crop for food and feed, was the expected rule. But what about those rural people who either worked their own small holdings or worked for landlords who had no commissaries or "staked" the tenant to food from crop year to crop year? The answer was found in the furnishing merchant.

The next selection, by Thomas D. Clark, a well-known historian of the South, explains how the furnishing merchant or country store keeper, with his credit arrangements, took care of the economic needs of poor people as well as of the farmers with the larger land holdings. Dr. Clark traveled throughout the South in 1941-1942 collecting and reading the old ledgers kept by these country merchants, and his findings reflect the careful study he made of the business practices of an earlier day.

• 39 • The Furnishing and Supply System

THOMAS D. CLARK

In the post-Civil War economy of the South the furnishing merchant was a key figure. He became the hub of the new system of agriculture, supplanting in many respects the factor of the earlier years. It was through his stores that goods were made available to customers on their home grounds, and it was he who facilitated the process of economic revival in the badly isolated regions of the South.

There were two big waves of store beginnings. The first came immediately after the close of the war, when high priced cotton, disruption of southern economy, and a general change in the distributive processes among the wholesale houses in the border and northern cities were influential in bringing about an organization of new stores. Southern boys coming home from the army, many enterprising Union soldiers, and a large number of Alsatian Jews saw in storekeeping a promising economic future. The second was in the 1880's, when cotton and tobacco culture were climbing to new peaks of production; and in the flurry of store organization during this period a majority of the more important stores were established.

Disorganization of the earlier supply system of the South brought about a new condition of trade which wholesale merchants were quick to sense and exploit. Instead of wasting energy on the restitution of the old factorage system of supply, they went to work to develop and expand the crossroads stores. They helped to locate desirable store sites, selected storekeepers, stocked the stores with goods, and supplied money and generous credit when it was needed. Actually they became stationary factors who used the southern merchant as a local intermediary for the distribution of a rapidly increasing quantity of goods. This was to be the merchant's most significant part in the building of the New South. Since there were few local banks, the local merchant was both a source of commodity supply to the people and a channel of capital outlet for extra-regional investors. It was he who served as a direct local contact man for the big wholesale mercantile houses, the fertilizer

[From "The Furnishing and Supply System in Southern Agriculture Since 1865," *The Journal of Southern History*, Vol. 12, No. 1, Gainesville, Fla., 1946. Pp. 24-44. Used by permission.]

manufacturers, the meat packers, and the grain, feed, and cotton speculators. A special credit system which was devised by wholesale houses and manufacturers also tied the local merchant up with the nation's banking system.

This system of farm supply and its method of credit-granting constituted a central theme for interpreting much of the history of the New South. Certain conceptions are regarded as standards in reaching an understanding of southern economy. Most of the observations and comments center around the issues of credit-granting, rates of interest charged, and business techniques of the merchants.

The most fundamental issue raised time after time in any discussion of the furnishing merchant's place in southern economy has been his method of doing business. Charges and countercharges have been made which accuse merchants of numerous bookkeeping abuses. . . .

From the customers' standpoint any system of bookkeeping, even the simplest single entry type, was beyond comprehension. They had no way of knowing whether merchants kept honest sets of books. Careful checking of numerous accounts reveals remarkably few errors, and such as have been found are minor slips in bookkeeping rather than intentional manipulation of accounts. These errors seem to have been made as often against the merchants themselves, as against the customers.

. . . Goods sold over the counter of the southern general store were nearly all of the cheapest obtainable quality. Order notes, such as these random samples, indicate clearly the customer's lack of interest in quality. "Please let Jennie Gaines have a hat," a South Carolinian wrote·T. G. Patrick, "She says you have one for seventy-five cents." Another wrote, "Please let Sam Moore have one pair of coarse cheap shoes & charge to Ike Yongue." Even orders for cheap molasses and biscuit crept into the notes. "Please send me six sacks corn, 50 lbs. cheap flour"; and "Please send me 2 gallons of cheap molasses."

Nearly always, customers bought goods with the price uppermost in mind. Getting possession of the article was the primary mo-

tive, and eighty per cent of the order notes were written in the form of supplications. Merchants knew this, and they bought stock for their stores accordingly. . . .

Goods were sold customarily at two prices. Cash prices were under those paid for goods charged on the books. Frequently notes came to merchants asking that no book charge be made on an order for goods with the promise to pay in cash within a week or two, and occasionally a landlord would request that his tenant be supplied goods at "high credit prices."

*   *   *

Accounts were closed generally during the months of October, November, and December, and the new books opened in January, February, and March. Accounts were listed just as the purchases were made. At the end of the year the debit entries were added together and an interest charge entered against the total account. The average rate was ten per cent, but a mere statement of the interest rate is only a part of the usury picture. It does not take into consideration either the time element involved or the ultimate interest rate which the customer was forced to pay. . . .

There was an additional interest factor which seldom shows up in store records. When a landlord "stood for" accounts, he often kept either a duplicate record or carried his tenants' charges in his own personal account, and instead of being allowed to settle at the store, the tenant was required to pay the landlord. The tenant was charged both the storekeeper's mark-up and interest costs, and he paid interest to the landlord for taking the risk by "standing for" the account. Occasionally the landlord increased his annual income by purchasing staple goods in bulk lots at cheaper prices and selling them at mark-up profit for himself.

*   *   *

The credit system in the South was largely a product of the sore lack of adequate transportation facilities. Perhaps the central theme of all comment on certain of the South's failures was that of diversification of field crops. . . .

Literally hundreds of editorials and special feature accounts of poor roads found their way into newspapers. Practically every southern farmer living as much as five miles from a town faced the problem of poor roads every time he hitched his mules to a wagon. State laws were cluttered with ineffective legislation relating to roads, and county officials strove with some degree of continuity, if indifferently, to build local highways. Yet in nearly all the condemnation of the one-crop system of agriculture and miry roads there is an absence of any practical sense of appreciation of the importance of improved and diversified market conditions. The critics themselves failed to understand the necessity for markets for new southern products. It was here that their crusading for reform hit a major snag, and failure to solve this made their pleas historically true, but impossible of realization. What was true of highways was likewise true of railroads and their connections with market centers, and railway freight rates on farm products were so high that often they erased any margin of profit farmers could rightfully expect.

Had transportation and market conditions been different it seems safe to assume, in the light of the facts of business operations and possibilities, that merchants would have welcomed an opportunity to broaden their income basis for their trading areas. There can be little doubt that the fluctuations of cotton production and prices held the same eventual fate for the merchant as for the farmer. Credit was restricted or expanded in many cases on the basis of whether weather, general crop, and market conditions were good.

Frequent notes found their way to merchants in late summer asking for permission to extend accounts. Dependence upon cotton alone, however, was dangerous for the merchant. At the last moment the cotton market was subject to serious and unexpected fluctuations, and cotton was a highly competitive crop because several sections of the South glutted the market and forced prices down at selling time. But with all of its disadvantages cotton had some marked advantages over other farm products. Where roads were universally poor and methods of hauling were still primitive cotton could be transported with relatively small loss to either producer or merchant. The problem of maintaining storage warehouses was simple, because the major problem was that of keeping the cotton dry and fires away. There was an established market with a long tradition behind it, and it was fairly easy to secure adequate outside capital to finance the trade.

* * *

Some merchants made money from their stores. Some of them were able to accumulate a considerable amount of cash savings. Others accumulated little money, but came to own large holdings of land. Most of them were able to build comparatively good homes, but it is doubtful that many of them ever grew rich in the business. When the boll weevil reduced the cotton crop, and when competition of cash stores developed with an expansion of industry, the old line furnishing merchant went into eclipse in the South. His end came only after he had committed countless sins against real southern agricultural progress, and had been properly criticized for it in the newspaper and periodical press, and even in books. But the question remains, what part did the furnishing merchant play? Actually he was never an originator of anything. He was the most direct means by which the lien laws were made to work as a source of credit and banking for his community. His safe bulged with thousands of liens and mortgages. His store was both a source of supply and a market facility. He facilitated the one crop system of agriculture, and as a special agent for the fertilizer companies he sold guano in April to be paid for at high November prices plus an exorbitant profit and interest charge. Also, he helped to channelize enormous amounts of extra-regional capital into the South.

On the credit side of the ledger he was to all outward appearances a stable citizen, often a school trustee, local bank president, postmaster, sometimes a railway agent, a source of character reference, official community "obliger," and a decisive voice in all other community affairs. His ledger books carried church and lodge accounts, and lists of subscriptions to build and support churches. He served on the board of stewards or deacons, and was often the member of the school board who was entrusted with the responsibility of selecting teachers and textbooks. But most important of all, he was only a cog in an economic machine which for the South was much larger than the individual influence of merely a simple form of mercantile business.

Even today in the Cotton South some furnishing merchants still do business in ways reminiscent of thirty years ago. But most of them have lost out with the coming of such government agencies as the Farm Security Administration in the 1930's, with the rapid spread of chain stores, which showed what a high mark-up the local merchant had been accustomed to, and with the growing practice on the part of landowners of paying farm laborers in daily wages rather than in a share of the crop.

But there is another important element in the changing rural scene of the Cotton South—namely, farm mechanization. How rapid has this been? What psychological and social factors now favor it? This is the theme of the next selection. To some extent the author of the next selection, Alvin Bertrand, a rural sociologist from Louisiana State University, repeats a little of what Dr. Woofter has discussed in his account of the plantation system of the 1930's, but this repetition gives much-needed emphasis to important points too frequently passed over. We have included two of Dr. Bertrand's footnotes since they explain basic terms for those not versed in some of the social-science vocabulary.

• 40 • Southern Farm Mechanization in Its Social Setting
ALVIN L. BERTRAND

INTRODUCTION

Much literature of late has been devoted to the general theme of "mechanization" in the South, with the plantation belt coming in for particular reference. These studies, as a rule, have been confined to the factual establishment of the phenomenal increase of machines on southern fields since 1930. Seemingly, social scientists have been too absorbed in the duty of chronicling this trend to indulge in more abstract analyses. At any rate, inventories of both the popular and scientific treatments of this subject reveal a conspicuous neglect by authors to construct a theoretical framework or, in other words, to analyze the role of the social processes in bringing about the change. This paper is an effort in that direction.

The terminology and concepts employed are the ones more or less commonly accepted.*

* Basically the social processes are considered as coming about from the interaction of individuals and groups. It has been pointed out that there are only two fundamental forms of such interaction, opposition and cooperation,

[From "The Social Processes and Mechanization of Southern Agricultural Systems," *Rural Sociology*, Vol. 13, No. 1, Raleigh, N. C., 1948. Pp. 32-39. Used by permission.]

Illustrations are taken only from the Southern Plantation System for two reasons. In the first place, the clear-cut identity of this system expedites analysis. Secondly, it is in these areas that the greatest change of this nature has and is taking place.

HISTORICAL BACKGROUND

It is common knowledge that the social structure of the Southern Plantation System had taken on more rigidity very soon after the Civil War. This makes it seem reasonable to assume that these "crystallized mores" were shed only when social processes were set in motion which altered or destroyed some social institutions and founded others. We propose to examine the contemporary scene, first to find out what developments were responsible for the departure from established practices; and second, to review insofar as is possible the evolving social fabric in terms of a theoretical

---

and that other processes derive from them. Opposition can be divided into either competition or conflict and broadly defined as a struggle against another or others for a good, goal, or value. Cooperation, on the other hand, is set forth as a joint striving for the above ends and may involve the combination of unlike effort as illustrated in the division of labor. Differentiation is designated as a type of cooperation which involves a division of social labor in terms of roles and status. Accommodation, compromise, toleration, or any other basis for working agreements between contending groups or individuals, comes out of conflict. From conflict and differentiation emerges the process called stratification. This process is closely related to accommodation and involves the formation of society into caste, class, or orders of status. Assimilation, or the merging of divergent groups into new and homogeneous associations, generally arises out of competition, conflict, and cooperation. Actually as the above definitions imply, the social processes are just another way of describing social functions and of looking at fundamental cultural phases of familial, economic, political, and other social activities. For a detailed discussion see: Kimball Young, *Sociology* (New York: American Book Co., 1942), pp. 643-867.

framework designed to show the causal relation between this behavior and the introduction of technology to the fields. Obviously many variant patterns in specific areas and special cases will have to be overlooked for the sake of brevity. . . .

The historical fact setting the stage for this treatment is that planters of the South generally ignored agricultural machinery many years after mechanization had become common in the North. This lag was related to several factors. Slavery was one of the more important reasons why the early South did not look to technology. The Southern planter of that time was so fully occupied with both slave management and the defense of slavery that he had little time to think of or experiment with new machinery.

Immigration differentials during the latter part of the 19th century give a clue to another reason why the South lagged behind the North and West in the use of machines. Land-hungry migrants with little cash but new ideas and tools did not find a welcome in the comparatively populated, socially stratified and culturally static South. Consequently, agricultural technology at the production level did not advance far beyond the limited knowledge brought over by the first settlers of this region.

A third reason why the South overlooked mechanization is found in the so-called "factory" system of the plantations. Agricultural endeavors, under this system, are characterized by non-laboring and oft-times non-resident entrepreneurs. It is not difficult to see how a non-laboring farm operator or owner might be slow to experiment with and adopt innovations which did not affect his personal comfort or well-being.

W. F. Ogburn's point (in his book *The Social Effects of Aviation*) that an important factor restricting the use of an invention is the existence of a substitute which is available at a lower price or which is simpler or more workable suggests a fourth reason. The presence of an abundant supply of labor undoubtedly retarded the adoption of machinery.

TRADITIONAL INTERACTIONAL PATTERNS

It is necessary to give a brief history of the plantation system in order to bring out the basic interactional patterns which characterized it until the early 1930's.

Emerging from the devastation of the Civil War, southern landowners were faced with the problem of getting their lands into production again. At the same time many former slaves were finding their new freedom woefully lacking in the essentials of food and shelter. It was inevitable that the two come to some kind of a working agreement. The system of sharecropping which evolved, following a brief trial of wage labor, has been attributed to both the scarcity of money and a disapproval on the part of the planters to the paying of cash wages. T. Lynn Smith, citing primary sources, has shown how this disapproval was a result of the planters' not being able to depend on work agreements with ex-slaves. During the busiest time the "hands" were apt to desert the fields as soon as they received their wages. At any rate, the system assured the planter, on the one hand, of a stable supply of labor and the sharecropper, on the other, of a relative security in the furnishing of food, shelter, etc.

Actually the above working agreement represented a truce from the oppositional interaction between planter and laborer developed during the Civil War. The terms of the truce called for a differentiation between groups which reset class lines and again stratified the society as in "antebellum" days. That the system was characterized by wide differentials in standards of living is not surprising. In a stratified society where the masses have no alternative but to gain their livelihood in competition with one another, living standards are bound to vary widely between the upper and lower classes.

With a class system three fields of interaction became possible; between the lower class members, between the upper class members and between the classes. Between lower class members the interaction can be described as more of a competitive process than anything else. Disparities in the fertility of land and variations in the policies of landlords were the basis for keen competition. The well-known residential instability of croppers can be attributed in part to this process. Oppositional interaction between white and non-white "tenants," because of race relations or cultural competition, often developed into open conflict.* It has been said that some planters aggravated this situation by openly expressing a preference for Negroes as sharecroppers. Though the main current of interaction, in an economic sense, was oppositional in nature, it is significant that cooperation was maintained to a fairly high degree in the religious and recreational activity.

Oppositional interaction between planters, when it was found, can best be described as simple rivalry. Little personalized competition or open conflict characterized social relationships between these upper class members. On the other hand social functions were the occasion for many cooperative efforts. A strong in-group feeling or class solidarity seems to account for these phenomena. Though landowners were not always on the best of economic relations with bankers, loan companies, etc., interaction between these groups does not directly concern class relations.

Inter-class relation, on the other hand, was something entirely different. With land giving them their license, planters, as a rule, felt free to adopt coercive practices in order to control the landless masses. This control usually was maintained by close supervision of the cropper's or tenant's crop as well as his holidays or rest periods. The laborer accommodated himself to such practices either by rationalizing that the situation could be worse, or inwardly compromising a present injustice to future revenge.

* As population pressure increased whites began to compete with Negroes for places on the land as tenants and laborers. By 1935 there were 368,408 colored sharecroppers as compared to 347,848 white sharecroppers, and in 1940 white tenants outnumbered Negro tenants 597,912 to 461,982 in the cotton belt.

In summary, it can be said that people connected with the Southern Plantation System, in 1930, were divided into two distinct classes. The ownership of land was concentrated in the upper class and vertical mobility up the agricultural ladder was virtually impossible for the masses. While the former class enjoyed a relatively high living standard, the latter class in many instances enjoyed no more than mere subsistence. Population pressure and economic dependence made competition a keen process in the lower class, while upper class members were too busy trying to carry on in the face of the depression to worry about labor relations. Such a system, as Smith has pointed out, has all the elements necessary for class struggle.

THE ROLE OF THE DEPRESSION

The coincidence of our last great depression with the first large scale observance of the machine on the southern fields may lead the casual observer to assign a direct causal relation between the two. No more exercise than a slight review of history proves the error of such an analysis. Though going through many previous periods of hard times the southern scene had retained its familiar one-horse technology intact. It is necessary to hold the fact of the depression as a constant and look for developments which it may have brought about as variables. Two such observations stand out as being characteristic of no previous crisis. They are the unionization, with resulting cooperative action on the part of agricultural workers, and the advent of the AAA with its specific definitions and policies. According to our hypothesis, close scrutiny of these developments should give us the answer to the enigma of why southern planters began mechanization only after 1930.

UNIONIZATION OF SHARECROPPERS RELATED TO MECHANIZATION

The organization, in 1931, of a sharecroppers union in Tallapoosa County, Alabama can be looked upon as the beginning of a series of incidents which changed the relations between "tenant" and landlord and paved the way for mechanization. Never before had these particular agricultural workers got together in anything like a cooperative organization. Since the first organizers were industrial workers, some reportedly Communist, it seems safe to say that the tenants and laborers themselves respected the existing class interactional patterns (whether because of tradition or fear of upper class retaliation is beside the point) too much to provide the necessary leadership for this kind of organization. At any rate, the speed with which the movement spread pointed out that these lower class members were in a potential state of revolt against the existing order. (Organizers were able, because the prevalent depression brought destitution among the croppers, to stress grievances to good effect. Such things as "tenants" being allowed smaller shares of cotton, less food furnishings, and having to pay exorbitant prices at the plantation store were thoroughly propagandized.) Strangely enough, though the first union's members were all non-white, the later Southern Tenant Farmers Union organized in Poinsett County, Arkansas in 1934 was composed of both races, a precedent seldom set in southern history.

Plantation owners and operators reacted immediately and violently when it became apparent what an organization of their workers could mean. Justifying their action on the grounds that the sharecroppers had violated the sacred precepts of class behavior, some landowners indulged in nearly every type of coercive behavior at their command. The situation was described by Howard Kester, one of the union leaders, as follows:

While violence of one type or another has been continuously poured out upon the membership of the union from its early beginning, it was in March, 1935, that a "reign of terror" ripped into the country like a hurricane. For two and a half months violence raged throughout northeastern Arkansas and in neighboring states until it looked at times as if the union would be completely smashed. Meetings were banned and broken up; members were falsely accused, arrested and jailed, convicted on trumped-up charges and thrown into prison; relief was shut off; union members were evicted from the land by the hundreds; homes were riddled with bullets from machine guns; churches were burned and schoolhouses stuffed with hay and floors removed; highways were patrolled night and day by armed vigilantes looking for the leaders; organizers were beaten, mobbed and murdered until the entire country was terrorized.

Despite all these efforts the unions thrived and managed through their own pressure instruments, strikes, to achieve some of their immediate aims. The effectiveness of these strikes is shown by the report that:

> On a given night the strike bills were distributed throughout the territory. So effectively were they distributed that many people thought an airplane had dropped them down on the cabins. On the following day a strange emptiness hung over the cotton fields. Most of the workers did not go to the fields and those who did soon returned to their cabins. . . . A labor official from Little Rock made a trip through the cotton country to see how effective the strike was. He reported that he saw two workers picking cotton. The strike was effective and the cotton hung in the bolls until the union told the men to go back to work. (Kester: *Revolt Among the Sharecroppers*)

This turn-about coercion served notice to all landowners that their labor supply was not assured and furthermore it could and would desert the fields at the most critical times to press any bargain it desired. Only when planters realized that they were unable to rely on traditional interactional patterns to assure them a continuous human labor supply did they begin looking toward the machine as a substitute. And more and more as conflict situations developed between laborer and landowner machinery was substituted for the former. The first part of our hypothesis finds justification in that fact.

THE AAA RELATED TO MECHANIZATION

In the previous section it was shown how some laborers and "tenants" overstepped the bounds of class convention to set processes in motion which precipitated mechanization. This section proposes to show how very soon after the labor movement began, one class of planters in turn was to behave similarly with like results.

In answer to the mounting surpluses and stagnant markets which were staring farmers in the face, Congress passed the Agricultural Adjustment Act of 1933. Under this act farmers entered contracts to reduce acreage in specified surplus crops in return for benefit payments, financed chiefly by processing taxes on the commodity concerned. The first cotton contract offer specified that "any producer who is owner, landlord, cash tenant, or managing share tenant and who operates a cotton farm" could be a party to a 1934 and 1935 cotton acreage reduction contract covering his farm. In other words payments were to be made to the farm operator if he could qualify technically as manager.

Since some "tenants" and sharecroppers could qualify as "managing tenants" they were entitled to a pro rata benefit payment for the land taken out of cultivation on their respective plots. Mere laborers, however, had no claim to these payments. Many landlords were quick to realize this difference and to take advantage of it by shifting from sharecropper or "tenant" to cash day labor or mechanized operation. A few, through the "Landlord's Code," were able to abide by the letter of the law with such maneuvers as declaring the tenant "non-managing" if he was "supervised" by a casual riding boss. It is not unfair to say that the "tenant" was left to bear the large share of acreage reduction while the landlord received the major benefits. The authors of *The Collapse of Cotton Tenancy* felt that:

> One obvious reason for the wholesale neglect of the tenant lies in the fact that the

Agricultural Adjustment Administration organized its program under the direction of the planters themselves. . . . The AAA as finally administered met the landlord's approval. If it effected any disorganization, that disorganization was not inimical to the planter's interest. Ultimately it proved to be a mere subsidy to planters.

As early as 1935, Frey and Smith were able to see what had happened and the reason for it. They wrote:

At the present time it is very apparent that the tenant, cropper, and laborer were pretty much overlooked in the cotton-control program. They were not the ones demanding a program of control in the first place; they had practically no voice in framing it in the second. The program devised was one entered into by the government and the landlord. The planter was left to work out his own arrangements with the families on his place, tenants, croppers, and laborers. It is small wonder that the cotton control program is often called a "landowners' program."

The extent to which the landlords managed to attract AAA benefit payments their way is shown by the Woofter study. [See Selection 38.]

They found that, "the landlord received an average of $822 per plantation, compared with $108 per plantation received by all tenants together." Tenants, then, became no more than pawns in the game between the AAA and landowners. They were either discharged completely as surplus labor when production curtailment took place, changed over to seasonal day laborers, displaced by "non-managing" machines, or ruled ineligible for payments through the use of legal strategy.

Obviously, action of the above sort violated traditional interactional patterns in that planters forsook customary arrangements for the express purpose of profiting at the tenants' expense. When the full significance of his "treatment" dawned on him the tenant was prone to be bitter and uncooperative. This in turn set in motion processes which ended in more displacement of workers by machines. In 1940, only those landowners who had abided by the "meant" conditions of the law and tenants who had obeyed the traditional class behavior code were operating under a semblance of the old system.

THE WAR AS A CLIMAX

If mechanization was rapidly taking place through the processes just discussed, the coming of the war can be looked upon as the event which capped the climax. A large share of the farm population literally deserted the land. Those who were not being pressed into the armed forces migrated to the industrial centers of the North and West. Thus, the plantations found themselves practically without manpower. As workers became more and more scarce, planters who had mechanized for one reason or another counted themselves very fortunate. On the other hand, landowners who had not turned to technology, in particular those who had lived up to the AAA law and retained their labor supply, found themselves in a predicament. Years of strict compliance with both the letter and the spirit of the law went for naught as the planters who had done most to safeguard the rights of the workers on their lands watched the laborers leave by the thousands at exactly the time they were most needed.

At this point it was impossible to substitute machinery for laborers because the manufacture of agricultural equipment had come to a virtual standstill soon after the National Emergency was declared. Their workers gone, unable to get machinery, and confronted with the relatively favorable situations of their less scrupulous neighbors, such planters resolved never again to be caught in such a dilemma, to free themselves from a dependence upon labor to the highest degree possible.

In this resolve they did and are turning to the relative security of the machine and in so doing are completing the breakdown of old behavior patterns and institutions and creating or adopting new ones. In their turn, sharecroppers, tenants and laborers of the former lower class have had an opportunity to evaluate their previous existence in the light of army travels and industrial "war wages." Neither will be conducive to their return to the areas in the first place, and to the old patterns of interrelationships in the second place.

In conclusion it may be said that the die is cast, the plantation system has or is changing to technology as a result of social processes set in motion by the unionization of agricultural laborers, strengthened by landlord adjustments to the AAA program and brought to a climax by the mass abandonment of the fields by the laborers during World War II.

As mechanization comes to the South, a large pool of potential industrial workers is made available. This, as the following news story will show, is one of the reasons why manufacturing concerns are being attracted to the South. But there are other reasons too. Compare the dramatic account of what is now going on in the Cotton South with Selection 33, which dealt with manufacturing before the Civil War. Such a comparison provides an interesting case study in social change.

• 41 • *The Enlightened Revolution*

The Old South, the land of cotton, sharecropping and mortgages, is the fastest changing region of the U. S. From the southern Atlantic seaboard west to Arkansas and Louisiana, trim, modern factories have sprung up in the cities, the small towns and the open fields. Since the beginning of World War II, industry has invested billions in the new Southern plants, put 2,000,000 Southerners on new, steady payrolls, and started the dynamics of history's first enlightened industrial revolution.

A GEORGIA CORPSE

The big change came with express-train momentum, but it was a long time getting started. The plight of the old Cotton South was well illustrated by Henry Grady, managing editor of the Atlanta *Constitution*. To a Boston audience in 1889, he described the funeral of a "one-gallus" man in Pickens County, Ga. Said Grady:

They cut through solid marble to make his grave, and yet a little tombstone they put above him was from Vermont. They buried him in the heart of a pine forest, and yet the pine coffin was imported from Cincinnati. They buried him within touch of an iron mine, and yet the nails in his coffin and the iron in the shovel that dug his grave were imported from Pittsburgh. They buried him by the side of the best sheep-grazing country on the earth and yet the wool in the coffin bands and the coffin bands themselves were brought from the North. They buried him in a New York coat and a Boston pair of shoes and a pair of breeches from Chicago and a shirt from Cincinnati. The South didn't furnish a thing on earth for that funeral but the corpse and the hole in the ground.

By 1920, the South's industrial revolution had begun—but in the ugly classical pattern that was set a century before in the textile mills of England. Cotton mills moved south to take advantage of hand-to-mouth labor conditions. The "lint-heads," as cotton-mill workers were called, huddled together in drab mill

[From "The South," *Time, the Weekly Newsmagazine,* Vol. 58, No. 24, New York, 1951. Pp. 22, 27. Used by courtesy of *Time,* Copyright Time, Inc., 1951.]

villages, chronically in debt to the company store. They worked a 55- to 60-hour week for around $15 (as compared with a 48- to 54-hour week in New England for about $19).

In the '30s, this classical agony of industrial birth came to a halt. The New Deal put a floor under wages, a ceiling on hours and gave organized labor enough encouragement to worry Southern mill owners. At the same time, U. S. capitalism itself was undergoing basic changes of attitude and method. More and more industries discovered that well-paid employees did better work and bought a lot more of everybody's products. It is the South's good fortune that the second phase of its industrial expansion comes in a period of enlightened industrial relations unprecedented in history.

FIERY CROSSROADS

What happened in Camden, S. C., is an example of the new kind of industrialization. In 1946, Camden's townspeople grew curious when small groups of tight-lipped engineers, labor specialists, tax experts, lawyers and power analysts began dropping from "the North." The visitors would take samplings through the length and breadth of Kershaw County, then fly mysteriously back whence they came.

It wasn't until two years later that Camden discovered that E. I. du Pont de Nemours had picked the town as the site for a $17 million plant for processing Orlon, a new synthetic fiber.

There was only one leading citizen of Camden who objected. He warned that the coming of Du Pont would ruin the town's winter-resort business. He wrote a letter asking Du Pont to stay away. When his fellow townsmen found out, three carloads of young bloods roared over to the man's house and—in a unique variation of a waning Southern custom—burned an oil-soaked cross on his front lawn.

By the spring of 1950, a handsome, air-conditioned Du Pont plant was ready to operate. Of the 950 employees, about half came from the town, half from the surrounding cotton land. One of the transplanted farmers was Cleatus Threatt, then 25, a World War II veteran whose 65 acres of sandy cotton land were mired in mortgages. One day in May 1950, he was astride his tractor, plowing under a hail-ruined cotton crop, when a friend ran from the neighborhood telephone to tell him that Du Pont had accepted his application for a job. Cleatus had never worked in a factory in his life.

OUT OF THE MIRE

Like most of the South's farmers, he turned out to be good at it. Du Pont put him through a two-month training course, then set him to work as a laboratory technician testing batches of raw materials. In 18 months, he missed only twelve hours of work. His pay climbed from $1 an hour to $1.62 ("I make more now in a week at the plant than I used to make in a month on the farm"). Fortified by this certain income, he kept the farm and bought another 145 acres of better land, built a new seven-room frame house, and bought enough fertilizer to push his cotton and tobacco to record yields. He began to plan a cattle-raising venture on the side.

The revolution brought political as well as economic changes to Camden. The town's voters went to the polls and turned out their old-line politicians, voted in an efficient city-manager government. They chose for their mayor Henry Savage, Jr., a 48-year-old lawyer who had worked hard to bring new industry to Camden. Old forms of negligence vanished under new forms of efficiency (sample: investigators found that a cottonseed plant had been drawing off unmetered city water for 20 years). Camden's municipal bonds, which had been discounting at 4% and 5%, gained a Class 1 rating: the latest batch discounted at 2%.

Out of the new city and county tax revenue and new efficiency came a new junior high school, enlargement of Camden's six cafeterias, and plans for a new Negro high school. Camden added Pontiac, Nash, Oldsmobile and Cadillac agencies, two new drive-in theaters, three new furniture stores, a radio station, supermarkets, a fourth farm-implement agency, and its first pawnshop. The town's white churches noted a 37% increase in membership (the Episcopal Church was highest: 52%) and paid off most of their debts. Contractors put up nearly 1,000 new houses and apartment units. New sewer lines prompted the removal of 675 outdoor privies. Even Camden's Confederate Monument, a 12 ft. marble reminder of the last Northern invasion, was transplanted from its old stand in the middle of Broad Street to a new, less trafficked site in the park.

NEW WHIRL

Camden's changes have only begun. By mid-1952, Du Pont will complete an additional $25 million expansion of its Orlon plant (one of 20 Du Pont plants in nine Southern States), will hire about 1,900 more workers, and start Camden's spiral whirling again by paying out an additional $7,300,000 a year in wages.

Among the factors in the South's industrial growth are cheap electric power from TVA and private utilities, natural gas piped from Louisiana and Mississippi, and a lowering of Southern freight rates, which used to be much higher than in the Northeast and Midwest.

Industry draws industry. Each new payroll gave the South more money to spend. Northern manufacturers had to decide whether it was cheaper to feed this market by freight or by a new branch plant. Ford moved an assembly plant into Atlanta, General Motors began building Chevrolets, then Pontiacs, Oldsmobiles and Buicks in Atlanta, too. Purchasing power brought refrigerator plants, refrigerator plants brought enameling plants. Dairy processors and meat packers came along as Southern workers began eating higher and higher on the hog. An estimated 14% of all U. S. industry now lies in the Southeastern U. S.

Contrary to legend, most of the big corporations which have recently built Southern plants were not primarily searching for cheap labor. Some Southern wages are still lower than Northern, but the gap is sure to narrow. Southern labor offers employers some other, solider advantages. The Southern labor pool is deep. (Mechanical cotton pickers, for instance, and other labor-saving farm machinery are expected to displace 2,000,000 field hands by 1965; many of them will be available for factory work.) The South's labor population is young and quick to learn. Employers who complain that they have to scrape the bottom of the labor barrel in the North find they can pick, choose and train the brightest of young Southerners.

GLAD HAND

The Southern glad hand has been quick to welcome industrial prospects. In 1936, Mississippi embarked on the "Balance Agriculture with Industry" plan which gave state assistance to local communities so they could build plant facilities. In return, the companies that moved in were supposed to maintain a minimum level of employment for about ten years. Nearly all Southern states borrowed some variation of this technique, or offered special tax reductions to help new factories get going. Favorite targets are industries which employ lots of people, e.g., the shoe factories (Arkansas got eleven in three years), and garment plants (heaviest in Tennessee).

Port Wentworth, Ga. built a new industrial water plant to attract the Southern Paperboard company. Natchez, Miss., "clarified" the state stream pollution law to get the Johns-Manville insulation board plant. In Greeneville, Tenn., some schools joined in educating the populace in the art of dairy farming to help the Pet Milk Co. build up a milk supply for its new processing factory.

Thus far in the revolution, the Negro is still the stepchild, although he is often an indirect beneficiary. Northern corporations, shunning discrimination in their home plants, usually yield to local pressure and restrict Negroes to menial labor. There are notable exceptions. In Memphis, the International Harvester Co. flatly announced that it would hire Negroes without discrimination as to type of job and with equal pay. Out of 2,425 production and maintenance employees, 641 are Negroes.

Industrialization and relative prosperity is stemming the tide of Southerners moving North. Southern college graduates are staying home. Scientific research and executive management will inevitably fall into the hands of young Southerners.

The South's new industry is there to stay. If the U. S. economy continues to expand, the South will stay in the forefront of the parade. If the national economy deflates, the South's new factories will be among the last to sag, because they are among the newest and most efficient in the nation.

Part of the revolution described in the preceding selection involves the relationship between management and labor. To what extent is the Southern worker becoming unionized? How successful has been the much-heralded Operation Dixie of the CIO, which set out over three years ago to unionize Southern labor? The author of the next selection points out that today the labor unions are engaged in a "defense of the beachhead." He indicates that "industrial democracy" is an importation to the South and that there are a number of traditional social traits supporting a different type of management-labor relations.

• 42 • *The Emergence of Organized Labor*

GEORGE C. STONEY

For the past decade the opposing forces of industry and organized labor have spilled dollars, ink, and on occasion even blood in a major campaign for control of the southern worker. At this writing it would seem that labor is fighting a holding operation, its "southern drive" converted to a dogged defense of the beachhead it gained during the early Wagner Act period and the first years of the late war.

This fact—and only a few labor people will question it—is to be regretted, for no one has benefited more from this competition for his loyalties than the southern worker himself.

The direction and financing of both the contesting sides has been largely non-southern, which is again a matter for regret. For this continues the colonial-paternal pattern: the autocratically benevolent plantation owner of a hundred years ago working off his indebtedness to a northern banker has simply

given place to the manager of a modern branch plant, equally tied and often just as autocratic and benevolent. In his wake have come south more recently the modern industrial unions, striving to maintain their influence on a national standard of wages and working conditions in a section of the country that knows little about "industrial democracy" and most of whose leaders have shown a distinct distaste for it.

Mean and unromantic though the struggle be, the economic benefits it has brought to the South are very real.

Those fortunate Yankees who motor to Florida or the Gulf Coast each winter must surely notice the difference—the television aerials on hundreds of small farmhouses north and east of Atlanta; the rows of shiny bicycles outside rickety clapboard schools for Negroes in Mississippi; the remodeled mill villages along the Piedmont range from Danville

[From "New Opportunity—in a New South," *The Survey*, Vol. 87, No. 4, New York, 1951. Pp. 149-154. Used by permission.]

south through Charlotte and Greenville; the flashy new store fronts around court house squares in Georgia and Alabama.

Ten years ago silk stockings blowing in the wind beside one of those chicken-coop houses that straggle along the highways outside most southern towns marked the home where a daughter worked in the mill. Now one looks for the new electric refrigerator and washing machine on the porch. For now it is more than likely two or three members of the family are bringing cash back from town each Friday afternoon.

Everywhere there are more painted houses and better dressed people. The traveling "outsider" (for the South is still a section apart, and thinks of itself as such) who has no prewar memories to use as a comparison may be distressed on occasion by the winter bleakness of the general landscape, the relative squalor of most towns once he passes through the better residential sections.

But as he drives on to that landscaped tourist court outside the next town (with more baths and inside toilets than the whole community had fifteen years ago) he should notice the new brick consolidated school, the swank drive-in theater, the streamlined mill. On Sunday the "mill-hand" children pouring out of the big new brick Church of God Tabernacle look almost as straight-legged and well dressed as the business men's children coming out of the Presbyterian Sunday School on the other side of town.

In sum, the South in 1951 looks, acts, and feels more like the rest of the United States than at any time in the past century. Most people still cook their beans and collard greens with a slice of salt pork, but now very often that side meat has a good wide streak of lean in it.

Though some mourn lost "charm," the South's new industrial gain is considered good news by most southerners. It should be considered good news by the rest of the country, too. For these thirteen states with roughly a fifth of the nation's population are producing a third of its children, a surplus labor force that—despite remarkable industrialization of

the home region—is sending to the North and Middle West millions of new citizens. The annual influx from the South is surpassed in size only by foreign immigration in a few peak years before or just after World War I. What these children have to eat and the way they are educated is obviously of national importance.

During the 1940's, while the country as a whole boosted its dollar income approximately 130 percent, all southern states did much better than that, with Mississippi actually making an increase in per capita income of something like 226 percent.

The South's per capita income in the early 1930's was well below half the national average. Today it is almost two thirds of the national figure. While a substantial part of this increase has come from higher farm prices, even more has come from higher industrial wages. For example, in textiles the average minimum wage has been boosted in fifteen years from 23 cents an hour to about 87 cents.

In every major field of manufacturing, the South's share of national earnings has gone up: in tobacco from 53 to 58 percent, in all textiles from 36 to 40 percent, in lumber from 33 to 37 percent, in automobiles and rubber products from 3 to 6 percent, in chemicals from 15 to 20 percent, in paper from 12 to 15 percent—and this trend is continuing.

Since the post-reconstruction days of Henry Grady, southern leaders have preached that their section's only path up from poverty is through industrialization. While an occasional politician might sound off against Wall Street money and people with "foreign" names, the best silver in the best homes would be polished up to entertain the traveling Yankee who brought either with him, if that visitor happened to be looking for a factory site.

Measured volume-wise, most southern industry has been developed by outside firms and outside capital and the proportion of outside control seems to be increasing. In a brilliant analysis entitled "Why Industry Moves South," published in 1948 by the National

Policy Association's Committee of the South, two economists, Glenn McLaughlin and Stefan Robock, state:

The extent of "foreign" control of southern industry is suggested by some 1939 statistics for the seven states of the Southeast. Nationally, 18.5 percent of all manufacturing establishments were branch plants and they produced about 56 percent of the total volume of manufactured products. In the southeastern region, 27.2 percent of all establishments were branch plants which produced almost 70.5 percent of the region's total volume of products. This dominance of branch plants also undoubtedly applies to new facilities constructed since 1939 although no exact measures are as yet at hand.

McLaughlin and Robock, basing their generalizations on eighty-eight carefully picked case histories, say three main things attract industry to the South: southern markets, southern raw materials, southern labor, in that order of importance.

These findings seem to have surprised almost everyone. For two generations southern leaders had assumed that "cheap, cooperative, native-born labor" was their section's main attraction, and advertised it as such. When the New Deal brought in federal minimum wage laws, southern congressmen led the fight against them, saying such laws would kill the South's chance to get new industry. State minimum wage laws are still conspicuous by their absence. Yet within a decade after total wages paid southern labor started up, the markets these extra dollars create have become the section's most important attraction for new industry.

McLaughlin and Robock found only a handful of their eighty-eight new plants—those in textiles, garment-making and shoes—were attracted south by the relatively lower wage scales they found. Even the textile and apparel makers seemed resigned to the fact that whatever differential in actual hourly rates of pay they might now enjoy would soon be done away with, leaving them only the differential (one found country-wide) between rates of pay in small towns against those paid in cities.

Why, then, does southern labor still stand as an important attraction to industry and is its unorganized status such a threat to unionized workers in the rest of the country? The most obvious reason is that there is a vast difference between hourly rates of pay and total labor cost per unit of output. In their new southern plants managers seem able to get more production for the dollars they put into pay envelopes. Let's see how this is possible.

The South's high birthrate plus the swift mechanization of agriculture is sending literally millions of new workers into towns. This makes labor considerably more plentiful than in the older industrial sections. When a manager opens a new factory he can pick his employes more carefully, concentrating on the younger age groups. Employes who have a background of underpaid farm work and little choice in industrial employment prove to be more amenable to the new work procedures, increased workloads, the major shifts in what might be called "factory customs" that usually come when a modernized plant is put into operation. This leads to less turnover and lower rates of absenteeism.

It is remarkable, given the widespread popular belief to the contrary, that not one industry studied by the writers of "Why Industry Moves South" had found southern workers less efficient than others and many reported them more efficient, more eager to learn, and—of particular importance—much more willing to work third shifts.

A textile engineer of my acquaintance explained why his chain had decided to open a new plant in South Carolina rather than nearer the main market area:

Land was cheap, he said, allowing them to use the more efficient all-on-one-floor layout. The milder weather made construction a bit cheaper, too. Since most of the workers have cars, the company was able to set their factory down in the middle of the country rather than in or near a town. But the main attraction, he said, was the ease with which they could get people who are willing to work the midnight shift.

Industrial improvements in his line, it would seem, are moving so fast one cannot build a new mill without considering that it may be out-of-date in twelve to fifteen years. So plants are planned for more or less continuous operation. Being able to get labor for a third shift whenever needed without paying a premium would, in itself, make the location of great advantage.

The beautiful synthetic fabric factory this engineer helped to build and landscape sits in the middle of a particularly woebegone stretch of gullywashed cotton country, though around it are well fertilized lawns and pastures, owned by the company. The plant is air conditioned throughout. The cafeteria, used jointly by workers and management, could serve as a movie set for a fashionable café. During their lunch hour, employes, most of them young women from the nearby farms, stroll along the hallways to see attractively decorated show windows in which the management displays its own products made into dresses by famous couturiers, with signs telling the girls where they can buy the materials and patterns at a discount.

At night floodlights add to the factory's glamour. What tenant farm girl, seeing this sight, knowing its promise to her of almost a dollar an hour, is going to be disturbed by the thought of night work? She who has often picked cotton all day in the hot sun to earn a dollar will be slow to believe the word of organized textile workers in the North when they say the pace at which she must work in the new floodlit mill may endanger her own health and put a strain on older workers for whom she is unwittingly setting the pace.

The willingness of such young women to spend their nights tending spindles in southern mills has already had a direct effect on work standards in New England, where both managers and union representatives have been forced by southern competition to agree to changes in laws that once protected women from night work in factories.

Until the late 1930's, textiles dominated the Southern industrial picture as completely as cotton and tobacco growing dominated its agriculture. About half the industrial wages earned in the southern states today comes from work in either textile or garment factories. Fortunately, this system of "one crop industry" is changing. In the last decade the expansion of heavy industries paying relatively higher scales of wages has outstripped textile expansion.

Many of these heavy industries have expected that the new employes would be unionized; a few have even encouraged this. Strong and very genuine industrial trade unions exist in the South today in papermaking, rubber, auto assembly, chemicals, and aluminum. They join the strong unions in southern steel and coal that fought their way to recognition in the 1930's.

Few of these new unions could have gained a foothold without extensive financial aid from the North. Most still lean very heavily for direction upon their national organizations. In general, the locals are conservative, their members often apologetic. It is not uncommon to find them explaining that their own peculiar situation demands a trade union but they are seldom ready to give personal assistance to workers in other plants who are fighting for a union of their own. Away from the shop they are reluctant to be identified with the union. Labor seldom maintains in these new branch plants the power it holds in the more central locations where members have a tradition of trade union activity and where local political and governmental controls are as responsive to their pressures as to the employers'. Throughout their study McLaughlin and Robock show the attention given by new industries in picking their site to the attitude of state and local officials on such matters and the town's reputation for "maintaining industrial peace."

Ruled by state and local governments who see unionism as a bar to the industrial expansion they desperately need, surrounded by the mass of poor farming people who have the fixed idea that high union wages are responsible for their own low standard of living, plagued by racial difficulties that bring the democratic policies of national unions into dangerous (and easily exploitable) conflict with local customs and beliefs, threatened constantly by the influx of fresh workers from the farms willing to take jobs at almost any price—it is remarkable that these trade unions have made the progress in the South that they have. It is even more remarkable that violence has played such a relatively minor part in their formation.

The situation in textiles is quite different. Here in the South's oldest and still most important industry unions have contracts in fewer than one fifth of the mills, and in many of these their hold is tenuous.

There are good reasons why the CIO unions, in announcing their jointly financed and directed "Operation Dixie," three years ago focused their attention on textiles and have expended most of their effort since that time on this one industry. For in the southern textile situation lies a hard economic lesson for all organized labor.

As long as forty years ago textile manufacturers began moving south out of New England to escape the higher wages and lower work loads being forced upon them there. Last year Seabury Stanton, president of Hathaway Manufacturing Company of New Bedford, Massachusetts, and spokesman for a group of New England mill operators, told a congressional committee that slightly more than 80 percent of the cotton textile industry is now located in the South. Organization in the New England mills is almost complete. Since the unions had not been able to force upon the southern mills wages and working conditions that would give the mills of New England some basis for fair competition, Mr. Stanton was asking Congress to set minimum wages and working conditions that would make it possible for the New England group to stay in business. The wage differen-

tials against which northern mills have to operate, said Mr. Stanton, amount to 20.7 cents an hour, when all "fringe" benefits are figured in.

This manufacturer was not speaking for the majority of textile chains whose largest holdings are already in the South and who are more and more limiting their expansion to this area. In some few instances manufacturers have moved machinery and facilities to escape union-imposed wages and workloads —"runaway shops" the union calls them. The vast majority of the shifts have a more complex background, but the results, in so far as the union is concerned, are the same.

With no strong union hold on their main production centers now, textile chains can play non-union plants off against union plants and vice versa. Recently, for example, [a certain cotton mill] announced general wage increases in all plants except the one having a union contract. After several months of delay the matter was adjusted, but the union lost its contract the following year. Early in February of this year, when workers threatened to strike the woolen plant of [a firm located] at Rockville, Connecticut, a notice appeared on the company's bulletin board saying the plant would shut down and move south if work loads equal to those in their southern plants were not accepted.

Until the federal government put a floor under wages with its NRA legislation in the early New Deal days, one found in southern textiles nearly the lowest wages and most appalling living and working conditions in the United States. Though there were outstanding exceptions, the industry was owned and run in small units. Competition was ruthless. Operations were sporadic—several months of day-and-night shift work and then equally long stretches of no work at all— while families used expensive credit at the company commissary to get side meat and corn meal.

The workers the textile plants attracted, again with outstanding exceptions, were people of little education whose childhood on tenant farms or in the back coves of the southern mountains had given them no preparation to fight in an organized way for their own betterment. The custom was to shut them off in mill villages where they continued to live in isolation, a bitter, violent, pitiful group whose towheaded children were taught their place as "mill-hand kids" whenever they ventured across the tracks in much the brutal manner that they, in their turn, taught Negro children the curse of being a different kind of outcast.

Fifteen years of prosperity have made a vast change in this picture. In the industry there has been a wholesale consolidation of the small, locally owned units into well financed mill chains, either by outright purchase or centralized financing and marketing. Modern personnel policies brought improved mill houses. Now the newer mills are not building houses at all. Workers travel in their own cars and live on small farms or in ordinary town neighborhoods.

Given another twenty years of prosperity, the old class distinctions between "mill hands" and other southern wage earners may disappear altogether. Today, however, these class differences remain strong and show themselves clearly in the textile worker's attitude toward himself and his fellows—his lack of self-confidence, his mistrust of his own leaders in dealings with such superior beings as the boss, his preference for leaders that come to him from outside the "mill-hand" group and at the same time his readiness to turn upon that leadership whenever he is cowed. The class concept can be seen, too, in the typical middle class southerner's sincere disbelief when confronted with the idea that a textile worker is capable of having anything to say about his own place in the economic scheme of things.

Sporadic union activity in southern mills has existed for two generations. Every few years long-suffered grievances would erupt into strikes that spread from one mill town to another, often with no reference to immediate causes. With little organization to guide

them, these protests were more like peasant uprisings than purposeful strikes and were so regarded by most communities where the police, and on occasion the state troopers, were dispatched to deal with them.

After a period of excitement, a show of solidarity, many bloody brawls and enough shooting to frighten all but the bravest, the orgy would be over. Strikers straggled back through the mill gate, where the foreman waited to blacklist out of employment in his or any other mill in the district the ones he recognized as ring leaders. And if the authorities did not deal with whatever "outsider" might have been a party to the disturbance there were generally enough disillusioned textile workers to do the job themselves, often the same men—and women—who a few days before were beating up their fellow employes who wanted to go back to work.

Such was the great uprising of the late 1920's, when a handful of Communists were blamed for the months of turmoil around Gastonia and other towns in the Carolina textile strip. Such was the uprising of 1934, with its flying squadrons. Calls would come to a striking group from those still working in the next mill village: "Come pull us out. We want you to shut us down, too." They wanted leadership. They wanted to hit back at the boss. The idea of gaining through unionism a chance to achieve a measure of independence, to gain for themselves as ordinary textile workers a chance to help determine their own destiny and to bear responsibility for their part in it was beyond them.

The strikes of 1937-38 were more solidly based. The CIO had begun the painfully slow process of educating in the fundamentals of trade unionism what textile workers it could reach in this climate notably unhealthy for union organizers. A few contracts were gained.

With the advent of the Wagner Act and the National Labor Relations Board it seemed a new era had come for the textile worker and his union. Under this government-sponsored arrangement there appeared to be a way for them to get union recognition and collective bargaining without resorting to pitched battles. For a brief time this was the case and though community opposition was still great certain headway was made.

Then war-born prosperity, new personnel policies of the larger mills, and those minimum wage laws organized labor itself had fought so hard to get through Congress began to make textile organization even more difficult. The "mill hands" found they were getting better wages and working conditions—as their employers kept informing them pointedly—"without having to pay tribute to any outside union bosses."

Still, grievances did keep popping up and locals were formed. Seemingly realizing the necessity for solid organization rather than emotional outbursts the CIO's textile union leaders set out on a policy of organizing through NLRB elections. Their first few victories brought demands for contracts giving wages and working conditions similar to those won in the northern mills. The industry massed to combat this approach with the same kind of determination.

While the textile union was able to win many elections in the mills, the full record shows that this peaceful means of organization brought very few actual contracts into effect. For the election results being legally sanctioned depended ultimately for enforcement not upon strikes but upon the actions of the courts. Court action means delay. While the lawyers squabbled and fenced there was plenty of time for the employer to show those workers taking an active part in the union's campaign the error of their ways.

Time after time, a year or two elapsed between the day the union won the right to negotiate and the day NLRB's staff could give a ruling on their protest that the employer refused to bargain in good faith. Meanwhile, the local chapter would have disintegrated, its membership frightened, or disillusioned, or simply fed up. Some hearings were stretched out over a five-year period, and when they eventually reached the U. S. District Court the employers found a remarkably simple solution. They would agree to negotiate, following another election, and the whole round would start over again.

[A certain large corporation] runs forty-five mills in the South. Union organization has been undertaken in fifteen of these. The NLRB has issued at least nine orders directing the company to cease and desist from unfair labor practices, such as interference with employes in their right to organize, discharges of employes for union activity, and refusal to bargain in good faith. In at least two instances the Board secured enforcement decrees in the federal courts. Though the union has been certified as bargaining representative in eight of [the firm's] mills over the last twelve years, not a single agreement has ever been negotiated.

This summary of [one corporation's] relations with the textile union appears in a recently released report of the Senate's Subcommittee on Labor-Management Relations. The report describes textile management's methods of defeating the unions in some detail. It will be sufficient here to say that, despite the still widely scattered ownership prevalent in the industry, methods used by various managements are strikingly similar. Warnings about closing down the mill if the union wins the election are included in almost uniformly worded letters from the manager to his employes; the same "national religious monthlies" carrying stories about the foreign birth and non-Anglo-Saxon lineage of union leaders appear free of charge in workers' mail boxes; the same pictures of CIO officials dining with Negroes are distributed on handbills; the same law firms are used as consultants in directing both the management's campaign before the elections and in handling whatever Labor Board cases might arise after they are over.

Since the southern textile employers did not give the Senate subcommittee the benefit of testimony, we do not have a similarly documented account of union tactics. It is obvious, however, that the industry group is matching labor's united southern drive with its own.

Industry's view is that the South—and the southern worker—does not want or need unionism and it is going to protect employes from what it considers dues-extortion. The CIO claims the southern worker is being exploited in the same way that northern workers were before they won union contracts and that they have never been given a chance to make up their own minds about unions, freed from the feudal domination of the boss, the local police, and hostile public opinion.

The unions are not going to cut off their southern drive. Money to finance it will still keep coming not only from textile unions in the North who see that every new unorganized factory in the South threatens their own standards but also from other unions who know that if the textile industry is able to shed its union-enforced standards in this way, other industries are likely to follow its example.

Tactics of organization may change, however. At present the textile drive is directed and manned by a group of dedicated young men. Matured in the New Deal decade, they operate on the principle that government and the courts will eventually respond to what they consider the needs and desires of the people with whom they work. They hold summer conferences where textile workers get training in community organization, labor history, and political action. They hold institutes in Washington where delegates from local unions hear speeches by congressmen, economists, experts on foreign affairs.

The older trade unionists who have come to the southern drive from coal, steel, and other unions who fought their way to recognition with the aid of brass knuckles, matching goon squad with goon squad, are growing impatient with these methods. The gradualists, they say, haven't any hope of getting legal justice in the obviously hostile southern courts or fair dealing from the obviously hostile southern law enforcement officers. They contend southern unions must make their own "justice" the way it has been made, for example, in the coal fields.

The CIO's textile union has many leaders of outstanding ability whose services are sought often by the federal government, universities, and foundations. Unfortunately this union is at present weakened by internal disputes, stemming in part from genuine differences of opinion over tactics but largely the result of frustration and discouragement as more and more employers, taking their cue from the success of the southern opposition, stand out against long established union agreements. Thus, a national union that was approaching mature responsibility in the field of labor-management relations is threatened at its foundations.

Strikes and more strikes can be expected in southern textiles; violence and more violence. The battle will go on between management and labor for America's newest labor market and the South will continue to improve its economic status in the meanwhile.

A new generation of industrial workers—better fed, in better health, more knowledgeable than their parents—will soon represent a majority of the southern people. Business is already beginning to flourish through their energy and spending power. And if some greater element of political and economic democracy can be made part of the South's new life, then the country as a whole will benefit from its renaissance.

The New South:

A Changing Social Structure

>>

Economic forces, as we have already seen, are having great influence in the South today. There are other forces, too, which are altering the older social structure and giving new directions to the dominant social processes. Sociologists use the following three concepts in attempting to understand these forces:

Change. Any alteration of a pre-existing element or complex. Culture change is any alteration of a culture trait or complex; social change refers to an alteration in social relations.

Social forces. The factors involved in a social process; elements that initiate and direct social phenomena. As commonly conceived they include attitudes, appetites, wishes, desires, motives, tendencies, habits, or other items that are assumed to underlie the patterned forms of conduct or to move men to action. Racial prejudices, the love of country, propaganda, scientific research, and so on, are social forces. Five of these were described in the Introduction to this volume.

Social process. The interaction of elements in social change and the transition from one social condition to another. (See footnote, Selection 40, for one method of describing the basic social processes.)*

Probably no one is better qualified to describe the current social changes in the South than Howard W. Odum, of the University of North Carolina, who carried through the pioneering investigations that give much substance to our knowledge of the South today.

* These definitions are taken from E. B. Reuter, *Handbook of Sociology*, Dryden Press, New York, 1941.

Odum's *Southern Regions of the United States,* published in 1936, was the outgrowth of years of patient research and represents a landmark in the literature of its kind.

In the article that follows, Odum takes up again the theme of industrial development but then goes on to list other significant social changes. Many of these will be dealt with in greater detail in the remaining selections of this unit.

• 43 • Social Change in the South
HOWARD W. ODUM

This discussion of the changing South undertakes to present those major recent changes which are clearly observable and, to a considerable extent, measurable. The theme, "Social Change in the South," finds its setting not only in the framework of a changing America but in the changing structure of modern society everywhere. It therefore is not only a theme of perennial interest, but of peculiar importance at this time in America's reconversion program of the future.

For the purposes of this symposium three main currents of social change in the South will be considered. The first is reflected in the larger area of social and economic changes, including public finance and technological advances. The second has to do with changes that have taken place among the Negroes of the South. The third has to do with changing ideologies and attitudes in the white South.

If we oversimplify our approaches to these three aspects of the South's culture today, we may anticipate our conclusions by noting that, in the first place, the South has changed more rapidly than has the rest of the United States. In the second place there has been an almost complete and revolutionary change in many aspects of Negro life and culture. In the third, except for isolated examples there has been relatively little change in Southern culture with reference to the traditionally Southern bi-racial culture, politics, and inter-regional cooperation, except that temporarily the South appears to have solidified its protest and de-fense attitudes. These have brought about relatively increased tensions in the structure of the South's total society.

* * *

. . . Thus, in our first category, the main changes are comprehended in the following areas: in the increase of wealth and of income; in the rise of the general standard of living with considerable improvement in rural living standards; in urbanization and therefore the bringing about of a better balance between the country and the city; in increased balance between agriculture and industry, and in a balanced agriculture; in increased mechanization of agriculture; in an awakening to the meaning of conserving resources; in great strides in technology, such as research, specialization in manufacturing, transportation, communication, in increase in public works and special public social services; and in increase in public education and public recreation, especially in athletics. Manifestly all these changes reflect an extraordinary transformation in the total Southern economy and culture.

With reference to the Negro, the main changes seem to be in the following areas: a large migration out of the South, and therefore a decreasing ratio of Negro people to the total population; a large migration from the rural South, tending to make the Negro an urban rather than a rural people; a considerable increase in educational opportunities; the

[From "Social Change in the South," *Journal of Politics,* Vol. 10, No. 2, Gainesville, Fla., 1948. Pp. 242-253. Used by permission.]

rise of a middle and upper class Negro; a rising standard of living; the rise of "the new Negro" and especially a "new" Negro youth; the development of an extraordinarily able Negro leadership; a changing attitude toward segregation; an increase of frustration and aggression; an increase of outside pressures upon the Negro and the South; changes in the Negro worker, especially the woman worker. All these changes, often little known and understood in the South, manifest a significant transformation in race relations and in the ratio of the Negro to the total cultural South.

With reference to the third current of change, namely the ideologies and attitudes of the white South, the story can best be told in terms of reaction and discussion. In general, however, there have been changes somewhat as follows: a freer discussion of all aspects of life and culture with fewer restrictions than formerly; a sharpening of defense and a reinforcing of opposition to changes in segregation practices; an increase in thought and talk about "racism"; revolt against the Supreme Court decisions with reference to voting and higher education and more articulate opposition to federal legislation affecting the South; the still solid South with minor threats of secession from the Democratic party; some progress in southern organization for civil rights; a relatively large number of young college students and returning G. I.'s advocating a more liberal practice with reference to race relations; considerable progress in organized labor advances; strong reaction among the young people who work on farms, in factories, and who operate the trucks and taxis; some recrudescence of the Ku Klux Klan; an ever-increasing pressure from the outside. The net result is reflected in an increasing tension and conflict, affecting all aspects of the South's life and leadership in the nation.

Returning to the assumption that the South is changing more rapidly than the rest of the nation in many of the social-economic aspects of its life and culture, we note that these changes may be measured in several ways.

They may be described in terms of absolute gains or losses. They may be measured in terms of relative gains or losses as compared with the rest of the nation. Further comparisons may be made with both the amount of gain or loss and with the rates of change. These may be observed in terms of the South's actual status as compared with the nation, or in terms of the ratio of each measured item's ratio to the South's total, again in comparison with the similar ratio of each item to the Nation's total. Thus, if we look at the situation with reference to urbanization we find that the South started with a low ratio of its population as urban, then increased its urban population more rapidly than the rest of the nation but still has a relatively smaller urban population (in terms of percentages) than the United States as a whole. This urban increase is not only greater than for the nation as a whole but its rate of increase in the South has been accelerated from decade to decade more rapidly than in the rest of the nation and is even more accelerated in the case of the Negro.

Or we may look at certain expenditures for public education. Starting with a low actual expenditure the South's rate of increase is greater than for the nation, as a whole, yet its absolute expenditures still remain far below the nation's average. So, too, the South's expenditure for public education, although constituting a larger ratio of its total public funds than the nation as a whole spends for the same purpose, is still, after its large increase, below the nation's average. Here again, special factors affect the rate of acceleration as in the case of Negro education, in which the South is spending more for Negro education in 1948 than it did for all education a few decades ago.

The nature of the present day trends in the South may be illustrated further by certain specific cases from which it is possible to observe a general pattern of change. Here the South's rate of change is greater than for the rest of the nation, although both its absolute and relative ratio to the total may be smaller. Thus, the estimated population of the three Southern census regions in 1945 was

32.3 per cent of the total for the United States. The total income payments for the same regions were 23.4 per cent, but the percentage increase from 1940 to 1945 was 147 for the South as compared with 116 for the nation. Salaries and wages in the South were 22.3 per cent of the nation's total but the increase for the South was 155 per cent as compared with 125.1 for the nation. The South has 16.9 per cent of total bank deposits representing an increase of 234 per cent, as compared with 142.8 per cent for the nation. In registration of private and commercial automobiles the South has 24.1 per cent, an increase of 2.2 per cent as against a decrease for the nation as a whole of 1.7 per cent. For truck and tractor registrations, the figures were 30.7 and 15 per cent as compared with 9 per cent. In receipts for motor fuel the South's proportion was 38.4 per cent of the total and its increase was 11.1 as compared with a national decrease of 4.5. There were similar large differences in the increase of both private and public telephones, in gross postal receipts and in expenditures for public education. The southern states' ratio for general expenditures for state governments for 1946 was generally greater than for the nation as a whole, including expenditures for education, safety and correction, health, welfare. . . .

These are adequate samplings to indicate trends which are described in more detail in various sources cited. There are other illustrations of changes of a different sort. For instance, there was an increase in the population in four southern states which greatly exceeded the increase for the United States as a whole. This increase manifestly indicated trends due to outside influences which concern the South's relation to the rest of the Nation. In the case of Florida and Virginia there is a clearly measurable flow of population from the Northeast. In Virginia it is an overflow from the District of Columbia and a "pattern of Virginia" appeal. In the case of Florida, it is clearly a case of Florida becoming an "Eastern State" with its winter climate and special urban recreation facilities. In the case of Louisiana, there are Middle America and the Mississippi River, together with the expanded port of New Orleans and the South American hinterlands. In Texas, there was the expansion of war industries and chemical industries and a tendency to become more a part of the West than of the South with an expansion similar to that of the Pacific Northwest's Seattle. These are important trends for the future.

Other trends of importance are the increase of certain industries in relation to the rest of the country. Thus in textiles the Southeast tended to supplant the New England advantage and in furniture the ratio of the South to the Middlewest was changing rapidly with increases in the South being greater.

There was thus a trend toward a better balanced culture through the widening range of occupational opportunity, with greater equilibrium between and among agricultural and non-agricultural workers, domestic services and industrial workers, and an increase of social services and scientific workers to approximate a better balance of skilled and trained workers. Alongside these changes, the increase in the population of high school and college students laid the foundation for a continuing increase in the enrollment and growth of higher institutions of learning.

Returning to the second current of social change in the South, there is no doubt that the Negro himself has changed tremendously. It is not only that he has developed important upper and middle classes; it is not only that he has developed a magnificent leadership, and that thousands have taken advantage of higher educational opportunities; it is not only that Negro youth, sensing the epochal spiritual change in racial attitudes and led by Negro leadership of the North and South, is willing to experiment with every type of equal opportunity; it is all this and more. It is as if some universal message had reached the great mass of Negroes, urging them to dream new dreams and to protest against the old order. It is as if there were pathos and tragedy in their misunderstanding of the main tenets of a bitter Negro leadership, and as if many of the northern Negro leaders of limited mentality have confused southern Negroes with the idea that any sort of word of courtesy or cheerfulness is an index of subservience to the white man. In all of this, whether it is pathos and tragedy or admirable idealism and noble effort, the net result is a "new" Negro facing the "old" white man.

In *Race and Rumors of Race* we have pointed out how there is a vigorous, lusty enthusiasm and an aggressive attitude and action characteristic of a whole new generation of Negro youth, much of which is as spontaneous and inevitable as would be the growth of the youth of any people, and we have indicated the results of the increasing education and experience of a race in the midst of a region and a nation that were going forward rapidly. A part of this enthusiastic aggressive attitude and action on the part of young Negroes is due, of course, to the new education and to the leadership and agitation of many of the Negro educational leaders in both North and South. But even if this had not been a great influence, the changing reaction and responsibility of Negro youth would have been an inevitable product of an evolutionary development. To this extent the situation in the South may be more indicative of growing pains and evolutionary development than of impending crisis, provided adequate regional-national arrangements to take care of the situation are available.

To those who would face reality, this relatively new and vigorous aggressiveness among young Negroes appears quite natural. In substance, this is what the Negro seems to say:

"We want equal opportunity to live in this the best land in the world. We want a chance to do the best work and to get the best pay. We want to express ourselves fully, and as youth in a youthful race perhaps we are considerably bumptious and noisy. We want the right to travel, to trade, to work without embarrassing segregation laws and customs, and we would like to live anywhere in the community whenever we can make the grade. In more specific instances and cases, we like to go into the drug stores, in the markets, and into other public places as a matter of fact just as other people do; perhaps we want this more because we have not had it, and we are a little immature and naive about it.

"And we like to dream of unreasonable things to be done and ideals to be attained, and we want to do this even as other people do without being considered presumptuous. In the long life line of human beings waiting their turn for service, achievement, privilege, obligation, we want to take our place regularly and not be always slipping back to the end of the line and giving way always to someone else. We are in a transitional stage, boisterous, vocal, unreasonable, and we don't give a damn if we are; we will be heard. And don't blame us if even the best of us talk big about what we are going to do when and if we do get what we want, and if we don't get it. And don't blame us permanently if in this stage of new transition and learning some of us do lose our balance and if we lose our patience and run amuck. We are eager, ambitious, and we get hypnotized with the feeling within ourselves."

There is another major field in which the behavior of Negroes is new as compared with the older southern patterns of work relationships. It is not only that Negroes could earn more money and insist on more pay and larger participation in work of all kinds, with shorter hours and more specialized division of labor. For here the Negro is following a new pattern everywhere. But there is, even among Negroes who have worked long and faithfully in the same fields, a tendency suddenly to change their attitudes and modes of work behavior. Sometimes they don't say much about it. They just change. And sometimes they grumble and just refuse to work in the old way at the old pay. And even though they follow the natural trend, their action results in a critical point of conflict, since it upsets the traditional southern economy of white-Negro work relations.

Even more radically changing the whole southern way of life is the new behavior of Negro women who for generations have been "servants" to the white women of the South.

The net result is that for the average white family the Negro servant is a thing of the past. Negro women are following a natural, logical, and fair cause in demanding more money and less work; in accepting work where they can get more money and have more time at home; or in not working at all, in view of the more nearly adequate pay of their husbands or sons. It is all logical, as is also their explanation to the white women who seek their help. "Your husband gets good money and you don't have to work out; my husband gets good money, and I don't have to work out." This illustrates the basis of the deep resentment by the white South so long conditioned to Negro help for little pay. It may even add to the resentment of the unthinking multitudes of white southerners that the Negro speaks the truth when she says she has been a slave for the white folks long enough.

The greatest over-all change in the Negro South might be described as the development of a high standard of culture and leadership in which achievements in business, literature, art, and education have become commensurate with high standards of culture anywhere. This development is, however, largely unknown and not understood by the white South which continues to discriminate against the Negro by default as well as by intention. Thus, programs will be made, conferences held, in which it is announced that all colleges or all community agencies are participating when, as a matter of fact, only white institutions are envisaged. This ignorance on the part of the white South and the unwillingness to re-examine the Negro's culture is a part of the unchanging South to which we refer next.

The reflection of the social changes in the South, with reference to traditional southern culture and ideologies, may be measured almost more by reaction within the framework of the other changes than by distinctive changes themselves. In the long run it means that the South in 1948 is a somewhat different South from what it was in the 1920's. The impression, at least superficially, is that there has been an increase in narrow sectionalism as opposed to earlier trends towards interregional arrangements.

During the 1920's and the early 1930's it was commonly assumed that "North" and "South" were no longer valid realities in the new America that was developing, except as they reflected a tragic past which the nation wanted to forget. The First World War had relegated the term "the War," meaning the Civil War, to an outmoded past that took its place alongside other epochs of "only yesterday," or that represented stepping stones on which the nation had already risen to higher things.

Before that, perhaps during the whole of the first third of the twentieth century, there were very substantial trends toward a genuinely realistic reintegration of the South in the nation as, in the regional balance of America, the southern states adopted higher standards of achievement and participated more completely in the total American culture. The South, as Southeast and Southwest, was taking a dynamic place in the nation, even as the Far West, the Northwest, and all the other regions were making America strong and united by developing their separate diversities of strength and seeking a new economic and cultural balance.

There were several reasons for these important trends, perhaps about equally balanced between the regions and the nation as a whole. The leaders of the South had inventoried her resources and her deficiencies and had begun to face the facts in preparation for genuine progress. A new school of historians in the North had rewritten the history of the nation, appraising the South fairly, and had also made realistic diagnosis and criticism of the northern administration after the Civil War. The South had also made extraordinary strides in nearly all phases of its culture and economy. It had developed industry, paved great highways, increased its urban civilization in both the Southeast and the Southwest faster than any other regions. It had pioneered in some aspects of public welfare, public health, and education, and had, with the cooperation and support of the Northeast, strengthened its colleges and universities. It had begun to develop research in both the physical and the social sciences and to apply the results to agriculture and industry, and it was increasing its representation in the national councils of leadership. The South had assumed a new sort of leadership in literature and had become the best documented of all the regions. In all this, the South had liberal cooperation from publishers and educational leaders and philanthropists in the Northeast. And there was pride of achievement not only in the South but in the other regions, particularly in "the Wests," for what the southern regions were doing.

All this was especially marked in the period immediately following the First World War, from 1918 to the early depression years. Then, once again, both the Southeast and the Southwest took larger and more positive part in the affairs of the nation as the Democratic administration developed the New Deal. This was true in two main ways. One that occurred naturally and logically was the larger southern share in the federal government under a Democratic administration. The other was the southern share in the measures of relief and reconstruction during the depression years when the region was in some instances worse off than other parts of the nation. At any rate, the southern states put their hands to the task, and through state planning boards, through various technical ways of cooperating with New Deal agencies, through public works, work relief, agricultural adjustment, through educational cooperation and other ways assumed a new kind of normal and logical participation in the total national effort. Southern personnel, both in political and in appointive arrangements, was large.

Then a strange thing happened, happened twice, once because of the depression New Deal pressure and once because of the pressure of war; namely, a sudden revival of the old sectional conflict and the recrudescence of the terms North and South. It would have been unbelievable if it had not actually happened that this, together with special and intensi-fied revival of the old race conflict, would bring the South to its greatest crisis and the nation again to one of its chief domestic problems since the Civil War.

First, the realistic researches into the resources, deficiencies, and needs of the South, and then the action of the New Deal administration, caused the nation to rediscover the South as a peculiar example of backwardness and later of badness, and to undertake to remake it overnight. The revival of the term "South," in so far as the national administration was concerned and in so far as it began to be used universally by editors and critics, came about in two ways. One was typified in the now famous slogan that the South was the nation's "Economic Problem No. 1." The South was Tobacco Road. It was again missionary territory. But, whatever it was, it was "The South." Secondly, the South came to be synonymous with conservatism or reactionary policies because southern senators and congressmen and state governors and leaders opposed many New Deal policies. "What else could you expect? He is a Southerner," came to be a common refrain. And then the South, with its usual sensitiveness, revived with a vengeance the term "North," charging that section with "trying to make the South over."

The second intensification of the North-South conflict was brought on by the War, which was expected to unify the nation, and in which the southern states led in enlistment and in all-out support, as a result of the South's racial segregation culture and laws. The nation realized suddenly that the American Dream guaranteed to all its citizens equal rights and opportunities and that while it had gone to war for global democracy, two of its own great regions contained a negation of democracy. It realized further that this negation and this segregation policy applied to the armed forces, because the Army and the Navy and the Air Corps were a part of a white man's world, where the Negro was discriminated against through no fault of his own. And so there was the ever recurring question, "What can be done about the South?"

Increasingly, individuals and agencies, private and public, set themselves to the task of "making" the South change. This is a long story which we have already discussed. Yet the net result was an unbelievable revival of the old bitterness attached to the terms "North" and "South."

It is not possible to estimate how long the present tensions will last or in what direction and at what rates they may continue in the future. At the present time they have a bearing upon all southern achievement and trends, limiting the full extent of economic and industrial development, of educational standards, and of national participation in American life.

Without a doubt, the South is changing, and in some respects changing rapidly. But will the North and the South soon be indistinguishable? Many people of both regions would consider any changes that brought such a result the greatest of misfortunes. However, our regional differences will certainly not disappear entirely, and the increasing similarities in such superficial matters as architecture does not mean that behavior and attitudes are correspondingly similar.

The following selection deals with regional differences of a basic kind and is important because it shows how closely the social structure and the social history of a people affect beliefs, ideas, and values. The term *ideology* is used to refer to the well-worked-out set of explanations accepted by most of the people in a society as the reason for supporting its various institutions and mores. It may or may not be "reasonable," and it is seldom "scientific," since it is rarely subjected to logical analysis. But the fact that people accept an ideology and cling to it stubbornly in the face of threatened change gives it great social significance. A society can hold together and function as an effective unit only if there is sufficient agreement among its members about the basic answers to the problems of life. Ideologies are the incorporation of those answers in a form which is passed from one generation to another, changing only slowly and imperceptibly as conditions change.

The author of this selection is a native of Georgia who has also lived in the North. He has distinguished himself as a sociologist, and here writes from a rich background of investigation in social science and of familiarity with the regions discussed.

• 44 • Ideologies of the South in Transition
WILLIAM F. OGBURN

Regions differ not only in climate, resources, production, and vital statistics, but also in customs and social attitudes, but being less accurately measurable these are often omitted from scientific studies of regions and left to the novelist and traveler for description. Nevertheless they are important and are among the most interesting of the characteristics which differentiate one region from another. Thus the inhabitant of the South is, in popular opinion, different because of a variety of attitudes, such as his chivalry toward women, his race prejudice, his hospitality, his leisureliness, his preference for the military life, his

[From "Ideologies of the South in Transition," *Social Forces*, Vol. 23, No. 3, Chapel Hill, 1945. Pp. 334-342. Used by permission.]

manners, and his acceptance of social classes. These attitudes contrast greatly with those in other parts of the United States where there is a strong belief in women's rights, where Negro children go to school with whites, where speech is frank, and where one social class is held to be as good as another.

IDEOLOGIES AND MORES

Social attitudes are very dear to the people who hold them. Indeed they become matters of belief and thus exert a strong influence like religious sanctions, and are binding like morals. Thus to behave like a gentleman is one of the highest attainments in the social values of a southerner. Honor is a shining virtue. To act ungentlemanly and dishonorably is condemned more than most sins. Similarly in northern cities, no one would dare to admit that he was undemocratic, that he belonged to a superior class. The brotherhood of man is his belief, without distinction of color or creed. Also high in his scale of values is efficiency, the measure and reward of which is success. Not to be efficient is to be dubbed a failure, no matter how kind or good one may be. What could be worse than to be called a failure?

So our social attitudes become rights and wrongs. They are cherished like the beatitudes or are condemned like the practice of the Philistines. We can hardly discuss them calmly. They tend to become eternal truths for all people at all times. Thus, it is good for everyone to follow the codes of conduct set for a gentleman. Everyone should in every age believe in the brotherhood of man and that all men are created equal.

Sociologists have sought to signalize this emotional binding force of our cherished social attitudes by calling them mores. Thus it is said mores make right and wrong. For instance, democracy is right and slavery is wrong. It follows that a person living under a particular set of mores cannot speak against them, any more than in the present war one could speak out in the United States in praise of Hitler. One cannot speak in favor of slavery, for our mores are against slavery, though slavery was held to be good among the Greeks and at various other times and places in the world. The mores tend to restrict our vision, to make us contemporary-minded. They narrow our view like a fog. Thus we cannot see how slavery could have been proper in ancient Greece. We cannot understand how polygamy could have been suited to any people.

The mores of the South and of the North are different on many subjects. One is the Negro. Since each region believes in its own mores, and since the mores are antagonistic, each is heartily condemned by the other. Segregation and social inequality of the Negro are held desirable in the South, while in the North such an attitude is considered most unjust. Which is right?

Furthermore these attitudes are changing. The South is becoming more liberal toward the Negro while in the Northern cities property owners in urban residence sections are active in trying to keep the Negro from living in the neighborhood. There is thus some confusion in regard to social attitudes. The South is not only in conflict with the North but also with itself. For new social attitudes are developing in the South which are antagonistic to the social attitudes of the Old South. Thus the sheltered daughter of the old days is today going to a coeducational college and sometimes her free and easy behavior is a consternation to the older generation. There is confusion over the proper place and conduct of women in society. The older generation and the new are in conflict. Which is right?

SOCIO-ECONOMIC SYSTEMS AND MORES

The purpose of this essay is to try to bring some clarity and order in this confusion. The first point is that there is a correlation between a socio-economic system and its social attitudes, and that the mores which are right for any one socio-economic system are not necessarily right for different systems. Thus in the Old South the system was agricultural; in the northern industrial cities the social order is based on the factory system. Each system has its own attitudes, for instance, on child labor.

In the Old South child labor was good. The old-time southerner was really astounded to hear that in the North they were not letting children work, and making laws to prevent it. For among self-sufficing farmers child labor, that is, the industriousness of children, is greatly to be desired. That is the way the young learned to become farmers and capable housewives, for there were no agricultural schools. It was necessary for the boy to learn to care for the animals, to plow, to harvest, to mend wagons and broken tools, and for girls to learn to cook, to sew, to spin, to weave, to make medicines, to preserve fruits, to manage a house. To keep a playful youngster at these tasks required considerable pressure. If a child played too much, or did not do his chores, he was likely to come to a bad end, it was held. "An idle mind is the devil's workshop." The apprentice system—child labor—whereby a youngster learned to be a wheelwright or a lawyer was admirable. These were the virtues that Benjamin Franklin praised. Loafing and play were condemned, much as frivolity is disapproved by college deans today.

This ideology regarding child labor was not, of course, peculiar only to families with children, or only to self-sufficing farmers. Like the clouds or the weather it covered the region, even the villages, towns, and the new cities, populated from rural regions. Also while this attitude toward the industriousness of children was particularly appropriate to the self-sufficing farm of pre-Civil War or pre-Revolutionary days, it hung over into the twentieth century. For the mores change slowly.

In the industrial North the situation was quite different. There were factories where children went to work before daylight, worked all day in rooms where the air was bad and where there was little sunshine. In winter they came home after dark. Their wages were low. The tasks were routine and did not call for the varied talents that were so useful around the farm. They were tired at night.

Their chief opportunity for play was on Sunday, but on the Sabbath recreation was tabooed. Therefore child labor was bad. Here the ideology was play and more play for children and no child labor for the young. The economic conditions were those of the factory system, and a new ideology on child labor arose, appropriate to this system.

Hence it is easy to see how the peoples of the urban States of the North, who were passing child labor laws which were good and moral, in their missionary zeal would want to impose them upon the agricultural southern States. When the southern States, with few factories and many farms, did not respond, they were considered by the northerners as benighted. The idea of the adaptation of the mores to the economic conditions was not appreciated by the editorial writers in the Boston newspapers. In the course of time factories came to the South and also child labor legislation.

In the case of child labor there are two ideologies, each appropriate to its own economic system. In this illustration there is observable the myopic influence of the mores. The vision is restricted to one economic system. The adherents of each system condemn the other. The southerner needed the labor of his child on his own farm and after all it was his child and not the State's. He resented implications as to his morality and he was astounded at the child labor laws of the North. The victorious North was for imposing its system on the South whether it fitted or not, and the northerner had scant understanding of the socio-economic system of the South. Each had his perspective limited. The northerner was on the winning side in this battle of the mores, for the old agricultural order was receding in the South, and factories with their new ideologies were coming to southern cities.

As the cotton factories came South, there was a lag in attitudes toward them. At first the factories were new and few, and the old mores of the need of industriousness for the young were all pervading. So the new mores of child labor, like all new social movements, had to fight their way against the opposition of the old.

THE FORCE OF TRADITION

It has been shown that each economic system has its own ideology. But this fact does not wholly explain the southern attitudes. The rural west is agricultural also and is quite different from the Old South in many of its attitudes. It is true that western agriculture is different from southern, yet this difference is not satisfactory as an explanation. For peculiarities of southern ideologies, it must not be assumed that agriculture in the southern States created them, as the factory system of the northern cities created the ideologies of the North. The South imported its attitudes from England. England of the eighteenth and earlier centuries was rural, too, with self-sufficing agriculture. The colonists came from England and brought ideologies with them. In the South with its predominantly rural life these attitudes of pre-industrial England took root and flourished better than in the non-agricultural North.

The southerner's attitude toward social classes, for instance, is much like the attitudes toward social classes held in England before the rise of cities, and also in France and other European countries. There are observers who think the southerner's views on social classes derived from his experience with the Negro. It is much more probable that they were brought over from England and persisted under the conditions of life in the South.

In discussing the ideologies of classes and democracy in the South and in the North, and indeed of other ideologies to be presented later, the purpose is not to present them scientifically and objectively. Rather they will be presented sympathetically with the idea of trying to show how the southerner feels toward his beliefs and what the social attitudes of the northerner mean to the city dwellers of that region. The reader should be able to see how each set of mores appears to be right and proper, even though they may be antagonistic. Also there is in this paper no particular interest in the extent to which the views are held in a region, such as might be collected from questionnaires. Instead a somewhat idealized statement will be presented, in order that the outlines may be seen more sharply.

SOCIAL CLASSES AND DEMOCRACY

The southerner never thought much about social classes because that is all he had ever known. He brought them over from eighteenth century England where they have persisted until the present, much as they have persisted in the South. The southerner took classes for granted, just as he takes the atmosphere around him for granted. It was not a matter for comment or debate. There were in the South three classes; the large upper class, a small class of poor whites, and the Negroes. The Negroes were slaves and were considered to be an inferior people. The poor whites were ignored. They were not good farmers. They didn't have much refinement. Many of them were illiterate. But a member of the upper classes seldom thought of his superiority. He had no occasion to strut; to have done so would have been bad form. The superiority of the upper class was obvious.

It never occurred to the southerner of the upper classes that he was socially responsible for the lower classes. That was their own problem. He believed in heredity and never thought that the upper classes were unjust to the lower classes.

In fact he had little idea of class; but he did of family. The families with which his family associated were really his conception of class. There was much pride in family. There were, of course, various degrees of prominence among families, as there were grades in the landed gentry of England or levels in the aristocracy of France. That one's family and their friends had standards, values, and achievements no doubt gave some sense of superiority, much as there are feelings of superiority among nations today. Thus the inhabitant of the United States has no shame in feeling that his country is better than Mexico. Family pride was somewhat like the pride one has today in his church, his club, his athletic team. There was a family stand-ard in courtesy, in skilled management, in fair dealing, in industry, in hospitality, in acquisition of the arts and learning. These the family name stood for. The family made every effort to maintain and improve its status. They brought their children up to honor the family name. If a member or rela-tive showed signs of weakening, the other members made efforts to keep him in line and not to allow dishonor to be brought on the family name. The family was the one agency of social achievement. Families of cul-ture, of education, of wealth were proud of their achievements or their standing and they wanted their children to associate with chil-dren of other families of culture, to inter-marry with them. The families one associated with were in the social class to which one belonged. The social classes were thus collec-tions of families.

The system was a stable one among land-holders in a settled agricultural society; more so than in a city where property does not remain in a family line for many generations in an age of great change.

The southerner was very appreciative of the importance of good associates. A mother knows that she does not want her boy to associate with bad boys. This idea is the same as that stressed by sociologists who speak of the influence of groups on personality. As Professor W. I. Thomas says, "A person can-not rise much above or fall much below the level of the group with whom he associates." This leads to a "consciousness of kind" so that members of one family like to associate with families of good standing. Therefore, family and class were good, matters of pride, nothing to be ashamed of.

What was the evil of such a system? Did it not maintain high levels of achievement? Did it not keep individuals from backsliding from standards? If other families did not do so well was it not their own fault, thought these self-sufficient farmers.

The southerner found it difficult to un-derstand how, in the cities of the North, the lower classes were glorified, how to be born in a log cabin or on the lower east side was something about which to boast, how the brotherhood of man meant that one's child should associate with any Tom, Dick or Harry, how a family with untrained taste in art, with no musical acquaintance, with no achievement in education, with no travel abroad could be rated on a par with a family which had these advantages. He thought it inconsistent that in northern cities superiority may be claimed for a college, a business, a city, a club, but not for a family or a social class. He found the cult of the common man and the democratic dogma, strange attitudes. The tastes of the masses were of the level of the tabloid, the wild western moving picture, the comic strip, the pulp magazine. His was a family system based on landed property in a stable agriculture with considerable belief in heredity and not much experience with the "uplift" of governments and social move-ments.

In the northern cities, a man may start life as a common laborer and wind up the head of a steel corporation. Hence one man is as good as another. If the common laborer was born in a log cabin, then the log cabin is a symbol of his achievement and hence a matter of pride. The cities are centers of opportunity. There are schools for everyone. A boy graduating from the grammar school can go to high school, which opens many opportunities, one of which is a college edu-cation. Thus class barriers are swept away. Ability rises to the top. A city family can hardly hold its wealth for several generations as landowners can do in a stable agricultural society. The factory has broken up the family system of agricultural times. The family name doesn't mean much. It is the individual that counts, not association of families. The family ceases to be the one great social institution for achievement. It is replaced by the civic organi-zation, by the government, by clubs. Civic pride replaces family pride. But above all democracy means that the lower classes are not to be held down to inferior positions by the powerful upper classes. The everlasting glory of democracy is that the poor need not remain poor but can rise in the economic and social scale. Democracy is supported by the sciences of sociology and biology which show no superiority of one race over another and which show the difference in ability of the classes to be much a matter of environment. The century of the common man does not mean so much a glorification of the standards and tastes of the lower classes, but rather a century of opportunity for the common man, freed from the obstacles of special privileges and unequal opportunities.

With the vote and the public schools and the purchasing power of high wages, the common man becomes very popular with the politicians, with the advertisers, with the newspapers, with the cartoonists, with the moving picture producers, and with the radio speakers and artists. There arises the ideology of the common man. Walt Whitman is his poet; Abraham Lincoln his political ideal. An ideology of the common man is built up resting upon freedom, equality, brotherhood, no privilege, no snobbishness, the virtue of honest toil, the rights of man, fair dealing, no distinctions of race and equal opportunity. The material values of the standard of living are praised more than spiritual assets. These virtues and values were supported by the powerful pressure of "Main Street." Democracy has all the compelling force of the powerful mores. None dare speak against it. To criticize democracy is no more permitted than to praise fascism.

From this point of view, the southerner with his poll tax disbarring the poor from voting, is an obstacle to progress. His treatment of the Negro is an indescribable injustice, as it denies to him the opportunities which democracy brings. The southerners are reactionaries who oppose the use of government to raise the lot of the common man. His pride of family and social class is seen as reactionary Bourbonism, as the entrenchment of special privilege, or it becomes the butt of ridicule. Southern aristocrats, along with moonlight and magnolias, plantations and Kentucky colonels were suitable material for the comic opera.

Thus, again we have two different and conflicting attitudes toward the social classes and democracy characteristic of the landed gentry and of the industrial cities.

FAMILY AND MARRIAGE

Attitudes toward the family are also different. In the Old South, the family was the main economic institution and the most powerful social one. It was the agency of attainment, of rising in the world, of care for dependency. As such, the family name was more important than the first name. It was the family rather than the individual. Marriage brought social status, property, membership in a social class, protection, associates for one's children. It also meant a business partnership, whose success rested on the ability of the husband as a provider and of the wife as a household manager. Thus in choosing a mate, romantic love was only one of many other factors. A young person should marry in the same class, into a good family. A marriage partner should be capable as well as good looking, and was appraised as a prospective father or mother of children.

The family being an economic institution, man and wife were business partners, with man as the head and woman a capable manager. There was a definite division of labor free of jurisdictional conflict. Divorce disorganized this economic institution. Virtue of women was a cornerstone of this type of family and there were just two types of woman, good and bad. Women's place being in the home, they were trained not only in skills, but in graces, manners, and charm to make the relationship work smoothly. Particularly were women brought up in the social graces to please men, economic heads, property owners, protectors and fighters.

In the new northern cities, young people marry as individuals, not as members of families. Family prestige means little, so great is the flux in the social scale. Family and relatives, instead of giving strength, status, and support, are troublesome and unwelcome in small city apartments where goods are all bought. Class lines are not much of an influence in marriage, for universal education and the rewards of efficiency in business mean that any individual is eligible as a marriage partner. There are not many household duties in a childless family living in a steam-heated apartment with a delicatessen store around the corner. Thus companionability and love tend to be the only factors determining the choice of mates. If a young couple love each other, they may marry, no matter what are the other conditions, and if a married couple do not love each other, to continue living together is a sin. So divorces are frequent. Women can get jobs in offices, stores, and factories. Hence they take on the attitude and practices of men. Comradeship replaces chivalry. Women are people, not just females. The family domicile is said to be a suite of rooms over a garage, a parking place for the night. Personality, happiness, companionship, and the giving of opportunities to children are the only goals of family life.

These antagonisms in the ideologies of marriage and the family of the landed gentry and of the city dwellers are illustrated by the abdication of the British throne by Edward Windsor to marry an untitled American divorcee. The royalty held to the status concept while the American point of view was that of romantic love, so adequately presented in the moving picture.

FRIENDSHIP AND ACQUAINTANCE

Among neighborly self-sufficing farmers there is little occasion for hypocrisy or pretense in personal relations. Friendship can be genuine, though there is an effort for such farmers to be friendly and neighborly, and perhaps some pretense is involved, but in a society with slow change the amenities are observed with good manners. There is, of course, dislike, even feuds, among rural families. Indeed, there are cliques of families; but these cliques are based upon choice. The right to choose one's friends or associates ranks high in the hierarchy of a southerner's values. This right of choice is a source of difficulty in the southerner's adaptation to democracy. Under the cult of the common man must he be friends with anyone? Has he no right of

choice, of preference under the dogma of the brotherhood of man? Among the self-sufficing landed gentry you like a friend for what he is, not for what you can get out of him. To "use" a friend for selfish purposes was very much condemned in the Old South. There were certainly limits to the extent to which one could impose on a friend.

This attitude toward friendship made it difficult for the southerner with his ideas of family and class to adjust to the new tools of democracy, particularly voting. The politician very quickly practices the art of exploiting personal associations and friendliness, if not friendship, in order to get votes, as for instance kissing the baby of a prospective voter for whom he has no special friendliness. Thus it was said in the Old South that a man could not be a gentleman and be in politics. A member of the landed gentry objected to "currying favor," as it was expressed. This conception of friendship is much in evidence in Sir Walter Scott's novels of social life in rural England, which were widely read in the Old South.

The southerners also found it difficult to adjust to the tools of the trader, as did also the English gentry. To the gentry the trader "curried favor" in order to increase his customers. He was ingratiating for ulterior motives. This conflict between the folkways of the trader and the landowner in England is well known.

It is not to be implied that the Old South had only beautiful friendships. The picture is idealized and not supposed to be representative. It was rather the code, and codes are not always strictly adhered to.

In cities, friendship is somewhat different. There it is surprising how many occupations depend upon the good will and friendliness of others. Thus the doctor must have patients, the lawyer, clients. The merchant needs customers and the banker depositors, whereas the independent farmer needs only to make his land produce. Consider the case with the salesman. His job is to make you buy something whether you want to or not, whether it is good for you or not. In cities, honors, rewards, and approbations go to extroverts who are popular and have the most "friends." One collects friends because they are useful. The model is the politician. The insurance salesman is another illustration.

Friendships in cities tend to become acquaintanceships. Indeed many city dwellers do not have a conception of friendship. A friend is someone who likes you well enough to let you use him. There is a reciprocity about it. You help me to get on and I will help you. Some years ago there appeared a book of great popularity called, *How to Win Friends and Influence People*. To a southerner of the old school, the title sounds iniquitous. It is immoral to influence people, except in religion and in the case of children and relatives. To influence people is to violate the sanctity of their personality, to interfere with their freedom. As to winning friends, in the old ideology, why try to win them? You have them or you do not, according to your temperament. If you are a solitary person like Thoreau, you do not need to have many friends. People who win friends are like the politician and the insurance salesman. This from the ideology of the old South.

From the ideology of the urban North, why not influence people? To sell them insurance is a good thing. If more people can be persuaded to buy automobiles, the world will be better for it. If people use you and your friendship for good purposes, then you can use them for the same reason. Thus progress is advanced. Cooperative and voluntary collective effort depends upon such "friends" in urban regions. Among independent farmers there is less need for such a pattern of friendships.

MANNERS AND MORALS

The differences in the mores of the North and the South are not always to be explained by the socio-economic system and by the heritage of tradition. Another factor is the rapidity of change. Thus in the Old South where cotton and tobacco were planted generation after generation and change was very slow, codes of behavior could be followed by each succeeding generation. Manners are codes of behavior laid out in detail to curb the selfishness and egotism in the little acts of life. Morals and law deal with more important curbs. Both morals and manners need to be learned in detail to fit any situation. Both are much easier to learn and enforce in a stationary society than in a rapidly changing one. Where there is rapid change, new sets of rules must be made to fit each succeeding change. These may be no sooner learned than they must be changed for another set.

Hence in the Old South, manners were much in evidence. Great care was taken to teach them to children. Less emphasis is placed upon manners in the cities of the North, necessarily, for there the rapidity of change following the new inventions and the waves of migrants makes it difficult to have good manners. Also the manners tend to be somewhat different. For instance, a southerner considers it bad form in making a business call to launch immediately into setting forth his proposition. First, one asks about the health of the other, the condition of his family (if he be known well), the state of general business, or even about the weather. Only after these preliminaries may one proceed to the business at hand. In the North, all the gestures are considered unnecessary, a waste of time, and inefficient. In the South, it is not good taste to appear too aggressive; for aggression is selfishness which is kept under cover by manners. In the North, aggressiveness is one of the most desired of all traits, for it spells efficiency, hustle, and success. People not schooled in manners are often confused by the niceties of speech, and have fears of making a *faux pas*. Hence manners are derided as excess baggage in favor of simplicity and directness. But the essential difference between the North and the South in manners is due to the different rates of change in the two regions.

SUCCESS AND VALUES

An outstanding difference in ideologies between these two regions, the South and the North, is in their attitudes toward success, and how much sacrifice in values one is permitted to make to attain success.

In the North success is worshipped like a god. This attitude flows from the abundance of rich rewards and the widely spread opportunities in the industrial North. These rewards come from the mass production of machinery run by mechanical power. In the twentieth century industrial regions are rich and agricultural poor, that is relatively so. The economic prizes of the factory system are much greater than those of fertile valleys. In 1820, before the era of factories, Charleston, South Carolina and New York City had about the same amount of wealth. Now the industrial states are where the wealth is. Universal education opens these opportunities to all. The race is on. Success is immeasurably desired. The plaudits are for the successful. As in the days of the Klondike gold rush the rewards are for the ruthless aggressor. The cult in the cities is efficiency, to be a "go-getter," a "live wire." The ideal for youth is to be a hustler, aggressive, "up-to-date." To be a failure is to be scorned, or to be ignored, to be passed by. Accomplishment, speed, production, efficiency, "stream lining," executive ability, aggressiveness, hustle are the particulars of these social values. Ruthlessness may be excused if it gets results. With the struggle to be first, moderation and balance cease to be valued in favor of the extreme, that is the best, first place. Boasting is not only permitted, but considered all right, even admired in the successful. Efficiency is beautiful; and the results are good, very good.

It is not surprising then that, in order to attain success, many values and virtues may be sacrificed. Thus one "uses" friends, or sacrifices friendship, recreation is neglected, health abused. Competition is of the cutthroat variety with a wreckage of neuroses following. Legislators may be bribed, and shady deals pulled off. The word "honor" disappears from usage. "Currying favor" of those who can help is common practice. The temptation is very great to forget the Ten Commandments and the Sermon on the Mount. It is as though in the ranking values success is at the top. But the ends justify the means. Think of the opportunities for doing good which come to the successful. Colleges may be endowed, cancer institutes supported, and art galleries set up. Then, too, most success is in doing something eminently worthwhile, as Henry Ford did in supplying tractors to farmers. So success becomes part of the new mores.

In the Old South of agricultural landowners, there were other values more important than success. Among the values a youngster learned at his mother's knee, the word "success" was seldom mentioned. A lad was urged to be good, noble, a man of honor, to keep his word, and to be a gentleman. To be a "Christian gentleman" was the ideal. Of course, everyone wants to be a success, that is they do not want to be a failure. But in an agricultural society of landowners, great and spectacular successes were rare. Property was fairly stable from one generation to another, and a prominent family might remain so for several generations. So success was desired but not extravagantly. If a person was trustworthy, reliable, truthful, considerate, lived up to his promises, respected women, did not boast, fought for the right, he was a success. So success was not a particularly important word in the lexicon. Above all one must not stoop to succeed.

Even leisure, a good time, horse racing, shooting quail, and the social amenities were not to be sacrificed in order to get rich. A leisurely social life with its pleasures and associations were values not to be put aside in a mad pursuit of wealth.

Then, too, it was not good, definitely not good, to love money too much. There was a contempt or ostracism of those who chased the "almighty dollar" too eagerly. To say of a man, "He will do anything for money" was an insult. To be stingy with money was the sign of littleness, of narrowness. On the other hand, generosity was praised. One said with pride, "This is something money cannot buy." To offer money for anything other than very standard materials, such as real estate, dry-goods, etc., or for other than standard services, such as a shopkeeper's supplies, was very likely to give offense. It was quite definitely necessary to warn the young against too much love of the "filthy lucre." Indeed, it was all right for a gentleman to have a contempt for money. A family without much money, if they had a good name, possessed the social requisites, and exercised the virtues, would be much more esteemed socially, than a very wealthy, newly-rich family without the proper tastes and manners.

The insistence on standards of goodness, character, and honor are found wherever a stable society exists, even among the primitive peoples. The lack of appreciation of success is correlated with a status and a stationary society, especially one where family standing and landed property are inherited. The attitude of hostility toward money is that of a self-sufficient farming society where money is little known and used only for a limited number of purchases. Money symbolized a strange, new economy in which riches were deified, and it was felt as a hostile intrusion into the scheme of values of the landed gentry.

These southerners who followed other values than success were viewed by the efficiency devotees of the North as lazy, pleasure loving, unprogressive, and inefficient. How could a southerner sit on his front porch contentedly drinking his mint julep negligent of the rich rewards of progress? His balanced life of moderation was measured against the single-minded pursuit of the extreme success, and was judged wanting. Thus in the scale of values in the social systems of the South and of the North, success was differently emphasized and the price to be paid for it was differently estimated.

CONCLUSION

A selected list of ideologies of the Old South and the urban North have been described and found to be different. Neither region appreciates the social values of the other. In general those of the South came from rural England of earlier centuries, and were products of an agricultural society not changing very rapidly. Though agricultural they spread over the towns and villages and somewhat to the cities. On the other hand, the ideologies of the North arose from industrial cities, changing rapidly, with great wealth, and a shifting population.

In the stream of social change cities are spreading, factories are coming to the South, and with them the ideologies of the North. At the same time the ideologies of the landed gentry are receding. Thus in the South the mores are in transition. There is conflict and confusion. The future will be clarified somewhat by recognizing the economic origins of these ideologies and why they have come about.

But the correlation of the mores and the socio-economic system is not perfect. The economic system is an important factor in determining some mores, but it is not the sole determinant. Otherwise the ideologies of English, German, and American industrial cities would be the same; and those of the landed gentry in France, England, and the United States would be all alike. But they are not. The existing tradition in any region forces some adjustment of the ideologies of the machine when it is imported. This adaptation comes about through choice, which rests on the attitudes of the people.

This is illustrated by a question I once asked a fencing instructor, an elderly man from France. Realizing that occupations often determine attitudes, I said to him, "I suppose you regret the passing of the duel?" "Well," he said, "isn't it rather disgusting to have your intimate affairs mulled over by the courts and their hanger-on lawyers, and to have your personal affairs spread before the populace in the pages of the yellow journals? Wouldn't it be better to settle them other ways?" Each group of mores has its own values, if we can only see them. It does not behoove a person of broad mind and education to fail to understand that the mores of other peoples and of other times have their good points. Intolerance toward the mores of other peoples shows a narrowness of outlook. The northern cities are centers of dispersal for the new conquering mores that are spreading over the land. But their missionaries show a narrowness of understanding and an intolerance of the ideologies of other regions. And in the South some of the sectional patriots are equally narrow and lacking in understanding of these new social attitudes and values that are being rapidly adopted.

The new ideologies of the democratic industrial cities will be modified somewhat as they spread to the South, adapted to the southern tradition. Here is where the choice of the southern people comes in. In the countries that had the duel among the gentry—England, France, and Germany—the daily newspapers publish very little of the intimate affairs of the people and scandals, much less than the press in the United States, where the duel never flourished, though dueling in its absence may not be the sole explanation. The ideologies of the South are in transition, the problem of the southerners is to preserve the best of the old values and to select from the virtues of the new. But there is not complete freedom of will, for the socio-economic systems are powerful forces in affecting ideologies. It is the old problem of free will and determinism.

We now move from the area of broad generalizations to the description of a small community, in which the social forces described by Odum and Ogburn can be seen at work.

In the 1940's, social scientists in the Division of Farm Population and Rural Welfare of the U. S. Department of Agriculture decided to study the reasons for stability and instability in American rural communities. They chose six places which were experiencing different degrees of change and observed the daily life in each for a period of several months. Studies were issued for Landaff, N. H., El Cerrito, N. M., Irwin, Iowa, Sublette, Kans., a Pennsylvania Amish community, and Harmony—a Georgia plantation community. It is from the last study that the next selection has been taken. The stress placed upon the social value system affords a key to understanding much about the social structure of any group. Some of these intangibles, or mentifacts, were explained in the preceding selection.

In the heart of the old plantation belt, which stretches across central Georgia from South Carolina to Alabama, is situated Putnam County. The little community of Harmony, in the northeast part of Putnam County, is composed of approximately 70 families—20 white and 50 Negro. The community extends for about five miles in all directions from its center, at which are located the schools and churches of both the whites and the Negroes. The residences of the white families are scattered, usually about a mile from each other, and near each of them usually live several Negro families.

Harmony is, in truth, two communities with little in common except the understanding that keeps each group to itself and the economic interdependence that requires each to cooperate continuously with the other. Sociologists term a situation of this sort a biracial adjustment, and the community of Harmony provides a good example of its actual functioning. In both communities changes that were set in motion originally by the onslaughts of the boll weevil are being hastened by the pressures of encroaching unbanization and industrialization. As the economy shifts from cotton-growing to dairy farming, the work habits, social relationships, and community structure assume different patterns.

Gradually the details of the biracial adjustment will change, but there is little doubt that it will continue to exist for many years to come.

• 45 • *The Community Pattern: Harmony, Georgia*

WALLER WYNNE

THE COMMUNITY

In the days before the boll weevil, Harmony Community had twice the population it has now, and then its institutions were larger and more numerous. Today, there remains an elementary school and a church for white people; an all-grade school, a church, and a Masonic Lodge for Negroes. Owing to the small number of white children, the community has had difficulty in holding its white school. In fact, the school was closed for several years, and was only recently reopened.

Formerly, the community had some trade services of its own, but now it is entirely dependent upon nearby towns, principally upon Eatonton, the county seat, which is about 8 miles away. To some extent, Madison, the county seat of Morgan County, which adjoins Harmony on the north, serves for trading purposes, and occasionally farmers go about 50 miles to Macon or Athens, the largest cities nearest to the community.

Although the relationship between Harmony and Eatonton primarily relates to trade, there is some social intercourse between residents of the two places, usually in the form of occasional visits between relatives or close friends. White children of Harmony attend high school in Eatonton, one farmer sometimes attends church there, and several farmers hold membership in a county-wide farm organization that meets at the county seat, but with these exceptions, Harmony folk do not participate in the social and institutional life of the town. Though dependent upon Eatonton for certain services, farm families do not thereby identify themselves with the townspeople.

The typical Harmony family is a highly cooperative unit, and all members of it except the very young contribute to the business of making a living on the farm. The woman's part varies, as between white and Negro families. Generally, white women do only the lighter outdoor tasks such as gardening and caring for poultry but sometimes, usually in emergencies, they help with the milking. Among owner-operators, women almost never do field work; class traditions are against it and the economic status of the family does not require it. Women in white tenant families do not work in the field as a general rule. Negro women, on the other hand, usually work in the field.

Women of the community feel strongly that they should help their husbands earn the family living and they proceed to do it. The wife of one owner said, "I have always thought that a wife should help out all she can, and I have kept some chickens ever since we were married." She contributes to the family income by selling poultry and produce.

Family ties among both white and Negro families are strong. Children leave home but their interest in members of their family and their concern for their family's welfare do not perceptibly diminish. Children who live relatively close to their parents visit them rather often; those who live at a distance come less often but usually come at least once a year if circumstances permit.

Children's interest in their parents includes a willingness to help with their sup-

[From *Culture of a Contemporary Rural Community: Harmony, Georgia,* Rural Life Studies, No. 6, Bureau of Agricultural Economics, U. S. Department of Agriculture, Washington, D. C., 1943. Pp. 37-43, 45-51.]

port although among white families only a few, if any, are really in need of assistance. A daughter of one white farmer on numerous occasions has asked her father, whose health is very poor, to give up dairying, saying that she could and would provide for him.

Negro children also are willing to help support their parents. One farmer's children have time and again urged him to give up farming because his health is poor. The earnings of this farmer's children, all but one of whom live in distant cities, are considerably above the average of most Negro sons and daughters in the community. Most Negro children, although willing, cannot contribute to the support of their parents. As a general rule, indigent Negroes are dependent upon public relief.

The strength of ties between closely related families is generally strong, especially between white families. But dissension between closely related families is not uncommon, and it sometimes greatly weakens the tie between them. On occasions, however, when some situation arises that calls for the united strength of the unfriendly families, differences are forgotten and the families stand as one.

Among white residents, Harmony Baptist Church is by far the most important institution in the community next to the family, and most families are members of it. A few of the families are Methodists, belonging to a church in an adjoining community, but they sometimes attend the local Baptist church.

People of Harmony are proud of this church which dates from 1828. The present wooden building was constructed in 1927 after a fire had destroyed the original building. Only a small amount of insurance had been carried, but former residents contributed generously to the rebuilding.

Church services are held one Sunday each month and revival services are held during 1 week each year. For many years the church has been unable to pay for the services of a trained preacher.

Those who had been accustomed to a trained preacher have felt keenly the need for such a person. The present pastor, who lives a considerable distance away, is present in the community only on the day he preaches. One person remarked of the services, "I listen very attentively but I think the while whether I can live through it." Some persons gave the lack of money as the reason the church does not have the type of preacher the members want; the preacher receives $10 each Sunday he preaches. On the other hand, another said that though the people have pride in their church, they are not willing to make the personal sacrifices that would enable them to pay a more highly trained man.

On the Sunday that services are held, the preacher arrives a few minutes before the hour of beginning. He leaves the community shortly after dinner, which he has in the home of one of the church members. The privilege of having the preacher to dinner is not sought after as it was in past years. One woman recalled that formerly a preacher "had to be triplets" to accept his many invitations to dinner. Nowadays the church has to have a committee whose duty it is to find a family that will ask him to dinner. The committee's task is often difficult, for members do not hesitate to say "no" to their request.

The church has three organizations: a Sunday School, a Young People's Union recently organized (1940), and a Woman's Missionary Union. The Sunday School and Young People's group meet every Sunday— the former before church and the latter at night—and both are attended by persons of all ages. The maximum attendance at either is about 40 persons. Sometimes during the winter when the weather is very wet and the roads are almost impassable, the Sunday School sessions are discontinued for a while.

The Woman's Missionary Union has few members. It is held together primarily by one woman, who has worked hard to keep the organization going. The local Union had its beginning in 1882, just 2 years prior to that of the State Union. The group meets once a month at the home of a member.

Most people are agreed that the church does not have the same hold on the people that it had in years past, and members do not attend church so often as they once did. Several explanations were given for the decline in attendance. One was that people are less religious today, though no one could explain why. The automobile was "blamed" by some: "People go riding instead of going to church." One farmer whose family does not go regularly said that he could not afford to dress as his neighbors do and that he was embarrassed to have people stare at him; another indicated that social differences kept him and his wife at home, though their children attended Sunday School rather regularly; one was critical of the gospel taught at the local church; several said they did not go as often as they should but they could give no reasons.

Among the colored residents the church—Jefferson Baptist Church, the only Negro church in the community—stands first among the formal institutions in the community. Almost all the Negroes join the church at the appropriate age. Some lose their membership through behavior the church does not countenance, because of playing cards for instance, but generally they are readmitted to membership when the Board of Deacons, the governing body of the church, becomes convinced that they have reformed their ways. As proof, the individual must describe the experience by which he regained his faith.

Preaching services for the colored people are held one Sunday in every month, prayer meetings are held every Saturday, and Sunday School services every Sunday. Members are required to attend church regularly. If one is absent he must later give a reason, and if he is absent on three consecutive Sundays he is deprived of his membership unless he offers an acceptable reason. Prayer meetings are generally attended only by adults and the older children, but all members of the family go to Sunday School. In addition to its usual services, the church holds, every August, a week of prayer meetings followed by a week of preaching. These events highlight the church year. On the Sunday that closes the 2 weeks of prayer and preaching, people are present from far and wide. These are persons who were born in the community but who have left it to live in other counties, in nearby States, and in distant cities—Chicago, Detroit, New York, and others. Their children who were born outside the community and have never lived there, come too. The old residents have retained membership in the burial society of the church in order to be buried in the churchyard of the community where they were born.

Negroes too are not so interested in their church as they were 50 years ago, according to the Chairman of the Board of Deacons. Then, "folks took a great interest in their church and attended with more regularity than now. They would talk about what the preacher had to say. Nowadays folks can't tell you on Monday what the preacher's text was on the day before." By way of explaining the change he said: "Folks are more sinful than they used to be." He explained this as part of God's plan. "He has a purpose even though we can't understand it." As evidence that folks are more sinful now than in the past, he stated that not so many members take communion now as in the past. According to that church's doctrine, only members without sin may observe the communion rite.

This man was critical of some things in his people's religion, saying: "I don't want the preacher to tell me about what I am going to do when I get to Heaven—if I do. I don't care about hearing about the golden slippers and the great wings I'll wear. I want to know what I have to do here on earth to get to Heaven. If I am saved, I think the Lord will tell me what to do when I get there. I don't worry about that. Getting happy and cutting up ain't religion to my way of thinking."

The Harmony Community is served by two schools—one for white children and one for colored. The school for whites is a one-teacher elementary school and has an enrollment of only 11 pupils, 3 of whom live in another community. The teacher does not live here. Harmony children who are of high-school age attend the nearest high school, at Eatonton. They are transported to town by bus at the county's expense, but transportation is not provided for children of grade-school age.

The enrollment at Harmony school has not always been so small. Years ago there were enough pupils to require four teachers, one of them a music teacher. The Harmony school then, older residents declared, was as fine as any in the county.

Residents of the community would consider the loss of the school a calamity to the community. "When you take the school away you kill the neighborhood." "When you take the school out of the community, the community goes to pieces."

A community without a school finds it difficult to attract new residents. "The first thing a man wants to know when he rents a place is how near the school is. Folks don't want to move into a community that does not have a school. The same thing is true of the church." This statement is typical of the feeling most people have about the school. Furthermore, the loss of the school frequently means the loss of residents who want their children to have all the school advantages possible.

Opinion was divided on the question of whether schools should be consolidated. Some people hold that "the consolidated school is wrong. It tears down one community to build up another." Such people do not think that the consolidated school offers children a better education or that it is cheaper to operate since the county must provide transportation. Some people, on the other hand, hold that the consolidated school is a fine thing. "I wouldn't send my children to a country school. You have to do justice to children. I took my children out of Harmony school and sent them to Eatonton so they could have a good education. I wouldn't send my children to a teacher that didn't have an A.B. degree." Sampling further: "The consolidated school is progress and it isn't. Children get a better education at the consolidated school but it educates them away from the farm. But if I had children, I would want them to attend." This person recognized what the loss of the school means to the community, declaring: "When you take away the church and school you take the heart out of the community."

Virtually all of the people of Harmony believe strongly that children should have the best schooling possible. The number of boys and girls sent to college is ample evidence of that fact. The ideal situation, in the opinion of nearly all, would be to have good schools in every community, but if that is not possible, then good schools somewhere near—even though the community suffers through the loss of its own school.

The school for colored children combines elementary and high-school subjects. Most of the children are enrolled, and most of them attend regularly. Among the Negro families interviewed, all want their children to have as good schooling as the community affords, but there was not the strong feeling relative to the importance of the school in the community as was found among white residents.

There are no farm organizations in the Harmony Community, and there is only one in the entire county—The Putnam County Farm Board. Only two residents of the community are members of it. Other residents have been invited to become members on several occasions but they have declined because they are unable, for one reason or another, to take a regular part in its activities.

The Putnam County Farm Board is a nonpolitical organization of white farmers and businessmen who have as their goal the improvement of agricultural conditions in the county. Virtually every phase of the farming life of the county is of interest to the Board: Terracing, subsoiling, growing of legumes, planting fruit trees, permanent pastures and pasture improvement, stock improvement, high-producing sires for dairy herds, cow testing, home raising of feed, one-variety cotton planting, etc. Although the Harmony Community has but little representation on the Putnam County Farm Board, residents are highly sympathetic with its objectives.

There is only one cooperative in the county—The Eatonton Cooperative Creamery. It is a mutual, nonprofit, cooperative, processing, purchasing and marketing association, which began operation in 1932. The creamery sells most of its milk—whole milk —on the Atlanta market. Most of the dairymen in the Harmony Community have their milk delivered to the creamery by trucks operated by individuals, as the creamery does not have its own trucks.

This creamery represents the most recent effort of dairymen in the county to operate a cooperative creamery successfully. The first attempt was made in 1909. This cooperative creamery failed through mismanagement, it is said, and a second was organized in 1911. Dissatisfaction with regulations governing the operation of dairies and the inability of farmers to produce an adequate supply of milk caused this one to fail. Several other attempts between 1911 and 1932 were made but these were also unsuccessful.

When the present cooperative was projected, most dairymen in the community gave it immediate support despite the failure of earlier cooperatives. They think that some organization is necessary if dairying is to be profitable. One dairyman said: "After the last cooperative failed, I said I would never sign again. But I did."

PATTERNS OF INFORMAL ASSOCIATION

Informal cooperation is not now, and never has been, a characteristic of either owners or tenants, whites or Negroes. Exchanging labor, farm tools, and machinery is the exception rather than the rule. This is probably explained by the fact that the plantation system of farming, which existed until fairly recent times, did not require cooperation among farmers, for it was highly self-contained with respect to labor and equipment.

But although farmers do not cooperate with one another in carrying on farming activities, they do rally as they have always done, to the aid of one another in times of stress or disaster. Thus, if sickness strikes, neighbors readily lend a willing hand; if a crop is damaged and replanting is necessary,

they are ready with equipment and teams and labor if the unfortunate farmer cannot cope with the situation alone.

The pattern of visiting within Harmony Community today contrasts sharply with that of 20 years ago. Then people—both white and colored—visited more often than now. The decrease in the frequency of visiting was attributed partly to a decline in the interest of neighbor in neighbor, but more to "changes of the times." Among white residents, the character of visiting has changed, also. For example, among white residents and to some extent among Negroes, the practice of paying a brief call while on the way to or from town in their automobiles has supplanted the more formal visits, or brief conversations at the trade center on Saturdays permit an exchange of information and so it does not seem necessary to visit each other in the homes. Most people agreed that automobiles have been a principal reason for less visiting. Whereas residents formerly went visiting on Sunday, they now go riding. "It's no use to visit on Sunday because you never find anyone home. They are all out riding," was a typical statement. But several persons said they are always at home on Sunday, especially for the sake of their children who find that day most convenient for visiting. Then a majority of the adult residents are well advanced in age and are not able to go around much.

In the past, white owner families frequently entertained guests, who, without previous invitation, would spend the entire day. Now to visit unannounced is to visit without being welcome although very close friends and relatives are generally welcome at almost any time. The decrease in all-day unplanned visiting was attributed to the fact that families do not have so many servants as they once had and therefore are not prepared to entertain friends on a moment's notice. Only one interviewed family employed more than one servant, and only a few families had even one servant regularly for most families cannot now pay the relatively high wages that servants demand. Spend-the-day guests today are generally persons not from the community but from places rather far away who arrange for the visit in advance.

Many people of both races expressed regret that there is now so little visiting, and acknowledged that they feel the loss of the companionship of friends but several said they were glad there is not much visiting as it tires them.

Commercialized amusement among Negroes is limited to an occasional moving picture in Eatonton. Although children attend more frequently than do their parents they do not go often because of the expense. Only one Negro—an owner—had a radio, but most of the colored people would like to own sets.

School, when it is in session, provides some recreation for the Negro children, and sometimes their parents attend the baseball and basketball games and other activities engaged in by their children.

* * *

LEADERSHIP

There is no well-defined pattern of leadership in the Harmony Community. In fact, there is virtually no leadership in the community as a whole, nor among either race. White members of the community are highly individualistic, have opinions of their own, and are inclined to independent action. At the same time, there are evidences of an informal leadership. That is to say, farmers, though they do not recognize an active leadership in the community and apparently think and act independently, are to some extent guided by the opinions and actions of several individuals who are held in high regard by them. In the whole community there is probably not more than one individual who could command the support of the entire community and behind whom the community would unite solidly.

The Negroes of the community are equally without leadership. Until a few years ago, however, there was one man—an owner—who was acknowledged by all as their leader. Since his death, they have not had, and do not now have, a leader, according to the statements of those interviewed. Closest to being a leader

among his people is the sole owner in the community. He occupies a high place in the Negro lodge and church and is held in high esteem by the colored people of the community and by whites as well. In a situation requiring leadership the Negroes of the community would unquestionably follow him.

YOUTH IN THE COMMUNITY

Among the white families there are only a few young people and there are not more than five single persons between the ages of 16 and 30 years. To appreciate the situation with respect to youth, it is necessary to understand that nearly all children that were born to persons now 50 or more years of age have migrated to the city. Of the few who have remained, only three are farming; the others work in towns or at non-farm occupations.

Most of the children who have migrated had some education beyond high school; many of them had a 4-year college course. Though many of them would probably not have followed farming in any event, all were virtually forced to leave the community because of the lack of opportunities there. The children who left are reported to have been rather successful; one or two have returned to the community, but not for economic reasons.

There are less than 20 white children who are younger than 16 years of age, all of them members of five families.

Among the Negro families there are a good many young people. Many have migrated to urban centers but some of them, particularly the younger ones, have remained in Harmony and have reared children.

Among these youth the most critical problem is the question of economic opportunity. The trend in farm enterprise in Putnam County is away from cotton and toward dairying, but the cultivation of cotton is the one base on which Negro youth can establish themselves as farmers here. The capital requirements for setting up a dairy farm are not within their means, nor, for that matter, within the means of white youth. Several relatively young men who are now establishing, or planning to establish, themselves as dairymen have not acquired capital from their parents nor through farming but have accumulated it over several years by day labor in industrial plants. The colored boys may not hope to do this because industrial opportunity is lacking; furthermore, successful dairying requires experience that they do not have. Cotton farming, on the other hand, requires relatively little capital, and the colored people have been trained in the methods of cotton cultivation from early childhood. Cotton is the one base on which the Negro youth could establish himself as a farmer but his chance to use it is small because of the limited acreage in cotton.

Moral standards among Negro youth in the community are apparently higher than they have ever been before. Vice and delinquency and crime are so infrequent as to be minor problems, if even that. There is practically no gambling. The shooting scrapes, very common in the past, are virtually unknown.

VALUE SYSTEM AND ITS SUPPORTING SANCTIONS AND ATTITUDES

Whatever disadvantages farming may have, farmers of the Harmony Community are almost unanimous in agreeing that such disadvantages are more than offset by the advantages attached to farming and that farming yields them a highly satisfactory way of life. This is equally true of both white and Negro farmers.

Among white farmers two of the most important values that attach to farming as a way of life are: (1) economic security and (2) freedom to manage their own affairs. A farmer may not have any or all of the "luxuries" he would like but "he can always make a living"—enough to eat. Self-sufficiency in that respect is a cardinal principle with every farmer. Each cherishes the freedom to manage his own farm according to his own way. "I am my own boss," is a typical statement.

Security and freedom are not the sole values farmers find in farming. They find enjoyment in it. Planting and cultivating and harvesting crops requires hard work; the milking of cows means confining labor. But they yield satisfaction: a good stand of a crop, a fine cow—in those things the farmer finds pleasure and most of the families take pleasure in well-kept yards with flowers and shrubs.

Among Negro farmers, the owner enjoys the same economic security and freedom as the white owners. The renters are their own bosses within obvious limitations, but the croppers have the status of wage hands, despite the fact that they have a share in the crop, and are no more their own masters than are employees of industry. Although neither the renters nor the sharecroppers among the Negroes may be said to have economic security, each does find a certain security in the self-sufficiency he practices. Almost all of these renters produce their own food. In contrast with some parts of the South where croppers are denied the chance to produce their own sustenance, croppers in the Harmony Community are encouraged by their landlords to be self-sufficient.

Although Negro farmers do not value security and freedom of action particularly, they do find satisfaction in farming and attach great value to it. "My glory is turning the earth," one Negro renter said. "I loves to farm, especially when I is encouraged. When my crops come up I got to be in the field day and night seeing 'bout 'em. I likes to see pretty fields all green." Many Negro families take pleasure in having a variety of flowers and potted plants.

The farmers admit certain disadvantages in rural life, but not so many as in the past, and they are not a serious drawback to his enjoyment of farm life. In earlier times the farm families felt keenly their isolation from the outside world. Now they feel this less, or hardly at all. Automobiles, radio sets, daily newspapers, and (just recently when a new system was installed) telephones—all have virtually erased any sense of isolation. "We don't seem so far away from things, with a car. We don't go to town very often, but it's good to know that you can go when you want to. You feel more in touch with the world when you have an automobile," one owner said. From another: "Most of the advantages of the city I can enjoy if I want to. I have an automobile and if I want to see a show or a football game I have but to climb in it."

The lack of many of the conveniences found in city homes is one of the disadvantages of rural life, but farm homes now have some of these conveniences—mechanical refrigerators, for example—and now that electricity is being brought into the community, farmers may be able to have the same electrical contrivances that their city friends have.

Despite the disadvantages of rural life—which are less for the white farm families than for the colored—few would exchange it for life in the cities. Almost without exception the farmers said that if they had the chance to live their lives again they would select farming as their way of life.

Prominent among the basic "virtues" held in high regard by the farmers is hard work. Most of them have always worked hard. Long hours—from light until dark—were customary. "I used to eat my breakfast at the plow so I could be ready to work when it was light enough. And we worked until you couldn't see. I worked hard." "I was always in the field before it was light and stayed there—except for dinner—until I could hardly see a step ahead of me." These statements are typical.

Not many farmers now work so hard as they did formerly, usually because they are not physically able to work long hours. "People don't work as hard as they used to," one farmer said, and that opinion was expressed by every farmer—white and Negro—without exception.

Farmers expressed a variety of opinions as to why people do not work as hard as they once did. One farmer believed that "the automobile and the fact that there are more things to keep people out late at night" were important reasons, but beyond that he was not sure about the explanation. Another said: "With the automobile people can get about more and they want to see something of the world. They are not content simply to stay home and do nothing but work." One owner

remarked that "some people are afraid they will dirty their hands. I am not ashamed to work and get myself dirty. No one need be ashamed of any work that is honest." One farmer said that people don't work hard any more because they have no wish to get ahead. The opinion most generally expressed, however, was that people are not inclined to work hard because they know that the Government will provide for them. But whatever the explanation, all the farmers agreed that the day of hard work from dawn until dark is past. The laborer has breakfast at home and the sun is high before he enters the field; nor can the owner "push" him without running the risk of having him leave. When the sun sets the laborer wants to be not in the field but at the barn.

Farmers are not so thrifty as they were in earlier years, according to general opinion. But even when thrifty, these families were never ones to deny themselves the things that made for as satisfactory and as complete a life as possible, they say. The planter's tradition of a luxurious life was too strong. Not all of the farmers have the planter background, but the philosophy of the planter has conditioned the life of the people to a considerable degree. Thought must be given to the future, but at the same time one must live today. Most farmers have followed and still follow that philosophy. "Money is made round so it will roll," one owner said; one should not squander money, he thought, but one should enjoy life, and therefore he had "never been one to save everything." He had recently bought a new automobile: "I could have made out with the old one, but there is real enjoyment in a new car, and I decided to buy one." Another owner said: "A man ought to save something, but he should also enjoy life. I figure how to save a penny but I don't deny myself a good time."

According to some people, there has been a marked decline in the habit of saving among these farmers. "Some wear silk that should wear cotton," one owner said. He thought that easy credit had encouraged people to spend freely and to save little. Another owner believed that people save less now than formerly because they have been encouraged to want more things. He thought, too, that the "various Government programs have encouraged people to spend." This opinion was the one most often given to explain why people are less thrifty now than formerly, but a few thought that "trying to keep up with the other fellow" has been one cause of the changing situation.

These opinions were those of white farmers who were thinking primarily in terms of white people—mostly those living in their own community, but also others within the range of their experience. But the colored people were not entirely excluded from these opinions. Few Negroes, however, have anything to save; most of them are marginal farmers, including renters who own their work stock and equipment. But even among the very few who could save something, however small, there is less inclination to do so now than formerly, according to general opinion. One Negro farmer accumulated more than $1,000 (and later lost it in a bank failure) but he is a rare exception.

Opinions among both white and Negro farmers varied as to the comparative honesty of people now and in the past. Some thought that people are as honest now as they ever were—perhaps, even more so; others, and they were somewhat in a majority, thought that people, generally speaking, are less honest than they used to be. For the most part, opinions on this subject were mainly based on feeling, sometimes on hearsay or circumstantial evidence, and only rarely on actual evidence of dishonest practices.

One of the most common bases for holding that the sense of personal honesty has declined is found in connection with the operation of Government programs. The charge was often made that some farmers, by falsifying figures, were able to obtain larger allotments than those to which they were entitled. Some charged that persons in Harmony are receiving work or relief benefits which they have obtained by misrepresenting their need. Others pointed to resettlement clients of the Farm Security Administration, charging that some of them accumulate large debts without any intention of repaying them.

Why people are less honest, farmers did not know. Some thought them more greedy than formerly and that this had led them to be dishonest. But the reason why people are more greedy could not be explained.

Success at farming, informants hold, requires that a farmer not only work hard but that he do his work when it should be done. To neglect plowing a field when the ground is right in order to have some certain pleasure is sure to lead to failure. Farmers have little respect for the man who neglects his work. They do not tolerate tenants who are not steady workers. The tenant is free from Saturday noon to Monday morning, but on other days he must be on the job. Farm owners are themselves steady workers; owing to age and declining physical strength a few are not capable of strenuous work for long hours day after day, but they work to their practicable limits.

White owners in the Harmony neighborhood are highly self-reliant. The success they have achieved has been through their own efforts and by dependence upon themselves. They solve their own problems and they seldom seek advice. Among Negro farmers, the cropper is dependent upon his landlord, and practically every decision with reference to farming is made for him. Renters, on the other hand, have to rely largely upon themselves. Even those renters whom the landlords "furnish" are on their own in the operation of their farms. As a general rule, renters seldom seek the advice of their neighbors.

A debt is a matter of honor among these farmers. The ravages of the boll weevil left many in debt, but instead of going into bankruptcy as they might have done, they declined to take that course and eventually paid all their obligations.

"Credit is a good thing, but some abuse it," one farmer said, and his statement is typical of these farmers' attitudes toward going in debt. Indebtedness incurred for a tractor or other farming equipment in order to carry on efficient farm enterprises is considered a perfectly legitimate use of credit, but to buy on credit goods that are not absolutely necessary—household goods, for example—is not considered an appropriate use of credit if the farmer is incurring a debt beyond his capacity to pay. The general practice is to use credit as little as possible.

Negro farmers, in contrast with their white neighbors, have very limited credit facilities and so are unable to incur any considerable debts. Generally speaking, their debts do not extend beyond those incurred for feed and seed loans, for rent, and for "furnish" supplied them. According to their white neighbors, most of them consider indebtedness a solemn obligation and make an honest effort to repay it.

Holding to the attitude that personal indebtedness should be consistent with sound farm business management and should not be incurred for non-essentials for which the individual cannot pay, farmers disapprove of the Nation's large indebtedness, and especially because they think much of the national debt represents wasteful expenditures. Generally speaking, most of them have taken the position that there is nothing they can do about the matter and so it is not for them to be concerned about it. "It's the Government that's doing the borrowing and spending, and if they want to waste it, there's nothing I can do about it. My protest doesn't count for anything."

The folkways of the Harmony people are strong, particularly in biracial relationships.

Long-established patterns of right and wrong behavior operate smoothly to control the individual in the interest of the group as a whole and of the dominant white group in particular. The local church is not an important force in social control among the white group, but among the Negro group it is. The possibility of legal penalties as a form of social control is ever present, but so strong is established behavior in the community that they are seldom invoked.

In biracial relationships the patterns of behavior to which Negro and white adhere in the community are essentially those that prevail in other communities of the cotton-growing South. In the realm of customary behavior, the Negroes, for example, address all white adult persons as Mr. or Mrs., or by some title indicative of superior status, as "boss man." Failure to observe this custom would classify a Negro as "uppity," and he would eventually be forced to move from the neighborhood because no farmer would hire him. On the other hand, custom dictates that a white person shall not address a Negro as Mr. or Mrs., and that white and colored people must not shake hands.

Social gatherings of whites and Negroes together are strictly taboo although there are some mixed-group contacts. On special occasions, whites attend functions and funerals at the Negro church. Negroes never attend functions at the white church, but their attendance at funerals of white persons is not uncommon.

In the Old South, society was stratified on lines of class and caste, and this stratification was accepted and firmly fixed. But how have events since the Civil War dealt with this class structure? Has it been revived and maintained on the old lines or has the New South become structured in an entirely different way? In the social scheme of the Old South, the institution of the family was dominant and we have already seen in previous selections how such diverse phases of life as politics, religion, and cotton growing reflected the central position of the Southern family. Has this dominance continued through the years, surviving the upheavals of war and Reconstruction?

For answers to these questions we turn to a book by Francis B. Simkins which traces events in the South from 1820 to the present, emphasizing both the changes that have taken place and the continuity that has persisted from the past.

• 46 • Social Class and the Family in the New South

FRANCIS B. SIMKINS

The most important development in Southern society after the Civil War was the shift of control from the agricultural aristocracy to men of industry and commerce. Earlier chapters described how the Civil War smashed the power of the great landowners and how that struggle was followed by the economic rise of merchants, bankers, and industrialists. The storekeeper assumed the position held by the planter, and Bourbon political leaders, despite their fine manners and old-fashioned oratory, were modern enough to heed the demands of business men, the actual masters of the counties and states they represented. Just as the enterprising citizen of the Old South aspired to become a planter with slaves and broad acres, his counterpart in the New South was eager to become a wealthy business man with holdings in town property and mortgages on farm lands. He knew that the continued pursuit of farming involved low prices and probable economic ruin, while a mercantile career might lead to material success.

This contrast explains the growth of commercial and industrial towns, and also the immense popularity of the New South movement with financial ambitions similar to those of the contemporary North. . . .

Most of the agrarian aristocracy that survived this change was shabby. . . .

The fortunate few who were able to adjust themselves to the post-bellum system of labor and land tenure still retained the old style. However, the majority of the former planter class took one of three possible courses: an escape into storekeeping, law, politics, or other non-agricultural occupations; like the characters in Ellen Glasgow's novels, the maintenance of old ideals, outward appearance, and the traditional way of life through rigid economy and heroic pretense, continuing to enjoy the fine old silver and furniture amid austere surroundings devoid of modern conveniences and luxuries; or adjustment to the ruins in the manner of William Faulkner's characters. Scattered over the South were hundreds of crumbling mansions, victims of the decay that had set in during Reconstruction, and inhabited by the discouraged descendants of once lordly planters. Roofs leaked, plastering sagged, porches rotted. . . .

Despite these harsh realities, the attitude of the agrarian aristocracy of the Old South continued to be a living part of Southern tradition, not only for the 35 years after 1865 but for the twentieth century as well. A war that destroyed most of the old regime at the same time attached so much tragic grandeur to it that this era could not be forgotten. Although the Old South would never reappear after the Civil War, it could still be dreamed about and imitated. . . .

The frustration of living on poverty-blighted lands was offset by proud boasts of relationship with departed leaders of the old days. Ancestor hunting became a vital part of the Southern social strategy. . . .

The survival of social ideals of the Old South prevented the new ruling classes from attaining a prestige equal to that enjoyed by the plantation aristocracy. Merchant, banker, and industrial groups of the New South won economic power without achieving that social

[Reprinted from The South Old and New: A History, 1820-1947, by F. B. Simkins, by permission of Alfred A. Knopf, Inc. Copyright 1947 by Alfred A. Knopf, Inc., New York. Pp. 283-295.]

dominance which America in all areas out-side the South accorded to business leaders. The spirit of community consciousness forced Southern business men to turn to the Bour-bons for political leadership. To win social prestige the successful merchant had to assume the trappings of aristocracy. This meant the purchase of land and the discovery of real or imaginary ancestors among once prominent slaveholders. The business men lacked distinc-tion of their own; they were overshadowed by the more successful industrialists of the North, whom they imitated in dress and economic concepts. Their progressive ways smacked too much of Northern values to win the wholehearted approval of the Southern masses. Moreover, the business leaders of the New South were without stability and fre-quently failed in business before they could establish families. Among them were few dynasties comparable to the great planter class of the Old South, or to the millionaire families of the industrial East.

*   *   *

Commercial developments of the Recon-struction period allowed the small town or country merchant to assume a position of power and prestige, in many respects like that of the ante-bellum planter. They gained wealth from the trade of the greatly increased number of farm operators and added to their fortunes by acquiring mortgages on farm lands and crops. The storekeepers built showy homes typical of the Gilded Age, and if not members of the plantation aristocracy by birth, they frequently married into it. The more successful merchants eventually became bankers and plantation owners and were sub-sequently honored with church offices and state senatorships.

. . . The whole system of merchant-farm credit was smashed by the depression of 1929. The chain store, with its cheap cash arrange-ments, replaced the local merchant, who was relegated to the status of the neighborhood grocer. Bankers were the only surviving local magnates comparable in importance to the older credit merchants. Those not wiped out in 1929 continued to enjoy a certain standing in the life of most Southern communities until the present.

Emerging later than the merchants were those who won fortune and prestige through the lumber industry. They cut down the huge forests of the South and shunted the logs behind dinky engines to sawmills, where they were made into building materials. This class did not secure a permanent place in specific communities, because its members wasted the forests or allowed them to be decimated by fires. . . .

The wealth created by the vast industrial development of the 1880's inevitably produced a privileged class. This was composed of in-dustrial capitalists, men who established and maintained the South's cotton and steel mills, its coal mines and furniture factories. Here was a new group to impose itself upon South-ern communities along lines already familiar to those who knew the history of English and Northern industry. The Southern factory owners built fine houses for themselves, de-manded and received favors from public au-thorities, and advocated social and political reform. Their power was peculiarly Southern. Unconsciously copying the planters, they es-tablished their workers in villages which resembled the slave quarters of old. In return for this "benevolence," they received a feudal obedience from their workers.

The quickening business enterprise of the twentieth-century South produced a crop of millionaires.

*   *   *

In a very real sense, the lawyers and poli-ticians who ruled the Old South continued to hold their traditional position after Recon-struction. In 1900, 1933, or 1945, almost as much as in 1800 or 1850 they were the only group able to achieve national fame along with local importance. The main reason for their continued prestige was their ability to retain exclusive possession of public office and direction of public expenditures and court procedures. . . . Of all Southerners they were the most adaptable to changing conditions.

When occasion demanded, they could assume the courtly manners of the plantation aristocracy—the long coat, the broad-brimmed hat, the flowing oratory, the Latin phrases; they also knew how to affect the rough dress and colloquial speech of common folk, or the smooth ways of the successful business man. They were indestructible, rich in the gifts all Southerners admired. The day seemed distant indeed when law and politics would fail to attract the more ambitious and talented Southerner.

It is evident that the cream of Southern society was composed of a variety of groups. There was the planter class whose contemporary importance had declined but whose heritage of manners and ideals gave tone to all segments of the upper classes. Added to this section were remnants of the storekeeper group, the lumber barons, the turpentine distillers. Then came the prominent millionaire families, their imitators, and the commercial overseers and their aides. And of course, there were the perennial lawyers and politicians. Supplementing these were doctors, dentists, higher public officials and also army officers whose importance grew as the social functions of government expanded. There were ministers of the Gospel, college professors, and newspaper editors who lent a moral and cultural note to discriminating social groups. A few Negro doctors, ministers, teachers, and business men might be considered in the "ruling" class because of their influence over the Negro masses.

Although the upper classes comprised no more than one-tenth of the Southern people, they formed an aristocracy all their own, and were an integral part of society as a whole. Like the governing classes of England, they adjusted themselves to changes, even receiving talented recruits from the lower orders. Unlike their predecessors of the Old South, these new rulers had no fixed institution to defend. They were either too wise or too practical to make themselves an object of attack by emulating their ancestors who had argued for slavery so strenuously. When they felt obligated to defend their position, they spoke in terms as acceptable to the twentieth century as the pro-slavery argument had been unacceptable to the nineteenth century. If their rule was tyrannical, it resembled the social domination of the contemporary North to such an extent that outside critics could make no devastating accusations.

Southerners knew how to make social distinctions—for example, who not to receive in the intimate circle of their homes or clubs. As genuine Americans, however, they did not know how to draw class lines in the cosmopolitan manner. In a society in which so many wore ready-made clothes and owned automobiles, those with exclusive tastes could not dress or ride very differently from others. There were few private schools where children of the upper classes could escape from the social promiscuity of public institutions. The South could not avoid the social confusion so typically American. A friendly critic notes "a feeling of neighborliness, and almost pioneer closeness among the people of all walks of life." The young man or the young woman of anonymous origin could enter the inner circles of society if he or she possessed a requisite amount of charm, good looks, and dancing ability.

. . . It was not socially demeaning for girls of good families to be stenographers or trained nurses, or for the boys of the best families of small towns to wait on tables or be filling station attendants. The pride of ancestry was so widely exercised that, paradoxically, it made for social democracy. Almost any Southerner could become an aristocrat of a sort by tracing his descent from genuine or spurious forebears of distinction.

Perhaps the most striking characteristic of upper-class Southern society was its almost complete absence of intellectual interests. Leaders of the post-Reconstruction era were Confederate heroes, primitive men whose strength lay in geniality and physical prowess rather than in mental attainments. The next generation of leaders grew up during the cultural famine of war and Reconstruction; some were city-bred with an aristocratic heritage, but the majority sprang from the uncultured yeomanry. Although members of the third generation of leaders were often college-bred, they usually specialized in "campus courses," football, and fraternities. They were induced by editors and professors to support museums and orchestras, but displayed little understanding or enjoyment of these institutions. Theirs was the company of the perpetual Philistines to whom it meant social suicide to discuss intellectual or esthetic subjects. The ladies of the upper classes often attended better colleges than the men and demonstrated little opposition to higher learning. Yet, after graduation, they found more satisfying activities than the pursuit of themes outlined for them in college lecture halls. Domesticity remained the chief obligation of the Southern wife and daughter. Less attractive members of high society—or those who were too old for dances or babies—went into women's clubs with their study groups and musicales. Not so the ladies of high personal charm and social standing, who were too busy with their many diversions to tolerate the tedium of lectures and recitals.

Inevitably, such cultural immaturity was reflected in much outright boorishness. Strangers found it difficult to converse with ladies who prattled about their neighbors and were too provincial to discuss topics of general interest. They were disappointed by the soft hands, pink faces, and general corpulence of business men as contrasted to the tanned countenances and lithe figures of the old-time planters. Nor were they prepared to find "hooch" in place of mint julep, the fox trot instead of the Virginia reel, and most of all, perhaps "the grafting of Yankee backslapping upon the normal Southern gentility."

Strangers also discovered that the chivalric code of Southerners meant one set of morals for women, another for men, with much talk about "feminine honor" and "Southern virtue" by those who tolerated a low legal age of consent for illicit relationships. Such shortcomings further indicated the immaturity of the newly rich and the backwardness of the lower classes. The discriminating minority sedulously preserved the aristocratic traditions of good manners and good morals. If money in this society, as elsewhere, was the final arbiter, pride in its possession expressed itself in terms of superior standards inherited from the Old South. Accordingly, impoverished old families could still dictate to the *nouveau riche,* and when a marriage took place between an old and new family, the standards adopted were always those of the old.

The governing families, then, possessed modesty and good breeding in ample measure; much informal geniality without familiarity; a marked social distinction that was neither deliberate nor self-conscious. Indeed, the best families of the South were the most delightful segment of the American elite. Southern charm reached its culmination in the Southern lady, a creature who, like her plantation grandmother, could be feminine and decorative without sacrificing any privileges except the masculine prerogative to hold public office. Count Hermann Keyserling in 1929 was impressed by "that lovely type of woman called 'The Southern Girl,'" who, in his opinion, possessed the subtle virtues of the French lady. What at times appeared to be ignorance, vanity, or hypocrisy, frequently turned out to be the innate politeness of the Southerner who sought to put others at ease.

To a greater degree than other Americans, Southerners practiced what may be regarded as the essence of good manners: the idea that the outward forms of inherited or imposed ideals should be maintained regardless of what went on behind the scenes. Southern ideals were more extensive and inflexible than those prevailing elsewhere in America. To the rigid code of plantation days was added, in the late nineteenth and early twentieth centuries, the repressions of puritanism imposed by the Protestant clergy, who demanded that the fiddle be silenced and strong drink eschewed "on pain of ruin in this world and damnation in the next." As the land outwardly became more moral, the Southerner expressed his primary love of play and conviviality by "sneaking into the woods with his cards, foregathering with his cronies over a jug behind the barn, slipping away over the river in the nighttime to a cockfight or a breakdown." Although Southerners were among the hardest drinkers in America, one reason they refused to vote for presidential candidate Al Smith in 1928 was because he openly defended drinking. Many critics called this attitude hypocrisy, even deceit; the Southerners, however, insisted upon making a distinction between hedonistic tendencies and long-established ideals. If such evasiveness did not create a perfect code of morals, at least it helped to repress the indecent.

Whether within or without the approved standards of chivalry and puritanism, Southerners have managed to extract the maximum pleasure from the 70 years that have elapsed since Reconstruction. This applied equally to the difficult decades that followed 1865 and the more affluent times of the twentieth century. During the earlier period materials were ingeniously utilized; old jewels, laces, fans and shawls were refurbished; mothers became expert dressmakers and devised refreshments of a simple type. Special stress was placed on the charm and beauty of the Southern girl and an aristocratic self-esteem which blinded the observer to the sound of a creaking floor or the sight of a faded garment. Twentieth-century wealth added material comfort to the social scene, a circumstance that did not necessarily blot out gentility. Some of the social diversions that grew out of these factors survived or developed during the post-bellum period, while others emerged from twentieth-century conditions.

In the decades after the Civil War, the family was the core of Southern society; within its bounds everything worthwhile took place. No one recognized to be a Southerner's social equal dined anywhere other than in his own house or in that of a friend. Good Southern dishes—hot biscuits, fried chicken, custards—could be had only in the home, and the sole type of architecture that appealed was domestic in nature. This absorption in household affairs explains why strangers, un-

acquainted with Southern home life, found the social scene so dismal. They saw ugly main streets deserted after business hours, and noted an almost complete lack of public entertainment. The hotels were poorly equipped, the restaurants so drab and filthy that they repelled persons of good taste. Southerners who preserved the traditions of comfort and good manners seemed altogether oblivious to these conditions.

After 1910 there were changes in Southern domestic life. Urbanization and industrialization meant an increase in apartment houses, and the abandonment of the family roof by youths seeking the opportunities of a changing economy. The Southerner was frequently lured away from home by the temptation of the automobile and good roads, and became itinerant like other Americans. Hotels became numerous and often achieved the standards of other American public places; restaurants multiplied, and the suburban and rural areas blossomed with community centers given to dancing, dining, and drinking. Public places continued to be almost as backward as in the nineteenth century. In the vast distance between Washington and New Orleans, only with difficulty could the traveler find a restaurant of distinction. The numerous roadhouses were places of bad food, raucous and indiscriminate conviviality, even ruffianism and immorality. They were merely centers of escape for young people tired of the gentility of the home. When these young people married, they joined their elders in losing interest in what happened along the roadside after dark.

There was no significant uprooting of family life. The home in the twentieth century remained the core of a social conservatism fundamentally Southern, still harboring "the tenacious clan loyalty that was so mighty a cohesive force in colonial society." This explains the interminable visits among brothers and sisters, the sheltering of elderly aunts and distant cousins, the care of old family servants, the seeking of favors from relatives in high places, and the tribal conferences whenever a daughter married or a son changed employment. A living symbol of the prevailing domestic stability was the front porch where, in the leisure of the rocking chair, the Southerner endlessly contemplated the past. Here nothing important had happened since the Civil War, except that the screen of trees and banisters had grown more protective.

It was, however, not only the white families of the South who painfully attempted, in the years after the Civil War, to achieve economic security and family unity. And it is not only among the white population that families with roots far back in the antebellum past have occupied places of high social prestige in their communities. Paralleling but quite independent of the new pattern of white social class in the South has been the growth of a pattern of Negro classes. Frequently, as is pointed out below, mulatto families of quite mixed ancestry had already achieved a degree of prominence and economic success before the Civil War, and some of these families have continued to occupy relatively secure and respected positions.

E. Franklin Frazier, the author of the next selection, heads the Department of Sociology at Howard University and has served as president of the American Sociological Society and more recently as chairman of a UNESCO committee studying race relations. Himself a Negro, he has been greatly interested in analyzing the ways in which Negro family life in the United States has changed and developed through the years. He has written authoritatively on the problems of Negro youth and on the Negro family. In the next selection he traces the background of some of the most stable Negro family groups. They form a small minority of Negroes, and in many ways are unlike the less-educated Negro proletariat, but as a group they have played an important part in the difficult passage of their people from slavery to citizenship.

• 47 • The Growth of a Negro Upper Class
E. FRANKLIN FRAZIER

Those elements in the Negro population that have had a foundation of stable family life to build upon have constituted in communities throughout the country an upper social class, more or less isolated from the majority of the population. Up until the first decade of the present century, their numbers were slowly increased by other families that managed to rise, as the favored families in the past, above the condition of the Negro masses. Generally, these families have attempted to maintain standards of conduct and to perpetuate traditions of family life that were alien to the majority of the Negro population. Where they have been few in numbers, they have often shut themselves up within the narrow circle of their own families in order not to be overwhelmed by the flood of immorality and vice surrounding them. In some places they have been numerous enough to create a society of their own in which they could freely pursue their way of life and insure a congenial en-

[From *The Negro Family in the United States,* revised and abridged edition, Dryden Press, New York, 1951. Pp. 190-195, 198-205. Used by permission of the University of Chicago Press.]

vironment to their children. Often, intensely conscious of their peculiar position with reference to the great mass of the Negro population, they have placed an exaggerated valuation upon moral conduct and cultivated a puritanical restraint in opposition to the free and uncontrolled behavior of the larger Negro world.

In general, homeownership since emancipation offers the best index to the extent and growth of this class of families in the Negro population. By 1890, or a quarter of a century after emancipation, 22 per cent of the families on farms had bought homes; while in the cities and small towns of the country a sixth of the families were living in their own homes. During the next decade homeownership increased slightly in both rural and urban areas; but after 1910 the proportion of farm families owning their homes declined and by 1940 had reached less than 22 per cent. This decline coincided with the rapid urbanization of the Negro and the increase in homeownership in cities. We find in 1940 the highest amount of homeownership among the rural-non-farm families, with one family in three owning its home. Variations in the extent and trend of homeownership during this period can also be observed in the different states. However, the statistics for the various states fail to give us any clue to an understanding of the character and role of this favored group in the development of Negro family life. We must see these families as a part of the communities in which they have been a leavening element for the masses.

We shall turn first to . . . two counties in the plantation regions of Alabama and Mississippi, [where] there has been very little farm ownership. In 1910 only 7.5 per cent of the Negro farm families in Issaquena County, Mississippi, owned their homes; while in Macon County, Alabama, where the situation was slightly better, 11.3 per cent were homeowners. However, even in the plantation region where farm ownership is at a minimum, the mulatto families have some advantage over the black families. The family histories of two of the mulatto owners in Macon

County will show how they are differentiated culturally in many cases from the majority of landless black tenants.

The head of the first of these families was a mulatto, fifty-eight years old, who was born in an adjoining county. His father, who was born a slave, was the child of a white man. The father managed to accumulate five hundred acres of land which his fifteen children helped him to work. He exchanged this land for land in Macon County a little more than forty years ago in order that his children might be near Tuskegee Institute, though none of them ever atttended that school. The father left his land to his fifteen children, nine girls and six boys. Three of the brothers, including our informant, are still on the land. Our informant, who has been in the present house forty years, is the father of eighteen children. He has kept a careful record of his children's births in a book. Twelve of them were by his first wife, who died in 1919, and the remainder by his second wife, whom he married soon afterward. All the children by his first wife are living, except two who died in infancy. His present wife continues to cook for a white family in which she was employed when she married. Three of the older children are married and live in Montgomery, while the remaining thirteen continue to be a part of the patriarchal household. The family occupies a large well-built four-room house.

The head of this family was the superintendent of the Sunday school connected with the Baptist church in which he has been a deacon "for years." Because of his superior education and position as a landowner in the community, he serves as a clerk in the church and conducts the prayer meetings.

His farm consists of a hundred and sixty acres, fifty acres of which are in cotton. He owns farm tools, including two sweep stocks, two turn plows, three cotton-planters, and a mowing machine. He also has two mules and four cows which give three gallons of milk a day. His family enjoys a varied diet of beans, peas, peppers, squash, collards, and cabbages from the garden. Though a landowner, he is nevertheless dependent upon the vicissitudes of the agricultural and credit system of the plantation region. Although he "came out even" in 1930, as he remarked, "back debts et us up." The local bank foreclosed on its thousand-dollar mortgage, and he has been making an effort to redeem his land. His two brothers were in the same situation with regard to their holdings.

The history of another family of mixed blood, that owns one hundred and sixty acres and rents four hundred acres of land which is sublet to tenants, will show how the stabilizing of family relations has been bound up with the growth of institutional life among this favored class. The head of this family was born in 1880. According to his story, he was the son of the mulatto daughter of a white man and "a pure Negro excusing him being mixed with Spaniard." Both of his parents were slaves. He was one of ten children and worked for his father until he was twenty-one. He married as soon as he was "emancipated" from the authority of his father. After working six years, he bought the farm in 1907. He attributed his success and desire to have a home to the example set by other colored people, particularly those at Tuskegee. He remarked:

> I guess it was the inspiration I got when I was quite a boy. You see I worked around white people and I always had the idea that I wanted something too; then I used to go to Tuskegee and see how other colored folks lived and that encouraged me to have the idea to own my own home. I felt like a man ought to own the very best home he could get. I just went to rural schools. My father farmed about a half a mile back east of here.

But we are able to get a further insight into the process by which this family has become stabilized and built up a tradition from other facts in the family history. His grandfather was one of the first deacons in the church which he helped to start right after the Civil War. He explained with considerable pride: "My grandfather was the first one to go there [the church], my father the sec-ond, I am the third, my children the fourth and I have some grandchildren who go there which make the fifth generation which practically have been going to that church."

There were seven children in the family, two of whom were boys, twenty-four and eighteen years of age, helping their father on the farm. The oldest daughter was teaching school, while two of her younger sisters were married and living away from home with their husbands. The remaining five children were living at home with their father and a stepmother whom their father had recently married after being a widower for eight years. The house, with its screened windows and rambling rose bushes and vines and potted plants on the porch, stood out in sharp contrast to the hovels inhabited by the multitudes of tenants on the surrounding plantations. Of the six tenant families—three on the rented land and the others on the owned land—five were working "on halves" with an "advance" of ten dollars a month. Although, on the whole, this landowner had been successful, during the previous year he had lost money, while during the current year his tenants for the first time had "come out in the hole."

The well-organized family of a sixty-one-year-old black landowner, who called himself "a pure nigger," shows how, in some cases, those families with a small heritage of stable family traditions and culture create about them communal institutions to maintain and perpetuate their ideals and conceptions of life. When, upon reaching maturity, this man was "emancipated" by his father, he followed the instructions of his father, who had been a slave, and bought his first twenty acres of land. From time to time he added to it, and, with what he received from his father, he owned one hundred and twenty acres in all. He and his wife had been married forty-one years and had an only child, a son, who was born a year after they were married. This son, who was married to a woman with whom he "was raised up," had seven children. Since he was the only child, the mother had wanted him to remain with his parents; but he had reasoned with her thus: "Mamma, papa went to work and bought him a home and when my children get grown, I want them to see something I have done." So the son acquired a place about a mile away. Nevertheless, he sends his children to the school which, like the community, has been given the name of the family, because his father gave the land for its construction. Although there have been no lodge meetings since the "Mosaics went down," and "community meetings are held mighty seldom," they still get together when they want to "transact any business about just one thing and another for the benefit of the school."

These families are representative of the relatively few families in the plantation area which have managed to forge ahead because of their superior family heritage and thrift. But, like the great mass of Negro tenants, they have been restricted in their development by the plantation system. Their numbers have remained practically stationary in spite of programs encouraging landownership and scientific farming. Individual thrift and a superior social heritage have, in the final analysis, been powerless in the face of the inescapable economic forces inherent in the plantation system. Migration has offered the only escape from the deadening effects of the poverty and the ignorance of the masses of tenants. The decrease, during the decade from 1910 to 1920, in the proportion of mulatto families in Issaquena County, Mississippi, is an indication of this selective migration. On the whole, it is only in those regions outside the plantation area that family life among the rural Negro population has reached a relatively high level of development with the support of an organized community.

*   *   *

... The mulattoes in ... [Hertford County, North Carolina] have shown, until recent years, considerable prejudice toward the blacks with the result that they tended to form separate communities. In two such communities in this county, one taking its name from a mulatto family of free origin and the other from a black family of slave origin, we can see how the rural Negro family has become stabilized under the two very different sets of traditions. Information concerning the origin and history of "Whitetown," (the name of this community, as well as that of the black community, has been changed) the mulatto settlement, was given by the present head of the settlement. Our informant's father, who was born in 1801 and lived within a half-mile of the present settlement, was married twice and had eighteen children in all. The hundred acres of land which he owned were divided among the nine children, who were living at the time of his death. Our informant, who was born in 1853 and has the appearance of a white man, is still active. Although he sold his share for thirty-five dollars, he purchased more land from time to time until he acquired seven hundred acres, the size of the present settlement. The settlement became known by the name of the family around 1860. There was a school in the settlement at the time taught by a member of one of the other mulatto families. Our informant boasted of the fact that, when the "grandfather clause" was passed in order to disfranchise colored voters, he was the only colored man in the near-by town who could vote.

At present there are in the settlement ten children and thirty grandchildren of our informant. His brother, who also lives in the settlement, has six children and one grandchild. Working under the control and direction of the head of the settlement, the children and grandchildren raise cotton, corn, peanuts, peas, and tobacco. In this isolated community with its own school this family has lived for over a century. There has been considerable intermarriage between cousins. They have refused teachers appointed by the county unless they have been very light mulattoes. The family attends a church which was established by a mulatto minister for their benefit. These closely knit families have been kept under the rigorous discipline of the older members and still have scarcely any intercourse with the black people in the county. Seeing these families with their blond and red hair and blue eyes working in the extensive tobacco fields, one would take them for pure Nordic stock.

The other community, composed of black families who boast of pure African ancestry, grew out of a family of five brothers, former slaves, and is known as "Blacktown," after the name of the family. Although the traditions of this community do not go back as far as those of Whitetown, the group has exhibited considerable pride in its heritage and has developed as an exclusive community under the discipline of the oldest male in the family. The founder of the community, the father of our informant, was reared in the house of his master. According to the family tradition the master, "Major Black," was "one of the best white men in the section." Just before he died he called around him all the Blacks, who had taken his name, and said, "I have treated you all right; if I have wronged you, I beg your pardon." The old mansion, which is still standing, is inhabited by the grandson of the major. The paternal relations of slave days are maintained by the grandson and other descendants of the major. When one of the brothers of the original head of the Negro community died, a son of the major came from Norfolk, Virginia, to be present at the funeral.

The boundaries of the present community are practically the same as those of the old plantation, a part of which is rented from the grandson of the major. But most of the land is owned by this Negro family. The oldest of the five brothers was, until his death fifteen years ago, the acknowledged head of the settlement. At present the next oldest brother is recognized as the head of the community. His two sons, one of whom was our informant, have never divided their 138 acres. He and his three brothers, with their children numbering between forty and fifty and their numerous grandchildren, are living in the settlement. Twelve of their children have left the county, and three are living in a near-by town. Our informant left the community thirty-four years ago and worked at hotel work in Boston and as a longshoreman in Philadelphia, but returned after five years

away because he was needed by the old folks and longed for the association of his people. One of the sons of the five brothers who founded the settlement is both the teacher of the school and the pastor of the church which serves the needs of the settlement.

These settlements are distinguished from similar clans of blood relatives in the plantation regions of the South by their higher economic status and their deeply rooted patriarchal family traditions. They represent the highest development of a moral order and a sacred society among the rural Negro population. This development has been possible because economic conditions have permitted the germs of culture, which have been picked up by Negro families, to take root and grow. This has been the case with the blacks, as well as with the mulattoes, who, on the whole, have enjoyed superior advantages. Although the mulattoes have less illiteracy, more home-ownership, and comparatively fewer broken families with a woman head, the farm-owners among both classes in this county and the plantation counties as well have a larger number of offspring and more children surviving than the renters and farm laborers in either class. There has been sufficient isolation to shield these families from the disorganizing effects of industrialism and urban life but not enough to produce stagnation. But, as we have observed before, roads and automobiles are gradually destroying the isolation of these regions in the South. Some of the younger generation are venturing into the outside. During 1931 a member of the younger generation in both the black and the mulatto settlements was arrested and punished for transporting illegal liquor.

From these rural communities we turn now to the towns of the South, where amid the shacks and hovels inhabited by the mass of Negro population, a homestead here and there gives evidence of higher aspirations and some heritage of culture. Negroes in the towns and small cities of the South have been constantly drawn from the plantations to work as laborers on road construction, in the mills and the factories, and as domestics in the white families. Usually in these towns and cities there has been a small group of families who have remained segregated from the mass of the Negro population because of their superior economic and cultural status. In some of these communities there has been a single family that has stood out from the mass of the Negro population and endeavored to maintain the standards of family life that were foreign to the masses. A young woman, a teacher, who came from one of these communities tells of the life of her family in a town in Georgia. Her father was the son of a Negro woman and a white man. His white half-sisters became interested in him and helped him to enter one of the Negro colleges established shortly after the Civil War. On her mother's side there had also been some cultural advantages that raised her above the masses of the Negroes. Her maternal grandmother had been a house servant during slavery, and her children were later given instruction by the family that once owned her as a slave. One of these children, her mother, had been encouraged to attend the same school which her father attended. The courtship between her mother and father began while they were in college. Two northern white women, who became interested in her mother and sent her to the Latin High School in Boston, gave her two buildings to start a school in the town of her birth in Georgia. Her father came to teach in the same school and married her mother. The story of her mother's efforts to establish the school and her family's attempts to maintain their own moral standards in the face of the degradation of the masses was related by her as follows:

Our life around M—— was very seclusive. Nowhere to go and nobody to associate with. We were taken away for the summer for vacation to see a little of the world. When my mother first established the school there was quite a bit of opposition. They thought it was at first a Congregational School and they sought to burn it down. She would have to sit up at night with a shawl around her shoulders to watch the buildings going up. Eventually a fire was started but some of the neighbors put it out. After it was erected they kept the children home—they were not going to have any "Congregations" in their families. The people in the community were mostly all Baptists. They said the Congregationalists were not Christians. Although the people there were thrifty and many of them owned their own homes, they had very low moral standards. Our mother and father kept us away from them. It caused hard feelings. We were not allowed to associate with the masses. There was a lot of factories there—canning factories and every child about fourteen years of age had to work. Every year about school time there would be so many illegitimate children born to these girls. My sister and I were the only two girls who didn't work there at the factory.

In the larger cities of the South where these families were more numerous, they were able to create a more congenial environment for their way of life. This was especially true of those cities where there already existed a group of families with several generations of free ancestry and where college communities were located. The development of Negro family life in New Orleans and in Charleston, South Carolina, had its roots among the colored people who were free before the Civil War.

In New Orleans the Civil War and emancipation and consequent industrial and social changes caused the disruption of the free mulatto caste. Many of the free colored people who had themselves been slaveholders were sympathetic toward the confederacy and in some cases participated in the conflict on the side of the South. A review of confederate troops held in New Orleans in 1861 included a regiment of fourteen hundred free colored men. Between the people of this class and the newly emancipated blacks there was little community of interest or sympathy. Some of the members of the free colored caste acquired positions of influence during the Reconstruction Period. One of them was state treasurer from 1868 to 1879. But, when white domination was once more established, the color line was drawn so as to include the former free people of color and their descendants and the former slaves in the same category, and both were subjected on the whole to the same restrictions. Although this brought about some solidarity of interest and feeling between the two classes, many of the descendants of the free colored caste withdrew to themselves, refusing even to send their children to the schools attended by colored people and Negroes of slave ancestry. One of the members of this class wrote concerning the broken morale of his group:

> Certain Creoles of our day are reduced to that point of moral impotence that they despise and repulse their kind, even their own parents. Instead of thinking of means of deliverance, they surrender to their weakness, without being able to determine what principles to follow or what resolutions to take, as if they wished to habituate their natures to absolute submission or the obliteration of their individualities. They live in a stage of moral enfeeblement which resembles the last stage of helplessness. In this state of deterioration they not only care little about raising their abased dignity, but they multiply their errors as if to increase their mortification.

The rehabilitation of these families was often effected when they became the leaders of the Negro group or when they intermarried with the ambitious and rising families in the Negro group and mingled their traditions with those of the latter. This was the case with the family of one of the political leaders of the Negroes in the South. Although he was a mulatto, his wife's family, who belonged to the free mulatto caste, objected to their daughter's marrying him because he was a descendant of slaves.

We can get some idea of the outlook of the free mulatto caste from the following excerpt from the family history as related by the daughter:

> Upon the death of my grandfather (who was a butcher and had been killed by his slave), my grandmother married an independent tobacco manufacturer. There were twelve children by this second marriage. He and grandma, of whom I have a picture, appear to be white. He looks like an old Confederate soldier. Grandma, when a widow, had refused to marry a man who had fought in the Union Army. She regarded him as responsible for losing her slaves. She consistently refused to salute the American flag. Once when she had to get a passport to go to New Orleans and was ordered to salute the American flag, she spat upon it and put it under her feet. She was not punished for this, either because she was a woman or because she was a beautiful woman. Until her death she regarded Abraham Lincoln as her enemy. Grandma strenuously objected to my father's marrying her daughter because my father was a descendant of slaves. All of her children who are living are now in the white race.

The conflict in traditions and outlook on life was further revealed when the politician wanted their daughter to attend a Negro college and his wife wanted her to enter a convent. As it turned out, the daughter, who married into the colored group and identified herself with them, became a leader of colored women in politics. Her daughter, who was completely identified with Negroes, married a successful businessman who has made a conspicuous success in manufacturing.

In Charleston the cleavage between the mulattoes of free ancestry and the emancipated Negroes, especially those of mixed blood, has never been as wide as in New Orleans. Doubtless . . . there was prejudice against admitting black Negroes into the "charmed circle of aristocracy," as one of the mulattoes referred to her class. But what distinguished these families chiefly from the great mass of the Negro population was not simply their light skins. They took pride in their economic and educational achievements and more especially their culture and purity in family morals.

The emphasis which this class generally placed upon morality in family relations is exemplified in the remark of a member of one of these families that migrated from Charleston to Philadelphia because of an assault during the slavery agitation. In speaking of the attitude of the old Philadelphia families toward the mulatto families from the South, she remarked: "The people there regarded all mulatto women from the South as the illegitimate children of white men, but in the case of our family we could boast of being legitimate."

A brief sketch of the history of one of these old Philadelphia families will throw some light on the origin of the puritanical outlook of this class. The family in question traces its descent from the brother of Absalom Jones, who with Richard Allen organized the Free African Society in 1787. After he broke with Allen, he founded St. Thomas' Protestant Episcopal Church. This pioneer minister's nephew, who was the father of our informant, lived to be ninety-two years of age. As a boy he was bound out, as was customary, to a barber. Later he became the proprietor of three barber shops in the business section of the city and served a select white clientele. Our informant took pride in the fact that his father was one of the founders of the Central Presbyterian Church in 1844 and later wrote its history. He married into one of the old families, one of whose members was appointed to a diplomatic post by the government. There were sixteen children, including our informant. Five of our informant's sisters became schoolteachers, one brother

a barber, another a painter, and the remainder went into business. Our informant, who had completed over forty-three years in the Post Office as a clerk, was also the secretary of a building and loan association. He was married to a woman who belonged to one of the old families in New Orleans. They have two daughters who are schoolteachers and a son who is a manufacturing chemist. Our informant still has the eyeglasses which Absalom Jones wore and a chair in his living-room which belonged to his distinguished granduncle.

In other communities of the North where these families have settled they have formed nuclei of family groups that have striven to maintain purity in family morals as well as external forms of respectability. Their numbers have been increased constantly by families that possessed the traditions of the rural families which we have given some account of in this chapter. This small group has been the custodian of the gains which the Negro has made in acquiring culture and civilization. In taking over the manners and morals of the whites, there has been in some instances a disharmony between form and content. But, in most families, insistence upon moral conduct has been supported by genuine sentiment. Where their moral vision has been out of focus and their conscious strivings to attain culture have produced artificiality, this has been the result of their seeing themselves as if in two mirrors. They have seen themselves both in the mirror of their own race, whose ways of life they shunned and disdained, and in the mirror of the white race, in whose image they vainly would have made themselves over. On the whole, these families belong to an age that is past, or before the Negro became a dweller in the modern city.

Religion in the Old South followed the lines of the social classes; thus, the beliefs and practices of the plantation owner and his family were hardly the same as those of his slaves or of the poor whites in the hill counties. On the still-expanding frontier, especially, there was a strong accent on revivalism. Olmsted, in Selection 29, described a revivalistic service he attended in 1853.

For insight into the religion of the New South we make use of a personalized document by Hodding Carter, a newspaperman from Greenville, Miss., who has become a nationally recognized interpreter of Southern attitudes and manners.

• 48 • Faith of Our Fathers
HODDING CARTER

The South may be described as the Bible belt in the same offhand and derisive way that the Eastern seaboard can be identified as the barbiturate belt, the roaring, raw cities of the Midwest the tommy-gun belt, and the West Coast the divorce belt.

But the religious identification goes deeper. Though the citadels crumble, the South remains the great western-world stronghold of Protestant, fundamentalist Christianity. As such it is the legatee of the spiritually zestful, mystic, and masochistic soul of its largely Celtic forebears.

In Tennessee, devout folk still sing praises to the hero of their brush with monkey-minded sons of darkness:

William Jennings Bryan is dead, he died
  one Sabbath day.
So sweetly was the king asleep, his spirit
  passed away;
He was at Dayton, Tennessee, defending
  our dear Lord,
And as soon as his work on earth was
  done, he went to his reward.
He fought the evolutionists, the infidels
  and fools
Who are trying to ruin the minds of our
  children in the schools,
By teaching we came from monkeys and
  other things absurd
By denying the works of our blessed Lord
  and God's own holy word.

In Mississippi, Tennessee, and Arkansas, the teaching of evolutionary theories is still technically illegal; and, in the spring of 1948, the University of Arkansas turned down a proposed course which listed the first chapter of Genesis under "Myths of Creation." The camp meeting, brought up to date with loudspeakers and cooling systems, can, in rural Southern localities, outdraw Betty Grable and break even with Jim Folsom, Herman Talmadge, and John Rankin. The political pressures, in certain material directions, of the Baptist and Methodist churches, and to some extent the Presbyterian, are powerful and not uniformly misapplied. New churches continue to be built, though it is somewhat more difficult now to fill the pulpits than the pews. There is in the South an unexhausted reservoir of simple piety, which, if directed toward true acceptance of the Sermon on the Mount and the Christian concept of man's brotherhood, could and may yet effect a more profound change in regional social-racial patterns than any legislation devised toward that end.

Few Southerners find it easy to look upon these facts with detachment. That thing called the old-time religion is in the blood of most of us, and if it is laughed at, the laughter has as accompaniment an almost inescapable inner, esoteric warning that the ways of God are not to be mocked by man. A little over a century ago, the South of the Scotch-Irish farmer and frontiersman was swept by an evangelical flood that submerged the gentlemanly Jeffersonian skepticism and Anglican liberalism, leaving on the Southeastern seaboard alone an isolated high ground of doubt and investigation.

Through the back country rode the indomitable Methodist circuit riders. Rough-tongued men and women were propelled

[From *Southern Legacy,* Louisiana State University Press, Baton Rouge, 1950. Pp. 27-37.
Used by permission.]

below the surface of rushing rivers and obscure streams by the sanctified hands of self-discovered Baptist preachers, and rose choking, to scream the glory of God and their temporary abnegation of red liquor, eye gouging, and painted Jezebels. This was the Second Awakening, primitive, democratic, and certain, and religious liberalism in the South died before its surge. Victim, too, but of secular and sectional considerations, was the early revivalist concern with the black man's freedom; the Protestant churches of the South became the inspired spokesmen for the institution of slavery, entrenching themselves the more solidly thereby, and Christianity, Northern version, a distorted, satanic misinterpretation of the gospel that doomed the sons of Ham. God had providentially placed the poor, heathen African in the charge of the South. God was on the South's side. It was as simple as that.

"The parties in this conflict are not merely abolitionists and slaveholders," proclaimed the Reverend James Henley Thornwell, Presbyterian divine and president of South Carolina College in 1850. "They are atheists, socialists, communists, red republican jacobins on the one side, and the friends of order and regulated freedom on the other. In one word, the world is the battleground, Christianity and atheism the combatants; and the progress of humanity at stake."

Organized religion in the South became the mighty fortress of the *status quo;* the revival exhorters assumed the dignity and the defense of the ruling classes, uncompromising as ever in their castigation of the sins of the flesh but equally adamant in their justification of man's ownership of man. A Calvinistic God had ordained slavery; those who rebelled against it were in rebellion against God. Narrow fanaticism, strict and literal interpretation of the Bible, defense of the established order and its apostles, orthodoxy discernible even among the anarchical multitude of sects—these were the South's religious answer to the abolitionist, the hell-damned skeptic, the new, restless scientist, and the worldly outsider.

And that, to a lessening and challenged degree, is the religious South's position today.

Yet, it is unfair to so limit the impact of Protestantism upon the South. God was an anthropomorphic Hebraic avenger, with terrible lightning in his eyes, but the Christ child was gentle and forgiving, loving man, loving even the least of these, even the retarded black, God-ordained to be a hewer of wood and drawer of water. A tribal God punished the wrongdoer, but it was the tender Christ who illumined the path of righteousness, who waited beside the still waters, who whispered in the ear of the tempted, who cried out in agony, "Father, forgive them; for they know not what they do."

I know both sides. My family was Presbyterian, not as rigid as the parents of my Baptist and Methodist playmates, for whom dancing and cardplaying were sins only surreptitiously indulged in, but rigid enough and to spare. Sunday school, church, Young People's League, prayer meeting. On Sunday, no funny papers, no movies, no ball games, no profane music. Family prayers every night during a prolific family's summer reunions, with a gay, emancipated aunt at the piano, making ragtime of the gospel hymns, while a horde of cousins, deliciously afraid that God might strike her dead for her rhythmic sacrilege, filled the seashore night with "Shall We Gather at the River," "Beulah Land," and "Stand Up, Stand Up for Jesus." We *knew* God was everywhere. The children's catechism said so. We knew, too, that a still small voice would report to us, and to God, of wrongdoing. And, best of all, we knew that the little Lord Jesus would get us out of trouble if we asked forgiveness. I have never heard a more beautiful phrase than my paternal grandmother's metaphor for the air itself. "God's breath," she said, "it is God's breath." I know, too, that none of us were untouched by the beauty of her faith, by her sureness as to good and evil, in the formative years when consciences grow or wither.

And now the other side. When I was fifteen and yet undisturbed by doubting, a revivalist came to town. Those were the days of

Gypsy Smith, for whom I once proudly passed and shamefully dropped a collection plate, and Billy Sunday and lesser but just as loud fighters for the Lord. This exhorter was in the category of the lesser, but he had a way with him, and within two days the news of his success with the town's sinners packed the chilly church for matinee and evening performances. Near the end of his week's visitation, when almost all except the most case-hardened had been saved, I went to a night meeting with two friends, partly out of curiosity as to how people performed publicly when they were saved, but certainly without any agnostic doubting of the message the revivalist would bring that night. The Bible was still the unchallenged word.

Our small, diffident group sat in the back of the church, around the wood stove, bunched nervously together while the revivalist worked himself and his audience to a numbing hysteria of devotion. We sang the hymns lustily enough, and at first I was awed by the man's intensity and his audience's response. Men and women, and even children whom I had never suspected of being damned, began hitting the glory trail, crowding to the foot of the pulpit, some crying and one woman gagging with nausea. I became conscious of a strange, sickening resentment, a disbelief that this performance had any basic relationship to religion. It was my first such feeling and it made me want to leave. I wish I had. But we stayed by the stove, watching the hypnotized converts move forward, until, at last, there were no more volunteers. Then the revivalist moved upon the rest of the worshipers, most of whom had undoubtedly been publicly saved on previous nights. He called upon everyone who knew himself to be a sinner to stand and acknowledge his salvation through the blood of the Lamb. As men and women and children began rising from their seats, the revivalist stepped down from the platform, walking up the aisles with arms upraised, to urge the slow or reluctant to get up or be forever lost. The members of our small group looked at each other. Something went cold inside me, and I shook my head

negatively to the others. I had decided I was not going to get up, and that this shouting man could not doom me with his alternatives. In a few minutes, everyone in the church was standing except the three adolescent boys around the stove.

We had hoped to remain undetected, being far in the rear and removed from the pews, but he spotted us and in another moment towered over us like the angel at the gates of Eden. He exhorted us to stand. I kept my head down, not daring to look at him nor at the incredulous faces that turned to stare at us.

The revivalist rejoiced in the challenge. He entreated us in the name of the forgiving God and warned us of hell-fire to come. He called upon our parents—happily none of them were present—to intervene. He laid hands upon us, commanding us to acknowledge our sinfulness. One of my friends, frightened out of his wits by now—as I was—rose, leaving two young sinners to face the wrath of God. And we stuck it out to the horror of everyone present. I wanted to kill that man. I was afraid of mortal punishment and of my parents' reaction when they heard of this spectacle we were making. But we sat and sat, our faces burning, our ears ringing, our eyes downcast, and finally the revivalist gave up.

My parents, quickly advised of their son's strange behavior, were shocked but sympathetic. They did not like the notoriety. The best thing to do, they said, was to stay away from such meetings if I did not like them.

I have never attended a revival since. There are easier ways to break with fundamentalism and the God of wrath.

The vengeful tradition persists. Once, years later, I suggested editorially that a Holy Roller revival in our town remove itself beyond the city limits because the noise was disturbing to Christians and sinners alike. The participants were handling snakes and white-hot coal-oil-lamp chimneys, getting the shakes and the shouts, and it was not pleasant. So, the next day it was noised around that I was to be denounced in the Unknown Tongue that night. I went to hear it. My Holy Roller friends made certain that their listeners would know who was being denounced. In the middle of the unintelligible jabber-jabber-jabber of the Unknown Tongue, they would occasionally shout my name or that of my newspaper.

Such performances mean religion yet to too many Southerners. Some powerful denominations in Mississippi still conduct state-wide days or hours of prayer whenever the legislature undertakes gingerly to repeal or modify our unavailing liquor laws; but I have not known them to concentrate similarly when forward social legislation is being considered. We have an eighteen-year-old printer's apprentice in my newspaper plant who, in the name of religion, refuses to go to a movie, play cards, dance, or drink even a Coca-Cola. And I know two Protestant ministers to whom inclusion of a rabbi in a ministerial alliance is repugnant because they hold the Jews eternally responsible for the death of Christ.

Tragedy lies in this mean dissipation of the tremendous Southern reservoir of faith. Fortunately, that tragedy is being increasingly perceived by churchmen and laymen, particularly the younger men and women, and from their awareness comes not only future hope but present action. In seeming contradiction to the constant evidence of misdirected zeal, many churches of the South—Protestant and Catholic alike—are far ahead of their memberships in the areas of social action, which is as it should be and must be. It is not uncommon today for ministers to espouse constitutional rights for Negroes or to bespeak applied Christianity in economic relationships. Some of them pay for their daring. There is much muttering in the South against radical tendencies in the churches, the Federal Council of the Churches of Christ and the YMCA and the YWCA being especial targets, and the spirit of schism is strong. But by the very fact that the minister is still a man apart, ordained by God, his courage and vision can command respect if not emulation. As an example, I can cite the experience of a devoted young clergyman, who less than a year after he came to our town preached a blunt, biting sermon on racial discrimination. He was violently criticized, some members left his congregation, and it was predicted that he would not last a month longer. He is still here and I know that he has won converts.

And where could be found more fertile fields for crusading than the churches of the essentially rural South? There the communal stream runs strong. There, as much as human frailties and human concerns permit, men and women dwell for a short time beyond themselves, seeking refreshment of the spirit, warming themselves in the bright sunlight of the churchyard beneath a brighter if uncomprehended sun. There, fleetingly, they are malleable to good; there the inheritance of ardent faith could pry open the hearts to the words of the preacher who finds his text in Galatians:

"There is neither Jew nor Greek, there is neither bond nor free, there is neither male nor female: for ye are all one in Christ Jesus."

Anyone wishing to understand the South today must know not only about its economy, family life, and religion but also something of its local government. Whereas the federal agencies spend much time in promoting social change, local government in the South—and particularly the county government—seems dedicated to resisting change. The fact that most county officials represent rural constituencies is a partial explanation of this resistance; another is the continuance of control in the hands of the larger landlords, who have innumerable political as well as social and economic connections. As we saw in Selection 36, this was also true of the Old South.

Also an influence, however, was the "populist" movement, which reached into the South during the 1890's and the years immediately thereafter. The tightly knit control of the "Bourbons," or privileged aristocratic minority, was shaken to such an extent that those of less "noble birth" had much more to say about affairs in the Democratic Party. Then, and periodically since then, "demagogues" arose to voice the discontent of the small farmers, to play up the race issue with considerable enthusiasm, and to capture control of various state governments. But such political events, though highly publicized nationally, have not done much to weaken the hold of "the courthouse clique," in which the voice of the old-time planter class still has most prestige in the cotton-growing South.

These are important points to bear in mind when reading the comprehensive and carefully prepared statement on local government which has been written especially for this volume. John E. Reeves, a long-time student of this subject, is a member of the Department of Political Science of the University of Kentucky.

• 49 • Government in a Community of the Cotton South
JOHN E. REEVES

INTRODUCTION

The people of a southern, cotton-growing community are affected by all levels of government, but it is rural-local government with which they are most intimately concerned and for which they are primarily responsible. The units of government in the rural South consist of county governments, school districts, and occasionally special districts for drainage or other specialized purposes. In Louisiana, the county is called the parish.

County government has declined relatively in importance during the last several decades, as measured by the percentages of the total tax dollar spent by the county, the state, and the nation, but as measured by increased county expenditures we find that in 1890 county governments in nine southern states spent 38 cents per capita and in 1945 the same counties spent $11.97 per capita. Actually the importance of the county depends in large measure on its performance of functions that have been determined to be wise by the Federal and state governments. The county is thus the first unit of government which contacts the average citizen and the only one

with which many persons ever have any contact. It is to county officials and county school officials that citizens of the cotton-growing community must look for educational services, library services, health services, and usually for welfare services and farm to market roads, not to mention many routine functions such as the recording of deeds and the issuance of various kinds of licenses. There is reason to suppose that the future of democracy may depend upon the proper performance of some or all of these services.

Government, including county government, is that organization through which the people, acting collectively, perform for themselves those functions which cannot be performed as economically or as efficiently in any other way. In the performance of its functions government can, as Lane W. Lancaster has said, "command the property, the services, and even the lives of those who support it." It is the only modern institution endowed with such power. County government must not be written off as an unimportant part of total government.

Government, although possessing far more coercive power than any other institution, is only one of the many institutions and organizations which play important roles in the life of a community of the Cotton South. Among other institutions and organizations, one finds the family, the church, farm organizations, women's groups, banks, cotton brokers, other business organizations, and, in some cases, private schools. The incorporated town or small city also has a major influence in the community. However, the county-seat town has its chief influence on the surrounding territory as a going economic and social organization rather than merely as a unit of government. It is to the courthouse and not to the city hall that the cotton-growing community looks for governmental services.

Throughout modern history, as society has become more complex and the demands for certain services on the part of all of the people have become more and more insistent, new services have been added to those already performed by government. It has not been very long since most of the public welfare services now performed by government were the concern of private charity; less than two generations ago many of the highways in the Cotton South were toll roads, owned and operated for profit by private corporations; and at the beginning of the history of the Cotton South, public education was unknown in that region —indeed, it was not until after the Civil War that public education had any considerable growth there.

The governmental institutions of the southern cotton-growing community were brought to this country from Great Britain. They were adapted to the American scene and have changed, usually belatedly, to meet the most insistent demands of a changing social order, but are still in many respects better suited to a more primitive society. For instance, the system of paying officials by means of fees (still in effect in most southern jurisdictions for the compensation of such officials as tax collectors, property assessors, county clerks, and frequently petty judicial officials) was well-suited to the time when there was not enough government business to keep officials fully employed. For example, the editor

of a local newspaper might serve as county clerk and issue marriage licenses, record deeds, and perform other similar county functions in his spare time for the fee involved. Now that most county offices provide full-time employment for a chief official and a few deputies, a much more economical and just method would seem to be to determine what each job is worth per month or year and pay the official and each assistant accordingly. Under such a system, whatever fees are still charged for services could be diverted into the public treasury, along with taxes and other income. Again, the area of counties was so devised as to enable a citizen in the most remote section of any county to go on horseback or by wagon or carriage to his county seat, transact his governmental business, and return to his farm the same day in time to do his evening milking. In the age of the automobile, several times the distance could be covered. The resulting duplication of public buildings and officials is quite costly. Many other instances where the government of the southern cotton community has lagged behind the needs of the times could be mentioned, but the above are sufficient to indicate that there are costly lags.

LEGISLATIVE ORGANIZATION

Government in this country is usually organized into three branches: the legislative, the executive, and the judicial. Roughly, this is true in the county, but typically there is a great deal of overlapping of functions and in many communities all three functions are performed by the same officials.

The legislative branch of government is weak in the county. This results naturally from the county being primarily an administrative arm of the state, enforcing state law and performing other state functions.

The legislative functions of county government in the Cotton South are performed usually by a county board or fiscal court which is also an administrative board. These governing bodies, by whatever names they may be called, are usually composed of three to nine members and are elected by popular vote, either from the county at large or from districts. In addition to passing a budget, functions of the county board which are legislative in nature are usually confined to (1) providing for certain new functions which the state legislature may make optional at the discretion of the board, and (2) approving land use planning measures which other governmental agencies may wish to put into effect.

OVER-ALL ADMINISTRATIVE ORGANIZATION

The county board, discussed above, is also the chief administrative agency of the county in the Cotton South. It is, however, not an agency which has supervisory authority over all administrative affairs in the county. Many functions may be presided over by independently chosen boards, chief among which are a school board and a health board. Still other functions are performed by popularly elected officials such as a sheriff, tax collector, property assessor, and probably an attorney, coroner, county clerk, and maybe others.

The hydra-headed type of administrative organization in effect in the Southern county is a direct result of the early belief, fostered by Jacksonian democracy, that the more officials elected, the more democratic the government. This belief has persisted despite the fact that practically all of the evidence points to the probability that democratic responsibility and the efficiency of democratic government are reduced by such disjointed organization. However, not only does "administration have its roots deep in the history of the people," but also in a democracy, it tends to find a way to accomplish the people's will without violating their beliefs. Until relatively recent years there was no great need for efficiency in county government, since it performed but few functions, the tax rate was not particularly onerous, and the average person was not greatly affected one way or the other by county inefficiency. The growing importance of good roads, public health, soil conservation and other services has changed this picture and now we find an increasing interest in making county administration more efficient.

JUDICIAL ORGANIZATION

All civil and criminal cases in the Cotton South are usually tried in the county court house, the city hall, or in the office of a justice of the peace. Traditionally, the justice of peace court (sometimes referred to as the magistrate's court) was at the base of the judicial system. Although this court still exists in many southern counties, it has been completely abandoned in some of the more enlightened jurisdictions, and functions only to a very slight degree in others. Formerly, each county was divided into magisterial districts ranging in number from three to ten or twelve. A justice of the peace and a constable were elected in each district, the constable to make arrests and serve court orders, and the justice of the peace to try petty criminal and civil cases. Trials were held in the local district thus eliminating the necessity of going to the county seat for the trial of petty cases. The progressive abandonment of the justice of the peace court has been a result in part of the automobile and is indicative of the fact that the social lag is not absolutely fatal to progress.

Next above the justice of the peace court is the county court, sometimes called the probate court. The county court usually has jurisdiction over petty civil and criminal cases, arising anywhere in the county, as well as performing the probate function—i. e., interpreting and enforcing wills, distributing the estates of persons who die intestate (without having drawn a will), and administering estates of deceased persons until the property is allocated to and vests in the heirs or devisees. Generally, too, the judge of this court has charge of all juvenile cases.

Above the county court is the chief trial court of the state. It is generally called the circuit court in the south, but is sometimes known as the superior court or by other title. It has original jurisdiction over all felony cases and over all important civil cases where the sum involved is in excess of a stated amount such as $200 or $300. A district for this court usually includes more than one county with the judge holding court periodically in the court house of each county in his district.

LOCAL POLITICS

Generally those who hold the top official positions in a southern county are beneficiaries of a county political machine affiliated with the Democratic party. The official party organization of the county usually consists of precinct representatives who, on paper, are chosen democratically at "mass" meetings or by secret ballot. However, so few voters participate in these elections that a small group of leaders of the party in the county is nearly always able to determine the choice of precinct representatives, who are, in turn, controlled by the leaders instead of the leaders being controlled by the precinct representatives and the people.

The precinct representatives usually choose a county chairman who is the formal head of the party in the county, but he may be only nominally the head. The real boss of the party in the county may be one man who may not hold any official position, but usually in a rural county ultimate control is lodged in a small group of three to six, some or all of whom hold county offices. By means of patronage and other favors this group can control key figures (rich farmers, country storekeepers and the like) in each precinct, who, by getting out the vote favorable to organization candidates and sometimes by less scrupulous methods, can carry the precinct. This group decides who shall receive the support of the county organization in state and district primaries. The organization may also support a full slate of candidates in the county primary, but where the organization's interests are not too deeply involved candidates for certain county offices may be allowed to fight it out on the basis of popular following.

Sometimes county political machines retain power for decades but upheavals are not unknown, particularly if a losing candidate for governor or other high office is backed.

There is often a skeleton Republican organization interested primarily in federal patronage if and when the Republican party wins a presidential election.

The Democratic organization in a rural county is likely to lean to the Dixiecrat point of view. Until recently Negroes have been barred from the ballot both by statutory means and by intimidation. They are still not voting in large numbers.

ADMINISTRATIVE FUNCTIONS

The county is frequently spoken of as an administrative arm of the state, and as a general rule it has far more discretion in the performance of administrative functions than it has in relation to legislative or judicial functions. Typically, the state authorizes the county to perform certain functions and makes provision for the administrative organization by means of which they shall be performed, but leaves the extent and the details of performance entirely up to the county. In some instances, however, both state and federal aid may be available to assist the counties in the furnishing of certain specified services, in which case a large measure of control may be exercised by either or both.

Financial Administration. One of the most important phases of public administration in a southern cotton-growing county is the administration of county finances. The county board is usually responsible for certain functions of financial administration. In addition to passing the budget, which is a legislative function, the board approves all expenditures, establishes salaries, and either directly or through a treasurer makes arrangements for the deposit of funds and the securing of loans.

In any particular southern county, it is almost certain that the county board will not have full authority in relation to finances, since the assessment of property and collection of taxes are usually the responsibility of independently-elected officials. It is in the assessment of property that the worst abuses occur. Practically everywhere the law requires all property to be assessed at its fair cash value, but nowhere is this done. Instead, some property is put on the tax rolls at a small fraction of what it would sell for, some is listed at more than its actual value, little, if any, is listed at its true value, and it is usually the rich and politically powerful who are favored. Most states exercise some control over assessments. It may actually assess certain types of property such as intangibles and the holdings of public utility corporations. The state tax department may review and check assessments of the counties, and in some states instructs the assessing official as to what his duties are. Such state supervision appears to have resulted in but little improvement, but at present there is a concerted effort on the part of state officials in some of the southern states to improve the situation.

Law Enforcement. The enforcement of the criminal law of the state is one of the oldest functions of the county—it is, indeed, as old as the county itself. The southern rural county's law enforcement machinery is still literally the same as in seventeenth century England. The sheriff is the chief police officer of the county, but he has many other duties as well. He is always charged with certain duties in relation to the court and he or one of his deputies must be in attendance at all sessions to wait on the jury, execute and serve writs and other processes, summon witnesses and the like. In most states he is given still other duties—being tax collector in some instances, jailer in others, and county librarian in at least one. The only other local law enforcement official typical of the rural south is the constable and he is rapidly disappearing from the scene. Where he exists, the constable still has the same function in relation to the justice of peace court as the sheriff has to the county and trial courts.

While the local organization for rural law enforcement has remained the same, the problem has changed drastically. Before the automobile came into use organized crime was confined in very large degree to the city and rural enforcement was concerned with petty gambling, an occasional drunken brawl, isolated cases of larceny, trespassing, and trouble arising out of such matters as boundary disputes. Organized crime still arises in large part from the city, but the automobile has made it possible for the professional criminal to transfer his operations to the small town, the open country, and the crossroads village, while making the big city his hideout.

The growth of rural law enforcement problems has brought about the establishment of state police forces in some states, and in certain others the highway patrol has general police power in rural areas.

Record Keeping and License Issuing. A county official, frequently the county clerk, is responsible for keeping all records of deeds, mortgages and the like. The same official usually issues various kinds of licenses such as marriage, automobile, hunting, and certain types of business licenses.

Highway Administration. Local roads leading to the county seat, and feeding into through highways, have been the responsibility of county government in the South for many years. However, during the last four decades there has been a revolution in the methods of constructing and maintaining roads and highways. There has also been a vast change in responsibility of the federal and state governments in this field. During the greater part of the nineteenth century these units of government did little about highways except that the state granted franchises to tollroad or turnpike companies. While the county was active, it usually required property owners to work on the roads so many days every year in lieu of paying taxes for their maintenance.

The coming of the automobile brought both the state and the federal government into the through highway field, and required the county to tax its property owners and begin road maintenance and construction in earnest. In recent years the county has received considerable funds from the state to be used on local highways and several of the southern states have inaugurated local or rural highway programs of their own.

Educational Administration. Although in the rural South the modern tendency is to think in terms of the county school system, and more frequently than not there is a county school superintendent with an office in the court house, actually the county government as such is not responsible for school administration. Formerly the superintendent was elected by popular vote and the tax rate and a few other policy matters were determined by a school board. Now, more frequently, the superintendent is chosen by the board which constitutes the governing body of a separate governmental unit—the county school district. Nevertheless, public education is one of the most important, if not the most important, governmental function performed by local officials and employees in the southern county.

Education is financed in part by taxes on local property and in part by state appropriations. Vocational and agricultural education is also financed in part by federal funds. Originally state funds were divided equally among the districts on the basis of the number of children or some comparable data but the modern tendency is to use a portion of them to equalize educational opportunity in the poorer counties.

The federal government sets up certain requirements (particularly in relation to personnel and teachers' pay) that must be met before its funds are available, and the state exercises more complete control. Supervisors from both state and federal agencies are likely to be in the district frequently, particularly in those districts where federal money is being used.

State laws may impose tax and debt limits and frequently require a minimum school term and minimum salaries for teachers. Although the limitations and the requirements are likely incompatible, at least in the poorer districts, the state department has to try to enforce both. Other controls usually exercised by the state department include approval of an annual budget, approval of all bond issues, and certification of teachers.

Health Administration. Public health work is one of the newer functions of county government, but a rapidly growing one; it is also a field in which both the state and federal governments are particularly active. It is usually optional with the county as to whether it will establish a health program, but if it does it must operate strictly according to state law. In general there are two types of county health organization: (1) a county board of health and a part-time health officer; and (2) a county health board with a full-time health department, under the general supervision of the board. Obviously the first type cannot operate very efficiently. The physician with a private practice who acts as part-time health officer cannot be expected to do more than make routine investigations, enforce sanitation laws, and enforce quarantine if declared by the board or state health authorities. Full-time health departments operate in a majority of the southern counties at present.

Most of the southern states permit two or more counties to cooperate in providing one public health department, and some progress has been made in actually combining counties for this function. Also, cooperation between a county and a city located in it is usually permitted and often practiced.

Public health work is financed by the local units of government, the state, the federal government, and by grants from such private organizations as the Rockefeller Foundation.

State supervision is exercised over local health work to a greater degree than any other local function. The selection of personnel is subject to state approval and the state department of health usually plans, coordinates and directs the work of the local department to such an extent that it is in effect a branch office of the state department. The recent growth and relative efficiency of health work may give the defenders of "local democracy" reason to ponder.

Welfare Administration. Traditionally the county was the one unit of government in the South which was universally responsible for public welfare administration. Until recently, however, it confined its functions to operating an almshouse for the aged poor, granting niggardly sums to the desperately poor and perhaps granting specified sums at regular intervals to certain classes of indigents such as pauper idiots and to mothers of dependent children. The work has usually been carried on by the county board itself or by a superintendent of the poor, acting also as the keeper of the almshouse.

The county almshouses are generally recognized as unsatisfactory, and Virginia has led the way in establishing district homes for the aged. The federal system of social security may make the almshouse unnecessary in the future. It is almost certain to make one for each county still more undesirable.

A great change came over public welfare administration after the passage of the Social Security Act of 1935. Every county in the land has citizens who receive aid under this Act, which is always contributed to by both the state and the federal government, with visits by officials of these governments being made for inspection or supervision of the work. In addition to the public assistance program for the benefit of the aged, the blind, dependent children, and in some cases, the permanently disabled, there is unemployment insurance which usually has an office or representative in the county, and the state employment service which either has an office in the county or in a nearby county so that it can serve the people of any particular county.

Agricultural Extension Work and Soil Conservation. The Federal Smith-Lever Act of 1914 provided for a system of grants-in-aid to the states for the promotion of extension work in agriculture and home economics. Under its provisions, county agricultural agents and home demonstration agents have been established in most cotton-growing counties. The county agent has made a real place for himself among southern farmers. At first the farmers were skeptical but as time went on they learned that the agent was generally right and came to take his advice on all agricultural problems. When farmers have problems of highly specialized nature the assistance of specialists from the state college of agriculture can usually be obtained. The home demonstration agents have also established a solid reputation with farm housekeepers.

The county and home demonstration agents are usually paid jointly by the Federal government, the state, and the county, with the local Farm Bureau Federation sometimes making a contribution as well. The agents are supervised by the extension officials of the state college of agriculture and personnel and other standards set by the federal government have to be met.

The Agricultural Adjustment Administration has an office in each county which supervises allotment control under the Federal Agricultural Production and Marketing Administration. This office works closely with agricultural agents in assisting the farmer to secure needed fertilizers and in other ways. It is through the Agricultural Production and Marketing Administration that farmers are compensated for staying within the allotted quotas of production.

The Federal Soil Conservation Service has a conservation officer with headquarters in each state and district offices at various places in the state. Under the stimulation of this office, several of the southern states have set up state soil conservation committees to supervise the establishment of local conservation districts and the choice of local soil conservation committees. These districts are usually coterminous with the county but may be larger or smaller than the county. In these districts, a majority of the farmers having agreed to cooperate, the local committee may formulate and enforce land-use regulations (usually with the consent of two-thirds of the land owners). Both the Soil Conservation Service and the county agents assist the district in planning and executing a soil conservation program including terracing and other means of preventing soil erosion, the use of fertilizers and legumes and the rotation of crops.

Great emphasis has been given to soil conservation in the Tennessee Valley states by the T.V.A., with its manufacture of fertilizer, its reforestation program and its emphasis on prevention of soil erosion and silting.

SUMMARY

In conclusion it may be said that county government performs many important functions for a southern cotton growing community. Among the functions performed by the county are county road construction and maintenance, public health and welfare work, record keeping and license issuing, the administration of petty justice, and agricultural extension and soil conservation work. Education is the function of a separate unit of government. County functions are usually performed by outmoded governmental machinery, better suited to an earlier more primitive society, but the people seem to like their county government as it is. Since the county is the unit of government nearest to the people it should be the one in which they are most interested.

Although all Americans are concerned with the problem of the relationship between Negroes and whites, and many thoughtful and useful studies of the problem have been made, it is impossible to find a common area of agreement on the subject among Americans. We are too easily caught up in a conflict between ideals and realities, between traditions and events, and few of us can be sufficiently detached to consider the question without letting personal feelings enter in. Hoping to get a fair, unbiased survey of the position of the Negro in the present-day life of the United States, the Carnegie Corporation, in 1937, asked the distinguished Swedish social economist Gunnar Myrdal to direct a comprehensive study. Aided by a large group of able researchers, Myrdal left no aspect of the subject untouched. The work was not finished until the end of 1942, and when it appeared in print it was recognized as one of the most significant books of its time.

Myrdal and his associates have dealt with the United States as a whole, since the Negro's place in a democratic country is a national problem and not a local one. In many ways the situation is more acute in the South, but basically there are few differences except in degree and in detail between one section of the country and another. Therefore, it seems appropriate to depart, in the following selection, from the focus we have maintained on the South and consider the Negro problem for America as a whole.

The conclusion reached by Myrdal can be summed up briefly. He sees the Negro problem as a dilemma between the democratic beliefs held by all Americans and the undemocratic treatment accorded the Negro. He makes no sweeping accusations and provides no simple solutions. Instead, he patiently explores each aspect of American life—jobs, living conditions, law enforcement, schooling, recreation, and so on—determining what Americans do and what they believe should be done, and then examines how the treatment and position of the Negro differ from the treatment and position of other Americans. Most of us are aware of some of the unpleasant aspects of Negro-white relations, and it is often easy to see how specific arrangements and habits have grown and become firmly rooted in American life. What is more difficult is to see the entire dilemma from a distant perspective, undistorted by opinions or prejudices.

In the following selection only a few of the topics covered in nearly 1500 pages can be touched on—and these briefly. Included here are parts of Myrdal's discussion of segregation in housing, of discrimination in economic opportunity and legal treatment, all of them crucial matters in the country as a whole, as well as the South. One of the most complex subjects, caste and class, is dealt with extensively in Myrdal's volume but is omitted here for lack of space. Myrdal found that Negroes in America form a lower caste, which they can never leave, and in which they suffer certain disadvantages regardless of individual ability. This is the nature of a "caste system" in any part of the world. Also, although Americans are often hesitant to realize it, we have a class system, in which every individual is expected to have the opportunity to climb to a higher level. Negroes, however, can climb only within a separate series of Negro classes, since competition for social prestige or status never occurs across the line dividing our castes. Actually, few Negroes are able to rise to the "middle" class level and almost none to the "upper" class, since wealth, education, approved occupations, and the other marks of middle and upper class membership are particularly difficult for them to achieve.

Myrdal concludes his volume with a note of hope that the relations between Negro and white in America will continue to show the lessened friction and increased tolerance that he noted during the beginning of World War II. But he also ends with the sobering warning that the entire world is watching our attempt to resolve this dilemma, for the world is looking to us for leadership in world affairs.

> . . . The great reason for hope is that this country has a national experience in uniting racial and cultural diversities and a national theory, if not a consistent practice, of freedom and equality for all. . . . Mankind is sick of fear and disbelief, of pessimism and cynicism. It needs the youthful moralistic optimism of America. But empty declarations only deepen cynicism. Deeds are called for. If America in actual practice could show the world a progressive trend by which the Negro became finally integrated into modern democracy, all mankind would be given faith again—it would have reason to believe that peace, progress and order are feasible. And America would have a spiritual power many times stronger than all her financial and military resources—the power of the trust and support of all good people on earth.

• 50 • *The Dilemma of the American Negro*

GUNNAR MYRDAL

MINORITY PROBLEMS AND THE NEGRO PROBLEM

For some decades there has been a tendency to incorporate the American Negro problem into the broader American minority problem. In the United States, the term "minority people" has a connotation different from that in other parts of the world and especially in Central and Eastern Europe, where minority problems have existed. This difference in problem is due to a difference in situation. The minority peoples of the United States are fighting for status in the larger society; the minorities of Europe are mainly fighting for independence from it. In the United States the so-called minority groups as they exist today—except the Indians and Negroes—are

[From *An American Dilemma: The Negro Problem and Modern Democracy*, Harper and Bros., New York, 1944. Pp. 50-58, 380-383, 391-392, 394-396, 523-526, 560-561, 565, 586-588, 599-604, 644-647, 650-662. Used by permission.]

mostly the result of a relatively recent immigration, which it was for a long time the established policy to welcome as a nationally advantageous means of populating and cultivating the country. The newcomers themselves were bent upon giving up their language and other cultural heritages and acquiring the ways and attitudes of the new nation. There have been degrees of friction and delay in this assimilation process, and even a partial conscious resistance by certain immigrant groups. But these elements of friction and resistance are really only of a character and magnitude to bring into relief the fundamental difference between the typical American minority problems and those in, say, the old Austrian Empire. Of greatest importance, finally, is the fact that the official political creed of America denounced, in general but vigorous terms, all forms of suppression and discrimination, and affirmed human equality.

In addition to a cultural difference between the native-born and the foreign-born in the United States, there was always a class difference. At every point of time many of those who were already established in the new country had acquired wealth and power, and were thus in a position to lay down the rules to late-comers. The immigrants, who left their native lands mainly because they had little wealth, had to fit themselves as best they could into the new situation. Their lack of familiarity with the English language and ways of life also made them an easy prey of economic exploitation. But as long as the West was open to expansion, immigrant groups could avoid becoming a subordinate class by going to a place where they were the only class. Gradually the frontier filled up, and free land no longer offered the immigrants cultural independence and economic self-protection. Increasingly they tended to come from lands where the cultures were ever more distant from the established American standards. They became distinguished more markedly as half-digested isolates, set down in the slums of American cities, and the level of discrimination rose.

The first stage of their assimilation often took them through the worst slums of the nation. Group after group of immigrants from every part of the world had their first course in Americanization in the squalid and congested quarters of New York's East Side and similar surroundings. They found themselves placed in the midst of utter poverty, crime, prostitution, lawlessness, and other undesirable social conditions. The assimilation process brought the immigrants through totally uncontrolled labor conditions and often through personal misery and social pressures of all kinds. . . .

From the viewpoint of the struggling immigrant himself, the harsh class structure, which thrust him to the bottom of the social heap, did not seem to be a rigid social determinant. In two or three generations, if not in one, the immigrant and his descendants moved into, and identified themselves with, the dominant American group, and—with luck and ability—took their position in the higher strata. Only because of this continuous movement of former immigrants and their descendants up and into the established group could the so-called "Americans" remain the majority during a century which saw more than a score of millions of immigrants added to its population. The causal mechanism of this social process has been aptly described as a continuous "push upwards" by a steady stream of new masses of toiling immigrants filling the ranks of the lower social strata. The class structure remained, therefore, fairly stable, while millions of individuals were continuously climbing the social ladder which it constituted. The unceasing process of social mobility and the prospect of its continuation, and also the established Creed of America promising and sanctioning social mobility, together with many other factors of importance, kept the minority groups contented and bent on assimilation.

Religious differences, differences in fundamental attitudes, and "racial" differences entered early as elements of friction in the process of assimilation and as reasons for discrimination while the process was going on. With the growing importance of the new immigration from Southern and Eastern Europe in the decades before the War, these factors acquired increased importance. They are, in a considerable degree, responsible for the fact that even recent community surveys, undertaken decades after the end of the mass immigration, give a picture of American class stratification which closely corresponds to the differentiation in national groups. This type of differentiation is one of the most distinguishing characteristics of the American social order.

The split of the nation into a dominant "American" group and a large number of minority groups means that American civilization is permeated by animosities and prejudices attached to ethnic origin or what is popularly recognized as the "race" of a person. These animosities or prejudices are commonly advanced in defense of various discriminations which tend to keep the minority groups in a disadvantaged economic and social status. They are contrary to the American Creed, which is emphatic in denouncing differences made on account of "race, creed or color." In regard to the Negro, as well as more generally to all the other minorities, this conflict is what constitutes the problem, and it also contains the main factors in the dynamic development. Taking a cross-sectional view at any point of time, there is thus revealed an inconsistency in practically every American's social orientation. The inconsistency is not dissolved, at least not in the short run. Race prejudice and discrimination persist. But neither will the American Creed be thrown out. It is a hasty conclusion from the actual facts of discrimination that the Creed will be without influence in the long run, even if it is suppressed for the moment, or even that it is uninfluential in the short run.

In trying to reconcile conflicting valuations the ordinary American apparently is inclined to believe that, as generations pass on, the remaining minority groups—with certain distinct exceptions which will presently be discussed—will be assimilated into a homogeneous nation. The American Creed is at least partially responsible for this, as well as for the

American's inclination to deem this assimilation desirable. Of course, this view is also based on the memories of previous absorption of minority groups into a dominant "American" population. Even the American Indians are now considered as ultimately assimilable. . . .

This long-range view of ultimate assimilation can be found to co-exist with any degree of race prejudice in the actual present-day situation. In many parts of the country Mexicans are kept in a status similar to the Negro's or only a step above. Likewise, in most places anti-Semitism is strong and has apparently been growing for the last ten years. Italians, Poles, Finns, are distrusted in some communities; Germans, Scandinavians, and the Irish are disliked in others, or sometimes the same communities. There are sections of the majority group which draw the circle exclusively and who hate all "foreigners." There are others who keep a somewhat distinct line only around the more exotic peoples. The individual, regional, and class differentials in anti-minority feeling are great.

In spite of all race prejudice, few Americans seem to doubt that it is the ultimate fate of this nation to incorporate without distinction not only all the Northern European stocks, but also the people from Eastern and Southern Europe, the Near East and Mexico. They see obstacles; they emphasize the religious and "racial" differences; they believe it will take a long time. But they assume that it is going to happen, and do not have, on the whole, strong objections to it—provided it is located in a distant future.

The Negroes, on the other hand, are commonly assumed to be unassimilable and this is the reason why the characterization of the Negro problem as a minority problem does not exhaust its true import. The Negroes are set apart, together with other colored peoples, principally the Chinese and the Japanese. America fears the segregation into distinctive isolated groups of all other elements of its population and looks upon the preservation of their separate national attributes and group loyalties as a hazard to American institutions.

Considerable efforts are directed toward "Americanizing" all groups of alien origin. But in regard to the colored peoples, the American policy is the reverse. They are excluded from assimilation. Even by their best friends in the dominant white group and by the promoters of racial peace and good-will, they are usually advised to keep to themselves and develop a race pride of their own.

Among the groups commonly considered unassimilable, the Negro people is by far the largest. The Negroes do not, like the Japanese and the Chinese, have a politically organized nation and an accepted culture of their own outside of America to fall back upon. Unlike the Oriental, there attaches to the Negro an historical memory of slavery and inferiority. It is more difficult for them to answer prejudice with prejudice and, as the Orientals may do, to consider themselves and their history superior to the white Americans and their recent cultural achievements. The Negroes do not have these fortifications for self-respect. They are more helplessly imprisoned as a subordinate caste in America, a caste of people deemed to be lacking a cultural past and assumed to be incapable of a cultural future.

To the ordinary white American the caste line between whites and Negroes is based upon, and defended by, the anti-amalgamation doctrine. This doctrine, more than anything else, gives the Negro problem its uniqueness among other problems of lower status groups, not only in terms of intensity of feelings but more fundamentally in the character of the problem. We follow a general methodological principle, presented previously, when we now start out from the ordinary white man's notion of what constitutes the heart of the Negro problem.

When the Negro people, unlike the white minority groups, is commonly characterized as unassimilable, it is not, of course, implied that amalgamation is not biologically possible. But crossbreeding is considered undesirable. Sometimes the view is expressed that the offspring of crossbreeding is inferior to both parental stocks. Usually it is only asserted that it is inferior to the "pure" white stock. The assumption evidently held is that the Negro stock is "inferior" to the white stock. On the inherited inferiority of the Negro people there exists among white Americans a whole folklore, which is remarkably similar throughout the country. . . .

Whether this concept of the inferiority of the Negro stock is psychologically basic to the doctrine that amalgamation should be prohibited, or is only a rationalization of this doctrine, may for the moment be left open. . . . Miscegenation is said to be a threat to "racial purity." It is alleged to be contrary to "human instincts." It is "contrary to nature" and "detestable." Not only in the South but often also in the North the stereotyped and hypothetical question is regularly raised without any intermediary reasoning as to its applicability or relevance to the social problem discussed: "Would you like to have your sister or daughter marry a Negro?" This is an unargued appeal to "racial solidarity" as a primary valuation. It is corollary to this attitude that in America the offspring of miscegenation is relegated to the Negro race.

A remarkable and hardly expected peculiarity of this American doctrine, expounded so directly in biological and racial terms, is that it is applied with a vast discretion depending upon the purely social and legal circumstances under which miscegenation takes place. As far as lawful marriage is concerned, the racial doctrine is laden with emotion. Even in the Northern states where, for the most part, intermarriage is not barred by the force of law, the social sanctions blocking its way are serious. Mixed couples are punished by nearly complete social ostracism. On the other hand, in many regions, especially in the South where the prohibition against intermarriage and the general reprehension against miscegenation have the strongest moorings, illicit relations have been widespread and occasionally allowed to acquire a nearly institutional character. Even if . . . such relations are perhaps now on the decline, they are still not entirely stamped out.

*　　*　　*

If we now turn to the American Negro people, we can hardly avoid the strong impression that what there is of reluctance in principle toward amalgamation is merely in the nature of a reaction or response to the white doctrine, which thus stands as primary in the causal sense and strategic in a practical sense. It is true that white people, when facing the Negro group, make an ideological application of the general Jim Crow principle —"equal but separate" treatment and accommodations for the two racial groups—and proceed from the assertion that both races are good to the explanation that there is a value in keeping them unmixed. They appeal also to the Negroes' "race pride" and their interest in keeping their own blood "pure." But this is a white, not a Negro, argument.

The Negro will be found to doubt the sincerity of the white folks' interest in the purity of the Negro race. It will sound to him too much like a rationalization, in strained equalitarian terms, of the white supremacy doctrine of race purity. . . . Even the Negro in the uneducated classes is sensitive to the nuances of sincerity, trained as he is in both slavery and afterwards to be a good dissembler himself. The Negro will, furthermore, encounter considerable intellectual difficulties inherent in the idea of keeping his blood pure, owing to the fact that the large majority of American Negroes actually are of mixed descent. They already have white and Indian ancestry as well as African Negro blood. And in general they are aware of this fact.

* * *

Every widening of the writer's experience of white Americans has only driven home to him more strongly that the opinion that the Negro is unassimilable, or, rather, that his amalgamation into the American nation is undesirable, is held more commonly, absolutely, and intensely than would be assumed from a general knowledge of American thought-ways. . . .

The intensity of the attitude seems to be markedly stronger in the South than in the North. Its strength seems generally to be inversely related to the economic and social status of the informant and his educational level. It is usually strong even in most of the non-colored minority groups, if they are above the lowest plane of indifference. To the poor and socially insecure, but struggling, white individual, a fixed opinion on this point seems an important matter of prestige and distinction.

* * *

This attitude of refusing to consider amalgamation—felt and expressed in the entire country—constitutes the center in the complex of attitudes which can be described as the "common denominator" in the problem. It defines the Negro group in contradistinction to all the non-colored minority groups in America and all other lower class groups. The boundary between Negro and white is not simply a class line which can be successfully crossed by education, integration into the national culture, and individual economic advancement. The boundary is fixed. It is not a temporary expediency during an apprenticeship in the national culture. It is a bar erected with the intention of permanency. It is directed against the whole group. Actually, however, "passing" as a white person is possible when a Negro is white enough to conceal his Negro heritage. But the difference between "passing" and ordinary social climbing reveals the distinction between a class line, in the ordinary sense, and a caste line.

* * *

THE THEORY OF "NO SOCIAL EQUALITY"

In his first encounter with the American Negro problem, perhaps nothing perplexes the outside observer more than the popular term and the popular theory of "no social equality." He will be made to feel from the start that it has concrete implications and a central importance for the Negro problem in America. But, nevertheless, the term is kept vague and elusive, and the theory loose and ambiguous. One moment it will be stretched to cover and justify every form of social segregation and discrimination, and, in addition, all the inequalities in justice, politics and breadwinning. The next moment it will be narrowed to express only the denial of close personal intimacies and intermarriage. The very lack of precision allows the notion of "no social equality" to rationalize the rather illogical and wavering system of color caste in America.

The kernel of the popular theory of "no social equality" will, when pursued, be presented as a firm determination on the part of the whites to block amalgamation and preserve "the purity of the white race." The white man identifies himself with "the white race" and feels that he has a stake in resisting the dissipation of its racial identity. Important in this identification is the notion of "the absolute and unchangeable superiority of the white race." From this racial dogma will often be drawn the direct inference that the white man shall dominate in all spheres. But when the logic of this inference is inquired about, the inference will be made indirect and will be made to lead over to the danger of amalgamation, or as it is popularly expressed, "intermarriage."

* * *

This theory of color caste centering around the aversion to amalgamation determines, as we have just observed, the white man's rather definite rank order of the various measures of segregation and discrimination against Negroes. The relative significance attached to each of those measures is dependent upon their degree of expediency or necessity—in the view of white people—as means of upholding the ban on "intermarriage." In this rank order, (1) the ban on intermarriage and other sex relations involving white women and colored men takes precedence before anything else. It is the end for which the other restrictions are arranged as means. Thereafter follow: (2) all sorts of taboos and etiquettes in personal contacts; (3) segregation in schools and churches; (4) segregation in hotels, restaurants, and theaters, and other public places where people meet socially; (5) segregation in public conveyances; (6) discrimination in public services; and finally, inequality in (7) politics, (8) justice and (9) breadwinning and relief.

* * *

SOCIAL SEGREGATION AND DISCRIMINATION

At the outbreak of the Civil War, most Northern states were nearly as far removed in time from actual slavery in their own realms as the Southern states are now. Their Negro populations were comparatively small in numbers. But slavery was a living institution within the nation. Though conditions were rather different in different Northern states, the general statement can be made that wherever Negroes lived in significant numbers they met considerable social segregation and discrimination. The Abolitionist propaganda and the gradual definition of emancipation as one of the main goals of the War undoubtedly tended to raise the status of Negroes somewhat. Still, one of the difficulties congressional leaders had in passing the Reconstruction legislation was the resistance in some Northern states where people found that they would have to change not only their behavior but also their laws in order to comply with the new statutes.

In the social field—as in breadwinning, but not as in politics and justice—the North has kept much segregation and discrimination. In some respects, the social bars were raised considerably on account of the mass immigration of poor and ignorant Negroes during and immediately after the First World War. In the latter part of the 'twenties this movement was perhaps turned into a slight tendency in the opposite direction, namely, an appreciation of "The New Negro." After a new wave of unpopularity during the first years of the depression, there seems again to have been a slow but steady development toward less social discrimination during the era of the New Deal. But quite apart from these uncertain fluctuations during the last couple of decades, it is obviously a gross exaggeration when it is asserted that the North is getting to be "like the South."

Even in the realm of social relations it is of importance that the average Northerner does not think of the Negroes as former slaves. He has not the possessive feeling for them and he does not regard their subservience as a mark of his own social status. He is, therefore, likely to let the Negroes alone unless in his opinion they get to be a nuisance. Upon the ideological plane the ordinary Northerner is, further, apparently conscious that social discrimination is wrong and against the American Creed, while the average Southerner tries to convince himself and the nation that it is right or, in any case, that it is necessary. The white newspapers in the North ordinarily ignore the Negroes and their problems entirely—most of the time more completely than the liberal Southern press. But when they have to come out in the open on the Negro problem, they usually stand for equality. Back of this official attitude, of course, is the fact that most Northerners are not in direct contact with Negroes. The patterns of social discrimination in the South have originally formed themselves as rural ways of life. In the North the rural sections are, and have always been, practically free of Negroes. Even in the big cities in the North, where there are substantial Negro populations, only a small part of the white population has more contacts with Negroes.

Lacking ideological sanction and developing directly contrary to the openly accepted equalitarian Creed, social segregation and discrimination in the North have to keep *sub rosa*. The observer finds that *in the North there is actually much unawareness on the part of white people of the extent of social discrimination against Negroes*. It has been a common experience of this writer to witness how white Northerners are surprised and shocked when they hear about such things, and how they are moved to feel that something ought to be done to stop it. They often do not understand correctly even the implications of their own behavior and often

tell the interviewer that they "have never thought of it in that light." This innocence is, of course, opportunistic in a degree, but it is, nevertheless, real and honest too. It denotes the absence of an explicit theory and an intentional policy. In this situation *one of the main difficulties for the Negroes in the North is simply lack of publicity*. It is convenient for the Northerners' good conscience to forget about the Negro.

In so far as the Negroes can get their claims voiced in the press and in legislatures, and are able to put political strength behind them, they are free to press for state action against social discrimination. The chances are that they will meet no *open* opposition. The legislatures will practically never go the other way and attempt to Jim Crow the Negroes by statutes. The federal Reconstruction legislation has taken better root in the North. When the Supreme Court in 1883 declared the Civil Rights Bill of 1875 unconstitutional, most states in the Northeast and Middle West, and some in the Far West, started to make similar laws of their own, while the Southern states, instead, began to build up the structure of Jim Crow legislation.

With the ideological and legal sanctions directed *against* them, social segregation and discrimination have not acquired the *strength, persuasiveness or institutional fixity* found in the South. Actual discrimination varies a good deal in the North: it seems to be mainly a function of the relative number of Negroes in a community and its distance from the South. In several minor cities in New England with a small, stable Negro population, for instance, social discrimination is hardly noticeable. The Negroes there usually belong to the working class, but often they enter the trades, serve in shops, and even carry on independent businesses catering to whites as well as to Negroes. They belong to the ordinary churches of the community, and the children attend the public schools. Occasional intermarriages do not create great excitement. They fit into the community and usually form a little clique for themselves beside other cliques, but nobody seems to think much about their color. . . .

In the bigger cities, even in New England, the conditions of life for the Negroes have probably never been so idyllic. Since the migration beginning in 1915, the status of Northern Negroes has fallen perceptibly. In the Northern cities nearer the Mason-Dixon line there has always been, and is even today, more social segregation and discrimination than farther North.

One factor which in every Northern city of any size has contributed to form patterns of segregation and discrimination against Negroes has been residential segregation, which acts as a cause as well as an effect of social distance. This fundamental segregation was caused by the general pattern for ethnic groups to live together in Northern cities. But while Swedes, Italians, and Jews could become Americanized in a generation or two, and disperse themselves into the more anonymous parts of the city, Negroes were caught in their "quarters" because of their inescapable social visibility; and the real estate interest kept watch to enforce residential segregation. With residential segregation naturally comes a certain amount of segregation in schools, in hospitals, and in other public places even when it is not intended as part of policy. Personal contacts become, as a matter of course, more or less restricted to Negro neighborhoods. As the Negro sections grew during the northward migration, it became more and more possible for Negroes to have their entire social life in Negro neighborhoods, and white people became conditioned to look upon this as a natural and desirable situation. In this process white Southerners who also moved northward have played a crucial role. To make a manager of a hotel, a restaurant, or a theater interested in trying to keep Negroes out of his establishment, it is not necessary that more than a tiny majority of customers object, particularly if they make a scene. Time and again I have, in my interviews with managers of various public places in the North, been told

this same story: that they, themselves, had no prejudices but that some of their customers would resent seeing Negroes around. The fact that most Negroes are poor and residentially isolated and, hence, do not patronize white places often, and the further fact that upper class Negroes, who could afford to, abstain voluntarily from visiting places where they are afraid of being embarrassed, solidifies the situation. I have also noticed that Negroes often have an entirely exaggerated notion of the difficulties they would meet. They are conditioned to suspect discrimination even when there is no danger of it. So they abstain from going to places where they actually could go without any trouble. When once this pattern is set by themselves the result might later be discrimination when some Negro tries to break it.

The migrating Negroes have probably been even more influential in spreading Southern patterns in the North than the Southern whites. The low cultural level and poverty of the average Southern Negro stand out even more when he comes North, where general standards are higher. If he comes without any other education, he is at least thoroughly trained in the entire ceremonial system of scraping his foot, tipping his hat, and using self-abasing vocabulary and dialect, and generally being subservient and unobtrusive in the company of whites. A Negro recently from the South is characterized as much by his manners and bearing as by his racial traits. He might get some ideas of a new freedom of behavior in the North and actually try his best to behave as a full man; and he might, indeed, easily succeed in becoming aggressive and offensive. But fundamentally it takes a radical reeducation to get him out of his Southern demeanor or the reaction to it. For a long time after migrating he will invoke discrimination by his own behavior. The submissive behavior of lower class Southern Negroes is usually not appealing at all to the white Northerner, who has not been brought up to have a patronizing attitude and who does not need it for his own self-elevation. The white Northerner also dislikes the slovenliness and ignorance of the Southern Negro. Thus the Negro often seems only strange, funny or repulsive to the white Northerner.

Even the poor classes of whites in the North come to mistrust and despise the Negroes. The European immigrant groups are the ones thrown into most direct contact and competition with Negroes: they live near each other, often send their children to the same schools, and have to struggle for the same jobs. Obviously attitudes among immigrants vary a good deal. Recent immigrants apparently sometimes feel an interest solidarity with Negroes or, at any rate, lack the intense superiority feeling of the native Americans educated in race prejudice. But the development of prejudice against Negroes is usually one of their first lessons in Americanization. Because they are of low status, they like to have a group like the Negroes to which they can be superior. For these reasons, it should not be surprising if now, since new immigration has been restricted for a considerable time, a study of racial attitudes should show that the immigrant groups are on the average even more prejudiced than native Americans in the same community.

I have an impression that the resentment against Negroes in the North is different from that in the South, not only in intensity, but also in its class direction. It does not seem to be directed particularly against the rising Negroes. In the more anonymous Northern cities, the Negro middle and upper classes do not get into the focus of public resentment as in the South. More important is the Yankee outlook on life in which climbing and social success are generally given a higher value than in the more static Southern society, and the ambitious Negro will more often be rewarded by approval and even by admiration, while in the South he is likely to be considered "smart," "uppity" or "out of his place."

Otherwise, the North is not original in its racial ideology. When there is segregation and discrimination to be justified, the rationalization is sometimes a vague and simplified version of the "no social equality" theory of the South which we have already discussed. It is continuously spread by Southerners moving North and Northerners who have been South, by fiction and by hearsay. But more often the rationalizations run in terms of the alleged racial inferiority of the Negro, his animal-like nature, his unreliability, his low morals, dirtiness and unpleasant manners. The references and associations to amalgamation and intermarriage are much less frequent and direct. . . .

In this situation, however, not only is intermarriage frowned upon, but in high schools and colleges there will often be attempts to exclude Negroes from dances and social affairs. Social segregation is, in fact, likely to appear in all sorts of social relations. But there is much less social segregation and discrimination than in the South: there is no segregation on streetcars, trains, and so on, and above all, there is no rigid ceremonial governing the Negro-white relations and no laws holding the Negro down. The fact that there are no laws or defined rules of etiquette is sometimes said to cause friction and bitterness because some whites in the North will want Negroes to keep away from them, and Negroes cannot tell which whites these are. But the absence of segregating laws also keeps the system from being so relatively locked as in the South. It allows Negroes to be ambitious. And since Negroes in the North have the vote and a reasonable amount of justice in court, and since they can go to good schools and are, in fact, forced to get at least an elementary education, they can struggle for fuller social equality with some hope.

* * *

ECONOMIC DISCRIMINATION

The picture of the economic situation of the Negro people is dark. The prospects for the future—as far as we have analyzed the trends until now—are discouraging. The main practical problem must be how to open up new possibilities for Negroes to earn a living by their labor.

Southern agriculture offers no such new

opportunities. It is, on the contrary, likely that Southern rural Negroes will continue to be pushed off the land and thus increase the number of job-seekers in nonagricultural pursuits. In Northern agriculture the main trend will also be a contraction in the demand for labor. The segregated Negro economy will never provide any great number of jobs. It is on the ordinary nonfarm labor market that Negroes have to look for new opportunities. In the nonagricultural pursuits, Negro job limitations, as we have found, are of four different types:

(1) Negroes are kept out of certain industries, North as well as South.

(2) In industries where Negroes are working, they are often confined to certain establishments, whereas other establishments are kept entirely white.

(3) In practically all industries where Negroes are accepted, they are confined to unskilled occupations and to such semi-skilled and skilled occupations as are unattractive to white workers. The main exceptions to this rule are in the building industry where the Negro had acquired a position during slavery but has been losing ground since then.

(4) Finally, there is a geographical segregation. Negroes in the North are concentrated in a few large cities. In the Western centers there is still only a small number of Negro workers. Negroes are even scarcer in the small Northern and Western cities.

Race prejudice on the part of the whites is the usual explanation given for these various types of job limitations. But to relate discrimination to prejudice means little more than to substitute one word for another. Leaving this problem aside for the moment, we may observe that race prejudice and discrimination, in the economic sphere, operate principally in three different ways:

(1) Many white workers, even if they think that Negroes generally should have a fair share in the job opportunities in this country, tend to be opposed to Negro competition in the particular localities, industries, occupations, and establishments where they themselves work.

(2) Some customers object to being served by Negroes unless the Negro has an apparently menial position.

(3) Many employers believe that Negroes are inferior as workers, except for dirty, heavy, hot or otherwise unattractive work. Perhaps even more important is the fact that they pay much attention to the attitudes of both customers and white workers.

All these conditions, in many different ways, are self-perpetuating. Let us, in this context, just point to one element in this circular process. Suppose that an individual employer would entirely ignore the race of those applying for work at his shop and would consider just the individual capacities of the job-seekers, white or black. The fact that most other employers exclude Negroes means that the individual employer would have a disproportionate number of Negroes applying for his jobs. The rumor about his unusual behavior would draw Negro workers from other localities, and he might soon find a majority of Negroes on his labor force. The consequence might be that his establishment would be shunned by white labor, and it is not impossible that the result would be an almost all-Negro shop. The best he can do if he wants to favor the Negro, without having to face such consequences, is to fix the percentage of Negro workers; but that means giving up the principle of selecting Negro and white workers on an individual basis.

* * *

Even in the North the Negro is generally believed to be inferior as a worker. White employees often are strongly against having any Negro co-workers. Yet these attitudes are less general and less well entrenched in the North than they are in the South. Many, perhaps even most, Northerners tend to be rather uncertain and vacillating on such matters. There is nothing in their general ideologies which would support economic discrimination against Negroes. There is no racial etiquette, little emotion about the "social equality" issue, no white solidarity for the purpose of "keeping the Negro in his place." On the contrary, the equalitarian principles of the American Creed dominate people's opinions in the North. Northern states and municipalities, as we saw in Chapter 15, usually uphold nondiscrimination in public relief as well as in politics, justice, and all other relations between public authorities and the citizens. People in the North are "against" economic discrimination as a general proposition. If the white Northerners had to vote on the issue, a large majority would probably come out for full equality of opportunities on the labor market: they would be in favor of making employment opportunities "independent of race, creed or color." The actual discrimination is, however, as we have seen, the rule and not the exception.

* * *

The vicious circle of job restrictions, poverty, and all that follows with it tends to fix the tradition that Negroes should be kept out of good jobs and held down in unskilled, dirty, hot or otherwise undesirable work. Residential segregation and segregation at places of work hinder whites from having personal acquaintance with Negroes and recognizing that Negroes are much like themselves. In the eyes of white workers the Negroes easily come to appear "different," as a "low grade people," and it becomes a matter of social prestige not to work under conditions of equality with them. The fact that Negroes actually work almost only in menial tasks makes it more natural to look upon them in this way. The occupations they work in tend to become déclassé.

When once the white workers' desires for social prestige become mobilized against the Negroes in this way, when they have come to look upon Negroes as different from themselves and consequently do not feel a common labor solidarity with them, "economic interests" also will back up discrimination. By excluding Negroes from the competition for jobs, the white workers can decrease the supply of labor in the market, hold up wages and secure employment for themselves. To give white workers a monopoly on all promotions is, of course, to give them a vested interest in job segregation.

Negroes, on their side, have to try to utilize every opening, even if it means working for lower wages or under inferior working conditions. The abundance of Negro labor, kept idle because of exclusionist policies, must always be feared by white workers. If given the chance, Negroes will accept positions as "sweatshop" competitors—something which cannot fail to increase the resentment of the white wage earners. Sometimes they may even work as "scabs" and so white workers get extra justification for the feeling that Negroes represent a danger of "unfair competition." The Negroes react by being suspicious of the white workers and their unions. For this reason, they are sometimes "poor union material" even if white workers choose to let them in on a basis of equality. White union members then resent the "ingratitude" of the Negroes.

The racial beliefs are conveniently at hand to rationalize prejudice and discriminatory practices. The whole complex of stereotypes, maintained by limited contacts, is an element in the vicious circle that perpetuates economic discrimination. With some difficulty, white people might be taught that there are all kinds of Negroes as there are all kinds of whites, some good and some bad, and that many—not just a few—individual Negroes are better than many whites. But here the separation between the two groups works strongly against the Negroes. Anyone having to fill a position or a job, having to select a fellow worker at his bench, or a neighbor in the district where he lives, by just drawing a white or a Negro man without knowing anything in particular about him personally, will feel that, in all prudence, he has a better chance to get the more congenial and more capable man if he selects the white. Here the stereotyped concept of the average Negro as it exists in the Northern white man's mind works as an economic bias against the Negro.

* * *

These observations have all referred to the

North. The situation in the South is not entirely different, but there are certain significant dissimilarities, some advantageous and some disadvantageous. The factor of ignorance and unconcernedness is important in the South, too. Many white Southerners would undoubtedly give their backing to positive measures to preserve a place for the Negro if they knew more accurately about his plight and about the unfavorable trends. But there is in the South an entrenched and widespread popular theory that the Negro should be held down in his "place." Discrimination in justice, politics, education, and public service creates an atmosphere in which economic discrimination becomes natural or even necessary in order to prevent "social equality."

On the other hand, there are, in the South, many people in the white upper class who feel, as a matter of tradition, that the whites should "look out for" and "take care of" their Negroes. As there are fewer and fewer personal ties between upper class whites and Negroes and the isolation between the two groups is growing, this factor is becoming less and less important as a protection of Negro employment opportunities.

The mere fact that there are many more Negroes in the South makes them less strange to white people. The white Southerner does not react so much, and for such flimsy reasons, as many Northerners do, to having Negroes around. The employers have more experience with Negro labor and are often not so prejudiced against using it. The fact that they are seldom prepared to treat Negro and white workers on a basis of equality often makes it easy for them to employ Negro workers without having any "trouble." The workers are more accustomed in many trades to work with Negroes.

The Negroes have also had a sort of protection in the traditional "Negro jobs." These job monopolies, however, have been largely in stagnating occupations and trades. As we have seen, white workers have always been pressing against these job monopolies. Job exclusion in all desirable and most undesir-

able jobs has, on the whole, been steadily progressing. The Negro's prospects in Southern industry are not promising. The very fact that there are so many more Negroes working there already means that the possibilities for expansion of Negro employment are slighter than they are in the North. The high natural increase of the white population in the South, and the likelihood that many white farmers will be pushed out of Southern agriculture, means that the white pressure to exclude Negroes from jobs will be strong even if there should be considerable industrial expansion.

Particularly in the South the concentration of Negro workers in the unskilled jobs is dangerous for their future employment, as mechanization means a constantly decreased demand for unskilled labor. Unskilled labor itself is changing character. Modern technical development means that formerly unpleasant jobs are becoming "suitable" for white workers. The entrance of women into industry not only means that Negro labor has a new competitor but also intensifies the issue of "social equality." All these trends have been going on for a long time in the South. They are bound to continue. Since there is so much Negro labor in the Southern labor market, and since the resistance against keeping Negro labor in skilled work and "nice" unskilled work is so strong, it is difficult to see much hope for the Negro in Southern industry.

* * *

LEGAL DISCRIMINATION AND LYNCHING

The American tradition of electing, rather than appointing, minor public officials has its most serious features in regard to the judiciary branch of the government. Judges, prosecuting attorneys, minor court officials, sheriffs, the chiefs of police, and in smaller communities sometimes the entire police force, are either elected for limited terms or are dependent for their offices upon political representatives of this uncertain tenure. In some places they can even be "recalled" during their terms of office, though this is comparatively rare.

The immediate dependence of court and police officials upon popular election—that is, upon local public opinion and political machines—instead of upon appointment strictly according to merit, and the uncertainty of tenure implied in this system naturally decreases the attractiveness of these important positions to many of the best persons who would otherwise be available. Professional standards are thus kept lower than those which could be attained under another system. The courts do not get the cream of the legal profession. The social prestige of judges in local courts is not as supreme as could be wished. Corruption and undue political influences are not absent even from the courtrooms. These facts themselves have the circular effect of keeping the best men from judicial positions.

But, apart **from** such general effects, the fact that the administration of justice is dependent upon the local voters is likely to imply discrimination against an unpopular minority group, particularly when this group is disfranchised as Negroes are in the South. The elected judge knows that sooner or later he must come back to the polls, and that a decision running counter to local opinion may cost him his position. He may be conscious of it or not, but this control of his future career must tend to increase his difficulties in keeping aloof from local prejudices and emotions. Of course, the judge's attitudes are also formed by conditions prevalent in his local community, but he has a degree of acquaintance with the law, and with public and legal opinion outside his community. This would tend to emancipate him from local opinion were it not for his direct dependence on it.

The dependence of the judge on local prejudices strikes at the very root of orderly government. It results in the danger of breaking down the law in its primary function of protecting the minority against the majority, the individual against society, indeed, of democracy itself against the danger of its nullifying, in practice, the settled principles of law

and impartiality of justice. This danger is higher in the problem regions where there is acute race friction and in rural areas where the population is small and provincial, and where personal contacts are direct. Under the same influences as the judges are the public prosecutors, the sheriffs, the chiefs of police and their subordinates. The American jury system, while it has many merits, is likely to strengthen this dependence of justice upon local popular opinion. If, as in the South, Negroes are kept out of jury service, the democratic safeguard of the jury system is easily turned into a means of minority subjugation.

The popular election of the officers of law and the jury system are expressions of the extreme democracy in the American handling of justice. It might, in spite of the dangers suggested, work excellently in a reasonably homogeneous, highly educated and public spirited community. It might also work fairly well anywhere for cases involving only parties belonging to a homogeneous majority group which controls the court. It causes, however, the gravest peril of injustice in all cases where the rights of persons belonging to a disfranchised group are involved, particularly if this group is discriminated against all around and by tradition held as a lower caste upon whose rights it has become customary to infringe. *The extreme democracy in the American system of justice turns out, thus, to be the greatest menace to legal democracy when it is based on restricted political participation and an ingrained tradition of caste suppression.* Such conditions occur in the South with respect to Negroes.

If there is a deficiency of legal protection for Negroes, white people will be tempted to deal unfairly with them in everyday affairs. They will be tempted to use irregular methods to safeguard what they feel to be their interests against Negroes. They will be inclined to use intimidation and even violence against Negroes if they can count on going unpunished. When such patterns become established, the law itself and its processes are brought into contempt, and a general feeling of uncertainty, arbitrariness and inequality will spread. Not only Negroes but other persons of weak social status will be the object of discrimination. . . . In the South there have been frequent occasions when the legal rights of poor white persons have been disregarded, and even when general lawlessness prevailed. When the frequency of law-breaking thus increases, it becomes necessary to apply stronger penalties than is necessary in an equitable system of justice. In all spheres of public life it will, of course, be found that legislation is relatively ineffective, and so the sociologists will be inclined to formulate a general societal law of "the futility of trying to suppress folkways by stateways." Lawlessness has then received the badge of scientific normalcy.

The Negroes, on their side, are hurt in their trust that the law is impartial, that the court and the police are their protection, and, indeed, that they belong to an orderly society which has set up this machinery for common security and welfare. They will not feel confidence in, and loyalty toward, a legal order which is entirely out of their control and which they sense to be inequitable and merely part of the system of caste suppression. Solidarity then develops easily in the Negro group, a solidarity against the law and the police. The arrested Negro often acquires the prestige of a victim, a martyr, or a hero, even when he is simply a criminal. It becomes part of race pride in the protective Negro community not to give up a fellow Negro who is hunted by the police. Negroes who collaborate with the police become looked upon as stool pigeons.

No one visiting Negro communities in the South can avoid observing the prevalence of these views. The situation is dynamic for several reasons. One is the growing urbanization and the increasing segregation of the Negro people. The old-time paternalistic and personal relationship between individuals of the two groups is on the decrease. Another factor is the improvement of Negro education which is continually making Negroes more aware of their anomalous status in the American legal order. A third factor, the importance of which is increasing in pace with the literacy of the Negro people, is the persistent hammering of the Negro press which, to a large extent, is devoted to giving publicity to the injustices and injuries suffered by Negroes. A fourth factor is unemployment, especially of young Negroes, with resulting insecurity and dissatisfaction.

Because of these changes, as Du Bois tells us, ". . . the Negro is coming *more and more* to look upon law and justice, not as protecting safeguards, but as sources of humiliation and oppression." He expresses a common attitude among Southern Negroes when he continues: "The laws are made by men who have absolutely no motive for treating the black people with courtesy or consideration: . . . the accused law-breaker is tried, not by his peers, but too often by men who would rather punish ten innocent Negroes than let one guilty one escape." To the present observer the situation looks far from peaceful and quiet, as white people in the South have tried to convince him. It has rather the appearance of a fateful race between, on the one hand, the above-mentioned tendencies which increase Negro mistrust, unrest, and asociality, and, on the other, the equally apparent tendency for the white group increasingly to be prepared to give the Negro personal security and equality before the law.

* * *

Lynchings were becoming common in the South in the 'thirties, 'forties and 'fifties of the nineteenth century. Most of the victims in this early period were white men. The pattern of lynching Negroes became set during Reconstruction. No reliable statistics before 1889 are available. Between 1889 and 1940, according to Tuskegee Institute figures, 3,833 people were lynched, about four-fifths of whom were Negroes. The Southern states account for nine-tenths of the lynchings. More than two-thirds of the remaining one-tenth occurred in the six states which immediately border the South: Maryland, West Virginia, Ohio, Indiana, Illinois and Kansas. Since the early 1890's, the trend has been toward fewer and fewer lynchings. The annual average in the 'nineties was near 200; in the 'thirties it dropped to slightly over 10. In 1941 it was down to 4, but there are already more than this in 1942 (July). The decrease has been faster outside the South, and the lynching of whites has dropped much more than that of Negroes. Lynching has become, therefore, more and more a Southern phenomenon and a racial one. Against the decrease in number of victims there has been a marked trend toward greatly aggravated brutality, extending to torture, mutilation and other sadistic excesses.

*　　*　　*

It is possible to speculate about the causes for the decline in lynching. If our analysis of the background factors is correct, the rising standard of living and the improved education must have been of importance. The fundamentalism and emotionalism of Southern religion have been decreasing. Cultural isolation is being broken by radio, improved highways and cheap motor cars. There is more diversion from the drab and monotonous small town life, and the sex taboos have been somewhat relaxed. The national agitation around lynching, strengthened after the organization of the National Association for the Advancement of Colored People in 1909, has undoubtedly been of tremendous importance in awakening influential people in the South to the urgency of stopping lynching. The sharp decline in lynching since 1922 has undoubtedly something to do with the fact that early in that year the Dyer Anti-Lynching Bill was put through the House of Representatives. It was later killed in the Senate by the filibuster of the Southern senators, and the sellout of Western and Northern senators, but the continuous discussion of the measure from then on has probably been of great importance. A prominent Negro leader confided to the present author that, as a force to stamp out lynching, the agitation around the bill is probably as effective, or more effective, than the law itself would be.

Southern organizations of whites have taken to condemning lynching. Some religious denominations of the South declare against lynching at their annual conventions and sponsor programs on racial matters for white youth. One of the most active fights of the Commission for Interracial Cooperation has been against lynching, and, under its auspices, the Association of Southern Women for the Prevention of Lynching has collected nearly 50,000 signatures of Southern white women and of a few hundred peace officers to a pledge against lynching. Other women's organizations in the South also have been active in the propaganda against lynching. One of the most notable changes has been in the attitudes of the press. Today the great majority of Southern newspapers will come out openly against lynching. State authorities usually try to prevent lynchings, and they have an instrument in the State police systems which can be readily concentrated in any community where people are congregating for a lynching. Behind this movement is the growing strength of Southern liberalism.

*　　*　　*

RECENT CHANGES AND OUTLOOK FOR THE FUTURE

Against the obstacles of the powerful interlocking system of social, judicial, political, and economic inequalities and disabilities, and in spite of the desire on the part of the majority of Southern whites that the Negroes remain in an inferior social status, and the great indifference and ignorance about it all on the part of most Northern whites, *the Negroes are rising*. They are rising most rapidly in the North, but their rate of rise in the South is not inconsiderable. It is one of the paradoxes of the American situation, ultimately due to the split morality of the nation on the issue of racial democracy, that this rise of the Negroes to a great extent is the result of education and other public efforts, which—solicited by the Negro leaders, pushed by a small minority of Southern liberals, and assisted by Northern philanthropy

—is largely provided by the Southern states themselves with the approval of the ordinary Southern whites in political power, acting in partial obedience to the American Creed.

The fundamental character of these efforts and their result have been to diffuse American middle class norms to the uneducated and crude Southern "folk Negroes," emerging out of the backwardness of slavery. Besides education, the persistent forces of industrialization and urbanization are having an impact on the Negro. Migration, occupational changes, the easy methods of communication, the Negro press, the growth of Negro organizations, the radio, the moving pictures, and all other vehicles of "modern life" are working upon the minds of Southern Negroes, gradually upsetting the older static tradition of compliance and introducing new thoughts and presumptions, dissatisfaction and unrest. In so far as the caste line remains comparatively fixed, one result of these changes is increasing isolation. The spiritual effects of segregation are accumulating with each new generation, continuously estranging the two groups.

One phase of the rise of the Negroes is the formation of a Negro middle and upper class. A nucleus of such a class was already forming among free Negroes in slavery times. Since then it has been steadily, but slowly, growing, partly as a result of segregation itself, which holds down the Negro masses but opens petty monopolies for a few. These middle and upper class Negroes, who have stepped out of the servant status, live mostly by catering to their own people. [See Selection 47.]

* * *

The behavior patterns and attitudes of the small Negro middle and upper class group are of greatest importance for the whole Negro people as they set the standards which are spread from the pulpit and the teacher's desk, by the influential Negro press and through social imitation. As has already been suggested, popular education in America is even more essentially directed on the dissemination of middle class views and ways of life

than in most other countries. The cultural rise of the Negro masses means their gradual approach to middle class standards. Negro education is now segregated in the South nearly to the limit and is, consequently, in the hands of this spiritually isolated Negro middle and upper class group. White people do not know much about what goes on in Negro schools or what is printed in the Negro press. They would be shocked if they knew. But more fundamentally, white people are caught in the contradictions of their own thinking. The white control of the Negro schools cannot check, and cannot be intent upon checking, the spread among Negroes of the middle class attitudes leading to Negro social withdrawal. This is what the whites have asked for. Racial pride and voluntary isolation is increasingly becoming the pattern for the whole Negro people. Lower class Negro parents now teach their children to keep out of the way of white people.

Meanwhile the old bonds of intimacy between upper class white families and their Negro servants have been breaking down. This process started immediately after Emancipation but is not yet fully consummated. . . . In so far as Negro professionals increasingly are taking care of the souls and the bodies of Negroes generally, the result is not only the creation of a culturally isolated Negro middle and upper class but also, on the other side of the fence, a new barrier to communication between white people and lower class Negroes. In their daily work also Negroes and whites have been becoming increasingly separated. The only exception in the South to the general trend of increasing separation is the recent coming together of Negro and white workers in the new labor unions.

* * *

The isolation we are speaking about— caused by all the barriers to contact involved in etiquette, segregation, and discrimination from the side of the whites and in voluntary withdrawal and resentment from the side of the Negroes—means a decrease of certain types of contacts between the two groups and a distortion of the ones that are left. It is useful here to put the reverse question: What contacts do remain? and what is their significance for interracial relations? To answer these questions there ought to be quantitative studies of the sort we have discussed previously. Since no such studies have been made, our observations have to be general, tentative, and in the nature of somewhat schematic hypotheses for further research.

Negroes constitute about 10 per cent of the American population, and since there has been little attempt to segregate them by region, there is naturally some contact. Of course, Negroes have been concentrated—for historical reasons—in the South, but there are enough Negroes throughout the North and in cities of the West for their appearance to be commonly recognized by the majority of the white inhabitants of these latter areas. The patterns of segregation and withdrawal are so effective, however, that even where Negroes are a common sight *there is actual contact with them in practically only three spheres of life: the casual, the economic and the criminal.*

By *casual contacts* we mean all those instances where Negro individuals and white individuals see each other but without the condition of recognizing each other as individuals, or at least for the whites to recognize the Negroes as individuals. Casual contacts would thus include passing on the street, passing or remaining briefly in the presence of each other in public buildings or public vehicles, having visual or auditory contact with each other by reason of independent relations with common third persons, or the like. Such contacts are the most numerous type, except possibly on the plantation and in other rural areas where either the Negro or the white population forms a small proportion of the total. Casual contacts are important in an urban civilization. But they are especially important in Negro-white contacts, since they are only slightly diminished by patterns of segregation and discrimination as compared to other types of Negro-white contacts. Since the casual contact is one in which

the participants have no occasion to regard each other as individuals but only as members of a group, *the main effect of the casual contact would seem to be a strengthening of stereotypes.* Negroes, but not whites, have something of an antidote for the casual contact in their economic contact with whites. The main effect of casual contacts is, therefore, to create and preserve stereotypes of Negroes in the minds of the whites. This is not to say that casual contacts are the only, or even the most important, cause of stereotypes of Negroes. But the impersonality of the comparatively numerous casual contacts allows whites to see Negroes as a relatively uniform biological and social type and to ignore the great variations that would become apparent if observation were more attentive. All Negroes come to look alike to the average white person.

Casual contact between Negroes and whites is probably increasing as Negroes—and whites—are becoming more mobile and as the scope of Negro activity is becoming broader. Also it has been taking on a slightly different character as it enters the urban environment. In a city it is sometimes impossible to avoid close physical contact. Negroes and whites jostle each other unconcernedly on crowded streets, and Negroes have been observed to be standing in the white sections of crowded Jim Crow buses. The increase of casual contacts in Southern cities is undoubtedly wearing away somewhat the strictness of racial etiquette.

The increased range of casual contacts in recent years is not unrelated to the growth of a Negro upper class. This is especially important in the North, where there are no laws against Negroes using public facilities. A well-mannered Negro dressed in good taste who appears in a restaurant, a white church, or a railroad station is likely to weaken unfavorable Negro stereotypes rather than to strengthen them. In the South the effect of the appearance of the upper class Negro is somewhat more problematical. In the long run this will probably have a favorable effect, but in many known instances it has led to violence from lower and middle class whites who felt that the Negroes were getting too "uppity." The Negro's physical appurtenances—that is, his home, store, or automobile—will serve as a casual contact in the same manner as his person.

The effect of increased casual contacts due to increased Negro mobility has, thus far and when considered alone, probably hurt the Negro in the North, even if other advantages for the Negro people as a whole from northward migration have more than compensated for this disadvantage. The Northern white man, who formerly felt little prejudice against the few Northern Negroes and was inclined to idealize Negroes as part of his Civil War heritage, reacted unfavorably when the Great Migration brought up thousands of illiterate, dirty, and poor Negroes from the Deep South. In Chicago in 1910, for example, a few Negroes were scattered all over the city, and they were invited to many ordinary white homes as neighbors. Now Negroes are forced to live in definite sections and practically the only white homes they are invited to are those of a few intellectuals and radicals.

Unlike casual contacts, *economic contacts,* though usually not intimate or protracted, are important enough for the whites and Negroes to see one another as individuals. In the great majority of economic contacts, whites see Negroes as economic inferiors, as when they are servants or other types of menial workers. More rarely they meet as economic equals, as when Negro and white workers work on the same level or when businessman meets businessman or salesman meets customer. Practically never do whites see Negroes as their economic superiors. This is due, of course, to the striking differential in economic and occupational status of whites and Negroes. In contacts arising out of economic relationships, the Negro partner is rarely employer, supervisor, skilled worker, merchant, or professional man. An additional reason for this is the fact that Negroes who occupy these higher economic positions tend to serve and to employ other Negroes. Of course, most whites are vaguely aware that there are Negroes in high economic positions. But it is probable that they everywhere underestimate the number of such Negroes, and it is certain that they rarely have enough contact with them to know them as individuals. From their side, Negroes have economic contacts with whites mainly as superiors and occasionally as equals. They thus tend to have their attitudes of inferiority and dependence—already in existence because of the slavery tradition—reinforced. The same can be said of their attitudes of resentment.

There is one sphere of economic relationship which is extremely important for several reasons. We refer to the Negro as a personal and domestic servant, a position in which he held practically a monopoly in the South until the depression of the 1930's, and in which he is numerically important in the North. The social importance of this relationship derives mainly from the fact that it is very intensive on one side. The Negro maid knows the life of her white employer as few white persons know it; and the Negro janitor and elevator operator knows a great deal of what goes on in his building. In slavery days the house servant learned the culture of his white master and—from a position on the top of the Negro class structure—transmitted it to the other slaves. Servants no longer have the highest socio-economic status among Negroes, but it can be safely said that Negroes know the white world very well, in its private, though not in its public, aspects.

The white employer, on the other hand, does not know the Negro's world just because he has Negro servants. The white employer ordinarily is interested mainly in getting his servant to work, and his attitude toward the servant is, therefore, usually impersonal. We have already commented upon the fact that this relationship has in the main lost in intimacy and personal friendliness. Even if the white mistress takes an interest in her servant's well-being, she seldom gets first-hand acquaintance with the Negro's living conditions, and Negroes show an extreme suspicion of inquisitive whites, who, even though friendly, have a superior and sometimes insulting attitude. In the South, there are also the barriers of etiquette: when the content of friendliness and mutual feeling of belonging is carved out from the system of etiquette, it becomes, to the Negroes, a cause for generalized resentment against the whites, and, to the whites, a formalization of their power over the Negroes. In both directions the etiquette works toward estranging the two groups. Even if, by some rare chance, a white employer should really come to know intimately his or her Negro servant, he would not thereby come to know the whole wide range of Negro life. What often happens in the employer-servant relationship is that—depending on the degree of friendliness or appreciation of the white employer and the degree of confidence felt by the Negro servant —the white man or woman makes an exception of his or her servant to the stereotyped conception of the "Negro in general." Similarly, the Negro servant might under happy conditions come to regard his or her employer as an exception to the general run of mean and exploitative white people. Too, the lower and dependent position of the Negro servant enhances the white person's belief that "the Negro is all right in his place."

The contacts between white and Negro workers were formerly of the same type. In the trades and handicrafts, the pattern in the South was, and is, that the white worker had a Negro helper. In factories the Negro workers are usually segregated or, in any case, held to certain jobs. As we have pointed out, the mixed trade unions are a new adventure with an uncertain future. It is commonly reported that white workers, if they become accustomed to working with Negro workers, tend to become less prejudiced, and consequently that the Negro workers become less suspicious and resentful. . . . Our general hypothesis is that everything which brings Negro and white workers to experience intimate cooperation and fellowship will, on the balance, break down race prejudice somewhat and raise Negro status. The possibilities for Negroes to rise to the position of skilled workers have, therefore, not only economic significance but also

a wider social import as this will tend to weaken the stereotype of the menial Negro.

There are other types of economic contacts between Negroes and whites in which the members of the two groups are of equal or near-equal status. Over a long time span Negro purchasing power has been increasing, and the number of Negro businessmen who can deal as economic equals with whites in a similar position has been rising. The long-run effect of this is probably to make more whites realize that some Negroes have as much capacity as they, although some whites feel nothing but irritation and resentment that can turn into violence at the thought of Negroes rising in the economic scale. The effect, as usual, is cumulative: white merchants and salesmen in the South are chipping away at the etiquette in order to please their Negro customers, and the absence of the etiquette in a social relation helps to create a spirit of equality.

Another sort of economic relationship in which Negroes have a measure of near-equality with whites is that in which the Negro is an entertainer or artist. The Negro as a musician, actor, dancer, or other type of artist is allowed to perform almost freely for a white public in the North—and to some extent in the South—in a way that he can in no other economic sphere outside of the service occupations. His excellence in these fields—cultivated by folk stimulation from earliest childhood and by the realization that other means of earning a living are closed—is recognized. In fact, it is even supported by the stereotypes: the Negro must make up for an intellectual lack by an emotional richness. Nevertheless, a Negro who achieves distinction or popularity in these fields is regarded as an individual, and there can be little doubt that he raises the general prestige level of the Negro population. What has been said of the entertainment and artistic fields is true also of the athletic field, in which Negroes have achieved notable successes.

*   *   *

We mentioned *criminal contacts* as the third most important field of Negro-white relationship. Ordinarily in American societies, as in practically all other societies, criminal relationships are minor. The fact that it is so important in Negro-white relationships has unique causes and unique effects. . . . Whites *believe* the Negro to be innately addicted to crime. The importance of Negro crime as a basis of social relations arises not only out of this fact, but also out of the fact that Negro crime gets great publicity. Even today a large proportion—perhaps a majority—of the news about Negroes that appears in the white newspapers of both South and North is about Negro crimes. When a Catholic or Jew, Swede or Bulgarian, commits a crime that is serious enough to get into the newspapers, it is not usual for his religion or nationality to be mentioned. When a Negro commits a newsworthy crime, on the other hand, only rarely is an indication of his race not prominently displayed. To many white Northerners, this crime news is the most important source of information they get about Negroes. To white Southerners, the crime news reinforces the stereotypes and sometimes serves to unite the white community for collective violence against the individual Negro criminal or the local Negro community in general.

Crime news is unfair to Negroes, on the one hand, in that it emphasizes individual cases instead of statistical proportions (a characteristic of all news, but in this case unfair to Negroes because of the racial association with especially disliked crimes) and, on the other hand, in that all other aspects of Negro life are neglected in the white press which gives the unfavorable crime news an undue weight. Sometimes the white press "creates" a Negro crime wave where none actually exists. In the latter part of the summer of 1941, Washington, D. C., was disturbed by a Negro "rape-and-murder wave," according to white newspapers throughout the country. Actually only one Negro was found to be responsible for the several crimes.

Crimes against Negroes outside of lynching receive no publicity in the white press. Lynching receives a wide but declining pub-

licity, especially in the North, and such publicity probably serves to raise Negroes—by contrast with Southern whites—in the attitude of Northern whites.

We have emphasized the most important aspects of the three most important spheres of Negro-white contacts—the casual, the economic and the criminal. The casual contact is inevitable if Negroes live in the same communities as do whites; the economic contact is the main reason for not wanting to send Negroes back to Africa or to segregate them in an isolated region and is, therefore, "inevitable"; the criminal contact is the result of a prejudiced but news-interested society. Besides contacts in the casual, economic, and criminal spheres of life, there are a few contacts between Negroes and whites in almost every other sphere. Usually they are unimportant numerically, but they may be important in bringing about change. The personal relations arising out of Negro activity in science and literature are restricted to a small proportion of the white population, whose prejudice—if not already low—is diminished considerably by such contacts. Indirectly the effect may be greater. The scientific discoveries of a George Washington Carver or the literary product of a Richard Wright will achieve nation-wide publicity and acclaim and will affect people as far down as the lower middle classes.

*   *   *

White Southerners are still proud of insisting that they "know the Negro," but the observer easily finds out that the actual ignorance about the other group is often astonishingly great. The average Southerner knows roughly—with many easily detected opportunistic gaps—the history of the Negro and the conditions under which Negroes live in the South. His lack of knowledge is of the Negro himself as an individual human being —of his ambitions and hopes, of his capacities and achievements. He zealously cultivates barren half-truths into rigid stereotypes about "the Negro race." Because of this pretentious ignorance, and because of the etiquette, the white Southerner cannot talk to a Negro as man to man and understand him. This, and the habit of living physically near this strange and unknown people—and resisting energetically the incorporation of it into the total life of the community—breeds among Southern whites a strained type of systematic human indifference and callousness. Although the Southerner will not admit it, he is beset by guilt-feelings, knowing as he does that his attitude toward the Negroes is un-American and un-Christian. Hence he needs to dress his systematic ignorance in stereotypes. The Southern whites need the sanctioning tradition: "the Negroes we have always with us." They need the ceremonial distance to prevent the Negroes' injuries and sufferings from coming to their attention. . . .

Under the old master-servant relationship, the white man's "understanding" of the Negro was not great, but with the disappearance of this relationship even this small amount of sympathetic knowledge declined. What remains is a technique of how to work Negroes and how to keep them "in their place," which is not a difficult task for a majority group which can dispose of all the social power instruments—economic, legal, political, and physical—and has made up its mind to use them for this purpose. But insight into the thoughts and feelings of Negroes, their social organization and modes of living, their frustrations and ambitions is vanishing.

* * *

The Northerner also is ignorant about the Negro, but his ignorance is less systematic and, therefore, often less deep. As he is ordinarily less inhibited from looking upon the Negro as a normal human being, and as his observation of the Negro is not blinded by the etiquette, he is usually more cognizant of Negro attitudes and capacities and is more willing to lend a sympathetic ear to the Negro's plight. But he is much more ignorant of the conditions which the Negro faces. If the Southerner's whole race philosophy and even his kindliest thoughts are insulting to the new type of Negro emerging out of the cul-

tural assimilation process, the Northerner is likely to insult him out of sheer ignorance. The average Northerner does not realize that to call a Negro woman a "Negress" is taken as an insult, and he does not understand in what high esteem the Negro holds the title "Mr." He does not see the discrimination under which the Negroes labor. Not knowing the patterns of violence and of laxness of law in the South, the Northerner does not comprehend the full reason for the Negroes' pathological bitterness and fear.

On his side, the Negro is inclined to be suspicious of the Northerner's good intentions and to retain in the North the cynical attitude and secretive manners that he has developed as a camouflage in the Southern race warfare. As a servant the Negro goes into middle and upper class homes even in the North and acquires a sort of knowledge about white people. But this knowledge is distorted, since it covers only the private life of the whites and not the public life. Seldom does a Negro know how white people on his own level live and think. In part, the Negro's ignorance is an effect of exclusion from white society. In part, it is the result of the Negro's having different interests and worries. He is preoccupied with Negro life and problems, and this makes him a little blind to the general American ones.

Mutual ignorance and the paucity of common interests is a barrier to, and a modifier of, social contact between even educated and liberal whites and Negroes in the North, even in the extraordinary circles where segregation and discrimination play no role. I have seen Negro and white social scientists together as friends and colleagues. But I know that when their minds meet it usually concerns some aspect of the Negro problem. The Negro is ordinarily not present—and if he is present, he is a stranger—when the whites meet to discuss more general problems. If this is true among liberal social scientists, it is still more true among prejudiced people in all classes. The Negro is an alien in America, and in a sense this becomes the more evident when he steps out of his old role of the servant who lives entirely for the comfort of his white superiors. Ignorance and disparity of interests, arising out of segregation and discrimination on the part of whites, increased by voluntary withdrawal and race pride on the part of Negroes, becomes itself an important element increasing and perpetuating isolation between the groups.

Negroes adjust and have to adjust to this situation. They become conditioned to patterns of behavior which not only permit but call for discriminatory observance on the part of the whites. The people who live in the system of existing relations have to give it a meaning. The Negroes have the escape, however, that they can consider the system unjust and irrational and can explain it in terms of white people's prejudices, material interest, moral wrongness and social power. They can avoid contacts and in the unavoidable ones have a mental reservation to their servility. It becomes to them a sign of education and class to do so and thereby preserve their intellectual integrity. Many Negroes succeed in doing this, and their number is growing. *But the unfortunate whites have to believe in the system of segregation and discrimination and to justify it to themselves.* It cannot be made intelligible and defensible except by false assumptions, in which the whites force themselves to believe.

So the social order perpetuates itself and with it the sentiments and beliefs by which it must be expressed. The lower caste may with some exertion release themselves intellectually. The higher caste, on the contrary, is enslaved in its prejudices by its short-range interests. Without their prejudices, white people would have to choose between either giving up the caste system and taking the resultant social, political, and economic losses, or becoming thoroughly cynical and losing their self-respect. The whites feel the Negroes' resentment and suspect new attitudes. Formerly the whites got some support for their false prejudices from the Negroes. This is becoming less and less true. Now they can hardly claim to "know their Negroes" and are forced to admit their ignorance. The social separation they

asked for is becoming a reality. Thus the tragedy is not only on the Negro side.

But the system *is* changing, though slowly. Modern knowledge and modern industrial conditions make it cumbersome. The South is becoming "normalized" and integrated into the national culture. Like every other "normal" province, it is beginning to dislike being provincial. The world publicity around the Dayton trial, for instance, did much to censor fundamentalism in Southern religion. A great part of the region's peculiarities in its racial relations is becoming, even to the Southerner, associated with backwardness. The Southerner is beginning to take on an apologetic tone when he speaks of his attitude toward the Negro. To insist upon the full racial etiquette is beginning to be regarded as affectation.

The South has long eagerly seized upon every act of prejudice practiced against the Negro in the North and, indeed, all other social ills of the other region. The visitor finds even the average run of white Southerners intensely aware of the bad slum conditions in Northern metropolises and of the North's labor troubles. Even the Southern liberal has the habit of never mentioning a fault of the South without mentioning a corresponding condition in the North. . . .

Southerners travel and migrate and are visited by Northerners and Europeans. They listen to the radio and read papers, magazines and books directed to the wider national audience. Southern writers—in social science, politics, and *belles-lettres*—aspire to national recognition and not only provincial applause. The thesis that the region is poor and culturally backward, and that this is largely due to the presence of the Negroes and to the Southern Negro policy, has been for a long time developed by Southern authors. The average Southerner is beginning to feel the need for fundamental reforms. Many Southern newspapers have become liberal. Interracial work is beginning to be recognized as socially respectable.

The diffusion of scientific knowledge regarding race cannot be regionalized any more effectively than it can be segregated along a color line. Racial beliefs are becoming undermined, at least for the younger generation in the middle and upper classes. Most of them never reach the printing press or the microphone any more, as they are no longer intellectually respectable. The educated classes of whites are gradually coming to regard those who believe in the Negro's biological inferiority as narrow-minded and backward. When a person arrives at the point where he says that he knows his views are irrational but that "they are just instinctive" with him, he is beginning to retreat from these views.

The capital N in "Negro" is finding its way into the Southern newspapers as it earlier did into books. It is becoming a mark of education in the white South to speak of Negroes as "niggras" and not as "niggers"— a compromise pronunciation which still offends the Yankee Negro but is a great step from the Southern white man's traditional point of view. In Southern newspapers Negro problems and Negro activity even outside crime are beginning to be commented upon, not only to draw Negro subscribers, but also because these matters are actually found to be of some general community interest. Letters from Negroes are not infrequently printed and sometimes the content discussed with respect. It would be no great revolution, at least not in the Upper South, if a newspaper one morning carried a portrait of a distinguished Negro on the front page. In liberal newspapers in the Upper South, Negro pictures have already occasionally been printed in the back pages.

The educated, respectable, self-possessed Negro is to the average white Southerner not so often as earlier just the "smart nigger" or the "uppity nigger." As the South becomes urbanized and some Negroes rise in status, it is becoming increasingly impracticable and, in some relations, actually impossible to bracket all Negroes together and treat them alike. Social classes among Negroes are becoming recognized. Titles of respect, the offer to shake hands, permission to use the front door and other symbols of politeness are more and more presented to certain Negroes who have attained social success.

We must not exaggerate these signs of wear and tear on the Southern color bar. *"Social equality" is still a terribly important matter in the region. But it is not as important as it was a generation ago.* One needs only to compare the tremendous upheaval in the South when President Theodore Roosevelt in the first decade of the twentieth century had Booker T. Washington to a luncheon at the White House with the relatively calm irritation the white South manifested in the 'thirties when President Franklin Roosevelt and his gallant lady did much more radical things. It even continued to vote for him. The South is surely changing.

But the changes themselves elicit race prejudice. From one point of view, Robert E. Park is right, of course, in explaining race prejudice as "merely an elementary expression of conservatism," as "the resistance of the social order to change." When the Negro moves around and improves his status, he is bound to stimulate animosity. The white South was—and is—annoyed whenever the Negro showed signs of moving out of his "place." And the white North definitely became more prejudiced when hundreds of thousands of crude Southern Negroes moved in. But conditions for Negroes are improving, Southerners are being jolted out of their racial beliefs, and the group of white people interested in doing something positive for the Negro has grown. The increase in prejudice due to the rise of the Negro is a local and temporary phenomenon in both the North and the South.

The Future of the South

>>

It is difficult to conclude the story of the South with any final summary, because changes are still taking place and the South will not be in the future what it is today or has been in the past. To an even greater extent than some other parts of our country it is beset with problems and is in the midst of difficult readjustments. It has been impossible in this book to cover every aspect of the South, and the careful reader will already have become aware of many omitted topics. But enough has been presented to show the central core of Southern life as a unified and consistent whole, in all its problems and its strengths, its weaknesses and its promises, its clinging to the old with one hand and reaching out to the new with the other. We have seen how social change comes to an agrarian society based on the plantation system, and how the question of racial relationships has changed from a "private" matter for the South to settle in its own way to a burning national issue.

A fitting way to close, we believe, is to turn again to the little volume by Hodding Carter, *Southern Legacy,* and present his summing up. Carter's search for the South's "way out" of its problems is reminiscent of the earnest questioning in Selection 19 by the Chinese sociologists seeking an answer to their country's rural problems.

• 51 • *Out of Inquietude*
HODDING CARTER

If the South had ever agreed with the rest of the nation that it is primarily a collection of unfavorable statistics, it would have lost long ago the self-esteem which is an essential requisite for cultural survival. But the price of ignoring the statistics is their certain perpetuation.

For a hundred years the statistics have

[From *Southern Legacy,* Louisiana State University Press, Baton Rouge, 1950. Pp. 176-186. Used by permission.]

been inexorably produced by invasion and political obliteration, by bankruptcy and a debilitating agricultural economy, by uninspired leadership and a spiritually destructive human relationship. The legacy they represent in sum total is one that has impoverished rather than enriched. It has been balanced in part by a stubborn, defensive pride and a regional devotion as baffling to the observer as they are nourishing to the Southerner himself. Love of region and self-esteem have been the South's emotional antidotes to otherwise inescapable degeneration.

As antidotes they have served their purpose admirably. As substitutes for reality they have been insufficient. The statistics remain. And the South of a mature purposefulness need ignore them no longer in fear that material fact may destroy spiritual certainty.

In the eleven states of the Southeast live some 35 million people, a smaller proportion of the nation's population than they represented fifty years ago. The out-migration quickens. During the war years, the South lost one million more inhabitants than it gained. Of its young men who served in the armed forces, one in seven found greener pastures elsewhere after demobilization. Of its young men who remained at home, proportionately more were rejected for physical and mental disabilities than in any other region of the nation.

The states which the one in seven forsook receive only 10 per cent of the nation's industrial wages, although they contain one fifth of the population. The average per capita income of their citizens has more than doubled in twenty years, to $883, but it is only 67 per cent of the national average. It is understandable that the young men are still restless, still intent on the distant field. Their migration has left in the South's labor force far more adolescents and old men than are present in the nation's labor force as a whole. And those who leave and those who remain at home are alike handicapped in their work, for only one third of the South's population has been educated beyond the eighth grade.

In this day of the machine, one Southerner in four has less than a fifth-grade education. The principal migration is from the farms of the South. Of the 160 million acres of American farm land which erosion has reduced to inutility, nearly 100 million, more than 60 per cent of the total, lie in the South. On the useful and useless land, two thirds of all Southern farmers try to make their livings by growing cotton and tobacco.

Two years out of three, the Southern farmer produces far more cotton than is consumed. Although he prides himself on his individualism and is suspicious of his distant government, the cotton farmer is solvent only because of Federal agricultural benefits. And the Federal government provides, principally through payments to farmers, 22 per cent of the South's total income.

Overproducing its field crops, the South does not yet produce sufficient dairy products, meat, poultry, eggs, vegetables, and feedstuffs to care for its own needs.

Nor is this agricultural instability balanced by industrial productivity. In the entire United States, 36 billion dollars in wages and salaries were paid in 1946, but the South's share was only a little more than 3½ billion. The average annual wages of the Southern industrial worker rose from $1,019 in 1939 to $1,798 in 1944, a greater increase percentagewise than for the nation as a whole; but the national average wage was $2,302. Although the South's rate of industrial growth surpassed the rest of the nation's during and since the war, industrial diversification is still distant. Textiles, wood products, food products, and chemicals account for nearly two thirds of the South's industrial output, with textiles making up nearly one third of the total. The South does not yet have industrial capital and management and a trained labor supply. It lacks the great life-insurance companies and investment banks necessary to provide capital investment. It is still primarily an exporter of raw products for processing elsewhere rather than a processor itself.

Against this background of agricultural

and industrial lags, other unfavorable statistics are inevitable. The South has the fewest doctors and the fewest hospital beds for each thousand of its population. Its venereal disease, tuberculosis, and infant and maternal mortality rates are the nation's largest. Its expenditures upon its educable children are the smallest and its illiteracy rate the highest. Less than 5 per cent of its rural homes have baths. Its people commit proportionately the greatest number of crimes of violence and escape with the least degree of punishment. They cast the smallest vote in relation to their numbers. And so on, throughout a somber catalogue.

All of this is well enough known. What is less known is that, except in population loss, the South is moving upward on every gauge by which the progress of a civilization can be measured. Ours is no longer a problem of direction but of acceleration.

More land is being restored in the South through terracing, crop rotation, and pasturing than anywhere else in the nation. Manufacturing income has almost tripled in ten years. In every Southern state, new hospitals are being built, state health departments expanded, disease reduced, school systems extended.

The giant turbines of the Tennessee Valley Authority put water to work for man. The white-faced Herefords graze where once the mined earth cried out for rest. Around the multiplying factories are lined the automobiles of workers from the gutted hills and the once-listless towns. The young saplings rise by plan from the land where the forests were planlessly slain. Everywhere the change is sure.

There is a material and a moral urgency to this Southern metamorphosis. Ours is a region surpassingly endowed and as wastefully negligent of its endowment. No other region has as generous a combination of equable climate, productive soil in spite of abuse, actual and potential hydroelectric power, timber and mineral reserves, and human resources. No other region has made as little productive use of what it embraces. No other region has destroyed so much of itself.

If the 35 million Southerners were to attain a standard of living equal to that enjoyed by the rest of the nation, their material demands would add 15 billion dollars in needed goods and services to the nation's consumption totals. Could they divest themselves of the searing heritages of mistrust and fear, they would subtract immeasurably from the bill of particulars by which the enemies of democracy seek to negate its meaning throughout the world. These are the South's twin mandates to itself. They cannot be carried out through the force-feeding of new practices and ideals. The realization of their urgency must come from within.

The statistics cannot be evaded. It is useless for Southerners to pretend that the region we love is not identical with the region whose faults and needs have been so thoroughly tabulated. But the statistics can be changed. They were created out of the Southern past and the past does not endure even when men insist that it is unending. The Southern legacies are not eternal and need not be accepted when reason suggests their rejection; but before rejection or retention, they must be inspected and evaluated and their sources understood.

So it is that the South must look behind even as it moves ahead, recognizing the fetters of an agrarian tradition which could have been altogether wholesome, but which was degraded through a one-crop economy, the enslavement of man, and the pitiable makeshift of tenancy on land that men had ruined and were in turn ruined by. The agrarian past must be honestly weighed. Against the manors it reared and the virtues it possessed must be balanced the flight of intellect which it impelled, the prejudices it inspired, the political miasma in which it was shrouded, and the quantitative limitations of the distinctive culture it produced. And we must recognize, too, its peculiar contribution to the American dilemma arising from the presence of the Negro, the abused, retarded, identifiable stranger of 300 years whose similarity of aspirations and dissimilarity of race have created in the white South a unity of resistance which is the principal cohesive element in its regional solidarity.

I have spent a good many hours, not altogether fruitfully, reading or listening to proposals for solving the South's problems. Some of them were convincing, some unrealistic, some downright absurd. Their principal point of agreement is that the Southern predicament has been primarily economic, a conclusion which requires no great wisdom to reach.

To these earnest blueprints I have nothing to contribute save a certainty that the mandatory first step today is to make the availability and the quality of public education in the South at least comparable to prevailing national standards, so that our man power may acquire equal productive capacities in the crafts and arts and sciences, and the wider social vision that is education's first obligation to society. But as this equal proficiency is attained it must concurrently find agricultural, industrial, and professional usefulness in the South, else the migration of the young and the talented will increase as skills are acquired which cannot be employed at home. The goal of agricultural-industrial balance must be set beside the goal of education. There is nothing profound in such observations. They have been made many times before, but as long as the goals are unachieved there is need for repetition.

Yet even the absolute attainment of economic objectives would not in itself resolve the racial dilemma that is not restricted to the South but aggravated here because of the numbers involved and attitudes generated by law and folkways for three centuries. Education, greater economic security, and protective legislation can soften the impact of racial antipathies, but there is no formula for ending them except the formula which man discovers within himself.

The best that can be expected in the ascertainable future from the South's attainment of national levels in income and education is a more rapid amelioration of the discrimina-tory aspects of the white-Negro relationship. The harshest manifestations of prejudice exist where the living standards of the dominant and the submerged groups are alike low, and where the numerical pressures of the submerged and dissimilar are interpreted by the dominant as constituting a political, economic, or social threat to the established controls. Since the living standards are being raised and the numerical pressures reduced throughout the South, greater and rapid amelioration appears certain.

Through migration, the Negro population in the South is decreasing in relation to the white population, so that in no Southern state and in less than 180 counties is the Negro in a majority. Until now this migration has been principally voluntary and motivated by ambition or resentment or both, but it is being quickened involuntarily as the machine replaces the man and the mule.

The admission that the reduction of the ratio of Negro to white in the South will hasten the South's over-all progress is also an admission of democratic failure; but as tragic as the implication is, the fact remains that if the Negro exodus continues, it will contribute at least as much to the South's economic transformation and to white acceptance of the Negro as a citizen as will any other presently foreseeable factor. The Negro vote, for example, is the least opposed in Virginia, North Carolina, and Tennessee, the states with the smallest Negro populations and the greatest industrial balance and agricultural diversification. Pigsty housing, inferior schooling, and inadequate medical facilities are the least condoned or accepted as inevitable in those areas of the South where the white majority is the largest.

But the South cannot wait for this bleak and negative impetus to development. Even if half of the nine million Southern Negroes were to leave, the remainder would constitute an unending reproach until they were recognized as citizens entitled to the same political rights and the same economic opportunity and capable of making equal contributions to democratic America.

Such recognition is the paramount necessity for the South today, and for all America. The integration of the Negro in our national life has an importance more immediately imperative than are domestic or even moral considerations. In the unresolved struggle between the democratic and the totalitarian concepts, the exclusion of the American Negro from full and uncontested participation in the democratic scheme provides the totalitarian protagonists with an effective weapon. The skin colors of three quarters of the world's population are black or brown or yellow. It is to this questioning, undecided majority that the Communist propagandist addresses his calculated disparagement of democracy as bearing a label "For Whites Only —All Others Keep Off."

I would like now to set aside the problems and the statistics and turn again to the legacy of regionalism. The Southerner does not love his country the less because of his self-identification with the comprehensible part of the whole. America is vast and many-sided, but a man's valley and hillside and state are near and intimate; and if there is any antidote to our mounting reliance upon distant, impersonal, and centralized power it is the regional attachment which, by virtue of long identification with his background, the Southerner possesses to a greater extent than do the rest of America's people.

I know that I am no better citizen than the immigrant's son, and it may be that I accept more lightly than he the privileges already won for us both; but I find serenity and sureness in the knowledge that to the river where we wait with guns for the mallard's winter flight my people came long ago with more purposeful weapons, some to prosper and some to lose what they found. Perhaps their small triumphs compensate for the later failures, perhaps their defeats remind us that there is nothing lost that cannot somehow be regained. I cannot travel through the valley of Virginia nor along the Mississippi without experiencing a quickening of the blood; if my sons or even strangers are with me, my tongue loosens and I want to tell them of the people who settled and fought and clung there, for they were my people; and if the allegiance is sentimental it is not shallow. I understand the forces that fashioned these men. I am at home with their spirits.

This may be provincialism, but there is nothing unhealthy in it. The sense of intimate identification with a region fortifies the will to make it more nearly perfect and secure; and as the part is strengthened so is the whole. It is only when loyalty makes the regional patriot blind to imperfection and resentful of inspection that it becomes a deteriorative force; the obligation to examine, to protest and to propose change must accompany affection, else devotion can destroy. Too many Southerners fail to perceive this corollary; defiant and resentful of the alien critic, they are even more enraged by the native censor, stigmatizing him as a nest-fouler and suggesting that he should go elsewhere if he is not satisfied with what he finds.

I prefer to remain dissatisfied. I hope that there will never come a time when my sons or their sons will look about them and be content; for the soul is nurtured on inquietude: the soul of a man, the soul of a region, the soul of a nation. Out of inquietude the South, so long bemused in the twilight of its self-satisfaction, stirs now before the dawn.

THE ENGLISH MIDLANDS

Left: The term *conurbation* has come into use in England to describe the immense, sprawling industrial cities which have swallowed up outlying towns and adjacent factory districts in their growth. But although they are highly congested, they have a great advantage: they bring together both the means of production, with its highly skilled labor, and a great body of consumers. Coal mining in England (*below*) is of immense importance in providing one of the basic materials for industry. It is hampered by the narrowness of many seams, which makes the use of machinery difficult, thus greatly reducing productivity per man.

Right: Here, as in many parts of England, a factory stands only a few yards from a picturesque old town crossroads. This wide dispersal of industry is as characteristic as is concentration in great urban centers. Among other things, it means that even rural areas are rarely far from factories, mines, or mills. It means, too, that sometimes the English worker lives very close to his place of work, and also very close to the countryside. Even with great industrial growth, farming is important in England, and every effort is still made to produce a substantial part of what the nation eats. *Below:* A harvest group takes a few minutes for the traditional cup of tea.

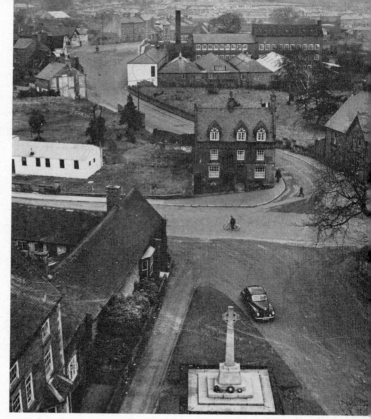

Top: A colliery, such as this one in the Midlands, is not a particularly pleasant place to work, with the landscape a jumble of buildings, machinery, and mine tailings. But even more serious has been the unplanned growth of such industrial areas in England, as well as other parts of the world, resulting in greater difficulty when industrial expansion and rebuilding is undertaken. *Bottom:* By contrast, the center of an industrial city is frequently attractively planned, with spacious parks and avenues. Even here, however, crowding and traffic congestion become a burden and there is little room for growth.

BRITISH MIDLANDS INDUSTRIAL AREAS

Scale of Miles

0   25   50   75   100

SCOTLAND

NORTH

SEA

Newcastle

NORTHERN
IRELAND

IRISH

SEA

Hull

Leeds

Liverpool   Manchester

REPUBLIC

OF

IRELAND

Sheffield

Stoke on Trent   Nottingham

Leicester

Birmingham

WALES   **E N G L A N D**

Bristol

London

Southampton

E N G L I S H   C H A N N E L

F R A N C E

Introduction

>>

Although it is the most complex of the three societies in this volume, the English Midlands should not prove the most difficult to understand, because we, too, live in an industrial society. Even our rural areas are closely caught up in the forces and complexities of what is smugly termed "modern civilization." The English Midlands can also be better appreciated when it is realized that industrial society has developed rather rapidly from the background of a society quite similar to that of Peasant China. The Cotton South, which has just been dealt with, represents a transitional and rapidly changing society and provides us with perspective for our analysis of the Midlands.

Nevertheless, at the outset of our study of the Midlands, some reorientation in our thinking may be necessary. We shall be dealing with one small part of an island only slightly larger than Kansas but with a population about 25 times as great. Furthermore, although the British have absorbed people of many and diverse origins through the centuries, they have not recently experienced such gigantic ethnic assimilation as we have in America. This gives the British people more common characteristics and more homogeneity, although they too have local loyalties and regional differences.

The English Midlands have to be seen in an accurate time perspective, too. When our republic was getting underway, the Industrial Revolution was already working out its transformation of English life. The roots out of which industrial society grew will be described in those selections that tell how the peasantry was transformed into a wage-earning class. But the story of the Industrial Revolution (and that means the story of the English Midlands) is also one of intelligent exploitation of natural resources, of a developing technology in textiles and metal work, and of such occupational specialization that labor unions eventually became an essential feature of the social landscape. A person's labor was transferred from the home to the factory, where centralized power ran many machines at once, where there was effective supervision and mass production. The expense of building a factory and equipping it with machines, of buying raw materials and employing labor meant that new ways of financing had to be worked out. The result was the business corporation, one of the major social inventions of Western society, which made it possible for many individuals to supply capital for an enterprise without acquiring any personal liabilities, in most cases, for the failure and default of the corporation.

Mass production called for increased markets as well as new supplies of raw materials. Profits accumulated to the point that businessmen had to look abroad for ventures in which to invest their idle funds—much of this capital coming to America to finance our transcontinental railroad construction and other enterprises which we now consider essential to our economy.

In the study of England it will be apparent that a democracy can exist within a monarchy, that marked social changes can occur by "evolution rather than revolution," and that the more complex and concentrated the economy, the greater the tendency toward centralized government control. In England, large sections of the economy have been taken over by the government, a process called *nationalization*. It also means *socialization* when viewed in terms of the theory that the people themselves should control the means of production, such as mines, utilities, and the like. This is in sharp contrast to the American emphasis on *private ownership* of utilities and the failure of any Labor Party to emerge in the United States as a politically significant force under the banner of governmental management of our basic industries.

Socialization, however, has another meaning. As we have seen earlier, it is the term used by social scientists to describe the process by which individuals are transformed into socially acceptable persons who know what roles are expected of them in given situations. Some of the selections which follow trace the influences brought to bear upon the growing English boy and girl. In reading of their school experiences, we must remember that in England a "public school" is really what we call a private school. Family life and recreational patterns have some minor differences from ours, but they reflect industrialization in much the same way as they do here. The city becomes an increasingly significant social factor and in its development has attracted the attention of community and regional social planners.

The English value system, though similar in many points to ours, has shades and nuances of its own which influence behavior in subtle ways. Selection 79 presents an excellent description of some of these fine points.

Although the focus is generally on the Midlands, some selections have had to deal with England as a whole, since they deal with the actions of the central government. We shall see, for example, the British plans for nationalization of the economy and of medical care. Even while this book was being prepared, however, a change in the British government has begun to reverse the program of nationalization, although the fundamental centralization of the British economy has not been greatly changed. In many social measures, the United States has followed Britain by a generation or two, and many are wondering whether the centralization there is the course that America will pursue some years hence. It is important to us, in this connection, to understand what the English patterns are, why they appeared, and what similarities and differences in American and British ways may influence the eventual extension of these English patterns to this side of the Atlantic.

It can be seen from the grouping of the selections that we have chosen certain topics for emphasis in connection with this industrial society: (1) the urban concentrations of the people (*conurbations,* in English terminology); (2) the extensive utilization of resources; (3) the historical roots in the Industrial Revolution; (4) the high differentiation of the economy; (5) the strong influence of the economy and the government on other aspects of the social system, such as the family, religion, recreation, social welfare, and education; and, finally, (6) the persistence of many social values even in the face of changes in many other phases of life.

The People

W_ho are the British? Of what diverse strains is their population made up? For the answer to these questions we turn to *The Face of Britain,* a booklet by the well-known British geographer L. Dudley Stamp. His summary begins with Paleolithic (Old Stone Age) man and his Neolithic successors, long before the coming of the Romans, and tells of successive invasions by tribesmen on the move.

For information about the British people in more recent times, we make use of Eva M. Hubback's *Population of Britain.* This selection will illustrate in detail how demographers (population analysts) go about their task of studying the statistics of birth rates, death rates, and other such data to determine the rates at which groups within the total population are increasing and decreasing. But the most significant fact about the population of Britain today is not the rate at which it is changing but the way in which it is becoming concentrated around a few major urban centers. This process was thoroughly investigated by a Royal Commission, whose report was issued in 1940; two brief passages from this report make up Selection 54.

The last of the selections on the people of Britain considers the urban concentrations of an industrial society, but from a less statistical point of view. Urbanization changes many aspects of a people's life and has had far-reaching effects, which have frequently been completely unforeseen. All towns are not alike, however, either in the reasons for their development or in their problems, and in the latter part of Selection 55 the variations among English towns are emphasized. It should be borne in mind that even peasant societies have town centers, but the growth of such centers into great metropolises is especially characteristic of industrial society; gradually even the outlying villages are drawn into the orbits of the conurbations or drastically altered by them.

• 52 • The Peopling of the British Isles

L. DUDLEY STAMP

Before the ice-sheets of the Great Ice Age overwhelmed this country Britain was still joined to the continent of Europe. Early man with his implements of crudely chipped flint came into the country by land and settled on river-banks where small clearings could be made, and where his implements are still found buried in gravel-beds. As the cold of the approaching Ice Age became more severe, men took to living in caves, and often disputed ownership with cave-bears, cave-lions, and the sabre-toothed tiger, whilst giant elephants roamed tundra-like lands outside the caves. In the latter part of the Ice Age the British Isles were cut off from the Continent —probably when ice-dammed waters overflowed southwards from what is now the southern part of the North Sea—and with the retreat of the ice the climate became milder and thick forests began to clothe the land. The fierce men of the caves with their heavy brow ridges disappeared before a new invader —neolithic man—who brought polished stone implements, and buried his round-headed kinsmen in round graves or barrows. Neolithic man probably arrived in Britain between 3000 and 2000 B.C., and started cultivating the land and domesticating animals. But about the same time—or perhaps earlier —long-headed people who came from the Mediterranean approached Britain from the south-west and settled in Wales and Cornwall. They brought with them the idea of building great stone circles, and these Megalith builders have left as their greatest monuments Stonehenge and Avebury—showing how far they penetrated towards the east. So even at this early age two strains of people inhabited Britain—the one group mainly in Lowland Britain, the other mainly in Highland Britain.

Then came the broad-headed Nordic-Al-pine peoples, also from the south-east, with their bronze and, later, iron implements, but even these were but indifferent weapons with which to attack dense forest growth. So these early people laid out their trackways on the ridges where the forest was thinner or absent.

The people of Britain at this time—between 1000 B.C. and A.D. 43—were organised in tribes, and are often referred to in British literature as the "ancient Britons."

In A.D. 43 the Roman conquest of Britain began by an entry in the south-east and a rapid advance north-westwards towards London. A Roman commercial centre was quickly established at the natural crossing-place (still the lowest bridging point) of the Thames, and the Romans imposed a uniform organisation over the whole of Lowland Britain. There they established cities and farms (villae) and made their long straight roads, which still form the basis of the British main road system. Two or three of these great Roman settlements—Uriconium and Silchester—have failed to survive, but generally the Romans realised the value of both local and regional site values. So the great Roman settlements such as Dover, Chichester, Winchester, Exeter, Bristol, Cirencester, Deva (Chester), Dindum (Lincoln), and Eburacum (York) have not only survived but have become foci of modern life. The Romans established their Civil Districts all over Lowland Britain, but never established themselves over Highland Britain or the Celtic fringe. In Wales, the Pennines, and the North they established military camps and military districts, and Hadrian's Wall from Carlisle to the Tyne (at Wallsend) marked for long the limit of Roman influence northwards. Beyond Hadrian's Wall the province of Valencia was but a temporary extension of the Roman domain embracing southern Scotland as far as the

[From *The Face of Britain*, British Life and Thought: No. 5, published for the British Council by Longmans, Green and Company, London, 1945. Pp. 11-14. Used by permission.]

wall of Antoninus from the Forth to the Clyde.

The withdrawal of the Romans, owing to the troubles at home, left Britain open to new invaders. The fifth and sixth centuries were the period of invasion, conquest, and settlement by the pagan Angles, Saxons, and Jutes. Lowland Britain became completely Anglo-Saxon, but Highland Britain remained Celtic and Christian, though there were extensive movements amongst the Celts themselves—notably an invasion of Scotland (where the Scots from Ireland drove out the native Picts) and Irish invasions of Wales and Cornwall. Whereas the Romans had imposed their control and to some extent their culture, but had eventually departed leaving mainly roads and cities to mark their four-centuries sojourn, the Anglo-Saxons both conquered and absorbed the native inhabitants of Lowland Britain. They established a number of Kingdoms —East Anglia (divided into the region of the North Folk and the region of the South Folk—now the counties of Norfolk and Suffolk); East Saxon land (now Essex); South Saxon land (now Sussex); West Saxon land (Wessex, now divided into a number of counties). Into the forested lowlands of the heart of England the Anglo-Saxons penetrated by river; their settlements were largely riverside settlements, and their chief towns (now the "county towns") nearly always on navigable waterways. The numerous place-names ending in -ham (home), -ton (town), -sted (farm), -hurst (wood), -ea or -ey (island), and other common terminations indicate Anglo-Saxon settlements or earlier settlements renamed by them. The Anglo-Saxons extended the use of the plough and laid the foundations of British agriculture: they gave England her name (Angleland), her language, and many of her institutions.

The Anglo-Saxons were followed by the Danes, who established a Danish Kingdom, but the Norwegian invaders of the eighth, ninth, and tenth centuries were seafaring Vikings who found in the coastlands of Highland Britain an environment more closely resembling that of their Norwegian homeland, and so established themselves as a Scandinavian fringe.

Thus the British Isles at the time of the Norman Conquest (A.D. 1066) comprised an Anglo-Saxon Lowland zone (by this time converted to Christianity), a Celtic Highland zone, and an irregular, Scandinavian fringe.

Like the Romans before them, the Normans spread over Lowland Britain, where they constituted a ruling minority crystallising and intensifying the feudal system. They gave to this part of the country many of the finest castles, cathedrals, and churches still extant, for the Anglo-Saxons previously had built mainly in wood. It was not until a century after the conquest of England that the invasion of Ireland began; it was not until 1282 that the Principality of Wales was added to the domain of the Plantagenet Kings. The remaining large portion of Highland Britain resisted both union and conquest until Scotland, in the person of her King James VI, provided the vacant English throne with a monarch who became James I of England in 1603.

At various times since the Norman invasion the cultural and economic life of Britain has been enriched by the arrival of groups of refugee immigrants—notably Flemings and Huguenots.

The visitor to Britain is often at a loss to understand the marked local variations to be found in so small an area in speech, manners, customs, and, to a less extent, in religion, dress, and even physical characteristics. These differences are often accentuated by an intense local patriotism, and their understanding is only possible through an appreciation of the diverse environments and their effect on the evolution of human groups of very different history and background.

In the following selection eight statistical tables have been included; these compress into little space what it might take many paragraphs of text to explain. The birth rate, as you have already learned in the study of the Chinese peasant, shows the number of children born every year per thousand of the population. For example, if 100 children were born within a year in a community of 5000 the birth rate would be 20. The death rate shows the number of people who die every year per thousand of the population. The difference, then, between the birth rate and the death rate is called the natural increase.

We begin to understand what some call "the dynamics of population" when we compare the birth rates and death rates between different social classes, occupations, ethnic groups, or regions. We also find out what effects industrialization has on a people.

• 53 • *The Population of Britain*
EVA M. HUBBACK

THE GROWTH OF THE POPULATION SINCE 1066

Relatively little is known about the size and growth of the population of England and Wales before 1801, when the first census was taken. Before that time the number of people in this country was largely guesswork. All we can say is that at the time of the Norman Conquest it was probably about 2 millions. It grew slowly, so that in 1600 it was about 5 millions. This slow rate of growth was due mainly to the fact that, although there was a high natural birth-rate and practically no emigration, there was, up to the middle of the fifteenth century, an almost equally high death-rate due to bad social conditions coupled with inadequate medical knowledge. Adam Smith's statement is often quoted to the effect that, although during the last quarter of the eighteenth century Highland women were each accustomed to having about twenty children, usually only two or three of these lived to grow up. Our knowledge of the families of the kings and queens, and the many family monuments in old churches, with their rows of little boys and girls, paint the same picture. Rarely do we hear of large surviving families. This is not surprising, since it is thought that before the Industrial Revolution about three-quarters of the children born in London died before they were 10 years old.

During the last half of the eighteenth century general prosperity grew rapidly; the introduction of the turnip family into our rotation of crops made it possible to keep cattle alive to produce fresh meat and milk in winter. Scientific discoveries, such as vaccination, and progress in medical knowledge generally greatly reduced mortality—especially infant mortality—and the death-rate began to fall considerably.

During the nineteenth century—although the birth-rate remained as high as it has probably ever been until 1871, when it reached 35 per thousand—the expanding industrial system, with its greatly increased prosperity, led to a much bigger chance of rearing a large family successfully. Improvements in housing, in sanitation, in nutrition and in medical knowledge continued; and we find, during this period, the combination of a birth-rate still high with a considerably lower death-rate.

This led to such a big increase in the population that it nearly doubled itself between

[From *The Population of Britain*, Penguin Books, West Drayton, Middlesex, England, 1947. Pp. 20-35. Used by permission.]

1801 and 1841, and more than doubled itself during the following sixty years. By 1900, therefore, it had reached 32 millions in England and Wales. But during the next forty years—up to 1940—the increase only consisted of another 10 millions, since, in spite of the death-rate continuing to fall from 1871, a startling change began to take place about that time in the birth-rate. It fell steadily from 35 in the seventies, until in 1933 it reached a record low level of 14.4. The consequence was that the number of babies born in 1931 to the 4,918,000 married women under 45 was less than three-quarters of the numbers in 1871, when there were only about 2½ million married women. For an equally small number of births we have to look back to the period before 1851, when the number of married women was about 2 millions all told and the total population only about 17 millions. There was thus a fall in the average number of children per family from over 5 in the 1870's to about 2 in the 1930's—a number obviously too small for replacement purposes. . . .

POPULATION GROWTH AND CHANGES, 1851-1938

As long as the birth-rate is higher than the death-rate there is a natural increase in the population, assuming this effect is not offset by emigration. The following table shows the birth- and death-rates per thousand of the population from 1851 to 1938. It will be noted that the birth-rate grew steadily till 1871, when it began to fall, and by 1938 was less than half what it had been in the earlier period. Suggested causes for this are given later.

The death-rate, which had dwindled, though intermittently, since the middle of the eighteenth century, began also to fall steadily from about 1871, when it was 22.3, to 1938, when it was 11.6. These figures, however, do not fully reflect what had actually happened; for—since the proportion of deaths is highest among young children and old people, and lowest among people between 5 and 50 years of age—the death-rate (like the birth-rate) is affected, not only by changes in social conditions and medical knowledge, but also by changes in the age-distribution of the population. The increase in the proportion of old people, from 9.4 per cent of the population in 1920 to 13 per cent in 1938, meant that the death-rate had not fallen as low as it would have done had the 1920 proportions between old and young been maintained. Had this happened, the death-rate in 1938 would have been 8.5 instead of 11.6.

The effect of changes in the death-rate at different periods can best be realised in

TABLE 1.—GROWTH OF POPULATION, BIRTH AND DEATH RATES IN ENGLAND
AND WALES, 1851-1938

Year	Numbers of Population (000's)	Birth Rate	Death Rate	Rate of Natural Increase
1851	17,928	34.1	21.8	12.3
1861	20,066	34.8	21.5	13.3
1871	22,712	35.5	22.3	13.2
1881	25,974	34.1	19.7	14.4
1891	29,002	30.8	19.7	11.1
1901	32,528	28.7	17.2	11.5
1911	36,070	24.5	13.8	10.7
1921	37,887	22.8	12.4	10.4
1931	39,952	15.8	11.9	3.9
1938	41,215	15.1	11.6	3.5

changes in the "expectation of life" at birth in the same periods. (The expectation of life means the average age in years to which a person is likely to live if the death-rate of the year when he was born remained unchanged.) The expectation of life for men increased from 43.7 years in 1881 to 61.8 years in 1938, and for women from 47.2 to 65.8 for the corresponding years. It serves as an admirable indication of changes in social conditions, and is everywhere higher for women than for men. This is partly because baby boys are more difficult to bring up than baby girls, and partly because men are more likely to follow dangerous pursuits than are women.

Owing to the fact that between 1851 and 1938 the birth-rate declined to a greater extent than the death-rate, the natural increase of the population, which is the margin between the two, fell from 13.2 in 1871 to 3.5 in 1938. This indicates the great slowing down in the rate of growth in the population during that period.

Even the rate of natural increase, however, cannot tell us very much about what is happening with regard to the replacement of any given generation by the next, as it does not take into account various other important changes. Neither can the birth-rate, since this relates births to the total population, whereas, of course, it is only women of child-bearing age who can have children. If, therefore, the proportion of women between 15 and 45 years old in the population changes, the birth-rate is bound to alter so long as the number of children produced by each woman remains the same. Since younger women are naturally more fertile than older ones, it will also change if there is a larger proportion of younger to older women within the child-bearing age-group.

We shall have a much better idea of what is happening, then, if births are related, not to the total population, but to every thousand women of child-bearing age. This gives us the *General Fertility Rate,* and shows us that whereas in 1871 1,000 women of these ages were having 154 children a year, in 1938 they were only having 62.1.

NET REPRODUCTION RATE

. . . The net reproduction rate gives the most faithful indication of what is happening with regard to replacement, since it takes into account, not only the birth-rate of the mothers, but also the death-rate of the daughters; and it will be remembered that a net reproduction rate of 1 shows that the present generation of women of child-bearing age are exactly reproducing themselves. The following table shows the course of the net reproduction rate in England and Wales between 1851 and 1938. The turning point came actually in 1922, and the rate became less than 1 from that date. By 1931 it had fallen so low that women of marriageable age were failing to reproduce themselves by a sensible amount. It only reached 1 again in 1946.

TABLE 2.—NET REPRODUCTION RATE IN
ENGLAND AND WALES, 1851-1938

Year	Net Reproduction Rate
1851	1.3
1861	1.4
1871	1.5
1881	1.5
1891	1.4
1901	1.2
1911	1.1
1921	1.1
1931	0.8
1938	0.8

CHANGES IN AGE COMPOSITION

Although the net reproduction rate was less than 1 between 1923 and 1946, there was still some natural increase in our population, as there were so many people, both in and after the reproductive age-groups, who were born at a time when the birth-rate and the number of births per annum were both very much higher. One of the most important effects of any fall in the birth-rate is the change in age distribution of the population. This can best be illustrated by the following table:

TABLE 3.—AGE COMPOSITION OF POPULATION
OF GREAT BRITAIN, 1881 AND 1938

Age Group	1881	1938
0-4	4,031,000	3,219,000
5-14	6,804,000	6,860,000
15-24	5,598,000	7,431,000
25-34	4,318,000	7,621,000
35-44	3,349,000	6,700,000
45-54	2,484,000	5,689,000
55-64	1,751,000	4,709,000
65 and over	1,375,000	3,979,000
Total	29,710,000	46,208,000

To compare 1938 figures with a date more recent than 1881 we find that in 1911 those under 45 were 32,125,000, and those 45 and over were 8,705,000. In 1938 those under 45 were 31,836,000 and those 45 and over were 14,377,000—a 65 per cent increase.

A glance at these figures shows that in 1938 the number of school-children, 6,860,000, was—even if they all lived—too few to replace the young people between 15 and 24, from whom productive workers are selected. These in their turn, being only 7,431,000, were too few to replace the group of potential parents between 25 and 34, who numbered 7,621,000. Of all women over 15, over 40 per cent had already passed the age in which they could have children. One person in four was already over 50 years old.

MARRIAGE RATE AND AGE OF MARRIAGE

So far, in referring to the birth-rate, we have not distinguished between married and unmarried mothers. But since in England and Wales legitimate births in 1938 were 96 per cent of the whole, it is these which constitute the overwhelming majority of births. We must enquire, therefore, into the marriage-rate, i.e. the number of persons married per 1,000 of the population. In this country it has always been high. In 1850, 859 out of every 1,000 women were married; in 1910 the number had fallen to 818, but rose again in 1920-22 to 860, dropping in 1931 to 826, but rising to 900 in 1938. (The marriage-rate in

each year is very closely related to the level of economic prosperity, so that the difference between the figures of 1931 and 1938 is due largely to the increase in prosperity after the worst years of unemployment in the early thirties.)

Women who marry young may well be expected to have more children than those who marry late in life, partly because they have more years of possible child-bearing ahead, partly because the power to bear children is greatest for women under 25, and becomes greatly reduced near the end of the child-bearing age. Contrary to the popular impression, the average age at which women marry has dropped in recent years. It rose slightly to about 26 years old in 1911, then declined slightly to 25.5 in 1931 and to 24.6 in 1938.

THE BIRTH RATE IN DIFFERENT SOCIAL CLASSES

Neither the birth-rate nor the death-rate is the same in all social classes. Take the birth-rate. As is common knowledge, since 1871 a high birth-rate has in this country generally gone hand-in-hand with poverty; and the birth-rate among unskilled workers was in 1938 probably about 30 per cent higher than among the richer and professional classes, who were, before the war, considerably below replacement level. Thus the poorer half of the nation's parents were producing perhaps two-thirds of the coming generation; and, in general the size of families was inversely correlated with the income level of those in a given occupation.

This difference in the birth-rates of various social classes was most marked when voluntary family restriction first began, since it was the richer classes who first adopted the new ideas and habits. Gradually these spread to the middle classes; later to the higher rank of the working classes and still later to the unskilled workers. This being so, it is not surprising that the difference in the rates between different social classes became less and less, and that recently the biggest fall has been among the lowest-paid workers. Can we in due course expect the present position to be reversed so that there is a direct instead of an inverse ratio between a man's income and the number of his children? . . .

The following table illustrates tendencies up to 1931. . . .

hardly changing, but all other classes showing a considerable reduction.

It is also of interest to compare the birth-rate of different occupations in 1911 and 1921, as shown in Table 5.

After 1921 the situation changed again.

TABLE 4.—BIRTH RATES IN DIFFERENT CLASSES, ENGLAND AND WALES, 1911, 1921 AND 1931

Class	Births per Thousand Husbands under 55; Wives under 45		
	1911	1921	1931
1. Professional and higher business ranks	119	98	94
2. Lower professional and business ranks	132	104	90
3. Skilled workers	153	141	120
4. Semi-skilled workers	158	162	133
5. Unskilled workers	213	178	153

It will be noticed that by 1921 the difference between Class 1 and the lowest two classes had narrowed, and that by 1931 Class 2 and Class 1 had changed places, Class 1

TABLE 5.—BIRTH RATES IN DIFFERENT OCCUPATIONS, 1911 AND 1921

Occupation	Births per Thousand Husbands under 55	
	1911	1921
Hotel-keepers and publicans	94	66
Nonconformist clergymen	96	76
Anglican clergymen	101	78
Authors and journalists	104	86
Teachers	95	87
Local authority officials	84	88
Directors and managers of businesses	120	103
Commercial travellers	125	105
Doctors	103	110
Textile workers	125	110
Civil servants	120	113
Bricklayers	158	118
Clerks	141	121
Farmers	141	131
Boot and shoe operatives	148	138
Agricultural labourers	161	155
Policemen	153	159
Furnacemen	198	179
Coalminers	230	202
Dock labourers	231	209

The practice of birth-control continued to spread downwards, but only reached the lower social groups mainly since that date. This tendency to reduce class differences can be seen in the following figures relating to the birth-rate among owners and miners:

TABLE 6.—BIRTHS PER THOUSAND MALES, 1921 AND 1931

Owners and employers	106	76
Skilled miners	174	126
Semi-skilled workers	200	101
Unskilled miners	156	81

Thus in ten years the fertility of the semi-skilled declined by 50 per cent, that of the unskilled by 48 per cent, and of mine-owners and skilled workers by only 28 per cent. This is not surprising if it is remembered that during these years unemployment, which results in fewer marriages, specially affected the semi-skilled and the unskilled. At the time of writing there are no figures of a more recent date.

DEATH-RATE IN DIFFERENT SOCIAL CLASSES AND REGIONS

The [next] table [7] shows the difference in 1930-32 between the death-rates in different social classes (as defined in Table 4).

It is in the infant death-rate (the number of infants per thousand born who die during the first year), however, that the greatest dif-

TABLE 7.—DEATH RATES IN DIFFERENT SOCIAL
CLASSES

(General death-rate = 100.)

	Men	Married Women	Single Women
Class 1	87	81	100
Class 2	94	89	64
Class 3	97	99	95
Class 4	101	103	102
Class 5	112	113	112

ference is found between the various social classes; and infant death-rates have therefore always been regarded as one of the best indications of social conditions. In 1932, in the case of infants during the first month of life, the death-rate among children of the poorest classes was 50 per cent more than among the children of the well off; in the first three months of life it was over 29 per cent more, and for the last half of the first year, when bad conditions had had more time to make themselves felt, it was nearly 50 per cent more.

In the general death-rate as well as in the infant death-rate there are strongly marked differences between the various regions; whereas the rates in the South-East and Eastern counties were in 1937-9 only 89 per cent of the general death-rate for England and Wales, those in Northumberland and Durham, Lancashire, Cheshire and South Wales were, respectively, 115, 116 and 117 per cent of the general death-rate.

The difference in conditions between South-East England and South Wales in 1937 was, in fact, almost as great as that in Britain between 1911 and 1939. If, before the war, conditions in Northumberland, Durham, Lancashire, Cheshire and South Wales had been as good as in the Home Counties, then these areas would have recorded in the average year not 130,000 deaths but only 100,000. In short, 30,000 people died there each year, not because of any gaps in medical knowledge, but because of local conditions. (Mark Abrams, *Condition of the British People, 1911-45*.)

There are also considerable differences in the infant death-rate between various parts of England and Wales. When, in 1938, the general infant death-rate was 52.7, the rural districts on the whole had a rate of 47.3. Of the county boroughs, whereas that in Greater London was just under 50, Sunderland, with its cold climate and its legacy of unemployment, had one of 85, and Canterbury, on the other hand, well off and in a sunny district, had a death-rate of only 30. It is interesting to know that during the same time (1936-9) Holland had reduced its infant death-rate to 37, and New Zealand in 1938-40 to the remarkable figure of 32. Scotland, on the other hand, still had in 1936-8 an infant death-rate of 77.

* * *

POPULATION FIGURES, 1939-46

During the war various startling changes took place in both the marriage- and birth-rates, though the death-rates have remained singularly little affected. It is desirable that these should be considered apart from the pre-war figures, as it is immensely important to try to estimate whether in the future it is the war-time or the pre-war rates which are most likely to hold the field.

Let us start with the marriage-rate. One reason for the startling increase in the number of marriages—especially between 1933 and 1942—has already been suggested. All over the world more people marry when times are good than when times are bad. During the period of worst unemployment in the early thirties, the difficulty of getting a home together was so great that it was not surprising that as employment became better—thanks to the steady increase in building and to rearmament—the rate began to rise.

When the war came, the heightening of the emotional atmosphere and the natural desire of young people to marry when they could still be together, combined with a period of economic prosperity unknown in their lifetime, resulted in a startling increase in the number of marriages. At the beginning of the war an additional reason for the high mar-

TABLE 8.—COMPOSITE TABLE TO ILLUSTRATE TRENDS FOR 1939-46 IN ENGLAND AND WALES*

	1939	1940	1941	1942	1943	1944	1945	1946
Live birth-rate	14.9	14.5	14.1	15.6	16.2	17.5	16.1	19.1
Total live births	619,352	607,029	587,228	654,039	683,212	744,843	685,544	820,268
Births per thousand married women, age 15-45	108	98	94	103	107	. . .	. . .	. . .
Death-rate†	12.1	13.9	12.8	11.5	11.9	11.6	11.4	11.5
Net reproduction rate	0.81	0.76	0.74	0.85	0.90	1.0	0.91	1.1
Infant death-rate	51	57	60	51	49	46	46	43
Marriage-rate	21.3	22.5	18.7	17.8	14.1	14.3	18.7	17.9

* [For full table see original source, page 33.]
† During the war years only civilian deaths were included.

riage-rate was that the "marriageable stock" itself had risen since 1931. The bumper crop of babies born in 1920 and 1921, when families were re-united after the 1914-18 war, had reached marriageable age, and a larger proportion of young people were marrying. An extra source of husbands for young spinsters was also to be found in the large numbers of young unmarried men in the American and Canadian Forces.

* * *

Since 1939 there has been a marked if intermittent rise in the birth-rate. This was probably partly due to the increased number of marriages, and partly to the desire felt by older married couples for a child before they were separated. The fact that married women could not be directed to employment if they had children under the age of 14 may have contributed to an increased birth-rate. But in spite of the fact that there were nearly a quarter of a million more marriages in the first three years of the war than there would have been if the moderately high marriage-rate of 1936-8 had persisted, nevertheless there were only 190,000 more births than there would have been had the average birth-rate of 1936-8 been maintained. Demobilisation has

been followed by the birth-rate rising to 22.7 for the first quarter of 1947.

The most significant figure from the point of view of our future population is the average family size. Further light is required on any possible changes; and an investigation for the purpose is being made by the Royal Commission. Up till the last few years the average family size had remained unchanged since 1930; and—this is the important point—at a size (about 2) lower than replacement level. But the high birth-rate of recent years would suggest that it is extremely probable that it has now increased, though not up to replacement level.

Fortunately the deaths in the armed forces in the recent war were less than half the number in the first world war. They amounted in all to about 300,000. As for the civilian death-rate, in spite of the loss of about 60,000 civilians by bombing, its satisfactory character was due in part at least to the fact that—owing to arrangements for the provision of milk and other food for mothers and babies, and to certain recent medical discoveries—there was, during these years, the lowest infant death-rate we have ever had. There was also a very satisfactory bill of health in the general population.

• 54 • *Distribution of the Industrial Population in Britain*

THE WORLD PHENOMENON OF URBANISATION

Two outstanding features of population growth have marked the last couple of centuries. The first has been the astonishing expansion of the nations of the Western civilisation. It is stated that at the present time peoples of European origin number approximately 625 millions, constituting about one-third of the human race. It is not clear how many people of European descent there were in 1800, or what proportion of the world's population they then constituted, but there is authority for the estimate that the increase in their number since 1800 has amounted to about 400 millions, while that of all the rest of the world has probably not been more than 200 or 300 millions. This clearly is a very remarkable expansion.

The death rate in Great Britain in the eighteenth century prior to the Industrial Revolution was undoubtedly high. In London it was probably as high as 50 per 1,000 in 1750, and it was still over 30 per 1,000 in 1800. In the smaller towns and rural districts of England there was a considerably lower death rate than in London and some of the other larger places, but, even so, it was probably not less than 35 per 1,000 in the middle of the eighteenth century for the whole of England. By 1800, it had fallen to between 25 and 30, leaving a considerable margin as compared with the birth rate even if that did not exceed 35 as may well have been the case, and when the second and third censuses had been taken (1811-21) the flood of new life had popularised the phrase, a "redundant population". This decline of the death rate was largely attributable to the Industrial Revolution itself: that Revolution removed two great positive checks which had been operative in greater or less degree until that time, namely, inadequate subsistence and the heavy incidence of disease

due to the lack of proper sanitation—sanitation which the growing wealth of the towns was in the succeeding years to provide.

The second remarkable feature of population growth has been the even more rapid proportional rate at which the great urban centres of Western civilisation have spread, overflowing their boundaries and forming sprawling agglomerations of humanity, many of dimensions without precedent in the world's history; this concentration of population in great units has been the subject of much scientific investigation in recent years, and Weber, writing in 1899, described it as the most remarkable social phenomenon of the nineteenth century.

Here again are traceable the effects of the Industrial Revolution. The world in the sixteenth, seventeenth and eighteenth centuries had known teeming cities of traffic and exchange: Venice, the Hansa towns, the City of London, were busy centres of merchandise and population long before steam and the power loom had revolutionised the conditions of industrial production, but the factory and the machine at once gripped, transformed and expanded existing centres of commerce.

Great Britain, the first country to receive the impact of the Revolution through the discoveries of her sons, was also the first to experience the phenomenon of uncontrolled urban growth. Up to the end of the eighteenth century, probably no city in the world had reached a population of a million, but at the census of 1801 Greater London is recorded as having reached a population of well over a million and since then it has retained its place as the most populous conurbation in the world.

* * *

The nineteenth century was marked by the persistent and rapid enlargement of the great cities and in Great Britain to-day ap-

[From *Report,* Royal Commission on the Distribution of the Industrial Population, London, 1940. Pp. 10-16, 29-30.]

proximately two-fifths of the total population dwell in the seven million-mark conurbations, while the corresponding proportion in the United States is only about one-fifth. Generally speaking, during the last hundred years the million-mark cities have tended to increase

which are of great importance. First, the acreage of Great Britain in comparison with other Western countries is exceedingly limited in proportion to the size of its population. This can be most easily illustrated by the following simple table:

Country	Square Miles	Population	Population per Square Mile
Belgium	11,750	8,250,000	702
France	213,000	42,000,000	197
Germany	229,000	81,000,000	353
Italy	120,000	43,606,000	360
U. S. A.	3,738,000	137,000,000	36
Great Britain	88,750	46,000,000	518

(For England alone the figures are even more striking:)

England	50,330	38,552,000	766

their populations at rates at least twice as great as the mean rate of increase for their respective countries; and especially is this characteristic of the capital cities.

This phenomenon of aggregation into great cities which developed so rapidly and so persistently in the last century or more, first in the West and eventually throughout the world, has a vast momentum behind it; the call of the city, and of the big city, to all classes of the community the world over is loud and compelling; it represents a tide of forces social as well as industrial in character, stimulated by men's need not merely for a livelihood, but for the best possible opportunities in respect of education, medical and surgical treatment, mental recreation, professional and business advancement and so forth. A tide of this volume is likely to be difficult either to dam or to direct, and attempts to do so will require the fullest and most careful consideration.

DISTINCTIVE FEATURES OF URBANISATION IN GREAT BRITAIN

The world-wide development of intensive urbanisation presents in the case of Great Britain certain distinctive features, two of

Thus, if England is taken as a unit, the pressure of population shows a figure per square mile of more than 60 in excess of Belgium, which is usually considered the world's most densely peopled national area. As a result of this limited acreage, the Commission's problem presents a picture set in a narrow background: in a country with millions of unoccupied or sparsely occupied acres, urbanisation can be considered in relation to much wider surroundings.

The second distinctive feature referred to above is the vast—and many would add alarming—growth of population in London and South-Eastern England, largely at the expense of the rest of the country. It is not necessary to describe this growth at length or to labour the figures here. It is sufficient to emphasise that one unmistakable modern trend which has emerged in evidence is the great drift of population from the North and West towards the South-East.

The concentrations of population in Great Britain may be divided into two groups, namely, the shipping and commercial centres and the centres of mining and manufacturing industry. The two main shipping centres, London and Liverpool, import commodities from all parts of the world, with the result that they have large docks, warehouses and other storage facilities, together with the remaining technical equipment required for unloading and distributing on a large scale. This commercial and distributing function alone provides employment for a considerable population, which in turn gives employment in local industries to a further group. But London, in particular, is more than that. In quite early days it became a centre of handicrafts and cottage industries that have since become factory industries, with the result that it is now an important centre of such industries as leather tanning and dressing; boot and shoe manufacture; the finishing sections of a number of iron and steel trades; tailoring, dressmaking, millinery, etc.; the production of paper and of chemicals, dye stuffs and drugs. As a port it was once largely engaged in the building of wooden vessels and it is still an important ship repairing centre; it has also become one of the chief grain milling centres. It is also the largest centre of the timber trade. Having always been the main commercial centre of this country London has grown to be a large factory centre. Its growth as a manufacturing centre has also been fostered by the fact that it is the capital city and the centre of the British commonwealth, the chief centre of the printing and publishing trades, and the Mecca of tourists both from within the country and from other parts of the world, with the result that it maintains public utility services and miscellaneous services on a scale unknown elsewhere in this country. Other large commercial centres, such as Liverpool and Hull, have also built up manufacturing industries, either industries of a local character or "basic" industries using imported materials.

The oil and oilcake industry, grain milling and copper production may be quoted as illustrations of such industries.

The second group of concentrations of population is based upon mining and manufacture. The main concentrations are the Clyde Valley, the North East Coast, East Lancashire, the West Riding and the West Midlands. Other less pronounced concentrations are to be found in other parts of the country, such as South Wales and the East Midlands. It will be observed that every one of these is situated on a coalfield. In the case of some, more particularly South Wales and the North East Coast, the economy of the community is largely based upon coal production and the sale of coal outside the area. In the case of others, coal is the foundation of manufacturing industries the products of which are the main products that are sold outside the area. Thus, for example, in West Yorkshire the supremacy of coal is challenged by the wool textile industry, which is itself largely based on coal; in South Yorkshire the mining industry has helped to build up a large and still growing steel industry; in the West Midlands the coal industry exists mainly as the handmaid of a large group of miscellaneous metal industries. Thus the coal industry performs a double function by providing a commodity for export to other areas or other countries and by attracting other industries to its own neighborhood. It may be broadly stated that throughout the nineteenth century coal acted as the great magnet to the industrial population other than that which was concentrated in the chief shipping and commercial areas.

The next selection is the result of the efforts of an organization called Political and Economic Planning, which describes itself as,

> ... an independent non-party group, consisting of more than a hundred working members who are by vocation industrialists, distributors, officers of central and local government, town planners, architects, economists, doctors and so forth, and who give part of their spare time to the use of their special training in fact-

finding and in suggesting principles and possible advances over a wide range of social and economic problems. . . . The group has . . . published full-scale reports on the coal-mining, cotton and iron and steel industries, housing and building, electricity supply, international trade, the Press, the health services, the social services, retirement pensions, continued education from the age of fourteen, and agricultural research.

Four years' work went into the preparation of the report, a small part of which is presented below.

It seeks to provide a comprehensive, balanced and up-to-date summary of the main factors affecting the choice of location of industry, and to supply a basis for a judgement upon the practicability and advisability of attempting conscious stimulation and guidance of industrial development in the national interest. The Report finds in favour of such a policy, but points out its difficulties and limitations, and shows where further examination is needed.

• 55 • Towns and Industry

Towns are among the oldest social organisms of civilization and have developed a complex life, many aspects of which are only remotely relevant to the problems of location of industry. Nevertheless, the town is, in most cases, the background of industry and is, to a large extent, moulded by the particular nature of its contact with industry, past and present. On the one hand industries, especially those with low location factors, have been established in towns in order to obtain services, labour and markets. On the other hand, towns have grown up round industries, especially those such as coal or cotton with high location factors. It is difficult, therefore, to say to what extent the present distribution of population is the result of, or the reason for, the present pattern of the location of industry. The industrial population and industry have, at any rate, to live side by side, if not intermingled, and it is therefore important to consider their interrelations. These interrelations are both social and economic. There are towns, notably London, in which families

from many other areas are eager to live and there are other towns which not only fail to attract outsiders, but fail to hold a number of their own most enterprising inhabitants. The success or otherwise of an industry may depend on the social vitality, the general planning and the efficiency of the services of the town in which it is established. It is easy in considering the location of industry to underrate the importance of this relationship, or even to omit all reference to it. Apart from those costs directly incurred by the individual business there are social consequences arising out of its operations which have to be borne by the community as a whole.

* * *

According to the Census, 80 per cent of the 1931 population of England and Wales lived in local government areas classed as urban—that is, in country and municipal boroughs and in urban districts. Up to 1901 there was a rapid rise in the urban percentage, and this was followed by thirty years of relative

[From *Report on the Location of Industry in Great Britain,* Political and Economic Planning, London, 1939. Pp. 148-168. Used by permission.]

stability, but, according to the 1936 estimates, the rise has now been resumed. . . .

. . . Thus at least four out of every five people in Great Britain are town dwellers. Moreover, areas which are for local government purposes distinct are often in practice parts of one large town. The population is, in fact, much more urbanised and much more concentrated in a relatively few large towns than the figures suggest. The evidence of the Garden Cities and Town Planning Association before the Royal Commission on the Geographical Distribution of the Industrial Population shows that in 1934 more than 20 million persons out of the 45.4 million in Great Britain lived in or very near the fourteen chief urban centres, 15¼ millions living in the six largest towns.

In view of these figures it is rather remarkable that hardly more than 12 per cent of the area of England and Wales is urban (1931), and much of this is not yet built up, although as an offset substantial tracts of land classed as "rural" are more or less built up. Towns from their very nature show a high density of population in relation to their area, but the actual density varies a great deal. . . .

ADVANTAGES AND DISADVANTAGES OF URBANISATION

. . . Land values in the central areas of the largest towns rise to remarkable levels. It was estimated by the President of the Surveyors' Institution in November, 1935, that properties occupying the best position in the City of London had about doubled in value during the previous fifty years, and Sir Charles Bressey, who quotes this in his "Greater London Highway Development Survey, 1937," states that the cost of comparatively insignificant street widenings sometimes works out at a rate exceeding £2 million per mile. As regards effects on housing, the Garden Cities Association shows that in Manchester the cost of land for the Hulme working-class rehousing scheme is over £7,000 per acre, and the total cost per flat, including site, is over £800; while in central London with land at up to £20,000 an acre, figures in excess of £900 per

flat are reached, compared with an average of about £400 for cottage houses with gardens in small towns. The natural result is that long-needed road facilities are not provided, and housing replacement has been either neglected or provided at a low standard of space per person in order to keep down rents plus subsidies to a not quite intolerable level.

The effects on traffic and health respectively are clearly traceable. An investigation for the Bressey Report showed that the average speed of a well-driven powerful private motor car on main routes through London during working hours in 1936 was not more than 12½ m.p.h., and on considerable stretches in the centre was forced as low as 3½-8 m.p.h., with frequent holdups lasting 1-2 minutes at points of intersection. On the North Circular Road, a suburban highway generally considered very inadequate for traffic needs, the average speed was 23.6 m.p.h., and it seems safe to say that in typical modern street conditions in the British large town, journeys by private car take at least four times as long as they would on unobstructed roads. The growth of towns and of traffic without corresponding improvements in facilities has now, in fact, more than offset in the central areas any speed advantage due to the invention of the internal combustion engine. A powerful car now takes longer to do many journeys than an average cab-horse of forty years ago.

Recent urban growth has meant that large and continually increasing numbers of people are forced by lack of accommodation, high rents, and unsuitable living conditions near their work to live at a distance and travel back and forth twice or in some cases four times every working day. In 1921, the latest year for which such figures are available, at least 800,000 persons were travelling daily to work in central London. The movement, however, includes many opposite currents. Thus Stretford, near Manchester, sent nearly a quarter of its population out to work in other areas, but imported in their place other day-time workers equal to almost half its population. There were already nearly twenty years ago many similar but less extreme cases not only in Greater London, but in most of the chief urban areas. According to the Garden Cities Association "in the year up to June 1937, the people of London made 4,250 million journeys in the London Transport area—436 per head or 2,340 per family. They paid in fares over £41 million or £16 3s. per family. The average journey cost 2.347 pence. In Birmingham in 1936 the journeys were 373 per head and the fares 1½d. per journey, or £8 17s. per family for the year," not counting in either case journeys by taxi or private car. In a small town the corresponding figure is estimated at only £2-£3, and in many cases it is less.

The time taken in such travel for many persons averages 1½-2 hours a day, and on a number of lines a majority of the passengers who travel at peak hours have to stand. The problem of excessive journey time and fares takes different forms in different areas, but is common to the mining valleys of South Wales and the newest industrial belts. A case is known of a large factory outside London, one-quarter of whose workers live an hour or more away from it. On the other hand, there are towns even in the 100,000 size-range, where almost all the workers can still easily walk or cycle to work and go home for their midday meal. According to 'The People's Food,' by Sir W. Crawford and H. Broadley, the proportion of husbands having their midday meal at home is between 50 and 60 per cent in the larger British towns, the proportion being lowest in London (30 to 50 per cent).

The effect of running very heavy traffic in narrow channels between tall buildings, or underground, is greatly to increase exposure to noise, which is very fatiguing and harmful to the nerves. In the carriage of a City tube train travelling at 30 m.p.h. the noise ranges from about 90 to 106 phons—a level at which an adult lion continuously roaring to capacity (105 phons at 18 ft.) would scarcely be audible. Many city streets produce continuous traffic noise reaching 80-90 phons, which is about the level of thunder 1-3 miles away and louder than church bells at 400 yards. The noisiest position by Niagara Falls is stated to yield an average of 105 phons.

Another effect of urban congestion is the very heavy atmospheric pollution already mentioned. An investigation by the Department of Scientific and Industrial Research (summarised in Cmd. 3989, 1931) showed that over a complete year atmospheric pollution from Norwich, a town about two miles in diameter, with relatively very clean air, was significant for a distance of five to six miles down wind from the centre of the city. With a town twenty-four miles in diameter, or a group of neighbouring urban areas twenty-four miles in diameter, pollution would be significant up to about sixty to seventy miles, or more in those cases where the air of the town concerned was dirtier than at Norwich. Smoke is annually responsible for damage measurable in money to the extent of about £40-£50 million—not to speak of an enormous amount of damage on which no money value can be placed. Here is an avoidable national waste equivalent to about 9d. on the income tax. The distorting effect of atmospheric pollution on town development is seen in the emergence of suburbs to windward of the worst affected areas as segregated communities of the richer local inhabitants. Thus smoke plays its part in aggravating class divisions.

A further problem particularly acute in large towns is public cleansing, which is described by the Ministry of Health in its 1936-37 Report as "one of the most costly services provided out of the rates," involving an annual total charge on England and Wales of some £11 million. The towns contribute the overwhelming majority of the 15 million tons per annum of solid waste matter which has to be disposed of in such a way as to avoid nuisance, including about 1 ton of household refuse from every house and about 3 million tons of debris (excluding snow) from 26,500 miles of streets in towns with over 20,000 population.

It is hardly surprising that in spite of modern improvements in sanitation and preventive medicine one of the characteristics of large towns is their unhealthiness. Care must be taken in interpreting statistics on this subject, because there is no standard of measurement for health, and such indirect indices as death-rates present pitfalls. The Registrar-General's Decennial Supplement for England and Wales, issued in 1936, offers something like a reliable yardstick, and shows that taking the national "expected" rate as 100, the actual male death-rate for all county boroughs is 111, and for all rural districts 86. That is, male death-rates in county boroughs are 30 per cent above those in rural districts. The northern large towns show relatively higher death-rates than the southern, and in Greater London the Outer Ring is conspicuous for the lightness of its death-rates as compared not only with inner London, but with other urban areas.

Large towns have usually proved a type of habitat in which the human species can live, but is unable to reproduce itself adequately to maintain its numbers. In the past this has been due mainly to comparatively heavy death-rates: now the same result is brought about largely by the towns' very low birth-rates. In England and Wales, however, there is much less contrast between town and country in this respect than in certain continental nations. In the past the deficiency of the towns has been made good out of the surplus of the country, but this is obviously difficult when the country is producing very little surplus and when its population is reduced to less than one-fourth that of the towns. The period in which it was frequent to find a very large proportion of country-bred people living in large towns has definitely ended, and the towns have increasingly to face replacing their own populations. Yet in many respects recent changes have made urban areas more unsuited than ever to the bearing and rearing of children—as a large number of the drawbacks already described are particularly unfavourable to family life. The large city tends to become a suitable environment only for the able-bodied and unencumbered adult.

Enough has been said to indicate that there are certain disadvantages in concentrating populations in large towns. What are the benefits of the practice and how far do they offset the disadvantages?

The most evident advantage of the town is that it brings large numbers of people, many at a high standard of living, closely enough together for the use of elaborate services and equipment in common. A rich enough family can maintain in an isolated country house its own electric light plant, its own access by metalled roads, its own passenger and goods transport, and its own extensive library, picture gallery, and even zoo, but for the vast majority of families such services have only been brought within reach by devices for their collective provision. The town enables a collection of families grouped together to enjoy a great number of services in common at a low cost.

There is an inherent economy, often of immense importance, in such collective provision, but the nature and extent of this economy is affected by technical changes. In two respects such changes have recently had an important influence. In the first place the old limitations on the size of an efficient town, which were imposed by the limits of walking distance and by difficulties of regular provisioning and water supply have disappeared. Motor vehicles, steam trains, electric trains, trams and trolley buses, and even bicycles, greatly widen the built-up area which one centre can serve. Telephones, quick efficient mails, and extensive delivery services can help to minimise the effects of distance. Methods of organisation in business and government make it possible to serve, police, and administer much larger aggregations without conditions becoming absolutely intolerable.

But it must be noted that the same developments which enable the large town to become larger also enable it to be more easily dispensed with. Science increases urban facilities and the size of group which can afford them, and also makes it possible to give the inhabitants of small towns and even of rural areas services formerly restricted to large towns. Electricity, road transport, telephones, wireless, piped water supply, retail delivery and other services are to a large and increasing extent available in rural as well as urban areas, although the cost is sometimes higher and the convenience or range of choice reduced. In a number of cases it is a deliberate policy to even out differences in cost and facilities as between town, suburb and country by making the consumer in the town sudsidise the consumer outside it. The result has been not only greatly to enlarge the size of towns, but to blur, sometimes to a surprising extent, the distinction between town and country. It is no accident that "rurban" development, or the creation in country surroundings of scattered settlements dependent on urban incomes and retaining urban outlooks and ways of life, has lately gone ahead as fast, or perhaps faster than, the growth of towns. . . . In some parts, towns in any clear-cut sense of the word can hardly still be said to exist: so far has the degeneration into built-up areas gone.

The same trend has led to other consequences. The old-fashioned town offered a relatively meagre range of services, whose effective enjoyment was confined to a small minority of its inhabitants. Lately there has been a progressive expansion, not only of the range of services, but of the proportion of the population which can enjoy them. This has involved in turn a great increase in the number of persons engaged in collective urban services, and has tended at the same time to reduce considerably the size of population needed to sustain a given unit of service. Certain services, such as electricity supply, tend to become available at lower cost the more densely their consumers are concentrated, but others, such as highways, increase in cost per unit of population beyond a certain density. Many of these, however, cannot be supported adequately by thinly scattered communities and they therefore become relatively more costly to provide both above and below certain densities. As the scale of use often varies directly with standards of living, a rise in standards of living may bring a small community up to the appropriate level for supporting a given service, or may push a large town into the zone of higher costs or increasing congestion.

A town which has an appropriate size of population for providing certain services to a privileged minority of its inhabitants may have a much larger population than is necessary or convenient for giving the same services to the whole or even a majority of its inhabitants. If, for example, two-thirds of the inhabitants of many of our large towns suddenly adopted the upper income-group practice of having a bath every morning, it would very seriously increase the difficulties and costs of the existing water supply, based on the assumption that most people have their bath, if any, not oftener than weekly, and on competitive exploitation of remote sources by rival water undertakings. Again, owing to the higher standard of living and the much greater use of road passenger transport, routes which could never have supported a service thirty years ago now do so comfortably, while services which were well used thirty years ago are in many cases hopelessly congested. Our urban street system, already chronically jammed with traffic when one person in twenty owns a car, would in most towns at once become virtually unusable if even three out of twenty started using cars, as in New Zealand. In fact, the economics of our towns would be fundamentally altered by even a moderate change in a single factor such as the attainment of the New Zealand level in motor car ownership relative to population.

Much of the confusion in contemporary urban life becomes explicable if it is borne in mind that the town represents, with considerable accretions and with only minor alterations, an organism created to serve a range of technical needs which has long since been outgrown, and a degree of privilege and differentiation in opportunity between sections of the community which no longer exists.

It is important in considering urban advantages to distinguish between those which are now, or shortly will be, shared by non-urban communities, such as telephones and electricity, and those which are likely permanently or for a long time to remain confined wholly or mainly to the town, such as department stores, art galleries, technical schools, and sewage disposal plants. One of the greatest material advantages of the large town is its capacity for low-cost, high-speed delivery of an immense range of goods, and its capacity to make instantly available a great variety of services, from permanent waving to advice on how to start manufacturing ball-bearings. For social purposes, again, towns have advantages which increase probably in direct ratio to their size, as between communities of similar character. There appears to be a tendency in small towns and in country districts for social groups either to cling to an excessively narrow range of interests, or to split up into fragments too small to follow out varying interests without a sense of frustration. In the large town a man can be and often is a member of several different social groups for several different purposes, but in the small town or the country there is an inevitable tendency, where different groups exist, for their memberships to overlap so heavily as to reduce their independent impetus and the sense of freshness gained from belonging to them. The advantage of the large town in this respect is, however, immensely increased by the smallness of the minority at present having the leisure, the education, and the will to take part in many significant activities, and by the overwhelming attraction which it can exert on people with minority interests owing to this and to economic factors.

With this general introduction it becomes desirable to analyse in more detail the general pattern of town life and the different types of contemporary town.

PATTERNS OF TOWN DEVELOPMENT

The sites of towns occupy considerable tracts of ground, ranging from a few hundred acres to upwards of a hundred square miles in the largest examples. By no means all this area is, however, built up. Even the most densely developed quarters contain a considerable acreage of unbuilt ground in the form not only of streets and railways, but often of vacant sites, yards, gardens, or open spaces, and open water.

The buildings in different towns and in different parts of a large town also vary greatly in size and character, and in the nature of their arrangement on the land. The simplest town plan is a row of buildings along both sides of one main street with few and unimportant side streets. This lineal plan is found not only in many villages, but in quite large communities occupying cramped sites such as the Rhondda, where 140,000 persons living in a narrow mining valley are grouped under one local authority. The same plan has reappeared in the modern ribbon developments along arterial roads, where the cost of road construction in conjunction with the operations of land speculators and utility services have canalised population as effectively as mountain slopes.

Another very common type of plan is the radial, which is essentially a series of lineal developments intersecting at a common centre. This is the natural pattern for a town site which has road connections in several directions. The village on a cross-roads is the simplest example. Where there is some special site feature the plan is modified accordingly: thus a seaside resort or a port fronting a wide arm of the sea is typically semi-radial in pattern.

The obvious weakness of the radial town is the excessive congestion of its centre which may be offset by elaborating it into a spider-web pattern. This has occurred naturally in many continental cities formerly girdled by fortifications, whose demolition has provided sites for wide ring roads. By-passes for large towns tend to become ring roads, and one of the main proposals for relieving London traffic congestion is by means of further circular roads to keep through traffic away from the centre.

While the lineal and radial patterns emerge almost unconsciously, and the spider-web pattern represents a primitive and partial planning, there are several other patterns which have been conceived and imposed in advance of development. Probably the simplest of these is the chequer-board or gridiron plan, used by the Romans and in certain medieval experiments, and in modern times common in North America and other new countries. There are relatively few British towns on this pattern: Barrow-in-Furness, laid out in mid-Victorian times, is one of the chief examples. Other mathematical or geometric patterns such as the hexagon, octagon or star are hardly represented in Great Britain and the monumental or formal lay-outs favoured in Rome, Paris and Berlin are also uncommon in the British towns with the outstanding exceptions of Bath and of Edinburgh New Town. On the other hand, England is the home of formalised informality, which is conspicuous in the winding roads and closes of the modern garden city and of many suburbs and housing estates.

Towns may develop either by ribboning, by continuous spread, by more or less open scattering, or by satellite growth with artificially preserved free zones between the groups of buildings. There is a tendency as a town grows for the main functions to become segregated in distinct areas and one of the main tasks of town planning is to anticipate, guide, and make provision for this segregation. Thus in London, finance and commerce gradually displaced other functions in the City, while theatres, restaurants, cinemas and certain types of shop gathered largely in a relatively small part of the West End. In both cases the process occurred in such a way as to cause extreme congestion and inconvenience to the large crowds brought in from other areas at the peak hours. The same problem occurs where factory industry is concentrated, as at Trafford Park, in large aggregations remote from the homes of many of the workers. The siting of industry in relation to other functions of the town takes many different forms, each raising its own difficulties. Some towns have grown up round old established industries or mines, whose modernisation is thereby hindered, while they in turn make it difficult if not impossible to improve the centre of the town. In other cases factories are mixed indiscriminately with dwellings and other buildings, sometimes in large numbers, or sometimes as isolated freaks or survivors of an earlier phase. The result usually is to lower the residential amenities and rateable value of the neighbourhood, and to create a good deal of friction. It is said that Queen Victoria strongly objected to the large brewery which still remains close by Buckingham Palace, and which can be smelt in favourable conditions for upwards of a quarter of a mile. "Borderline" industries, such as laundries, bakeries and garages or vehicle service stations, have a more legitimate place among dwellings, but often cause friction, especially on account of night use. On the other hand, industries which go right outside the town into undeveloped areas, and which usually raise local rateable values, often cause a different set of difficulties by injuring rural amenities, by requiring uneconomic development of services and by competing with agriculture for limited land and labour supplies.

Perhaps the most successful solutions have been found where industry has been segregated in units large enough to permit planning for its special requirements, but not so large as to involve long journeys to homes and places of recreation. Examples of this are found in some of the newer garden cities and satellite towns where provision is made for both living and industry, in some medium-sized older towns where a separate industrial zone has naturally developed, and in some light industry zones on the borders of larger towns, where adequate workers' housing is available close at hand and where development has not become excessive.

TYPES OF TOWN

Differences in function lead not only to the emergence of distinct quarters serving different functions within a given town, but also to the emergence of distinct and specialised types of town.

Only in extreme cases is the character of a town so clearly marked that it can be classed without reservation as, say, a pleasure resort or a mining centre, and nothing more. Most towns are of mixed composition and function, and impressions of dominant local characteristics formed from observation often prove to be over emphasised when checked against surveys and statistics. Moreover, towns may change their character very rapidly—the university town or fishing port of a few years ago may already have become primarily a manufacturing centre or a seaside resort before the extent of the transformation is appreciated even locally. It is, nevertheless, useful to attempt an outline classification of some of the contemporary types of community in Great Britain, bearing in mind that most towns fall into at least two of the categories, and that some embrace nearly all of them, although in varying degrees and often in geographically separate quarters. Strictly speaking, the following analysis is of broad elements in towns, but it is more convenient and pictorial to speak, for example, of a town in which the season-ticket holder is the most pronounced element as a dormitory town than to describe it in more abstract terms. Moreover, so long as it is used with discretion and a sense of proportion, the pictorial approach may give at least as true a picture as that based strictly on statistical analysis, for different towns have different atmospheres which often influence largely even such matters as the location of industry. It by no means follows that the importance of the various elements in determining the direction and rate of development is truly indicated by, for example, the numerical proportion of the persons engaged in different occupations.

It should therefore be borne in mind that the following categories are only distinguished as a basis of analysis, and that in practice they frequently overlap. Many who are familiar with some of the actual towns named will no doubt disagree at times not only with the classification, but with the putting of certain towns in certain categories. Very often a good case could be made out for placing a single town in any or all of several categories, but this does not necessarily indicate

either that the classification or the method of using it is misleading. One of the main characteristics of modern towns is that they try to serve several different and often incompatible purposes. On the other hand, almost all towns specialise to a marked degree, and their specialisms conform more or less closely to a fairly small number of distinguishable types. Some specialisms, such as the military and the mining specialisms, often dominate the towns where they are found, while others, such as the cathedral or the school and the university specialisms, habitually exist side by side with other substantial activities.

The analysis begins with the simplest current types of community and ends with the most complex. In each case there is a description of some salient characteristics of the type, followed by a discussion of some of its principal advantages and drawbacks, with special reference to economic and social vitality and attractiveness.

The village, the simplest form of group settlement with division of labour, still flourishes. It provides elementary essential services such as a meeting place for worship and often also for social activities, a public house, a general shop or shops, a petrol-filling station, and a post office. The modern village often possesses communications in the form of a telephone box, and often such utilities as a bus service and an electricity supply. The housing of the farm population may either be concentrated in the village or scattered, but in any case the typical village is concerned wholly or almost wholly with the everyday needs of people living within walking distance—it does not serve the population of any other grouped community, but simply provides for the needs of individuals in its immediate neighbourhood. Among the professions, clergy and teachers are distributed in the great majority of villages. Services of doctors and nurses, banks, hairdressers, and some others are usually shared between a group of villages or supplied, like all the more specialised services, from a neighbouring country town. Local recreations, such as cricket, football and the hunt, almost inevitably involve co-operation over an area includ-ing several villages, although for the popular games each village will have its own team. The normal size of a village is between about 100 and 1,000 inhabitants.

The village typically benefits from a strong community sense and excellent integration with its surroundings. On the other hand, close personal contact may easily degenerate into lasting feuds, and the leadership of the community is almost inevitably identified with the local employing class, possibly eked out by some workers on their own account such as small farmers. There is no focus in the village for upper and middle class social life outside private houses: its typical meet-ing place, the "pub," is a working class insti-tution. While responsibility for leadership is clear and is not easily evaded, and while the risk of unemployment is light, such stability as exists tends to be bought at the price of economic and political domination by a small minority, and of a material standard of life so low that by urban tests almost every village is a depressed area. Collective services and community centres, although increasing, are still in most cases relatively meagre.

The country town, in addition to serving the everyday needs of its own population rather more elaborately than the village, typi-cally provides for the weekly or occasional needs of the inhabitants of a number of sur-rounding villages and parishes. The most obvious of these needs are buying and selling of supplies, and the country town therefore tends to have a high proportion of shops, some of them specialised for various crafts and regular markets. It also has one or more representatives of such professions and serv-ices as auctioneers, estate agents, veterinary surgeons, solicitors, banks, and cinemas, which are absent or rare in villages. Moreover, it is a point of transshipment for passengers and goods between the main railway and road network and the surrounding district. It is very frequently the headquarters of one of the smaller units of local government, such as a rural district council or a drainage au-thority. The typical country town, unless its

size is inflated by other factors, usually has between 1,000 and 5,000 inhabitants.

The country town possesses, like the vil-lage, a fairly deep-rooted community sense and effective integration with its surround-ing district, without suffering to anything like the same extent from the disadvantages outlined above. It enjoys very much fuller services, but these often operate on much too small a scale for full efficiency and many which are taken for granted in larger towns are absent or very poor. There is less of a pro-nounced class barrier, and a much larger share of leadership falls to professional and business men.

Factory industries are sometimes attracted to or develop in relatively small country towns. The danger, where these are too suc-cessful, is that they may come to dominate local life and turn the area into something resembling the "mining camp" type described later.

The traffic town possesses to a high de-gree what geographers term nodality—that is, it commands a number of routes of some importance, and thus enjoys relatively good transport services and road access from a fairly wide area. All towns are to some extent traffic towns, but it seems convenient to dis-tinguish those which owe their location and their growth primarily to this factor, even though most of them also have a claim to a place in one or more other categories.

Railway junctions and depots, or ports, are often prominent features of a traffic town, but the mere existence of such facilities does not constitute a traffic town in the sense here described, unless there is sufficient servicing of the passengers or handling of the goods to provide something more than transit business.

The most characteristic locations for a traffic town are at the limit of tide-water navi-gable for seagoing vessels or at the lowest suitable bridge position on a river or inlet, near the entry to a convenient route through or round some major natural obstacle such as a range of mountains or hills, or a chain of lakes, or at a rail-head serving a considerable area. London is one of the chief examples,

and others which have always had importance on this account are Exeter, Norwich,
Gloucester, York, Carlisle, and Stirling. As
the factors on which a traffic town bases its
importance are natural and strategic it is rare
for a new site to become of first-rate importance or for an old one to shrink into
obscurity. Manchester is perhaps the most
striking example of a rise and Cirencester of
a fall in importance as traffic towns since
Roman times. There is no visible upper limit
to the size of a traffic town, and the development of this type has been enormously stimulated by the modern possibility of provisioning economically and supplying with water
any size of population, and by the tendency
not only for the growing services to develop
in such towns, but for the growing light industries to be attracted by the rich market
they offer.

Traffic towns are often administratively
important as capitals of counties, assize towns,
and divisional headquarters of national services. The employment and income arising out
of these activities are of growing importance
to them as the range of public services expands.

The traffic town, as it varies greatly in
size, is a peculiarly difficult subject for generalisation on advantages and drawbacks.
Typically it shows a high development of
professions and services, including commerce,
banking, transport and communications, and
public administration. Therefore it can support a fairly lively and progressive intellectual
life, and has rarely an acute problem of leadership. It has a much richer growth of voluntary associations than the country town, such
bodies as rotary clubs being characteristic. In
many cases, despite recent growth, a fairly
strong civic sense and effective contact with
the life of surrounding districts persists from
the time when the town was smaller and
more closely knit. It also tends to show a relatively good balance: towns of this type, until
they grow immensely large, are rarely divided
crudely into great tracts inhabited by members of a single social or income group. On
the other hand, the very nature of its basic

functions gives it a serious obsolescence problem over street and parking space, terminal
and exchange facilities and general layout.
Wastes at this point can often be successfully
passed on to the consumer, but this is not true
for export trades and may not be true indefinitely even of home market activities.

The port is a special type of traffic town,
and many of the largest traffic towns owe a
good deal of their importance to the possession of a port, although they would not be
classed here as traffic towns if they had not
considerable importance on other grounds as
well. The general freight and passenger port
for ocean-going vessels is most often combined with a large traffic town, as in the case
of London and New York, but a number of
important general ports such as Hull and
Liverpool, and to a less extent, Southampton,
occupy sites which would have little importance for traffic if the port facilities did not
exist.

*　　*　　*

The port combines a very stable and often
traditionally-minded nucleus and a highly unstable floating element of transients and of
temporary activities. Few types of town suffer
so much from long-run insecurity, and history is full of examples of once great ports
reduced to insignificance, not only by silting
or erosion, but by geographical and other
changes in the balance of industry, by labour
disputes, and by political action. Although
there is no recent case of the decay of a major
British port, the position of the port of Liverpool, for example, has recently been much
reduced relatively to Southampton, and the
docks of Penarth have actually been closed.
Apart from long-run insecurity, ports are particularly susceptible to short-run fluctuations,
especially when, as is often the case, they are
closely concerned with shipbuilding, ship-
repairing, or other export industries. From
its nature the port tends to be rather weakly
integrated with the life of its surrounding territory except where, as in the case of London,
Bristol, and Manchester, it is also an important traffic town for its region. Ports have

frequently acute social problems, due to mixed populations, often without local roots, security of income, or an adequate standard of life. The growth of amalgamations and combines in road and rail transport, shipping, shipbuilding, flour milling, sugar and oil refining, and other characteristic port industries gives rise to a problem of absentee ownership and control of the main economic assets, which is only beginning to be offset by a growing awareness, in flour-milling and one or two other industries, of their local social responsibilities. Community sense is encouraged by the sharp fluctuations in prosperity to which ports are subject, but the social balance is often one-sided, and in the absence of one or two exceptional and wealthy families leadership tends to be weak.

The mining camp town is a convenient expression not only for all towns based on an extractive industry, but in a wider sense for towns whose chief reason for existence is or has been a single factory industry or works. Most but not all such towns are products of the past century or so, and they are still being created—Billingham with Norton-on-Tees, Corby, and Kinlochleven are recent additions —while towns such as Scunthorpe, Fort William and Northwich have been so enlarged and altered in character as to approximate to this type. Railway locomotive and rolling stock workshops have given rise to similar settlements at Swindon, Crewe, Eastleigh, Ashford (Kent), Wolverton (Bucks), and elsewhere. Towns of this type are mainly of small or medium size, among the largest clear examples being Middlesborough (iron and steel) of 140,000 population, and Merthyr Tydfil, now reduced to 63,000. Swindon had just over 60,000, and Crewe under 50,000 in 1931. Although some towns in this class have become county boroughs, they tend to be unimportant as administrative and commercial centres in relation to their size, and their amenities are not such as to encourage development into resorts or residential areas.

The mining camp town has had the opportunity of a new plan, free from medieval street-lines, but this opportunity has in many cases been very poorly used. Towns based on one industry are often also inhabited very largely by one income and social group over large areas, and show a tendency to excessive class segregation even where many different occupational grades are present. Integration with the life of the surrounding district is typically weak, and there may be downright hostility between "natives" and "immigrants" persisting for remarkably long periods. Community sense may be very strong, owing to ties of common occupation, or very weak, but in either case there appears to be a characteristic "garrison" atmosphere extending to all social grades. The identification of local leadership with economic power is often pronounced, reaching its climax in the "company town." Short-run fluctuations in prosperity may be negligible or severe, but no town of this character can be considered immune from long-run risk of dereliction and many of the worst depressed areas are in this category—Merthyr Tydfil and the Rhondda, Brynmawr, and other South Wales mining and iron towns, Cleator Moor and Jarrow. It is hardly surprising that towns of this type share with certain ports the chief part in returning to Parliament and to local councils candidates of extreme Left Wing political views. The proportion of males is often exceptionally high.

The military town dependent largely on a garrison, dockyard, R. A. F. station, arsenal or other military establishment is a variant of the last type, with certain peculiarities. In Great Britain the naval centres are much the largest and the aviation centres the smallest, partly because some of the naval ones happen also to have other important interests. . . .

The military town has little to distinguish it from the mining camp town, except that it enjoys rather greater security as many of its workers are entitled to State pensions, and if it is injuriously affected the matter can be pressed in Parliament. The limitations of this security are, however, visible in the case of Pembroke, where the docks were completely closed by the Government some years ago, leaving a depressed area ever since. Owing to the extent to which military service transfers able-bodied men, with their dependents, to different parts of the country where some of them take root, and to the pensioner element, military towns tend to develop a residential character, which is assisted by their class composition and their peculiar amenities, for instance, in recreation facilities and parades.

The cathedral city also has its "garrison," but it has proved of a much more enduring character and is much more intimately bound up with the social life of the region. In many cases the cathedral town is also conspicuously a traffic town and a residential town, while several have had a substantial "mining camp" element grafted on at a late stage in their development. The purest examples of cathedral cities appear to be: Canterbury (25,000), Chichester (16,000), Winchester (25,000), Wells (5,000), Durham (18,000), Lichfield (9,000), and Ely (8,000).

The cathedral city has typically great stability, a strong community sense, considerable intellectual resources and leadership within somewhat narrow limits, and close relations with its surrounding district. The classes are often well mixed geographically, but differences in income and status are substantial and sharply defined. Partly owing to residential attractions the average age of the population is apt to be high, and its outlook unprogressive.

The school and university town is only found in anything approaching a pure form in very small examples, such as St. Andrews, Fife (8,000), Sedbergh, Yorks (2,000), and Oundle, Northants (3,000). This element is, however, conspicuous in association with others in medium-sized towns such as Oxford (88,000), Cambridge (75,000), Cheltenham (49,000), and Bedford (41,000).

The school and university town is worth distinguishing owing to the peculiar difficulties arising from the marked seasonal fluctuations in numbers of persons in its upper income group according to school and university terms. In a number of cases this is partly offset by a different seasonal peak for tourist visits, and by a relatively large resident population of well-to-do retired people, or persons with unearned incomes. Towns in this category and the next are the chief competitors for the entertainment of annual and other conferences—an industry which in the United States has reached enormous proportions, and has led to intense rivalry between cities seeking to attract lucrative bodies of guests.

The resort. The most conspicuous form of resort is the seaside town, which in the largest examples (Brighton, Bournemouth, Blackpool) reaches over 100,000 population. Many seaside resorts are of quite recent growth, and share a number of the characteristics of the "mining camp" town. Others are grafted on older ports. Of inland resorts the most clearly marked are the Spas. . . .

The resort typically suffers from a conspicuous seasonal fluctuation between "rush" and "slack" periods, and in the small and extreme examples may be virtually closed down and left to caretakers at certain times of the year. The growth of indoor attractions, provision of extensive equipment such as all-weather promenades, concert and dance halls, and swimming baths, the development of the conference industry and the increasing numbers of pensioners retiring on small incomes to resorts have helped to overcome this disadvantage, especially where the resort is large and the climate favourable, but the problem remains. From its nature the resort is almost inevitably involved in large municipal expenditure, while the average size of its private businesses, measured in terms of persons regularly employed, is relatively small, partly owing to the absence of large productive plants or transport depots and partly because of the migratory nature of much of the labour. Labour standards tend, therefore, to be low, and in spite of the development of municipal enterprise, politics are usually well to the Right. The average age of the population is high. Most resorts show signs of suffering from too rapid unplanned growth, and this problem threatens to become accentuated as a result of the increase of holidays with pay.

The residential town from its nature almost invariably develops by using a resort, a school or university town, a military town, or some other type as a nucleus. Thus Buxton, Bournemouth, Oxford and other towns have added a strong residential element to their earlier functions. A few examples such as Haslemere (9,000), and Crowborough (6,000), are almost purely residential.

The importance of this type is likely to grow as the population becomes more elderly, and as the effect of superannuation schemes becomes more substantial. It develops most readily out of the last three categories, and many which were once classed under these heads appear destined to become predominantly residential. One feature of the residential town is a high proportion of relatively large incomes, and unless other factors, such as schools, provide an offset, it usually has a high average and a large percentage of females.

The dormitory town is a fairly recent development. In most cases it is physically attached as a suburb to the town for which it serves as a dormitory, but there are numbers of detached towns which serve to a substantial extent as dormitories for towns at some distance, such as, e.g. Southend-on-Sea for London, Chester for Liverpool, Ilkley and Harrogate for Leeds-Bradford, and some of the Clyde resorts for Glasgow. Dormitory towns are essentially residential towns, but differ in depending mainly not upon unearned incomes, but on profits, salaries and wages, which have to be obtained by a daily journey of their earners into a metropolitan centre or other large urban area. Towns of this type have gradually spread downwards through the income grades, but still tend to be dominated by the middle and upper groups who can most easily afford the luxury of spending an hour or more a day and a considerable sum of money in travel in overcrowded vehicles.

The dormitory town is distinguished by a daily and weekly rather than a seasonal rhythm, the number of adult males being strikingly low in working hours as compared with the night and week-end population. The average age of the population tends to be low

and the proportion of children higher than anywhere else except in mining areas. Dormitory towns are frequently of recent growth, and often consist largely of small houses "owned" by their occupants through building society payments. They are therefore in process of acquiring expensive social equipment, and of meeting liabilities to which they have been in effect committed by the developers. Local politics are therefore liable to be dominated by "rate-payers'" questions. There is no incentive to take an interest in the affairs of the surrounding neighbourhood, which may even be hostile to the newcomers, as in the case of the "mining camp" town. The inhabitants of some of these areas have been aptly described as being refugees who do not realize that they are refugees.

The planned town needs a category of its own. Most English towns developed during the long interval in which planning was neglected, but Salisbury (1220), and the fragment of Winchelsea (c. 1290), Letchworth (1903), and Welwyn Garden City (1920), are examples of towns whose sites were deliberately chosen and planned from the outset, with results clearly visible to-day. . . .

The planned town has in its early stages peculiar problems in the advance provision of equipment and amenities, the purchase and control of land, and the enforcement of regulations which in other towns would only arise gradually when the need for action became apparent to all, and when, incidentally, the benefit to be obtained from it had been sharply cut down. The fact that so much has to be done at once and that the whole population for some years consists of immigrants from elsewhere, raises difficulties over finance, leadership, and the community spirit which older towns do not have to face. The age of the population naturally tends to be low during the early stages, and its outlook progressive or "advanced," although uneven rates of growth may later lead to unusual age compositions.

The metropolitan centre is almost invariably a very large example of a traffic town or port, and is usually also part of an urban cluster, its main distinguishing characteristic being that it provides or controls governmental, professional, technical, financial, distributive, communications, and other specialised services over a considerable area, including other substantial towns which come within its orbit for these purposes. Metropolitan centres are the largest type of town, often reaching populations of a million or more. The largest British examples are London, Glasgow, Greater Manchester, and Birmingham, but a number of smaller cities such as Edinburgh (440,000) fall in this class.

The metropolitan centre enjoys naturally an exceptional range of services and facilities, but is apt to pay the penalty in congestion and in rapid obsolescence of equipment and layout. It is relatively well provided with amusements and with social and cultural facilities, but owing to the extent and variety of its interests it is liable to be poorly integrated as a community and with its surrounding districts. There are enormous potential resources in leadership, but these are often largely diverted owing to the concentration on national and international affairs, characteristic of a metropolis.

The urban cluster, often described as the "conurbation," is a group of several or many towns or built-up areas growing from different centres, but with fringes merging into one another and sometimes giving place to new common centres. The seven greatest British urban clusters are Greater London, Greater Manchester, Greater Birmingham, Leeds-Bradford, and surrounding West Riding towns, Merseyside, Glasgow and its neighbours, and Tyneside. The populations of these range between one and ten millions each. . . . The characteristic of an urban cluster is a growing confusion of function and interchange of population between different parts of the urban area. The main nuclei tend to become metropolitan centres with commercial, administrative and amusement quarters, displacing householders and industrialists, who shift to the subordinate centres or to cheaper land on the fringe. Typically the central area of an urban cluster ultimately finds

itself with a small night population consisting mainly of caretakers and a huge day population of adult or juvenile wage-earners and salary-earners mostly in commerce, distribution and services. This stage has actually been reached in the City of London, and to a smaller extent elsewhere.

The urban cluster is composed mainly of types of town whose problems have been reviewed under other heads, the most characteristic pattern being a metropolitan centre surrounded by dormitory towns, "mining camp" towns, and often a port, and other types. Its most pronounced problems are obstinate housing troubles, both from slums and overcrowding, expensive and congested transport, lack of open-air recreation facilities and access to open country, and polluted air and rivers. As the various centres are usually separate local government units, often in two or more counties, waste, overlapping, and friction in local government are pronounced.

* * *

The object of this analysis is to stimulate discussion regarding the town as a background of industry and as a social organism whose development can be, and is being, shaped by human wills. The question before the nation now is whether to accept the types of town resulting from the blind play of economic and social decisions, all taken regardless of the type of town they will produce, or whether to examine the different possible types of town, to agree on the merits and demerits of each, and to make economic and social decisions within a framework which will ensure that the towns of the future combine the maximum advantages and the minimum drawbacks of their various types. The time has passed when the patterns and sizes of our towns can be accepted as Acts of God. It is no more necessary to put up with towns growing together into one congested and characterless urban cluster than to put up with leprosy or bubonic plague. By any reputable standard our towns are, with few exceptions, deformed and diseased organisms. When public opinion begins to regard them

dispassionately the demand for a national fit-
ness campaign for our towns will become
irresistible. While there is scope for endless
diversity of opinions it appears to be fairly
widely accepted that the least successful types
of towns are at one extreme those dominated
by a very narrow range of interests, especially
industrial interests and at the other extreme
those which attempt a little of everything
without giving scope for any one aspect to
achieve anything like full development. These
two extremes are both created in Great Britain at the present time.

The Habitat

>>

Sometimes it is best to be technical in order to be clear. This is especially true when references in succeeding selections speak of Britain, Great Britain, the United Kingdom, and the British Isles. Just how do these terms relate to one another?

Great Britain (or Britain) is the large island that consists of Scotland, England, and Wales. Northern Ireland (frequently called Ulster), the Channel Islands, and the Isle of Man, in addition to Great Britain, make up the United Kingdom. The British Isles is the most inclusive term, since it includes the United Kingdom and also southern Ireland or Eire, formerly called the Irish Free State, which zealously asserts its independence from Britain.

In Great Britain itself, our major interest is in the Midlands, but before considering them we shall look at the major geographic features of the island as a whole. Industrialization has not blotted out the attractiveness of many regions or overwhelmed them with the monotonous uniformity that has come to industrial and urban sections. In fact, the habitat of Britain is remarkably varied, and, as L. Dudley Stamp points out in Selection 56, there are many kinds of scenery within a short distance of most cities

The geography of Britain is complex; many relatively small areas are recognized and their distinctive features are familiar to Britons. Some of the most important of these will be mentioned, and a few of the common English terms used in describing them will appear, such as heath, fell, moor, fen, and weald.

To some extent, the people of an industrial society appear less directly dependent on the physical features and resources of the land on which they live. But, on careful examination, the influence of the land can be seen to be as powerful as for simpler societies. The selections which follow contain many references to the location of natural resources, such as coal and iron, around which great industrial developments have taken place. Likewise, the development of agricultural areas, main highways, and seaports has been fundamentally affected by aspects of the habitat. In a separate selection the climate will be

439

briefly described and an attempt made to counteract the unfavorable opinion that Americans are supposed to have about it.

THE BUILDING OF BRITAIN

It would be difficult to find an area of comparable size anywhere in the world which exhibits quite such marked contrasts as may be found within the very limited area of the British Isles. A journey of twenty-five miles in Britain will often afford as much variety of scenery as one can find in two hundred and fifty miles in many of the newer lands, and within her hundred thousand square miles may be found an epitome, sometimes beautifully modelled by Nature in miniature, of most of the scenery of Europe. Too often the visitor, with but a few days to spare, sees only Lowland Britain—it may be Liverpool and London with perhaps a side trip to Edinburgh —and so fails to appreciate the contrasts between the wild, almost inaccessible fiords or sea lochs of the north-west Highlands of Scotland, the Dutch-like scenery of the drained fens of the Holland division of Lincolnshire, the rolling downland of Salisbury Plain, the secluded, heather-covered glades of the New Forest, the rugged crags of North Wales, the smiling orchardland of Kent, the grimy, narrow, congested valleys of South Wales, and the desolate almost uninhabited moorland of Sutherland. These scenic contrasts are often within easy reach of the great centres, so that a Londoner born and bred can still thrill at the discovery of new bypaths within twenty-five miles of the city, whilst the Glasgow slumdweller has the finest combination of sea and highland scenery within the same radius.

The charm of Britain lies in no small measure in these contrasts, thrown as they are into even greater prominence by the fickle yet fascinating moods of British weather. The London pea-soup fog is a creation rather of fiction than of fact: without it novels of Victorian London or the exploits of Sherlock Holmes would lose much of their flavour. Actually the fog records of the worst of British localities compare favourably with most parts of the world. The vagaries of spring may be trying, but they have their compensations

*Whan that Aprille with his shoures sote
The droghte of Marche hath perced to the
rote.*

Chaucer recognised these vagaries six centuries ago as an essential prelude to the bursting forth of spring flowers and leaves. Nor would the Emerald Isle of Ireland deserve her adjective except for the frequent procession of mild damp days throughout the year.

The variety of scenery in Britain is largely a reflection of the complex geological history of the islands. Geologically, Britain is almost a museum model. Within the islands are found samples of the rocks laid down in each of the great ages of the earth's history. This is a fortunate circumstance in that many of the pioneer geologists were British, and, as they gradually pieced together the fascinating story of the earth's history, naturally named the great periods from British localities. The period that saw the dawn of life for so many of the great zoological groups—the Cambrian— takes its name from Cambria or Wales, whilst the succeeding Ordovician and Silurian perpetuate the names of ancient British tribes of

[From *The Face of Britain*, British Life and Thought: No. 5, published for The British Council by Longmans, Green and Company, London, 1945. Pp. 7-11, 15-16, 19-21, 27, 41-44, 51-52. Used by permission.]

the Welsh borderland which might otherwise have been almost forgotten.

A line joining the mouth of the Tees on the east coast of England to the mouth of the Exe or Tor Bay in Devonshire divides approximately Highland Britain from Lowland Britain. There are many fundamental distinctions between these two divisions. Not only do all the major highland masses lie to the north and west of the line whilst the chief lowlands are to the south and east, but the rocks which make up Highland Britain are mostly the older rocks which break down but slowly into somewhat poor, stony soils, whilst the rocks of Lowland Britain are younger, less resistant to weathering, and afford richer soils. As a result man has been able to utilise effectively only the better parts of Highland Britain—the valleys, the coastal plains, and the lowlands—and his farms or his villages are often separated from one another by wide stretches of uninhabited upland moors. In other words, human settlement tends to be essentially discontinuous in Highland Britain.

In Lowland Britain, on the other hand, the land is more kindly, gently rolling and undulating rather than flat, though rarely reaching a thousand feet above sea-level. Ploughed lands and grass fields, farms and villages, form an intricate but continuous pattern. Land unsuitable for farming and settlement is limited in extent, and occurs as isolated islands. Human settlement is essentially continuous, and individuals form members of communities which are but rarely isolated.

It is not surprising that Lowland Britain, essentially Anglo-Saxon, has had an entirely different history from the Celtic fringe or Highland Britain. To this day the Highland peoples—the Scots, the Welsh, the Cornish, and indeed the Irish—are distinct in traditions, dialect, and outlook from the Lowland English. Excluding Ireland, six persons out of every seven live in or on the fringe of Lowland Britain, yet the Highlanders have played, and still play, a very large part in the life of the country, a part out of proportion to their numbers.

Since this distinction between Highland Britain and Lowland Britain is so fundamental, it will be of value to notice at once the parts of the country which lie in the two divisions.

Highland Britain includes the whole of Scotland, which itself comprises three contrasted parts. The northern half of Scotland is formed by the Highlands, to the south of which are the Central Lowlands, in turn cut off from England by the Southern Uplands. Although the Highlands and Southern Uplands cover three-quarters of the country, they have less than a quarter of the people: the Central Lowlands, which most closely approach Lowland Britain in many characters, have only a fifth of the area but four-fifths of the people. The Southern Uplands are continued by highlands across the border into northern England, where the broad upland of the Pennines form the so-called backbone of England (a misnomer, since it is foolish that only the northern half of England should have a backbone) and where also is England's mountain playground, the Lake District. The Lake District forms actually the northernmost of three westward-projecting peninsulas. The central and largest one is Wales; the southern one is occupied by the counties of Devon and Cornwall.

Lowland Britain comprises the hill and valley land of the southeast; the rich farming land of the east, and the rolling grassy plain of the Midlands. The latter has a north-westerly prolongation into the plain of Lancastria, and a north-easterly one into the plains of Yorkshire.

Almost everywhere in Britain the major coalfields occur in the borderlands between Highland and Lowland Britain—where mountain or hill-mass gives place to the plain. In some areas, notably in South Wales, coal has been the magnet which has drawn a dense population, largely of Lowland origin, into the otherwise unattractive valleys of the great moorlands.

* * *

Enough has been said to make clear the great contrasts of physical environment to be found in Britain, and it is scarcely surprising that these varied environments have played a marked part in moulding the characters of their human inhabitants, an influence which has persisted throughout British history, and is still very apparent today. It will be wise, therefore, to examine briefly the part which these physical features have played in the peopling of the islands.

* * *

ALBION AND THE GARDEN OF ENGLAND

Four out of every five of the peace-time visitors who approach Britain from the continent of Europe see, as their first glimpse of the country, the high white cliffs formed where the chalk of the North Downs reaches the shores of the Strait of Dover between Folkestone and Dover, or where the chalk of the South Downs is breached by the inlet on which stands Newhaven. This familiar sight is perpetuated by the name "Albion", often applied to Britain as a whole. The journey from Folkestone or Dover to London is inevitably by one of the routes through the Garden of England, the beautiful county of Kent. Kent is one, the largest, of the three counties of the south-east (Kent, Surrey, and Sussex) which lie south of the Thames and share that famous region known as the Weald. To the geologist the Weald is a denuded anticline, with its axis from west to east and then from west-north-west to east-south-east, pitching at both ends, and with its eastern end breached by the sea. To the layman the Weald may be described as a varied and gently undulating lowland with a core of low hills and sometimes with other lines of low hills and the whole almost completely encircled by the steep inner faces of the chalk hills—the North Downs on the north and the South Downs on the south. These hills are cut through at intervals by river-gaps, which not only afford well-used routeways for road and rail but which are usually guarded by historic towns and cities dating back in many cases to Roman times.

The word "Weald" (Anglo-Saxon) is actually the same as the German *Wald,* and refers to the once densely forested character of the Weald. The ancient routeways follow the more easily cleared uplands; as late as Elizabethan times (1558-1603) the oak forests of the Weald were supplying timber for the ships of the British Navy. The final destruction of the forests came through the use of the timber in the making of the charcoal for the once great iron industry. Round St. Paul's Cathedral in London were, until recently, heavy iron railings made from Wealden iron, but the industry has long since been killed by the competition of the coalfield and seaport iron centres. The Weald still has the appearance of being well wooded: on the heavy soils the small pasture fields are separated by narrow "shaws" or belts of woodland only a few yards wide. In the heart of the Weald the Forest Ridges have a dry sandstone soil and support patches of pine forest and heathland. But the traveller from Folkestone or Dover to London is most likely to travel through the more fertile part of the Weald where rich loamy soils support numerous hop gardens and where the old "oast-houses", formerly used for drying and storing the hops, are a feature of very many farms. Part of the Kentish orchard country—of apples and cherries— is on such land near Maidstone. Other parts of the Weald have sandy ridges notorious for the infertility of their soil, but equally famous now for the attractiveness of their pine-forest and heathland scenery. A large tract of land of this type is found around Haslemere and Hindhead, another at Leith Hill, and both tracts are preserved as public open-spaces.

Some of the most beautiful scenery in Britain is associated with the Chalk Downlands.

* * *

EAST ANGLIA AND THE CORN-LANDS

Nowhere else in Britain are the general conditions so favourable to arable farming. Over a low plateau of chalk and other rocks, the ice-sheets of the Great Ice Age deposited a mantle of varied boulder clay and other glacial "drifts". Sometimes these are coarse and sandy, and give rise to infertile tracts such as Breckland (now extensively planted with coniferous forests), but over most of the region the glacial soils are deep, rich, easily ploughed, and well-drained loams. The hard frosts of winter break up the soil after ploughing, and help to kill obnoxious insects; the dry, sunny summers ripen well the grain crops. In this region was evolved the famous "Norfolk four course" rotation—wheat, root crops, barley or oats, fodder (clover or beans) —which spread to other parts of England and made Britain a great corn-exporting country in the early eighteenth century. [Corn in England is small grains, not maize.] Before that East Anglia had long been famous for its wool (from sheep fed on root crops) and most of the small ports round the coast were busily occupied in shipping the wool to the mills of Flanders. It was but a step for the skill of the Flemish weavers to be emulated by the people of East Anglia themselves, so that Norfolk and Suffolk became the premier wool-manufacturing counties of Britain. This they remained until the industrial revolution gave an economic advantage to the woollen manufacturers on the Yorkshire coalfields, and the competition killed the East Anglian industry. But the wool merchants and the woollen manufacturers, waxing rich, had shown their thankfulness to God by building noble churches in the style of the sixteenth and seventeenth centuries, and scarcely a Norfolk village cannot boast a beautiful parish church, with a lofty square tower, very often built of flint from the chalk.

In spring and early summer Norfolk and Suffolk present a pleasing picture of rolling brown fields, varied by the fresh green of the young corn, with picturesque villages nestling by streams in the sunken valleys. Norwich itself is typical in its situation, in a valley at the junction of two navigable streams, its castle on an artificial mound looking across to the slender-spired cathedral on the one hand, and the largest sheep and cattle market in England on the other. The countryside is perhaps even more attractive in August, when the great fields of golden grain, separated by green hedges, are ready for cutting, and patches of poorer land are picked out by the brilliant hue of the wild red poppies—beloved of the artist, hated by the farmer.

North-east of Norwich a number of sluggish streams meander slowly through drowned valleys which are partly occupied by rich pasture-land, partly by reed-swamps, and partly by broad, shallow stretches of water. This is the famous Broadland, and the "broads" form a peace-time playground for all who love sailing, or an unconventional holiday of which fresh air and water are the chief ingredients. Some of Broadland is only protected from the sea by lines of sand dunes, and a disastrous breach during a high tide and north-east gale resulted in the flooding of 7500 acres in 1938. By way of contrast to Broadland scenery, the visitor should cross the desolate heaths and young forests of Breckland in the west and see also the varied parkland scenery around the royal residence of Sandringham in the northwest. On the east coast Great Yarmouth and Lowestoft are two of Britain's greatest fishing ports, invaded in normal times during the season by thousands of Scottish fisher-girls whose nimble fingers "gut" the herrings.

HOLLAND IN ENGLAND—FENLAND

On the east coast of England is a broad shallow inlet of the sea known as the Wash. Into this inlet there empty several rivers—the Witham, Welland, Nene, and Ouse—which formerly meandered through a vast waste of marshland—the Fens. Here and there low islands rose a few feet above the marsh-level and formed refuges for those who sought peace and isolation from the world. Most notable of these is the Isle of Ely on which the monks of the Middle Ages built their great cathedral church of Ely—a cathedral to hold 3000 people in a country town which today has only 5000 people all told. For centuries the shallow Wash has been gradually silting up, so that Fenland has been reclaimed for the land of Britain in two ways—partly from the fresh-water fens and partly from the salt-water marshes. Between these two marsh areas a low silt ridge afforded slightly firmer ground. Along this ridge is an artificial bank attributed to the Romans and still called "Roman Bank", and protected by it from sudden inroads of the sea are the chief of the old villages of Fenland situated in what are appropriately called Townlands.

* * *

WALES AND THE WELSH BORDERLAND

South Wales consists essentially of a great plateau deeply trenched by river valleys, and underneath lies the great South Wales coalfield. In the eastern part of Central Wales, between the coalfields and the mountains of Central Wales, is a triangular area occupied by Old Red Standstone. Part of this forms one of the wildest and most desolate upland areas in Britain—the Brecon Beacons and Black Mountains—but the eastern part ranging into Herefordshire is a sheltered basin with orchards and smiling cornland and hop gardens. The eastern margin of the Welsh borderland is a line of hills stretching from north to south from the Wrekin, through the Malvern Hills. There is a small fragment of South Wales, the Vale of Glamorgan, which is quite different from the rest of the country and really belongs to the agricultural regions of Lowland England.

* * *

THE LAKE DISTRICT

England's Lake District lies in the three north-western counties of Cumberland, Westmorland, and northern Lancashire, and forms the northern of the three blocks of Highland Britain which project westwards as peninsulas. The core of the Lake District is geologically ancient, consisting as it does of slates, shales, and volcanic rocks of early date highly folded by the Caledonian earth-movements. But the district owes its distinctive features to a comparatively late uplift in the centre. As a result its rivers radiate from the centre; the

river valleys were widened and smoothed by tongues of ice during the great Ice Age so that they are now occupied by lakes arranged like so many spokes of a wheel about a central hub. The central hub has some of the most rugged if not the highest mountains in the British Isles, with well-known rock-climbs which have served as a training-ground for many a world-famous mountaineer.

Though two of the major lakes serve the city of Manchester as a supply of water and the Lakeland hill-slopes or fells afford summer grazing for many sheep, Britain needs the Lake District more especially as a recreational area, and it is the great hope of many that it will form the second of Britain's "national parks"—the Forest of Dean having become the first in 1939. It has the advantages of healthy scenic beauty combined with ready accessibility—in the north of the same county that harbours the depressing cotton towns, just across the Pennines from the Northumbrian coalfield and almost as accessible from the Yorkshire industrial regions.

* * *

LANCASTRIA AND THE COTTON WORLD

Lying between the Irish Sea and the mountains of North Wales on the west and the Pennine Uplands on the east is an extensive plain. In the south it is some forty or fifty miles wide, and in the south-east is linked with the Midland Plain through what is often called the Midland Gap. In the north the plain narrows and is interrupted by broad spurs from the Pennines—the Rossendale and Bowland Fells—and in the extreme north only a few miles separate the hills from the sea of Morecambe Bay.

This plain occupies most of the county of Lancashire, nearly the whole of Cheshire, and the northern half of the county of Shropshire or Salop. As in other lowlands in the north of England, a thick mantle of glacial deposits hides the solid rocks; and the red Triassic marls which underlie the heart of the plain are rarely seen though ridges of Bunter sandstone may rise above the general level. Largely the boulder clay and glacial deposits are of local origin and wrap around the Pennine spurs; in other places material swept from the floor of the Irish Sea has been spread over the land. In consequence Lancastria enjoys a very wide variety in soils, but, having climatic conditions relatively mild as a result of the sheltered position, and a low rainfall for western England, it is a region of great importance agriculturally. This is often forgotten, because industrial development has overshadowed agriculture.

In the south the retreating ice-sheets left shallow lakes on heavy boulder clay in the hollows, separated by mounds and ridges of more sandy material. Some of the lakes, locally called meres, remain, but most have dried up, leaving wet boulder-clay hollows now covered with rich grass meadows and with numerous small ponds which afford a ready water supply for animals. The heart of the Cheshire Plain is therefore under grass; the cropped land on the ridges is mainly devoted to the raising of feed stuffs for animals. Cheshire (with northern Shropshire) is world-famous for its dairy pastures and its dairy cattle and its output of cheese. The cheese is marketed in normal times as C.C.C.—Choice Cheshire Cheese. Here and there in this southern country, patches of woodland and heath on the sandy ridges give variety to a charming, quiet countryside.

Northwards, as the Mersey is crossed, glacial loams have given a very fertile, easily worked soil. Hollows in the surface once occupied by marshes and bogs (locally called "mosses") have been carefully drained within the last two hundred years and now have that rich black soil so well known in the English Fenland and used for the growing of potatoes and vegetables for the Lancashire towns. So, side by side, the visitor may see the grimy manufacturing and colliery towns and rich market gardening land, as well as stretches of the best corn in western England. Northwards and eastwards, towards the Pennine slopes, the soil becomes poorer and more stony

and is mainly under grass, but grass of indifferent quality when compared with that of Cheshire.

*   *   *

THE PENNINES AND YORKSHIRE

The Pennine Upland is sometimes called the backbone of England. Generally it is a flat-topped or rolling upland with a steep high edge to the west and a long gentle slope to the east. It is broken into a number of blocks by transverse gaps or valleys. The Cheviot Hills with their old, rounded, volcanic hills link the northernmost block with the Southern Uplands of Scotland, and both the Cheviots and the northern Pennines consist of sheep moorlands. The first great gap is the Tyne or Haltwhistle Gap, affording ready communication between Carlisle on the west and Newcastle on the east.

Between the Tyne Gap and the Stainmore Gap, a flat-topped sandstone plateau separates the Durham coalfield from the Lake District and reaches its highest point in Cross Fell (2930 feet), from which there is a drop of 2500 feet direct to the fertile Eden valley. Southwards from Stainmore the Pennines consist partly of sandstone, partly of limestone. In consequence of the latter, there is some fine limestone scenery, especially near Settle and Malham, but the streams draining from the Pennines are streams of hard water. This has been quite sufficient to prevent the growth of industry on either side, since most industry demands, particularly, supplies of soft water. The limestone extends as far south as the Aire Gap—a connecting link between the cotton-weaving towns of Lancashire and the woollen towns of Yorkshire. The Aire Gap is used by one of the six railway lines across the Pennines, as well as by a main road. It is also used by a canal, but the number of locks required has effectively prevented the development of any large traffic. To the north of the Aire the Pennines are drained eastwards by the Swale, Ure, Nidd, and Wharfe, which eventually join to form the Yorkshire Ouse. Their upper valleys form the famous Yorkshire dales, where from such centres as Richmond visitors may enjoy unrivalled scenes of moor and valley.

South of the Aire Gap the Pennines form a narrow belt of sandstone (Millstone Grit) upland separating the main cotton district of Lancashire from the great woollen district of Yorkshire. The Pennines here have a threefold function. They are utilised as the gathering-ground for the water supply of the innumerable towns on the flanks—supplies of fine soft water—they give pasture to a few sheep, and they serve too as a grand open space where those from the smoky towns below may enjoy clean, pure air sweeping straight across from the mountains of Wales.

The southern block of the Pennines really begins at the flat-topped mountain known as the Peak. From there the streams flow southwards, eventually joining the Trent, and have carved for themselves valleys of great beauty. The limestone hills are covered with short grass turf, the grit-lands with heather moor; the valleys are largely wooded. Many of the most attractive parts of this country are now owned or controlled by the National Trust (the National Trust for Places of Natural Beauty and Historic Interest) and so are open to the public for recreation. In the heart lies the town of Buxton, a spa, situated at a thousand feet above sea-level.

The Pennines are flanked on either side by coal-fields. Those of Northumberland and Durham and Lancashire have already been considered. But on the eastern side of the Pennines from the Aire Gap southwards is Britain's largest coalfield. It lies in four counties and is worked in three—Yorkshire, Nottinghamshire, and Derbyshire—and from its economic development really falls into three parts: the woollen districts, the steel districts, and the southern area.

Like nearly all the great British industries, the woollen industry of the West Riding of Yorkshire has its roots far in the past. The Pennines provided natural pasture for sheep; the many small streams of soft water provided not only the water for scouring and dyeing of the wool but also innumerable sites for water-wheels.

• 57 • *The Climate of Britain*
ALICIA STREET

Although only about three times as many people live in the United States as in England, Scotland and Wales combined, the United States is nearly thirty-four times as large as the island of Britain. Britain is only a little more than half the size of California. It is triangular in shape, its eastern side from the northern point called John O' Groats to Dover, Kent, measuring only five hundred and fifty miles, while the southern side from Dover to Land's End, Cornwall, measures three hundred and twenty miles. England and Wales taken together are about the same size as the state of Georgia. No place in Britain is more than seventy-five miles from the sea; even in the most inland sections farmers often look up to see flocks of sea-gulls wheeling over their plowed fields and say to themselves, "High winds at sea since the birds come inland; God help the sailors in their ships."

But although the British, and more particularly the English, are crowded very closely together in a very small country with smaller natural resources than the United States, there is one respect in which they are very fortunate. That is in their climate. This is perhaps a surprising statement because almost every-

[Reprinted by permission of the publishers, J. B. Lippincott Company, Philadelphia, from *The Land of the English People*, by Alicia Street. Copyright, 1946, by Alicia Street. Pp. 15-18.]

one has heard how annoying the weather usually is in England. Because of the frequent clouds and the moisture that hangs in the air even on fairly clear days, England has less sunshine than most countries, and its sunlight is weaker than in other places where the air is dry and clear. What is worse, the sunshine rarely lasts long enough for a person to have time to enjoy it. The weather changes constantly. If it is raining when you get up in the morning and you put on a raincoat and rubbers when you go out, the sun is almost sure to be shining by lunch time, and the raincoat and rubbers will seem a nuisance. But if you go out without them after lunch, you will probably be caught in a shower by four o'clock. Picnics ought to be fun in England because there is so much beautiful scenery and almost no mosquitoes. Instead they are often disappointing because although the day may have been bright and warm when you packed your lunch, a chilly drizzle is likely to be setting in just when you are ready to eat it. To add to the difficulties of the weather forecasters, a day in January may be as warm as a warm day in July, and a day in July may be as cold as the coldest day in January.

But although the English weather is as troublesome as any in the world, the English climate—meaning average weather—is a good one. After all, there are many places in the world where Nature seems to fight against men—where rivers overflow their banks, where cyclones and hurricanes tear away towns, where plagues of insects destroy crops, where men die of extremes of heat or of cold. By comparison with these, Nature is very kind in England. What men have made during the past two thousand years has been as safe from the violence of her fiercest moods as from the violence of land warfare. Earthquakes have not leveled the ancient cathedrals nor have tornadoes uprooted the trees in the century-old orchards. In dozens of little ways the mildness of the climate affects daily life. Men ride to work on bicycles all through the year. Houses do not need storm windows for winter or screens for summer. English gardens contain yuccas and begonias, and along the south coast, even occasional palm trees. Wheat is often planted in the fall and most of the plowing is done in mid-winter. Cattle rarely have to be kept in their barns.

Obviously, English winters are seldom very cold and conversely, the summers are seldom hot. Whereas at a given point in the United States, the temperature may range from 5 below zero in the winter to 100 degrees F. in the summer, the change at a given point in England is likely to be from 30 degrees to 80 degrees F. Naturally, anything above 70 degrees is called a heat-wave, and if the temperature of a room approaches 68 degrees people are likely to rush about opening windows and doors to let a breath of cool air into the place.

The most celebrated feature of English weather, the London fog, is very much exaggerated in reputation. Many sections of the United States have far more fog than England, and what makes a London fog thick is not so much the moisture in the air as the soot from millions of coal fires. Fortunately bad fogs are really infrequent in London. In the course of several years' residence there, I have only once been caught in a fog so thick that for a long time I could not find my way home. The people who gave London its reputation for fog were the writers of fiction who discovered that a "pea-souper" made a weird and exciting background for a story. London housewives who have to wash all their curtains after a real fog are glad that most London fogs exist only in the story books.

But it is not only the frequency of the London fog that is exaggerated; it is the quantity of rain in England. England seems to have a great deal of rain because there are so many showers. But usually very little rain falls at a time; often the rain is hardly more than a floating mist in which you can walk for hours without getting really wet. Once in a while the sky opens and there is a downpour lasting ten minutes, but in most parts of England it soon dwindles into the usual drizzle. Western Scotland is another matter. New York, Chicago and Los Angeles have nearly eighty inches of rainfall per year. [In attempting to correct misconceptions concerning rainfall in England, the author grossly exaggerates figures from the United States. The 1941 Yearbook of the U. S. Department of Agriculture, *Climate and Man,* gives the following 40-year averages for rainfall: New York 41.63 inches; Chicago 31.85 inches; Los Angeles 14.76 inches. Only in small areas of the Great Smoky Mountains and of western Washington and Oregon does U. S. rainfall average as high as 80 inches per year.] Areas of heavy rainfall in western England have about sixty; London averages about twenty-five. No section of Britain is dry like the American desert but if there is a period as long as two weeks without rain farmers become very seriously worried about this "drought." They know that with such a light rainfall there can be very little water stored in the soil to carry the crops over a long period of dry weather. But they do not often have such cause for worry.

The most astonishing thing about the English climate is that it exists in an area which lies so far to the North. England lies directly across the ocean, not from the United States, but from icy Labrador. How strange is the contrast between Canada's Arctic blizzards and the winds that blow lightly across English gardens where roses bloom until Christmas time. What is the magic source of the warmth which gives the British Isles their beauty and their wealth?

It is the Gulf Stream, that mysterious great warm river that flows through the ocean. The Gulf Stream flows in a northeasterly direction, bringing warmth to the islands in the North Atlantic and making their climate different from that of Labrador or even that of the continent of Europe. The winds that blow off the Gulf Stream keep Britain warm in the winter and cool in the summer. Once in a while a storm blowing down from the Arctic and over the cold North Sea may sweep over England's green fields, but again from the south and the west comes the warmth that soon melts snow and ice and brings back to life the frost-nipped vegetation. The Gulf Stream is Britain's best friend for the wind that blows over its warm blue waters is really the breath of life to the people who live in the British Isles.

But habitat consists of more than location, surface features, and climate. It also is made up of mineral, plant, and animal resources. The purpose of Selection 58 is to show the close connections among resources, technology, and the growth of industry. Before taking up this selection on the Black Country, which is just north of Birmingham, we ought to get firmly in mind two other of the important regional specializations of England, the Lancashire cotton industry and the Yorkshire woolen industry, since each region boasts different resources and a different historical development.

Most of us, when thinking of the rise of the Industrial Revolution, tend to think first of the developments in spinning and weaving machinery which, together with new sources of power, led to the factory system. As a matter of fact, the textile industry developed outside the Midlands—the focus of our study—but, as the next selection will show, the inventions occurring in the Midlands had considerable effect on the growth of factories elsewhere. Lancashire, to the northeast of the Midlands, was and still is the center of cotton-textile manufacturing. As A. Demangeon, in his book *The British Isles* (London: 1939) has pointed out,

> Owing to its proximity to a great seaport trading with the whole world (Liverpool), to its coalfield, its fast-flowing streams, its damp climate, and its long

traditions of industrial skill, Lancashire soon concentrated in its area nearly the whole of the cotton industry of Great Britain. In 1838, it contained three-fifths of the cotton workers in the United Kingdom. . . .

For woolen goods one turned to Yorkshire, which is north of the Midlands. About it Demangeon also writes:

The West Riding (in Yorkshire) stands in nearly the same relation to the woolen industry as Lancashire does to the cotton. Its lead in the industry dates from the end of the 18th century, when the manufacture of wool migrated to Yorkshire from the eastern and southwestern counties. There it was in touch with Lancashire and its progressive district which had created the great cotton industry. West Riding supplied water power for the mills, clean water for washing the wool, and, above all, coal which was lacking in the eastern and southwestern counties.

If space permitted, it would be of considerable interest to trace the various steps which were taken to give these two areas their worldwide pre-eminence in the manufacture of textiles. For a specific case study of a different industry, however, we have chosen another area—the Black Country, which will be described at greater length in Selection 70. The technological development here is related to the natural resources of coal and iron ore, as well as to the borrowing of numerous scientific ideas from other places. Attention will be given to metallurgy, together with the numerous discoveries and inventions that made the Black Country "black by day and red by night."

• 58 • Development of Industrial Technology in the Black Country 1700-1900
W. K. V. GALE

There have been two main phases in the industrial history of the Black Country—the growth and decline of the iron and coal trades over a period of a century and a half, and the development of the area during the last fifty years or so into a centre of light engineering. The iron and coal trades were responsible for the existence of the Black Country as we know it today. Later changes have been incorporated into a structure already existing. It is with the first phase of industrial development, and in particular with its technical aspects that we are concerned here.

Definition of the Black Country is not as simple a task as may at first appear. The Black Country has neither physical nor political boundaries, and although it is a concentration of industrial towns, industry alone will not serve as a basis for definition. For if manufacturing industry is taken as the sole consideration, the Black Country could be said to include Birmingham, which it certainly does not. Yet a basis for definition exists in the causes which brought the Black Country into being. In the main there were two causes—the great natural mineral wealth of

[From *Birmingham and Its Regional Setting: A Scientific Survey*, Buckler and Webb, Birmingham, 1950. (From a reprint. Pp. 3-20.)]

the area, and the technical developments which made possible the use of that wealth. Economics have played their part in the changes which have affected the area, but the simple fact remains that until it became possible to use the natural resources on a large scale, the Black Country could not develop. Technically, two things were needed to start the growth—a method of smelting and working iron with mineral fuel, and some form of mechanical power to operate the machinery.

The eighteenth century provided both. When they became available, industrial growth began, and proceeded at an ever-increasing rate for many years. The district, which had contained a number of scattered towns and villages, some old, but none of much importance, expanded until it became the conurbation it is today. The earliest date which can be assigned to the beginning of the Black Country is the mid-eighteenth century. Half a century after this the Black Country, "black by day and red by night" with its great concentration of furnaces and smoking chimneys was truly in being.

It is only necessary to mention some of the technical effects of the natural conditions in which the minerals were found. For iron making, it is not only necessary to have ample supplies of ironstone and fuel, because the blast furnace consumes great quantities of limestone as a flux. Refractory clays and sands are also needed to build and repair the furnaces themselves. The Black Country was fortunate in that it possessed all these requisites. Large supplies of ironstone and fuel alone might have been sufficient cause to import the remaining materials from a distance and so establish an iron trade, but the area had no need of such expedients. Everything necessary for large-scale iron making was to hand; coal existed in various qualities, which were admirably suited for several different purposes. None of the minerals was very difficult to work. The thick coal in some parts cropped out at the surface, and could be won by simply quarrying or adit working. All over the district, coal could be found at reasonable depths, and as the outcrops became exhausted, technical progress enabled the deeper seams to be worked.

* * *

Charcoal was the only fuel suitable for iron smelting and refining [during medieval times, and even later]. As time went on charcoal became scarce. The use of raw coal was out of the question on account of the sulphurs in it, which produced 'red short' iron—metal which would crumble whenever the smith attempted to forge or weld it at a red heat. Coking the coal was a solution to the problem, and this is in fact how it was solved, but the introduction of such a process was far ahead. It also became possible at a later date to use raw coal in the blast furnace, but this was not until 1828, after the hot blast had been invented. No immediate answer to the fuel problem being found, the charcoal shortage developed into a serious famine. Suitable timber was being used faster than it could be replaced, and the threat of coming to a complete standstill confronted the iron trade.

* * *

Towards the end of the seventeenth century it becomes possible to get a clearer picture of the South Staffordshire iron trade, for, in 1686, there appeared the first detailed account, that of Dr. Plot. He was observant and painstaking, and his remarks on the iron trade are of considerable value. From his description of blast furnace practice it is of interest that most of the terms in use today were by then current. The blast furnace had many of its essential features well established by that time, and for many years it remained but little altered, except as regards size.

* * *

That process which so many had sought was found at last by Abraham Darby (1676-1717), when he succeeded, from 1709 onwards, in smelting iron with mineral fuel. . . . Darby first coked the local Shropshire coal, and with the coke obtained, he produced a usable pig-iron. He was primarily an iron-founder—a maker of cast-iron pots—and the iron he made was suitable for his purpose. He did not patent the process, and it was open to anyone to use it. . . .

In the meantime, the iron industry had been growing, if only slowly, in South Staffordshire and Worcestershire. In 1740 four furnaces were in blast in the area, two of them fairly large for the period. By 1788 the number had increased to six, with three building and—significant fact—they all used coke as fuel. The charcoal furnaces were no more. Thus one foundation of the Black Country had been laid, and the development of canals, which was taking place at about the same time, was paving the way for further progress.

THE STEAM ENGINE

The events so far chronicled had set the stage for a new development—the introduction of mechanical power in the form of the steam engine. They had in fact done more—they had rendered its need imperative. The iron trade could expand no more, so long as it was dependent upon water power, and the mines could not be deepened to reach the unworked minerals until they had efficient means of drainage. In these respects the Black Country was, of course, neither better nor worse off than many other areas, and on that score alone not particularly worthy of note; but it was here that the steam engine was developed, and a start was given to that revolution in industry which was to have such a profound effect upon the whole world.

*   *   *

It is worthy of note that somewhere between Wolverhampton and Dudley (the exact spot has not been identified), was the site of the first successful steam engine of what we might call a recognisable type. Thomas Savery (1650-1715) had produced a form of steam pump in 1698, but the engine which Thomas Newcomen (1663-1729) erected near Dudley in 1712, was not only his and the Black Country's first, it was the first workable engine in the world to have a piston and

cylinder. It worked by producing a vacuum beneath the piston, which caused the pressure of the atmosphere to force the piston down into the cylinder, and so, through the medium of a rocking beam, lift the bucket of a pump. It is correctly known as an atmospheric engine. Steam was used to produce the vacuum, and the Newcomen engine is the direct ancestor of the steam engine of today. Newcomen's engine, being at first capable of reciprocatory motion only, could do nothing more than operate a pump, but this it did with considerable success. . . .

Following the work of Newcomen came the epoch making inventions of James Watt (1736-1819).

*   *   *

At first, Watt's engine, like that of Newcomen, was only capable of effecting reciprocating motion and was thus limited in application to pumping water or working a blowing cylinder. Consequently, its main appeal was on the grounds of increased efficiency over the Newcomen engine and it found particular favour in the districts where coal was expensive. In the coal mining centres, economy in coal consumption was of little importance, and the simplicity and cheapness of the Newcomen engine enabled it to survive in face of the competition of the Watt engine.

When the initial difficulties of single-acting engine construction had been more or less overcome, Watt tackled the problem of obtaining rotative motion from his engine. There was no doubt about the demand for an engine which would drive rotating machinery and Watt was not the only one to realise the fact. A Newcomen engine with a crank and flywheel had been set to work in Snow Hill, Birmingham, in 1779, at a mill belonging to James Pickard. The builder of the engine, Matthew Wasborough of Bristol, was granted a patent for the application of the crank to a steam engine in 1780, and Watt was thus prevented from using the simple crank on his own engine.

*   *   *

In place of the crank, Watt devised the well-known sun and planet motion, and in 1782 he took out a patent for a rotative engine. This year is an important one in the history of the steam engine, for Watt also patented the principle of double-acting and expansive working. Two years later Watt introduced and patented an improved method of connecting the piston-rod to the beam—his celebrated parallel motion—and the engine was complete in the form in which it was to remain for about half a century. . . . The effects upon industry of the availability of almost unlimited mechanical power are too well known to need more than a passing reference.

* * *

THE EARLY NINETEENTH CENTURY

Tremendous strides were made by the Black Country iron trade in the first quarter of the nineteenth century. Some idea of this expansion can be gained from the fact that while in 1796 the area contained only fourteen blast furnaces, by 1830 there were no less than 123. From a primitive condition the iron trade had progressed to a highly organised industry and its plant and products had developed greatly. . . .

Until about 1832, the average blast furnace was small, judged by present day standards, and increase in output had been achieved as a result of an increase in number, rather than size, of furnaces. Changes had already taken place in material handling, however. Until the advent of the steam engine, furnaces had, perforce, been literally 'hand charged.' The hoisting of the materials to the furnace top was simplified by building the furnace alongside a natural bank if one was available; if not, as was generally the case in the Black Country, an artificial ramp was provided.

Steam power made it possible to elevate the materials mechanically. . . .

The materials for the charge—coke, ironstone and limestone, were stocked near the back of the furnace. They were loaded by hand into barrows, which were then hoisted to the furnace top, and the contents tipped through one of the apertures (usually four) in the 'tunnel head' or short stack which carried the fumes and flames above the charging platform. Except as regards increase in size this remained unchanged as the method of charging Black Country furnaces. Mechanical charging apparatus came too late to have any real application in the Black Country, though some local furnaces have been so equipped.

An important development which had begun to spread throughout the Black Country was the introduction of the vertically integrated concern. Though one proprietor had sometimes owned all the mines and works involved in the making of iron, it now became possible for every process to be carried out on the same site. Previously the positions of the furnace and forge had been largely dependent on the availability of water power, and the production of pig-iron and wrought iron had been sometimes widely separated owing to the inadequacy of the available stream or river. Now the only consideration was easy access to coal and ironstone and the furnaces and forge were located together. Not infrequently, limestone, clay and sand were available too, and several works carried out the entire process of iron manufacture from mine to finished product, being entirely independent of outside sources for practically all their needs.

* * *

The iron and coal trades developed along similar lines so far as the employment of labour was concerned, and well before 1850 both had their firmly established customs. The coal mines were operated by charter masters (locally 'butties') who contracted with the owner to work the mine and provide their own labour. If the mine was a large one several butties would be under contract to the owner, each having his own 'district' or section of the mine.

In the iron trade a similar system prevailed, though owing to its greater complexity there were more divisions in each works. At the blast furnaces, all the owner did was to provide the furnaces and machinery, and employ a manager and two principal assistants. Of these, one, the 'bridge-stocker' took charge of the top of the furnaces, being responsible for handling all raw materials, hoisting them to the charging platform or 'bridge,' and charging them as required. The preparation of the pigbeds and all work at the bottom of the furnaces, including tapping and slag or 'cinder' removal, was the responsibility of the 'stock-taker.' Both these individuals hired whatever labour they required, and in this respect were not answerable to the furnace owner. At the ironworks, the master engaged the puddlers, who themselves employed an 'under-hand' and, usually, a boy to help at the puddling furnace. Each rolling mill (a large works often had several), was operated by a 'roller' working (usually on a tonnage basis) for the master, and, again, employing whatever labour he needed.

Such arrangements, which had grown up slowly, were firmly established by custom, and remained with the trade until recent years. Disadvantages included the ease with which the charter masters could operate the truck system, paying their employees partly in cash and partly in goods. Such a system was open to abuse, and abused it certainly was, though it was no worse in the Black Country than elsewhere.

In 1865 the average output of a blast furnace in the Black Country was 130 to 150 tons per week, although a few made as much as 250 tons, and about twenty furnaces in all were using waste gas to heat the blast or fire the boilers. No less than 2,100 puddling furnaces were then in operation, and although the production of pig iron had fallen somewhat, the trade might have seemed in a wholly healthy condition.

Some of the more far-sighted of the iron- and coal-masters had sounded a note of alarm. William Matthews of Corbyn's Hall, near Dudley, had, in 1860 estimated the duration of the coalfield to be about forty years (in which he was remarkably accurate) and others had referred to the approaching ex-

haustion of the ironstone mines, and to the increasing difficulty of providing adequate drainage for what mines remained profitable to work.

In the case of ironstone, available local supplies were already insufficient and ores were being obtained from Northamptonshire and other parts of the country. Non-local ores had, in fact, been used as a part of the blast furnace charge for many years.

By far the most important development of the nineteenth century, as far as the Black Country was concerned, was the introduction of a process for making cheap mild steel. In 1856, Bessemer introduced his acid converter process, and cheap steel became a practicable proposition. It came in when the Black Country was enjoying its greatest prosperity. Few people at the time realised its implications, but it had a far reaching effect on the local iron trade. Wrought iron was made in several grades, and by far the greatest output was of the cheaper quality, used for all sorts of purposes where a superior grade was not necessary. As the mild steel process spread, the makers of the lower-grade wrought iron found the new material a formidable competitor.

*   *   *

Just as two principal causes, one the natural mineral wealth, and the other the development of the steam engine had brought the Black Country into being as an iron producer, so two other causes were to bring about decline. The exhaustion of the mineral resources caused the coal trade and the mining of ironstone to become virtually extinct, and the production of pig-iron to follow suit.

The technical developments which made cheap mild steel possible took away a great part of the wrought trade. In the last 30 years of the nineteenth century a great number of ironmasters closed their works. . . .

By 1900, coal production had dropped to about a half of what it had been in 1865, and in the next few years the fall was much more rapid. In 1913 the number of puddling furnaces was estimated at 661 and a further reduction must be recorded since.

ANCILLARY TRADES

The earliest of the ancillary trades was the manufacture of hand-wrought nails, which was probably as old as the iron trade itself. By the eighteen-twenties it employed about 50,000 people, but from then on, the competition of the machine-made nail became increasingly severe. Although it lingered on for many years, the hand-wrought trade is now extinct as far as the Black Country is concerned.

In the case of chains, chain cables and anchors, the Black Country is still the principal centre of production. The making of chains is of considerable antiquity, but the making of anchors was introduced to the district by Noah Hingley, of Netherton, Dudley, in 1848 as an addition to his already existing business of wrought-iron and chain making. There have been changes in technique, but the Black Country today turns out, by modern methods, chains, chain cables and anchors which are without equal.

*   *   *

Engineering is worthy of special note, for the Black Country was the birthplace of many notable engineering achievements. The steam engine underwent most of its early development in our area, and it was in Smethwick that the world's first factory designed and built solely to make engineering products— Soho Foundry—was built. The engineers of the Black Country were equal to all the tasks set them, and steam engines, rolling mill plants, machine tools, and marine engines, all have their place in Black Country history. Locomotives, too, have come from the Black Country, and if the district has not made many, it turned out a very famous early one —the 'Stourbridge Lion.' This locomotive, which was built by Foster and Rastrick at the works of John Bradley and Co. at Stourbridge, was the first to run in the United States. Even shipbuilding was not unknown! In 1822 the Horseley Iron Company of Tipton built and engined one of the first iron steamships, the 'Aaron Manby' which was sent in sections to London and assembled there. It traded across the Channel to France for many years.

Some brief reference to the changes since the area ceased to be a major producer of coal and iron may be made. Many new industries have come to the Black Country, which is now a recognised centre of light engineering. The inherited skill and adaptability of the inhabitants have proved fully equal to all the changes. In working and fabricating iron for a multitude of purposes the Black Country excels, and where once there was a great outward traffic in pig- and finished-iron, there is now a large but opposite, inward traffic of the same materials, which are used in innumerable products. The Black Country still produces pig-iron for foundry and steelworks use, though its output is very small compared with other districts, and its ores and fuel come from outside the area.

Of high grade wrought-iron it is still the premier producer. Though mild steel has superseded wrought-iron for many purposes, the latter is still supreme in some fields, and its use has increased rather than diminished in recent years.

'Made in the Black Country' is still recognised as a hallmark for many products, and by no means the least of these is wrought-iron.

The previous selection on the Black Country has already introduced the Midlands, the area with which we are concerned in this part of the book. But thus far the question of where the Midlands are has not been answered with precision. By combining many people's ideas, the author of the next selection, which was prepared especially for this book, was able to arrive at a composite which comes as close as possible to defining something about which opinions vary greatly. There is little doubt, however, as to the central area included in the term, and the drawing of sharp boundaries is often deceptive in geography as well as in other spheres.

• 59 • The English Midlands
CATHARINE K. HAYNES

LOCATION OF THE MIDLANDS

The English Midlands—the very use of the term implies the existence of an area which is somehow to be distinguished from the rest of England. We have only to look at the long list of organizations beginning "Midland . . ." in the Birmingham phone directory, to read headlines in a Nottingham paper such as "East Midlands and Festival," to look at such government reports as *North Midlands Coalfield,* or to hear the broadcast of the "Midland News" and the "Midland Quartet" from Droitwich to realize that the Midlands represents something distinctive.

Yet as one goes about trying to discover just what the Midlands is, one finds vagueness on the part of the ordinary person and confusion among the enlightened. A compartment mate (from Newcastle), as the train rolled from London to Leeds, commented, "Oh, the Midlands? I think it's further south, but I don't really know where it is." A woman who had lived in Birmingham twenty years remarked, "I guess it is sort of in the middle. It certainly would include Nottinghamshire, Derbyshire, and Birmingham." A teacher in the North Country asserted, "If you ask me there is no such thing," while a London engineer said, "No one has ever actually defined the Midlands." Wading through the professional literature, one is greeted with a variety of usages, not to mention contradictions. A regional geography uses "North-East Midlands" to describe the territory referred to elsewhere as "East Midlands," sometimes known as "North Midlands." *North Midland Country,* a guide book, cuts a northern slice from the areas more commonly re-

ferred to as "West Midlands" and "East Midlands." Still more common is the use of "The Midlands" to describe only one half of the area.

As one delves beneath what appears on the surface to be confusion, however, one finds a core of consistency in the definition of the Midland region. (At this point you will probably need your map of England.) In the early eighteenth century we read in Daniel Defoe's *A Tour Through England and Wales,* "I came forward to view the midland counties of England, I mean such as may be said to lie between the Thames and the Trent." In the early twentieth century, C. B. Fawcett, in his book *Provinces of England* (a milestone in the development of a regional geography in England), divided the Midlands into three provinces—the Severn, the Trent, and Central England. According to Fawcett, the Severn and the Trent Provinces lay

. . . between the southern limits of the Lancashire Peakdon and Yorkshire Provinces to the north and a line drawn across the Fenland from the western corner of the Wash to the Northampton Heights, and thence along the edge of the Cotswolds and westward across the lower Severn . . .

Central England, or South Midland, according to the same authority was

. . . surrounded by the Severn and Trent Provinces to the northwest and north, East Anglia to the east, London to the southeast, Wessex to the south and Bristol to the southwest.

Parallel with this development of regionalism in geography has come the increasing use of regional divisions by the central government and nation-wide organizations for administrative purposes. During World War I the Ministries of National Service, Labour and Munition in their regional mobilization of the country had a district which was called "West Midlands." Since this time, the "Midlands" has been used to identify the central part of England in an overwhelming proportion of cases where administrative districts were designed. With the nationalization of some of the basic industries of Great Britain, there has been even more regional administration, with reliance on some form of the term "Midlands" for this central portion. Although these administrative units have not sprung up from the grass roots but have rather been superimposed from the top, there can be little doubt that geographical, economic, and social factors have been taken into account as many of these divisions have been made.

An examination of seventeen maps using the Midlands as an administrative unit is quite revealing. The counties, or parts of counties, included on these maps are tabulated below with the frequency of their incidence:

Cheshire	1	Derbyshire	14
Shropshire	17	Nottinghamshire	17
Herefordshire	15	Leicestershire	17
Worcestershire	17	Northamptonshire	14
Staffordshire	16	Rutland	14
Warwickshire	17	Lincolnshire	9
Gloucestershire	7	Buckinghamshire	4
Wiltshire	2	Bedfordshire	3
Oxfordshire	4	Huntingdonshire	2

If we were to rely on this table we might pick out the counties which appear most frequently and call them the Midlands. Using this as our basis, we should spot Derbyshire, Nottinghamshire, Rutland, Leicestershire, Northamptonshire, Warwickshire, Staffordshire, Shropshire, Herefordshire, and Worcestershire as our Midland counties.

Our task, however, is not so simple. The northern boundary appears to be fairly well-defined, for Yorkshire is not listed at all while Cheshire appears in only one case. We might guess, by looking at the physical map, that the Pennines provide a natural break here. The situation becomes rather complex, however, when we discover that the Peak area reaches into northern Derbyshire and northern Staffordshire. The fact that these parts are sometimes eliminated from the Midlands would give support to the theory of the Pennines serving as a barrier; it also shows that our boundary is not so precise as we thought at first. To the West, we see that the Midlands invariably stops at the line dividing England from Wales. We would expect the natural barriers, the differences in language, in social and economic patterns to drive a wedge here. Yet, we are told that near the boundary of Wales there is a great deal of mobility of the people, that the dialects in the western edge of the Midlands are mixed with Welsh. On the East, we learn that East Anglia (Norfolk, Suffolk, and Essex, broadly speaking) seems to have a cultural tradition of its own and is relatively self-contained. Lincolnshire, however, is a rather debatable matter, for it is included on about one-half of the maps of the Midlands. To the south and southeast, the situation again becomes complicated, for Gloucestershire, Oxfordshire, Buckinghamshire, Bedfordshire, Wiltshire, and Huntingdonshire are sometimes counted. The infrequency of their occurrence indicates that they are marginal to the Midlands.

The student with a need for definite answers will find no satisfaction in this fuzziness at the boundaries. It is of primary importance to emphasize that though we may locate a core of the Midlands, it is impossible to draw sharp lines around it. One geographer comments, "From the geographical point of view any attempt to define the exact boundaries of a region is usually a failure." This would appear to be particularly true in a country as small as England, so hemmed in by the sea, so bound together by common tradition, so interwoven by a highly developed network of communication, and so united—in recent decades—"by the overwhelming dominance of urban life."

It becomes clear as one examines these maps of administrative regions that in most cases a division between the East and West Midlands is acknowledged. On occasions, the East Midlands is called North Midlands, but the dichotomy between the two seems to be accepted by administrators. One administrative unit which did not divide the two, the British Broadcasting Corporation, recently witnessed the difference between East and West Midlands. For some time the BBC broadcasted from a station near Birmingham to the whole of the Midlands. So centered in the interests of the West Midlands were its programs that the newspapers of East Midland cities began to complain loudly in their editorial columns. As a result, only recently a station has been set up in Nottingham. This division seems to be reinforced by rather poor communications and transportation between the East and West Midlands, as compared with that between northern and southern points. There is no geographic barrier between the two, though perhaps they fall roughly into two river basins—the Severn and the Trent. One possible explanation is that the heavily populated Birmingham conurbation, lying west of center in the Midlands, has exerted a very heavy pull on the country surrounding it whereas to the East the areas have been more attracted to such cities as Nottingham, Leicester, Derby and have developed their loyalties and economic bonds accordingly.

THE WEST MIDLANDS

First, let us take a closer look at the West Midlands. Perhaps the most commonly accepted definition of the West Midlands today includes the counties of Shropshire, Herefordshire, Worcestershire, Warwickshire, and Staffordshire. These are the counties set by the Civil Defense Office during World War II, by the West Midland Group for Post-War Reconstruction and Planning, and are in current use in the Regional Office of the Ministry of Town and Country Planning. In 1942, George Cadbury said of this district,

thus defined, "The West Midland region is considered by us to be as nearly a natural planning unit bounded by reasonable lines of demarcation as any other that could be devised."

To characterize the West Midlands as a whole, however, would be quite difficult. One writer has said of the Midlands, "Even today many people regard it mainly as a place they cross in order to get somewhere else." Indeed, the picture called to the mind of many an Englishman is that of dingy factory row houses, air grimy with industrial smoke, and vast smouldering heaps of factory and mining waste. This picture is most characteristic of the Black Country, though other industrial areas in the West Midlands have many of these features to a lesser degree. There are contrasts in industrial areas—the Potteries of North Staffordshire are quite different from the industrial Birmingham, for example. One observer speaks of Kidderminster, the center of the carpet industry, as having "distinct problems which occur nowhere else in the West Midlands." Even the coal mining districts vary. While in the Cannock Chase region the miners are isolated from the rest of society in their grim and straggling mining communities with few amenities and almost no recreation facilities, the miners in the East Warwickshire coal field are drawn from urban areas of mixed communities and enjoy a more varied existence. Turning west, we find the agricultural counties of Hereford and Shropshire, not to mention the more rural parts of Warwickshire and Worcestershire. Some of these areas remain rather untouched by the changes urbanization has wrought on the landscape of other sections. Stratford-on-Avon, for example, lies in as idyllic a country setting as is to be found in England; perhaps here the American tourist trade has fought a successful battle with industrialization.

Attempts to generalize on the characteristics of the people of the West Midlands is so spurious that conversations on the subject can easily degenerate into arguments such as this one:

Mr. T. (a Southerner): The Midlanders are more materialistic than are the people from the South. Here, when a man buys a bicycle he volunteers the price he paid for it to anyone who will listen. People in the South would never think of such a thing.

Miss P.: I don't think you can say that at all.

Mr. T. (unperturbed by this dissension): Midlanders are more pushing—they don't wait in queues like people do in other parts of the country.

Miss P. (vigorously): That's just not true. I don't think you can generalize about the people here. The population is too heterogeneous—too mixed. You have all kinds here.

Perhaps Miss P. would find consolation and support from these observations:

As for the people who live in these counties of central England, what sharp differences they show between one and another, what contrasts in temperament and outlook. Even in speech there is no gradual fading from one variation of a dialect to another as in the North and West, but distinct, abrupt changes in cadence, pronunciation, and words themselves. . . . It has been truly said that in no part of England is the population more heterogeneous.

Another commentator echoes:

No part of England has a character so difficult to assess as this group of loosely united counties. They do not fit into a mould as do, say, East Anglia, the North, or the West Country. They consist of so many dissimilar elements.

Perhaps the very dissimilarity of the people and the rich contrasts within the area serve to distinguish it from other regions in England, more finely drawn.

From all that can be gathered from impressions, the people themselves do not tend to identify themselves with the Midlands. A middle-aged woman, the wife of a professor, remarked, "You never hear anyone say 'I'm from the Midlands.'" In answer to the question, "Are you from the Midlands?" the woman, who had lived in Birmingham for twenty years, said, "No, I'm from the North Country—I was born in Barnsley." Indeed, county pride seems a rather important factor here, as Mr. George Cadbury indicates:

County loyalties are very strong, and the county regiments of the Army, county cricket teams, and the like have very considerably fostered this loyalty in recent years. The intrusion of new urban centres, like Birmingham, has blurred the lines a little, but in that case has provided a central regional capital which does not decrease the validity of the county lines at their outer extremities.

There are other indications of localized loyalties, not in the county unit as such, but in a district united around a particular economic pursuit or some other pervasive factor. We see local patriotism quite markedly in the Black Country and the Potteries. Whatever the loyalty, it seems in the light of present information that the West Midlands is an entity of discrete parts, rather than a region strongly bound together by common tradition and marked regional loyalty.

There is one unifying factor which cannot be denied; this is the dominating influence of the Birmingham Conurbation. There can be no doubt that this, the third largest conurbation (and the second largest city) of England, serves and is served by the area around it. Its industry is interlocked with that of the surrounding territory; it draws labor from these districts. It serves as a center of trade and commerce for the area; it draws much of its food from the neighboring farms. Its newspapers are delivered on a wide circle of doorsteps outside the city; people from all around find excellent travel facilities into Birmingham to satisfy their taste for the theatre, music, the pantomime, and the like. The University of Birmingham not only gets strong support from the West Midlands, but also serves it through regional research. As one gets further out on the periphery of the circle of influence, one finds pulls in other directions; such as the pull of Derby on Burton-on-Trent, the attraction of Manchester for the Potteries, the competition with Bristol in the southwestern extremes of the West Midlands. So significant is the dominating influence of Birmingham, however, that some would appear to use it as the primary criterion for inclusion in the West Midlands.

Let us now turn the spotlight on some of the areas within the West Midlands in order that we may not only see something of the variety of flavor to be found there but also that we may view the relationship of a few of the parts to the whole. It is not within the scope of this summary to give a complete analysis of any or all of these districts; these statements are, rather, to be taken as thumbnail sketches. They represent impressions of astute observers rather than summaries of scientific research—with some exceptions.

BIRMINGHAM

Birmingham, the regional center, is a comparatively young city, as cities go in England. It rose rapidly with the Industrial Revolution; today it enjoys a peculiarly healthy and resil-ient economy with its great variety of industry—predominantly light engineering. One observer comments that the recent rise of the city has meant relative freedom from the tradition of the landed aristocracy and acute class-consciousness that have been more common in other parts of England. The co-authors of the *West Midland Plan* have this to say:

> During the 19th century Birmingham was preeminently the home of the small man; the skilled artisan and the small manufacturer were the characteristic figures. Movement from one social stratum to another was relatively easy and common; the workman could set up on his own account. The result was a preponderance of the middle classes.

As the city has developed, it has extended outward to accommodate its bulging population; in this process many of the middle class have moved out with industrial and commercial development at the center. This seems to be the rough pattern of the city at the present time.

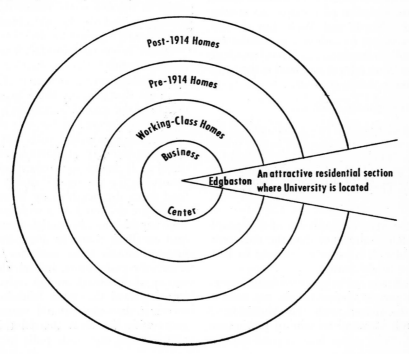

Post-1914 Homes

Pre-1914 Homes

Working-Class Homes

Business

Edgbaston   An attractive residential section where University is located

Center

With regard to the general appearance of the city, Peter Self has this to say:

> Insofar as the early horrors of industrialization have permitted, the town is reasonably well-planned, open space is fairly widely distributed, and most of the housing estates are compact and accessible. Birmingham is no model of beauty, but at least most of its land is put to appropriate purposes and little of it is wasted.

It is noteworthy that Birmingham was the site of the pioneer effort in model housing for employees, Bournville, built upon the plan of George Cadbury. [For a description of it see Selection 70.] Even today, Birmingham is the center of activity for planning in the region, for it was from here that many of the members and the financial support of the West Midland Group on Post-War Reconstruction and Planning were drawn.

THE BLACK COUNTRY

North and northwest of Birmingham lies the Black Country, an area of some 87,000 acres and with a population of somewhat under a million. It has a density of population of around half that of Birmingham—but this does not mean that there is more room for better living conditions or amenities, for mining, industrial development, and population growth have combined to despoil the land. An observer in 1843 wrote of this area:

> The traveler appears never to get out of an interminable village, composed of cottages and the very ordinary houses. In some directions he may travel for miles, and never be out of sight of numerous two-storied houses; so that the area covered by bricks and mortar must be immense. These houses, for the most part, are not arranged in continuous streets but are interspersed with blazing furnaces, heaps of burning coal in the process of coking, piles of ironstone calcining, forges, pit-banks, and engine chimneys; the country being besides intersected with canals, crossing each other at different levels, and the small remaining patches of

the surface soil occupied with irregular fields of grass or corn, intermingled with heaps of the refuse of the mines or of slag from the blast furnaces. Sometimes the road passes between mounds of refuse from the pits, like a deep cutting on a railway; at others it runs like a causeway, raised some feet above the fields on either side, which have subsided by the excavation of the minerals beneath. . . . The whole country might be compared to a vast rabbit warren.

Even today, it is described "from an aesthetic viewpoint . . . (as) hideous in the extreme." The principal trades of the Black Country have been heavy industries—mining and heavy metal works. This industrial organization "either demanded heavy capital as with the iron foundries and heavy metal trades, or next to none, as with the nailers and small independent miners." This structure also called for unskilled and heavy labor; "there was little place in the economy for the middle classes or indeed the skilled artisan," in contrast to Birmingham. Today the Black Country is preponderantly working-class and for the most part, with the exceptions of Wolverhampton, Smethwick and perhaps West Bromwich and Walsall, is extremely poor. As a consequence, the Black Country towns have almost invariably

> . . . grown up with little provision for middle class or upper class housing and still less for the amenities which these classes require. . . . Recreational facilities reflect this one-sided development. Theatres and large public halls scarcely exist at all; and even the provision of cinemas is poor. The Library service is, with one or two exceptions, conspicuously bad. . . .

It would seem from the above evidence that the Black Country is relatively homogeneous in its landscape, industry, and character of its population. It has, characteristic of working-class areas, a high birth rate and large family size. Perhaps this homogeneity has contributed to the strong sense of identification with the area. Behind this sense of community, moreover, is a body of Black Country fables, customs and the like. It is observed that Black Country men have a distinctive quality about them, reflected not only in their unique dialect but also in such things as a "Black Country humor, with a peculiarly acid character." It cannot be doubted that there is a strong sense of patriotism in this area, but, at the same time, the ties with the Birmingham Conurbation are represented not only by the continuous ribbon of settlement extending from Birmingham but also by marked economic interdependence.

NORTH STAFFORDSHIRE

From the Black Country we continue north to the northern part of the county of Staffordshire. Here we find two industries predominant—pottery and mining. The Potteries have their center in Stoke-on-Trent, which combines the famous Five Towns so vividly pictured by Arnold Bennett. In 1908 he wrote in *The Old Wives' Tale:*

The Five Towns seem to cling together for safety. Yet the idea of clinging together for safety would make them laugh. They are unique and indispensable. From the north of the country right down to the south they alone stand for civilization, applied science, organized manufacture, and the century— until you come to Wolverhampton. They are unique and indispensable because you cannot drink tea out of a teacup without the aid of the Five Towns; because you cannot eat a meal in decency without the aid of the Five Towns. For this the architecture of the Five Towns is an architecture of ovens and chimneys; for this it burns and smokes all night, so that Longshaw has been compared to hell; for this it is unlearned in the ways of agriculture, never having seen corn except as packing straw and in quarter'n loaves; for this, on the other hand, it comprehends the mysterious habits of fire and pure, sterile earth; for this it lives crammed together in slippery streets where the housewife must change white window-curtains at least once a fortnight if she wishes to remain respectable; for this it gets up in mass at six A.M., winter and summer, and goes to bed when the public-houses close; for this it exists—that you may drink tea out of a teacup and toy with a chop on a plate.

Perhaps in the nearly fifty years that have passed since this was written, there has not been too much change in the Five Towns. One critic describes Stoke as "a shapeless conglomeration with no real center," marked by "extremely poor living and working conditions." With its lack of diversity of industry, it has had a great problem of unemployment. There is a great amount of part-time work, in which women figure prominently. There is a heavy out-migration from the area because there is so little opportunity for young people and so little selection of occupation. The two industries of the area—pottery and mining—have attracted largely working-class people.

There has been some question about the inclusion of North Staffordshire in the West Midlands for purposes of planning. In contrast to the South Staffordshire coalfields, which is in the heart of the West Midlands, the northern fields belong to the Pennines, "being the western counterpart of the Yorkshire-Derbyshire-Nottinghamshire coalfield which lies to the east of the Pennine range." "Its unique pottery industry, and the sturdy independence of its people have tended to make it self-contained." It appears to be pulled in two directions—towards Manchester and towards Birmingham—for various purposes. For shopping, services of medical specialists, entertainment, and the like, the people of North Staffordshire usually seek Manchester, while administratively they are definitely tied to Staffordshire. In 1942 one observer commented that North Staffordshire was too small for a subregional planning unit, that "much quiet absorption" into the Midlands was taking place; yet in the process of investigation, preparatory to suggesting the West Midland Plan, Sir Patrick Abercrombie and Herbert Jackson, only a few years later, decided that North Staffordshire should be a separate planning unit in the light of its differences from Birmingham and the Black Country.

As we leave this industrial strip from Birmingham to North Staffordshire, we find the industrial development more dispersed. Shropshire, Herefordshire and the southern part of Worcestershire are predominantly agricultural Though there seem to have been no questions as to the inclusion of Shropshire and southern Worcestershire in the West Midlands, there has been some doubt about Herefordshire. George Cadbury, discussing this doubt, says of Herefordshire:

> It is in an entirely separate drainage area down the valley of the Wye, and is cut off from Worcestershire by the barrier of the Malvern Hills. It also has many close affiliations with South Wales and draws many of its supplies from Gloucester. On the other hand, there is no doubt that Hereford folk look to Birmingham, not Bristol, as their metropolis, and the existence of the reasonably good Birmingham-South Wales and Shrewsbury-South Wales railway services, which converge at Hereford, do tend to bind it to the region. Though Hereford traders tend to draw supplies from Gloucester, Hereford farmers tend to send their produce to Birmingham. . . . It is interesting to note that Birmingham University receives grants from all the counties except Herefordshire, and even in this county the Teachers' Training College at Hereford chose to be associated with the Midland Joint Board and is therefore linked with the headquarters at Birmingham University.

To counterbalance Mr. Cadbury's inclination to include Hereford, we find that, a few years later, the counties of Hereford and Shropshire did not join forces with the other West Midland Counties in working out their plan for the Ministry of Town and Country Planning. One commentator stated that these two counties had become wary of cooperating with the more urbanized and industrialized sections, because they felt they had lost ground in past "co-operation."

As we retrace our steps in the direction of the East Midlands, let us return to Staffordshire and enter the East Midlands via Burton-on-Trent, the brewing center. In this city, we have an illustration of the pull between the East and the West Midlands. Administratively, it is a part of the West Midlands, since it is located in Staffordshire. It is, however, only ten miles from Derby and buses run every quarter of an hour from Burton to Derby—a fact which illustrates their close ties. On the other hand, though thirty miles from Birmingham, Burton people seek this larger center for amusement, cultural activities, and more extended shopping. An excellent railway service makes Birmingham with its greater diversity readily accessible to the people of Burton. Here then, we see one instance of the lack of definitiveness in the transition from the West to the East Midlands.

THE EAST MIDLANDS

The East Midlands is even more difficult to define and describe than the West Midlands. Geologically, the East Midlands is linked, via a continuous coalfield with only a minor break, to southern Yorkshire. Northern Derbyshire, part of the Peak area, is really closer to the Pennines than to the East Midlands. Foundries and other heavy metal working industries provide a bond with the Sheffield area. The emphasis on processing textiles tends to bind the East Midlands to the textile areas of the North. Perhaps less isolated in the past than was the West Midlands, the East Midlands has been more in the flow of English life and has been more under the influence of the traditional social structure.

The East Midlands has equally as much cultural and economic diversity as has the West Midlands, but it lacks the unifying factor of a dominant regional center. In the place of a Birmingham, the East Midlands has several cities with their satellite environs— Nottingham, Leicester, Derby and Lincoln— to mention the most prominent. These cities, unlike the more recent Birmingham, are county towns with a long history and tradition, tending to bind the loyalty of the surrounding areas, but dividing the influence within the region. In this division of power between the various centers, Nottingham has perhaps the edge. A planning official remarked:

Nottingham likes to think of herself as the queen of the Midlands and nothing makes Leicester madder. When Nottingham and Leicester have financial drives for the same cause, all they have to do is put up two barometers—one showing Nottingham results and the other Leicester's. That encourages competition all right.

In 1919 C. B. Fawcett wrote of the Trent Province (East Midlands) and the Severn Province (West Midlands):

In comparison with the Severn Province, the Trent Province may be said to possess much greater physical and historic unity, but distinctly has less economic unity. The last fact is primarily a result of the relative equality of its principal towns. . . . The central position of Nottingham would probably enable it to unify the life of the province; but it is not likely to be able to dominate that life to any great extent.

In 1928, Paul Bryan acclaimed Leicester as the rising power in the East Midlands because it was more favorably located in regard to transport facilities and had been less seriously affected by industrial depression than had Nottingham. In 1950, however, it appears that Nottingham is rather generally accepted in administrative circles as the headquarters of this region. K. C. Edwards marks in Nottingham the assumption "of many of the functions of a regional capital as envisaged by Fawcett . . . in 1919." It is interesting to note in this connection that some West Midlanders explained the fact that there was no group such as the West Midlanders group in the eastern half of the district because of this lack of a dominant regional center, whereas an East Midlander, keenly interested in planning, said that the reason was the lack of funds to support such a group's activities.

What the East Midlands lacks in unity, it makes up in prosperity. Though there are some areas, such as the declining towns and villages of south-west Northamptonshire and a depressed cotton district and the older part of the coalfield in Derbyshire, which are rather depressed economically, for the most part the area enjoys economic well-being. During the depression, Fogarty writes: "Unemployment in all of the counties except Rutland, and in one or two years Lincolnshire, was well below the national level." One factor in this, we are told, is the excellent balance between industry and agriculture; another factor perhaps lies in the diversity of industry itself. There are rich and fairly recently opened coal resources. The East Midland coalfields have the highest productivity per man as well as the most modern of facilities of any coalfield in the country. The iron resources of the section produce one-third of the nation's foundry iron. The close proximity of these resources to coking coal sources has fostered the growth of foundries. Textiles, boots and shoes, light engineering are but samples of the diversity of industry in this area. There is considerable economic interdependence among various sections of the Midlands and, within reasonable distances, much interchange of labor. One example of this is to be found in the women who come from the mining districts, where there is almost no work for women, into Nottingham to work in the textile industries or cigarette factories.

Informants on the East Midlands would venture few generalizations. One commented that the Non-Conformist Church (such as Baptist, Congregational, Methodist, etc.) is quite strong in the East Midlands as well as in the West Midlands whereas the Anglican church is stronger in the south and particularly in areas where the landed aristocracy hold forth. This section, he ventured, "has a tradition of nineteenth century liberalism, of the small business man's worth, of free trade." For the most part, stress was laid upon the diversity within the area. As in the case of the West Midlands county ties again loom large; in many cases rivalry between counties waxes quite keen.

The Midlands, we must conclude, like the English custard, lacks definitiveness and cohesion. The Midlander does not, as does the Southerner in the United States, feel a strong loyalty to his region. Perhaps he is more like the Mid-Westerner who is less aware of the Mid-West than of his state and his nation. This lack of regional consciousness is possibly responsible for the dearth of regional research until quite recently, and in turn, perhaps the current extension of regional services and studies on the part of universities and other agencies is indicative of a new Midland awareness. People are mailing more and more questions and reports to regional capitals; in the future, the effect of this may be noted in ordinary people saying more frequently, "I'm from the Midlands."

The Emergence of

an Industrial Society

>>>

Since an industrial society is inconceivable without industry, it is necessary to trace the growth of what has been termed, for want of a better term, the Industrial Revolution. In England, the Industrial Revolution was preceded by agricultural and commercial revolutions, also of great importance. Furthermore, it was not merely technological but social as well, and it actually represented a cumulative social change rather than merely a sudden inventive achievement. That is, those responsible for the development of various types of machines combined principles and parts which others had already worked out in different connections. Such combinations are possible on a truly revolutionary scale only when there has been a sufficient accumulation of culture traits or individual elements to be successfully put together into new working arrangements.

In order to show the Industrial Revolution in some time perspective, we shall quote, first, a description of the Old Midland Village, a nostalgic and even sentimental picture of what Midland rural life was like before the large-scale growth of industry. It turns back the clock to the early eighteenth century. In reading this account, we must bear in mind that there are still many Midland villages today whose inhabitants live in the old brick and stone houses described, although their outlook differs considerably from that of their forebears who built those houses.

• 60 • The Old Midland Village
WILLIAM G. HOSKINS

The great landlord, the country-house, and the spreading timbered park with the sub-servient village at its gates, are only one side of the Midland scene and one, moreover, of recent growth. Before the sixteenth or the seventeenth century they were not characteristic of the Midlands at all, for more than any other part of England—except, perhaps, East Anglia, that immemorial home of free men and women—the Midlands were mostly a country of "free" villages. Only a minority of villages had a resident lord or squire; most contained a numerous class of peasant proprietors, small owners of the soil whose title went back often into the mists of pre-Conquest days. It is this class of men and women who created the Midland village, who chose its site, cleared its natural woods and heath, built its farmhouses, cottages, and barns; built its lovely stone church and the mill beside the gentle willow-fringed stream; carved those leaning, lichened headstones in the church-yard; gave names to the woods and spinneys, the fields and brooks; trod out the roads and lanes, and built the bridges:

Here they went with smock and crook,
Toiled in the sun, lolled in the shade,
Here they mudded out the brook
And here their hatchet cleared the glade.
Harvest-supper woke their wit,
Huntsman's moon their wooings lit.

From this church they led their brides,
From this church themselves were led
Shoulder-high; on these waysides
Sat to take their beer and bread.
Names are gone—what men they were
These their cottages declare.

It is to these ordinary men and women, and the old villages in which they lived out their sober and quiet lives, that I now turn.

A COUNTRY OF VILLAGES

Midland England is more than anything else a country of villages, of compact villages gathered round the church or the green, or strung along a winding street; sometimes perhaps of even more ancient shape—ring-fence villages whose houses, built around the four sides of a hollow square (like the formation of the covered wagons in American frontier days of Indian attacks) reflect the early days of forest and danger on all sides. But whatever the size and shape of the Midland village, we find all the farmhouses and cottages of the parish, the inns and the smithy, are gathered along its streets, and none lie away out in the fields, lonely and remote like those of the wild Devonshire parishes. South-western England is a landscape of isolated farms and hamlets: one may go for miles without seeing a single clustered village: the church stands alone, and the farms and cottages are dotted singly all over the sides and shoulders of the massive hills, and in the deep combes. The parish and not the village is the unit.

But in the Midlands the isolated farm and hamlet can hardly anywhere be found: only in the anciently wooded districts that long remained cut-off, like Charnwood Forest in Leicestershire, and in the old wooded parts of Bedfordshire and Buckinghamshire, do we find farms and hamlets away from the parent village, and the characteristic road-pattern of country that has been enclosed direct from the forest. But here, too, the village is still the most prominent type of human grouping.

It is true that even in the counties where the compact nucleated village is most apparent on the Ordnance map, one occasionally comes across red-brick farmhouses in the fields between the villages, but these betray their late appearance by their names—New York Farm,

[From *Midland England: a Survey of the Country between the Chilterns and the Trent,*
B. T. Batsford, London, 1949. Pp. 61-69, 71-73, 75, 79. Used by permission.]

THE EMERGENCE OF AN INDUSTRIAL SOCIETY

Bunker's Hill Farm, Quebec Farm, Newfoundland Farm. They are the creation of the enclosure awards of George III's day, that revolutionised the old village life all over the Midlands, creating large fields and compact farms, in place of the multitudes of scattered strips in the open fields; but even these isolated farms are few in number, and the enclosure awards, though they transformed the life of the old villages, did not disintegrate them physically. They leeched out all the heart and spirit of the village but left its shell intact.

And so, apart from the industrial districts that mostly lie along a narrow belt of country from the Nene to the Trent where the Victorian prosperity of the hosiery and footwear industries has swamped the old agricultural villages and reduced them to a soggy shapeless mess on the landscape, the Midland village has kept its shape and old likeness. The houses of the village lie all along the streets, mostly facing the street and butting straight on to it without any garden or railings intervening, but sometimes, and usually these are the oldest houses in the place, standing at right angles to it, presenting a blank gable end directly on to the road. The "ancient homesteads", as they are called in the enclosure awards, lay on the village street, or ran back from it; at the back or to one side there was always a small paddock of pasture called "a croft", generally an acre or so in extent (rarely more), and behind the farmhouse was the yard with its buildings (barns, stables, outhouses of all sorts) grouped round it. Somewhere to the side lay the garden and perhaps a small orchard also. All up and down the village streets one finds this constant pattern, with cottages interspersed here and there between the farmhouses, which were well detached from each other; and all over the Midlands, from north to south, this is the familiar pattern—the ancient homesteads clustered within the ring-fence of the village.

BUILDING IN BRICK AND BUILDING IN STONE

In Leicestershire, the farmhouses and cottages will be built mostly of local red brick, especially in the west and south of the county, but here and there in the back lanes the more ancient mud walls can be seen, and less frequently a timbered house of Elizabethan or Stuart times, though these are scarcer in Leicestershire than anywhere else in the Midlands. But the red-brick, which came in generally for village building in the Midlands shortly before 1700 can be, and is, very pleasant in its early styles, with its mellow colouring, slight hand-made irregularities and rough texture, its interesting mouldings and ornament, and the delicate curves of garden walls. There is some excellent building in brick in the Leicestershire villages . . . and a great deal that is seemly and decent, ranging in date from the 1680's to the 1830's. It is only after 1840 that the real horrors of red-brick as a building material were increasingly explored and, since this coincided with the rapid growth of the two staple Midland industries with their demand for workers, we find in the towns and villages street after street of shiny machine-made brick capped by smooth and shiny Welsh slates, on which no moss or lichen will ever grow: streets and "terraces" proudly dated 1877 or 1884, or some such placid year, rich with lace curtains and large pots of aspidistra blocking the view into the period parlours; streets and roads named after the Jubilee or the Scottish Highlands, or the builder's daughters (Clara Terrace and Laura Villas) or Poplar Avenue which leads briefly to a factory-wall where poplars have long since ceased to blow.

* * *

Though the Midlands are mostly overlain with clay, the stone foundations are not far down in most parts. Between the Trent and the upper Welland . . . and again between the Nene and the Ouse . . . the overlying clay is of such thickness as to make the stone inaccessible, and in this district we find villages built of mud and timber (the so-called "wattle and daub" construction) up to the time of James II, and after that of brick. But in the broad belt of country between these claylands the stone—limestone and ironstone mostly—is near the surface, and here we find some of the most beautiful villages in England. There was a time when every village in Northamptonshire, which is the heart of this stone country, had its own quarry, and probably many more than one, for medieval quarries were generally small; and Rutland is even more beautiful in its stone-built farmhouse and cottage architecture, for it has had no manufacturing industry to ravish its old villages. Hardly a single village in Rutland is not worthy of admiration, in whole or in part, and some are outstandingly good.

* * *

The Northamptonshire villages and country towns fall into two groups, according to the stone they stand on: those of the north and east of the county are mostly of the grey limestone, extending into Buckinghamshire at Olney, which is largely built of stone; and those of the west and south are built of the even lovelier ironstone or marlstone, as it is variously called. Where the two stones meet, we get some charming mixed colours.

* * *

Wherever you go, however, one thing is inescapable from one end of this Stone Belt to the other, and that is that nearly all the best building in every village and country-town falls into the seventeenth and eighteenth centuries, and that within this period there were two generations in particular in which building was at its height, both in quantity and in quality—the two generations between about 1590 and 1650.

* * *

THE FIELD SYSTEM AND VILLAGE GOVERNMENT

There were two reasons, perhaps largely peculiar to the Midlands, why this peasant civilisation reached its zenith in this part of England, as well as two other reasons that were common to the whole country. First, that the open-field system, which called for continuous co-operative effort on the part of the village as a whole and so gave a peculiar colour to Midland life, was more characteristic of the great middle zone of England than of any other part. And further, that the Midlands, especially north of Watling Street, but to a lesser degree to the south also, were the home of a large class of peasant proprietors, owning from twenty to fifty acres most of them and subservient to no squire or landlord. So we have a social system from early times founded on the whole village as the unit of work and play and government, and on a considerable class of free men and women who owned at least some of the land they tilled.

The cultivation of the open fields was bound to be a communal affair, governed by a multitude of detailed rules passed at the annual meeting of the whole village. There are numerous references in local records to the existence of such an annual general meeting at which resolutions were debated and changes made, if a majority thought it desirable, in the rules. The old system was by no means as inflexible and unchanging as the textbooks so often repeat. And any changes were recorded in writing in a book kept by one of the village officials for the time being, and read out in church on the next Sunday or two for the benefit of those who had not attended the meeting, so that no man could thereafter plead ignorance of a new rule. The rules for managing the open fields at Wymeswold, in north Leicestershire, drawn up by a village meeting some time in the early part of the fifteenth century, have been preserved among the manuscripts of Lord Middleton and printed by the Historical Manuscripts Commission, for anyone who cares to read them.

Not only were all the lands of the parish—common pasture, meadows, and leys, as well as the great arable fields—used according to the rules prescribed by a completely democratic assembly, but the village governed itself through its own officials, elected by the same assembly, and every man of any standing and responsibility was expected to take his due turn in the rota of officers—constable (most important of them all, for he was the link between his village and the majesty of the general law of the country), churchwarden, overseer of the poor (from 1601 onwards), field-reeve, pinder (keeper of the village pound), and the lesser offices of village business: every man took an office according to his capacity to serve it well and there are few, very few, references to men who decline to take their share in the government of the local democracy. This combination of a physically unified village, surrounded by open fields that could not be cultivated except by agreed and common action for which all adult persons had some sense of responsibility, was a good foundation for any civilisation.

Not only that, but the open-field system had another important attribute. Besides calling for a truly democratic kind of society, providing opportunities for all men to share in the government and good management of their native villages, it provided opportunities for all, however lowly, to "get on" in a modest way. The man with little or no capital but a pair of strong arms and the will to work was not shut out from economic security and independence as he is today in practically every country in the world (every one at any rate, that has been infected by Western European ideas); but he had his foot on the bottom rung of a ladder which, with his own energy and skill, would take him, not necessarily to the top (few nourished that restless ambition) but to a level of modest comfort and self-respect, to some sort of standing in his own little society. I have read many hundreds of manuscript inventories of Midland villagers, attached to their old wills from Henry VIII's time onwards, and among these one continually finds men who are described as "cottager", "labourer", or "shepherd" who die leaving a decent competence in worldly goods, to which they had been helped by their own employers more often than not, as the employer's will, when one turns it up, shows. Yeomen and husbandmen, even the more modest among them, not infrequently left to their shepherds or their labourers a few sheep

or lambs, or a half-acre or so of crops in the village fields, sometimes apparently not only the crop but the land on which it grew as well.

* * *

. . . There is no shadow of doubt that the open field system did afford opportunities to anyone with a good pair of hands, however poor his start, to advance himself a few rungs up the ladder towards security and independence and in this respect alone, even if it had no other attribute, it was a better form of society than that in which most men toil fruitlessly today.

THE PEASANT ECONOMY

I said . . . [above] that besides the two characteristics that were together more strongly developed in the Midlands than in any other part of England, there were two other characteristics of this old peasant civilisation which were more or less common to the whole country in former days, and which were the very essence of the old way of living: I mean its intense "localism", to put it in a word, and (what follows from that) its balanced economy.

As to the first of these, I cannot put it better than George Bourne did in one of his best books, *Change in the Village*. "It was of the essence of the old system", he says, "that those living under it subsisted in the main upon what their own industry could produce out of the soil and materials of their own countryside. A few things, certainly, they might get from other neighborhoods . . . but as a general thing the parish where the peasant people lived was the source of the materials they used, and their well-being depended on their knowledge of its resources." All over England, country people had this local knowledge of where everything was to be found and how to make the best use of it; and not only did this give them a minute understanding of the soil and of the whole of their immediate surroundings, and a pride for the skill required in using difficult materials where none others were to be had; but because everything that went into them came out of their native soil, their buildings, which are the only remaining sign of that "home-made civilisation of the rural English", look as though they had grown out of the very earth they stand in, so well matched they are and resting so comfortably on it. They belong to it, just as their builders belonged to it and would in due course mingle their bones with it.

* * *

SKILLED CRAFTSMEN

Because the old Midland village aimed at being self-supporting so far as was humanly possible, it found employment for a host of skilled craftsmen within its boundaries, men who lived as much by the land as did their fellows who tilled it and fed their animals on it—the smith, the miller, and the wheelwright (the three most important men of all); the carpenter, the mason, the tailor, the shoemaker, the butcher, the baker, and the saddler and harness-maker. This kind of balanced economy in the old village—and it was an *economy* in all senses of the word to have all these things made or done within the village itself—this kind of economy goes back a very long way, for we find it well developed even in the fourteenth century. The poll-tax returns of 1381 for certain Leicestershire villages, for example, show us a remarkable list of craftsmen. At Hallaton we find carpenters, a brewer, tailors, a barker, a baker, butchers, cobblers, weavers, a cook, a wheelwright, an ironmonger, a shearman, fisherman, in addition to the purely farming households; and at Medbourne, three miles away, the list includes a miller, a mason, skinners, a carpenter, a butcher, and a "belman". Not all villages were as self-sufficient and as various as this, but most had their smith, wheelwright, miller, mason, and carpenter, and so it was all over the Midlands. If one village had no mason or miller, he could be found in the next surely enough: there was plenty of inter-village traffic, but in general people found all their earthly needs and wants met within a radius of three or four miles at the most, within sight of their own church spire.

Not only was there this balance of activity within the village itself, but the craftsmen themselves kept a similar balance in their own working lives. All, almost without exception so far as I can discover, had a little land near their homes and farmed in their spare time or when, as was inevitable at certain times of the year, trade was slack. There was no enforced idleness for reasons beyond their control: there was always another occupation at hand, always plenty to do, always a pleasant change of occupation and scene there in the background. In the old Midland village, for example, the smith was not only the most important craftsman of the community, but often farmed a small freehold also. . . .

The wheelwright was hardly, perhaps, as exalted a personage as the smith, though he was equally necessary to the life of the village, and he, too, like the carpenter, the tailor, shoemaker, baker, freemason, and weaver had some land and farmed as a side line.

* * *

The village baker appears quite early in medieval records in the Midlands, perhaps because in many parts fuel was becoming exceedingly scarce and it was a necessary economy to get bread baked down the street at the bakehouse rather than at home.

* * *

THE PEASANT WORLD

Every village was a little organism, with a life of its own and a flavour peculiar to it alone, very nearly self-sufficient and always aiming at being so. Around the village stretched the two or three thousand acres which were the basis of its life, the open fields which were more characteristic of Midland England than of any other part. This was the peasant's world outside the few streets and lanes that constituted his village, and he knew every inch of it *by heart*. Outside these fields he rarely ventured far nor, for the most part, ever wanted to.

From long experience—experience older than his own, and traditional among his people—he knew the soil of the fields and its variations almost foot by foot; he understood the springs and streams; hedge-row and ditch explained themselves to him; the coppices and woods, the water-meadows and the windy heaths, the local chalk and clay and stone, all had a place in his regard—reminded him of the crafts of his people, spoke to him of the economies of his own cottage life; so that the turfs or the faggots or the timber he handled when at home called his fancy, while he was handling them, to the landscape they came from. Of the intimacy of this knowledge, in minute details, it is impossible to give an idea. I am assured of its existence because I have come across surviving examples of it, but I may not begin to describe it. One may, however, imagine dimly what the cumulative effect of it must have been on the peasant's outlook; how attached he must have grown—I mean how closely linked—to his own countryside. He did not merely 'reside' in it; he was part of it, and it was part of him. (George Bourne, *Change in the Village*.)

* * *

Truly it was at its best a peasant civilisation, a rich many-sided culture. It had its darker side: one could enumerate its many faults soon enough; it was far from perfect. But it "took care of a few fundamental things". Men lived in a place that had meaning and significance for them; their roots went down deep into the cultural humus formed by centuries of ancestors before them on that spot; they "belonged" to that place. "Men are attached to places", says Lewis Mumford, "as they are attached to families and friends. When these loyalties come together, one has the most tenacious cement possible for human society." . . .

Not only did men live in a place that had meaning for them but they worked in it also, all their lives: home and work were synonymous. And, further, they saw the beginning of their work and the end of it and could therefore take a deep pride in doing it well. But their experience was even wider than this, for they saw their work long before it reached them and long after it had left them. The wheelwright on his evening walk was already marking down in his mind particular trees still growing and planning their use in years yet to come; and when he had finished his cart or wagon he saw it round about the parish for the rest of his life and could still feel the same pride as on the day he turned it out, the best he was capable of. This old qualitative civilisation, disparaged and derided as it is by those who have never troubled to understand it, limited though it was in scope, aimed, not at power, but at perfection and now and then achieved it.

We turn now to a short account of the worldwide changes that lay behind the transformation of the Midlands and, indeed, much of England, from a rural to an industrial region. John L. and Barbara Hammond, who wrote the next selection, are well-known social historians, whose writings reflect a sensitive awareness of the interconnections between social and technological events. In the book quoted here they detail many facets of the fundamental changes that have accompanied the growth of industry in England and the world as a whole. For additional information on the rise of the textile industry, mining, pottery making, and the iron and steel industry their book can be consulted with profit.

• 61 • The Birth of the Modern World
JOHN L. HAMMOND AND BARBARA HAMMOND

The Industrial Revolution has created societies in which the plainest lives are ruled by forces that are as wide as the world. In the Middle Ages a man's neighbors were those who lived near him; his outlook was bounded by his village; he could watch the growing of his food, and the spinning and weaving of his clothes. This life, with the charm and the danger of its simplicity, was extinguished by a series of changes, of which the most dramatic were the great mechanical inventions that began in the eighteenth century and have succeeded one another with extraordinary rapidity from that time to this. The new industrial system has been associated throughout the world with the name of England, because the English people played the leading part in making and using the first discoveries. It was from England that the new processes, the new machinery and the new discipline passed to the continent of Europe. . . . England, unlike Germany and the United States, passed through a revolution of great importance before the introduction of the railway. That revolution was marked by the dissolution of the old village, by the transformation of the textile industries, by changes of a different kind in the Pottery industries, and by a great concentration of capital and power in the industries connected with iron, steel and coal. Its effects were important enough, and decisive enough, to alter the character of English life. . . .

. . . By the middle of the [eighteenth] century it is possible to discern the contributions that England was to make to the solution of the problems created by these new conditions. The immediate confusion has passed; society makes its first efforts to adapt its arrangements to its new life; the distinctive features of a new civilization are emerging from the shadows. Decisions have been taken, institutions have been created, a temper has been formed, beliefs have assumed solid shape that are to influence, for good and for evil, throughout the nineteenth century, first the life of the English people, and later the life of all the most active of the races of mankind.

*   *   *

The Industrial Revolution was in one sense catastrophic, since it had effects that were immediate, and spectacular; in another it was gradual, for it was the climax or the sum of a series of developments, none of them peculiar to England, some of them later in time in England than elsewhere. Any definition of this new society would make it clear that it could not have been called into being by any single set of forces. Its men and women, in Mr. Hardy's phrase, serve smoke and fire rather than frost and sun; they produce for commerce and not merely for subsistence; they use in their daily lives the products of different countries for which they make payment by an elaborate system of exchanges; they live by an economy in which occupations and processes are sharply specialized; they rely for most of their production on the help of machines; the mass of persons taking part in this production have no property in the land, the capital, or the instruments on which it depends. It could not be said of a society so complex as this that it was created by Watt, by Arkwright, by Crompton or by Stephenson. All that can be said is that the inventions by which those names are known throughout the world were decisive events in its history: decisive, because mass production depends on those inventions, and mass production is an integral part of the new system. Those inventions were essential, but among the causes that made the English people what they became, other events were not less significant.

*   *   *

[From *The Rise of Modern Industry*, 5th edition, Harcourt, Brace, New York, 1937. Pp. 1-4, 21-23. Used by permission.]

The discovery of the Atlantic routes marked or caused a revolution . . . that took some centuries to produce its full effect. Commerce began to assume not merely a new scale, but a new character; it did not merely employ larger vessels and greater capital, it shipped popular cargoes. When the Dutch and the English first competed in the East, the Spice Islands were counted the chief prize; by the end of the eighteenth century the Spice Islands and India had changed places, and it was doubted whether the cost of keeping those islands was repaid by their profits. For commerce had begun to provide for the many; to depend on popular consumption; to enter into the daily life of the ordinary man. India and America sent new delicacies to England, and in the course of a century, owing to a number of causes—the growth of commercial capital, the development of the arts and machinery of trade, the improvement of transport, changes of habits and manner of life—those delicacies were brought within reach of the poorer classes and passed into general consumption. Tea, sugar and tobacco took the place of pepper, spices and cloves, as the chief articles of commerce.

Tea, when first imported by the East India Company, was a highly priced luxury, but by the middle of the eighteenth century it was a popular drink. A writer complained as early as 1742 that "the meanest families" in the Lowlands of Scotland had given up beer for tea. Cobbett and Hanway, the philanthropist, agreed that tea-drinking was robbing the English people both of their health and their beauty. "Your very chambermaids," wrote Hanway, "have lost their bloom by sipping Tea." By 1828 the yearly consumption of tea in these islands had reached 36,000,000 lb. Sugar grew rapidly in favor. In the Middle Ages the Englishman sweetened his food with honey. Until the seventeenth century sugar was a rich man's luxury; at the beginning of the eighteenth century England imported 20,000,000 lb., and by 1782, 160,000,000 lb. Rice was another novelty brought from America. In a cookery book printed in 1734

there is not a single recipe for the preparation of rice; in another, printed at the end of the century there are twenty-two.

Thus ships were now sailing across the Atlantic, or rounding the Cape of Good Hope, bringing cargoes destined, not for palace or cathedral, but for the alley and the cottage. Capitalist commerce was providing for the wants of the peasant and the workman, as well as for the taste of noble or cardinal, rich merchant or prosperous lawyer. Owing to new resources, new products, new materials, new habits, the expansion of wealth and the development of finance, commerce increased rapidly in volume and scale, and this change in degree was accompanied or followed by a change in kind. The day when more profit was to be made by carrying tea for the poor from India, than by carrying pepper for the rich from Java, marked an important stage in the progress of the world to the modern system.

The commercial revolution of the fifteenth and sixteenth centuries was an essential preliminary to the industrial revolution of the eighteenth and nineteenth centuries. For capitalist manufacture on the modern scale was only possible when capital could be applied to the production of goods that were consumed by the mass of the people, and it was the use of capital for this purpose that gave the Industrial Revolution its sweeping character. Commerce and production take the same course. As pepper gives way to tea, so silk gives way to cotton. The relations of Europe and the world outside are reversed: Europe that had drawn on Asia for manufactures takes the lead in production. The conditions arise that make possible so strange a spectacle as that of a Lancashire town using a raw material, not grown on English soil, to produce goods that are exported for popular consumption to India or China. England has learnt how to make greater fortunes from clothing the poor in the simple fabrics of Manchester, than had ever been made from clothing the rich in the gorgeous fantasies of Babylon or Damascus.

The change from peasant to industrial civilization may be described in another sequence. The wants of the ordinary man were supplied in the early Middle Ages, as in the days of Greece and Rome, either by himself and his family, or by his neighbors; in the next stage these wants were supplied by special persons plying a craft, in a village or small town, organized sometimes in guilds; in the third stage the provision of those needs became the business of individual or group production and large scale merchanting; in the fourth it became the business of large scale production. At that point the world passes to the industrial age: to an age in which commerce and finance are no longer aspects, growing in importance, yet still aspects of its life, but the basis on which a society depends. The English people were the first to develop this system, to enjoy its wealth, to suffer its evils, to struggle with its problems, and to build on this foundation an imposing place and power in the world.

Herbert Heaton, in his article on the Industrial Revolution in the *Encyclopaedia of the Social Sciences,* takes an attitude somewhat different from that of the Hammonds, whom we have just quoted. He shows, for example, that it took 150 years for the Industrial Revolution to get started and another 150 years for the economic transformation to work itself out; and he wonders whether the process can accurately be termed "revolutionary." He does admit, however, that there was a change in tempo about 1750.

Heaton's discussion also reminds us of the contributions that many people and nations made to the preliminary conditions necessary for the Revolution. Heaton indicates, furthermore, that even though the laboring people may have had a hard time of it, the entrepreneurs, or employers who took the risks and managed various business ventures, did not have such an easy time themselves. We include below, as Selection 62, Heaton's summarizing paragraphs. The author was born in England but has taught in American universities for a number of years, at present at the University of Minnesota.

• 62 • *The Industrial Revolution*

HERBERT HEATON

. . . In all lands where it came to displace an established industrial structure the industrial revolution ran a roughly similar course. The textile industry was usually the first to be affected, then the making of clothes, metal articles and foodstuffs; the large scale manufacture of iron and of steel represented often a distinct step forward but one not easy to take, while the manufacture of machines and producers' goods generally was a hazardous venture. Indeed it is this final step toward complete industrialization which has been most difficult for more recently industrialized countries. In lands coming late to industrialism the easiest success has been won in industries which process the natural or farm products, which produce simple wares such as blankets or plain cotton pieces or which enjoy the natural protection of distance from possible competitors.

Migration of industry from manual domestic or shop conditions to the factory varied

[From "Industrial Revolution," *Encyclopaedia of the Social Sciences,* Vol. 8, Macmillan, New York, 1937. Pp. 10-12. Used by permission.]

in speed from industry to industry. Spinning went quickly; weaving, knitting and some metal trades passed through a transitional workshop period, in which workers were gathered under one roof but continued to use the old equipment. In the clothing industries the sewing machine could be used in the home, and many women clung to the putting out system but had to submit to sweated conditions. The shoemaker and hand loom weaver put up a long fight, and the victory of the laundry and bakery is still far from complete in Europe.

Dependence on coal and water power led to industrial concentration on the coal fields, river valleys and such belts as the fall line in America. Water power had only a limited effect in causing concentration, for it strung the factories all along the banks of rapidly flowing rivers, and for certain textile washing processes an ample supply of water was almost as important as a supply of fuel or power. Where water and coal were found together, as in the Pennine valleys and eastern Belgium, industry was spread over the whole region in villages or towns. For the metal industries location was determined by the coal supply, since it was easier to bring the metal to the coal than vice versa; but this involved the construction of adequate transport facilities, such as the railroad between Lorraine and the Ruhr.

The movement of population to the industrial areas still needs further study. But for England it is now evident that there was no simple mass transfer of people from the south and east to the north and west. The industrial towns grew by drawing workers in from the hinterland, and the void thus made was filled by people from slightly further afield. Journeys were generally short, except in the case of the Irish who swarmed across the Irish Sea to Lancashire, Glasgow and Yorkshire. Only later, when the railroads made longer journeys easier, was there any serious long distance migration. In newer countries, such as the United States, native population was for long streaming away from the eastern industrial centers and a continual

inflow of immigrants was necessary to insure an adequate labor supply.

Problems of urban health and housing were probably most acute in those towns which were the homes of the early spinning factories. In looking at them it should be remembered that until 1835 many British manufacturing centers had no adequate municipal government, that knowledge about the essentials of public health was scanty, that cheap production of pipes, bricks and woodwork did not come until about 1840, that house building depended on the willingness of someone to sink capital in dwellings and that the rate of interest current or the profits to be made in industry might be more tempting than the return on house property. A glance at the housing of the poor in nonindustrial towns of the eighteenth century and at the difficulties which have surrounded the provision of working class dwellings since 1914 should provoke a more merciful judgment of the "jerry builder" of the early nineteenth century. In the United States living conditions in the early textile towns of New England were very good; only with the coming of wave after wave of foreign laborers did the worst slum conditions appear.

Of labor conditions no easy generalization is possible. Long hours, child labor, employment of women, insanitary conditions, payment in truck, unemployment, low wages, capitalistic tyranny, labor unrest, industrial fatigue, occupational diseases and the "cash nexus" were not inventions of industrial factory capitalism. Night work was a new thing in the textile industries; but the only novelty about child labor was that children now worked in large groups, were subject to factory rather than parental discipline, discharged more responsible tasks, had to leave the hearth to work and were kept vigorously at their day or night tasks. It should be noted, however, that child labor was universally regarded as natural and that the children's earnings were larger in the factory than they had been at home. When child labor was forbidden, something else—education—had to be developed to fill the waking hours of the young. The hazards to life and limb might perhaps have been prevented before they were attacked by legislation but they had first to be recognized as such, and the apathy toward them was as marked among the operatives as among employers. Such conditions and attitudes repeated themselves in most countries or regions where the factory system was introduced.

As to wages and employment light and shade alternate. In the early stages the new industries, especially cotton and pottery, seem to have paid much higher wages than were prevalent in the older industries, and the demand for hand loom weavers to cope with the flood of machine made yarn raised the rates paid for weaving. In England the long war with France lifted many nominal wages and some real ones, but the slump after Waterloo lowered levels in industry and agriculture alike. The hand loom weaver and some other manual workers suffered when they stuck to their benches in face of the machine; but elsewhere conditions seem to have improved because of rising wages and falling prices after about 1820 or 1830. Some occupations passed from male to female hands, but new occupations were opened up and old ones expanded—metallurgy, mechanical engineering, the construction and operation of railroads, shipbuilding, mining, building—and the opportunities for skilled well paid work multiplied accordingly.

In short, the industrial revolution increased rather than decreased the material welfare of the mass of the population; but some sections suffered from the transition, war and business fluctuations disturbed wages and prices and the dangers latent in the employee's lot became apparent. Unfortunately much of our view of the social aspects of the revolution is drawn from reports of official investigations, which in their very nature are full of complaints and grievances. From them one can paint the industrial revolution as "an orgy of soulless cupidity" (Tawney) and assume that to be the whole picture. But quantitative studies such as that by Clapham; detailed business studies of Oldknow, Owen, Wedgwood, Boulton, Gott, Krupp and others; and a more detailed knowledge of pre-revolutionary conditions tone down the picture and make at least some of the industrial leaders appear more like human beings and less like incarnations of ruthless self-interest. Moreover it is still far from certain how much the revolution was "a triumph of the spirit of enterprise" (Tawney). Enterprise there was but not always triumph, and the industrial field was strewn with the wreckage of men who failed. The trouble with machinery that broke down, with workmen who refused to use it, with customers who demanded long credit yet refused to pay their debts, with booms that burst, with banks that refused any more loans, with wars that closed markets, all made the road stony. Inadequate supplies of working capital wrecked many a venture, and when a successful period came the profits had to be plowed back into the business. The industrial revolution has not yet been studied through the records of bankruptcy, but enough is known to show on what a treacherous sea the entrepreneur of the early machine age launched his boat.

Making a Living

THE ENGLISH MIDLANDS

>>

The complexity of any society depends upon the number of special activities entered into by its members. This specialization, when considered in connection with economic activities, is called the division of labor. In England as a whole, and in the Midlands in particular, the division of labor is carried to its greatest extreme. A Midlands factory worker may spend his productive life span operating two or three similar machines. Even the Midlands farmer is a specialist in the sense that he produces almost entirely for a market rather than for his own subsistence and relies upon that market to satisfy many of his needs.

Every specialist has to depend upon others to supply at least some, and often nearly all, of his basic needs. The division of labor operates through the market. Hence, so much trading is needed because of the division of labor that England has been called a "nation of shop-keepers."

A more accurate generalization views England as the workshop of the world. In an international division of labor, England is the artisan and trader. England usually depends, as the individual specialist does, upon others to supply most of its basic needs. During the two World Wars, such supplies were sharply curtailed, and the postwar years have proved little better. A specialist, whether an individual or a nation, is particularly vulnerable to changing conditions.

In the selections that follow, several aspects of the British economy will be dealt with: first, agriculture; then, industry; and, finally, labor. Each is intricately organized and operates in a delicate balance of relationships with other economic activities, both contributing to and depending upon them. One result of this elaborate interdependence has been the recent governmental efforts toward nationalization, aimed at achieving better all-round effectiveness. That nationalization is not felt by all of the British to be the complete or the most satisfactory solution to problems is indicated by current reversals of the program in regard to certain industries. On a smaller scale the daily problems of the housewife also reflect the intricacies of a modern industrial economy, particularly when complicated by the strains of a recent and devastating war.

The story of Britain's farming and farmers begins with the most primitive practices and leads to the most modern development. As the next selection points out, Britain's farms today are among the most efficient in the world, being highly mechanized, with good crop yields and with stock breeds that remain at the top of the list.

Wilford Smith, in his *Economic Geography of Great Britain* (Dutton, 1948, p. 173), writes of the agriculture of Britain:

> The agricultural pattern of Britain is exceedingly complex, a mosaic of infinite variety, the country presents as great a variety of landscape as any other land of similar size, farming systems are frequently highly specialized and varied in kind, and present land utilization is strewn with relics of former land use, adapted to past economic conditions, existing side by side with others more closely adapted to the present economy. . . . The physical environment offers possibilities and sets limits, but within these the farmer has an infinite variety of choice open to him and he has not answered the question of what to do with his land always in the same way. There have been striking revolutions in land use.

A brief but authoritative account of some of these changes through the centuries is presented as Selection 63. In reading this and other selections by British authors, we must bear in mind that to the British *corn* means the important small cereal grasses of the country (wheat, especially, and also rye, barley, and oats) and does not refer to *maize*, as it does in American usage. The second of the selections on agriculture shows how farming continues, with certain modifications, in the area closely surrounding a large conurbation, or metropolitan center. These two selections together reveal the part that agriculture plays in the British economy.

• 63 • *The Development of Agriculture in Britain*

About four thousand years ago men in Britain first began to farm. They kept flocks and herds and grazed them on whatever herbage was available. Then they learned to plant crops by pushing a pointed stick into the ground and dropping seed into the hole.

When the Romans came they taught the Britons how to farm the fertile valleys, using the plow and oxen. It remained for the Saxons, however, to establish villages, and from this emerged the Manorial System with its three-field plan, under which the tenants held a number of strips in each of three communal fields. This system remained until the fourteenth century when the need for enclosing land for sheep-raising, due to the expanding wool trade, began the modern field system. These fields were either owned outright by freeholders or farmed by tenants paying a money rent.

The enclosure of the land made possible a further development in arable farming

[From *Agriculture in Britain*, British Information Services, New York, 1947. Pp. 3-33. Used by permission.]

which took place about 1720. The earth was improved by the use of various forms of lime and by the adoption of a four-course rotation of wheat, turnips, barley, clover, a system of farming encouraged by the great landowners of the time, designed to keep the soil permanently fertile. Britain took its place as the most successful farming country in the world.

British inventions came to the farmer's aid with Jethro Tull's Corn Drill in 1701, James Smith's Reaper in 1815, and Patrick Bell's Reaper in 1828. There followed chaff-cutters, steam cultivators, steam plows, binders, scarifiers, etc.

At the same time, livestock was improved. Robert Bakewell (1725-95), by the most careful methods, changed the large-boned, coarse, slow-maturing sheep of his era into the well-fleshed animal which he called the New Leicester, whose blood runs in many of the famous sheep breeds of today. The annual sheepshearings were the forerunners of our modern agricultural shows. In 1720 Benjamin Tomkins, a yeoman farmer, was left in his father's will "one cow called Silver and her calf." The descendants of Silver and her calf were selected and improved by the Tomkins family for more than a hundred years, and became the great Hereford breed which thrives equally on the pastures of its native Herefordshire and the ranges of Texas and Australia.

From Yorkshire, at the beginning of the nineteenth century, came Shorthorns, which are found in more places in the world today than any other breed of cattle. A poor Yorkshire weaver named Joseph Tuley, earning less than $5 a week, reared a pig which was to become world famous. Tuley and his wife went short themselves so that their pig might have all it wanted; they washed it and took it for walks on fine days, and in 1851 they entered it at the Royal Show. They were well rewarded. Their pig was the forerunner of the Large White, the most renowned breed of pig in the world.

Of the twenty breeds of cattle, sheep, pigs, and horses of world-wide reputation today, *all but three originated in England.* When the war began in 1939 Britain was the world's leading exporter of livestock.

In 1822 John Lawes inherited an estate at Rothamsted which he used for scientific investigation of fertilizers and their effects on crops. The successful results of his experiments led to the development of the fertilizer industry, in which Lawes himself had a direct part. Eighteen months before his death in 1900 he left $500,000 to endow the estate so that its work could continue, and Rothamsted is now among the world's leading agricultural research centers.

But, ironically, the Industrial Revolution—which prompted so many inventions to benefit the farmer—was also responsible in some part for the decline of agriculture towards the end of the nineteenth century. By then food could be brought from abroad more cheaply than it could be grown at home. Between 1867 and 1913 the arable acreage of Britain fell from 17,700,000 to 14,500,000 acres but the demand for more milk and meat for the new urban centers was responsible for increased numbers of livestock. Thus, with the coming of World War I and the ensuing U-Boat campaign Britain faced a serious food shortage. The farmers were appealed to in this crisis and responded by increasing the arable acreage by nearly one and a half million acres in two years, from 1916 to 1918.

The period between the two wars was necessarily one of readjustment. Grain prices fell owing to the large world production and reduced industrial demand, and British farmers had to adapt themselves as best they could to the new situation. Ways and means of helping the farmer during this period were sought. In 1924 subsidies were introduced by the British Government and from that year they were paid on sugar, from 1932 on wheat, from 1934 on milk and cattle, and from 1938 on oats and barley. Successful marketing schemes were also introduced for hops, milk, bacon, pigs, potatoes. These schemes ensured benefits of collective bargaining for members and the raising of standards and quality of products. They also improved collection and supply to distributors, and increased consumption by means of publicity.

Of further help to the farmer was the passing of the Land Drainage Act in 1930 which created Boards to control the use of water over areas of as much as 2½ million acres at a time. In this way it now became possible to deal with the drainage of a river system as a whole. By the end of 1942 schemes costing the equivalent of $64 million had been approved under this Act.

During this period Sir George Stapledon's experiments produced improved strains of grasses. It was he who advocated "ley" farming, whereby pastures were renewed every few years by plowing up and reseeding. Farmers began to appreciate more fully the value of good pasture. Even barren hilltops came under the plow for reseeding to grass. With the production of new grasses and careful livestock breeding Britain became, and still is, the "stud" farm of the world.

By 1939 agriculture was still Britain's largest industry, occupying 70 per cent of the land area of England and Wales, and providing employment, directly or indirectly, for over one million people. Yet, despite this fact and all the measures taken during the between-war years, Britain was producing less than one-third of the food she consumed. Moreover, British agriculture was unbalanced. While arable farming had sunk to 12,000,000 acres (the lowest in history), the number of dairy cattle, sheep, pigs, and poultry had never been higher. In order to feed this livestock Britain had to import between seven and eight million tons of feeding stuffs annually: one out of every three tons of food consumed by animals was imported.

Thus, with the outbreak of World War II, British farmers were faced with the greatest task ever set before them. With U-boats again active in the Atlantic and with all available shipping urgently needed for military purposes, Britain was forced to curtail imports of food for the people and feeding stuffs for animals. There were only two ways of doing this. First, a drastic control of food consumption by the people, which was achieved by rationing. Secondly, a maximum increase in home-grown food.

The first step was clearly to increase the acreage of arable land. But this could only be done at the expense of livestock. A question of priorities had to be decided—meat or milk? It was agreed that milk should be priority No. 1, and foodstuffs were accordingly rationed on this basis. Milk prices were subsidized and prices for agricultural produce were fixed in such a way as to encourage the production of foods considered most essential.

Everything humanly possible was done to help the farmer. War Agricultural Committees were set up in each of Britain's counties, and under these were established 478 District Committees, the members serving voluntarily and without remuneration. In the hands of these committees was placed the responsibility of translating policy into concrete achievements. The task involved was immense, for Britain is a land of small farms. In 1940 the Ministry of Agriculture closed down many of the peacetime agricultural colleges and attached the staffs to the new County Committees. These experts went out into the fields to spread the new ideas and teach the farmers new methods.

A Farm Survey was undertaken in 1941 with the purpose of improving the worst farms and those deficient in some respect, e.g., in management, machinery, capital, or land drainage. The Ministry issued advisory leaflets, produced films, and organized lectures and broadcast talks, and in 1942 arranged demonstrations on the farms themselves. These proved extremely popular and very helpful to the farmer.

One of the worst problems was the gradually increasing labor shortage. Farming was a reserved occupation and the bulk of the men stayed on the farms, but even so about 40,000 went into the armed forces or industry. In order to keep men on farms, a national minimum wage was fixed for the first time in Britain's history, and men were "frozen" as agricultural workers. To ease the situation further a Women's Land Army was recruited, which reached 70,000 at its peak. Workers were transferred, where necessary, from one farm to another. An emergency Land Corps and voluntary Land Clubs grew up and school children were also allowed to help. Men from the armed forces were used when available, as were prisoners of war.

Most startling were the advances made in the use and development of machinery, two-thirds of which was manufactured in Britain. The County Committees set up pools of machinery, and depots were established from which farmers could hire implements at reasonable rates. As a result, British agriculture is now one of the most highly mechanized in the world.

The land itself was improved through drainage schemes (for which the Government undertook to pay half the cost) and by encouraging the use of fertilizers. Already, four months before the outbreak of war, a campaign had been launched and a bonus granted to farmers for plowing up seven-year grass land. Very soon the tillage area was increased by over 60 per cent.

All these measures combined to enable Britain to produce 70 per cent of her wartime rations despite the fact that her population had greatly increased owing to the influx of Allied Armies and refugees from Europe.

• 64 • Agriculture in the West Midlands
W. B. MERCER

FARMS VS. FACTORIES

The industrial complex of the Birmingham area has been built up in the space of some two hundred years around mining, smelting and quarrying. Each generation has been content to labour amidst the detritus of its predecessors, to take what the earth would yield and to leave to its successors whatever of spoils its industry created. In the end an appalling area lies under colliery and quarry wastes, factory dumps, derelict workings or in depressions filled with water. . . .

Further afield, urban influences are indirect and nearly always a mixture of good and evil. Roads occupy much land and bear mainly alien traffic, but they bring also all the paraphernalia of modern farming to the farm gate. Electric pylons straddle the fields and add to the ploughman's yoke, but bring current to within measurable distance of the homestead and cottage. The huge water-mains that come in from Wales and branch out to a dozen little towns are a sore hindrance to the farmers in whose land they are sunk, but they carry supplies to farms—or at

least have that potentiality—as well as to towns. Alternative occupations are open to almost every farm-worker's child, and, equally, work on the farm is open to scores of thousands of urban dwellers; the towns do indeed furnish an immense pool of casual labour for fruit and hops and potatoes. Finally, from the towns there proceeds a stream of claimants for agricultural land, the stream varying greatly in volume with fluctuations in economic prospects, but always of considerable size. Three types of component may be recognized. At all times and in all places there exists a large number of men anxious to obtain a patch of land somewhere within reach of their urban homes, on which to carry out part-time cultivation. At all times, too, some young men and women with an urban background want to establish themselves as smallholders. They are most numerous after great social upheavals caused by war, and they have in the past been all too numerous in times of industrial depression. Thirdly, there is the business-man who wants to invest the fruits of industry in farming. This type is peculiarly susceptible to economic

[From *Birmingham and its Regional Setting, a Scientific Survey,* Buckler and Webb, Birmingham, 1950. (From a reprint.)]

changes. In lean times nobody wants a farm; in good times everybody wants one.

For one reason and another, therefore, it is scarcely possible to shake off the influence of Birmingham within fifty miles of Birmingham. Within that circle there are indeed areas of singular natural beauty and even some areas in which seclusion can be found if one's tastes lie that way, but in truth the town is always just around the corner. If no factory chimney can be seen, its effluents are in the air, while the traffic of the roads and of the railways plainly bespeaks the industrial area.

Within the Birmingham-Black Country Conurbation 37,000 acres are officially classed as agricultural land. The West Midland Group on Post-War Reconstruction and Planning put the area of undeveloped, "largely-agricultural," land at 68,970 acres. The traveller by road over the thirty weary miles that lie between the northern and southern extremes may well wonder where these acres are. Here and there a stretch of . . . pasture surrounds a dilapidated set of farm buildings; here and there a green paddock betokens regular mucking and mowing, a sward . . . breaks the succession of factory, mine, drab streets and wilderness of colliery spoil. Here and there, indeed, a farm seems in process of creation out of the waste; for some reclamation is going on, thanks to the bull-dozer and profits of other industries. Even an occasional field of corn may be encountered.

The type farm consists of the remnants of what was once a holding, together with a few odd bits of others, with rough grazing on a spoil bank; the buildings a poor little set, the stock a herd of nondescript milking cows. The cow is a placid sort of beast that can be schooled to graze almost anywhere, indifferent to human trespass and, within reason, to molestation by dogs. She can turn to good account a variety of by-products; if need be, and the funds of the owner allow, she can live entirely thereupon. Moreover, urban dwellers have faith in the milk of cows they can see; be the conditions of production what they may, the producer-retailer is always sure

of a market for his wares. And he may be able, while on his rounds, to sell a few potatoes, swedes and eggs. The area is, however, not noted for its poultry-keeping; by the standards, say, of Lancashire, there are few fowls. Milk is the mainstay of such farmers as there are. In recent years agricultural production has been swollen by the output of parks and other municipally-controlled land. Birmingham, for instance, grew more than 1,000 acres of potatoes during the war years.

Most of the agricultural land within the urban area lies, naturally, in the peripheral parishes. Here milk production vies with corn-growing, potatoes and market-gardening. The fringe farms, like their counterparts within, are often rumps whose obliteration has been checked only by the war, occupied by men who have been content to see their horizon shrink as the town swelled out to engulf them. . . .

Market-gardeners cluster around the outskirts. They are a varied band, shading by easy stages from the Saturday afternoon allotmenteer, through the lorry driver whose pal has got a greengrocer's shop, the post-office sorter whose life's ambition is to occupy a smallholding, the petrol-cum-café man who gardens when he is not pumping, the retired policeman, the man who used to be a saddler, and the young fellow but lately in the R. A. F. who has embarked his all in a couple of acres, up to the established nurseryman with a regular pitch in the market and the small firm with shops to feed with home-grown tomatoes.

* * *

VEGETABLE GROWING

It seems preferable to describe . . . [the next] section as vegetable-growing in order to distinguish it from the market gardening of the suburbs, since it is carried on further afield, though, in truth, many of the subjects are identical with those of the suburbs.

Three major areas are concerned—Lichfield, Kidderminster and the Avon or Evesham Vale.

. . . [In Lichfield] more than ninety per

cent of the vegetables are grown on holdings exceeding five acres; the farmer has become the gardener at least in respect of the major crops. There has indeed been some exchange of function; on the one hand, farmers, with livestock and corn interests tending to reduce their cereals to find room for vegetables, on the other gardeners by origin acquiring land for stock-keeping. . . . Recently, farms have become largely mechanized and there has been much bull-dozing of hedges. Potatoes, roots and green crops occupy anything from a quarter to as much as half of the total area of some farms; potato-growing has indeed been carried to a point which gives cause for alarm, for there have been many evidences in recent years of the build-up of eel-worm populations. . . .

Standard practice in years gone by has included winter-feeding of cattle in yards. The practice still obtains on many farms, despite the relative prices of stores and fat beasts; but two divergent movements are now discernible. Some farms are abandoning feeding in favour of maintenance of store stock only, with sale in-calf or for grass-feeding. Others, borrowing a leaf from neighbours a little farther north, are turning to a policy of arable dairying. . . .

The Kidderminster area differs from Lichfield chiefly in respect of the beet crop. There is a factory in the town, and throughout the district beet is grown on level terms with potatoes. Peas form also a notable crop. The crop is often sold to merchants who pick them.

*   *   *

. . . [The Avon Valley] district figures prominently in monastic accounts of gardening, and doubtless fruit-growing started here at a very early date; but it was primarily a corn-growing area until the construction of the railway in the middle of last century opened up contacts with the fast-growing population of Birmingham and the neighbourhood. Since then development of fruit and vegetable-growing has been rapid, and there has been much deliberate creation, by land-owners and public authorities alike, of small-holdings out of corn-growing farms. Simultaneously, specialised farming by capitalist enterprise has developed. As a result there is now in the valley an enormous aggregation of tiny holdings intermixed with farms of 50 to 500 acres.

*   *   *

The small-holdings are unique. In Evesham itself and two adjoining parishes there are 900 holdings. In another parish, of 1,100 acres, 350 growers occupy 900 acres between them. Practically all the cultivators live in the town or surrounding villages. Fields are small, but, even so, nearly every one is divided like the medieval open field, by paths or ditches, into tiny flats, the total holdings of many growers being made up of parcels in different fields, often in two or three parishes. Nearly every type of vegetable is grown, the most notable being, perhaps, asparagus.

*   *   *

Intensive market-growing originated in Evesham and Pershore. The two centres have long ere this linked up and the industry has spread far afield on both sides of the river, up to Stratford and beyond. Developments in the latter direction have been chiefly amongst capitalist farmers and business men, often with interests in fruit and produce marketing.

THE DAIRYING AREA

The great crescent of Triassic outcrop which enfolds Birmingham has long been noted for its dairy-farming. The output of milk from this region—the so-called "milk belt"—is sufficient to affect materially the nation's supply, and its farmers have rightly enough played a leading role in the development of modern milk marketing. (The first chairman of the Milk Marketing Board—Sir Thomas Baxter—was a Staffordshire farmer.) It is characterised by flat or gently undulating surfaces. . . .

The area is heavily stocked with dairy cattle. The county of Stafford, for instance, with 550,000 acres of grass and fodder crops, carries a stock of about 116,000 dairy cows and a total of 240,000 stock units—the equivalent, that is to say, of one stock unit to 2.3 acres. That is perhaps an average for the whole belt; the densest stocks occur in the west, and there is a general tendency to ease off towards the east.

MILK AND BEEF IN WARWICKSHIRE

Warwickshire farming before the war was a depressed industry. Eighty-five per cent of its land was in permanent grass, mainly of third-rate quality. On scores of farms, buildings and fixed equipment were steadily becoming derelict. Like other Midland counties it had once been a region of mixed farming, with 80,000 of its 460,000 acres in wheat and 160,000 in tillage; but when the decline in corn prices came in the 1880's, its farmers did not intensify their dairying to the same extent as their western neighbours; they continued sheep and cattle-feeding—enterprises excellent in their way but incapable of yielding high income, prone to lead to economies which take the form of discharging labour, to the merging of fields by the neglect of fences, and thus to ranching, dog and stick farming. Dispensing with labour is the first step in an insidious spiral, which ends with uninhabitable cottages, neglected homesteads, ditches, drains and fences. No land can be farmed in an husbandlike manner without husbandmen.

There were other deep-seated causes of decline. It had been a county of country seats *par excellence,* affording wonderful hunting. From the turn of the century the days of the country landlord were over and the break-up of estates began. Many farms were "bought" by tenants with insufficient capital to maintain equipment, and agriculture was not then a sufficiently paying proposition to attract Birmingham business interests. In a sense Birmingham did come out into the country, but it came out in search of dormitories only and thereby induced, over a wide area, that curious paralysis of agricultural enterprise which over-spill housing seems fated to cause.

*   *   *

A development of considerable interest in recent years is that of seed growing. There is no doubt that Warwickshire is well suited to the production of most sorts of grass seed and to white clover also, though the latter is a speculative crop. It seems quite possible that grass seed growing can be blended with winter maintenance of cattle, but experience alone can show in what proportion of our winters cattle can graze drills in February, with advantage alike to themselves and the ground.

GRASS LANDS

The Triassic outcrop—mainly of Bunter Sandstone—to the west of Wolverhampton has given rise to a big stretch of predominantly light land extending nearly to the Severn and, in a north-south direction, from Market Drayton to Stourport. The valleys of the streams are usually broad and moist or marshy, well suited to grass. This is the traditional home of arable farming, sheep folding and winter fattening of cattle.

Almost all of it has been heathland enclosed direct in the interests of wool production towards the end of the fifteenth century. A few commons of poor and marshy type remained open until Napoleonic times.

Though it is customary to speak of it as an arable area, it is in truth an area of mixed arable and grass. Farms are in general larger than in most districts in the Midlands; homesteads are conceived on generous lines befitting what may be called a good farming district, though population density is smaller than in the dairying area.

It is good barley land. Though it will grow wheat, this crop competed but poorly with barley until the necessities of the times compelled an extension of the bread grain. Had modern spring wheats been available in pre-war days, possibly bigger areas would have been grown. . . .

The barley, beef and sheep-folding system was at a very low ebb when the sugar beet subsidy was introduced. The new crop "took on" quickly, and its development affords a classic illustration of the forces that come into play when a new industry arises. A new technique had to be devised, methods of cultivation worked out, labour trained to new tasks. Cultivation methods were built up from those traditionally used in mangold-growing. It took farmers some years to learn that seed could be sown on the surface and covered up, instead of beneath the surface of a ridge; it took them longer to learn what violent treatment the seedlings would stand. Local industry contributed new ideas; the original Gower-drill was a godsend. Later on, with the coming of row-crop tractor tools, there developed amongst workers a degree of precision in mechanical work which made that of horse-tool days look clumsy indeed.

. . . Factories at Wellington and Kidderminster facilitated marketing, and the area under the crop grew steadily—with a brief setback when the sugar subsidy was reduced in 1932—down to the outbreak of war. Beet rather than corn became the keystone of farming. The area under arable cultivation was maintained at a high level.

* * *

MIXED FARMING IN THE WORCESTER PLAIN

Worcester is a densely populated county, with a general atmosphere of fruitfulness and modest prosperity. The close-set villages, often developed round what once were small commons and connected by a maze of narrow lanes, are plainly ancient settlements. Early man recognized Worcester as a delectable spot, and the Ridgeway which divides the county from Warwick was a well-worn track when the legions first sighted it. A considerable number of village commons still remain, the most noteworthy on the western side of the Severn.

* * *

The chief difficulty in appraising the farming of the Worcestershire Plain, however, lies in its diversity, in the number of enterprises commonly found on one farm. Everyone grows some wheat and some potatoes. . . . There are often a few acres of beet and some fruit is grown on every farm; usually some milk is sold; calves are reared for drafting into the herd, for sale as stores or for fattening, and they may be joined by others purchased for sale later in store or fat condition; there are usually a few pigs and a flock of hens in battery or out on free range, and one field may be let out for the season to a market-gardener who will grow sprouts thereon. All this on 60 acres. If it is a sizable farm there is a small flock of ewes as well, and autumn lambs may be brought in for feeding on the maiden seeds. . . .

In so far as one motif is dominant, it is milk supported by rearing, the emphasis falling on milk where water supplies and buildings are suitable, and on rearing where these facilities are poor. . . .

Vegetables and fruit undoubtedly contribute a big quota to farm income. Fruit is grown everywhere on scales varying from an acre or two of grass orchard, up to the specialist venture of the fruit farmer, pure and simple. It is a long-established enterprise which has evolved slowly. The county, therefore, is full of orchards planted to types of by-gone days, now in various stages of senescence, ill-suited to modern technique yet yielding too high a return to justify the cost of clearance; and sharply distinguished therefrom, modern plantations of bush and half-standard. Vegetables seem to have developed as a variant of the green crop for cattle; depending on situation and individual choice of the occupier, cultivation of these crops is either restricted to a portion of the normal root-break or extended to a major crop involving a quarter or a third of the arable land, as in the area on the light soils of Kidderminster.

As has already been mentioned, a complex industrial system must be fed with raw materials from many lands. At first, local resources are usually sufficient but, as they become depleted, they must be supplemented by imports. As industry becomes more highly specialized, there is greater demand for particular kinds of products for which there may be no domestic substitutes; there is also more need to discover new markets for goods produced in almost endless quantities by mass-production methods. Thus, commerce expands and flourishes, illustrating the "dynamic" character of capitalism.

In Selection 65, which follows, mention is made of the goods which pass through London and Liverpool, illustrating the *entrepot* character of these ports. Where goods are moved from one ship to another or from one type of conveyance to another, there is employment for local people and an important source of income.

But commerce and all the technological activities described in previous selections require capital. Thus, financial institutions take deep root in an industrial society, and banking on an international scale provides the mechanism by which worldwide trade can be carried on. Therefore, it is appropriate that the next selection carries the title of Industry (since it presents a bird's-eye picture of manufacturing centers in Britain), Commerce (since it emphasizes shipping and the exchange of commodities), and Finance (since it discusses the balance of trade and Britain's pecuniary resources).

• 65 • *Industry, Commerce and Finance*
PHILIP CARR

What are the foundations of the industrial, commercial and financial greatness of England, and what are the conditions which are essential to its existence?

The foundations are two—first, maritime transport, and then, coal. The essential conditions are also two—first, the freedom of the seas, and then, the maintenance of purchasing power.

Before the industrial age of the nineteenth century had given coal its enormous importance, London had already become the chief trading center between Europe and the other continents, and afterwards, as a natural consequence, the financial center of the world; and London had attained this position owing mainly to the fact that the goods exchanged between Europe and these other continents were carried almost entirely in British ships. There were geographical and historical reasons for this. The British Isles were favorably placed at the door of Europe and in the tem-

perate flow of the Gulf Stream. The British Navy had successively driven other competitors off the seas—first the Spanish, then the Dutch and then the French.

Thus, by the end of the eighteenth century, England had firmly established herself as a great commercial nation.

In the nineteenth century, she became a great industrial nation as well; and she became so largely because she possessed coal in enormous quantities, in excellent quality and in readily accessible places, so that she had, under her hand and cheap, the power for driving the steam engines, which she had herself invented for her factories, her railways and her ships, which, in turn, provided her with cheap delivery abroad.

The industries were built up in close proximity to, and indeed on the top of, the coal fields; and these coal fields were within easy distance of the seaports—there is no place in England which is not within easy distance of the coast, and the English coast is dotted with good seaports. As sea transport is always much cheaper than land transport, the shortness of the land journey to the factories from the sea for the raw material and from the factories to the sea for the manufactured goods was of great importance in keeping down the selling price of the finished article.

Consequently, by reason of having good coal at hand, and therefore cheap, and by reason of being close to sea transport, English manufacturers commanded two important elements of being able to sell cheaply abroad.

This double advantage was so great that it counterbalanced the fact that all except two of the chief raw materials used for the manufactures, which Great Britain exported overseas, had first to be imported from overseas.

These conditions remain the ones which govern the situation today.

*   *   *

With regard to raw materials used in manufacture, it is still the fact that only two of the important ones, iron and wool, are obtained to any considerable extent at home; and even they are not obtained to the full extent that is required.

The great iron industry of Great Britain was built up in the past by using exclusively British ore, and in time of peace Great Britain does still produce two thirds of the iron ore which she needs; but she imports the remaining third. Fortunately, there are considerable natural reserves, both of Jurassic ironstone in Northamptonshire and Lincolnshire and of hematite in Cumberland; but the Jurassic ironstone, although it is relatively easy to extract, and represents over 90 per cent of the British production, is low in metal content, and the hematite, while consisting more than half of metal, is rather difficult to mine. So that in normal times the resources of Scandinavia, French North Africa and Spain are drawn upon, while, during the war, a part of the difference is being made up by collecting scrap-iron.

As for wool, it used to be one of the most famous products and exports of England, and the best qualities are so still. Yet hardly more than a tenth of the woollen yarns and cloths which come from the mills of Bradford, in Yorkshire, or Paisley, in Scotland, and are exported all over the world, is made from the wool of sheep raised in Great Britain, but from the wool of Australia, and to a less extent from that of New Zealand, Argentina and Uruguay.

Several of the metals other than iron have been mined in Great Britain for hundreds of years—the Cornish tin mines, for instance, date back to the Romans—and important industries owe their foundation to these earlier deposits. However, the production has, in all cases, long been insignificant principally because the foreign ore could be obtained more cheaply; and it is upon imported ores that the industries originally created to work the metals of Great Britain have grown to rely. Thus, the relatively small output of lead and zinc from Derbyshire, Durham and Scotland represents only a fraction of what comes from Australia, India, and Canada.

It is from Canada and Northern Rhodesia that copper is obtained, as well as from Spain. Tin comes from British Malaya, Nigeria, Bolivia and Chile; manganese from India and Russia; nickel from Canada; chromium from Southern Rhodesia. Bauxite, from which aluminum is made, used to be imported to England from France and also to some extent from Hungary, Yugoslavia and Italy. It must now be sought in Guiana, the U. S. A. and Russia. Other non-metallic minerals, such as asbestos, magnesite, potash and phosphates, have equally to be imported, and the first and last of these, which England used to obtain from France and French North Africa, must also be drawn from the U. S. A.

Finally, all the mineral oil, used to make motor and aviation petrol, as well as for lighting, has to be imported, the U. S. A. being by far the largest producer, but considerable supplies being under British control in Iran and Iraq.

When we pass from the minerals below the soil to what is grown above it—animal as well as vegetable—we find that Great Britain is no less dependent upon imports from abroad.

Virtually the whole of the wood used in the country arrives from overseas, as well as the pulp used in paper making, to say nothing of newsprint paper itself. Canada, Scandinavia and Russia are the sources of supply for soft woods, while hard woods are brought from South America and Asia.

All the cotton, which is spun and woven in the mills of Lancashire, is imported—chiefly from the U. S. A., but also from India and Egypt. Much of the flax which is made into linen in Belfast comes from Russia, though much is also grown in the North of Ireland, and it is being increasingly cultivated in England.

All the tobacco which is smoked in Great Britain is imported, chiefly from the U. S. A., though 24 per cent of it comes from the British Commonwealth.

In the matter of food, the percentage of imports to the whole consumption is no less great—80 per cent of the cereals (mostly from Canada, but also from Australia and Argentina); 78 per cent of the sugar (chiefly from Cuba and Australia); 88 per cent of the butter and other fats (the butter principally from New Zealand, but also, until the war, from Denmark); 50 per cent of the meat (chiefly from Argentina in regard to beef, and New Zealand in regard to mutton, but also from Uruguay and Australia); 33 per cent of the milk (in condensed form, mostly from Holland until the war); 50 per cent of the fresh fruit (oranges from Palestine, Spain and Brazil, apples from Canada, Australia and the U. S. A.).

In addition, Great Britain imports the whole of her enormous consumption of tea (most of it from British India), her small consumption of coffee (mainly from Costa Rica and British East Africa) and her considerable consumption of cocoa (nearly all from British West Africa).

It will have been noticed that, in many cases, the country which is the principal source of supply is itself a member of the British Commonwealth of Nations. This is of considerable importance under war conditions, where finance is concerned, as I shall explain later. At the same time, these imports have to be carried over the ocean no less than if they were purchased from a foreign country, and the necessity of keeping the seas open and the ships of the merchant service constantly travelling over them remains as vital as ever.

British shipping is therefore at the very foundation of the commercial and financial greatness of the country, and it is also the life line of Great Britain.

* * *

I have spoken of shipping to begin with, because that is Great Britain's most essential activity in the sense that if it collapsed, Great Britain could not live. There are, however, other occupations which employ far greater numbers of workers. Look first of all at the productive industries, as they stood before war diverted the activities of so many factories from their normal course. Textiles and clothing, taking cotton and wool together, show the largest figures, the number of the women employed being double the number of the men—the totals in 1931, when the last detailed reports were made, were 1,200,000 women and 600,000 men. The industry in which the greatest number of male workers is occupied is that of metal trades and engineering (1,500,000), followed by agriculture (1,200,000), then by coal mining (1,000,000) and then by the building trades (950,000). Transport of all kinds, including ships, railways and road vehicles, accounts for a larger number of workers (1,750,000) than any of the industries just mentioned; and commerce of all kinds is responsible for almost as many (1,600,000); but these last are rather arbitrary groupings, and are of relatively little interest as an indication of the productive efforts of the country.

The enormous number of people who depend upon the textile industries shows what a great factor these industries are in British prosperity. As far as England is concerned, they are concentrated in South Lancashire for

cotton and in West Yorkshire for woollens—
that is to say, looking northwards at the map,
in that part of the country where the island
begins to get definitely narrower. The products of these industries are among the most
important of British exports; and it is significant that not only has the demand for
Yorkshire woollens and Lancashire cotton
goods been maintained since the beginning
of the war in such important foreign markets
as South America, and has even been increased, but that Great Britain has been able
to make regular deliveries to meet the demand.

The metal-working industries follow the
Yorkshire coalfields southwards from Leeds
to Sheffield and then to the neighborhood of
Nottingham, and are found again, rather to
the southwest, on the Midland coal field—
Wolverhampton, Birmingham and Coventry.

Around London and Liverpool are other
industrial areas, producing various kinds of
goods; but they are to be found there, not
because there is coal—for there is none—but
because, for various reasons, it is more convenient for them to be immediately in touch
with a great seaport, where the raw materials
arrive and whence the finished goods are
despatched, than to be on a coal field.

The shipbuilding industry is established
on the estuaries of the Clyde and the Mersey
on the West Coast and the Tyne and the
Thames on the East.

Among the British industries which manufacture for export, and make the economic
greatness of the country, I have spoken of
only one or two of the most important; but
there are many others. There are ships, locomotives, aircraft and motor cars, the value
of whose exports, taken together, was only
exceeded, in 1938, by two exports, machinery
and cotton, and exceeded that of iron and
steel and that of woollens. There are chemicals and dyes whose normal export is worth
more than £22,000,000. There are electrical
goods, pottery and cutlery, each of which ex-

port far more than £9,000,000. There are
high-class paper goods, the value of whose
export in 1938 was £7,000,000, manufactured
oils £5,000,000, and leather goods, £4,000,000.

As for the foreign buyers of these exports,
the largest buying country in 1937 was the
United States, closely followed by South
Africa, Australia and India. France, Germany,
Canada and Eire formed a second group. A
third group was composed of New Zealand,
Argentina, and Russia. In 1938, the United
States took less than three quarters of what
she had bought in 1937, but otherwise the list
was unchanged.

I have mentioned some of the manufactures, whose export in normal times helps to
pay for Great Britain's enormous imports of
food and raw material. How is the remainder
of these imports paid for, and how is the
balance created, which enables British foreign
exchanges—in normal times, once more—to
show a profit instead of a loss?

Of course, the transactions take place in
terms of money; but nowadays so many people understand the elements of economics
that it is hardly necessary to remind them
that money only represents something else.
In dealings between independent countries,
it immediately represents gold; but there is
no country whose gold reserve—even when it
is very great—would last very long if it had
to be drawn upon every year to liquidate even
a small adverse trade balance. Besides, drawing upon it at all would mean that the country is trading at a loss.

When a country really is trading at a loss,
it in fact pays for the adverse balance only
to a very small extent by exporting gold, and
chiefly by three methods—first, by exporting
materials, which do not represent production,
but are a drain upon the country's possessions
of capital values; second, by parting with the
ownership, at home, of property which represents capital values, and, third, by parting
with the ownership of property which its
nationals possess in other countries.

Many communities in the United States today are looking for economic salvation in the coming of more industry to their localities. Chambers of commerce and numerous other organizations are on the alert to persuade expanding business firms to establish plants in their locality. We are learning in this country, as the British learned some time ago, that there are many social factors, such as housing, schools, community spirit, medical services, which influence the decision to move into a specific community. But there are also the economic factors which, in the opinion of industrial management, will promote or hinder the financial success of the enterprise. Some of the factors have been studied and reported on by Political and Economic Planning, a group which has been described previously (see page 424). Notice that much of what is said in the report would apply equally well in America.

• 66 • The Location of Industry

. . . In order to avoid, on the one hand, saddling the community with unnecessary burdens and wastes, and, on the other hand, saddling industry with higher costs in the supposed interests of the community, it is necessary to know what determines economic location.

The main primary factors appear to be (1) raw materials, (2) suitable labour, (3) site and services, (4) access to market, and (5) finance. *Raw materials* range from those hardly processed at all to those very highly processed, and many may be home-produced or imported. One industry may use several, and what matters is the total cost of all its raw materials delivered at the works. Some factories depend on raw materials which are only handled at a few ports; others are financially linked with certain raw material suppliers and get a favourable price; while other raw materials are too bulky and low in value to justify transport beyond very short distances. Reliability of supplies is a factor, as well as their price.

LABOUR

Nationally, the proportion of female to male workers is about 4:10, there being relatively few women employed above the age of

30. It is difficult to find exactly what types of suitable labour are available in a given district, and every fluctuation or transfer of industry alters the position. A few industries are still localised by a pool of skilled labour in a traditional centre or centres, but changes in the nature of "skill" and of the training required for manufacture are making for less and less localising influence of the labour factor. Trade unionism has had an effect on location. Certain areas have, often unjustly, come to be regarded as under "unreasonable" labour leadership, and some employers have preferred newly industrialised districts where they can start with a clean slate. In many of the newer districts very mixed industries, long journeys to work, more leisure interests and, in some cases, higher pay, have much increased the difficulty and reduced the incentive for trade union recruiting, but employer-trade union antagonisms have declined, and in some industries the employers actively encourage their workers to join the appropriate unions. Wage agreements providing different rates for different zones have had a powerful influence in localising some industries, notably printing, much of which has become centralised in smallish towns such as Cheltenham, Frome, Beccles, Aylesbury, and Rochester. In

[From *Report on the Location of Industry in Great Britain,* Political and Economic Planning, London, 1939. Pp. 7-11, 64-65, 82-83. Used by permission.]

some areas certain types of new industry have to face considerable local prejudice—e.g. the making of consumer goods in a centre of heavy industry—while there is a marked tendency for any office work to prove more attractive than almost any comparable factory work. Differences in security of employment may be a decisive consideration.

SITE AND SERVICES

Steep slopes, liability to floods or subsidence, and, to some extent, climate, limit the choice of sites for industry, and further limits are imposed for certain manufactures such as brewing, by an inadequate quality or quantity of available water supply, and sometimes by the need for dumping of solid waste or disposal of liquid effluents. Apart from natural conditions there is much variation in the policies of local authorities in this respect.

Certain industries are incompatible as neighbors: for instance, a biscuit factory could hardly be operated next to a works emitting black smoke. A few "offensive trades" are subjected to special control, and the same applies to explosives works and petroleum refineries.

Accessibility of site by road and rail is usually an important consideration, but is sometimes offset by, for example, a need for avoiding vibrations or dust. The cost, terms of contract, and efficiency of utility services locally available are also an important consideration, although there is a tendency to even out some of the local variations as a result of competition and of national co-ordination.

The incidence of local rates [taxes] is often mentioned as a factor, but since de-rating, its importance as a cost burden has been very slight: for instance, all Birmingham industries combined contribute only some £240,000 a year towards local rates. Local authorities, however, also influence location in other ways, for example, by the degree of strictness or laxity with which they interpret the many regulations regarding building plans.

* * *

Industrialists have sometimes been persuaded to go to a place where a bargain site was available—for example, a factory already built and vacant through liquidation. Locations so determined are not always justified by operating experience, while the cheaply-acquired buildings may soon need expensive adaptation.

MARKETS

Access to markets, always important, has become more important than ever, partly because technical needs of production are satisfiable in more locations, and partly because of the more dominant position of the consumer, who has grown to demand rapid and regular delivery of small consignments from stock, and considerable after-sales service. The decline in relative importance of heavy industries and the growth of suppliers of consumer goods has had a similar effect. In some cases organizations serving a national market, such as the Co-operative Wholesale Society, have set up two or more duplicate factories to supply different parts of the country. This has the additional advantage in some industries of making each factory less unwieldy to run than a single, very large plant. The important consideration is no longer merely the cost ex works [a term similar to our f.o.b.], but the cost delivered to the consumer.

FINANCE

The mechanism for finance of new industries has a powerful effect on industrial location. Until recently it was almost impossible for finance to be found for a new industry in a depressed area. A region is depressed because it needs industries to employ its work-people, but because it is depressed it is a poor market for consumer goods, and therefore an unattractive location for a light industry.

As well-to-do and enterprising people can most readily leave depressed regions, and have in many cases done so, a further obstacle to revival has been created. Men who have the resources and temperament to be financial backers of a new enterprise tend to live in the South, and to favour mainly, if not exclusively, projects in that part of the country, so that they can keep in touch without the inconvenience of long journeys.

* * *

TRADING ESTATES

In the past each factory had to make separate arrangements for its site and buildings, transport, electricity, gas, water, heating and other services, including workers' welfare. Recently the trading estate has been developed as a means of providing some or all of these services on a commercial basis, and often also of renting the premises instead of compelling the industrialist to own them. In what circumstances, if any, is the trading estate economically inferior to the old system? That it has some advantage is indicated by the fact that the two oldest British trading estates have kept many industrial tenants and made fair profits over long periods. Trafford Park has paid an average return of nearly 4 per cent since its foundation in 1896. Among advantages of trading estates are that they enable new works to be started quickly without locking up much capital in land and buildings and without risk of finding that some necessary services cannot be economically provided on the site, that they give a lower cost both of erection and of supplying the factory with services, owing to bulk facilities on one spot, and that they can raise capital for development at low rates of interest. Such services can, however, only be economically provided if the estate is above a certain minimum scale—including, say, at least 75 factories of average size. Factories of all sizes occur on trading estates, but it is not clear whether certain works needing very extensive sites may not be more economically located elsewhere. Perhaps the most serious defect of existing trading estates is the inconvenience of many of their sites in relation to workers' housing.

* * *

SPECIAL LOCAL SKILLS

The need of particular skill is gradually losing its relative importance as a localising factor, for although skill is still required in industry, it is of a different kind from that of, say, fifty years ago.

A good example of an industry located almost entirely by skilled labour—it might almost be said in spite of certain other disadvantages—is the pottery industry. To quote the Board of Trade evidence before the Royal Commission on the Geographical Distribution of the Industrial Population:

The manufacture of china and earthenware is highly localised in "the Potteries" district of Staffordshire. According to Stamp and Beaver, there are certain difficulties in explaining why the industry should have become concentrated there. There appear to have been no records of pottery works there before the seventeenth century. "In the Middle Ages the making of rough earthenware pots was a typical domestic industry widespread over the countryside; in fact, carried out wherever there was clay together with wood for firing. In the seventeenth century coal replaced wood for firing, but on practically all the coalfields there are belts of clay suitable for rough pottery manufacture. It would seem that the industry was favoured in the North Staffordshire Coalfields because of its isolation, and the comparative poverty of the region agriculturally. The agricultural land was in the main occupied by small-holders, and the industry grew up as a sideline to agriculture. Pots were made in a shed at the side of the dwelling-house or the cowshed. The men dug their own clay, often in their own garden, and at least some of the families dug the coal with which to fire the ovens. Lead for powder glazing was obtainable from Lawton Park, six miles north in the carboniferous limestone. And thus there grew up amongst the agricultural population a large number of skilled master potters." It is noteworthy that the Potteries have maintained their dominant position in the industry notwithstanding that it is an inland district and much of the raw material has to be brought from a distance, e.g. china clay from Cornwall. The explanation is probably to be sought in the type of men, the Wedgwoods and others who, through generations, served the industry. Technical progress was rapid and the industry was ready to experiment; but the underlying motive was that the potters' trade was "a skilled trade with a tradition to follow" and new inventions were made "supplementary to skill and not subversive to it. The Staffordshire potteries by native skill improved their own earthenwares until they put other centres out of business."

* * *

LINKAGE WITH OTHER INDUSTRIES

Many industries are so linked to others that their location cannot be considered independently—for instance, the manufacture of textile machinery has to be near the cotton and woolen centres of Lancashire and the West Riding. There is also a continuous process of industrial evolution. . . . This process is often almost unrecognized at the time, but in some cases offshoots are purposely developed in order to offset slackness in another branch of the business, or to keep a labour force employed at off-peak periods. The chance location of the initiator often decides location, and sometimes the proprietor of a new works may deliberately place it to suit his leisure occupation, like the keen yachtsman who chose to manufacture iron piano frames at Burnham-on-Crouch.

Choice of location is therefore a complex blend of factors, some conscious and others unrecognised, some directly and others only very indirectly economic. Generally a site which is advantageous in some respects is disadvantageous in others, and whether or not all the considerations are weighed there remains great scope for the individuals in control to make the ultimate decision according to personal preferences.

Many of the Birmingham industries provide excellent examples of location by linkage, the relationship existing chiefly in materials and processes; for instance, brass and copper goods required by the electrical industries.

The usual reason for juxtaposition of linked industries is to minimise transport costs, but this may sometimes be effected at the expense of being compelled to employ more costly labour. In such circumstances it might be advisable to choose a location elsewhere, the increased cost of transport being offset by cheaper labour. For example, works making moulded plastic products for use in motor cars might, perhaps, be profitably situated at some distance from the assembly works. On the other hand, local loyalty often results in preferential placing of orders with local firms.

LOCAL EVOLUTION

Finally, mention must be made of . . . the process which has been called industrial metabolism, though industrial evolution would perhaps more accurately describe the changes which actually take place.

One of the best examples of this process is provided by Coventry, where a watchmaking industry developed into the manufacture of bicycles, which in turn gave rise to that of motor cars, and more recently aero-engines and aero-planes. This kind of development is based partly on the similarity of the skilled labour required, and partly on ability to use at least a proportion of the same plant for the old and the new manufacture. It also depends on the fact that these industries usually have a number of skilled workers working more or less independently, with a wide range of adaptability. It follows that industries which employ labour and plant of a highly specialised character peculiar to themselves, or depend largely upon some geographical feature, are less likely to produce this kind of development than others which are not so specialised. Thus coal mining is extremely unlikely to undergo evolution in the foregoing sense, while the manufacture of electric light fittings, for example, could quite easily do so. Again, leather manufacture (tanning and dressing) is less likely to develop in this way than, say, cotton weaving, which has already given rise to the weaving of rayon, staple fibre and other similar materials.

An extreme example of a rapid change in industrial composition by this process is provided by Wolverhampton, where it is stated that scarcely a single person is employed in the same work as he was ten years ago. This kind of development, assuming that the necessary conditions exist for its progress, can originate from several causes.

In the preceding selection it was mentioned that labor is one of the primary economic factors in the location of industries, and that employer-worker antagonisms have declined. The selection that follows will present a brief picture of the three main sections of the British Labour Movement—industrial, trading, and political. This is followed by a more detailed statement of the industrial side, leaving for later consideration the trading, or cooperative, aspect and the political power of labor.

Anyone familiar with the American labor movement will see many similarities between it and the British trade-union movement. We, too, have the craft unions (forming the American Federation of Labor) and the industrial unions (the Congress of Industrial Organization). But, as in England, the distinction between the two types sometimes becomes vague, although the arbitrary boundary is preserved in the formalities of organization. In both countries the collective agreement, or contract, results from collective bargaining between management and labor; when the two cannot agree, the matters in dispute may be left to an impartial arbitration board for decision. In other instances, a mediation board may step in to try to work out a compromise between the two parties.

One striking difference is apparent. In England, labor has gone actively into politics with its own political party, but in the United States the leaders of organized labor have preferred to offer support to one or the other major party in return for expected sympathetic treatment. Also, in England there is one central body, the Trades Union Congress, which represents all labor, although it has no power to bind the constituent unions. Another important difference lies in the fact that a far greater proportion of English than American workers are unionized. But in both countries labor—and often this means organized labor—must be considered a major factor in the economy and a group of utmost importance in the society.

• 67 • *Trade Unionism*
G. D. H. COLE

The British Labour Movement has three main sections—industrial, trading and political. For collective bargaining and common action to protect the workers as wage-earners or producers, there exist Trade Unions, covering altogether about 9½ million workers as compared with a total 'occupied' population in civil employment of about 22 millions. For the protection of the workers as consumers, mainly by means of mutual trading and the

[From *The British Working-Class Movement,* Fabian Publications, London, 1949. Pp. 5-11. Used by permission.]

co-operative organisation of the production of essential goods, there are Co-operative Societies, with a membership of about ten millions, representing a considerably larger total number of consumers. The political organisation, which exists to further workingclass aspirations towards a better social and economic system, is a good deal more complicated, as it is based largely on the Trade Unions and Co-operative Societies. The Labour Party is partly a federation of Trade Unions with certain other bodies, of which the Fabian Society has been one ever since the Party was formed; and there is also a Co-operative Party which, though separate in organisation, works in close alliance with the Labour Party. We have, moreover, to take separate account, in the political field, of the Communist Party, which has its own organisation and policy, and has steadily been refused admission to the Labour Party as an affiliated body, and also of the Independent Labour Party, formerly affiliated to the Labour Party but now outside it and greatly reduced in numbers, and of a number of other small bodies standing for some form of Socialism, or setting out to organise the workers politically for some special or limited purpose.

*   *   *

The three main sections—Trade Union, Co-operative, and Political—have each their own central co-ordinating bodies. The Trades Union Congress is a federation of national Trade Unions representing the various industries and occupations, and claiming to represent the collective standpoint of organised Labour in industrial matters. The Co-operative Union, which organises the annual Co-operative Congress, links together not only the local distributive Co-operative Societies, or Stores, but also Co-operatives of other types —the Wholesale Societies, the Producers' Societies, and the 'auxiliary' bodies, such as the Co-operative Women's Guilds. The Labour Party includes, in addition to the Trade Unions and other national bodies affiliated to it, the Local Labour Parties organised on a constituency basis, with individual members

as well as locally affiilated Trade Union branches and other bodies; and closely associated with it is the Parliamentary Labour Party, consisting of its elected representatives in the House of Commons and the small contingent of Labour peers.

These three main bodies are linked up in turn in the National Council of Labour, which issues from time to time major pronouncements on Labour policy and is designed to promote closer unity between the three sections.

*   *   *

TYPES OF TRADE UNIONS

There were in all, in December 1947, 730 Trade Unions in Great Britain, with over nine million members. The Trades Union Congress had, in the same year, 188 affiliated Trade Unions, with nearly eight million members. . . .

There are three main types of Trade Unions—*craft* Unions, organising skilled workers belonging to a particular trade or group of trades; *industrial* Unions, setting out to enroll all the workers in a particular industry, skilled and unskilled together; and *general workers'* Unions, enrolling mainly less skilled workers from a wide range of industries, but also organising skilled workers for whom no recognised craft Union exists. Typical examples are the London Society of Compositors, the United Pattern-makers' Association, the Amalgamated Association of Operative Cotton Spinners (*Craft* Unions); the National Union of Railwaymen, the Iron and Steel Trades Confederation, the National Union of Mineworkers (*Industrial* Unions or close Federations); the Transport and General Workers' Union, the National Union of General and Municipal Workers (*General Workers'* Unions). Not all Unions will fit neatly into this classification. For example, the Amalgamated Engineering Union is basically a Union of skilled men in a number of kindred crafts, but has also latterly opened its ranks to include less skilled male workers and, since 1943, women. The National Union of Public Employees resembles a general workers' Union, but is limited to employees of public authorities. The Associated Society of Locomotive Engineers and Firemen is mainly a craft Union of footplate workers, but includes also engine cleaners, most of whom hope to become drivers or firemen later on. There is a good deal of friction between mainly *craft,* or *kindred craft,* and *industrial* Unions over the organisation of both skilled and less skilled workers in some industries— for example, in the railway engineering shops and in the engineering industry generally, and between the National Union of Railwaymen and the Associated Society of Locomotive Engineers and Firemen over the organisation of the footplate grades. This friction, however, is a good deal less acute than it used to be a generation ago; and in many cases rival Unions have reached some sort of working accommodation—e.g., the Mineworkers and the Amalgamated Engineering Union about colliery craftsmen, and the N.U.R. and the Transport and General Workers' Union about the employees of railway-owned omnibuses.

In 1948 there were four Trade Unions with more than half a million members (Transport and General Workers, 1,264,000; General and Municipal Workers, 824,000; Amalgamated Engineering Union, 742,000; National Union of Mineworkers, 572,000). Two others (National Union of Railwaymen, 462,000; Union of Shop, Distributive and Allied Workers, 343,000) had more than a quarter of a million; and there were four more with over 100,000. The six largest Unions included well over half the total membership of the Trades Union Congress; and of these six, the two largest were *general workers'* Unions, three *industrial* Unions, and one (the A.E.U.) betwixt an *industrial* Union and a Union of *kindred crafts.* Craft Unions tend in most cases to be relatively small, as there are not many very numerous skilled crafts. The largest is the Amalgamated Society of Woodworkers (200,000).

In general *craft* Unions have higher contributions and benefits than others, usually including sick pay and sometimes superannuation as well as dispute benefit. *Industrial* and other Unions catering for a wide variety of workers sometimes have several scales of contributions and benefits, for different classes of members, or provide for voluntary contributions and benefits for sickness. Dispute benefit is provided for in all Unions except some in the public services, which do not use the strike weapon. But in recent years not very much has been spent on this benefit, as authorised strikes have been few ever since 1926. A large part of the expenditure of most Unions has to go on administration costs, including all sorts of services to members in collective bargaining, organization, and defence in legal cases (e.g., workmen's compensation).

TRADE UNION STRUCTURE

The basic Trade Union unit is the local branch (or lodge, among the miners), of which a big Union may have several in a single town. In such cases, the local branches are usually grouped round a District Committee, which is the main local body for handling industrial questions. Many Unions have District or Divisional Councils covering wider areas, usually with a full-time District Organiser; and some of the largest Unions have also full-time local officers. But most local Trade Union work is done voluntarily, or in return for small payments to cover expenses and lost time. Full-time officials are usually employed by the Union nationally, even when they serve a local area, and usually work under the orders of the National Executive.

National Trade Union Executives usually consist of persons working at their trades, and meet only occasionally (quarterly or monthly, with special meetings in case of need). Members are paid small fees ('delegation') to cover expenses and time lost. Most Unions have also Delegate Conferences, annual, biennial, or even triennial, which finally determine policy and make or alter rules. Executive members are sometimes elected by the Conference, and sometimes by ballot vote of the members. Some Unions use the ballot of members as a frequent means of settling policy issues. This applies especially to the Miners, and to some of the craft Unions. In the general workers' Union the Executive usually has very large powers. The chief full-time officials are often elected by ballot of the membership, but some Unions elect their officials at Conference. Lesser officers are sometimes elected by ballot, but more often chosen by the Executive. Trade Union constitutions differ greatly, in the main according to the organisation of the industry concerned. In some cases—e.g., building, printing, engineering—bargaining is largely local in the first instance, usually with an appeal to a national joint body, and arbitration or strike action in reserve in case of failure to agree. In other industries, from the nature of the case, bargaining is mainly national (e.g., railways, post office); and in many some questions are dealt with nationally and others locally (e.g., coal mining). The central issues of bargaining are standard rates of wages, hours of labour, holidays, overtime pay, and 'recognition' of Trade Unions for purposes of local or factory as well as national bargaining. A good many Unions have *shop stewards* in the factories, to see that membership is kept up, and to take up workshop grievances; but usually such stewards are not given much negotiating power, which is mainly reserved for District Committees and for the national Unions and their officers. One object of this is to prevent works agreements in conflict with national or district agreements; another is the fear that shop stewards may be inclined to throw over Trade Union 'discipline' or to act in violation of agreements not to strike until certain procedures have been followed. During the war, Joint Production Committees were set up in many war factories, for the purpose of improving organisation and output, but these were distinct from Shop Stewards' Committees. After 1945 many of these bodies were discontinued; but there has been a revival since, encouraged both by the Government and by the T.U.C.

Trade Union branches are usually based more on where members live than on where they work, and where there are several branches of a Union in a town the members working in the same factory may be scattered over the branches. Some Unions, however, take the place of work as the unit (e.g., to a large extent Miners, Iron and Steel Workers, Newspaper Printers, Distributive Workers). Those who favour more 'workers' control' in industry usually advocate the extension of shop stewards, shop stewards' committees, Joint Production or Consultative Committees, and branches based on the place of work.

Attendance at Trade Union branch meetings, and also frequency of meetings, differ greatly from Union to Union. In most cases only a small proportion of the members attend, unless there is some special excitement such as a dispute or wage-claim on foot. Many Unions collect subscriptions at branch meetings; but others have collectors who go from house to house, and others collect largely at the place of work, so that members need not attend the branch to pay. Normally, therefore, votes at branch meetings represent directly the views only of the keen minority, though they may, of course, correctly interpret the general opinion.

COLLECTIVE AGREEMENTS

In most big industries there are nowadays national agreements laying down both certain basic conditions of employment and the procedure to be adopted, locally and nationally, in adjusting differences. These agreements usually run for a term of years. In some cases they provide for reference to impartial arbitration in case of failure to agree. A good many Unions use the Government's Industrial Court as a tribunal for this purpose (or the National Arbitration Tribunal—set up during the war, to deal with disputes when strike action was forbidden—and continued since 1945). In a good many cases agreements cover a number of Unions in the same industry; and these Unions are often federated for common action (e.g., National Federation of Building Trades Operatives, National Printing and Kindred Trades Federation).

Strike action was limited up to 1947 (apart

from wartime limitations) by the Trade Union Act of 1927, which outlawed the General Strike and any sympathetic strike held to be designed to 'coerce the Government'; but this Act was repealed in 1947, and in general strike action is now limited only by the temporary continuance of the requirement to refer disputes to the National Arbitration Tribunal or to some other court of arbitration. The 1927 Act also prevented Civil Servants from joining with workers in private employment, either in the Trades Union Congress or in the Labour Party, and severely restricted picketing; but the Trade Unions have now recovered the freedom they enjoyed under the Trade Disputes Act of 1906.

THE T.U.C. AND THE TRADES COUNCILS

The central Trade Union body is the Trades Union Congress, with its General Council elected by the delegates as a whole to represent the main industries and groups which act as nominating sections. There are also two seats reserved for women. The General Council acts as the central body to represent industrial Labour, but has no power to bind the affiliated Unions. Neither the General Council nor the T.U.C. itself can call a strike: this has to be done by the separate Unions concerned. The General Strike of 1926 was called by a Special Conference of Trade Union Executives convened by the T.U.C. General Council. There is no general negotiating body to deal with wages and conditions. The General Council has, however, a joint committee with the Employers' National Confederation and the Federation of British Industries for discussion of general industrial questions; and it is represented on a number of general advisory committees of employers and Trade Unionists and on other official bodies set up to advise the Government both on labour matters and on wider questions of production, prices, rationing, etc. Locally, Trade Union branches are federated in Trades Councils, which exist to deal with general questions in their areas, but have no negotiating functions. They are chiefly organising bodies, and agencies of protest against local grievances. The Trades Councils have County Federations, a National Advisory Committee, and an Annual Consultative Conference; but these federal agencies have little power. The central Trades Councils machinery is in the hands of the T.U.C. General Council.

WOMEN

Of the total of about 9½ million Trade Unionists, about 1¼ millions are women—a rise since 1939 when there were just under a million women in Trade Unions, mostly textile and distributive workers. Women are harder to organise than men, partly because many of them leave employment on marriage, and partly because they are largely employed in less skilled work. Female membership rose greatly during the war, but has fallen since, as many war workers have retired from 'gainful employment'.

By now we should see clearly that an industrial economy has many kinds of occupations and that people demand of it numerous services. Great Britain has moved far toward the socialization of its economy by its nationalization of a number of industries, which is one way of saying that the government undertakes to manage for the people large segments of the economy. The problems that such a program encounters are discussed by Warren Haynes, an American economist who, as a Fulbright Fellow on leave from the University of Kentucky, made a firsthand study of the coal industry in Britain. He has prepared the following summary of his findings especially for this volume.

• 68 •   Nationalization in Great Britian
WARREN HAYNES

Nationalization is not a difficult word to define. A nationalized industry is a publicly-owned one; nationalization is the process of converting private assets to public ones. It follows that there is nothing peculiarly British about nationalization; in the United States we have a nationalized post office; the Tennessee Valley Administration was the means by which some assets of private enterprise were nationalized.

In Great Britain the overwhelming victory of the Labor Party in 1945 made it clear that an extensive program of nationalization would be carried out. The Party's platform, "Let Us Face the Future," called for public ownership of a number of industries: coal, gas, electricity, inland transport, iron and steel. It also promised to take over the Bank of England. As soon as it went into office, the Labor Government, headed by Clement Attlee, proceeded to draw up bills to fulfill these promises.

What was the purpose of nationalizing these industries? The Labor Party hoped public ownership of the "basic" industries would assist it in several ways:

1. Through control of investment in these industries, the Party felt it could more readily carry out an economic plan which would eliminate unemployment and assure that resources flowed into socially useful channels.

2. Public ownership of these industries would eliminate private monopoly in their sphere (replacing it, of course, with public monopoly) and would help break down the concentration of economic power in the hands of a few private individuals.

3. Nationalization would be a step in the direction of socialism "which can not come overnight as the product of a week-end revolution." It should assist in the redistribution of personal incomes, an item which has high priority in most socialist programs.

Nationalization of industry, at least for the immediate future, was to be restricted to "basic industry," which Labor leaders estimated at 20 per cent of all industry. At some future date further measures might be taken. On this, the Party was divided. The extreme Left wished to move rapidly to take over the insurance companies, the shipbuilding concerns, the joint stock banks, the docks, the aircraft industry, the automobile industry, cement, chemicals, and wholesaling. A much larger section of the Party favored a more moderate program; the goal of 20 per cent of industry was quite sufficient for it. There was even a section of the Party (Herbert Morrison was rumored to be its leader) which was opposed to taking over iron and steel, on the grounds that the Government had quite enough on its hands.

Before moving on to specific measures, several points should be made clear. First, nationalization is not a new thing in Great Britain. The Post Office had long been governmentally owned, and the Post Office had owned the telephone systems of Britain since 1892. The British Broadcasting Corporation, a government agency, had a monopoly over broadcasting. The London Passenger Transport Board, the Port of London Authority, and the Central Electricity Board were all examples of government enterprise before 1945. Many of these agencies were established by Conservative governments.

Second, it should be made clear that nationalization of the coal, electricity, gas, and other industries does not in itself constitute "socialism" as defined by the Labor Party, though perhaps it may be considered the core of the Party's platform. Many other measures, springing from the socialist creed, were put into effect between 1945 and 1950. The Health Insurance program, price control, rent control, supervision of monopoly, subsidized housing, town and country planning, and extended social insurance are but a few of these. This report proposes to discuss only a part of the Labor Government's achievement—the progress of the new publicly owned industries.

THE NATIONALIZATION ACTS: 1946-1950

The election of 1945 was followed by a series of complicated nationalization acts, which altogether take up hundreds of pages and have been elaborated by thousands of pages of regulations. The following summary of these acts must of necessity be highly simplified; later sections will go into one of the acts in greater detail—the Coal Nationalization Act of 1946 and will attempt to spell out what nationalization means in practice. For the present, let us summarize all the acts briefly.

1. *The Bank of England Act, 1946* This Act provided for the vesting of the stock of the Bank of England in the Government. This would be comparable to nationalizing the Federal Reserve Bank in the United States; the member banks were left untouched, except that government ownership of the Central Bank perhaps meant closer supervision of their activities. This Act was by no means a revolutionary measure for Britain; the Bank of England had already worked closely with the Treasury. The Conservatives put up little opposition to this measure, recognizing that a small change was involved.

2. *The Coal Industry Nationalization Act, 1946* This Act established a National Coal Board, which was to be responsible to Parliament through the Ministry of Fuel and Power. The Coal Board was to take over the assets of the private coal companies, except some very small unimportant ones. This act will be discussed more fully in later sections.

3. *The Cable and Wireless Act, 1946* This Act provided for public ownership of the stock of Cable and Wireless Ltd. It had the support of all the parties in Parliament and received a unanimous vote. Since the telegraph lines within Great Britain were already publicly owned and had been since 1870, this Act, which took over lines to some foreign countries, was not a radical step. The object of the Act was to unify all the telegraph services into one coordinated system, so that cooperation with Commonwealth and American systems could more readily be attained. The directors of Cable and Wireless were to be appointed by the Government and to come under the Postmaster-General.

4. *The Electricity Act, 1947* A large step toward nationalization of the electricity supply had been taken in 1926, when the Central Electricity Board was set up to coordinate electricity supply. The Central Electricity Board took over control of the generation and long-distance transmission of electricity, but the distribution of electricity was left to the old private companies and municipal systems. The new act provided for public ownership of the whole electricity supply industry: generation, transmission, and distribution. The British Electricity Authority, consisting of ten to twelve members appointed by the Minister of Fuel and Power, was to be the overall coordinating agency. Fourteen Area Boards were also established to distribute the power —thus much authority was delegated to regions. It is interesting that the chairman of the Electricity Authority has been Lord Citrine, formerly a Trade Union leader and General Secretary of the Trades Union Congress for many years.

5. *Gas Act, 1948* Under this Act, the Government took over the gas production and distribution facilities of Great Britain. A Gas Council was established at the center, and twelve Area Boards in the various regions. The organization differed from that in the electricity supply industry in that much more power was delegated to the Areas under the Gas Act. In fact, each Area Board is an almost completely autonomous public corporation, and the Gas Council is primarily a central discussion agency. The Council and Area Boards all come under the Minister of Fuel and Power. The trend towards decentralization, carried even further in the Iron and Steel Act, is one of the most significant developments since 1946.

6. *Transport Act, 1947* This Act established a British Transport Commission con-

sisting of from four to eight members appointed by the Minister of Transport. As in the Electricity Act and the Gas Act, powers were delegated to lower agencies but in this case these agencies were functional rather than regional. The five executives under the Transport Commission are known as the Railway Executive, the Docks and Inland Waterways Executive, the Road Transport Executive, the London Transport Executive, and the Hotels Executive, all of whom are appointed by the Minister of Transport.

The Transport Act is an extremely complicated one. All the railroads were taken over, but only part of the trucks (called lorries).

7. *Iron and Steel Act, 1949* The Iron and Steel Act did not become effective until February 15, 1951. It has been the most controversial of the nationalization measures. The Conservative Party has denounced this Act as unconstitutional, since it feels that the majority of the people do not want it. Accordingly, the Conservatives have promised to reverse the Act when they are restored to power. [Since this was written, early in 1951, the Conservatives have been able to take steps toward accomplishing this reversal.] Furthermore, it is clear that the Labor Party is split on the issue, though Labor Party Members of Parliament voted together for the bill to maintain party unity. This Act differs from the others in that the old firms were left intact as individual units, with their old names, the Government taking over the controlling stock. As far as possible, it was hoped that the same Directors would remain in charge.

An Iron and Steel Corporation was formed to supervise the activities of the individual firms. Small firms, producing under 20,000 tons of iron and steel, were not nationalized. The Iron and Steel Corporation consists of from five to eleven members appointed by the Minister of Supply.

SOME COMMON FEATURES OF THE NATIONALIZATION ACTS

While the above acts have of necessity had to be varied according to the conditions of each industry, there are a few things to be said that apply to all or almost all of them.

1. The Acts demonstrated the belief of the Labor Party that nationalized undertakings should be run by public corporations; that is, instead of having a government department run the industry, as is done in the case of the post office in both Great Britain and the United States, the authority would be delegated to a special corporation set up for this purpose. In this, these corporations are like the Tennessee Valley Administration or the Reconstruction Finance Corporation in the United States. However, unlike the T. V. A. and the R. F. C., the autonomy of the British public corporations established since 1945 is somewhat limited by the fact that each comes under a Cabinet Minister, such as the Minister of Fuel and Power, the Minister of Transport, or the Minister of Supply. The Minister in each case has substantial powers over general policy, but can not interfere in day-to-day matters.

2. In each act provision was made for parliamentary control. Various control devices are in use: the Minister is always subject to questions from Members of Parliament; occasionally the activities of the boards are subject to open debate; the boards must all present detailed accounts to Parliament which are discussed and debated. In general, Parliament is not supposed to debate day-to-day activities of the boards, but so far it has been found difficult to separate routine affairs from broader policy. For example, there was a considerable discussion in Parliament over the health of Ned, a pit pony (used in mining), who some M.P.'s (Members of Parliament) felt was not receiving proper treatment.

3. In each act there were provisions for compensation to the former owners. The calculation of the amount of compensation has necessarily varied in method from act to act, because each industry involved special considerations. Compensation was paid partly in cash, but mostly in the form of Government securities, which in some cases were to be non-transferable. The amount of compensation has been subject to arbitration and in

most cases there is little basis for attacking the fairness of the amounts. The most controversial aspect of compensation has been the nontransferability of some of the Government bonds issued.

4. In most of the Acts, Consumers' Councils have been set up to represent the interests of consumers. These report over the heads of the boards to the Ministers, and each Minister has power to put recommendations of Consumers' Councils into effect. To date, the general feeling, even among Labor Party Members, is that the Consumers' Councils have been ineffective for the most part.

THE COAL INDUSTRY: A CASE STUDY IN NATIONALIZATION

In order to give a more concrete picture of what nationalization is all about, it is proposed to go into detail on one of the nationalized industries—the coal industry.

Conditions of the Coal Industry before Nationalization. Perhaps it would be best to give a picture of the industry before nationalization, since accomplishments and difficulties under public ownership can not be understood without some knowledge of what went before. It is fair to say that the British coal industry was in extremely bad shape before nationalization, especially in the 1930's. Some of the major problems were:

1. *Instability in the demand for coal.* The markets for coal were falling off rapidly in the late 1920's and 1930's. The level of unemployment went above 25 per cent, not for just a few months, but for year after year. The miners slowly began to leave the industry; between 1920 and 1940 the number of workers fell from 1,227,000 to 749,000. Even so, every once in a while there would be a shortage of workers; both in World War I and World War II there were not enough men to meet the nation's need and coal shortages prevailed.

2. *Bad labor relations.* The labor relations were worse than in any other major industry. Strikes were numerous; over half of all time lost in strikes in all industries between the wars was lost in coal mining. The workers were generally hostile to the owners, but,

of course, this pattern varied from area to area.

3. *Low productivity.* Output per manshift (O. M. S.) is the usual measure of productivity in the coal industry. Output per manshift in British mines was less than one third of that in American mines. Moreover, Great Britain was not increasing productivity as much as continental countries between the wars. While O. M. S. in Holland rose by 118 per cent and in the Ruhr by 81 per cent between 1925 and 1936, the rise in Britain was only 14 per cent. And in World War II, the O. M. S. actually fell. Two reasons for low productivity can be stated: the best seams of coal in Britain had been worked out and it was necessary to work thinner, deeper, gassier, and more faulty seams; also, mechanization in British mines had fallen behind, partly because geological conditions were unsuited to some of the new methods.

4. *Lack of integration in the coal industry.* It has been generally agreed that the coal industry before 1947 was broken up into too many small units. It is not possible in this brief paper to go into the technical advantages of larger scale production; it is sufficient to state that most economists agree that the coal industry was not making the most of these advantages. Also the industry was not working cooperatively in attempts to stabilize prices and wages. Strange to say, in the 1930's the Government tried to force a degree of monopoly on the private owners and these owners refused to accept this power.

5. *Unsatisfactory working and living conditions.* The low wages of miners between the wars, the harshness of their working conditions, the high level of accidents, and prevalence of industrial disease are all too well known to deserve further comment. Unfortunately, most miners found little relief from hard working conditions in the home, since housing was usually inadequate, and mining towns were dreary places marred by nearby mountains of slag. All this contributed to the bitterness of miners.

Arguments for the Nationalization of the Coal Industry. The arguments of the socialists for public ownership of the coal industry follow from the above description of conditions under private ownership. It should be noted that the coal royalties, that is rights to underground seams, had been nationalized in 1938, but the big issue was whether the mines themselves should be run by the Government instead of the seams being leased out to private companies.

The socialists argued that nationalization would make possible a more economic organization of the mines; pits could be amalgamated; the government would be able to finance massive projects of mechanization; and uneconomic pits could be abandoned.

The public would benefit, it was claimed, from lower costs and prices and from elimination of what the socialists considered to be exorbitant profits. The public, through the government, would be able to control the industry and abolish undesirable practices.

One of the major claims was that human relations would be improved under public ownership. The workers would no longer be face-to-face with the owners they so long had despised; they would have a greater sense of participation in the running of the industry. It was further claimed that government ownership would bring a sounder conservation program, so that the rapidly depleting coal would not be wasted.

Structure of the National Coal Board. The Coal Act of 1946 set up a National Coal Board, originally of eight members but now more. This Board was appointed by the Minister of Fuel and Power, to whom it was responsible. The Board itself is a "public corporation," by which we mean that it is not a mere subdepartment of the government, but has a life of its own. In theory a "public corporation" is supposed to have a great deal of independence; it should be very much like a private corporation except that the government owns all the assets. In practice, the independence has been limited by the powers of the Minister of Fuel and Power to issue regulations governing the industry and to veto decisions of the Board, and also by parliamentary control.

The Chairman of the Coal Board has been Lord Hyndley, a former coal owner and director of one of the largest private coal concerns. Two trade union leaders were appointed to the Board, one of them a former miner. Two well known mining engineers, several business men, a college professor of physics, and an eminent civil servant were appointed to the other positions. It is of interest that there has been some conflict between the labor members and the engineers, and both engineers have resigned in a huff.

The Board could not run its 1500 mines directly from London. It set up eight (now nine) Divisional Coal Boards and, under them, forty-eight Area General Managers to help manage the industry. As much as possible the Coal Board tried to use the old managerial personnel, and the staffs of the mines themselves were left untouched in most cases.

Results of Nationalization. How has nationalization changed the coal industry? Has it solved the human and technical problems that have so long plagued the industry? The following comments are brief and tentative, but should help answer these questions.

1. *Employment and unemployment.* Unemployment has been virtually wiped out in the post-war period. Where uneconomic pits have been closed, the workers have either been moved to other pits or paid compensation. There have been plenty of jobs available; in fact, the difficulty since the war has been to find men to fill the vacancies in the industry. In a sense, full employment in Great Britain has been a curse to the coal industry, making it difficult to draw men from other industries and making it easy for coal miners to find more pleasant jobs outside. One of the major jobs of the Coal Board has been to hold on to its work force; in the first two years it succeeded in increasing the number of miners; in 1949 and 1950 the wastage has been greater than recruitment. If the rate of loss of men experienced in 1950 were to continue, there would be no coal industry in 27 years. However, in the first few months of 1951, workers are again moving to the coal mines, perhaps partly because of recent wage increases and

partly to avoid the draft from which miners are exempt.

The elimination of unemployment and the difficulties of holding on to the work force can not be attributed to public ownership. Almost all British industry has known high employment since the War. Wastage was severe under private ownership and it is likely that without nationalization there would be even fewer miners and a much more severe coal shortage.

2. *Wages and working conditions.* Miners' wages have been increased markedly since nationalization. An index of weekly wage rates in the industry rose from 208 in July 1946 to 294 in September 1950 and further increases have been granted in October 1950 and January 1951. Since 1939 miners' wages have moved from among the lowest to among the highest in British industry. One must beware of giving all credit to public ownership, however. The wage increases under private management during the War doubled wages; private management would have had to increase wages substantially in the period 1947-1950 to try to keep the miners from leaving the industry. It is probable the wages would have been just as high without nationalization.

The biggest advance made by the miners has been the granting of the five-day week in May 1950, a reduction from the former five-and-a-half days. Since the miner was to get six days' pay for five days' work, provided he stayed on the job all week, this was considered a great victory. It is unlikely that private owners would have granted this benefit quite so readily. Some observers have questioned whether the country could afford this reduction in hours in a period of coal shortage, but certainly the move has increased the attractiveness of mining and has undoubtedly encouraged miners to remain in the pits.

A number of other benefits were granted: increased welfare activity, special payments for injured miners and dependents of those killed in accidents, etc. With modernization of some of the pits, working conditions have improved slightly, and the accident rate has fallen.

3. *Labor relations.* It would be expected that miners would be highly pleased in winning the public ownership they have so long desired. If one asks a miner if he is better off under nationalization, the reply is almost certain to be "yes." The satisfaction does not run very deep, however. Most miners evidently expected some kind of dramatic change. But on vesting date (the day the government took over), the miner left his home at the usual hour, walked or took a bus to his pit in the usual way, went through the usual routine of putting on pit clothes, and descended into the mine. He found that the same deputy was in charge and above him the same overman, under-manager, and manager. His pay was the same (for the first few months) and his daily task no less.

Most miners seem to be somewhat disappointed by nationalization. Many expected that the workers themselves would be running the mines. While a few former miners and union leaders have been placed on the National Coal Board and on regional boards, the workers do not control the industry, though the workers' viewpoint is more actively sought than ever before.

The miners continue to grumble about past abuses. Many miners still complain about "capitalism" in the industry and seem unaware of the changes that have been made. Then there is criticism of the Coal Board itself; the miners in general have very little real loyalty to the Board; to some of them it seems remote and inhuman.

One would expect that better labor relations would be manifested in lower absenteeism and fewer strikes. Absenteeism in mining has been extremely high since the middle of World War II. In 1945 and 1946 it reached a peak at a rate of 16 per cent for all workers and 19 per cent for face workers. Since the government has taken over the mines on January 1, 1947, absenteeism has fallen slightly, but disappointingly so, especially in view of the shorter work week. Absenteeism is an extremely complicated subject, and there is not sufficient space here to analyze it. One interesting point to be made is that higher wages among British miners do not seem to encourage longer hours of work; in fact, many miners appear to want to buy leisure with their higher pay; the same is probably not true of American miners.

The number of man-days lost in strikes since nationalization has certainly been less than in the 1920's or early 1930's. There has been no "official" (that is, union-led) strike since vesting date; but there have been numerous small "unofficial" strikes carried out against the union's wishes. In fact, there were over 1000 strikes per year in the first three years of public ownership. Less than one per cent of total production was lost in these strikes, but in these years that one per cent was extremely important.

It appears that to date no revolution in human relationships has come about; perhaps in a longer period the habits of the past will break down.

4. *Production and supply levels.* In January and February, 1947, the most serious coal shortage in Britain's history took place, partly because insufficient stocks had been built up in the years preceding and partly because the winter of 1946-47 was the most severe in 50 years. Transportation was tied up so that coal stocks could not be moved. This coal shortage can not be attributed to nationalization; it could not possibly have been avoided with the Coal Board's heritage from an earlier era. It was clear, however, that the downward march in coal production would have to be halted.

In the first few months a small but encouraging rise in production took place, and, despite the five-day week, production has continued to increase ever since. Output per manshift has risen from 1.03 in 1946 to over 1.18 in 1950. The 1938 O. M. S., the prewar peak, was 1.14, so that the losses of the War have more than been met. The picture is not so bright as it might at first appear, however. Large sums have been spent on moderniza-

tion of the industry. Britain still lags behind most other countries in output per man, even behind countries where geological conditions are equally difficult.

How is it that Great Britain at present (February, 1951) again finds herself with a coal shortage despite increases in production? Britain has been trying to build up foreign markets for her coal; in 1950 she tried too hard. The rapid decline in the number of miners in 1949 and 1950 was unexpected, so that production did not rise as much as was expected. Moreover consumption of coal in 1950 rose more rapidly than was anticipated, especially because of increased use of electricity and gas. The country is barely scraping through the present coal crisis; industrial production has not suffered as yet but railway services have been cut.

5. *Costs, prices, and profits.* Costs have risen under nationalization, partly because of the higher price of supplies but even more because of higher wages. The cost per ton was 41 shillings in 1947 and rose to 45 shillings in 1949. In 1947 prices were not enough to cover costs and the Coal Board lost £23 millions. By the simple capitalistic device of raising prices, the losses were turned into profits in the following years: £1,650,000 in 1948, £9,470,000 in 1949, and probably about the same in 1950. Not too much emphasis should be placed on profits or losses, since the monopoly position of the Coal Board makes it possible to make a profit whenever it desires. The Board's policy, however, is to break even—to balance profits in some years against losses in others.

Coal Nationalization in the Midlands. Perhaps a more concrete picture of nationalization will be possible, if we look at the outcome in a particular region—the Midlands. As was pointed out earlier, the National Coal Board set up eight (now nine) Divisional Coal Boards. Two of these are in the Midlands; the West Midlands Divisional Coal Board and the East Midlands Divisional Coal Board. These Divisions were in turn broken down into Areas: four Areas in the West Midlands and eight in the East Midlands. Every area, then, contained a number of mines, each run by a colliery manager—in most cases the same manager as before nationalization. Altogether there were 60 mines in the West Midlands and 102 in the East Midlands on the vesting date.

Of all sections in the country, the East Midlands has had the greatest success in increasing production. Production has risen from 33 million tons in 1946 to over 40 million tons in 1950; O. M. S. has risen from 1.45 in 1946—already far above the national average of 1.03—to 1.73 in October, 1950. If all the British coalfields had had this experience, Britain would not be faced with a coal crisis. Indeed, she would be a heavy exporter of coal; costs of production would be lower in most industry; it might even have been possible to avoid the most severe aspects of the "dollar shortage."

The success of the East Midlands can be partly attributed to the more satisfactory geological conditions there: thicker seams and fewer faults, with more possibility for the newest types of mechanization. But credit must also be given to better labor relations in the region and the absence of many of the restrictive practices found in other sections. The managerial leadership in the East Midlands appears to be more dynamic and progressive; Sir Hubert Houldsworth, the chairman of the Division, is extremely active in putting new ideas into operation and winning the miners' support of these ideas. Paradoxically, absenteeism in the East Midlands is higher than elsewhere. Again it is suggested that the higher wages may be a factor.

The West Midlands has also increased production, but not to the same degree. The West Midlands was a larger producer of coal before the Great Depression, but now produces less than half as much as the East Midlands. Under nationalization, production in the West Midlands has risen from 16 million tons to 18 million tons. The West Midlands has also been relatively free from strikes, compared to the British total. O. M. S. was above the national average on the vesting date, but has not risen as rapidly as in the East Midlands, and today is around 1.33. The West Midlands is an older producing area and the best seams have already been worked out.

The East and West Midlands have been the most profitable regions under public ownership. It might be said that the profits of the Midlands are used to subsidize the losses of other regions, such as Durham and South Wales.

CONCLUSION

After four years of public ownership, three major issues face the National Coal Board and the other nationalized industries. To date no simple answer to these questions has been found.

1. The first question has to do with decentralization: how far should the Coal Board and other public corporations attempt to delegate powers to local agencies? We have seen that the Electricity Act and especially the Gas Act provided for greater degrees of decentralization than did the Coal Act, but even those acts have been criticized for centralizing too much power in London. The advantages of decentralization are numerous: decisions can be made more readily at the local level; more attention can be given diverse local conditions; there is less chance for red-tape and slow moving bureaucracy to develop; and labor does not feel that its masters are quite so remote. But decentralization is not so simple a question as most critics of the National Coal Board think. There are definite economies in centralizing such things as research; someone has to coordinate coal production plans for the whole industry; if the national Exchequer is to be a source of funds for the industry the national government must have some control; some agency must answer to Parliament for industry; and the workers themselves insist on nation-wide bargaining.

Despite the difficulties, the National Coal Board has been moving toward greater decentralization. Perhaps this development has been too slow; those who have worked in government or army agencies know that it is much harder to break a large unit into small ones than to reverse the process.

2. The second question facing the Coal Board and the other corporations is that of the position of the workers in nationalized industries. On one extreme are those who argue that the workers should have complete control; this might endanger the interests of the general public. Others argue that the workers should have representatives on the Boards, not a few ex-trade-unionists as there are at present, but real representatives voted upon by the workers. The objection to this is not only that such boards might place the workers' interest above the general public interest, but also that such representatives would have a split loyalty between the government on the one hand and the workers on the other. In fact, a large part of the trade unions are opposed to such representation, feeling that the unions must maintain their independence. The alternative that has the greatest support is the proposal that the present separation of management and worker representation through the unions be maintained, but that both management and the workers be educated to work more cooperatively than in the past. The National Coal Board, like the other boards, has set up an elaborate joint consultation machinery through which it is hoped that the workers and managers will be able to communicate their desires and anxieties more effectively. A great deal of experimentation on worker participation in public corporations is likely. So far, no satisfactory formula has been found.

3. The last question has to do with the relation of the public corporations to Parliament. One group argues that the industries should be made departments of the government and that any attempt at autonomy is hopeless. This view recognizes that Parliament is going to snoop anyway so why put up the pretense of independence. The opposite group argues for even greater independence than now exists, to keep the boards as far as possible from politics and so that strictly business, as opposed to civil service, methods be adopted. This issue is still open.

Thus we see that the final form of nationalization has not been achieved; much more experimentation will take place. It will pay us to watch the public corporations in Great Britain, for similar experiments are being carried out in the United States. Each country may learn from the successes and failures of the other.

The selection that follows was prepared especially for this book, to present the impressions of an American housewife (who is also a trained sociologist). She was impressed, as any American visitor would be, with the queues, the rationing, and the extensive and difficult shopping expeditions necessary to obtain various household essentials.

It should be kept in mind that Mrs. Haynes was in England during the winter of 1950-1951, and that since then some changes in the economic and political scene have taken place. Austerity remains, and rationing of some items continues, but there have been attempts to remove as many items as possible from the rationed list. Also, the reduction of subsidies has resulted in some price rises. The new Conservative Party Budget, formulated by Mr. Richard Austin Butler, the Chancellor, has cut imports by some 600 million pounds, even at the risk of further highly inconvenient shortages.

• 69 • An American Housewife in Leeds
CATHARINE K. HAYNES

I am sure that if I had come to England on a flying tour, stayed in London a week, then spent a night in a quaint inn in Stratford-on-Avon, and perhaps stopped over in York on the way to Edinburgh, my impression of the country would have been entirely different. I should probably have gone home and commented, "What beautiful green country! What a feeling of history! What picturesque little inns!" I should have been enthralled with the little I saw for one quickens to the beauty, to the sense of the past evidenced on all sides. Any guide book will confirm this.

It has been my good fortune, however, to have a more intimate and prolonged view of this country by living and keeping house in it. At first it **was** the many differences in our ways of life that struck me, and with my American bias and open curiosity, it was toward these things that my attention was turned. Now, after only a few months, I find that the curious has somehow melted away. For example, just the other day, I realized that I no longer noticed a difference in speech.

When we first moved to Leeds, a northern industrial city, we started to look for a flat (no one uses the word "apartment" here, but it is the same thing). We did not have to look long to confirm the guidebook's hint that there was little or no central heating here. The first flat we looked at had a coal grate in the front room and bedroom; the water was heated by electricity. The second flat, which we took, had a small coke stove in the living room and a coke heater for the water. There was a gas poker to start the fire —this was simply an open-ended poker attached to an outlet. This was to save much trouble for we did not have to lay the fire with paper and wood to get it started; there have been many times on particularly cold days, however, when it has taken as long as two hours to get the fire started. Generally we can count on about two and a half hours to get enough hot water to take baths; it does not take long to understand why the English are not so bath-happy as are Americans.

One common means of supplementing the heat is by electric fires (heaters). We have a small one in our bedroom which is a very large room; you can imagine that the heat is dispelled quite as rapidly as it comes off the wires. We have been in homes where the living room was heated entirely by electric fires. At first, when you come in out of the cold, you feel quite toasted, but later even a heated argument fails to take away the chill that gradually permeates your bones.

The heating of the bathroom proved to be somewhat a bone of contention. We found that few bathrooms in England are heated; ours was no exception. We asked our landlady about the possibility of putting an electric fire into the bathroom, but she was quite alarmed over the idea since a number of people had been killed by wet contact with electric fires. This alarm was echoed by several other people, so it was with a feeling of being a saboteur that I crept to the electrician's shop and bought a utility fire. (In England, there is at present a utility line of goods, which is generally low cost and serviceable, not subject to purchase tax. The purchase tax on more decorative and luxury articles is very high—this tax has been as high as 100 per cent.) Now after a half-hour of current running through the heater, one can no longer see one's breath in the bathroom.

When we first came to Leeds, I noticed that women invariably carried little satchels, or small suitcases, or shopping bags. I was curious about this until I went to the grocery for the first time. The grocer had no paper bags but was willing to sell me a paper carrier bag for three pence. After wearing out several of these in rapid succession, I joined the ranks of women carrying baskets or leatherette bags.

This was my first indication of the paper

shortage in England but I was to encounter this many times over. I recall shopping for some towels in one of the leading department stores in town; my purchase was wrapped in used paper. My grocer has wax paper for the meat, but around that goes newspaper. At the bakery, biscuits (which can mean anything from soda crackers to cookies) are usually put in paper bags, but quite frequently the bread is not wrapped at all. I notice that many women bring used bags with them. Perhaps the shortage is most noticeable in the size of the newspapers. *The Sunday Times* is ten pages long; compare that with the Sunday edition of the *New York Times* or Louisville *Courier-Journal*. There is very little advertising in the papers—much of it appearing in the fine print section like our classified ads sections. Typing paper is very hard to find. Yesterday when I finally found some copy paper, the clerk told me that they had received a shipment the day before and I had bought the last ream. A clerk the day before had told me that he expected their next shipment in from four to six months. Around this shortage, there have developed certain accepted practices. Envelopes are used a second time; government envelopes bear a printed suggestion to slit the envelope on the side and use it again. Clerks in the shops frown if you do not pop the article into your shopping bag, rather than wait for it to be wrapped. There is a regular collection of clean waste paper to which you are expected to contribute.

The lack of paper is just one of the features of English shopping that one notices to be different from ours. In America, it is becoming more and more common to go into a huge super-market, wheel a large basket through the store, and load it with staples, meat, fruits, and vegetables. Not so in England. You go to the green grocer for fruits, vegetables and fish; to another shop, for your staples; to the butcher's for your meat; to the bakery, for bread; to still another, for sausage and luncheon meats. I never do my weekly shopping without going to at least four shops—and this is not "shopping around."

The shops are very small and I have yet to find a self-service store.

In shopping, of course, one must have ration books. Meat, lard, eggs, butter, margarine, sugar, tea, yellow cheese, bacon, and candy are still rationed. To get our ration books, we had to present ourselves at the local office of the Ministry of Food. Here we had to wait in a queue. (The English have become famous for their queues. One falls into them automatically at the grocer's, in offices, at the streetcar stop, everywhere. There is no pushing or shoving. I have yet to see anyone break a queue.) A courteous official filled out numerous application forms with great efficiency and explained to us that we would have to register with a grocer and a butcher for our rationed goods. This meant that we would have to buy our goods from these people for at least eight weeks; after that time we could make a change if we so desired. When we registered, the grocer sent in a form to the Ministry of Food office; this enabled him to get the supplies for us. The ration points are marked off in the book rather than cut out in most cases.

Just to give an idea of what the ration is, here is an approximate list of purchases made for *two* people in the last week of January, 1951:

8 oz. butter
8 oz. margarine
3 oz. lard
3-4 oz. cheese
1 pound sugar
2 eggs
4½ slices of bacon (about twice the size of a slice of bacon in the United States)
¼ pound tea
1s/10d (about 25 cents) worth of meat—four lamb chops in this case

Frequently, the egg ration will be more; sometimes I get four eggs and once I got six. The most frequent number, however, is one per person. The meat ration is to be reduced even further from the above figure, as just announced by the Minister of Food, Mr. Webb; it has been reduced to 8 pence (9-10 cents) per person. (This is the lowest meat ration yet, even counting war time, and Mr. Webb says that he sees little hope of the situation markedly improving for years.) On the other hand, the bacon ration has gone up from 3 ounces per person to 4 ounces.

There are, however, numerous things which one can use to fill in this gap—tinned luncheon meats, rabbit, poultry, pork, and beef sausage. The famous pork pies are not rationed. Fish is a common substitute for the English. It has been interesting to note that non-rationed foods are much more expensive than rationed meats. When one could get a juicy rationed roast, it cost about 50-60 cents (for an exceptionally good one), whereas a chicken for two might cost as much as two dollars. One feels that rationing has meant that everyone could get his share. Tourists, fresh from the more austere England, have raved about the availability of steaks and the like on the continent. What they fail to see is that the tourists and the well-to-do there have meat which is far beyond the purses of the ordinary person.

Marketing, attempting to get variety and balance in meals takes infinitely more time and skill here than it does in the States. Tinned foods are not so commonly used here and frozen foods, though obtainable, are rather out of the reach of the usual budget. It is not surprising, therefore, to find that people in this part of the country rarely entertain with dinner. Coffee at the after-dinner hour and, of course, afternoon tea are the more common invitations.

For cooking, many people still use coal stoves. Quarry Hill Flats, a huge housing project in Leeds, has coal stoves for cooking. Gas and electricity are probably used more commonly, however. Fortunately, we have a gas stove, for during the recent power cuts, many women found themselves without heat as they started to prepare the evening meal. For a number of weeks in the fall and winter, our lights would go off for an hour every day or so. These power cuts increased in frequency in this area until they reached a climax on what was known in the North as "Black Monday," when there were seven power cuts, taking up almost the entire day. England generates almost all of her electricity from coal; the country is not only short of generators but of coal as well. During the day when industrial demand for power reached its peak, the generating plants would indulge in "load-shedding" (power cutting), primarily in the residential areas in order to enable industry to go on. Even so, industry seemed to suffer loss of production at times.

The shortage of fuel has been felt everywhere. With one week's supply of coke left, we find the coal dealer saying, "We'll do our best to get it to you, but we are five weeks behind in our orders as it is." We were, however, never without fuel. One family had to get a doctor's statement to get coal enough to heat a patient's room. Our landlady was invited to tea and told to bring her fur coat to wear during tea. A housing estate manager told me that many people on the housing estate were low on fuel; some even had to stay in bed to keep warm during a part of the day. Many people undoubtedly have sufficient fuel but all have to conserve carefully. The need to conserve fuel recently led the Minister of Fuel and Power, Mr. Noel-Baker, to ban display lighting. This has not made as drastic a change in the night landscape of the city as an American might imagine, for there are not the lavish displays of neon lights in English cities that there are in America. Piccadilly Circus, in the heart of London, is the only brilliantly lighted section I have seen in this country.

In the present crisis people are hoping that the weather will not become cold again. The cold weather, which is fairly persistent through the winter months, is penetrating, particularly because of the dampness. The coldness is nature's way of keeping foods here, for "fridges" are rare, but the dampness has no assets. It creates quite a problem in drying laundry. I remember hearing a young mother complain that the baby's laundry never seemed to get dry. I find wool socks, for example, taking about a week to dry in the kitchen, which is the warmest room in the house. The warm moist air in the kitchen is continually condensing on the walls, so that the walls appear to be sweating. Toothbrushes never dry; towels hang limp and damp on their racks day after day.

These are a few of the things that the British housewife—indeed, the whole family —has to put up with. In addition, the average middle-class English housewife has far fewer labor-saving devices than has the equivalent American woman. Formerly, she probably had a servant, but now she no longer competes with the attractive wages factories can offer girls. Perhaps the presence of servants generally through the middle-class homes of the past may be part of the explanation for the lack of gadgets and the like. Now, few people can afford them; some perhaps remain loyal to the old way of doing things as well.

Perhaps all this has sounded like an American grumbling about the differences in another country's way of doing things. It is meant as nothing of the sort. At first one finds things different and even hard at times, but one gets tips from the women here and forms habits without even being aware of the adjustments. This, however, is undoubtedly facilitated by the fact that this is a temporary set-up and not a life-time pattern. I am writing this more to tell a little told story of the English woman. I think we used to think of her, with her beautiful complexion, sipping tea out of Wedgwood cups while a maid catered to her every whim. She sips her tea all right, but she has to work harder than the average American housewife to take that break so universal in the English home. Moreover, one never hears a complaint. One housewife told me, after Mr. Noel-Baker had called upon the housewives to conserve fuel, "The housewife is always called upon to make the pinch, but she must never complain. It just isn't done."

It was indeed fortunate that this trip did not whisk me through the tourist centers of the land and let it go at that, for the England I have had the brief opportunity of seeing is not only rich in beauty and history, but stout in heart.

Social Organization

and Process

>>

An industrial society develops a complex political and social life. In our study of the Chinese peasant we found that the family was the chief pattern of association and thus played a major role in regulating life. In the old Cotton South, also, the family held an important central place, although the relationships among individuals and among groups within the society were considerably complicated by the patterns of stratification resulting from slavery. The New South is today taking over the economic and societal patterns of the rest of the United States and is cooperating in a network of governmental programs of national scope. Thus it has come about that even the traditional speeches on "states' rights" by Southern politicians sometimes have a hollow ring, for the local patterns of control have long since begun to give way to national patterns.

England affords us an example of a country in which government, as the agent of the whole (nationwide) social group, has come to the fore and exercised dominant control over many phases of the economy—and, either directly or indirectly, over many of the social patterns and activities. In the United States, on the other hand, we are still heatedly debating the extent to which the "public" federal government should exercise powers formerly or still held by "private" economic groups. But in both England and the United States there is no question that the individual's life is dominated by government or business or both, and that the family and the religious group no longer exercise their former degree of authority and control throughout the whole society. Furthermore, in both these societies many activities have come to be oriented toward some aspect of buying and selling or of money-making. Education, for example, is regarded by many people as primarily a matter of teaching people how to make a living, a function it used to perform to only a very slight degree. As another example, the commercialization of recreation is familiar to us all.

As we read the selections that follow, the influences exerted by economic organizations and by the government through those who hold statuses in connection with them will become apparent. We can note, too, how the value system tends increasingly to enlarge such statuses, while legislative bodies and public opinion both seek to limit the ways in which these people in positions of power and trust may behave. The banker as well as the bureaucrat finds himself bound by many more restrictions than formerly, but these are simply a reflection of these individuals' increasing prestige and power. Also, we can try to discover the relative importance of competitive and cooperative activities and the degree to which the compromise or accommodation is accepted in social relations. We shall see, too, the extremely assimilative character of an industrial society. Later selections will also treat of the motivational processes of socialization and social control.

It is well known that social scientists, who try to deal with phenomena systematically, are not the only people who have examined the society in which we live with great care. The travel book and the novel may present much the same information, though in a quite different way. J. B. Priestley, one of the foremost English men of letters, took an extensive trip through England in 1933. What he saw in his visit to the Midlands is presented in the next selection. Priestley's interests ranged widely, touching on not only the physical appearance of places but the work and the recreation of the people there. The nonconformists, whose religious activities interested him, are the Methodists, Baptists, and other Protestants who do not belong to the Established Church of England. Priestley is amused that young people use the Birmingham Corporation Art Gallery as a trysting place, and he tries to decide whether the model town of Bournville is a blessing or a curse to the workers in the chocolate factory there. His observations are revealing, and his ability as a professional writer gives them a vividness that is often lacking in the less personal accounts of the overserious scientist. It should be kept in mind that Priestley made his trip during the depression of the 1930's. Its devastating effect on the people, which is reflected in conditions he observed, was a major factor behind popular demand for the nationalization of certain industries.

• 70 • *To Birmingham and the Black Country*
J. B. PRIESTLEY

BIRMINGHAM

. . . I caught the bus that runs between Coventry and Birmingham. It was very full and so very uncomfortable. The weather was still fine but colder than it had been, with a sharp nip in the wind. We trundled along at no great pace down pleasant roads, decorated

[From *English Journey*, Harper and Brothers, New York, 1934. Pp. 60-90. Used by permission of publisher and author.]

here and there by the presence of huge new gaudy pubs. These pubs are a marked feature of this Midlands landscape. Some of them are admirably designed and built; others have been inspired by the idea of Merrie England, popular in the neighbourhood of Los Angeles. But whether comely or hideous, they must all have cost a pot of money, proving that the brewers—and they seemed to be all owned by brewers—still have great confidence in their products. At every place, however, I noticed that some attempt had been made to enlarge the usual attractions of the beer-house; some had bowling greens, some advertised their food, others their music. No doubt even more ambitious plans for amusement would have been put into force if there had been no opposition from the teetotallers, those people who say they object to public-houses because you can do nothing in them but drink, but at the same time strenuously oppose the publicans who offer to give their customers anything but drink. The trick is—and long has been—to make or keep the beer-house dull or disreputable, and then to point out how dull or disreputable it is. It is rather as if the rest of us should compel teetotallers to wear their hair long and unwashed, and then should write pamphlets complaining of their dirty habits: "Look at their hair," we should cry.

In the midst of a russet solitude, we came upon a notice board saying, *This is the City of Birmingham*. There was nothing in sight but hedgerows, glittering fields and the mist of the autumn morning. For a moment I entertained a wild hope that this really was the City of Birmingham, that the town had been pulled down and carted away. Not that Birmingham had ever done anything to me. I had never been there; this was my first visit. I knew very little about it. The little I did know, however, was not in its favour. I had always thought of the place, vaguely, as perhaps the most typical product in civic life of nineteenth-century industrialism, as a city of big profits and narrow views, which sent missionaries out of one gate and brass idols and machine guns out of another. It made a

great many articles, chiefly in metal, but so far in my life not one of these articles had gained any hold over my affections. I had never said, "Good old Birmingham!" myself, and never heard anybody else say it. In my limited experience, *Made in Birmingham* had been a dubious hallmark. And the Chamberlain family had supplied no heroes of mine. Then there were jokes about a foolish Watch Committee there. On the other hand, any guide-book could offer a great many facts on the credit side. In the eighteenth century, Birmingham had a Lunar Society that met every month, and among its members were James Watt, Matthew Boulton, Joseph Priestley, Josiah Wedgwood, Erasmus Darwin, Sir William Herschel, and Samuel Parr: a good all-around team of talents. The number of important inventions, from the steam engine to gas lighting and electro-plating, that either first saw the light or were first brought to perfection in this city, is very impressive. Its commercial success has not been merely a matter of geography and geology, the fact that it has been the centre of a district rich in coal, iron, wood, and sand. History comes into play here. Not being a place of any importance in the Middle Ages, Birmingham was not controlled by the guilds and did not suffer from the various restrictions imposed upon the then larger towns. It was not a chartered borough and therefore Nonconformists were free to settle and work there, and as the industrial revolution was largely nonconformist, Birmingham was able to take full advantage of it. Thus, when you hear jokes about the Birmingham Watch Committee and chorus girls' stockings, you are really at the end of a very long chain of historical cause and effect. Having allied itself to the black slavery of industry, the city managed to strike one or two stout blows for liberty in other directions, for which it must be given credit. And now it is the second city in England. By the time I had considered these matters, the fields had gone and we were passing houses and shops and factories. Did all this look like the entrance into the second city in England? It did. It looked a dirty muddle.

Where the bus finally stopped, a Birmingham citizen asked me if he could carry my two bags to the hotel. He was a young man, this Birmingham citizen: he was dressed in a ragged brown coat and a pair of patched and torn flannel trousers and the wreck of a pair of boots; his face was swollen and it was so long since he had shaved that he was well on his way towards wearing a matted tow-coloured beard. On our way to the hotel, I asked him a good many questions, but many of his replies I cannot give you because he spoke so badly that I could not catch them. But he was twenty-two, had been out of work since he was sixteen, was not receiving the dole, had a father but no mother, and his father was also out of work. It was a fair step to the hotel, and one of my bags, I knew, was heavy; so I told him to put them down and rest the moment he was tired; but there must have been good blood and bone somewhere in that ruin of a young fellow, for he never stopped or even slowed up but moved on at a good pace until he came within a yard or two of the hotel porter, who looked at him in a fashion that most of us would hesitate to adopt in talking to a mongrel that was snapping at our heels. However, I gave him a florin, which was what he usually made, with luck, in a whole day, and he went off delighted. There was a sudden access of civic dignity in the place. Here in Colmore Row you could imagine yourself in the second city of England. There is a really fine view at the end, where the huge Council House turns into Victoria Square. You see Hill Street mistily falling away beneath the bridge that the Post Office has thrown high across the road. If there is any better view in Birmingham than this, I never saw it. For a moment, as you stand there, you believe that at last you have found an English provincial city that has the air and dignity that a great city should have, that at last a few citizens who have eyes to see and minds to plan have set to work to bring comeliness into the stony hotch-potch, that Birmingham has had the sense to design itself as well as its screws, steam cocks, and pressure gauges. This is an illusion, and the only way in which to keep it would be to hurry away from that corner in a closed vehicle and see no more of Birmingham.

I could not do that, but I did the next best thing: I entered the Corporation Art Gallery and Museum, of which I had heard a good deal. The Director of the Gallery assured me that Birmingham had always had its craftsmen too and proved it by showing me case after case of local silver ware, some of it of tasteless design but all of it admirably executed. He also showed me some drawings done by young students—one of them only a boy of fifteen—at the local school of art; and these were surprisingly good. He assured me too that Birmingham could be very generous towards its Gallery and Museum. There were two cases of exquisite Chinese porcelain, and he told me that the necessary sum—I think it was between two and three thousand pounds—to buy these objects of art, which are quite useless and will never declare a dividend, had been raised in a few days. Oddly enough, two other cases of Chinese porcelain, equally exquisite, had been lent to the museum by a famous comedian, whose jests about Birmingham's prudery I still remember. The Picture Gallery is famous for its wealth of examples from two English schools, the old water-colourists and the Pre-Raphaelites. I did not spend much time with the Pre-Raphaelite collection, which is particularly rich in drawings, because I get very little pleasure these days from the work of Burne-Jones and his friends. . . .

. . . At the entrance to this art gallery and museum, they put up the daily returns of visitors. The recent average was about eight hundred a day on week-days, with a sudden leap into thousands on Sundays. This is not, I was told, because Birmingham has a passion for art on Sunday afternoon, but because then all the young people promenade up and down the galleries, not looking at pictures but at one another. Apollo has to serve Venus. But what of it? The boys and girls have to begin mating somewhere, and they could obviously begin their acquaintance in much worse places. And you never know. Venus may be a strict task-mistress, but no doubt Apollo is allowed a word now and then. A picture will occasionally catch an eye, then hold it; and so the old leaven of art will start working. There may be new masterpieces presented to this gallery in twenty years' time because a boy and girl were promenading and "clicking" there last Sunday afternoon. The director, a wise man, is of the same opinion. No doubt there are protests in Birmingham as there are elsewhere; and probably from those people—who must hate the whole commerce of the sexes—who protest with equal vehemence against the youngsters going anywhere else on Sundays, and when they have finally driven them out into the streets, protest against their being there too. They forget, these protestors, that both cities and the Sabbath were made for man. If the social arrangements do not fit in with the time-old desires of ordinary decent human nature, it is the social arrangements that should be changed.

I had lunch in one of those buffets that are so popular now in the larger provincial towns. There is a chef in a tall white cap, whom everybody calls Joe or Fred, and a white-jacketed waiter or two; and you sit on tall stools and have a slice or two of cold meat, a little salad, and perhaps some cheese. All very pleasant, and useful in preventing one from eating a larger lunch than one needs. But I take this opportunity of declaring that these places seem to me to charge a great deal more for their food than it is worth. After having a very light lunch, you find you have as much to pay as if you sat down and demolished three or four solid courses. Why?

So long as you keep within a very narrow limit in the centre, Colmore Row, New Street, Corporation Street, Birmingham has quite a metropolitan air, and on the fine afternoon I first explored them, these streets had quite metropolitan crowds in them too, looking at the windows of the big shops and hurrying in and out of cafes and picture theatres. The city has a passion for arcades, and I never remember seeing more. It also has a passion for bridging streets usually by joining two tall buildings somewhere on the third or fourth story. When you get to the end of New Street, you can cross into Paradise Street and then arrive in Easy Row. There you find the white Hall of Memory, built to commemorate the 14,000 Birmingham men who were killed in the great war, some of them possibly with bits of Birmingham metal. Behind this Hall of Memory is Baskerville Place, called after the great printer, John Baskerville: and I should like to think there was something symbolic and fateful in the conjunction of this war memorial and the famous printing press. Among the many statues in this part of the city there is one to Joseph Priestley, whose house was sacked and burned down by the mob not long before he himself was compelled to leave the country altogether. It is a pity that some of the charred remains of his library and laboratory were not kept to be exhibited by the side of the statue.

Tired of walking round, I climbed to the top of a tram. I did not know where it was going, and when the conductor came for his fare, I said I would go as far as the tram went, and took a threepenny ticket. As if it knew what was about to happen, the sun immediately went out. This treachery did not leave us in a kindly dusk—it was too early for that—but only in the middle of quite a different day, lowering and sullen. Then followed one of the most depressing little journeys I ever remember making. No doubt I was tired. And then again the electric tram offers the least exhilarating mode of progress possible. It is all very well for the Irish poet "Æ" to call them "those high-built glittering galleons of the streets"; but no man inside a tram, no matter how he strains his fancy, really feels that he is inside a glittering galleon. The people show a sound instinct when they desert the tramway for any other and a newer kind of conveyance. There is something depressing about the way in which a tram lumbers and groans and grinds along, like a sick elephant. Undoubtedly the tram helped. But it was Birmingham itself that did most of the mischief. In two minutes, its civic dignity, its metropolitan airs, had vanished; and all it offered me, mile after mile, was a parade of mean dinginess. I do not say that this was a worse tram-ride than one would have had in Manchester, Liverpool, Glasgow, any of our larger cities, or smaller ones either for that matter; I am not making comparisons between cities now. I only know that during the half-hour or so I sat staring through the top windows of that tram, I saw nothing, not one single tiny thing, that could possibly raise a man's spirits.

Possibly what I was seeing was not Birmingham but our urban and industrial civilisation. The fact remains that it was beastly. It was so many miles of ugliness, squalor, and the wrong kind of vulgarity, the decayed anaemic kind. It was not, you understand, a slum. That would not have been so bad; nobody likes slums; and the slum hits you in the eye and you have only to make an effort to get it pulled down. This was, I suppose, the common stuff out of which most of our big industrial towns are made. And those of us who have not to live or go shopping or amuse ourselves in such a thoroughfare as this probably do not notice it at ordinary times; we are on our way somewhere else and we let it slip past us, outside the motor or the tram-car without ever having a good look at it. But I was there, on that tram, to have a look at it, and if I was tired and perhaps a little low-spirited when I began, I was still more tired and far lower spirited before I had done. For there was nothing, I repeat, to light up a man's mind for one single instant. I loathed the whole long array of shops, with their nasty bits of meat, their cough mixtures, their *Racing Specials,* their sticky cheap furniture, their shoddy clothes, their fly-blown pastry, their coupons and sales and lies and dreariness and ugliness. I asked myself if this really represented the level reached by all those people down there on the pavements. I am too near them myself, not being one of the sensitive plants of contemporary authorship, to believe that it does represent this level. They have passed it. They have gone on and it is not catching up. Why were the newest and largest buildings all along this route either picture theatres or pubs? Because both of them

offer an escape: they are bolt-holes and safety-valves. Probably not one person out of a thousand along that road would roundly declare, "All this is a nasty mess, and I'm sick of it." But it is my belief that at least six hundred of them out of that thousand entertain an unspoken conviction that is constantly troubling them inside and that calls for either the confectionery drama of the films or for a few quick drinks. I think I caught a glimpse then of what may seem to future historians one of the dreadful ironies of this time of ours, when there never were more men doing nothing and there never was before so much to be done.

The conductor announced the terminus. I had arrived. I got out, to find that we had climbed to the top of a hill and that a cold wind was blowing over it, bringing dust and grit and filthy bits of paper. On one side was a stretch of high brick wall, which some posters told me was a sports ground. On the other side were some patches of waste ground and some decayed allotments, where the last green rags of gardening were shivering. Further along was a yard filled with rusted parts of motors and scrap-iron. I walked to the end of the brick wall and saw below and afar the vast smoky hollow of the city, with innumerable tall chimneys thrusting out of the murk. The wind dropped, and all along the edge of the pavement the filthy bits of paper settled for a moment before beginning to rustle uneasily again. A tram came making its ponderous moan, and I signalled it like a man on a raft seeing a sail. On the way down I looked at nothing, but some little things caught my eye. One of them was a notice outside a grimy tabernacle: *Get the Brotherhood Spirit.* What would happen, I wondered, if we did. Surely the result would startle those mild folk who put up that notice, for there would first be such a burning down and blowing up and wholesale destruction. Or so, in that depressed hour, it seemed to me.

Having some work to do, I stayed in my room and tried to collect my thoughts and some words for them. It was difficult because of the shattering noise. Are we breeding a race of beings who find it possible to think or rest or sleep in rooms vibrating with the roar of changing gears and accelerated engines, rooms that do not merely admit noise but that shake and ache with dreadful sounds? I stayed in this hotel bedroom several days, paying handsomely for the privilege, and the quantity and quality of rest and sleep I obtained in it were pitiful. Only the small hours were reasonably quiet and by that time one was often too tired and fretful to take proper advantage of the silence. If we are not breeding these new sound-proof beings, then this idiocy cannot go on or the nervous system of the race will break down. If I were dictator, I would insist upon a series of noiseless inventions and sound-proof devices, and threaten with exile any ingenious but misguided fellow who invented anything that added to the din. Perhaps I ought to have said all this to the page-boy I sent out for cotton-wool, which still remains the best aid to quiet, better than clever little gadgets of rubber or plaster. It was late when I went down to dinner, and much later when I wandered out into Colmore Row for a breath of air before bed. It was not quite eleven o'clock, however, and the look of these Birmingham main streets was very queer, for they were all blazing with light and yet almost empty. Victoria Square was like another Place de la Concorde. Never have I seen such brilliant illumination in a provincial city. But the old habits had prevailed; the theatres and picture palaces had closed; the crowd had gone home to bed; and central Birmingham emptily sparkled and shone as if it expected the arrival of a new and more nocturnal set of citizens. No doubt they are already on their way.

BOURNVILLE

I spent the next day, which was fine and warm, at Bournville. There were several good reasons for doing this. To begin with, I was interested in the manufacture of chocolate, having bought and eaten in my time great quantities of the stuff, and having several times, when I was about ten, tried unsuccessfully to make it myself. Then I wanted to see

another highly organized giant works, and Cadbury's was one of the biggest in the country. Again, Cadbury Bros. were renowned as employers of the benevolent and paternal kind, and I wanted to see what it was they did. And again, there was Bournville itself, the village. So out I went, through dignified Birmingham, messy Birmingham, to planned Birmingham, which had put on its autumnal colouring and was looking charming.

There are a good many things to be said about Bournville, the village. The first is that it has nothing whatever to do with the firm of Cadbury Bros., Ltd. This came as a surprise to me—as I imagine it will to many people—for I had always thought that the firm built the village for its work-people, on a sort of patriarchal employers' scheme. Nothing of the kind. Here are the facts as they are set out in one of the Bournville publications.

The Bournville Estate was founded by the late George Cadbury in 1895. In 1879, he and his brother Richard, who were partners in business as Cocoa and Chocolate manufacturers, moved their works from the centre of industrial Birmingham to what was then an entirely rural area, four miles from the city. The removal gave George Cadbury an opportunity to put into practice ideas he had long in mind, the result of his contact with working men as a teacher in Early Morning Adult Schools, with which he was connected for over fifty years. He had been led to the conclusion that the root of most social evils lay in the bad housing conditions in which all too many had to live. He was himself fond of country life, and knew its material and spiritual advantages over life in crowded industrial areas, and when the factory was thoroughly established in its new environment he began to see ways and means of giving more and more people the opportunity to enjoy it. He did not, however, contemplate a scheme only for the benefit of his own workpeople; rather, his idea was to make what he called 'a small contribution to the solution of a great problem'—the problem of housing as affecting large industrial towns.

He bought land in the neighbourhood of the factory, and in 1895 began to build Bournville village. Five years later—in 1900 —the estate covered 330 acres, and 300 houses had been built. At that time, in order to secure the perpetuation of his ideas, he handed over the whole property to a body of Trustees—the Bournville Village Trust —on behalf of the nation. He thus gave up entirely his financial interest in it, and secured that all profits—for it was set up on a sound commercial basis—should never accrue to any private individual or body, but be devoted to the development of the Bournville Estate, and to the promotion of housing reform elsewhere.

These then are the facts. It is worth noticing that this Quaker manufacturer, fifty years ago, talked about something that the newspapers and the government are just beginning to talk about now, namely, bad housing. And he not only talked, but he did something. And what he did has proved very successful. His Trust Deed was really a housing plan that could be legally enforced. Thus, he laid down that each house was not to occupy more than a quarter of its own site, that factories were not to take up more than a fifteenth part of any developed area, and that one-tenth of the land, in addition to roads and gardens, should be given up to parks and recreation grounds. Since then, the Trust has really acted like a local authority. It has leased land to Public Utility Housing Societies, which are on a co-partnership basis. These societies—and there are four of them—build houses and then rent or sell them to their members. Some experimental bungalows—each made of different material—have been built, as a test of costs and durability. There are some tiny bungalows, for single persons. There is also a residential club for business women. Some of the owners and tenants work for Cadbury Bros. Others come to Birmingham, and are clerks, artisans, teachers, and so forth. The vital statistics in the booklet I have before me

are of some importance. They are taken from an average of the seven years ending 1931. Death-rate per 1,000: England and Wales, 12.1; Birmingham, 11.6; Bournville, 6.5. Infantile mortality per 1,000 live births: England and Wales, 69; Birmingham, 72; Bournville, 56. Some years ago, the heights and weights, age for age, of Bournville children and children from one of the bad areas in Birmingham were compared, and the Bournville children were from two to four inches taller and between four and nine pounds heavier. And the Estate is flourishing.

I saw the whole of the village; if it can still be called a village for now it has the size and population of a small town. Its tree-lined roads, pleasant spaces, villas and gardens are not, of course, the eye-opener they must have been thirty years ago. Nevertheless, they are still infinitely superior to and more sensible than most of the huge new workmen's and artisans' quarters that have recently been built on the edge of many large towns in the Midlands. For example, in many of these estates, no provision whatever has been made for recreation, whereas in Bournville you see everywhere recreation grounds and halls. Model yachting is very popular in this district and it was decided to make another small lake in one of the recently developed areas. A gang of unemployed was brought out from Birmingham to do the digging and draining, and most of these men were not professional navvies at all. For the first day or two they worked with raw and bleeding hands; but they stuck it, and out of the whole fifty or sixty, only one dropped out. And now the little lake is there; I saw it myself, ready for whole fleets of model yachts. (I mention this for the benefit of those people—and there are still plenty of them—who think that most unemployed men are unemployable, or, if not that, at least not very willing to go very far out of their way to find work. I should like to set some of these people on a long digging job in heavy clay.) The village would look prettier if it did not consist almost entirely of detached and semidetached small villas. I would prefer houses arranged in small courts and squares. I do not understand this passion for being detached or semidetached, for you can have gardens just the same if the houses are built in little rows. The most charming houses in England, excluding manors and the like, are built in rows and not detached. (And so, of course, are the least charming, all the horrors.) There is something at once fussy and monotonous about a long road on which tiny villas have been sprinkled, as if out of a pepperpot. I am sorry Bournville has not been able to experiment more with rows, courts, quadrangles; but I was assured by those who know that their tenants greatly prefer to be semidetached. Within these limits, Bournville has done its work very well. If it has rather too many public halls of religion and too few frivolous meeting places for my taste, after all I am not one of its tenants. And its real importance is as an example of what can be done by some careful planning and an absence of the jerry-builder's motives. It is neither a great firm's private dormitory nor a rich man's toy, but a public enterprise that pays its way. It is one of the small outposts of civilisation, still ringed round with barbarism.

This is the age, among other things, of chocolate. Think of the number of chocolate shops you see in a day's journey. A very large proportion of this chocolate is made in the Cadbury factory at Bournville. I seemed to spend hours and hours being rushed from one part of this colossal works to another. It is really a small town engaged in the manufacture of cocoa and chocolate. I was shown a warehouse in which more than a hundred thousand bags of cocoa beans can be stored. These bags are mechanically hoisted to the top of a building, and then their contents pass from floor to floor, are shelled, winnowed, baked, crushed, refined, pressed, and finally pack themselves neatly into tins, which tins have been made by some busy little machines in a neighbouring room. Everywhere is the sickly sweet smell of cocoa and chocolate. I was told that an old foreman, who had spent fifty years in this atmosphere, still had his two cups of cocoa every night. The manufacture of chocolate is a much more

elaborate process, and though I could make a shot at describing it, I see no reason why I should. But there were miles of it, and thousands of men and girls, very spruce in overalls, looking after the hundred-and-one machines that pounded and churned and cooled and weighed and packed the chocolate, that covered the various bits of confectionery with chocolate, that printed labels and wrappers and cut them up and stuck them on and then packed everything into boxes that some other machine had made. The most impressive room I have ever seen in a factory was that in which the cardboard boxes were made and the labels, in that shiny purple or crimson paper, were being printed: there is a kind of gangway running down the length of it, perhaps twenty feet from the floor, and from this you had a most astonishing view of hundreds of white-capped girls seeing that the greedy machines were properly fed with coloured paper and ink and cardboard. In some smaller rooms there was hardly any machinery. In one of them I saw a lot of girls neatly cutting up green and brown cakes of marzipan into pretty little pieces; and they all seemed to be enjoying themselves; though I was told that actually they preferred to do something monotonous with the machines. I know now the life history of an almond whirl. There is a little mechanical device that makes that whirl on the top, as deft as you please. I saw thousands of marshmallows hurrying on an endless moving band of silvered paper to the slow cascade of chocolate that swallowed them for a moment and then turned them out on the other side, to be cooled, as genuine chocolate marshmallows. It is part of the fantastic quality of our time that what seem trifling bits of frivolity to most of us are of terrific importance to some people. I saw departments where solemn specialists sit in conference over a bit of cocoanut dipped in chocolate or whatever the trifle may be. Men with learned degrees, men with charts, engineers from all quarters of the world, have to be called in to decide the fate of that bit of chocolaty stuff. When you buy a box of these things, you have also bought the services of a whole army of people. It is all very strange, rather frightening. You have to shut your imagination off or you might go mad. Even I will never feel quite the same now about a box of chocolates.

There was a girl whose duty it was, for forty-two hours a week, to watch those marshmallows hurrying towards their chocolate Niagara. "Wouldn't that girl be furious," I said to the director who was showing me round, "if she found that her Christmas present was a box of chocolate marshmallows?" But he was not at all sure. "We consider our staff among our best customers," he told me. Other people there told me the same thing. Such is the passion now for chocolate that though you spend all your days helping to make it, though you smell and breathe it from morning until night, you must munch away like the rest of the world. This says a good deal for the purity of the processes, which seemed to me exemplary, but what it says for human nature, I cannot tell.

As it is human nature and not the manufacture of chocolate that really interests me, I will take leave now of Messrs. Cadbury as ingenious organizers and consider them as employers. They have of course long been in the top class of the school of benevolent and paternal employers. Their workpeople are provided with magnificent recreation grounds and sports pavilions, with a large concert hall in the factory itself, where midday concerts are given, with dining rooms, recreation rooms, and facilities for singing, acting, and I know not what, with continuation schools, with medical attention, with works councils, with pensions. The factory is almost as busy in the evenings as it is in the daytime. Games, music, drama, lectures, classes, hobbies, conferences, all keep the place in full swing. Once you have joined the staff of this firm, you need never wander out of its shadow. I saw a club-room, fitted up with billiards tables and draughts-boards and the like, where old employees who have been pensioned off come to spend their leisure, playing while their younger comrades are working all round them. The membership of the various clubs

and societies is about seven thousand. No form of self-improvement, except those that have their base in some extreme form of economic revolution, is denied a person here. No pastime, except the ancient one of getting drunk, is impossible. Here, in a factory, run for private profit, are nearly all the facilities for leading a full and happy life. What progressive people all over the world are demanding for humanity, these workers have here. Those in charge insist that the firm uses no compulsion whatever and never moves to provide anything until it knows that a real demand exists. It simply offers facilities, they say. And here let me add my conviction that whether all this is right or wrong, the employers themselves have acted in good faith, and genuinely prefer spending a good part of their money on their factory and its employees instead of racing stables and yachts and Monte Carlo.

Is it right or wrong? This is a very pretty problem. It is easy for some academic person, who has never spent an hour in a factory and does not really know how people live, to condemn it on philosophical grounds, but this may possibly be the result of turning off one's imaginative sympathy and not turning it on. We will assume now that our goal is other people's happiness, that what we want is that the mass of people should have a chance of leading the sort of life we lead—or should like to lead—ourselves. Now there is no getting away from the fact that here, owing to this system of paternal employment, are factory workers who have better conditions, more security, and infinitely better chances of leading a decent and happy life, than nearly all such factory workers elsewhere. They have, at least in part, what we should like everybody to have. Thanks to good management and an ever-increasing public passion for chocolate, a goal of some sort has been reached. It is easy, when you are sitting in a pleasant study and you know that it is unlikely that you will ever have to apply for work in a factory, to say that all this will not do; but could you honestly say as much if you found yourself a factory hand, and a factory hand who worked in bad conditions, who had no security, and whose employers did not care a rap if their people did nothing but drink themselves silly in their leisure? If you strike a balance of ordinary human happiness, in a class that has had all too few chances of it, then here is a definite and enormous gain. The Russians, in their plans for a proletarian millennium, are only taking aim at such a goal as this. What has been promised in Russia—in such matters as hours of work, food, housing, education, amusement—has been actually performed here. No factory workers in Europe have ever been better off than these people. And I doubt if America, even during its very prosperous years, could show us workers of the same kind who had such opportunities for a full, active, healthy life. On any sensible short view, the experiment must be praised.

It is when one takes a longer view that doubts begin to creep in. Is it good for people to see the factory as the centre of their lives, even if that factory offers them so much, and so much that is genuinely significant? Does this system of paternal employment suggest (as Hilaire Belloc pointed out, years ago, in his *Servile State*) the decay of genuine democracy? I believe that this very firm, when it opened a branch factory in Australia, tried to pursue the same policy there but met with a decided rebuff from the Australians, who, whatever their faults, are at least in practice the thoroughgoing democrats they pretend to be. "No," said these Australian employees, in effect, "we don't want your recreation grounds and concert halls, for if you can afford to give us these things, you can afford to pay us higher wages, and we'll take the wages." I do not say that this leaves the paternal employer without a retort, for he can reply: "Very well, if you don't want my welfare schemes, you needn't have them. I will follow the examples of other firms and not give you any recreation grounds or concert halls. But neither will I give you any higher wages. I'll put what I've saved in my pocket." But though he may be worse off in other respects, it is clear that the Australian employee as a political being is occupying the sounder position. He is selling his labour, and nothing else. He is not acknowledging that his employer is a superior creature, whose benevolence may fall upon him like the rays of the life-giving sun. A workman whose whole life is centred in his factory has put all his eggs into one basket. He may enjoy many unusual luxuries, but there is obviously one luxury he cannot enjoy and that is—a spirit of independence. Moreover, he is in danger of believing what his employers are anxious for him to believe and what, in all sincerity, they may believe themselves, namely, that the particular work of that factory is the most urgent and the grandest of human activities, that cocoa is not made for man, but man for cocoa. Pensions and bonuses, works councils, factory publications, entertainments and dinners and garden parties and outings organised by the firm, these are all very well, but they can easily create an atmosphere that is injurious to the growth of men as intellectual and spiritual beings, for they can give what is, when all is said and done, a trading concern for private profit a falsely mystical aura, can drape its secular form with sacramental cloths, and completely wreck the proper scale of values. Very soon, when this atmosphere has been created, you begin to hear talk of "loyalties" that soar high above the common and reasonable fidelity of a decent man trying to do the job for which he is paid. Business cant swells into business mysticism, as it did in the United States before the slump, and there was no end of rubbishy talk about "service" and "loyalty," the kind of talk we get here chiefly from advertising men in their windy conventions. And no institution is fit to dominate men's lives unless it is solemnly dedicated either to God or the commonwealth; and by the commonwealth I do not mean the State, which may be simply a number of selected persons or a dictator and his friends who happen to have collared the army and the police force. If one of these paternal factories were taken over by the State tomorrow, only one weakness of the system would disappear, the fact that the whole organisation is there for private profit; all the other weaknesses and dangers would remain, for the individual workman would still be compelled to look only in one direction for all the benefits of his life, would run the same risk of losing his independence, could still believe that he was made for his factory and not his factory for him, could confuse and mislay all his values, even though the directors had now to report to a public ministry instead of to a body of shareholders. (Many people easily avoid the pitfalls of business worship or mystical commerce only to fall into the trap of the mystical State, which makes them imagine that a group of institutions and a rough-and-ready organisation for political and economic purposes—let us say a combination of the British Museum, the Metropolitan Water Board, and New Scotland Yard—are somehow more important, of deeper significance to the wide universe, than the sum total of the human beings concerned. And I take this to be the most fashionable and potent illusion of our times; perhaps the father of those warring children, Communism and Fascism.) We must return, however, to the paternal factory system as it is working here and now.

I would say then, in a desperate attempt to conclude the matter and continue my journey, that workers in such places as Bournville have so many solid benefits conferred on them, benefits that must inevitably raise their status, both physical and mental, that in spite of the obvious dangers of the system, they are better placed, as citizens of to-day or to-morrow, than the ordinary factory worker, who is probably not so content either at work or play. (Though I cannot help wondering whether a girl or boy, put to some monotonous characterless task, then exercised, amused, and educated, will want to continue working at that monotonous characterless task. In short, the system may be sowing the seeds of its own destruction.) On the other hand, I for one would infinitely prefer to see workers combine to provide these benefits or a reasonable proportion of them, for themselves, to see them forming associations far removed from the factory, to

see them using their leisure, and demanding its increase, not as favoured employees but as citizens, free men and women.

And now, back in Birmingham in the dusk, I must offer a score of apologies to Messrs. Cadbury and their busy ten thousand, good hosts all of them and benefactors of the sweet tooth, for using them all as pegs when they had used me as a man and a brother.

BIRMINGHAM

Here are two glimpses of Birmingham life. The first is of the public whist drive I attended on Saturday night. It is worth remembering that card games, like almost everything else in this land of social hierarchies, are not without their class distinctions. Whist was once the favourite card game of the upper classes. Now that those people play bridge, auction or contract, whist has found its devotees in a very different set of people, chiefly the small shopkeeping, artisan and working classes. Why don't these people too play bridge, which is, after all, a much better game? We can only guess. Some of them think bridge much too complicated for them. On the other hand, many of them play a good game of solo whist, which demands considerable initiative and skill. (I have often thought that some of its devices—such as the *misère* call, the contract to lose tricks instead of making them—might have been profitably adapted to bridge.) Probably a second and weightier reason is that many of these people do not play bridge because they shrink from imitating the wealthier classes and do not want their friends and neighbours to think they are suddenly "trying to be posh." After all, there is more than one kind of snobbery. We hear a lot about the man who dresses for dinner in Central Africa; but that must not make us forget the existence of a much larger number of men who would die of shame if they were discovered by their acquaintances conveying soup to their mouths above a stiff white shirt. But whatever the reason may be, the fact remains that whist is still the favourite card game of the mass of the English people.

The whist drive I attended, one of several advertised in the evening paper, was not a private social function, the equivalent of a bridge party, but a public affair, a combined entertainment and gamble, run by some astute person for profit. (And a very nice thing he must make out of it, too.) It seemed from the advertisement to be the largest and most swaggering. You paid two shillings to compete, but there were money prizes amounting to twenty-three pounds. I concluded, rightly as it turned out, that a man who promises to part with so much prize-money must be fairly certain of getting a great many patrons at two shillings a head. The whist drive, one of a tri-weekly series, was held in a certain public hall and began at eight-fifteen. So I raced through my dinner and hurried on to it.

The hall was large, austere in colouring and decoration, and lighted in the most uncompromising fashion by unshaded bulbs of high voltage. It had about as much intimate charm as the average big railway station. I guessed at once that we were in for a formidably business-like evening. Suspended from the ceiling, about a third of the way down the room, was a large indicator, showing the four suits. The remaining two-thirds of the hall, beyond this indicator, was filled with very small chairs ranged round very small tables, most of them not proper card tables but mysterious objects covered with what seemed then, and afterwards, squares of rather dirty blanket material. When you paid your two shillings, you were given a scoring card, either black or red. (Mine was black.) On this card were the rules, the numbers of your first table and then spaces for the numbers of your succeeding tables, the tricks you made, and your totals. There were several hundred people there, and most of them seemed to be regular patrons and to know one another. They were mostly middle-aged decent working folk, with only a sprinkling of younger men and women. Nearly all the men smoked, and a fair proportion of the women; but there were no ash-trays. I knocked my pipe out on my heel. What the cigarette smokers did, I do not know. After ten minutes, a man shouted at us through a megaphone and we all went to our tables. The indicator told us what were trumps by lighting up a gigantic ace of clubs. We started. There followed what seemed to me one of the most strenuous hours I have ever spent. To begin with, the games were played at a tremendous speed, aces being banged on kings without a moment's hesitation. Then there was so much to do. You had to fill in your card and to initial the card on each table. If you were the losing man arriving at a new table—and I nearly always was—you had to shuffle the cards before the cut for deal. And three times out of four it seemed to be my fate to deal, and as the packs at each successive table appeared to be older and older and greasier and greasier, so that they were about four inches thick when they were stacked ready to be cut, dealing was an unpleasant business. Never in my life, not even in the trenches, have I ever seen dirtier and older packs of cards. It was not pleasant to hold them, even when they showed you a smudge of aces and kings; and it was a downright penance to be continually shuffling and dealing them. So what with shuffling, cutting, dealing, playing, gathering tricks up on those bits of blanket, clerkly work with the table card and your own card, changing tables, pushing past enormous fat women, I was kept so busy that after about half an hour of it I was fairly perspiring. And there was never a minute to lose. The whistle blew, as a signal to change tables, the indicator lit up its new suit of trumps, and if you had not finished your game, there were people waiting and looking very cross about it. There was practically no time for conversation, hardly time to smile. What conversation there was about the game, if for once it finished before the whistle blew, I could not understand. Three times my various partners said to me, "I'd a good back hand," and I could only assent feebly, for I did not know then and do not know now what a good back hand is. As I have not played whist, which is a very different game from bridge, for twenty years, and as all these games are run off at such a colossal speed, I cannot tell you whether these people played well or badly. I suspect that most of it must have been very perfunctory play, with no nonsense about finessing in it. All my partners were either very big fat women, who bulged over their chairs and the tables, and sweated good-humouredly, or else little witch-like females with sharp noses, tucked-in mouths, and iron spectacles, who held their cards very close to the brooches they wore, hardly ever spoke, and looked very cross, though I do not actually think they were. There were two distinct types among the men: the solid hearty chaps who sat bolt upright, puffing out clouds of smoke and banged each card down as if sheer force might win the trick; and the little thin cunning fellows who sank down and down and half-closed their eyes as they played, like so many Nibelungs. When the whistle blew after the twelfth game, everybody made a rush for the top end of the hall, and reappeared a few minutes afterwards, eating fruits, tarts, and slabs of cake.

This was the interval and by this time I had had quite enough whist-driving, but it seemed to me that if one player disappeared the whole elaborate organisation would be flung into disorder. So I stayed on and played another twelve games, nearly always losing and so going from table to table and shuffling packs of cards greasier than any I had ever seen before, cards that ought to have been thrown into the dust bin months ago; and I found myself in a far corner where the tables were almost touching one another and enormous women were unable to extricate themselves, and it was sweatier and hotter and smokier than ever. My total score was one hundred and fifty-five, which was some thirty or forty below the best. But there was still a chance that I might win a prize for a "mystery number," which was drawn by the promoter, after he had given the prizes for the winning scores. There was no excitement at the end, no cheering, no applause. It was all as brisk and business-like as the whole evening had been. When the last prize had

been awarded, everybody cleared off, rather as if they were leaving a factory than making an end of a night's pleasure. I suppose they enjoyed it—which was more than I did—otherwise they would not regularly attend these functions, as they undoubtedly do, but anything superficially less like a night's pleasure I never did see. Considering that many of them must be engaged all day in work that must be at once bustling and boring, it is surprising that they should choose this method of passing the evening. I do not believe that it is card-playing that attracts them there, for nobody could enjoy playing cards at such a speed. The secret is the gamble, the chance of winning two or three pounds for your two shillings. The purely social side of the whist drive was negligible; or at least so it seemed to me, though of course I was a stranger and may have missed some quiet fun. At the end, two impressions remained with me. It is difficult to find words for them here without appearing unpleasantly patronising; but I must take that risk. First, I was struck by the extraordinary ugliness of most of the people there. Nobody has ever called me handsome, and I do not ask for a very high standard of good looks in other people. It is not that these people lacked regular features, fine figures, bright eyes, and so forth. They were, for the most part, downright ugly, really unpleasant to look at closely. The women were either much too fat or far too thin. The men looked like lop-sided oafs, gnomes, hobgoblins. Nearly all looked as if life had knocked them into odd shapes, taken the bloom out of their faces, twisted their features and dulled their eyes. The few native races I have seen could have shown one far better-looking specimens of humanity than these. Possibly the people who go to whist drives are among the least handsome of their kind—this would obviously be true of young women—but even when that allowance has been made, that ugliness remains startling. In twenty years' time, I believe it will have gone. But it does not say much for our way of living that it should be there now. The second impression that remained was of a very different character. These people might be ugly to look at but they were not ugly to be with; in other words, they were surprisingly good-mannered and good-humoured. I never saw one exhibition of bad temper all the evening. Some were obviously much better players than others, and there was money at stake, but nevertheless there was never an embarrassing moment. Even the witch-like, iron-spectacled little women were never actually rude to anybody. They were all patient, decent, good-tempered folk, and they compared extremely favourably, startlingly, with the well-nurtured people I have often seen giving a show of bad manners and egoism at bridge tables, not merely in private but also in functions such as this. The sharp contrast between appearance and manner was very curious. I could make a text of it but will refrain, if only because I want these two impressions to be free from any suspicion of being forced, when actually they were simply what remained to me after an arduous evening.

The second glimpse of Birmingham comes from the following morning, Sunday. I awakened in a strangely quiet hotel, quite unlike the weekday place. The spell of an English Sunday is terrifically potent; even the weather is different. The whole city was blanketed in silence. The streets were wearing their Sunday look: few people in them, hardly any traffic, but a more than week-day allowance of mist hanging about, as if the country had been given permission to send a bit of its autumn weather into town. I ate my customary Sunday morning sausages in an almost empty dining-room, where the waiters were beginning to move like church wardens. You had a feeling, obviously shared by the head waiter, the reception clerk downstairs, the lift attendant, and the two yawning page-boys, that a slab of time like a vast suet pudding had been thrust into your hands, that before Monday dawned there would be time to write an epic poem on the Fall of Jerusalem or to work out successfully every different kind of patience. But I had not this embarrassing wealth of hours because I had decided to do some-

thing I had not done for many years, and that was to attend the morning service in a Nonconformist chapel. Birmingham has long been one of the chief strongholds of Nonconformity, and I felt that I could not pass a Sunday in it without visiting one of its places of worship. I found one about ten minutes' walk away. It did not belong to the particular denomination that had claimed me, willy-nilly, when I was a boy, but nevertheless my first discovery was that this service was almost exactly like the ones I remember from thirty years ago, and that the people taking part in it had not changed a great deal. The chief difference in the congregation was that there were fewer young people in it, and especially young men. I doubt if there were half-a-dozen men under thirty-five in the chapel. If there were any boys present, they escaped my eye. There were a few little girls, a sprinkling of older girls and young women, and all the rest of the congregation and the choir were middle-aged. But I suppose that in my chapel-going days, there would actually have been twice the number of people at this service. And though there was a certain amount of nodding and smiling before, and some hand-shaking after the service, I did not gather the impression that for most of these people this chapel was the centre of their social life; though the notices read out by the minister still suggested that it was.

Nevertheless, when one considers that we are generally supposed to have plunged or blundered into a new world since the war, that vast changes are taking place in every department of our lives, the likeness between this service and the ones I remember was astonishing. The organist looked the same and played the same stuff in the same old way. The choir, with its preponderance of rustling females, its one piercing tenor (I spotted him: eyeglasses and a grey moustache), its uncertain but hopeful basses, its trick of turning everything it sang, no matter how thunderous the music, how wildly oriental the words, into something neat and respectable, the rent garments of prophets converted into a pair of dark striped trousers, was the familiar choir of my boyhood. The deacons who carried round the collection plates were the immortal deacons of my memories: cashiers and shop-keepers, with pointed beards, gold-rimmed spectacles, morning coats, of a terrific respectability, whose very walk, as they returned the collection plates, obliterated the whole doctrine of original sin. Time had not withered them, though in truth they had always been a little withered. As I watched them, I knew that old as I am, a ratepayer and the father of children, I had only to go to the following Saturday's tea and concert and see these mysterious beings suddenly secular and waggish over ham sandwiches and lemon cheese tarts, to be as startled as I was in 1903. We sang as we had always sung. The minister prayed as he had always prayed, not perhaps quite at the same length but still as if he were sternly addressing some powerful but uncertain potentate from the East, who had to be talked to in this fashion before he knew his own mind. There was, as there had been, a children's address, which began by the minister, as ever, suddenly putting on a smile so false and sickly that it was frightening, looking down at three little girls in the second row, and then beginning in an odd voice to talk of some determined whimsicality. When I was a little boy I wriggled in embarrassment at these addresses, and I found myself wriggling all over again that morning in Birmingham. The sermon itself, which was not a bad one, had not changed much; there was the same trick in it of taking a tiny and apparently meaningless text—such as *Then Saul went up* or *These likewise cast lots*—and then finding an astonishing number of deeply significant meanings in it; a method that would soon turn any book, a *History of Rutlandshire* or *Commercial Guide to Sweden,* into a work of the profoundest wisdom. The minister, who had the merit, common among Nonconformist clergymen, of being able to read and sermonise in a sensible manly fashion, had a long dark face and the arched and restless eyebrows of a comedian. Indeed, his whole face was that of a comic

actor, probably French; and humor seemed continually to play over it like a breeze ruffling a pond; yet the man behind this face had not a glimmer of this comic spirit and was clearly a very solemn Nonconformist clergyman. Somehow, he had taken to wearing the wrong face, that was all. He fascinated me. Looking as if he were about to speak some terrific drollery out of a comedy by *Labiche,* he would announce the hymn and gravely recite its first four lines.

There was another contrast, however, queerer than that between the minister and his face. And I had not noticed this as a boy at these services. Then I had taken the general atmosphere of the service and the sect for granted. Now, returning to it after a long absence, I saw how odd it was that these mild Midland folk, spectacled ironmongers, little dressmakers, clerks, young women from stationers' shops, should come every Sunday morning through the quiet grey streets and assemble here to wallow in wild oriental imagery. They stood up in rows, meek-eyed, and pink-cheeked, to sing modestly about the Blood of the Lamb. After a few little coughs, they announced that certain sacred names and symbols induced in them fits of incredible ecstasies. They sat with bent heads listening to accounts of ancient and terribly savage tribal warfare, of the lust and pride of hook-nosed and raven-bearded chieftains, of sacrifice and butchery on the glaring deserts of the Near East. They chanted in unison their hope of an immortality to be spent in cities built of blazing jewels, with fountains of milk and cascades of honey, where kings played harps while maidens clashed the cymbals; and one could not help wondering what these people would do if they really did find themselves billeted for ever in this world of the Eastern religious poets. What, in short, had these sober Northern islanders to do with all this oriental stuff? What did it, what could it really mean to them? Could anything be less aptly shaped and coloured to match their own lives? If this was the time when their thoughts turned to the creator of this universe, when they were asked to consider the deep truths of life, to face their consciences and search their hearts, why should they be dragged into this far-away fantastic world of goats and vines and deserts and smoking sacrifices and tribal kings? It was almost as if instead of the familiar black-coated minister there had appeared in the pulpit a whirling dervish. Must God, I asked myself, remain forever in Asia? Are these people always to assume that He is still brooding over Babylon? What if He is now brooding over Birmingham?

THE BLACK COUNTRY

From Birmingham I went to have a look at the Black Country, which lies to the north and west of the city. This notorious region was strange to me. Now I have seen it, but of course it is still strange to me. You have to live some time in these places to understand their peculiar qualities. All I can do is to offer a few sketches, probably not at all accurate nor free from a certain subjective colouring, for in retrospect it is difficult to disengage the scene from the mood. But perhaps that does not matter: the record of a journey of this kind may be more important if it chronicles a succession of moods than if it captures a succession of scenes. Here, I think, I ought to say a little more about myself. It happens that during the last few years I have been away from industrial districts and have spent most of my time in far pleasanter places. But the first nineteen years of my life were passed in the industrial West Riding, in the shadow of the tall chimneys; and even yet I am not unduly fastidious about my surroundings. So you may take it that throughout this book I am not adopting some absurdly high standard that would make life in half of England impossible. I am not shocked because an iron foundry or a wool-combing mill has little in common with an author's drawing-room or study: I have long known what kind of places men have to labour in. My standard may be rough and ready and somewhat uncertain, but you can assume it is a reasonable one. If I declare that Coketown is a horrible hole, I do not merely mean that it cannot be fitted in to some private fairy-tale Merrie England of my own: I mean that it is a damned horrible hole. And I hope you will take my word for it.

I spent the better part of two days staring at this Black Country. The first day was fine and fairly bright. I went from Birmingham through Smethwick and Oldbury to Dudley, which seemed to me a fantastic place. You climb a hill, past innumerable grim works and unpleasant brick dwellings, and then suddenly a ridiculous terracotta music-hall comes into sight, perched on the steep roadside as if a giant had plucked it out of one of the neighbouring valleys and carelessly left it there; and above this music-hall (its attraction that week was *Parisian Follies*) were the ruins of Dudley Castle. I climbed a steep little hillside, and then smoked a pipe or two sitting by the remains of the Keep. The view from there is colossal. On the Dudley side, you look down and across at roofs and steeply mounting streets and pointing factory chimneys. It looked as if a great slab of Birmingham had been torn away and then tilted up there at an angle of about forty-five degrees. The view from the other side, roughly, I suppose, to the north-east, was even more impressive. There was the Black Country unrolled before you like a smouldering carpet. You looked into an immense hollow of smoke and blurred buildings and factory chimneys. There seemed to be no end to it. In the vague middle, dominating everything, was an enormous round white tower, which I afterwards learned was a new gasometer. It looked bigger than anything else in sight, and as nothing had dimension that could be measured, it was any size you liked to imagine it. You could think of it, without unduly straining your fancy, as the temple of some horrible new religion. The only sounds that arrived from this misty immensity below came from the tangle of railway lines that gleamed in the foreground of the scene, and these noises were so clear that they might have been picked out and then amplified. There was the scream of a locomotive; there was the clanking of the bumpered wagons; there was the long pu-u-ushing of a train gathering speed. I never remember hearing these railway sounds so clearly. Nothing else came from that enormous hollow. You could easily believe that there were no people down there, that a good locomotive was probably the most playful inhabitant of the region. I was glad that I did not know the names of the towns down there in the smoke; I felt that I was not looking at this place and that, but at the metallic Midlands themselves, at a relief map of a heavy industry, at another and greater exhibition of the 'fifties. No doubt at all that the region had a sombre beauty of its own. I thought so then, and I thought so later, when I had seen far more of its iron face lit with hell fire. But it was a beauty you could appreciate chiefly because you were not condemned to live there. If I could do what I liked with the whole country, I would keep a good tract of this region as it is now, to be stared and wondered at; but I would find it difficult to ask any but a few curators to live in it.

I descended into the vast smoky hollow and watched it turn itself into so many workshops, grimy rows of houses, pubs and picture theatres, yards filled with rusted metal, and great patches of waste ground. There was a cynical abundance of these patches of waste ground, which were as shocking as raw sores and open wounds. In my own West Riding, industry of the grimmest and most uncompromising kind has long been allowed to work its will on the countryside. There, however, the countryside itself is grim and uncompromising. Sometimes the mills, the rows of little houses, the cobbled streets, all seem like natural outcroppings of the Pennine rock. Huddersfield and Rochdale, Keighley and Nelson, may look grim, but the high lands that still separate them look even grimmer. But here in these Midlands, the countryside is mild and friendly. It is on the border of Arden itself. Industry has ravished it; drunken storm troops have passed this way; there are signs of atrocities everywhere; the earth has been left gaping and bleeding; and what were once bright fields have been rum-maged and raped into these dreadful patches of waste ground. And nothing I saw there, not even the slums, impressed me more painfully.

The places I saw had names, but these names were merely so much alliteration: Wolverhampton, Wednesbury, Wednesfield, Willenhall, and Walsall. You could call them all wilderness, and have done with it. I never knew where one ended and another began. I remember noticing in Wolverhampton, after half an hour of dingy higgledy-piggledy, the new building of the *Midland Counties Dairy,* white and trim and with immense windows, and thinking how alien it looked there, like the outpost of a new civilisation. I remember arriving at the very end of the earth, where the land appeared to have been uprooted by a giant pig and where there were cottages so small and odd that they must have been built for gnomes, and this end of the earth was called Gornal, and there the women, returning home from the brickworks, wore caps and shawls. The shawls were like those that the weavers used to wear in my own town, but our women had worn their shawls over their heads. Here, however, they wore caps as well, and looked as outlandish as the place they lived in. Afterwards I ran right through the Black Country and came out at the other end, almost within sight of the potteries. On the way back, somewhere between Stafford and Rugeley, I came to a bit of heath country, glowing with autumn, that was as pleasant as you could wish. There the sun went down. It was dark long before I got back to Birmingham; the ravished waste ground, the miserable houses, the muddle of dirty brick, the whole battlefield of industry, sank down and disappeared, and in their places appeared mysterious red gleams of fire and a pretty tracery of lights, so that I was happier staring about me than I had been all day.

My second day there was a Sunday, and in foul weather. Sometimes the raw fog dripped; sometimes the cold rain steamed; but throughout it was thick and wet and chilled. I lunched in one of the smaller towns with a man in the metal trade. There were several Black Country business men there, large hearty fellows, sturdy eaters and drinkers. There had been a sudden flurry of business in the metal trade, and my friend was going back to his office and warehouse in West Bromwich after lunch. I went with him, and on the way was shown, among other things, the last dairy farm in the district. It stood there surrounded for miles by the grim paraphernalia of industrialism; I had only a glimpse of it, a solitary surviving farmhouse in the wet fog, with a few ghostly fields on either side. My friend's warehouse was in— shall we say?—"Rusty Lane," West Bromwich. He keeps sheets of steel there, and no doubt any place is good enough to keep sheets of steel in; but I do not think I could let even a sheet of steel stay long in Rusty Lane. I have never seen such a picture of grimy desolation as that street offered me. If you put it, brick for brick, into a novel, people would not accept it, would condemn you as a caricaturist and talk about Dickens. The whole neighbourhood is mean and squalid, but this particular street seems the worst of all. It would not matter very much—though it would matter—if only metal were kept there; but it happens that people live there, children are born there and grow up there. I saw some of them. I was being shown one of the warehouses, where steel plates were stacked in the chill gloom, and we heard a bang and rattle on the roof. The boys, it seems, were throwing stones again. They were always throwing stones on that roof. We went out to find them, but only found three frightened little girls, who looked at us with round eyes in wet smudgy faces. No, they hadn't done it, the boys had done it, and the boys had just run away. Where they could run to, I cannot imagine. They need not have run away from me, because I could not blame them if they threw stones and stones and stones and smashed every pane of glass for miles. Nobody can blame them if they grow up to smash everything that can be smashed. There ought to be no more of those lunches and dinners, at which political and financial and industrial gentlemen congratulate one another, until something is done about Rusty Lane and West Bromwich. While they still exist in their present foul shape, it is idle to congratulate ourselves about anything. They make the whole pomp of government here a miserable farce. The Crown, Lords and Commons are the Crown, Lords and Commons of Rusty Lane, West Bromwich. In the heart of the great empire on which the sun never sets, in the land of hope and glory, Mother of the Free, is Rusty Lane, West Bromwich. What do they know of England who only England know? The answer must be Rusty Lane, West Bromwich. And if there is another economic conference, let it meet there, in one of the warehouses, and be fed with bread and margarine and slabs of brawn. The delegates have seen one England, Mayfair in the season. Let them see another England next time, West Bromwich out of the season. Out of all seasons except the winter of our discontent.

Priestley's illuminating comments have proven the point that in centers of industry *the job* is the thing. A growing economy provides more jobs; a shrinking economy leads to unemployment. Recreation frequently becomes an escape from the job rather than a pursuit enjoyed for itself alone. Even family life becomes greatly affected not only by adequacy of income but by the employment of women in industry and commerce. The single woman is given an economic freedom which she never enjoyed when she was dependent on an aging father or a considerate older brother. She can now become her own "breadwinner" and, should she marry later on, she takes into the home something of the independence which she has tasted.

In the selection that follows, Philip Carr describes this changed status of women in England—particularly in the middle-class home. How does this compare with the status of the Chinese woman?

• 71 • The Status of Women
PHILIP CARR

. . . Home life—for the town dweller at least—is gradually becoming flat [apartment] life; and what used to be an important part of home life, that is to say entertaining friends, takes place elsewhere, in clubs and restaurants, while even the recreation of members of the family chiefly consists of going out. They go out to the cinema, they go out to the theatre, they go out to the country for weekends, they go out to play golf or lawn tennis, or merely for a drive in the car—the car having almost taken the place of the home as the principal interest of many a family.

Home life is still further reduced by the fact that in an English town the head of the family does not return for lunch. He certainly has his breakfast with his wife and his children, if they are old enough not to have theirs in the nursery; and it is a meal taken in the dining room. But breakfast—at least on week days—is not a very conversational meal in England. Father reads his newspaper, which is propped up in front of him on the table. Mother probably does the same; and the children are not encouraged to be chatty. Besides, every one probably has to hurry off to be in time for business.

Home life on ordinary days therefore means dinner in the evening and the hour or two before and after it; and the hour before dinner is probably the only time when a busy man sees his younger children, for they are not allowed to "sit up" for the evening meal, but have their tea in the nursery and are put to bed early.

On Saturday afternoon and on Sunday, the family is—or at least can be—more united; but I have already pointed out that they are not likely to be at home.

When people live in the suburbs or the country, the picture will probably be quite a different one. If they want to receive their friends, they must do so at home; for there are no restaurants to which they can invite them. Besides, the garden is likely to have enabled the home to recover its importance. It may induce the head of the family to spend his leisure there, if his hobby is gardening, which it very likely is. In any case, the house and the garden together will have more personality than can ever be acquired by the town flat.

The position of women in the middle-class English home is in some ways different from what it would be in a Latin country. I have already suggested that perhaps the innate shyness of the English character prevents husbands and wives from easily becoming the familiar associates—almost the business partners—which they so often are elsewhere. Perhaps the reason is partly that English husbands think it is unfair to burden their wives with their office worries. In any case, I fancy that it frequently happens that a wife knows little of her husband's affairs; and the jest about her being able to say no more about his occupation than that "he is something in the City" is not entirely an absurdity. She has been brought up to regard marriage rather as a romantic adventure than as a contract, and her husband is often inclined to encourage the assumption that all the responsibilities are his and none of them hers.

Some people might be tempted, after being present at an English wedding, to imagine that we also treat the whole thing rather as something comic. Throwing rice over the bride and bridegroom as they leave the church has a certain air of carnival although it is really a very ancient custom. Tying a satin shoe to the back of the carriage in which they are driven away is also justified by tradition; but no such excuse can be found for the practical joke of adding a card with a large capital letter "L," as they do on motor cars, which are being driven by learners, who have not yet obtained their driving license.

However, it need hardly be said that although marriages are never arranged in England by parents, nor is there any close bargaining over marriage portions and allowances, and although the great majority of girls who marry in England have no dowry at all, and are not expected by their husbands to bring one, there are young Englishmen who are fortune hunters, and there are plenty of English girls, as well as men, who take a realistic view of the situation, and plenty more who are quite aware that a wife has duties as well as privileges.

This is especially the case since so many young women are now independently earning their living before they marry—since, in fact, the revolution in the social, economic, and political status of women, which began about 1900, but reached its full development only after the other war.

*   *   *

As far as industry and even commerce are concerned, the employment of women has not been brought about solely by the superfluity of the unmarried. It is largely the result of mechanical progress. In factories, human intervention has been reduced to such simple movements that they can be performed after very little training, and, for business offices, young women can soon learn to manipulate a typewriter.

Therefore women are employed in each case, because they do the work as well or even better than men—certainly better and quicker in the case of typewriting and in that of certain deft movements of machine minding—and also because women are nearly always paid less than men for any particular work. They are paid less because they are willing to accept less, and they accept less for two reasons. The first is that at the age at which they begin, they do not depend upon their employment for their living, or at least the whole of their living, as they are generally still at home with their parents. They also accept less, because they regard their employment as merely a provisional affair until they are married—for at that age they assume that they are going to get married. Indeed, they usually do get married, and they usually give up working when they marry. This produces the further result that the great majority of employed women are young. It has been calculated that whereas 80 per cent of the girlhood of England between the ages of eighteen and twenty is earning money in some way, the percentage drops sharply to 65 between the ages of twenty-one and twenty-four and still farther later on. Those who disappear are replaced by another generation of young girls.

I have said that these young girls accept relatively small salaries; but in fact they are not badly paid for the work they do, and probably many boys of their age would be glad to be paid as well. Most boys, however, would hesitate to accept a job which is never likely to lead to anything better; and the field is left open to the young women, of whom there is always a great mass in employment. In the business quarters of the City of London, the whole aspect of the streets has been entirely changed, in hardly more than a generation, by the influx of girl clerks and typists. What was an exclusively male preserve, with hardly a woman to be seen, has become a crowd, in which—at least at the hours when employees arrive and depart—the feminine note predominates.

The disappearance of these women when they marry is not always voluntary on their part. It is often the deliberate policy of the employers to dismiss women on marriage, not because they become less competent, but because they are supposed then to be supported by their husbands, and no longer need to earn any money; and the married woman is obliged to give up her job, in order that it may be passed to an unmarried girl who is out of work. This policy is adopted by the Civil Service and by other public authorities, such as Education Committees with regard to school teachers, and private employers are encouraged to follow it.

In the industrial North of England, female labor dates much farther back, back to a period when nobody thought of protecting the girl mill-hand from the competition of the married woman; and in the textile industry, even today, nearly half of the women employed are married. However, in factories of other kinds, the practice of not retaining women after their marriage has been established.

This invasion of commerce and industry by what may be called the rank and file of the army of women workers has been accompanied by the entrance of women into the higher as well as the lower branches of the Civil Service and also into several of the liberal professions. It is that of medicine which has attracted the greatest number, and it is there that women have attained the highest distinction. Medicine is also the first profession into which women succeeded in gaining admittance. This happened as long ago as 1870, when the London School of Medicine for Women was founded; but for many years, women doctors were few. Even now, when they are accepted as students in most of the London hospitals, there are one or two which still refuse to take them. The great majority allow them to study and to qualify, however, and in 1918 there was a military hospital in France, where the only males were the soldier patients, all the staff—doctors, surgeons and nurses—being women.

Women can now become barristers in England, but only since 1920, while in France they have been able to do so since 1900. They can also be solicitors; but in neither branch of the law has any woman yet risen to any considerable practice. They have been far more successful as architects, as decorators, and also as expert designers of kitchens; and in literature, journalism, painting, sculpture and the theatre they have achieved success and more. They have won fame. Some of them had indeed done so more than a hundred years before any feminist movement was thought of; but it is only in our own time that the number of women successfully practicing any of the arts has been such that the rise to eminence of one of them is no longer a rare phenomenon.

It is also only in our own time that women in England have achieved the full rights of citizenship—that is to say, the right to vote, on an equality with men, at parliamentary and municipal elections, the right to be elected as members of the House of Commons, and the right not to be disqualified, by reason of their sex, from the exercise of any public function. The pressure of demand for these rights became insistent at the same time as the feminine pressure upon the employment market, that is to say, at the beginning of the present century; and it was the result of the same set of circumstances, the excess in numbers of women over men and the consequent mass of unmarried women. The rights were granted immediately after the other war—the parliamentary suffrage in 1918 and the eligibility to the House of Commons a year later—there are now fourteen women members of that Chamber. It was also in 1919 that was passed the Act abolishing the sex disqualification for any Government post. Even now, however, the exercise of these rights in practice cannot be said to be complete. Although a woman can be a member of the House of Commons, it has been decided that she cannot sit in the House of Lords, even when she is a peeress in her own right; and although a woman might in theory be made a Judge or an Ambassador, it is highly unlikely that such an appointment will be made in our time.

The two selections that follow deal primarily with young people and describe the circumstances under which they grow up. If we were to make a detailed study of the socialization process, we would need to know a great deal about early childhood and even infancy, but we nevertheless gain considerable insight into a society by seeing it from the standpoint of the adolescent.

The first selection deals with young girl workers, telling of their housing conditions, their appearance, their jobs, their relationships with their parents, their schooling, and their use of leisure time. It is a revealing, intimate sketch, prepared for this book by Pearl Jephcott, who has written a number of sympathetic studies on the English working girl. There are many references to actual costs of permanents, bicycles, admission to the cinema, and the like. The English monetary terms can be translated fairly easily into dollars and cents. A pound (£) is roughly equivalent to $2.80; it consists of 20 shillings, (each worth 14 cents); a shilling is made up of 12 pence, each worth slightly more than one cent; £2.10 means two pounds, ten shillings, or about $7.00. Shillings and pence are written as 17/6, or $2.46—the cost of a permanent. Pence alone are written 3d. or 6d., about 3 cents or 7 cents, the weekly dues in some of the young people's organizations. This brief explanation does not include all of the intricacies of the English monetary system but it should help us understand the article which follows.

• 72 • *Young Girl Workers in English Towns*
PEARL JEPHCOTT

There are about one and a half million girls aged 15 to 19 in England and Wales. These notes, however, concern only those girls (though they are the majority) who start work at 15. Most of them are engaged in manual work and are the children of manual workers with the social background that this, broadly, implies. Most of them, too, are town, not country, bred. These two points must be borne in mind and the fact that the picture is a little weighted on the side of the poorer, less intelligent youngster from the less favoured background. Not many of the girls of these notes have been born with a silver spoon in their mouths.

The essential characteristics of adolescent girls are, of course, much the same in Alabama as in Middlesex, in a Chinese village as in a Marseilles tenement. We are familiar enough with these characteristics since all of us have had the experience of being an adolescent, and half of us have our own femininity

as a guide to help us interpret younger women. Most of us can recall incidents in our own adolescence when we laboured at good works for three days and were bone idle for the next four. Such reflections help us to sympathize with the adolescent's chameleon-like changes, her emotional heights and depths, her insecurities and her bursts of over-confidence. What we know much less about, and are less sympathetic towards, is the social conditioning that overlays the common framework. We know remarkably little about the differences in the compelling home patterns that each of us has smelled and tasted from the cradle—the differences in family feeding habits and the variations in leisure time customs absorbed through street games and fights and friendships. If it is hard to pin down differences induced by social conditioning in a society with which we have always been familiar, it is a much more hazardous business to try, as these notes are doing, to assess the significant points of the English working class girl for those who know the English scene chiefly at second-hand.

What do English girls look like? That, obviously, is a treacherous question to ask. However, since appearances do reveal the man, and since most girl adolescents spend a lot of time and thought about personal appearance, and since there are definite fashions in faces as well as in clothes, it may be helpful to try to describe one or two actual girls. Take Maggie Barnes, for example, who lives at number 20 Durham Avenue, along with three older sisters. All four girls work in local factories, two as machinists of children's clothes, one at a printer's on a feeding machine. Their father was a Corporation dustman but, through bad health and age, he has now finished with any regular work. Mrs. Barnes is a typical old-fashioned English working woman, country born, a servant until she was married and now the mother of seven grown-up children. The boy whose photo is on the sideboard was drowned in the war and she talks about him often. She is a heavy-bodied, thin faced woman, with wispy grey hair. She wears a black stuff dress, green print apron, wrinkled grey stockings and grey sandals cut away to ease her bunions a bit.

Maggie is the youngest of the family and is 15. She left school four months ago and works at the same firm as two of her older sisters, but she is not yet on a machine. She mostly does odd jobs: giving out work, bundling up the finished vests and knickers, etc. She is round faced and rather heavily built, with medium brown hair. She had a 17/6 perm at Christmas and puts her hair in curlers, but not with much success. Nor does she bother with make up. In the house she wears old white runners, with a hole in one sole, and a red marocain frock with a dipping hem that her Mother bought for 5/- from the bargain shop at the street corner. Over this she wears a royal blue cardigan, a hand-down from her eldest sister who knitted it a couple of years ago. Her spending money, from her £2.10. weekly pay, is 10/- a week.

It mostly goes on ice cream, sweets, fares and bits of clothes.

Things are different down the street. The girl there is a year older than Maggie. She is tall, fair and has a fresh complexion on which she spends a good deal of money and time. Her hair is fluffy so she has no perm. She washes it herself, on a Tuesday, at the kitchen sink. She is a capable girl, was in the "A" stream at school, and earns, on piece work, up to £4.10 at the same factory as the Barnes girls work. She hands her pay packet in to her Mother on a Friday night and gets £1 back for her own use. Her Mother takes 30/- for her keep and puts the rest by for the girl's clothes. Her present street costume is a lemon yellow two-piece, bought for £4, with a 12/6 pair of nylons "on a club" at a local shop. She paid for her handbag with her own money, and also her hat, a 24/- riding shape with a draped chiffon bow, in brown. Her name is Pauline Spree.

The artisan home tends to be tightly packed, both inside and outside, but more often than not it is still occupied by only one family. In Maggie's home, for instance, the front of the two ground floor rooms is kept for best. Coats, new bikes, and household goods in general are stored there. The other ground floor room is the hub of the house. It has an open coal fire, on which part of the cooking is done, supplemented by the gas stove in a very small scullery leading off the living room. There is a hooky mat made by Mrs. Barnes in front of the fire-place, a set of photos on a sideboard, and bits of treasures (stuffed birds in a glass cage, china dogs, a model aeroplane made by an R.A.F. son-in-law) on the mantelpiece. Whatever time of day you go in, part of someone's meal is on the table. The stairs lead off this room up to two floors and three bedrooms. This means that all of the bedrooms and beds in the house are shared. There is no bathroom so people wash in the scullery. The lavatory is outside the backyard. There is a bit of garden also in this yard but it is not cultivated because Mr. Barnes has an allotment. That, roughly, is a sketch of an old house. Its characteristic feature is compression, and the fact that any personal privacy is almost impossible. At the same time it is snug and if it is in good repair is not too inconvenient to run, from the housewife's point of view. The new council houses are, of course, a different matter. A much appreciated feature of these is that practically all of them have a garden. But the houses themselves, though modern in equipment and design, are still small in scale and permit much less personal privacy than is normal in the home of a professional family.

The working class girls give the impression, by and large, that they have more brothers and sisters than the girl from the professional home. This impression is borne out by population figures which show a fairly close correlation between size of family and social plus economic status. [See Selection 53.] The girls also give the impression that their family life is more closely knit than that of the professional home. The boys, and more so the girls, often show great reluctance to the idea of leaving home to get a better job. Girls, when marrying, will fairly often jib at the idea of having to live even in another part of the same city. The housing shortage has tended to encourage this reluctance. Many couples do not set up house now when they marry but have to live in one or a couple of rooms at an in-law's, a situation which has a good deal of bearing on the younger sister's attitude toward her own future marriage. The attachment to home and neighbourhood is strengthened by another factor, and that is that working class families tend to have more of their relations living nearby than does the professional family. Past experiences too, help to account for the reluctance to move. The recollection of generations of poverty and general insecurity has not yet faded. And in the bad old days one had, in the last resort, nothing to fall back on for help but the family. Even today school girls often show a very real sense of responsibility towards their home. "Her first duty was to her family" is a headmistress's comment on one girl. "If that required

absence from school, lies to cover absence etc., and large gaps in her work, well, Jean was sorry but the family came first." Starting work, too, is looked forward to partly because it means that now you will be able to help your mother. When schoolgirls take on paper rounds after and before school, or Saturday morning 6/– shop assistant jobs they often work more to help the family budget than for the sake of their own pocket money. The idea of part-time work while you are still a school child, unless driven to it by home needs, is relatively new in this country, and one does not find many of the school children of professional homes taking on paid work.

The great majority of boys and girls, and most of those with whom this article deals, leave school at the end of the term after their 15th birthday. In a normal 15 to 19 years old population there would probably be about 13% still at school. The 1949 figures for the 82,000 age 14-20 population of the City of Birmingham, for example, showed that 16,700 adolescents were still attending full time schools and colleges while 23,000 were having some form of part time education, possibly chiefly in evening classes.

Schooling in England proceeds in three stages, primary, secondary and further education. These stages were laid down in the Education Act of 1944 which provided more equal opportunities for all children, raised the leaving age to 16 (this to be brought into operation as soon as circumstances permit; and 15 to be the immediate leaving age) and initiated major reforms in buildings, staff and the organisation of schools. Broadly speaking, children go to a primary school from 5 to 11 when, on tests and school records, they pass to the type of secondary school best suited to their abilities—grammar (for the more academic), technical, or secondary modern school. Further education may be taken at evening classes, which many girl clerical workers attend, or at part-time day release schools to which an increasing number of employers now send their juveniles, particularly the boys, for non-vocational education. This generally takes place on one full day a week.

Small boys and girls are generally taught together in mixed schools. At the secondary stage also the same number go to single sex as to mixed schools. Further education which in any case is largely technical, is generally given in separate classes for boys and girls. English schools are relatively small in size as compared with American ones. The secondary modern school attended by many of the girls whose life is described in this article is the largest secondary modern girls' school in the city of 300,000 but has only 440 pupils. It was built 70 years ago and is typical of the older schools in which many town children are still housed. It is a red brick, Neo-Gothic three-storied place with a lot of white tiling and large, rather gloomy class rooms. Its asphalt play ground is cut off from the streets by a high brick wall and iron gates. A mile away, however, is one of the city's new secondary modern schools, a single story glass and concrete building, grouped round two gardens. It is light, gay and functional and is set off by its grass playing field.

Most people were glad when the school leaving age was raised. Certainly most girls seem to enjoy their time at school well enough even if some of them feel that the last year did not advance them very much in actual learning. A girl just starting work says that she feels more grown up and better able to tackle her job at 15 than she did a year ago. Many parents, too, are rather concerned because they seem to feel, as is probably true, that the secondary modern school in general has not really decided what the extra year should give these children. They deal largely of course, with the non-academic type, and carry a burden of children with low I.Q.s and of those who are handicapped by unsatisfactory homes. The present syllabus concentrates on widening the child's interests and making her aware of the community in which she lives, by visits to civic institutions, factories, etc. All girls in secondary modern schools get

a good deal of domestic training and this is a subject that girls who have left school often say they would like to go on learning.

Although reforms in the 1944 act have helped to democratise education, some correlation between social class and education still persists. The children of working class parents, by and large, still go to the secondary modern or technical rather than the grammar school. There is also still some correlation between the social class of parents and the amount of education beyond the compulsory minimum that parents give their girls as compared with their boys. On the whole the working class girl, unlike the girl from the professional home, tends not to get as long or as good an education as her brother.

> Young girls leaving school wanted to train in cutting and finishing departments, canteen, hot meals. . . . [Gown Manufacturer] Ltd.

This advertisement, one of many in the "Work girls wanted" column of a Midland evening paper is typical of the kind of job that a girl leaving the "B" stream class of a modern secondary school would consider. The large number of advertisements that appear regularly reflect the present state of the juvenile labour market when employers are driven to use every possible device to get hold of young workers. This means, of course, that the adolescent can now pick and choose her job and change it in a way that was unheard of before the war. The staff of the Juvenile Employment Bureaux give vocational guidance to all school leavers of secondary modern schools and very many children get their jobs through the Bureaux. On the other hand, some of the more enterprising girls and parents go after jobs directly. A good many girls, especially the shy ones, try to get their first job at a firm where a relative is working, or where the girl's own particular friend is employed.

Roughly speaking, there are three main types of employment that the secondary modern school girls follow. The first is as manual workers in industry; the second as workers in the distributive trades, and the last as clerical assistants in shops, works' offices, etc. To put this in other words—in the year ending June 1948 of all the new girl entrants into insurable employment, about eight went into industry as manual workers, for five who went into shops and seven into all other types of work. It is the children of the larger families who tend to go into industry and to get into the lower grade jobs. There is more job change too in manual than in shop or office work. Though frequent job changes, on the whole, are frowned on by those interested in the welfare of the adolescent (and are equally obnoxious to the employer), there is some case for those adolescents in very routine jobs who almost unconsciously seem to be looking for self education by at least changing the environment in which they have to do the dull and petty job.

With the shortage of labour, and with a more humane outlook in industry, firms now-a-days pay much more attention to conditions of employment. They are beginning, for example, to consider initiation schemes by which the young employee is made conversant with the operation of the firm's work as a whole. A good many firms, too, are introducing training schemes by which the girl is taught (as, for example, in the spinning mills of the Viyella firm) how to work a variety of machines. During a seven weeks training her abilities and aptitudes are carefully noted before she goes into the mill itself.

Such schemes, however, are still relatively infrequent. For very many girls unskilled factory work is of an extremely routine nature. She does such things as working a button-holing machine, wrapping electric light bulbs in their cardboard cases, picking out the broken edged biscuits from the whole ones as they roll out of the electric oven. This is the kind of job which requires almost nothing more than agile fingers. Unskilled work of this kind, in which even the three R's are not used, does nothing to exercise the wits. There is probably a certain proportion of girls with low I.Q.s whom routine work suits and who would be unhappy in any other environment, but for the majority of the secondary modern school girls, jobs of this kind, even if the girls do not consciously dislike them, have almost certainly a stultifying effect. The repercussions are demonstrated in many ways, particularly in the girl's personal attitudes and in the way in which she spends time after work. She feels frustrated and makes up for this by aggression and cheek. Neither her actual job nor her working environment, often an all feminine one, gives her enough new things to think about. Trivialities assume ridiculous proportions and the girl becomes engrossed in her personal relationships, particularly in those with the opposite sex.

In addition to this, such girls very often have no clear conception of any career before them. They see their job merely as a stop-gap until the day they marry. The idea that a girl should have a career, which she may or may not give up when she marries, has not really taken root in the working class family. This, and the fact that her prospective husband, if he also is in manual work, is probably earning as big a wage at 24 as he ever will, leads the working girl to expect marriage at a relatively earlier age than the girl in the professional home.

Not much material exists on the marriage age pattern of different social levels but the Registrar General's Statistical Review gives the ages at which all women in England and Wales marry, of whom the great proportion will come from working class homes. In the decade before the war 23 was the age at which the largest number of girls married. During the war the peak age dropped, to 20 in the early days of the war, to 21 for 1941, 2, 3. The 1947 figures reflect the immediate post-war conditions of course, but they are not very different from the earlier picture. They show that *more* girls married at 21 in 1947 than at any other age, and that 22 and 20, in that order and in about equal weight, were the next most frequent ages for girls to marry. With this pattern before her the girl is perfectly justified in thinking that she is likely to marry within a few years' time. The expectation influences the whole of her outlook and, in particular, the ways in which she considers it proper to spend her leisure.

Before commenting on the ways in which girls do spend their leisure it is useful to consider how the adults of the girl's family reckon to spend their spare time, and what sort of pattern she observes among her older friends. The immediate point that such a question calls to mind is that adult working class recreation, on the whole, is an informal affair. Visiting relations bulks largely in the programme. Visiting the local pub, particularly at the weekend, is another regular activity. Older men too, spend a lot of their free time working in their gardens and allotments. The younger ones take part in various sports, either watching or playing, and for men of all ages watching professional football, particularly on Saturday afternoon, is an almost universal activity. Television has not yet become a serious rival to the cinema, and the latter is one of the major recognised ways of spending a free evening. There is a good deal of family cinema going, to the cheaper cinemas, and some families, or perhaps a mother and adolescent daughter, go regularly to the local variety theatre, which exists in most of the larger towns.

The above suggests that many adults among the girl's acquaintances take their pleasures in an informal and unorganised way which does not necessitate joining any society. Of societies that are joined, the churches are of major importance from the point of view of numbers alone. It is a safe bet that more people take part regularly in the social activities provided by the churches than those provided by any other type of body. There is, however, an infinity of these other bodies—clubs and organizations for good works, for games, for hobbies and for cultural activities. But although these are so numerous, social surveys suggest that, on the whole, there are more adults who belong to no leisure time society than those who do belong to one, and that women on the whole belong less than men.

Numerous surveys have been made recently into the way in which adolescents spend their increasing volume of leisure. Most of these enquiries have been directed to the leisure time occupations of working adolescents, implying that those who are still at school at 16 and 17 are presumed to be occupying themselves in ways which adults regard as satisfactory. Three motives seem to have inspired these surveys. In the first place a good many of the seeds of juvenile delinquency seem to sprout during leisure that is aimless. In the second place adults have noted that the girls in very frustrating jobs tend to be the people who fritter away their evenings and week-ends in a very narrow set of activities. And thirdly there has been a growing conviction that it is an adult responsibility to see that all youngsters are given facilities to play the games and practise the hobbies that are recognised as giving so much pleasure and sensible recreation to the boys and girls from more ample homes.

These surveys suggest that on the whole adolescent girls who are at work from 8 A.M. to 5.30 P.M. probably spend the major part of their free time in their own homes. Apart from regular domestic chores, minding the smaller children, etc., they have their personal things to see to and can get enjoyment from hair washing, ironing, etc., in a way that the boys cannot. Not many girls seem to do much actual dressmaking, but knitting is an almost universal occupation. Serious reading of books, as distinct from magazines, is an occupation which seems to run in families and is practised by only a minority of girls who leave school at 15. On the other hand, many still buy the comics regularly and continue to read them, as indeed do the grown ups in their homes. Most of the girls as schoolgirls have read *Girls' Crystal* regularly, and the lower intellectual level of adolescents do not rise much above the level of *Red Star*, *Miracle* and *Glamour* type of magazine. The only newspapers that seem to be widely read much by this kind of girl are picture papers like the

Daily Mirror and the *Graphic,* Sunday papers of *The News of the World* type, and the local evening or weekly paper which every home takes.

After about 14 not many girls seem to "play out" or to take part in the street games, "Hot Rice," "Hadrian's Wall," skipping, etc., on which, as children, practically all of them spent a good deal of their leisure. They still go out onto the street, but for slow walks round with a girl friend, for long doorstep talks with a boy, for street corner gossip with other boys and girls, or for milk bar gang meetings with their particular set.

The girls probably go to the cinema more often than to any other type of paid recreation. About two nights a week seems a typical pattern for a girl with 10/- a week pocket money. Quite often girls will go with their mother or will treat a small brother to a special film, like *Mr. Ichabod and Mr. Toad.* In most artisan districts one cinema makes a point of catering for child and adolescent audiences with serials such as *Jungle Girl* and a generally unsophisticated swashbuckling programme. One cinema in the locality, too, generally runs a children's cinema club to which nearly all the girls have belonged but by the time the girls leave school they are growing out of this kind of programme.

Dancing is much less universally practised than cinema going but is generally regarded as a more dashing way of enjoying yourself. An ordinary popular dance hall in a provincial city charges 2/- for 3½ hours of dancing. Young girls often start their dancing under the wing of an older sister, and later on two girl friends will go together. Not very many girls seem to go in a group to dances. Old-time dancing has had a considerable revival recently, and is surprisingly popular even among the Bebop fans.

Cycling is another very regular form of recreation. Most girls manage to get a cycle of their own by the time they leave school probably paying for a £20 cycle by 8/9 weekly installments. There are hundreds of cycling clubs for the real enthusiasts who go in for racing and for 70 mile runs on a Sunday, but for the majority of adolescent girls cycling means not more than going out into the country with a friend for short rides. The popularity of ice and roller skating depends, of course, on what rinks are available. It is regarded as an expensive hobby. A girl who is earning up to £4 a week however will probably afford the 3/6 entrance fee and will save up to buy her own boots. Sports like hockey and tennis are relatively unpopular among working girls. The secondary modern schools are only just beginning to play games of this kind and girls on the whole seem much less able than boys to organise themselves informally into the teams, or even the fours, that such games demand. Swimming probably owes a good deal of its popularity, though it is said to be less universal here than in the States, to the fact that it is a pastime that you can pursue alone. The facilities vary greatly from place to place, but most town youngsters have a swimming bath relatively near to their home and the charges are not high, perhaps 1/- with reductions for people under 15.

More than half of the adolescent boy population and a rather smaller proportion of girls, spend some of their evenings at a youth organisation. These are societies for and of young people but sponsored by adults. The latter are concerned to help boys and girls obtain the sort of recreations they enjoy and at the same time try to provide some informal education, particularly for those who have left school at 15. Probably most of the adults connected with youth organisations see the latter as one method of training future citizens of a democratic state and members of a Christian community.

English youth organizations have a long history. Some of the national bodies like the Y.M. and Y.W.C.A., the Boys Brigade and the Girls' Friendly Society date back to the last quarter of the 19th century. These organisations were primarily intended to help the under-privileged young workers of the great cities. The Scout and Guide movement, started before the 1914 war, extended the scope of the youth organisation on, broadly, educational lines. At the beginning of the last war the statutory authorities got into co-operation with the many existing voluntary organisations for young people and, together, a great drive was made under the title of the Service of Youth. This aimed to increase the number of units, to raise their standard and generally to try to get more adolescents linked up with some type of organisation. The liaison between the official education authorities and the voluntary organisations, begun in 1939, still exists and has much strengthened the Youth movement. Funds, premises, and adult leaders are provided from both sources. Organisations, for example, meet in Local Education Authority owned schools and in Church owned Halls. The local boys' clubs arts festival may be run by the National Association of Boys' Clubs while the football and swimming leagues which the same clubs enter for are arranged by the youth organisers of the L.E.A.

All this sounds as if the youth organisations are very much an adult affair. In fact, in the well run units, the young people themselves are asked to take on as much as possible of the responsibility for their own organisation. The relatively small scale of the majority of the units makes this not too difficult. Most organisations have their own, elected Members' Committee. The boys and girls almost invariably pay a subscription, about 3d. or 6d. a week. They decide on programmes, are responsible for the canteen and, under a skilled leader, have a very definite training in democratic methods of control. A fair test of the good unit is how far the boys and girls do really regard the society as their own show.

There are many "boys only" organisations, including the pre-service ones which often have social clubs attached to them. A growing number of societies, especially of the club type, are open to both boys and girls. A decreasing number seem to exist for girls only. The most flourishing of this latter group seem to be for schoolgirls of 12 to 14. The sort of club that some of the girls described in this article belong to has one room with comfortable chairs where people can just gossip; a little canteen serving such things as tea and soft drinks, hot baked potatoes, slices of fried bread, and cheese cobs. It also has one hall big enough for a tap dancing class, for table tennis and for badminton. There is a stage that is a great asset to the drama class, one of the most popular and most valuable activities. One other room is kept for class work under an L.E.A. teacher. Crafts like leather work, embroidery and puppet making and art take place here.

Out of doors the clubs run tennis and cycling sections and camping week-ends, perhaps at a camp house up on the moors owned by all the organisations of the locality. To sum up: the present youth organisations have many weaknesses. They are subject to a good deal of justified criticism and they still fail to attract a large number of those young people who, so far as one can judge, would probably benefit from joining. At the same time, more than half the 14 to 18 population of this country finds it worth while to join voluntarily one or another of the youth organisations which suggests that the latter are meeting a genuine need. Individual youngsters' own enthusiasm and delight in the friendships, the adventures and the activities of their own Brigade or Troop or Club is the most convincing testimonial to the value of the youth movement.

For a somewhat different view of English social organization and processes, we turn to an article by Stephen Spender, the prominent poet, writer, and playwright. Spender presents a picture of the English adolescent as he is influenced through his education by the attitudes and traditions of his society. Particularly important are the development of class consciousness and sex attitudes, and the transmission of spiritual values. It should be kept in mind that in England a "public school" is one that in this country would be referred to as "independent," "private," or "non-tax-supported." Spender's article is based on a lecture he delivered at the Summer Seminar in Education for International Understanding, at Paris in 1947, under the auspices of UNESCO.

· 73 · The Adolescent and the Schools
STEPHEN SPENDER

I am not asked to speak about schools, but about the adolescent. One cannot think of the English adolescent without thinking of a little fragment of human material confronted by a great hierarchy of educational machines through which his young life is going to pass, and from which he will emerge as a member of a community. And the first point to make is that those machines select their material. There are the Elementary Schools, the Secondary Schools, the private Preparatory Schools, the Grammar Schools, the minor Public Schools, the great Public Schools, like Eton and Winchester, Harrow and Charterhouse, and then there are the Universities, Oxford and Cambridge, and what are called, I believe, the provincial Universities. Then, also, a class apart, there are the Girls' Public Schools. There are also the small progressive schools for rich children, which are in revolt against the Public School system.

And Eton and Harrow do not select the boy who goes to the Elementary School. English education is on a class basis. Indeed class feeling is more deeply ingrained in our educational system than anywhere else. I can illustrate this by drawing attention to what I know to be a fact; that many middle class parents who consider that in their own lives they have shed all traces of class feeling, and who may even wish to belong to the working class, yet, when it comes to educating their own children, send them to the public school against whose values they have rebelled themselves. The reason for this is not merely, I think, that such parents consider the Public School the best possible education; they also

feel that having a public school education is the sign of belonging to a social class, and they do not feel entitled, just because they have withdrawn from spiritual membership of that class themselves, to impose the choice which they have made for themselves on their children.

Thus, the main social experience of the English child and adolescent is that he belongs to a social class. The child of poor parents is forced continually to think of the job which he will do when he leaves school, the job that will grade him for life. He can only obtain the higher education which will make it possible for him to enter a profession by winning scholarship after scholarship, which will take him to the secondary school and finally to the University. If he wins sufficient scholarships to get to a University and then to pass beyond the University into a profession, he will then be absorbed into the broad middle class which is the main stream of English social and cultural life.

The poor are thus in a practical and empirical way made conscious of their place in society during their adolescence by their education. This does not mean that they recognize the superiority of the rich, but it does mean that they realize their own limitations. The social history of the poor man or woman is his or her education. The sons of those who can afford and who do send their children to public schools are conscious of their social position in quite a different way. They know that they belong to a privileged class, and they are conscious of social superiority. In between the public schools and the completely

[From "The English Adolescent," *The Harvard Educational Review*, Vol. 18, No. 4, Cambridge, 1948. Pp. 229-239. Used by permission.]

state-supported schools, there is a kind of limbo of minor public schools, day schools and grammar schools, which, unlike the genuine working class schools, have a real consciousness of social inferiority. This attitude is very noticeable amongst those grammar school boys who come up to Oxford and Cambridge: they feel ill-at-ease with the Public school boys. The sense of social superiority of public school boys is only equalled by the energy with which members of the upper-middle class in England sometimes pretend that it does not exist. Here are two examples. In 1928 I went to visit a friend who had just arrived at New College for Oxford. He was giving a tea party to six or eight other Etonians all of whom had also just come up to Oxford. They were all convulsed with amusement for a reason which they quickly divulged to me. To their amazement one of their contemporaries, who had come up with them to New College, was a boy—I shall call him X—whom they had known and laughed at all their time at Eton, because he was the son of the school grocer; he often waited on them behind the counter of his father's shop.

The year, 1928, may seem very long ago, but the second story is more recent. In the autumn of 1940, before I was called up (for military service), I taught for a term in a West-country public school. The boys at this school were mostly the sons of clergy, doctors, and other professional men. This school, in common with several other public schools, supported, as an act of charity, a mission which did good work amongst poor boys in one of the large neighbouring towns. It was suggested that as a revolutionary measure which fitted in with the mood of a country fighting a war alone for the salvation of world democracy, the school should offer two scholarships to be given to two working class boys so that they might be educated together with the sons of the parsons, doctors, and schoolmasters. As an experiment, another master and myself asked all the boys in certain houses of the school to write a short essay on their reactions to this proposal. The results of this inquiry amazed me. There was not a single boy who treated the suggestion as simply an invitation to two other boys, with a rather different background perhaps, to enter the school. To all of them it seemed outrageous and revolutionary. The answers were divided between (a) those who thought that it would lower and vitiate the school to have these two working class boys and (b) those who thought that the shock of such a social environment as that of our school on the working class boys would be such that they would never find their places in their own world again, would never be happy, and would probably be ruined in their later lives.

There is a saving grace in both these illustrations. Neither the undergraduates at Eton nor the boys at the school showed hatred or intolerance of the working-class boys. Their attitude was, rather, one of surprise to find that such people existed in the same sense, with the same ambitions and potentialities as themselves. And as a matter of fact the Etonians took well to X, the school grocer's son, when they had got over the shock of discovering that he was rather cleverer than themselves.

This is important, because English class feeling is deep rather than narrow. It derives from profound and utmost self-confidence of the ruling classes in themselves, and it has a depth which can absorb newcomers when they have proved that they can also belong to the middle class. This depth and breadth rather than narrowness derives from the fact that we are in a middle-class society with a middle-class culture. The working-class boy who wins scholarships makes his way up until he enters the middle class. Of course, politically, he may remain a revolutionary proletarian, but even such a political attitude does not alter the fact that the revolutionary writer or the trade-union leader inevitably enters into the middle class of traditional England. The trade unionist and socialist leaders who now appear to be in power in England have worked their way up through the educational system through self-education, into the middle class, which to some extent has broadened itself, by becoming aware of their existence, and absorbing them.

Perhaps I may seem to have strayed from the subject of the adolescent. But I think it is essential to bear in mind that there is a great difference between the experience of the adolescent of working-class parents in England and that of parents who can afford to send their children to the schools where one pays for an expensive education. This difference goes to the very depths of English life. In experiencing this class difference the adolescent experiences a social reality in effective action, which is more or less concealed in adult life. When I say that the poor child who had only a primary education is experiencing the class system, I mean that he is excluded by it from the middle-class tradition which is the main social and cultural stream of English life. And if the poor child gets scholarships and educates himself into one of the professions, into the arts or into politics, he enters culturally into the middle class, and is accepted by it. So we have in England this situation: that class counts very much in so far as the poor and the uneducated are excluded by poverty or ignorance from the middle class, and very little in so far as the middle class has a broad and deep culture which is capable of absorbing into itself every explicit and educated point of view even when it appears to be politically opposed to it. England is an evolutionary rather than a revolutionary country because it has a protean middle class.

Thus, also, we find that the class difference leads to entirely different forms of characteristic adolescent experiences of children of different classes. When we come to physical and physiological development, we find that the difference is very striking, because the public schools take the children away from their homes for nine months in the year and board them. The boarding-school life is undoubtedly healthy, rather spartan-like, and toughening. The poor children do not leave their homes, where, though they may be very poor, they may nevertheless be pampered and spoiled far more than richer children. Sometimes periods of pampering alternate with periods of poverty.

The atmosphere of the English working class or lower-middle class home, especially in large towns, cannot be said to be conducive to good physical and physiological development. During the early part of the war, as a nation, we were shocked into awareness of this. In the first place the medical examination of hundreds of thousands of young men and women for the services showed how deplorable the physical condition of the poor was. In the second place, people in the country became aware of the often verminous and nearly always unhealthy condition of children from the towns, when the towns-children were billeted on them during the period of evacuation of towns for fear of air raids. A report on the condition of these children was published by the Women's Institutes Association of Great Britain. This is an appalling document containing a great deal of information for whoever wants to read it.

When I asked my fellow-firemen how they brought up their children, nearly always I found that they preferred giving them tinned to fresh milk, that their children drank large quantities of beer and of tea, and that their most frequent meal was fried fish and chips. The elementary and secondary schools can hardly fight more than a losing battle against such conditions at home. The boarding schools, however, with their simple diet and their emphasis on the importance of games can certainly claim that physically, if not mentally, they produce a healthy type of adolescent.

Another great difference between the education of the upper and lower class adolescent is in the development of his attitude towards courtship, marriage, and sexual problems. Here again the child of poor parents takes his or her attitude from the home. The problem for the children who go to boarding schools is that, except in a few schools such as Bedales, where there are both girls and boys, the sexes are artificially separated from each other, at an age when the poor boy is probably walking out with his first girl.

In the English public schools there is no

training for courtship and marriage; there is simply a problem called sex, of which everyone is uncomfortably aware. In so far as there is an attempt to deal with this problem, it is pushed on to the science master, who is supposed to explain the biological functioning of sex to the boys, probably by a process of first explaining to them the amours of flowers, then frogs, and so on through the animal kingdom, until the possibility of such a relationship between human beings is indicated. The housemaster, or even the headmaster may be called in, if the sexual problem threatens to break out of this scientific test tube, where the school likes to keep it, and infect the emotional atmosphere of a boy's mind. It is no exaggeration to say that the attitude of most English school masters to sex is simply that it is not a question that should arise in a public school. It should do so after the boy has left school, and then it should solve itself without any previous training through a miracle of love.

The attitude of a headmaster of a minor public school is illustrated by the following story, which he told me himself. He said that one day he had walked down a lane near the school and he had seen two of the older boys sitting on a bench with their arms around the waists of two girls. I asked him what he had done. He said that he had sent for the two boys the following day and had said: "I saw you two boys with two girls yesterday. Now in certain countries, such as France, it would be thought that there was nothing wrong with the idea of two boys aged sixteen and seventeen sitting on a bench with their arms around the waists of two girls. However, we in England do not believe in that sort of thing. And on the whole, I think that the English way is the best." He seemed very proud of this reply, and no doubt it cowed the two boys. The only trouble is that the English way has met with the criticism that in some cases it perverts the normal development of the relations between the sexes.

* * *

A young woman who went to one of the "Girls' Public Schools," and to whom I had shown this paper, commented: "Sex education for girls, as far as I know or have experienced, is pretty well parallel with that of boys. The Botany mistress drops embarrassed hints, or the biology mistress makes a better job of it. Games, hobbies, and all the rest are terrifically encouraged to counteract any nascent interest in boys. At the same time *schwaermerei* on other girls is persecuted by authority—a fact which I am sure does much to stimulate it. . . . In the upper-middle classes I think the education of girls, with its emphases on games, Girl Guides, heartiness and unsentimentality, does tend to produce much too high a percentage of gawky and frigid women who—now that arranged marriages are no longer the fashion—have not the slightest idea how to approach the other sex. 'The English spinster' is, of course, proverbial abroad and is largely the product of bad education in adolescence, which still goes on.

"On the other hand this only applies to the middle class. The working class girl does not seem to have the same difficulties, probably because she imbibes the facts of life and a natural attitude in her more congested home life and while 'helping mother.'

"Against this I think that English middle-class women have in a very high degree the same attitude of responsibility as English men and are—in spite of these inadequacies as *women*—better citizens than most European women, because more generally emancipated, and taught from childhood to think themselves in no way inferior to the opposite sex."

It seems to me that our trouble in England in these matters is that we do not have an ideal of chastity or even restraint; we insist simply on a complete negation of the instinctional life of children, which often we succeed in killing or perverting. We do not accept the senses and then discipline them: we simply deny them and the consequence of this denial is to drive some English men and women into a pursuit of sensual reality which they have lost. Here we pay the price of belonging to a protestant tradition, and there is no doubt a great deal that we have to learn from the

Latin and Catholic countries, as well as from the psychologists.

The English public school is really a kind of small city state, and I think it is only if one sees it in this way that one can really understand its weaknesses and its merits. Like the city state, it is a community small enough and old enough for public opinion to be regarded as impersonal and almost sacred. The floggings, lines and other sensational punishments for which public schools are famous are only really border-line penalties for those who run outside the boundaries of the discipline of the inner city which is created by the extraordinary seriousness with which masters and boys take the school and themselves. A public schoolboy from Winchester who will soon, I am sure, be a cabinet minister, once said to me: "At Winchester, when I was head of my house, I was a greater man than I shall ever be again in my life, even if I live to be a Prime Minister." An appalling remark, from an appalling man, I thought at the time, "but he will certainly be an excellent prime minister!"

Thus the important thing about the public school is that the boys regard all its institutions, all its offices, as sacred; and the masters and parents do also. For a housemaster the choice of prefects and of the boy who will be head of the house is as serious as the choice of a new cabinet for a country, and the boys chosen for these functions take them as seriously as any task they will undertake in the rest of their lives. Of course, there are prefects and head boys who fail, but such failure is parallel to the scandal attaching to a cabinet minister who reveals to his friends the secrets of the Budget.

If one teaches at a public school, one finds it difficult to regard the boys just as boys: they are carried along, as on invisible lines, by the inner discipline of the school-state: if one punishes them, that is just like putting them back onto the lines from which they may have slipped.

I think that the explanation of the extraordinary civic sense of responsibility of England is to be found in the English education

which teaches boys to take themselves seriously as functions of an institution, before they take themselves seriously as persons or as individuals. This really explains a great deal, both of the merits and defects of the English. It explains why the English are so suspicious of anyone who takes himself as a person seriously, why they mistrust any machinery of thought, such as psychoanalysis, which directs the attentions of the individual too much onto himself and yet why, as responsible members of a community, they show a deadly earnestness about their own positions which leaves no room for cynicism.

The schoolmasters who persuaded a boy of sixteen at Winchester that he was a great man, were, in a sense, taking him far too seriously, or letting him take himself so; and in another sense they were not taking him seriously enough, because they were ignoring the fact that his psychological development at this time could have been that of a Pericles. Perhaps they were doing him an injury and yet they were giving him qualities which the ruling class of a society, such as the British Empire has been until now, undoubtedly needs.

Thus, I think that the English civic sense is not learned by giving children lessons in how local government works, but in forcing onto them in their youth the responsibilities of a very old tradition.

The upper class English adolescent, who is looked upon sometimes by the outside world as cold and impassive, often has nevertheless a tormented adolescence, which may be followed by a permanent inability to grow up in certain ways, or by a stifling of his emotional life, or by a rare capacity to learn and to develop throughout the whole of his life. The chief problems which may disturb him are sexual ones—which I have discussed—or a religious crisis, or a crisis in his relationship with his parents. In none of these things is he really helped in his upbringing, which tells him to suppress his sexual life, which cuts him off from his parents at a time when he should be getting to know and adjust himself to them in a mature relationship, and which teaches him a conventionalised tepid religious faith which seems only to be taught in order that it may be blown away by the first fresh winds of scientific knowledge.

As I have suggested, the strength of the Public School is its power to make boys take their activities which help the life of the school and live out its traditions, very seriously. The effect of the school city-state is to produce a type, what most public schoolmasters would call 'the public school type.' The characteristic of this type is that mixture of good qualities summed up in the minds of schoolmasters by the phrase: *Mens sana in corpore sano.*

The weakness of the system is that it becomes too easy for the masters and the boys themselves to value every activity of the members of the school in so far as it contributes or fails to contribute to the School State and School Type. Games can be regarded in this way. The school team, if it wins matches, contributes to the glory of the school; the discipline of games is a sacred rite within the school tradition; and, moreover, games are supposed to help the boys to lead asexual lives. It will be noticed here that games are not regarded, as they might well be, in part at least, as being valuable because they provide an escape from school ritual. The result of this attitude has been that a good many boys have revolted against games, precisely because they realize that they are being used as a means of preaching and practicing the school dogmas, instead of as play.

Religion, just as much as games, tends to become a part of the school ritual, instead of a window on to a wider, more universal valid order outside it. I am sure that headmasters do not intend this to happen, but nevertheless it does happen. The boy who shows an interest in religion which threatens to take him beyond the spiritual boundaries of the city state is regarded as unhealthy, dangerous, just as much as the boy who takes too great an interest in the arts. The religion that is taught in school strengthens the school code which may give a boy certain ethical standards that will last him all his life, but it does not give him an understanding of Christian charity or

the faith in an invisible world which will last him for a week after he has left school if he is brought in touch with the violence and crudity and passion of the real world.

If my analysis is even partly correct it will be seen that our public school education, whilst it instils us with a sense of responsibility to the community, does so at considerable cost to our personal psychology and relationship. In fact, it tends to perpetuate the adolescence of the Englishman, by discouraging the interest in spiritual life for its own sake which leads to spiritual maturity, by teaching us to treat as irrelevant physical instincts which lead men and women to understand each other in a mature and full relationship, and by neglecting the problem of the relationship of the growing child with his parents.

At the same time, if we are a people who never recover from certain adolescent weaknesses, we also acquire in adolescence certain virtues, such as reasonableness, adaptability, generosity, adventurousness, and an astonishingly open mind, combined with a pious attitude toward our institutions. England is supremely the country where the people respond to a national emergency and are capable of that kind of illumination which can see beyond self-interest to the need of the whole country, when it is explained to them, or which can reverse a long-established national policy towards some part of the empire within a few days. Most surprisingly of all, the very class of people who, according to a materialist view, should be most tied up with their own interests, the wealthy public school boys, are the first to sacrifice their lives in a war. Probably, if, in addition to having material interests, they were capable also of developing deep relationships with other people and their families, this capacity for sacrifice would not be so great. The philistines of the undisciplined and undeveloped heart have been among the first to save England in two wars.

In this sketch, nearly everything I have said has tended to emphasize the difference between the adolescent experience of the social classes in England. On the one hand, there are the public school boys, artificially withdrawn from parental affection, and indeed from nearly all affection, during the long years of adolescence; on the other hand there is the poor boy who is a home boy, who is often surrounded by an almost stifling family affection, and who regards 'leaving mum' as the most supremely difficult decision of his life. If I may appeal to the English novelists again, D. H. Lawrence, who was himself the son of a Nottingham miner, shows in his novels a classic picture of his own transition from his working-class origins to his later middle-class environment as a literary artist. His early novel, *Sons and Lovers,* is a heart-rending account of a working-class boy (Lawrence himself) breaking away from his mother's love; whilst his later novels show him lost in a world of the upper classes and trying to recreate the passionate atmosphere of the clinging relationship with his mother in a febrile sexuality.

Perhaps it would be true to say that if the English adolescent who goes to the boarding public school suffers from lack of affection, the working-class boy (the boy more than the girl) suffers from an excess of it. In the difficult lives of the poor, the home, unless it is a complete failure, as may happen, becomes the centre and supreme compensation for all the disappointments of life. And often there is a touching and perhaps rather oppressive emotional dependence of the parents on the children. With the girls this takes the practical form of loading them heavily with responsibilities, making them become, for example, at an early age, the mother of the younger children; with the boys it is more likely to be an emotional burden of the kind so poignantly described by D. H. Lawrence.

I think that many witnesses who have been in the services during World Wars I and II would agree that, on the whole, the public-school boys are tougher than the working class stay-at-home boys, and that this was very evident between 1914 and 1918, and still evident, though less so, between 1939 and 1945. Perhaps here we have a clue to the unity of English morale: that the upper-class adolescents have retained, to a considerable extent, their toughness and their capacity for leadership. However, toughness is not in itself a sufficient explanation. One has to add to it a few characteristics which really, I think, make the English adolescent exceptional, and which are certainly of value as an experience not to be submerged under the social changes which are taking place all over the world.

The first characteristic, I should call innocence! The English public school-boy is set aside from the experience of the world during his growing years, and plunged into a tradition which has to a great extent remained islanded from the surrounding world. The result is that, with all his faults, he remains to some extent an innocent, and his very defects are based on this innocence. Thus, as I have explained, his snobbishness is based on an almost incredible unawareness of the conditions and existence of the working populations in an industrial civilisation. Now snobbishness is certainly not a virtue, but the fact that this fault is one of innocence instead of one of narrowness and self-opinionatedness means that it can be remedied. So that there exists side by side with the English narrow-mindedness an equally strong open-mindedness, a capacity to see the other person's point of view.

This innocence is not a specially public school virtue. It is a virtue of other centuries, a country virtue of the country-side. But per·haps because the Public Schools are situated in the country-side, they have become, almost accidentally, transmitters of this quality of saving youth from the corruption of the towns. And the other virtues—tolerance, courage, modesty, adaptability, and the rest—are only consequences of this fundamental innocence.

Toughness and an integrity which, with all the faults of the English educational system have not been betrayed, are the contributions of the upper classes to the unity which has enabled English youth to unite for the desperate struggles of two wars. And with all the differences of background and training, the poor recognise and have, themselves, these values. Different as their experiences and environment are, they are given a schooling based on the same idea that education is a training which can create good citizens and strengthen character, and not just a machine for making youths pass examinations. The teacher is responsible, not just for the learning of his pupil, but for his whole development, his physical and moral well-being.

The contribution of the English adolescent experience to the planning of the adolescent education of a world citizen, might well be the idea that a certain isolation of the adolescent from the modern industrial civilisation is necessary. The problem is to isolate him, without at the same time making him unable to deal with the harshest realities of our existence, and of giving him the strength of his virtues. As I have suggested, a weakness of the English Public School system is that the energies of the boys are too often only directed towards the school itself. This has the result that emotional problems of adolescence which conflict with the discipline of the school-state are treated as though they do not exist; and the result of that is the protraction throughout the life of many Englishmen of unsolved emotional problems of adolescence. Again, the school chapel, which, like the school football field, produces a self-worshipping kind of Public School religion corresponding to Public School games, neglects the fundamental educational problem of our time: that is, how, during the period of adolescence, to strengthen in the mind of youth a faith in spiritual values and in human values capable of resisting the materialism and the power policies of the world of enormous conflicting social interests in which we live.

I cannot introduce phrases such as *spiritual values* and *human values* without attempting more precise definitions. By spiritual values I mean the sense that the structure of society exists for the sake of a purpose which is a spiritual purpose, and not just for its own sake. It is simply the sense that all material and social structures exist for the sake of an aim, and that that aim cannot be simply the structure and the material well-being of the society itself, but its vision of a purpose in life. It is the recognition that no civilisation is judged good because its members were of a certain social class or a certain race, but by the values which that civilisation produced; and those values are not just the material conditions within which members of that civilisation lived their lives.

By human values, I mean the realization that human beings, human individuals are each one of them sacred. A business, or a nation, or a political party, or a world organisation, which treats human lives as though they are chattels which can be moved about or cast aside or destroyed without regard for their sacred nature, or as though they were the mud which is dug out of a river bed, when the course of the river is altered, is dehumanising the human spirit, because the whole of humanity, even the humanity of the people who commit crimes against humanity, is involved in acts directed against any section of humanity.

Therefore, I believe that, in the world of to-day, it is necessary that the adolescent have a far greater degree of realisation of himself as a spiritual and also as a physical individual being than exists within the English adolescent experience. At the same time, I think that during this period of transition, the English experience has much from which people in other countries may learn.

This picture of English society would not be complete without a consideration of the role of the church. There is not sufficient space to discuss in detail the numerous organizations through which religious activity finds an expression in Britain, but a look at the membership figures of the major groups will suggest the extent of their importance. The Established Church of England, which is Protestant Episcopal in its form of government, numbers about 2,300,000 full members in England and Wales; the Roman Catholics number more than 2,500,000. Other denominations (Nonconformists) in England and Wales include Methodist, with nearly 1,150,000 members; Congregational Union, 370,000; Baptist, 340,000; Calvinistic Methodist, 230,000; Presbyterian, 80,000; Society of Friends, 20,000; and Churches of Christ, 14,000. In Scotland the Established Church is Presbyterian in form and has 1,250,000 members, the Episcopal Church has 56,000 members, and the Roman Catholic Church 620,000. The Jewish faith in the United Kingdom (which includes Northern Ireland) numbers about 385,000 members. (Statistics from the *American Encyclopedia Yearbook* for 1950.)

Something of the historical background and relationships of these groups will become apparent in the next selection. It was Henry VIII who led the break with the Roman Catholic Church and set up the Anglican, or Established, Church. But even after that break the Catholic Church continued to play a prominent role in English history, its avowed "universality" in contrast to the nationalism which the Church of England encouraged. It was only slowly that opposition developed within England to the doctrine that to be a good Englishman was to be a good member of the Anglican Church. The struggle to divorce religious loyalties from state loyalties led to the Nonconformity movements and eventually spread to the American Colonies, where it contributed significantly to their later Revolution. One of the interesting aspects of the development of Puritanism is the extent to which it may have provided a moral and intellectual atmosphere favorable to the rise of the special economic system we know as capitalism. This and other topics are treated briefly but expertly in the next selection.

• 74 • *The Churches and the Rise of Modern England*
ERNEST BARKER

THE FIRST REFORMATION: THE ANGLICAN

There were two Reformations in England —the Reformation which issued in Anglicanism, and that which issued in Nonconformity; and the dualism of the two—reflected, from the end of the seventeenth century, in the opposition of our political parties—has been one of the most peculiar and one of the most potent influences in our national life. It has not only reflected itself in the political organization of parties: it has also appeared in a social division. Anglicanism has been the religion of the gentry, the land, the villages:

Nonconformity has been the faith of the middle classes, of commerce and industry, of the towns. The one has fostered the love of tradition, the sense of historical continuity, the passion of national unity; the other has cherished an ideal of the purity of original Christian truth, a belief in the need for basing religious order newly and freshly upon that truth, a doctrine of the indefeasible right of the individual soul to make its own peace with its Maker. To the one the past has been sacred; to the other it has been suspect. The one was naturally drawn to a belief in two parallel and interconnected divine rights— the divine right of the king and the divine

[From *National Character and the Factors in its Formation,* Harper Brothers, London, 1927. Pp. 195-213. Used by permission.]

right of the bishop. It stood for authority, and it believed that authority, alike in Church and in State, had two attributes—the attribute of a divine origin and the attribute of a continuous historic tradition. . . . The philosophy of Nonconformity was colder and more rational. The foundation of authority, ecclesiastical or political, was human institution. It was men who had erected presbyters or kings, for ends of edification or protection: it was on a compact between men that their authority rested; and if that authority were not duly used for the ends prescribed, the compact was null and void, and what had been given by men could by men be taken away. . . .

In the Anglican system the king was more than parallel with bishops. He was the bishop of bishops—the supreme head on earth of the Church as well as the State—or at any rate (in Elizabeth's milder phrase) "the only supreme Governor of the realm . . . as well in all spiritual or ecclesiastical things or causes as temporal." Royal supremacy is thus of the essence of the Reformation. The king adds a new province to his existing territory, by acquiring control of things ecclesiastical (hitherto subject to the Pope) in addition to the things temporal which he has always controlled; and he gains at the same time a new consecration for his whole state and position, and a new appeal to the hearts of his subjects, by becoming, as it were, the chief priest of his people. Loyalty assumes a new fervor: "God bless the King" comes from men's lips with a deeper resonance; "Church and King" is a compelling toast; the principles of the Cavaliers, which became the principles of the Tory party, are launched on their long voyage. The conception and practice of royal headship, which may seem to lower the Church, had for its complement the fact of Establishment, by which the Church was exalted. If the king, who is the symbol of the State, is also the head of the Church, it is inevitable that the Church should be brought into a special relation with the State. On the one hand, the State will guarantee and protect the Church, by acts of legislation or executive process, in its powers and its properties; on

the other, the Church will consecrate the State, and, as it were, hold up its hands, in the course of its earthly activities. Establishment means both of these things; but it means particularly the latter. . . .

The conception which underlies establishment is a conception of a single society, which in one aspect we call a State, and in another we call a Church, but which in itself is one and undivided. . . . Before the Reformation there was an English nation, and that nation was organized as a State; but in matter of religion its members belonged to another and wider society, which was the general society of the Latin Church of the West. After the Reformation . . . the nation . . . is now conceived not only as a State, but also as a Church. It receives a new consecration; and the State, as the secular expression of its life, shares with it in that consecration. . . .

This was an ideal; but it never became a fact. Two grave questions occupied the minds of the leaders in Church and State as soon as they attempted to translate the ideal into practice. What was to be the basis of religious unity, and how much was it to include? What was to be done with the dissidents who refused to accept the basis and declined to belong to the single national society in its form of religious expression? . . .

The attempt to make the Church coextensive with the nation, and to use external religious observance as a drill to form the habits of Englishmen and to shape national character, encountered an invincible opposition. The ideal of uniformity was answered by the fact of Nonconformity. The Church could not be coextensive with the nation, when a large part of the nation refused to belong to the Church; and there could be no general external drill when thousands insisted upon a free right of internal choice. Nonconformity had always before it the example of Scotland, where, instead of the nation being drilled by external rule into a single religious society, religious society, regarded as something independent and prior, shaped a nation by its inner spirit in the image of its own unity. . . . As the *plebs* established itself in ancient Rome by the side of the *populus* so the Nonconformist congregations established themselves in England by the side of the Established Church. Like the plebeians in early Roman history, they suffered grave disabilities. They could not hold office, municipal or national; and by various statutes they were deprived even of the social right of maintaining schools and giving instruction. . . . It is the Church— the Establishment of the Church, and the Royal Headship of the Church—that is the essence of the Tory party which came into being during the reign of Charles II, just as it is the voluntary religious society, the independence of its congregations, and the general conception of the free Church in the free State, that is the essence of the Whig party which came into existence at the same time. . . . Our party system, almost to the end of the nineteenth century, and until a new third party emerged under the name of Labour, was a legacy of ecclesiastical policies. . . .

THE SECOND REFORMATION: NONCONFORMITY

Nonconformity, like Anglicanism, bequeathed a political party to the nation; and like Anglicanism, but in its own way and with its own quality, it has been a social force in the process of national development. . . . It has spread itself over the world, and made its home in the meeting-houses of Massachusetts no less than in the austere chapels of England; it has steeled our qualities, and accentuated our angularities; it has affected our economic life, and influenced the direction of our foreign policy; it has done much to determine the aspect we have presented to the world, and the judgment which the world has passed upon us.

English Nonconformity has two main streams. The first we may call by the general name of Puritan. Its great period runs from the accession of Queen Elizabeth to the Revolution of 1688. It included (down to 1662) Low Churchmen as well as those who were definite dissidents from the Church; it is represented to-day by Presbyterians, Congregationalists, Baptists, and Quakers. Perhaps

its numbers were never very great during the seventeenth century; and when William III attempted a religious census, immediately after the Revolution, he only enumerated 108,000 male Nonconformists to nearly 2,500,000 Conformists. The volume of Nonconformity was greatly increased in the eighteenth century, when the stream of Wesleyanism was added to its current; and at the present time the Nonconformists of England and Wales (who taken together are almost equal in number to the members of the Church of England) are evenly divided between societies which took their origin from the Puritan movement of the sixteenth and seventeenth century, and those which are derived from the Wesleyan movement of the eighteenth. Remembering this division, and the successive stages in which Nonconformity has played its part and exerted its influence, we must distinguish between the effects of the first and fundamental, and those of the later and secondary period.

Puritanism was rooted and grounded in a positive belief; but there is a sense in which we may say that, in English history, it has been the spirit "which constantly denies." From its beginnings it was engaged in a protestation against the State and a negation of its claims in matter of religion. . . .

There were other ways in which Puritanism fostered political liberty. Its basis was religious individualism; and it fostered a general temper of individualism. Its doctrine of the responsibility of the lonely soul for its own salvation readily allied itself with parallel tenets of secular philosophy, and it helped to encourage their general diffusion. It was the air in which ideas of the Englishman's legal "birthright and inheritance," and even more drastic ideas of the natural rights of all men, flourished in the seventeenth century. . . . All in all, we may say that Nonconformity served as a gathering ground of the various influences (religious, political, and economic) which produced the Liberal or Manchester philosophy of the nineteenth century—a philosophy which not only inspired a party, but determined in no small measure the general life and aspect of Victorian England. "Way for individual enterprise"—this was its teaching; and backed by the manufacturing and commercial classes, which had always been the stronghold of Nonconformity, its teaching triumphed. . . .

If the Puritans were driven, as a tenacious minority, in opposition to the State, to develop the more negative qualities of a minority, there was none the less in their creed a positive quality which was the ground and the rock of their resistance. Puritanism was something more than a challenge to the State. It was the practice of a firm and resolute will ("will . . . is the essence of Puritanism"), set sternly to the kingdom of God and His righteousness; it was a rigour of self-control, and an unrelenting process of self-discipline, by which the will of man was made to fulfil the apprehended purposes of God. It was not for the Puritan to steep his mind in the warm comfort of historic tradition; nor could his spirit float suspended in a cloud of encompassing witnesses, sustained by the communion of an inspired and inspiring Church. His was a new and solitary soul, projected into a bare world for an arduous and lonely struggle; and he must wrestle alone, in the night, with the angel of the Lord. He lived in a spiritual solitude; but he was not a solitary. He could not renounce the world and its works, or embrace the life of the hermit or anchorite; he had been sent into the world to do his Master's business and to fulfil his calling; and it would have seemed to him a surrender of the will and an act of cowardice to flee temptation or to shun struggle. . . .

Loneliness was one of the Puritan virtues, as it was also one of the Puritan defects. They dared to be alone, and they cultivated the high virtues of solitude. Solitude is the preparation and the parent of achievement. . . . But the loneliness of the Puritan was also a defect. He carried a lonely self-reliance to the verge of a lonely selfishness. He rejected any comfort or consolation of society, because he desired to lean on nothing but his own strong will; but he also forgot the just claims of society. . . .

Besides the practice of will, and the cultivation of solitude, the Puritan had a passionate zeal for work which, acting upon an energy natural, as we have seen, to the English stock, and fostered, as we have also seen, by the conditions of the English climate, raised it to a height at which it may sometimes seem almost daemonic. Work was conceived as something sacramental—the outward and visible sign of an inward and visible struggle to do the will of the Lord. The Parable of the Vineyard and the Parable of the Talents were ever before the Puritan's eye. He did not love the Book of Common Prayer, but there was one of its phrases which he took to heart; and he set himself, with all his power, "to learn and labour truly to get his own living in that state of life to which it should please God to call him." The doctrine of Calling . . . was a cardinal doctrine of Puritanism. God had called and "elected" men spiritually to the grace which comes by faith. He had also called and chosen them temporally for some particular employment or business, in which they must labour with diligence, making themselves known by their fruits. . . . Work was thus spiritualized and made an end in itself. . . . It is for this reason that more than one writer has regarded Puritanism as the parent of capitalism. Set together (the argument runs) the Puritan emphasis on work and production, and the Puritan challenge to the State with its consequent claim of a free way for individual initiative—and you have compounded the elements which constitute the capitalist system. The argument has been challenged by Mr. Tawney [R. H. Tawney, *Religion and the Rise of Capitalism,* 1926] on two main grounds. In the first place, we can trace the origins of capitalism back to an earlier age than that of the Puritan Revolution, and we can find its spirit and its methods already present in the Italian cities of the later Middle Ages. In the second place, Puritanism, in its earlier phase, and down to 1660, opposed itself to the unlimited accumulation of wealth, and its preachers maintained the old mediaeval doctrines of "the just price" and the prohibition (or at any rate the strict limitation) of interest. But if capitalism was earlier than Puritanism, and if Puritanism, in its first beginnings, challenged its methods and its principles, we must also admit (as Mr. Tawney readily admits) that the spirit of later Puritanism was an air congenial to the accumulation of wealth. It was not only that the Puritans were devoted to production in virtue of their doctrine of work and calling. Their discipline of daily life, in itself, and apart from doctrine, was calculated to lay the foundations of success in commerce and industry. They mortified themselves of joys—of luxuries and even of comforts; and a sparing habit of life was productive of saving, which led in turn to banking and the accumulation of capital. The regularity of Puritan life, its stern economy of time, the sense with which it was vested of working in the Great Taskmaster's eye, all tended to produce men of business capacity, ready for the management of affairs and the conduct of large undertakings. In both ways—by supplying the means and by providing the men—Puritanism prepared the way for commercial and industrial greatness, and was a forerunner of the Industrial Revolution.

* * *

Down to the end of the seventeenth century Nonconformity was a leaven, small in amount, which yet stirred and moved the whole nation. It grew in volume during the eighteenth century, when Calvinistic Methodism spread through Wales, which in the seventeenth century had been Anglican and Royalist; when Wesleyanism began to count its adherents in hundreds of thousands; and when the Nonconformist bodies generally, by their labours among the new population which was pouring into industry, began to make the volume of their membership more nearly equal to the settled Anglicanism of the countryside. Nonconformity, as we have seen, had always been strong in the towns, among the commercial and industrial classes; and the growth of industrialism and of urban life, which marks the latter half of the eight-

eenth century, was naturally favourable to the growth of Nonconformity. In that growth it was Wesleyanism which played the greatest and most conspicuous part, affecting not only its own immediate adherents, but also a large section of the Anglican body from which it sprang and which it eventually left. The social influence which it exercised was profound and far-reaching. Wesley and his followers consciously carried their mission among the working-classes, and especially and particularly among the miners. They carried it in the form of a gospel of "enthusiasm" (detestable to the older and more cultivated intelligences of an age of reason) which caught the popular imagination and stirred a popular emotion. But neither their mission nor their influence was confined to a single class. If they went to the poor, they also made converts among the upper classes, and they had their stronghold in the middle class. They gave to that class, which might otherwise have stayed complacent in a fat and dull prosperity, the stimulus of ideals—the aiding of missions; the spread of education; the reform of prisons; the abolition of the slave-trade and of slavery itself. They knitted the middle to the poorer classes in the common bonds of a religious organization: they united them both in the services of the chapel, in which laymen might play their part, and in the common social gatherings of which the chapel was a centre and focus. In this way Wesleyanism stopped the widening of that social gulf which had existed, it is true, before the Industrial Revolution, but which the Revolution, without any counteracting influence, might have made both broader and deeper. By what it did to draw classes together, and by the fact that it supplied a religious channel for the satisfaction of cravings and demands which might otherwise have run into the secular channels of French Revolutionary doctrine, Wesleyanism helped to keep the nation stable in the period of convulsion which marked the passing of the eighteenth into the nineteenth century. But it was not merely a stabilizing force, nor was it content that the comfort of religious enthusiasm should serve to divert men's minds from a sense of social injustice. It supplied, especially from the ranks of its lay preachers, men who led and spread working-class movements for better things—men who could rise above hatred or materialism, and connect ideas of social reform with a keen religious faith. The strength and the hold of the Trade Union and the Labour movement have depended, in no small degree, upon this connection. In other ways it has to be admitted that Wesleyanism inherited and accentuated national defects. It had some of the intolerance of the older Puritanism. It had something of its anxious discipline of life; and it diffused the same cloud of painful observance of the rules of external religion. It did not love the free course of thought, and it was dubious of human science. The tradition of the letter was strong in its teaching; and if the righteousness which it sought to teach was beyond that of the Scribes and the Pharisees, the enlightenment which it attained provoked Matthew Arnold to the adjective "Philistine."

It is possible that the Christian Churches will not exercise in the future the direct influence on national life and character which they have exercised in the past. In particular the influence which Nonconformity in its various forms has exercised during the last three centuries—an influence particularly deep and pervasive—is not likely to be so marked in this century. . . . It is not that Nonconformity has lost ground to the English Church, or, again, that both are losing ground to another Church: it is rather that both have handed to the teacher, and to the school, a torch which was once kept burning by the preacher, and uplifted in church and chapel. When schools and teachers were few, religious bodies had a double duty. They had to mould the characters and to awaken the intelligence of men by their teaching, as well as to touch and move their spirits by their preaching. The spread of a general system of national education may be said to relieve the churches of a part of their ancient duty. It was they who laboured first at the institution of that system; and its foundation stones were laid, over a hundred years ago, by Anglicans and Nonconformists alike, when the different voluntary societies set their hands to the provision of Sunday schools and the founding of day schools. . . .

A system of social relationships and institutions that has had, in the past, a far less complex pattern of organization than religion is *recreation*. In industrial societies the amount of time which an individual must devote to his job—making a living—is often drastically reduced, in contrast to peasant and tribal societies. One result is the emergence of "sport" as one of the important forms of recreation available to fill this new-found leisure time. Although an industrial society develops other forms of recreation, we have selected only this one for consideration here.

To those who know England well, the following selection may seem one-sided, since there are many leisure-time pursuits besides those described below. Many an Englishman takes pride in his garden; others are extraordinarily fond of excursions into the country by auto, by bicycle, or afoot. The pub, too, is an important center of social life. Nevertheless, we can better understand industrial society when we are aware of its emphasis on mass spectator sports and the role that athletic "games" play in the lives of millions of people. It can well be questioned, however, whether such sports are the ideal "safety valve" for the tensions and monotony of our mechanical age.

• 75 • Organized Sports for Leisure Time
PETER WILSON

A NATION OF SPECTATORS?

Almost every member of the 45,000,000 population of Great Britain has at one stage or another either played, watched or read about some form of sport. If the individual has escaped obligatory games at school, he or she can scarcely have avoided some contact with one or other of the sports—either through the medium of personal participation, newspaper reports, the cinema, the radio or television.

The game still traditionally associated with Britain is cricket, whereas in Scotland, Ireland and Wales there is only one first-class cricket county, while in all these countries, as well as in England, soccer is played and certainly watched by ten times as many people. Accurate statistics are difficult to discover, but through the soccer season, of approximately thirty-five weeks, an average of about a million people a week go to watch the forty-four English league matches which take place at least every Saturday.

Soccer is probably the supreme example of the watched rather than the played game—although, of course, those figures do not include the scores of minor league matches which take place throughout the length and breadth of the four countries and which are designed more for the competitor than the spectator. But neither do they include the Scottish professional leagues, which are equally or more for spectator than players.

Various games lay claim to having the greatest popularity amongst actual players. Bowls, for example, with its appeal for both sexes, probably has as many as three million devotees. But I imagine that the sport which has the largest number of active participants is snooker. Estimates vary, but I have been assured by a reliable informant—who is also a snooker enthusiast—that 12,000,000 people annually meander around the green baize table in the clubs and public saloons throughout the country.

It is difficult for the individual totally disinterested in sport to understand the attraction which the different forms of it have for their "fans." But in a largely mechanical age where, of necessity, the average individual has to exist in an urban community with few opportunities of self-expression, sport is the ideal safety-valve—and even watching sport provides the ideal opportunity for blowing off the steam accumulated during a week of repetitive and restrictive work.

One of the unhealthy symptoms of the vast attendances which throng with an almost religious fervour to their local football ground each week is the fact that many of them are people who are forced to lead the lives of automata at their work and who, nevertheless or therefore, seem to prefer the mass hypnosis of losing themselves in a giant assembly on what is supposed to be their afternoon of relaxation—when they might be following more individual pursuits.

THE CONSEQUENCES OF WATCHING

For years Britain was supposed to have been the world's schoolmaster in sport, but recently the pupil nations have equalled, and currently surpassed, the originator of most of the more popular international sports. The reason is not hard to discover. The more people who watch, and the fewer people who take part in, the various athletic pursuits obviously affect the general standard of games in any country.

With the possible exception of the U.S.A., British sport probably attracts more spectators, per population, than any other nation. Foxhunting has been described as "the pursuit of the uneatable by the unspeakable," and

[From "Sport and the Public," *Current Affairs Pamphlet,* No. 59, Bureau of Current Affairs, London, 1948. Pp. 3-10. Used by permission.]

an equally harsh criticism might be applied to the vast crowds who congregate for their Saturday afternoon soccer-watching, since it could be said that it is the muscular minority being watched by the "miniature" majority.

Certainly the old tradition of British sportsmanship is not exemplified by the home-club-supporting crowd at the average football match. There is blind and unswerving support for the local side and considerably biased opposition to both the visitors and the referee. But this is a transitory emotion, for once the actual excitement of the game has passed, the comments of the spectators streaming out of the average football ground are on the whole intelligent and well-informed about the game.

Yet, with all the criticisms which can justly be levelled against the mass spectator sports, the interest in games like association football is distinctly more healthy than unhealthy. Gambling, through the Pools, has certainly increased the attendance and the interest in soccer. But I have never heard it suggested, by even the most disgruntled punter, that the honesty of individual teams or players has been affected by the vast sums of money involved.

On the credit side is the fact that supporting games—even in the role of a spectator—means a few hours in the open air; and if only a small percentage feel the urge to emulate their heroes, by going out on common land and kicking a ball about however desultorily, there is at least that advantage over the surrender to the other manufactured entertainments like the cinema or the radio.

An interesting development in sport crowds is the astonishing increase in recent years among women "fans." The more obviously spectacular sports, where little specialized knowledge is required, are clearly the most popular. Outstanding among them is speedway racing, where there must be nearly a fifty-fifty ratio between the sexes. Few women have either the patience or the technical appreciation to attend three-day cricket matches—unless they are very fond of their fiancés or husbands—but at speedway, to a lesser extent at soccer, and in a different way at boxing, the female fan is on the increase and is making her voice heard in more than one sense.

Speedway, although one of the most artificial, is in fact one of the healthiest sports of all from the spectator's point of view. There are few stories of its "crookedness" which have a vestige of truth in them, and although it is an evening sport and many of the arenas are sited inaccessibly, it is the most truly family affair amongst all the major spectacular entertainments.

If the 1940's are to be known as the Atomic Age, the first third of the twentieth century might well be sub-titled the age of sport. Before that time sport was comparatively simple. There was cricket played on the village green and on the private grounds of the great country houses. There was football which was by no means an essentially proletarian game until well into the twentieth century. Prize-fighting was a hole-and-corner business. Track and field athletics were essentially local affairs, and most other sports were largely regional, creating little interest outside the district in which they took place.

The era of speedway racing, ice hockey, cycling, lawn tennis and golf, was still either unknown or far beyond the ken and interest of the man in the street. Horse racing of course there was—but difficulties of transportation and lack of the publicity which nowadays is taken as a matter of course made all but the most famous events relatively unimportant. One sport which attracts its millions nowadays was then completely unknown—dog racing. In the country districts, particularly in the North, fanciers coursed their whippets, but the mechanical hare which was to introduce "roulette on four legs" was not seen until the late nineteen-twenties.

Nowadays it is difficult to decide what is or is not sport. I have seen as much tense concentration on the face of a player gambling for five cigarettes in a pin table arcade as I have seen on the face of a punter operating in fivers at the Derby. Purists would restrict "sports" to hunting, whether the fox, the stag, the hare or the otter, shooting or fishing. More liberal minded interpreters would include the wide variety of athletic pastimes which the spectator can practise to some degree himself. But even that restriction, except for a small minority, would cancel out speedway racing, horse racing, boxing, ice hockey and a number of other sports.

It is difficult, if not impossible, to draw a distinction between sports and pastimes. Fifty years ago you would have been laughed at as a lunatic had you suggested that ping-pong had any function in sporting life other than as a mild *divertissement* for the ladies of the house. Today hard-headed commercial sports impresarios put table tennis on in their ferro-concrete stadia, and attract entrants from more than a score of countries and crowds of over ten thousand.

On the other hand, today croquet is a standing joke to many people; yet Wimbledon, which is one of the most famous names in the world of sport, is still the home of the All England Lawn Tennis and Croquet Club —although I must admit that among all its gracious lawns one does not often notice the one reserved for croquet. Fashions in games, as well as in clothes, alter with rapidity.

If the preceding selections are looked over, it will be apparent that quite a few patterns of association have been discussed, some fairly thoroughly. These include the community, treated in Selections 54 and 55 primarily as a settlement pattern rather than as an area of unified social relationships. Other patterns are work and economic groups, particularly the trade union, the family, age and sex groupings, and educational, religious, and recreational organizations.

The next selection turns to quite a different social institution, the British government, and briefly sketches the relations of the Monarchy, the Parliament, and the local government. The enormous importance of the government as an agency of economic control has already been pointed out in the discussion of nationalization, and in Selection 77 its paramount position in the fields of public health and welfare will be shown.

• 76 • *The British Government*

The British Parliament has two Houses—the House of Lords and the House of Commons. Great Britain has no written Constitution; Government is based on liberties won and Acts passed throughout the generations. Today complete legislative power is invested in the hands of the elected representatives of the people of Britain. The history of Parliament dates back to the thirteenth century when it first became the maker of laws and levier of taxes. The power of Parliament— and with it the liberties of the people—grew throughout the centuries: the law of Habeas Corpus passed in 1678 (by which people could not be held in jail without trial) and the Bill of Rights of 1689, were landmarks.

The result of this long history is that the Government of Britain is a blend of modern democracy, traditional customs, survivals and precedents which is sometimes hard to understand. The principle and practice of government is entirely democratic but certain traditional organs and practices have been retained because they are believed to be useful and

[From *A Picture of Britain: Background of a People*, British Information Services, New York, 1946. Pp. 39-46. Used by permission.]

practical safeguards. An example of this is the function of the House of Lords. By the Parliament Act (1911) most of the real legislative power of the House of Lords was removed. It no longer has an ultimate veto on Bills passed by the Commons. The most it can do is to delay a money Bill for one month, and return an ordinary Bill for reconsideration by the House of Commons three times. The House of Lords provides a valuable debating chamber and a "second thought," while the Commons is the active legislative body.

THE KING

Great Britain is an hereditary monarchy. The King is the head of the State and fulfills a very important practical function in providing continuity and helping the smooth working of the Government system. He is also in constant consultation with members of his Government and his experience may contribute much to their deliberations. Most of the King's traditional powers, however, were delegated to the Government or are now unexercised. For instance, the King has a theoretical power to veto Bills but never now exercises it: Ministers are appointed and dismissed in the name of the King, but always on the advice of the Prime Minister. The same applies to the dissolution of Parliament. The King does not enter into party politics but remains above politics as a symbol of the nation as a whole.

THE HOUSE OF LORDS

The House of Lords has the power to introduce Bills, but confines itself to introducing Bills dealing with uncontroversial and, often, with specialized matters. In addition to the peers who owe their title to birth, a large part of the membership of the House of Lords is made up of peers who have been given titles in recognition of valuable public service in such spheres as law, administration, science, or education. The House has thus a valuable function as a body of experts. Twenty-six bishops, sixteen Scottish representative peers (elected from among the total number of Scottish peers), twenty-eight Irish representative peers and seven Law Lords sit in the House of Lords. This House is also the Highest Court of Appeal, but only the seven Law Lords and other peers with judicial experience, take part in this aspect of its activity.

THE HOUSE OF COMMONS

The House of Commons is made up of the directly elected representatives of the people from 640 constituencies. In normal times the maximum duration of a Parliament is five years, at the end of which a General Election must be held. General Elections are also held when the political party in power loses the confidence of the House and wishes to appeal to the country. By-Elections are held in any constituency where the seat becomes vacant through the death of the Member or other cause.

Members of Parliament get a salary of $2,400. Anyone can stand as a candidate for Parliament provided he or she can get eight electors to sign his nomination. He then pays a deposit which he forfeits if he does not get one-eighth of the votes cast. This ruling is to discourage frivolous candidates. A candidate need not live in the area he wishes to represent. A limit is set to the amount which a candidate may spend on his election publicity. Candidates usually stand as the representative of one of the recognized parties, approved both by party headquarters and by the local party committee. They then benefit by the party organization and publicity. In Britain a General Election may come at any moment, so political parties have to consider the wishes of the public in their constituencies all the time; political meetings therefore play a large part in British life. When the voters go to the polls on election day they vote simply for a candidate to represent them in Parliament. Usually they can choose between two or three men representing different parties.

THE CABINET

The leader of the political party which has a Parliamentary majority usually becomes Prime Minister and he forms a Cabinet—that is, a group of Parliamentary leaders belonging to his party—most of whom he appoints as heads of Government Departments, responsible for their administration. In addition to its executive function, the Cabinet is responsible for initiating legislation sponsored by the Government.

The Cabinet is responsible to Parliament, and the responsibility is collective: if a measure of major importance for which one Cabinet Minister is responsible is rejected by the Commons, then the Government falls, and a General Election will probably be held. Cabinet Ministers are members of the Lords or Commons and have to face constant questions in Parliament concerning the way the affairs of their Department are being conducted. "Question time" in the House of Commons represents one of the most important of Parliament's functions—the regular checking up on Ministers so that they have always to be ready to explain and defend their activities to the satisfaction of Members.

LOCAL GOVERNMENT

Local administration is carried out by the Local Authorities who have very extensive powers in the application of laws and in making local bye-laws. They work very closely with such central Government Departments as the Ministry of Health, the Ministry of Education, and the Home Office. Members of Local Councils are elected by direct vote. They receive no salaries.

For the purposes of local government England is broken down into County Boroughs (the largest towns) and Administrative Counties. Under these come County Districts, Urban Districts, and Rural Districts, and under them again, Parishes. Each of these subdivisions has its own council and its own clearly defined responsibilities. Much of the work is done by special Committees of Councillors. Local Authorities derive revenue from local real estate taxes known as "rates," and they also receive considerable grants from the Central Government. They handle Health, Housing, Education, the Police, and often, also, Public Utilities and Transportation in their area.

LAW

Trial by jury is a basic principle of English law. All major criminal cases in England are tried by High Court judges in the district in which they were committed. For this purpose circuit judges travel round the country holding courts, which are called "Assizes." There are two courts of appeal from the High Courts, the House of Lords being a final court of appeal. All judges are appointed for life or until retirement. Minor offenses are heard in Quarter and Petty Sessions by honorary Justices of the Peace or paid magistrates who may send the accused to trial, or, for minor offenses, impose a limited penalty.

The Scottish legal system differs in many respects from the English, Scots Law being derived ultimately from Roman Law, while English Law has developed independently.

Before the days of the Industrial Revolution, welfare needs were met chiefly in the family or the neighborhood or else by some charitable, religious organization. But with the rise of the factory system and the insecurities which it brought, increasing attention has been paid to the care of the needy, the ill, the injured, and the aged. The old Poor Law approach was to make poverty a disgrace and regard it as almost entirely the fault of the individual; the newer approach in Western Europe and in the United States is to make use of insurance programs into which wage-earner, employer, and the government participate. Where insurance, governmental or private, is inadequate, some other public funds are distributed.

England has gone farther in recent years than any other Western country in its efforts to provide for the emergencies and uncertainties which its citizens face. This new program to provide for the individual's welfare "from the cradle to the grave" has been described as follows in an official information bulletin:

> On July 5, 1948, there came into force in Britain five important acts of Parliament dealing respectively with national insurance, industrial injuries, a national health service, the care of children, and a scheme of national assistance for those in acute need. Taken together they constitute what might well be called a new charter of social security, and enable Britain to claim that her system of security for the individual is second to none in the world.

The National Health Service has been the most widely discussed of the Acts because of the debate which has occurred in the United States over "socialized medicine." Both sides to the controversy cite the British experience to prove their points, the medical profession claiming that the quality of medical service in Britain is inferior under state supervision and that government intervention in this area is contrary to the American tradition; proponents of the proposed health bill suggest that many American people are not receiving proper medical attention owing to the concentration of doctors in the cities and the high costs of hospitalization, drugs, and physicians' fees, and that something should be done. And so the arguments run on. The issue can certainly not be settled here, but some light is thrown on the controversy by Rebecca West's calm but penetrating comments on the situation in Britain. She is one of Britain's most distinguished writers and, of course, has a firsthand familiarity with current health problems there, as well as in the United States.

• 77 • *The National Health Service*
REBECCA WEST

It is . . . [a] fact that the vast mass of the British people, Tory and Labour, doctors and laymen, accept the principle of the National Health Service. They are sometimes disconcerted by the way that that principle works out in practice, grumble noisily—and so they should, or wrongs would never get righted. But I think that few of them would consider it possible to abandon the principle. . . . For it is really true that the National Health Service was called into being because it was what was generally felt to be the only means of fulfilling a useful purpose; or, to be exact, certain useful purposes.

I can best show you what those purposes are by telling you how various people have been affected since July 5, 1948, when the Service was inaugurated by the Minister of Health, in pursuance of a duty laid on him two years earlier by an Act of Parliament.

Ever since then all of us except children and the old have paid certain contributions to the state under an Insurance Act. (When I give figures I will pay no attention to the devaluation of the pound.) On an employed man's insurance card the employer sticks a stamp for which he pays just under $1 and for which the employee pays $1—a total contribu-

[From "Can a Nation Afford Health for All Its People?", *Ladies' Home Journal*, Vol. 67, No. 9, Philadelphia, 1950. Pp. 139-140, 142, 144, 150, 156. Used by permission.]

tion of almost $2. On an employed woman's card the employer sticks a stamp for which the employer pays 65 cents and the employee 75 cents. Boys under eighteen have to have stamps on their cards amounting to rather more than half the value of those on men's cards, and the girls have to account for rather more than half the value of the stamps on a woman's card; and their employers have to pay their share. A self-employed man has to pay $1.25, a self-employed woman has to pay $1. A man who does not follow any employment has to pay just under $1; such a woman has to pay 75 cents.

I sneak in without paying, under the provision that the wife of a self-employed man can participate in certain benefits, of which the National Health Service is one, on his card.

Of these contributions an average of 10 to 15 cents is allocated to the National Health Service. The rest goes to provide such benefits as old-age pensions and maternity benefits. But the sum of the contributions thus provided for the National Health Service defrayed, at the beginning, only one fifth of its cost. The proportion must be much lower now that the cost has mounted. The deficit, which was originally four fifths and must now be more, is provided from income tax and from indirect taxation, such as the duty on tea, spirits, tobacco, and so on.

The state goes off with this insurance and taxation money in its hand and enters into a contract with the doctors and surgeons and nurses and druggists and hospitals of the land, by which it agrees to pay them certain fees if they give the population free service. So now we all can consult a doctor without paying him, get all medicines prescribed by the doctor without paying the druggist, and go into a hospital without paying for the use of the bed or the operating theater or the radiological or any other department.

Let us first see how it works at the receiving end: on the patients.

You are not being at all realistic if you imagine that the National Health Service is the product of an idealism which will no longer suffer it that people shall be sick and uncared for just because they are poor.

The National Health Service does not make any earth-shaking change in the position of the sick poor. If anybody tells you about little English children in garrets who are now borne away in ambulances to be operated on by world-famous specialists and be nursed back to health by nice starched nurses in hospital wards, and suggests that these children would have been left to die in those garrets until July 5, 1948, put him down as a political propagandist and an unreliable reporter.

The lot of the sick poor has been improved in many secondary ways; but the primary situation of the patient struck down by acute illness when not possessed of means to pay doctors or nurses or hospital authorities has not been dramatically altered.

This is not a criticism of the Service. It simply means that the medical and surgical treatment and hospitalization of people with yearly incomes below $1700 was so well looked after in most parts of England that, though we would all like to make it better still, it would hardly be possible to do so in our present economic circumstances.

*   *   *

The British had no reason to be ashamed of the medical provision they made for their lower-income groups. First of all, they had a useful insurance system. It was introduced by our great statesman, David Lloyd George, in 1911, with the intention of taking care of employed persons who made just enough money to meet their current expenses, but could not be expected to put by the savings which would enable them to cover the cost of sickness. He put the ceiling of this section at $650 annual income. That ceiling has had to be raised twice since; now it is $1700.

This system gave the insured person the right to register with the doctor and go on his panel, as his list of patients was called, and get his medical attention free. The weakness of the system was that it made no provision for the dependents of the insured person; not their wives, not their children, not their old folk. But this was less of a hardship than might appear. Many doctors organized clubs by which insured persons on their panels could get medical attention for their families, by paying something like a quarter a week. Many other doctors never sent in a bill for services rendered to the families of their insured patients, and calculated the extra work as part of the duty they had to fulfill to get their insurance fees.

There was also the district-nursing system . . . which sent out trained nurses to visit people with low incomes in their homes and give them whatever treatment was prescribed by their doctors, even up to midwifery service. This was a remarkable success, attracting a very fine type of nurse. There were also various units for taking care of special classes among the dependents, such as maternity and child welfare, school medical inspection, and school dental services. But there is no doubt that some dependents got left out of any scheme, particularly among women past the childbearing age, and old people. They have benefited enormously from the National Health Service, under which they have the same rights as anyone else.

* * *

But where the National Health Service makes a dramatic appearance is in another field: in the middle classes. For them it is as if the sun had come out from behind the clouds, and their relief is a promise as to the state of a happier future.

Take Charles and Joan as an example of the intensity of this relief, and its social purpose. . . . Charles is an officer in the regular army, and therefore they have a house near an army post where Charles is a lecturer, not far out of London. . . .

The other day Charles said, "We have good news for you," and Joan explained. "We're going to have a third baby. On the Health Service, bless it, so I don't mind a bit."

No political philosopher could possibly want a higher testimonial to a piece of social legislation.

Charles's army pay is between $4000 and $5000 a year, out of which they have to pay $1000 in income tax. In order to be near the army post, they have to pay a large rent for the only house which was vacant in the district.

They had their first child a year after the war ended; and it cost them, with doctor and nursing home and a nurse who had to stay two months because Joan was seriously ill after her confinement, over $500. Charles was getting less pay then and this amounted to one-fifth of the spendable income left after he had settled his income tax. Fortunately, he had his war gratuity and that met the bills. Their second child was born in the autumn of 1948, and this time there was no gratuity to fall back upon.

"We don't know what we would have done," says Charles, "if the National Health Service hadn't been set up in the meantime. We can't save off what I get. I suppose we would have had to borrow money and be slaves for the rest of our lives. As it was, we hadn't a headache. We just sat back and were glad the baby was coming."

* * *

The main trouble which afflicts the people who use the National Health Service arises, strangely enough, out of its very success. It arises out of the time factor.

* * *

If a person's time has more than a certain value it does not pay him or her to use the National Health Service. So many people are resorting to the doctors' offices and to the hospitals that the queues seem endless. Here is one instance in which the poor are actually getting less satisfactory medical attention than they had before the institution of the Service, for in many out-patient departments the time of waiting is doubled or trebled. And it is no joke sitting in a hospital waiting room when you are feeling ill.

* * *

This is at present a real defect in the system, and it would be dishonest not to admit its gravity. But time will cure it.

For one thing, these new queues of patients consist partly of people who are seeking medical attention because they do not have to pay for it. Now some of these people really do need medical attention, and could not pay for it; and they may be expected to recur in the queues. But there are others who do not need medical attention, and come simply because they like getting something for (apparently) nothing. Of these some will weary. It is not really very amusing, consulting doctors and going to hospitals. If you object that there have always been paying patients who found it amusing to consult doctors and go to clinics, and never seemed to weary of it, you are forgetting that now that doctors and clinics are no longer paid by these patients, they will probably throw them out.

Certain districts can be named by the Medical Practices Committee, which consists of seven doctors and two laymen, as "closed areas," and the committee may refuse any practitioner permission to set up in such an area if they think that it already contains too many doctors competing for the care of the sick. When this system has been working for some years the existing number of doctors will be fairly distributed all over Great Britain, and there will be no need for any doctor to have more patients on his panel than he can treat without reasonable delay.

But the transitional stage is uncomfortable; and how it could have been avoided I cannot see.

The doctors made a great fuss about coming into the National Health Service, but that was largely because the Minister of Health, Mr. Aneurin Bevan, made a dogfight of the negotiations with the British Medical Association over the terms on which they were to come in; and the secretary of the British Medical Association, Doctor Hill, is a bit of a bulldog himself. But there are working on doctors exactly the same forces which reconciled their middle-class patients to the Service.

I know very well how it used to be in the medical profession, because my sister is a doctor. With the help of the scholarships which Andrew Carnegie, of Pittsburgh, gave to his native Scotland and the self-sacrifice of my mother, she went through Edinburgh University with hardly a penny at the back of her. So, though she was the top of her year in surgery, there was no question of her becoming a surgeon, which is a much more common activity among women in Great Britain than it is in the United States. She had nobody to finance her through the long period of working without reward which was the necessary preliminary to a surgeon's career. She could not even raise the money to buy a practice. Some of the women in her year had parents rich enough to start them as surgeons; nearly all of them, after a few years, had practices bought for them. And notoriously parents have less money to spend on their daughters than on their sons.

Now times are changed. So the National Health Service looks very pleasant to a young doctor who wants to be a general practitioner. He takes his degree, holds some hospital posts, goes into practice in some area that is not "closed," and can have as many National Health Service patients as he can get up to the number of 4000 at an annual capitation fee of $3.50, and a payment for patients in outlying districts based on the mileage he has to cover to get to them, and fees varying from $25 to $35 for obstetric cases. He can also take private patients if he can find the time. He cannot cultivate these better-paying cases at the expense of his National Health Service patients, because he is strictly supervised and his National Health Service patients can file complaints against him before a stern and impartial tribunal. No doctor is engaged by the National Health Service on terms that make him a full-time servant of the state, for that is held to be dangerous. He might become a slave of the state.

* * *

On the whole, however, the general practitioner is not displeased by his financial position under the Act. He has security. But how does it affect his work?

Well, this business of overcrowding, of overwork, though it is temporary, is feared by some doctors to be doing permanent harm to medicine. They say that the doctor who finds himself faced with a mob of patients tends to send all of them who have anything but the simplest maladies off to hospital, and so tends to become a diagnostician on a very low level of diagnosis. It is partly, they say, the doctor who yields to this temptation who is responsible for the hospital outpatient queues.

He is also making barren a most fertile field of medicine. For the general practitioner, and only the general practitioner, can get thorough views of illnesses in relation to the whole life of the individual who is suffering from them.

* * *

. . . The real charge against the National Health Service [is] that it costs too much.

* * *

. . . When the Act was introduced in 1946 it was estimated that it would cost $508,000,000. By the time the Service was inaugurated, two years later, the estimates had risen to $832,500,000. In 1949 the estimates rose still further, and this year we are landed with an estimate for 1951 of $1,600,000,000.

Now it is possible to be too badly frightened by these figures. A great proportion of these sums represents money that would have been spent anyway on medicine, whether the Service had been introduced or not. Individuals would have spent it by direct payments to doctors, nurses and hospitals; now they first pay it to the tax collector, who pays it to the doctors, nurses and hospitals on their behalf. The worry is how much money is wasted on administration costs by this indirect method and whether this wastage is counterbalanced by the quite real saving effected by bulk buying of medical care.

But it is only sane to feel some fright, and indeed considerable fright, at these figures.

They mean that Great Britain is paying out $32 a head for medical care. Now, you cannot pay out what you do not earn. If you consider that out of our population of 50,000,000, 10,355,000 are under nineteen, and that another 5,250,000 are over sixty-five, you will see what a load this bill is on the producing adults between these ages.

You can gather what our plight is by comparing your expenditure with ours. Our national income a year ago was about $42,-480,000,000; yours [U.S.A.] was about $221,-500,000,000. You have more than five times as great a national income as we, which means considerably more margin. But 40 per cent of our income and only 24 per cent of yours goes in taxation. I again beg you, please do not put down that difference just as thriftlessness. We have had two world wars; we really are trying to work out an economy in which all citizens can be guaranteed full employment, which is not a contemptible aim. But it makes life difficult. The mere fact that 16,000,000 of our population—that is, 32 per cent of it—are too old or too young to be in full production explains why it is very difficult for us to have only 60 per cent of our national income at our own disposal as private persons.

The part of the taxation which goes to the National Health Service takes 5½ per cent of our national income.

It is misleading to consider it as an isolated payment. To get its full unpleasantness, consider it in conjunction with another tax—our defense tax. You lay out 3.5 per cent of your national income on that; we lay out 7 per cent of ours. That and the National Health Service account for 12½ per cent of our national income. And that percentage is increasing.

Now, why does the Service cost so much? Partly, of course, because some silly people are rushing to take advantage of a service which appears to give them something for nothing, and are seeing doctors and buying medicines which they do not really need. But that will wear out in time. . . .

But there is one item which, alone and inevitably, even if every person connected with the giving and receiving end of the National Health Service had behaved like angels, would have made it enormously costly. The Service had to take over the hospitals. They were in such a desperate condition that the National Health Service would have had to be created to get them on their feet, if for no other reason.

Any hospital, in any country, is a frightening economic portent today. Ours were especially frightening because of what happened to them during the war. A hospital is a very delicate and complicated organism and it would have to be a very hardy specimen to survive what was done to nearly all of them between 1939 and 1945.

*   *   *

CONCLUSION

I have left out so many aspects of the Service I wanted to describe, but I hope I have convinced you that the British National Health Service is not just a folly. It is not meaningless. It is a muddle and a monster and a premature baby. It can never work out to everybody's satisfaction, even if it is un-muddled and grows up normal and gets out of the incubator looking fine. Remember this: A National Health Service must be a disappointment, however successful it is. It is bound to be taken as a promise to give the whole population first-class medical and surgical treatment. Well, it can't do that. There are not enough first-class doctors, surgeons, dentists, oculists or nurses to go round, and not enough hospital beds. You are up against a natural insufficiency here; and if you quarrel with it you will have to quarrel with the same insufficiency which makes it impossible to guarantee every citizen a wife as beautiful as Elizabeth Taylor, and a Park Avenue apartment. In any National Health Service a large proportion of the population will have to make do with second-rate attention, and maybe some that is not so good as that. But that would be more grimly true without a National Health Service, and we are better off with one, for it has a purpose, and unless there is another war and unless we all fail in our duties, it should fulfill it.

There are four points which the Service has impressed on me, and I think it may be useful to Americans to hear what they are:

1. The National Health Service of Great Britain is not a piece of Socialist freakishness, but a necessity recognized by intelligent citizens of all parties. The bulk of the population came out of the Second World War unable to pay for medical attention on the scale which was necessary if doctors and nurses were to make a living, and the hospitals were tottering toward insolvency.

If the pressure of history acts on the population and on your hospitals in the same unkind way, you Americans will need, not want —it won't matter whether you want it or not, you will need it—a National Health Service of your own.

2. Start examining the medical landscape early to see if that need is appearing, for the chief thing necessary for the establishment of an efficient health service is time. It has to be based on calculations beyond the power of any community to collect or consider quickly. It is an enterprise comparable to the mobilizing of the Army or Navy or Air Force after the outbreak of a war. Its accountancy alone presents catastrophic possibilities of waste. Ask anybody whose wartime work lay in the finance department of any war-created unit of the Administration if you want confirmation of this statement.

3. It is necessary to frame the conditions of the National Health Service so that it is easy for the persons drawing benefit to understand how much it costs, and who pays for it, and what their own contribution to that payment, direct or indirect, is. Children should be taught the mechanism of the fund in schools, and the figures should be displayed in public places. When people overspent in the old days, they knew it because their purses were empty. Now they can overspend and never know it, because their purses are empty anyway, as they hand over most of their money to the tax collector, and they cannot tell when his purse is empty. This is a new problem arising out of a new and complicated way of living and it has to be met by education.

4. A National Health Service should be lifted out of the political field, because it will be a success or a failure according to the degree to which it is regarded objectively. In America you have a bipartisan foreign policy, and it is just as necessary to have a bipartisan health policy. Nobody should be allowed to cheer or boo anything connected with such a service. The only demonstration allowable is a slight knitting of the brows, such as might be provoked by the working out of a mathematical problem.

In spite of the obvious fact that all these points spring from my sense that our National Health Service is not so good as it might be, I invite you Americans with confidence to come to Great Britain ten years from now and look at it. By then it will be something to be proud of; and you may think we were not so foolish for frankly admitting when times have changed and the old arrangements for meeting the physical crises of life had broken down, and setting about making new ones. There are many different sorts of pioneering.

Throughout this study of the Midlands there has been emphasis on the numerous and profound changes that have taken place in a few generations. The most conspicuous have been in the way the people make their living, in the growth of industrial enterprises, and in the rapid concentration of population in great conurbations. Such changes as the replacement of the wagon and stagecoach by railroads, cars, and trucks have been dramatic in their suddenness and have tended to focus attention on the technological aspects of the recently developed industrial society. But changes have also been marked in the area of social relationships. The changed status of woman from the eighteenth century to the midpoint of the twentieth is a good indication of the way in which the whole of society has had to adjust to the new forces. Community life has become much more complicated, particularly in contrast with the village, which was once prominent in the social scene. Governmental pressures are now observed on every hand, although in England—and particularly in the Midlands—there is strong resistance by local governmental authorities to any encroachment from Whitehall (the executive seat of the national government). One-time religious functions, such as support of the needy and promotion of education, have become less important; family life is less centered about the home; and recreational pursuits are much more commercialized.

Paralleling changes in the social organization are modifications in the value system and in the beliefs and ideologies of the people. We have noted in each society described in this book a close correspondence between the status system and the set of social values. In England, status is centered in the social classes, whose importance shifts as new ideas and new values prevail.

The last pattern of association to be discussed is social class. The ramifications of English classes are complex and at times contradictory but C. Arnold Anderson has identified five basic divisions. The top class consists of the royal family. One member of this family, usually a man but sometimes a woman, is the titular head of the British Empire and the symbol of its unity. The second highest class is the nobility, with specific titles which represent social divisions among the nobles. The gentry come next. Sometimes they are called the landed gentry because many own fairly large estates. Some members of the gentry are related to various nobles but do not themselves have titles. The gentry might be called junior-grade nobility. Ranked below the gentry is the middle class or, as an indication of the divisions within it, the middle classes. It consists mostly of city or town people who own small businesses or hold the more responsible positions in business and industry. At the bottom is the lower, or working, class. The most highly skilled workers rate highest within this group and sometimes are counted as lower middle class. Semiskilled workers generally rank below the skilled, and unskilled and casual laborers are at the lowest level of the lower class.

It is generally believed that there is less social mobility in England than in the United States, though exact figures for comparison are lacking. Class distinctions are sharper in England, and hence it is more difficult for an individual to pass gradually from one class to another. On the other hand, a title of nobility may be inherited by one of the gentry, or a middle-class man may be granted a noble title. Some workers manage to move up into the middle class. Downward movement in the social scale is also possible, usually as the result of economic circumstances.

A study of postwar Britain is a clear case study of how a social structure can be made to harmonize with shifting values, all the while reciprocally influencing the value system so that moderate rather than extreme values are accepted.

The selection that follows has been prepared for this book by Margaret Stacey, who is connected with the first rigorous investigation of social class in England. This investigation has taken into account some of the recent research done in the United States and has sought to apply the latest social-science techniques. The conclusions set forth here are tentative, for the study has not been finished. They supposedly hold true for a single South Midlands market town which has been increasingly industrialized since the 1930's. What happens to a staid agriculturally oriented community, with some light industry, when an aluminum plant opens up and a flood of managers and workmen come in from outside? This article analyzes the changes chiefly from the standpoint of social class and, in doing so, reveals much about the changes in individual attitudes and social organization.

• 78 • Industrialization and the Class System in Market Town
MARGARET STACEY

Market Town is in the South Midlands of England, but does not form part of that industrial belt known as the "Black Country." It is, in fact, in the English scale, surprisingly isolated. There is no town of comparable size within a radius of 20 miles. It lies in a hollow, protected to the west and north by a line of hills and commands a plain which opens out to the south and east. As a market town it serves an area of approximately ten miles radius, which will be referred to as the Survey Area. For the villages in that area the pull of Market Town is greater than the pull of other neighbouring towns. The frontier of the Survey Area has been defined by those villages which respond equally to these two pulls.

The site is ancient. It was on the frontier of the Danish-occupied area in the ninth century and was a fortified outpost. In the early Middle Ages there was a large and prosperous manor, and by 1150 the township had been granted a market and fair charter. The Borough Charter was granted in the reign of Mary and was later confirmed by James I. Until the middle of the nineteenth century, the town was strictly a market town, a centre of distribution and exchange. Its industries were ancillary to the agricultural activities of the surrounding country area—flour milling, brewing, and hand-loom weaving for example —and it provided commercial and other services. In 1848 its first industrialisation took place, when a new works for the manufacture of agricultural implements was founded. A canal had been cut earlier (in the 1770's) to link the Midlands to the north with centres of population in the south. In 1850 the first railway was opened. These activities led to the first large-scale influx of "alien" workers, some Irish, but most probably from other parts of this country. The town, therefore, began at that time to take on a modern industrial complexion, but it should be emphasized that its main new industry was connected with agriculture and, while its products were sold further afield than the Survey Area, nevertheless it stood in a functional relation to the main activity of the area, agriculture. The agricultural implement industry flourished, and the town with it, throughout the last half of the nineteenth century. In the opening years of the twentieth century, however, it failed to maintain its position (largely, as far as one can tell, because the founder had not passed on his business acumen to his son). From about 1911 onwards there is evidence that the town was stagnating. The increase in the population was small and less than the natural increase. It did not share the population expansion of those years that took place in the rest of the country. At the 1931 census, there were some 13,000 souls living in the Borough. In that year an important change

began, the results of which form the basis for the present study. A big new aluminium factory began to be built to produce sheet and extruded aluminium. By 1933 it began production and by 1935 large numbers of workers were coming into the town to man the new industry. In a period, therefore, when large areas of the country were suffering from heavy unemployment, Market Town began to prosper and expand again, and to change its nature. A most important symbol to the inhabitants of the beginning of this change was the removal, about this time, of the cattle market from the streets to a large modern covered market towards the eastern edge of the town. The domestic market where greengrocery, fish, grocery, drapery, etc., are sold is still held twice a week in the open in the market square. The town now has a population of between 18,000 and 19,000 and about 5,000 houses.

In the town itself, about one-third of the working population is now employed in the aluminium factory. The factory is part of a large combine, its ownership is largely Canadian, its raw material is imported, its products have no particular relation to the area and go elsewhere to be finished. The great majority of its senior executives are not natives of the town, and many of its workers are immigrants of 15 years standing at the most. It forms, in fact, a complete contrast to the traditional economic activities of Market Town, based as they were on goods and services produced locally or for local consumption, and run in the main as family concerns or small limited companies. In the inter-war years, other similar changes in the economic structure also took place. Other firms, parts of national or international combines, opened factories in the town, and, a change which has altered the physical appearance of the town, more and more shops were sold to chain stores, some large, some small, but all making the shopping streets of the town centre lose their peculiar Market Town character, and look more like those in any other English town. This process continues.

Figures of employment in the major industrial groups may summarize more concisely the economic structure of the town today:

Industrial Group	Total
Metal processing (chiefly aluminium)	3,300
Distributive trades, hotels, catering and food processing	2,400
Agriculture and horticulture	1,600
Building	1,600
Transport, including railways and storage	1,500
Other manufactures	600
Domestic service (nonresident)	500

The income structure is also interesting. No one in Market Town receives a net personal income of over 2000 pounds per annum, and very few over 1000 pounds. This compares with a national distribution in which, in 1948, 175,000 received net incomes of over 2000 pounds, and 760,000 over 1000 pounds out of a total of known incomes of 3,210,000 (the numbers of people who earn under 250 pounds per annum are not known nationally and are excluded from this total).

To complete this introductory description it may be well to say something about the physical layout of the town. At its widest point it is not more than two miles across. A main north-south trunk road runs through the town meeting a less important east-west road at the Market Town Cross. The two main streets of the town run east from the main trunk road and here is found the shopping, commercial and professional centre of Market Town. The town is not large enough for these activities to have distinct areas of their own. Some good class residential property is still found near this centre, but all the best of the new houses are now built on the higher ground to the south and west of the centre. Indeed, many of the better-off now live in villages just outside the town, again particularly to the south and west, some of which are becoming dormitory areas. Clustering around the centre of the town, particularly near the north-south railway and the canal, which cut off the eastern part of the town, are three areas of nineteenth century working class terrace houses. There are four main areas of inter-war and post-war housing on the edges of the town. In these areas there are three Council housing estates and three estates of small owner-occupier houses. The aluminium factory lies over a mile to the north of the town beyond the last of the houses. The other factories and workshops are 'round about the old central part of the town. (See diagram.)

The purpose of this study of Market Town is to analyse the effects of the immigration into the town; more precisely to test whether the town is split into two groups, native and immigrant, and if so, whether this division is deeper and more important than other social divisions. Of other social divisions in the town, social class is one of the most profound. The importance of grouping into social classes has been shown for America by the work of the Lynds, Lloyd Warner, Davis and Gardner and others. No comparable work has yet been completed in this country, but it is clear from common observation that in England, too, social class groupings are of the first importance in social structure and social behaviour. There exists, however, no reliable index of social class in this country. One end result of the present work will be to attempt to provide a definition of social class and an index for its measurement. The nature of social class is known in general. It is a horizontal grouping with no clear boundaries, and upward and downward mobility continually takes place. But how many classes there are and where are the boundaries is not clear. The factors that go to make up the concept, such as occupation, income, education, residence area, manners and, in some cases, family connection, are also fairly clear, but in what proportion these factors combine to determine membership of a social class is unclear. However, it is quite clear that, except at the extremes, income alone is now practically meaningless as a guide to social class in England. During the course of this survey we are observing social class divisions as they operate in Market Town and are collecting also the objective data. On this

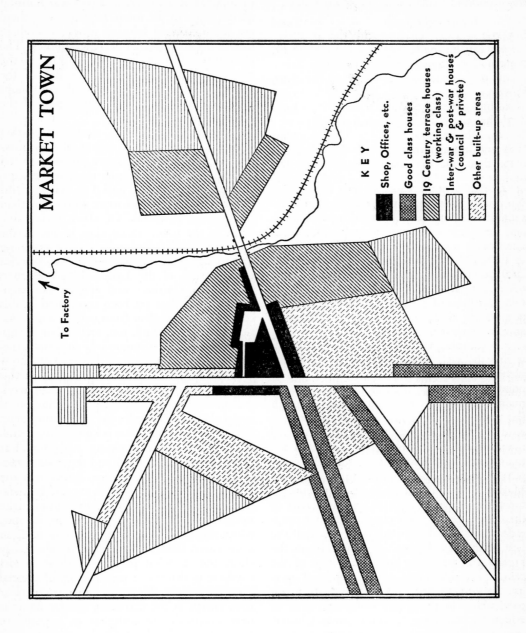

MARKET TOWN

To Factory

K E Y

Shop, Offices, etc.

Good class houses

19 Century terrace houses
(working class)

Inter-war & post-war houses
(council & private)

Other built-up areas

information we hope to base our definitions. The work has not yet reached the stage at which the cross-check between the functioning social class groups and the objective factors can be made. Any conclusions must, therefore, be tentative at this stage. Some points of interest have already become clear, however.

It has generally been considered in England that there are three main social classes: Upper, Middle, and Lower or Working, but that within each of these divisions there is more than one division, particularly in the middle group which is almost always referred to as the Middle Classes. The significant factor which divides the Upper and Upper Middle from the rest would seem to be the possession of a Public School (in the English sense) education. This forms the limit to a man's upward mobility. He may have achieved all the other necessary factors, but he can never quite qualify for the Upper Class without this educational background. If he gives it to his children they will be received into this class so long as they, too, qualify on the other grounds. The significant divide between the middle class and the working class seems to be not so much one of education, but of occupation. Here two factors operate: whether one is employer or employee and whether one's work is manual or non-manual. To be a professional worker, an executive, an owner of industry or shop places one in the middle class; to be a manual worker places one in the working class. On the margin are the low-grade clerical workers.

On this basis in Market Town one finds only two main social classes: the middle and working classes. The upper class in the national sense are absent from the Borough. They are to be found, however, living in the survey area, in the large houses, often but not always, with considerable land attached. At the top level are those with titles who may be wealthy industrial magnates or who may have few possessions apart from house and title. (It must, of course, be remembered that nowadays a small number of working class peers are created, but as yet this would not

seem to have affected class structure at all.) In this group, too, are the "County" families, who, while they may not be titled, qualify for membership of this group. Market Town itself not only has none of these people within its boundaries, but the senior executives of the large-scale industries of the town live outside, too. With the exception of one or two professional workers who qualify for the frontiers of the upper class on grounds of education, the upper class of Market Town itself is part of the national middle class. It is composed of professional men, doctors and solicitors, and the better-off owners of shops and small works in the town. From this group downwards all the shades of the social class pattern are reflected in the town.

Some interesting changes have taken place in the class structure of the town in the last twenty to thirty years. Twenty-five years ago there were one or two "County" families living in the town. Now all are gone. Furthermore, with one or two exceptions, members of the Upper Class living in the surrounding area now play no part at all in the life of the Borough. Managers of chain stores who have come into the town in this period have not been accepted as members of the shop-owning elite. They in some ways form a group on their own and to some extent group with the lower middle class, the responsible clerical worker, and the skilled craftsman. The managers of government departments which have opened new offices in the town again have not fitted into the existing class pattern. Nor have the junior executives of the aluminium industry and of other concerns. Again, and this has occurred throughout the country, there has grown up a new group of clerical workers which has complicated the class pattern.

Any attempt to divide the town rigidly into classes at this stage would be rash. But with all the limitations perhaps the attempt might be worth while. One's impressions and evidence to date would give the following scale. (Occupation, because it seems to be the most important factor, has been used to illustrate the type of people one might expect to

I. (Outside the town)

II. (Outside the town in the main)

III. (In the town and in surrounding villages)

IV. (In the town)

V. (In the town)

VI. (In the town)
VII. (In the town)
VIII. (In the town)

Upper Class: Public School education, possibly title.
Upper Middle Class: Senior executives of large-scale industry not included in I.
Middle Class: Professional men; owners of all except smallest shops and small factories. Bank managers, and senior executives of industry.
Middle Class: Small men working on their own account; junior executives. Managers of chain stores.
Lower Middle Class: Managers of chain stores. Routine clerical workers. Some skilled artisans.
Working Class: Skilled.
Working Class: Semi-skilled.
Working Class: Unskilled.

find in the groups which comprise the scale. It should not be inferred from this that occupation is thought of as the only, or the finally decisive, determinant of class membership.)

This scale for what it is worth must be read as a continuum with much overlapping at the boundaries. The tests which give stronger divisions than any others are:

(*a*) Public school education.
(*b*) Employer or employee.
(*c*) Manual or non-manual work.

Not only is the class pattern of the town as a whole changing, but people move from one social class to another. Competition to move upward, to "keep up with the Joneses," to spend visibly, is not so open as one gathers from social studies that it is in the U.S.A., but pressure is nevertheless there. This pressure is not overtly admitted. To state openly one's upward aspirations is not done; indeed, the pattern is rather to deny such aspirations and to deny the existence of social class altogether (a factor which makes it very difficult to study). The pressure to "get on" is often resisted; working class informants have explained how they refused an opportunity to set up in business on their own account, or are worried that their child has obtained a place in the grammar school be-

cause it may unsettle him. They prefer a secure place in the working class to the difficulties and insecurities, both real and imagined, of attempting to climb up. Neither is there in Market Town a general conviction that anyone can get to the top if he tries. Those who have "got on" or have "bettered themselves" are admired, if grudgingly; but the general philosophy, particularly in the working class, is to recognize that one is a member of that class and to attempt to improve the lot of the class as a whole, rather than of oneself as an individual, in competition with other members of the class. That mobility is an important factor is, however, clearly observable and a few illustrations may help to make its nature more plain. One man, in a small way of business, quite suddenly some 30 years ago, made a considerable sum of money. He left his brothers with whom he had been working and set up on his own. He prospered, but, although he became one of the richest men in the town, he was not accepted by the elite. Twice he applied to join the best bowling club in the town and twice he was refused. Then, having been a useful supporter of his political party, he became in the course of time Mayor of the town. He again applied for membership of the club. This time, as he was Mayor, the "first citizen," he was accepted. But he plays now with the other club. His children he sent away to school; they are now grown up and living in the town and are being accepted by the group that always cold-shouldered their father. In general, it would be true to say from this and other evidence that if one stays in Market Town it takes two generations to reach the elite from the lower middle class or the working class. An example of downward mobility is provided by a family who were skilled coach builders in the nineteenth century, when they would have ranked lower middle class. They did not learn a new craft or adapt themselves to new skills and are now all unskilled laborers.

To assess what effect social class has on the life of the town is difficult, but must be attempted. In the first place, if you are a child in Market Town, your father's social class membership will determine the education you receive, which will in its turn set limits to the amount of upward mobility that is possible for you.

If your father is working class or lower middle class, you will almost certainly go to the State primary school. You will then stand a chance at 11 years of age of winning entrance to the State secondary grammar school. Given equivalent intelligence, your chance of doing this will be greater the higher on the social scale your father is, partly because you will have a better environment for study and more encouragement and partly because of an unconscious bias on the part of the selectors. Despite the aim of the 1944 Education Act to provide "secondary education for all" with its implication of equality and its overt aim to provide education fitted to the "age, ability and aptitude" of the pupil, there is a clearly marked status system. Within the State secondary schools in Market Town, as in the rest of the country, this status grading is in the order grammar, technical and modern, and is related to the status grading of the occupations that pupils from these schools obtain. If you reach the grammar school and do well and your parents are prepared to sacrifice to keep you there beyond

the compulsory school-leaving age of 15, you stand a chance of a scholarship or grant to any university in the country, but it is more likely that you will go to a provincial university than to Oxford or Cambridge. Then a great deal of upward mobility would be possible for you short of breaking into the upper class itself.

If, on the other hand, your father is in the middle class, you may be sent to a private school. Here you may get a better or a worse education than you would have at a State school, but you may gain in social prestige. Or the school you go to may be an independent or endowed fee-paying school where you will get an education at least equivalent in merit to a State grammar school and rather more social prestige than if you had gone to the State secondary grammar school.

Again, if your father is a professional man or in the upper middle class, you may well be sent to a Public School, which ranks highest in the social status grading of English schools, although, as has been pointed out, within the Public School system there is a clear status grading again.

In these ways the education most people receive will be determined by their parents' social class and will set some limits to the amount of upward mobility possible for them: not because education is the most significant feature of social class in Market Town, but because of the close connection between education and occupation. This relationship between a parent's social class on the one hand and his child's education and subsequent occupation and, therefore, ultimate social class on the other is becoming to some extent blurred by the increase in opportunities for scholarships, but the pattern remains essentially the same; now more people can go further, but not yet can anybody go all the way.

The second important way in which social class operates in Market Town is in limiting the people one may meet and who, therefore, may become one's friends. This is shown in the membership of formal organizations in the town. By formal organizations we understand any institution which has a formal membership. It therefore includes churches and their ancillary institutions, trade associations and unions, social clubs, cultural organizations and the like. In the main these organizations (excluding the churches) can be divided into two main groups, Middle Class and Working Class. It is only on Government- or Borough-sponsored committees, deliberately balanced, that these two groups meet. Although I have excluded the churches from this description, within them the class pattern is also found. There is a tendency for people higher on the social scale to be in the Church of England and for people lower to be in the smaller non-conformist chapels, but this should not be over-emphasized; it is not necessary to transfer from a non-conformist chapel to the Church of England in order to move upward. It is worth noting, however, that three of the Church of England churches were developed consciously in response to the status system and still reflect it.

Thirdly, where one lives and in what kind of house is closely connected with one's social class position. This again limits one's possibilities for social contact, although Market Town is still small enough for the residence areas not to be so clearly demarcated as one would find in a city. The ideal to which the town aspires seems to be to own a detached house in its own ground, screened from prying eyes by walls, hedges or trees, on the higher ground to the south or west or in one of the neighbouring villages. Generally, however, a large semi-detached house is what the elite of the town finally achieve, or an old good class house, sometimes in a terrace. Most of the rest of the middle class and a few of the skilled workers live in semi-detached three-bedroom houses built between or after the wars, and which they buy by instalments. The workers are housed for the most part in Council houses, which they rent, or in nineteenth-century terraced houses.

In sum, therefore, one's social class membership determines the education one's children will receive, the organizations it is possible for one to join, the place one will live and the friends one can make.

Having attempted to assess the extent and importance of social class in the life of Market Town, some attempt must now be made to assess the effect of immigration. One difficulty is immediately encountered in this attempt. It is not enough to say that certain things were before the immigration and certain other things are now, and so the differences are the results of the immigrants coming to Market Town. Along with the arrival of immigrants came an increase in the size of the town. Some of the changes that one observed, therefore, may merely be a response to the increased scale of the town and not to the influence of immigrants as persons. Again, some of the changes may be reflections of changes in the national pattern and not be at all directly connected with the immigration into Market Town.

About half of the inhabitants of Market Town were born and brought up elsewhere. These newcomers came from Yorkshire and Lancashire, from industrial Wales and industrial Scotland, in fact from all those areas that suffered severe depression in the early 1930's. Many came, too, from surrounding villages and small towns and represent part of the "rural drift" of the inter-war years. It is difficult to put one's finger on the tensions that resulted and remain from this influx, partly because it is a technique in Market Town of dealing with the outcast not to make an open breach but just to leave him alone. Objections to new people, new ideas, or new organizations are rarely, if ever, expressed in public. In general terms it seems that, in the early stages of immigration, it was the immigrants who felt the tension; they complain that they were "left out," did not get service in the shops, and so on. Now it seems to be the old inhabitants who are on the defensive; they give the impression of withdrawing into their own groups and pursuing a policy of noncooperation. Tensions are now revealed over the allocation of Council houses (other things being equal, long residence in the town counts in an applicant's favour); in the fear of Trade Union organizers that in the event of a strike the native inhabitants would not stand solid; in the refusal of owners of shops and small works to follow a lead given by the new large industries.

Apart from changes in the social class pattern which have already been described, there have been changes in the social structure since the recent industrialization of the town. New organizations have been formed, notably a Rotary Club and a Trades and Labour Club. Immigrants play a large role in both of these, which leads one to conclude that they are immigrant organizations, but how far it is simply that the town is now large enough to carry such organizations is difficult to assess. For the rest, the immigrants appear to join organizations rather less than do old inhabitants.

A difference between the immigrant and the old inhabitant is that the latter have many more relations in the town, have family and kin to fall back on and which provide a "ready made" social group. The immigrant has to make his own social group or remain an isolate. For this reason, at one time, we expected that the final analysis would show more immigrants than old inhabitants in formal organizations, but this does not now appear to be the case. A surprisingly large number of immigrants, too, have been shown to have relatives in the town—brothers or sisters, whom they recommended to come, or parents who have retired and taken a house near their children who work here. This may show that the strength of kinship ties is rather greater than one expected in a geographically mobile urban population. But these ties are still clearly stronger for the old inhabitant.

Immigrants show some interesting behaviour differences from the old inhabitants. They go to church or chapel less frequently.

It is not simply that they come from places with a less church-going tradition, although this is so in some cases, but that by moving they have broken a habit learned in childhood and connected with one particular church or chapel and have not transferred the habit to a new church in a new town. Some even go so far as to say that they always go to church when they go back home for a visit, but have never been inside one in Market Town. In general, immigrants tend to be rather less traditional in their behaviour than the real Market Town people; they have broken with the traditions of their old town and have not accepted the traditions of Market Town. Again, they are less worried about large-scale organizations. The man brought up in Market Town distrusts a concern which is larger than he can see at one glance. He does not open branch shops on the new housing estates, leaving the field clear for the Co-operative which he dislikes intensely. He considers that a limited liability company is not private enterprise. He understands a face-to-face group, knows where he is in it and will assume leadership of it; but anything larger, more abstract in concept, he distrusts and therefore dislikes.

The aim of this study was to assess to what extent the town was divided into two groups, native and immigrant, and whether this was the most important social division. The tentative conclusion which has been arrived at is that while there is such a division, and that tensions result from it, it is a less profound division than the social class division; less profound because membership in the native or immigrant group does not affect one's total life situation to the extent that social class membership does.

Enduring Social Values

>>

Before we read the concluding selection on the English Midlands, it will be worth while to consider for a moment longer the importance of the consciousness of social class. It seems strange to many Americans that the strict adherence to such a status system would not divide English society into conflicting groups and open the way for deep rifts in the national unity. On the contrary, there is relatively little clash or conflict along the lines of the class structure. The reason, to a great extent, is to be found in the almost complete adherence to a set of permanent *values,* a set of attitudes as to what is right and proper and what is expected of an individual in all circumstances. The elements making up the English system of values are numerous, but C. Arnold Anderson has selected the following as among the most significant in making English society stable and unified.

First, English ideals are epitomized in the phrase "For God, King, and Country."

Secondly, England developed, early in her history, a strong sense of patriotism, a sense of being a nation, and a sense of the people's being subjects of her monarch. This has been constantly reinforced in her literature and is reinforced and complemented by the strong local patriotism toward county and village.

Thirdly, the royal family, and especially the king or queen, are symbols of English ideals.

The Church—that is, the Established Church, to which the upper classes belong—has always exerted a strong influence in English life, even after the extensive development of nonconformist churches.

Propriety, respectability, and diligence are stressed. Ambition and hard work are admired, but they must be tempered with an avoidance of display, with careful conformity to one's "proper" social position, and with morality.

Finally, but by no means of least importance, there is the strong sense of good sportsmanship and fair play, as voiced in the expression, "Let the best man win."

With all this in mind, we can appreciate the final selection by a well-known American historian. It forms a fitting close to our discussion of an industrial society because it is important to remember that, although numerous and rapid changes occur, there must be a considerable degree of stability if a society is to endure. In this selection, by Henry S. Commager, we note the persistence of certain social values and the way in which they give the society a consistency—serving as a social cement. Social change is characteristic of industrialized societies, but it need not result in complete disorganization as long as people perform their roles in terms of widely accepted social values.

• 79 • English Traits
HENRY S. COMMAGER

It is a little over a century ago that Ralph Waldo Emerson landed at Liverpool, spoke famously at Manchester, visited and lectured throughout England, and began writing that wonderful essay on English traits which remains the most astute and penetrating analysis of the English character in our literature. We expect perspicacity from the wisest American of his day: even from Emerson we have no right to expect prophecy, yet what is perhaps most remarkable about "English Traits" is its instinct for the permanent rather than for the transient. For if we review those traits which Emerson distinguished as peculiarly English we find that most of them persist today, flourishing vigorously after a century which has changed profoundly the position of Britain in the world, flourishing defiantly in an England dedicated to austerity and prudence as a century ago she was dedicated to luxury and power.

And not only do English traits persist, but the reasons which Emerson submitted for American interest in them. For it is still true, as Emerson observed, that "the whole world is an interested party," and particularly the American world. It is still true—as all whose memories go back to 1940 will acknowledge—that "the stability of England is the security of the modern world." It is still true that "what lures a solitary American in the woods with the wish to see England is the moral

peculiarity of the Saxon race—its commanding sense of right and wrong." It is still, we may hope, true that "let who will fail, England will not fail." It is still true, in short, that the American concern for the English character is lively, personal, interested, and justified.

National character is, to be sure, everywhere wonderfully tenacious, but nowhere is it more tenacious than with the English, who have, after all, something of a patent on tenacity. And this is the first and most obvious of English traits—the stability and permanence of the English character. Come hell or high water, the Englishman remains imperturbably English. He is, it would seem, less affected by the currents and crosscurrents of history than people of any other nation; he is less affected, too, by passing fashions whether of literature or of dress or of food. Nothing will make him false to his word or discourteous to his guest; nothing will keep him from his tea or change his cooking.

For a hundred and fifty years—from John Adams to Frank Dobie—Americans have been busy describing the English. That they have so largely repeated each other is a comment not on their lack of originality but on a persistence of national traits almost monotonous. It makes, perhaps, for dullness, but there is this to be said about England: you can count on her, you can set your sights by

[From "English Traits," *The Atlantic Monthly,* Vol. 182, No. 2, Boston, 1948. Pp. 61-65. Used by permission.]

her, you can almost set your watch by her. "What kind of people do they think we are?" cried Churchill at a fateful moment in history, and those who forgot what kind of people they were—the Germans and the French, for example—paid heavily for their failure.

Yet what is interesting about all this is that while the underlying character has remained palpably the same, that character itself is no simple thing, but wonderfully complex and even paradoxical. "England is the land of mixture and surprise," wrote Emerson, and the mixture has perplexed most of the interpreters. For the English character is not only stable and uniform, but various and heterogeneous; it is at once obvious and elusive, and almost every generalization must be not so much qualified as confounded.

A materialistic people—who can doubt it? —the English have produced more than their share of mystics and poets, of idealists and transcendentalists, more than their share of the Donnes and Herberts, the Blakes and Shelleys, the Wordsworths and Coleridges, the Foxes and Penns. The greatest colonizing people of modern times, they confess the most passionate attachment to their own country, their own county, their own community: they are at once the most indefatigable globe-trotters and the best gardeners. Their wealth and their wanderlust have enabled them to know the best of all other nations, but they remain true to their own: they carry their language with them wherever they go, and though every Englishman delights in French cooking, none permits his chef to imitate it.

A small nation, with a population highly mobile and highly urban, their differences in idiom and dialect and accent are the despair of foreigners; Vermonters and Texans can understand each other better than men from Devon and Lancashire, or from Glasgow and London, and if the observation that the best English is spoken in Dublin is an exaggeration, it is interesting that it should be made: no one ever suggested that the best American was spoken in Toronto. A unified and harmonious people, the English have persisted in

class distinctions and divisions far more ostentatious than those to be found in most other countries; while politically they have achieved as great a degree of democracy as any other people, they remain class-conscious, and every Englishman is branded on the tongue with his class mark.

A peaceful people, tender and kind, they are, when aroused, the most belligerent of men, good friends and bad enemies, with the indomitable qualities of the bulldog. Allegedly without a sense of humor, or with a belated one, they have produced, after all, the greatest humorists of our time, and the nation which boasted Herbert Spencer boasted, at the same time, Gilbert and Sullivan. The most law-abiding of people, they write the best of all detective and mystery stories and their literature is stained with violence. Monuments of conformity—no sin is more grievous than to do what is not done—they are at the same time passionate individualists, and the nation where nonconformity is a term of rebuke is that in which eccentricity flourishes unrestrained.

This is all paradox, and it is perhaps an additional paradox that the English character, though sometimes paradoxical, is rarely puzzling and never unreliable. The broad traits are clear enough; they persist through the years, they run through all classes of society. The qualities that tend to unify are far stronger than those which divide. What, then, are the traits which have persisted?

They are a law-abiding people. Probably no other people confess the same profound respect for the law, no other conform so instinctively to the rules and regulations of government or of any organization that has authority. They do not smoke where smoking is forbidden, or walk on grass in defiance of signs, nor do they dabble in the black market or try to evade payments on their income tax, or get out of place in a queue. Property is safe, women and children are safe, life is safe, and the critic George Orwell has recently suggested that the trait which distinguishes the English from all other people is their habit of not killing one another. Nor does all this rest upon law, or upon the police force: the whole of society is one vast law-enforcement agency and public opinion is fiercely hostile to law-breakers and rule-breakers.

That the English pay a price for this trait cannot be doubted. They are, if anything, too law-abiding and too acquiescent. They do not revolt readily enough against bad laws and troublesome regulations, but where law is concerned, they take the attitude that theirs is not to reason why.

The English have a highly developed sense of justice and of right. No phrase is more commonly used, by the ordinary people, than "it's right" or "it's not right," and that pretty much concludes the matter. They want to know where they stand, and they usually do. They believe in fair play, on the playing field and in the law courts and in business. They have little patience with subtlety or cleverness: they do not want rights that can be argued about. They hate all chicanery, all evasiveness and slipperiness. They are upright and down-right, foursquare and simple and stanch. They carry their sense of justice over into the political realm—in large matters of national or international policy, in small matters which have their day as questions in the House. Their law is at once just and heartless, and in matters outside the law they are philanthropic but not charitable.

They believe that every man should have his due, neither more nor less, and they have contrived a complex and rigid system to see that each has his due—and no more nor less. The English instinct for observing laws should make most controls superfluous, but much of English life seems organized on the basis of suspicion rather than of trust, and an expensive and pernicious system of checks and controls permeates life. No Englishmen cheat on their railway tickets, yet where in America a single functionary looks at a ticket, in England there are no fewer than three to perform this unnecessary service. When you ride on a bus or in a subway, you must be ready to prove that you have paid for your ride. Accounts are kept scrupulously; the crossed check is an English invention, and a man could as easily burgle the Bank of England as cash a check where he is not known.

The insistence that every man have his due extends from formal arrangements, like food rationing, to informal relationships, like gratuities: it is the enemy not only of favoritism but of carelessness. Before he will admit you to his libraries or his schools, before he will trade with you even, the Englishman wants to know who you are and what claims you have on him, and he will make clear, too, what claims he has on you.

In all this the English are at once the most courteous and the most discourteous of people, and the combination has confused observers for two centuries. It is the courtesy that is instinctive and pervasive, displaying itself formally in the ease of all social relationships and the quiet efficiency of all public ones, and informally in a thousand little acts of thoughtfulness. It is in part the product of training and habit—no children are more courteous than the English; it springs from respect for the individual; it is inspired by natural kindliness. It is to be found alike in individuals, in organizations, and even in crowds; it is habitual but rarely, as with the French, ostentatious.

The discourtesy is a more complicated matter, a mixture of suspicion, indifference, and arrogance, and it is, as often as not, calculated. Its explanation, like that of so many English traits, can be found in the class structure and class-consciousness of English society, and the danger to that structure from anything either incomprehensible or inharmonious. Once an individual is placed, whether as publican or gentleman, as charwoman or lady, all is smooth, but the social sport, whose position and whose claims threaten the structure of the class society, is subject to endless rebuffs. For until he has presented acceptable credentials, the stranger is suspected of asking more than his due, usurping a position which is not his by right, making claims which may be unfounded. Nowhere is the accredited visitor received more hospitably, nowhere is the unaccredited stranger—one whose dress or accent betrays a dubious position—so coldly rebuffed.

The English are an intensely practical people, infatuated with common sense. They have produced few great speculative philosophers but many practical ones: Bacon and Locke, Bentham and Mill, Spencer and Huxley, are their typical products, not men like Spinoza or Kant. They like to see a program, and they judge by results. In politics they have a wonderful feeling for the practical and the actual, an instinctive repugnance for the doctrinaire. They distrust all extremes: their Conservatives are liberal and their Liberals conservative, and even their socialism is a bundle of compromises. They will not waste their votes, and they will not waste their time on men or parties that are too subtle or fanatical, and no people are less susceptible to demagoguery.

For all their open-mindedness and their tolerance, they are an intensely conservative people. They hate innovation, wrote Emerson, and their instinct is to search for a precedent. Even where they are forced to make changes, they change the substance rather than the form, and though English law is certainly as modern as American, the English judge still wears a wig and a King's Counsel takes the silk. They know the advantages of steam heat but distrust anything quite so modern; all the propaganda of the Food Ministry has failed to introduce experiments in cooking, and they still have, as a French wit put it a century ago, but one sauce. Where to an American the fact that something has always been done a certain way is sufficient reason for changing it, to an Englishman it is sufficient reason for retaining it. When asked why Britain does not print an air-mail stamp instead of requiring two stamps to be pasted on every air-mail letter that is not written on air-mail stationery, one of the most unconventional of British scholars answered simply that they never had printed special stamps—and thought the answer conclusive.

For all their conservatism the English are progressive, and it is a peculiarity of the English character to achieve revolution through evolution. Those who speak in the House of Commons are still required to wear a hat, but what they say is rather more radical than anything that can be heard in the American Congress, and if top hats are still required at Eton, education there seems to produce men fit for the responsibilities of the new day. Oxford and Cambridge are still, to all appearances, aristocratic and even feudal institutions, yet they select their students on the basis of talent and each takes a larger percentage of its student body on scholarships than any American university. Everywhere this process of evolutionary adjustment can be seen: ostentatiously in the realm of politics, less spectacularly in the church, in education, in the relations of labor and industry, in the military.

For all their conservatism, their phlegm, they are one of the most adventurous of people. What other nation boasts a comparable galaxy of explorers, mountain climbers, navigators; what other could maintain a Hakluyt Society? From the day of Drake and Frobisher to that of Doughty and Burton the English have led the way to the strange places of the earth—always carrying with them their Englishness, even their afternoon tea, for while they are wonderfully adaptable in large matters, they make no concessions in little ones. They penetrate every river, conquer every mountain, levy upon the whole globe for their collections of flora or fauna, or of esoteric lore, and the adventures of Richard Hannay were not wholly imaginative.

Although they are the greatest explorers and colonizers, and have spread the English language and laws throughout the earth, they are the most parochial of people. Even their patriotism is parochial rather than imperial, and Englishmen would find it hard to sing the praises of things they do not know as Americans of the prairie states sing the praises of rocks and rills, of woods and templed hills. The English love their own country rather than their nation, and every acre of England has its historian and its muse. The London *Times* and the Manchester *Guardian* give adequate attention to world news, but few other papers do, and English journalism, generally, is far less cosmopolitan than American.

Though proud of their Empire, the English know little about it, and they know even less of America. More Canadian history is taught at Columbia University than at Oxford, and over a period of a century and a half no English scholar has contributed anything of lasting importance to the study of American history or literature. In matters of language, too, they are parochial. They do not take readily to foreign languages, expecting foreigners rather to learn English, and they are still inclined to think the American language a sort of debased dialect.

English conservatism and parochialism are not unconnected with self-satisfaction. On the whole the English approve of themselves, as well they may. Instinctively, rather than intellectually, they know that theirs is the best of societies, and their highest compliment is still that a thing is "so English." Recent events have, superficially, shaken this Gibraltar-like assurance of superiority, but it persists in little things, subconsciously as it were. Thus English scholars acknowledge the achievements of Harvard or Columbia or the University of Chicago, but they know in their hearts that Oxford and Cambridge are better, and when they are not on guard their pens slip into the assertion that their higher education is the highest in the world. Most of them are still convinced that the *Times* is the greatest newspaper in the world and that if a book is not in the Bodleian it is not literature. It was equally characteristic that an Oxford don should gravely inquire if any American law library had as many books as the library of his college, and that some passengers from Grimsby should refuse to touch any of the wonderful variety of fish prepared by the chef of the De Grasse because they knew no fish could compare with the fish of Grimsby.

The English have, needless to say, ground for complacency. It is still true, as Emerson remarked, that they make well those things which are ill made elsewhere in the world.

It is not skill alone that accounts for the superiority of their automobiles or their moving pictures over the American, but certain traits of character. They believe in durability, and make things to last—cars and boots and houses, for example. They take pride in their work, and have infinite patience. They carry into affairs even of business their standards of integrity and propriety: if their books are not always exciting they are almost always well written; if their advertisements rarely lure, they do not outrage decency.

They are a thrifty people—thrifty of property, of speech, of their emotions above all. It is not merely that they prefer understatement to exaggeration; they suspect any public expression of emotion, verbal or by gesture. There is far less public love-making in England than in either America or France, and far less public manifestation of family affection. The English do not shout themselves hoarse at games, but are content to murmur "Well played," and are careful to applaud the play rather than the team. They dislike a fuss and, above all, a scene; they will endure any discomfort rather than complain about it publicly, will waste an hour looking for a road rather than accost a stranger for information.

They are thrifty of the products of their minds, as well. They prefer, on the whole, a performance that is not too brilliant, a conversationalist who is not too clever. Churchill has been suspect, all his public life, for his incomparable oratorical gifts. They distrust the ready speaker, the facile actor, the brilliant player, as they distrust men or women who are too well-dressed. They resist styles, prefer old clothes to new, and have made tweeds and the umbrella national emblems.

They have created a masculine country—a society made for men and run by men; the contrast, here, with either France or America is striking. The English home belongs to the man, not the woman—belongs legally, as far as the ownership is concerned, and psychologically, where furnishings and conveniences are concerned. In the United States, advertisements are directed to women, in England to men, and the advertisers know what they are about. England has few magazines designed primarily for women, and English banks are not fitted with special rooms where women can transact their business. The whole tone of English society is masculine: the importance of clubs, the role of the pub, the concentration of family money on the education of sons.

There are no girls' schools with the standing of Eton or Harrow or Westminster, and only this year is Cambridge University conceding degrees to women. Of twenty-one Cambridge colleges, two are for girls; when it was observed recently that the number was scarcely sufficient, there was prompt agreement: there should be, said a young don, at least four. An American would have said, almost automatically, that there should be eighteen. Yet it should be added that all this has nothing to do with politics, or with literature and the arts. There are more women M.P.'s than Congresswomen, and for a generation, now, the best English novelists and critics have been women.

Not the most important, but the most pervasive and the most pernicious of English traits is class consciousness. It is not political, it is only in small part economic; it is social and psychological and philosophical. Its persistence is a tribute to the tenacity of traditional ways of thinking and acting, for it has resisted, stubbornly and successfully, the whole twentieth-century movement of democratization. Originating with the privileged classes, it is retained by the underprivileged, and class sentiment today is stronger with the lower than with the upper classes, and strongest perhaps with the middle.

It reveals itself in a thousand ways, most of them insignificant in themselves, but cumulatively not only important but controlling. In England, alone of English-speaking countries, accent betrays class. There are not only dialects for every section of England, but for each class, and the dividing lines are all but impassable, in less than two generations. The terms "lady" and "gentleman" still have meaning, and have not yielded to the leveling

process; other terms, too, confess a special class significance—"top drawer," for example, while the innocuous phrase "not quite" is loaded with dynamite when applied socially. The distinctions between officers and privates in the Army, officers and ratings in the Navy, are more decisive than in the American services, and even in the recent war a public school accent was helpful in obtaining a commission.

Nowhere else have domestics played a comparable role, nowhere was the hierarchy of the domestic staff more implacable, nowhere was Thorstein Veblen's theory of conspicuous waste more fully validated than in pre-war England. The use of the phrase "master and servant" to cover the field of labor relations derives from the Common Law, and there is a social as well as a professional distinction between solicitor and barrister.

Class distinctions extend even into the intellectual realm, where they are least justifiable. The intellectual pre-eminence of Oxford and Cambridge may be challenged, but never the social: it is interesting to note that though both are located in the provinces, it is the other universities—those at Manchester and Birmingham and Liverpool—that are called provincial. Any man can get a good education at the provincial universities, but if he has social ambitions he might as well cut his throat as go to them. A comparable hierarchy prevails in secondary education, and it is little exaggeration to say that half a score public schools, with Dartmouth and Sandhurst, dominate England socially. The class distinctions in newspapers and journals is sharper than elsewhere: the *Times* and the Manchester *Guardian* appeal to a small and select audience, as does the *Spectator* or the *Economist*. Even religious affiliations have a class tincture: the Church of England is the church of the upper, and perhaps the lower, classes, and the term "chapel" still has social connotations. Socially it is almost as fatal to be a Wesleyan as to have gone to a council school or to pay your tailor in pounds. For England alone of all countries has a special

coin for social purposes. The guinea is fictitious, to be sure, but no fiction was ever more
real, and the distinction between schools,
doctors, writers, tailors, who are paid in aristocratic guineas and those who are paid in
vulgar pounds is profound.

Logically this pervasive class-consciousness
should poison English society, but in fact it
does no such thing. English social relationships seem, in defiance of all logic, easy and
even happy. Ease, good nature, and happiness characterize English social life.

Crisis tests character. The English character is made for normal times and enables
the English to jog along cheerfully from day
to day. But it is made for crisis, too. Honor,
courage, tenacity, pluck, ability, practicality,
fortitude, integrity—these have ever been English traits.

*Come the three corners of the world
    in arms,
And we shall shock them. Nought
    shall make us rue,
If England to itself do rest but true,*

said Shakespeare, over three centuries ago,
and Emerson's memorable speech at Manchester concluded on the same note:—

Is it not true that the wise ancients did
not praise the ship parting with flying colors
from the port, but only that brave sailor
which came back with torn sheets and bat-
tered sides, stript of her banners, but having
ridden out the storm? And so, gentlemen,
I feel in regard to this aged England, with
the possessions, honors, and trophies, and
also with the infirmities, of a thousand years
gathering around her, irretrievably committed as she now is to many old customs
which cannot be suddenly changed; pressed
upon by the transitions of trade, and new
and all but incalculable mores, fabrics, arts,
machines, and competing populations—I
see her not dispirited, not weak, but well
remembering that she has seen dark days
before;—indeed, with a kind of instinct
that she sees a little better in a cloudy day,
and that in storm of battle and calamity,
she has a secret vigor and a pulse like a
cannon. I see her in her old age, not decrepit, but young, and still daring to believe in her power of endurance and expansion.

Who that knows England today, struggling
so gallantly to pay for the grandeur and
misery of victory, can doubt that she is at
her best in adversity, or refuse to have faith
in her power of endurance and expansion?

Conclusions

IRWIN T. SANDERS

>>>

There can be no really final conclusions in an introductory book in the social-science field, but it is appropriate to note a few suggestions about further study. First, we can approach new courses and further reading with a high degree of assurance, since we now have an outline of how a society is put together and how its many aspects intermesh. We have considered, at least briefly, the people of which any society is made up, the connections between the habitat and the society which occupies it, the complex of social relationships which make up an economy, and some of the other patterns which, when added to the economy, make up a society. It has been emphasized that all societies give their own distinctive and individual flavor to the groupings of people and activities that they all contain (for example, family, neighborhood, religion). Each society tends to preserve its distinctiveness as part of its cultural heritage.

Furthermore, some of the basic terms used to describe the nature of society should now be familiar. New "source material" is at hand in every newspaper, book, motion picture, or trip, and analysis of these new situations by means of the appropriate terms and labels can add greatly to an understanding of them. In addition, these basic terms are essential for the effective communication of ideas about the nature of societies or details concerning them.

Finally, reading about differences in the attitudes and behavior of other people forms a good basis for becoming aware of one's own attitudes and values. What is the "right" way to do things? When is an act proper or improper? Are some norms absolutes, which hold true in all circumstances and in all places? What kind of family life or religious belief is "most desirable"? What should be the relation of the individual to the government and to the society as a whole? An individual's "social philosophy" is made up of the total of such value judgments and, if they are consistent and firmly held, they make for meaningful, harmonious behavior.

The Scientific Method

The mention of value judgments calls for a comment on their relation to the method of science. Even a beginner in the social sciences must recognize a value judgment, and realize that it is a subjective, personal affair in contrast to the objectivity that is the aim of the scientist. Biases and personal factors can creep into even as simple a laboratory operation as reading a thermometer, and attempts must be made to eliminate them. In the interpretation of data about a society, either our own or another, it is even easier for preconceptions and other biases to introduce errors. The scientist is searching for truth, and the scientific method is the means that has been found most satisfactory for arriving at the truth.

In simplest terms, the scientific method consists of accumulating information (data, or facts) about a subject and then using this information in order to arrive at an interpretation or "explanation." The conclusions can be no better than the facts on which they are based, and it often happens that the discovery of new facts requires modifications in the conclusions. Thus, the scientist's "truth" is subject to change, always in the direction of a better fit between the facts and the statements based on them. In this process of gathering facts, analyzing them, and finding "answers," the scientist tries to state nothing as "truth" which the facts do not fully support. When he goes further, he labels his statement a hypothesis, an opinion, or a value judgment, and it should be realized that such a statement will reflect both the social heritage of the individual's society and his own scientific training.

It is an entirely normal and proper thing to go "beyond the facts" and express value judgments, since, in one's role as a citizen, decisions must be reached for which we have no scientific testing. But it is the chief purpose of the social sciences to help us find laws or principles governing the operation of social forces; as these become known, man can act more rationally in the areas of activity to which they pertain. Also, we shall have additional knowledge, based securely on facts, from which to derive the judgments which will still be necessary.

Seven Social Sciences

Although the social sciences have been mentioned by name from time to time in the foregoing pages, they have not been defined or described in detail. The way in which each approaches the subject of human society will be discussed briefly here, but the only method of thoroughly understanding the content and techniques of a specific science is to read widely in it and if possible undertake research in it. An introductory book such as this cannot, of course, make its reader a social psychologist, an economist, or a political scientist. Only specialized work can do that. But it is also important to realize that society and the culture of which it is a part "come all of a piece." There is a fundamental unity in man's social world, and if we learn a great deal about a specific aspect of it, we run the risk of overlooking this unity—the wholeness of the social universe in which we work.

Since the central theme of this book is social change, we shall try, in discussing the social sciences, to note particularly the way in which each deals with the processes, relationships, and events that make up social change.

1. Cultural Anthropology (also called Social Anthropology)

As would be expected, the chief area of study of the cultural anthropologist is culture, which has been briefly characterized on pages 8-12. There are at least four cultural processes which apply to social relationships, and therefore to social change.

The first of these is *invention*, which can be social as well as material. The origination of a new trait or custom—whether it be the slit wooden goggles of the Eskimo or the ancestor reverence of the Chinese—is invention. Analysis of any invention will reveal how complex the process is, with each component part of the custom sometimes being a separate invention in its own right.

A second cultural process is called *borrowing* when seen from the point of view of the culture receiving a new trait from another culture, and is called *diffusion* when studied simply as the spread of a trait from its point of origin to a second or third place. Most traits within any culture are borrowed; those societies with greatest access to other societies are likely to do more borrowing, thus leading to accelerated social change. A mere listing of all the traits the English have borrowed—even the traditional cup of tea—is convincing evidence for the relationship between accessibility to borrowing and receptivity to new traits on the one hand and the growth of complexity in relationships on the other.

A third cultural process is *integration*, or the adaptation and incorporation of the new trait into the existing culture pattern. This, too, is a complex process which may involve varying degrees of modification. Somehow or other the rough edges of a new trait have to be rubbed off; it must pass the test of being useful to its new possessors.

Loss of traits, or the discarding of traits no longer needed or suitable, may be listed as a fourth cultural process.

Acculturation is sometimes listed as a fifth cultural process and is used in a dual sense: in the more inclusive sense it means one people's adopting in place of their own culture that of another people so that only minor vestiges of the replaced culture remain; in the less common sense, it denotes the process whereby an indi-

vidual acquires the culture traits of the society into which he is born. It can thus
be seen that in this second sense socialization, with its emphasis on society, is a
part of the broader process of acculturation.

With such processes in mind we can appreciate the role of the archeologist,
who reconstructs past cultures and thus learns what they borrowed, invented, and
modified. The linguistic expert, by analyzing the structure of a language as well
as its vocabulary, can not only find clues to the kind of idea systems which a given
people have now and had in the past but can also trace the history of these systems and point out relationships among them. The ethnologist works almost
entirely with recent or contemporary societies, examining their artifacts, sociofacts,
and mentifacts. The field of anthropology also includes the physical anthropologist,
whose work lies outside the social sciences. He considers man as a biological
species, and pays particular attention to the inherited physical traits which make
up racial variations. By joining the cultural approach, which is the study of man's
works, with the physical approach, the anthropologist obtains an over-all view as
the basis for developing a "science of man."

2. GEOGRAPHY

Like anthropology, geography combines the physical and social sciences, although its whole subject matter is the earth's surface. Physical geography, as its
name implies, analyzes and describes the natural environment. Surface features
(and their origins), climate, and the distribution of natural resources, to mention
but a few topics, can be studied with little reference to man. But geography does
not entirely ignore man. Human geography examines the relationships between
various physical details of the habitat and man's life. With such an approach, and
with the inclusion of regional geography and economic geography, it becomes one
of the social sciences.

The human geographer's chief concern, therefore, is with mankind's process
of adjustment to his physical environment. This is a two-way process: not only
is man strongly influenced and limited by the natural environment, but he in turn
acts upon and modifies the natural environment. What he does to a forest is reflected in changes in a river's floods and its deposits of sediment. Man's killing
off of game animals, such as the buffalo, sets up changes in the vegetation patterns. Some geographers have specialized in the study and classification of the
possible resources of livelihood, in terms of "adjustments" such as pastoralism,
which is an adjustment to grass (which man cannot eat) by means of sheep (which
man can eat, milk, and shear). Social change can then be interpreted as one kind
of adjustment giving way to another—agriculture yielding to industry in the case
of the English Midlands. Work patterns change and family relationships are
affected; centralization of economy and government tend to follow, with a loosen-
ing of community bonds. This is not due entirely, of course, to man's relation to

the habitat, but there is no doubt that the processes of adjustment to natural resources must be considered in any analysis of social change if economic development is to be included. The economy becomes the contact point between the rest of society and the natural environment.

3. HISTORY

History is the study of man in time. Some historians consider themselves humanists rather than social scientists and conceive of the writing of history as being more akin to the humanities—literature and philosophy—than to the sciences. Their canons of scholarship are strict, and their work is sound, but they leave to those who call themselves social historians the task of introducing the scientific method into the study of history. Social historians, too, show a greater interest in changing social relationships through time than do many who concern themselves with the philosophy of history. Archeologists, mentioned above, may also contribute to history, deriving information through excavation of sites where man lived and buried his dead. The historian, however, takes as his primary data man's written records and builds his science on them.

The historical process may be likened to the flowing of time. In its simplest aspect the work of the historian means determining the sequence of events so that we can know what happened where and when. This is fundamental for tracing social changes. All social science depends at times upon the analysis of this historical process. Sociologists specializing in the family, for example, are interested in knowing what conditions in the past have been associated with the decline of family life. To the extent that the historian can help them read the record straight, to that extent their conclusions are likely to be valid. But social historians seek to go beyond the chronicling of the order in which things happened; they like to see what kinds of changes are simultaneous or associated. For example, they want to know if an autocratic family system is invariably associated with an autocratic state. Or they may want to know, as Thomas D. Clark demonstrated in Selection 39, just what the relationships and functions of some specific occupational group, such as the Southern country storekeeper, really were. With great care they hunt up the contemporary records and come out with the best available answer to such a question. Social historians, therefore, who seek to arrive at some of the uniformities observed through the study of the historical process in several societies are contributing to the understanding of social change.

4. ECONOMICS

Many economists define economics as the study of how man satisfies his wants—chiefly the material wants (such as the desire for a nourishing meal or a new car) but also "psychological" or nonmaterial wants (such as the desire for greater social prestige, which might be attained by going to an expensive restaurant or owning a car). In this book we have described the sets of social relationships within which the economic mechanism operates, but we have not tried to describe how a complex economic system functions.

An introductory economics course would take up the three most important processes connected with satisfaction of man's wants. The first is *production,* or "maximizing the total national dividend"—that is, providing those goods and services which people want in as great quantity as possible. The second process is *distribution,* or the sharing of production. It does not mean distribution in the simple sense of getting products from a factory through a wholesaler to a retail store. Rather, it means who receives what, out of all that is available. What will the investor get for his capital, the manager for his direction, the farmer for his crop? The third process is *consumption,* which is analyzed in terms of customer preference among the many ways in which he may satisfy his wants. Consumption underlies demand, which in turn effects production.

The Cotton South has provided a good case study of the effects throughout the social system when technological changes occur in the production process. Mechanization of agriculture calls for greater capital investment, which the marginal farmer cannot afford; it demands skilled rather than unskilled labor; and it even leads to a change in the distributive relationship between employer and employee. The social changes which result can be seen in migration, in the shifting of landlord-tenant ties, and in new community relationships.

5. POLITICAL SCIENCE

As its name suggests, political science is the study of government, or of the distribution of power in society. In Western societies it is customary for us to divide governmental structures into local, state or provincial, and national levels, and to determine within a given society the allocation of power at each level. Power distribution can also be studied, however, in terms of vertical rather than horizontal channels, by a threefold division into the legislative, executive, and judicial functions of the government. The processes by which political power is redistributed vary from the revolution, which results in a sudden and violent shift of power, to such regulated processes as an election, by which certain officials are replaced. Any of these processes not only bring about changes in political structures but have effects upon many other relationships. In one sense, even taxation is a process for redistributing economic power, since certain groups may be favored at the expense of others.

In societies different from our own, power can be found distributed in forms which we are not accustomed to think of as "government." Such groups as the family or the clan, or organizations with religious functions, may also "govern," in the sense of exercising control over the individual members of society. Until recently, political scientists had scarcely considered nonliterate societies, but the techniques of analysis can be as profitably applied to them as to our own society.

6. SOCIOLOGY

Sociology focuses on the study of society as a system and tries to describe and understand the interrelationships among all the parts of society in terms both of structure and function. The sociologist is interested in seeing, for example, how the government and the economy are intermeshed, or how the family, the class system, education, and religion fit in with one another, first in specific societies and then in human society in general. He need not become a specialist in political science or in economics in the sense of probing all the inner workings of these institutional arrangements, but he must understand them well enough to be able to see what part they play in a society.

The social processes, or forms of interaction, which the sociologist considers in his analysis of change include cooperation, conflict, competition, accommodation, and assimilation. Introductory courses in sociology deal with these in detail, as well as with the concepts of values and norms, which also become altered as social relationships change.

For example, a labor dispute between employer and employees which ends in a strike is a conflict situation. The social relationships are disturbed, sometimes to such a degree that a state or national government steps in to help work out a settlement. Through what is called conciliation, or a phase of the process of accommodation, each party to the dispute eventually yields on some points and an agreement is reached. This agreement may be written up in a collective-bargaining contract which describes how relationships between the employer and employees are to be conducted for a fixed period of time. Thus, social change occurs as people who are dealing with one another—sometimes cooperatively, sometimes competitively, sometimes antagonistically—move from one social situation to another.

Sociologists are trained to view such social phenomena as strikes, race riots, family life, social climbing, or religious organizations as involving people in relationship to one another. Knowing what is happening to these relationships aids greatly not only in working out the next step in a given social situation but in seeing the possible effects of any proposed solution upon those participating in it.

Although the subject matter of sociology and anthropology can be seen to overlap to a great extent, sociology is the older of the two disciplines and has concerned itself far more with the study of our own and other highly complex societies. Anthropology has tended to be limited to a consideration of simpler societies, although in recent years it has begun to show as great an interest as does sociology in the literate peoples of the world.

7. Social psychology

With social psychology we conclude this brief account of the social sciences. Social psychology is claimed by both psychology and sociology, and is sometimes said to belong to neither. This discipline seeks to describe the individual at the level of social action. Psychology contributes the knowledge about the individual which general psychologists (usually classed as biological scientists) have gained through experimental work. On the other hand, sociology brings to this new hybrid discipline the necessary knowledge of society. The anthropologist also contributes what he has learned about the connection between the culture of a society and the personality of its members. The processes of social psychology, therefore, depend on the point of view from which the individual is studied. One view is in terms of the role-playing process, which leads into a consideration of motivation and socialization. How does a society train its members to play the roles appropriate to their statuses in given situations? How are the social values internalized—made a part of the personality structure of the individual? How are deviants, those who will not conform, made to get into line through the techniques of social control? The connection between such processes and social change is close, whether there is resistance to or acceptance of change.

There are many allied fields—such as demography, law, ethics, religion, education, and philosophy—which make important contributions to the social sciences, but they are outside the strict limits of this group of studies and cannot be discussed here.

Summing up, then, we have disciplines dealing with man and his works (anthropology), man's record in time (history), man and his environment (geography), man and his wants (economics), government or power in society (political science), society as a social system (sociology), and the individual and society (social psychology).

It is sufficient for us at this point to learn the central core of each field without attempting to determine its precise boundaries. In the present state of the social sciences every one of them overlaps at many points with several others. Each has numerous unsolved problems, but each gives great promise of future achievements in our search for a better understanding of mankind.

Such categorical descriptions as the ones above can come no closer to expressing fully what the social sciences are like in content, aims, and methods, than a verbal description can tell how water tastes. It will depend upon the thirst of the drinker, the source of the water, and the container from which it is drunk. We have tried to provide the opportunity to make a start, but from here on the reader will have to do the sampling.

INDEX